Politics and the
Papacy in the Modern World

Politics and the Papacy in the Modern World

Frank J. Coppa

PRAEGER

Westport, Connecticut
London

Library of Congress Cataloging-in-Publication Data

Coppa, Frank J.
  Politics and the papacy in the modern world / Frank J. Coppa.
    p. cm.
  Includes bibliographical references and index.
  ISBN-13: 978–0–275–99029–9 (alk. paper)
 1. Christianity and politics—Catholic Church.   I. Title.
  BX1793.C565   2008
  262'.130903—dc22   2008012984

British Library Cataloguing in Publication Data is available.

Library of Congress Catalog Card Number: 2008012984
ISBN-13: 978–0–275–99029–9

First published in 2008

Praeger Publishers, 88 Post Road West, Westport, CT 06881
An imprint of Greenwood Publishing Group, Inc.
www.praeger.com

Printed in the United States of America

The paper used in this book complies with the
Permanent Paper Standard issued by the National
Information Standards Organization (Z39.48–1984).

10 9 8 7 6 5 4 3 2 1

Contents

1

Introduction: Rome and the Powers in the Modern Age

At the dawn of the modern age, when Giovanni Angelo Braschi assumed the triple tiara (1775), which some believed symbolized papal authority on earth, heaven, and the underworld, the new pope, Pius VI, seemed oblivious to the winds of change shaking its claims at home and in the international arena. In educated circles and among the political elite of Europe, rationalism, empiricism, scientific analysis, philosophical speculation, and reliance on historical inquiry challenged the universal role of the papacy. This criticism was reinforced by papal behavior, for while Pius VI advanced transnational claims for his office, he remained preoccupied by provincial concerns and developments within the Italian peninsula, and petty personal matters. This led him to largely ignore the broader intellectual climate, which disdained ecclesiastical assertions and derided papal pretensions. Like many of his predecessors, he relied upon the goodwill of the Catholic powers to sustain the papacy and its mission, and preserve his state and temporal power, which extended from Ravenna in the north to Terracina in the south, and stretched from the Mediterranean to the Adriatic.

Early on Italian nationalists such as the poet Vittorio Alfieri (1749–1803) complained that the Papal State's presence and policies since the eighth century had blocked Italian unification. Outside the peninsula, contemporary critics had a broader catalog of complaints. They grumbled that the clock of Europe had stopped in Rome, which was seen to combine feudal pretensions with Renaissance extravagance and whose rigidity and isolation led to stagnation, lamenting that while the world had

changed, the church and its leaders had not. The papacy, in their perspective, represented a relic of the past, finding its persistence to the present
ironic and unacceptable. They judged this institution to be in conflict with
reason, science, and historical criticism, as well as the emerging liberties
and national ambitions championed by an increasingly secular world.
Their critique was directed against both the temporal power and spiritual authority of the Holy See, and the pope proved unwilling or unable
to effectively refute these charges, while his personality, diplomacy, and
private life provoked criticism at home and abroad.

During his early pontificate the aristocratic and worldly Braschi pope
was seen to wallow in pomp and luxury, dabble in art and antiquities, and
restore favoritism and nepotism while clinging tenaciously to ceremony
and tradition. He rejected criticism by asserting the religious authority and
political power of his office, but failed to persuade critics who found his
vision neither balanced nor universal. Preoccupied by Joseph II's efforts
to restrict the "rights" and privileges of the church in Austria (Josephism)
and more frivolous considerations at home, Pius VI seemed to disregard
broader contemporary developments: the philosophical revolution, which
provided a critical perspective on political and religious traditions; the
Industrial Revolution, which altered economic and social life; and the
political revolutions in America and France, which introduced new ideologies and challenged prevailing structures. Despite Roman isolation and
apparent papal indifference to the mounting discontent, the revolutionary age unleashed a succession of storms for the Holy or Apostolic See,
the pope and the officers and bureaus through which he, along with the
Roman Curia, governed the church and the Papal State.

Some observers inside the church, and many more outside, invoked
change for the bishop of Rome, who claimed to be "Vicar of Christ and
Pastor of the universal Church on earth." This papal primacy, celebrated
by Catholics in the "Feast of the Chair of St. Peter," asserted at once the primacy of Peter over the other apostles, as well as the authority of the popes
as his successors. In an age when liberalism and nationalism made great
strides, the papacy remained the western world's oldest transnational
institution and in the eyes of some, one of Europe's remaining absolute
rulers. It is true that unlike other monarchs, the pope—the visual symbol
and virtual head of the Catholic Church—has been elected for centuries,
but the process that evolved was deemed both clerical and elitist. Peter,
as well as the early popes, designated their successors, but by the second
century the Christian community of Rome elected their bishop.

It was not until the pontificate of Nicholas II (1058–1061) in 1059 that
the cardinal bishops were designated to choose the papal successor, and

only in 1179 that Pope Alexander III (1159–1181) granted the cardinals the exclusive right to elect the pope. Sixtus V (1585–1590) fixed the membership of the college of cardinals at 70—which remained their number until 1993—when John Paul II (1978–2005) set the number of voting cardinals at 120. In 2007, in announcing his second consistory, Pope Benedict XVI set aside the limit of 120 papal electors.[1] The practice of sequestering cardinals, *conclave* (Latin for "with a key") harks back to 1241 when the cardinals could not decide upon a successor. Theoretically, any baptized male Catholic could be selected as pope, but current canon law stipulates he must become a bishop before assuming the office. Since the close of the fourteenth century, the cardinals have without exception chosen one of their own. Urban VI (1378–1389) was the last pope chosen who was not a cardinal. The story of Pope Joan or Joanna is a myth.[2]

Presently presiding over an organization of more than one billion souls, and the largest of the three major branches of Christianity, the papacy has aroused widespread interest and its share of suspicion, fueled by its tendency to shroud its affair in secrecy.[3] The inaccessibility of its archives for the recent past has frustrated historical inquiry. In 2006, for example, Monsignor Sergio Pagano, the current Prefect or director of the Vatican Archives, stipulated that the papers of Pius XII (1939–1958) would not be available for at least two more decades! In fact, Rome long has seemed to think in terms of decades and centuries, not sharing the preoccupation with the present displayed by the modern age. Perhaps this is so because the church predates most institutions and its leadership is an enduring entity; the papal annual lists over 260 popes from Peter to Benedict XVI. Revered by millions of the faithful, the papacy has been maligned and spied upon by others.[4] Some claim that this ecclesiastical institution's nature resists change and innovation, remaining *Semper Idem*—always the same—and while it has experienced progress it has resisted change.

Others disagree, pointing to change sanctioned by the papacy along with its continuity over the centuries, noting that while Gregory I, the Great (590–604), branded Mary Magdalene a penitent prostitute, John Paul II has hailed her as the "apostle to the apostles." Then too, early in the second millennium, Pope Urban II (1088–1095) launched a crusade in 1095 for the liberation of the Holy Land from its Islamic conquerors. However, at the opening of the third millennium, in the year 2000, John Paul II denounced violence in the name of religion as an offense against God. This stance has been supported by his successor, Benedict XVI.[5] In addition, a series of Vatican documents recently made available reveal that Pope Clement V (1305–1314) originally absolved the Knights Templars of Heresy, but under pressure from Philip IV of France—whose hospitality he enjoyed at

Avignon—the Pope reversed his decision and dissolved this religious and military order in 1312.[6] The works of Nicolaus Copernicus were placed on the Index of Forbidden Books (*Index Librorum Prohibitorum*) in 1616 by Pope Paul V (1605–1621) in 1619 and only removed during the pontificate of Pius VII (1800–1823) in 1822. Although it has taken some four centuries, Pope John Paul II in 1992 finally and formally proclaimed that "the Roman Catholic Church had erred in the seventeenth century for condemning Galileo for holding that the Earth was not the center of the universe."[7]

Furthermore, the Second Vatican Council embraced the religious freedom previous popes had condemned as "indifferentism" and even the papal stance on the use of condoms has been reexamined, if not revised. More recently, Pope Benedict XVI (2005–) stipulated that a two-thirds majority is always necessary for the election of a pope, overturning the more flexible provision introduced by his predecessor, John Paul II.[8] This follows a series of other changes in the papal electoral process over the years. The papacy has sanctioned theological as well as procedural changes, and during the course of 2007 reconsidered the long-held belief that unbaptized babies were excluded from entering heaven and confined to limbo. Indeed, this reconsideration forms part of a long-term process. St. Augustine in the fifth century argued that children who were not baptized were condemned to hell—although they did not endure all of its anguish. In the middle ages, theologians mitigated Augustine's assertion, arguing that the unbaptized children were relegated to limbo where they enjoyed a natural happiness but excluded from the Beatic Vision. Presently, the notion of limbo has been reconsidered and unbaptized children are included in God's universal salvation.

Papal involvement in political affairs has likewise evolved during its two thousand year history, and especially during the last two centuries—the scope of this volume. At the close of the eighteenth century, the papacy confronted a host of problems at home and abroad. The "Petrine Doctrine," claiming authority for the popes, was questioned and sometimes ridiculed as a grandiose delusion and flagrant fabrication. Increasingly, religion was no longer an affair of the state and the state no longer consecrated by religion. The emerging secular framework in Western Europe, which focused on man rather than God, presented a threat to the Catholic Church and its leadership. In turn, a series of nineteenth- and twentieth-century popes challenged what they perceived as the novel dogma of human freedom and the assumption that society and state existed for the fulfillment of the individual. What the liberals praised as self-maximization, the nineteenth-century papacy perceived as selfishness and license. Rome rejected the doctrine of egoism and hedonistic philosophy, which it charged made a gospel out of indifference to the plight of others, internally and internationally. While some claimed that humanity was perfect and society sick, the Vatican countered that human nature, corrupted by sin, required the redemption of religion and the traditional morality. This papal critique would later provide the foundation for the Church's social program.

The triumph of nationalism likewise challenged the transnational church and its leaders, who confronted a world order dominated by sovereign states in the nineteenth century, and menaced by totalitarian ideologies in the twentieth. During the course of the last two centuries, the papacy has perceived a determined, often violent, assault upon its temporal and spiritual authority by the champions of state omnipotence. The occupants of the Chair of Peter responded by launching an energetic counteroffensive, sparking a new political role for Rome. "The Catholic Church, more than any other religious denomination, cannot confine itself to a merely religious sphere," it has been observed, for its spiritual mission "brings it immediately into contact—and very often conflict—with fields adjoining religion."[9]

Some have deplored the blurring of the distinction between the papacy's strictly spiritual agenda, and its corresponding diplomatic actions to fulfill its religious mission. It is widely acknowledged that throughout the past two centuries the Holy See found itself embroiled in political and diplomatic affairs, including its determined opposition to the fruits of the French Revolution, which provoked the capture of two popes, its campaign against the excesses of nationalism and other nineteenth-century ideologies, the crusade against socialism and communism, its attempts to prevent the outbreak of the two world wars, its appeals for peace in the Middle East, its opposition to the use of the atomic bomb and other weapons of mass destruction, and at the opening of the twenty-first century, its unsuccessful effort to stop the "preventive war" launched by the United States against Iraq.

The 17 popes from Pius VI (1775–1799) to Benedict XVI (2005–) have had to confront the conflicts and crises, which have troubled the modern world, aided by their apostolic nuncios, the officially accredited representatives to the various powers. At times, when and where they had no official representative to the civil power, the Vatican has had recourse to its apostolic delegates, who officially represent the pope to the faithful and the hierarchy of the country, but very often transcend this religious role to assume diplomatic duties. Since the latter are officially entrusted with a spiritual mission and are supposedly involved in internal church matters, they do not require the consent of the governments of the countries to which they are assigned. Nonetheless, the Holy See usually assesses the reaction of a particular government before dispatching these religious representatives, who like other Vatican diplomats receive their training in the Pontifical Ecclesiastical Academy. The papal position is sometimes presented outside the formal diplomatic framework by means of a papal letter or encyclical to the faithful. Generally, an encyclical letter is sent to all the bishops and addresses a universal issue, while an encyclical epistle has a narrower focus, and is directed to a particular group of the hierarchy, usually focusing upon a national or regional concern.

Through these and other mechanisms, at the opening of his pontificate in 1775, Pius VI condemned the attacks on the faith by the spirit of modernity, and in 1798 denounced the replacement of the Papal State by the French-crafted first Roman Republic. The Age of Revolution was followed by one of Restoration, during which the states of the church were returned to papal control. Conservatives in the curia called for more, demanding the total restoration of the old political and diplomatic order with all the privileges and immunities it conferred upon the church and its clergy. This course was not favored by Cardinal Ercole Consalvi, the papal secretary of state, who recognized that the world had changed and believed the church and the Papal State had to make some accommodation with the modern age. Consalvi's moderation was anathema to the *zelanti*, the reactionaries in church and curia who championed traditionalism and favored the centralization of Catholicism in Rome. In 1821 they pressured Pius VII to condemn the *Carbonari*, as "a multitude of wicked men" who sought national unity in Italy.[10] His successor Leo XII (1823–1829), who collaborated with the conservative states of Europe against the so-called liberal menace, denounced religious toleration and Freemasonry in 1825. The Benedictine monk, who became Gregory XVI (1831–1846), condemned the indifferentism (1832), which claimed that all religions revealed divine truth, along with freedom of conscience and of the press, as well as the separation of church and state.

The papal counteroffensive against liberal culture and modern civilization reached a high point during the long pontificate of Pius IX (1846–1878), who after 1849 supported the ultramontism centralization of church doctrine and the absolutism of the Holy See. His "Syllabus of Errors" (1864) cataloged the 80 principal errors of the times, including the belief that "the Roman Pontiff can and ought to reconcile himself with progress, liberalism, and civilization as lately introduced."[11] The Vatican Council he convoked in 1869 proclaimed papal infallibility in 1870, affecting both the political arena and the religious realm. As the papacy's temporal power was progressively whittled away, it took steps to assure its religious primacy by the centralization of the faith in Rome. Some appreciated this development as a necessary consequence of the time of trouble confronting the church. The papacy's alignment with conservative political forces and traditional ideologies at once undermined liberal currents within the church while contributing to the disappearance of the papal state in the decade from 1860 to 1870, creating the Roman Question, which embodied the papal refusal to recognize the loss of their state or recognize the Italian Kingdom that emerged.

These problems, and especially the estrangement between the religious realm and civil society, confronted the nine popes of the twentieth century who continued to wield considerable influence in the church even though they remained somewhat separated from the broader society. These popes, like their predecessors, possessed the sole right to convoke an ecumenical council and only they, or their delegates, could preside over it. Although they could no longer appoint a successor as early popes had done, they could and did indirectly affect the outcome of the subsequent papal election by their selection of additional members of the College of Cardinals. Their primacy in matters of faith and morals was assured by the 1870 proclamation of papal infallibility.

Pius IX's more moderate, if not more liberal, successor Leo XIII (1878–1903) made a valiant effort to end the diplomatic isolation of the papacy, which had emerged in the last decades of Pius IX's pontificate. He also sought to make some accommodation with contemporary society in 1891 by issuing the encyclical *Rerum Novarum* (Of New Things), on the condition of the working class. In it the Bishop of Rome, who was also primate of Italy and pope, sought to apply traditional Catholic teaching to the changes introduced by the Industrial Revolution. By this and other means, Leo transcended the clash between church and state by focusing on church and society, seeking to end the alienation between the latter two. Despite this partial reconciliation with the modern world, Pope Leo XIII condemned socialism in 1878, and Americanism—the attempt to adapt Catholicism to contemporary ideas and American culture—in 1899. His successor, Pius X (1903–1914) in turn, denounced Modernism (1907), which challenged traditional Catholicism with its scientific approach to biblical scholarship, and in 1910, he imposed a Modernist oath on the clergy, constraining them to disown this liberalizing movement.

The need to transcend internal church developments and strictly religious issues was pronounced after the pastoral pontificate of Pius X, as the prospect of a catastrophic conflict cast a shadow over Europe. Not surprisingly, the subsequent popes from Benedict XV (1914–1922) to John Paul II (1978–2005) have all shared a diplomatic background. Pius XI (1922–1939) and Pius XII (1939–1958) concluded a series of concordats or agreements between the Holy See and political bodies, to protect church interests—including the controversial concordats with Fascist Italy (1929) and Nazi Germany (1933).[12] The concordat concluded with Mussolini led to the creation of the miniscule Vatican City State of some 108 acres, the world's smallest independent state. More important, it brought an end to the "Roman Question" by providing the papacy with the claim to temporal power without most of the burdens and responsibilities of sovereignty.

John XXIII (1958–1963), who convoked the Second Vatican Council (1962), and Paul VI (1963–1978), who brought it to a successful conclusion (1965), sought *aggiornamento,* or updating of the Church and an accommodation with the modern world. Among other things the council's pastoral constitution on the Church (*Gaudium et Spes*), called upon the church to enter a dialogue with contemporary civilization—and it did to some extent. Some found this too little, too late; others too much, too soon. There was criticism of Paul VI's unilateral action—three years after the collegial council—in imposing the church's traditional opposition to birth control in his encyclical *Humanae Vitae* (1968).[13] Liberals were further antagonized by the 1984 report of Cardinal Joseph Ratzinger—who became Pope Benedict XVI in 2005—which criticized Catholics embracing an "uncritical openness to the world."[14] In 1992, the Congregation for the Doctrine of the Faith—the Vatican office formerly known as the Inquisition, presided over by Ratzinger—dispatched instructions to the bishops of the United States on participation in political life, noting that those involved in lawmaking had an obligation to oppose laws attacking human life. In his message, Ratzinger explained that Catholic politicians might disagree with the Holy Father on the waging of war and the application of the death penalty, but not on abortion and euthanasia. Critics as well as admirers acknowledge the crucial political role of John Paul II at the end of the twentieth century, which has been amply analyzed and documented.[15]

Following his predecessors, Benedict XVI has interjected the papacy in the political debates raging over such issues as abortion, the death penalty, stem cell research, contraception, gay marriage, and the teaching of evolution. Like his predecessor, Benedict has denounced the attempt to create designer embryos. In 2007 the Vatican even involved itself in the mundane matter of issuing road rules and guidelines for the drivers of automobiles in its "Ten Driving Commandments."[16] Although the Cold War had passed into the realm of history at the opening of Benedict XVI's pontificate, a *new* Cold War had emerged as terrorism, among other problems, has troubled the papacy, as has the unilateral response of the superpowers to the perceived threat and their recourse to force. The papacy has long preferred collective action and the use of moral means to combat violence, and some have heeded its call. The pope "has a big influence on what happens in the world, not just in the Catholic community," said Moshe Katsav, President of Israel, adding, "I am sure that a clear voice from the pope against anti-Semitism against suicide bombing (and) terrorism . . . will echo widely and have a big influence."[17] In fact, the efficacy of the papal intervention against prevailing political, diplomatic, and ideological problems has been variously judged during the past two centuries.[18]

During the negotiations for the 1801 concordat regulating church-state relations in France, Napoleon cautioned his envoy to Pius VII that he should treat the pope as if he had two hundred thousand troops at his disposal. However, Stalin later proved less impressed, indeed rather dismissive of the papacy's impact. In 1935, when a French visitor asked the Soviet dictator if he sought Pius XI as a potential ally, Stalin supposedly responded "How many divisions can the pope supply?" Historically, there have been obvious limits to papal influence. The efforts of Pope Leo XIII to prevent the outbreak of the Spanish-American War of 1898, proved futile. Later, Pius XII's mediation attempts proved no more effective during World War II than Benedict XV's had been in World War I. Hitler, who distrusted Pius XII, during the German occupation of Rome in 1943 considered ordering his forces into Vatican City, making the pope his prisoner, as Napoleon had done over a century earlier. Warned of the national and international repercussions of this action, and the moral outrage it might provoke, the Fuehrer relented and respected the person of the pope and the territorial integrity of his tiny state. The dichotomy in assessment of papal action and influence is reflected in the literature with some studies apologetic and others polemical—particularly in the twentieth century.

The historiography on Pius XII is especially contentious, and partly cataloged in two recently published volumes.[19] Despite the controversy surrounding Pius XII's silence during the Holocaust, and the failure of papal mediation during World War II, the international image of the papacy has improved in the postwar period.[20] Among other things the papacy has been seen to play a role in the creation of the Irish Free State and the collapse of Communism in Eastern Europe. More recently, some have claimed that the traditionalism of John Paul II helped to decide the U.S. presidential election in 2004. At the end of the long pontificate of John Paul II, interest in the institution was reflected in the convergence of millions of pilgrims to Rome following this pope's death in early April 2005. Along with interest in the institution there has emerged a mounting curiosity in the person of the pope, with the media reporting on his dietary habits, dental visits, and even shoe preferences! This curiosity has been spurred by a number of factors including: Rome's greater recourse to Vatican Radio, established by Guglielmo Marconi in 1931, Pius XII's embrace of television, the stance assumed by the Vatican in the Cold War, and John XXIII's *aggiornamento,* which sought to bring the church into greater harmony with the modern world and whose convocation of the Second Vatican Council in 1962 captured international attention and generated unprecedented media coverage. The worldwide apostolic journeys of Paul VI, continued and multiplied by John Paul II, have contributed to the international status of the papacy.

Paul VI's interventionist policy and international outlook led him to speak out on a number of moral and political issues, while providing the Holy See with a voice at the United Nations. Subsequently, John Paul II, who traveled more than all the other popes combined, garnered a global reputation and extended the reach of the papacy. He is generally acknowledged to have had a crucial role in the collapse of communism in Poland and Eastern Europe. The Holy See, functioning as a spiritual force, political organization, and international entity, presently maintains relations with over one hundred governments. Even the United States, overcoming a longstanding anti-Catholicism and suspicion of the Holy See, reestablished formal diplomatic relations with it in 1984 during the pontificate of John Paul II.

In his first meeting with the diplomatic corps, Pope Benedict XVI expressed the hope that those countries without formal ties to the Vatican would soon establish representation,[21] and a number of countries did. In the spring of 2007, the Holy See established full diplomatic relations with the seven states forming the United Arab Emirates. During the second year of Benedict XVI's pontificate, the Vatican continued its outreach to the non-European and non-Christian world by offering a course "The Catholic Church and International Politics of the Holy See" to familiarize Muslim governments of the methods and mission of Vatican Diplomacy.[22] Reportedly, at the dawn of the twenty-first century the Holy See was seriously considering applying for full membership in the United Nations, transcending its current nonmember permanent observer status and thus enhancing its international outreach.[23]

The present volume focuses on Rome's response to developments during the past two centuries, exploring the papacy's religious, social, political, and diplomatic roles during the troubled period from the revolutionary upheaval of the nineteenth century to the collapse of communism in Eastern Europe at the end of the twentieth, and beyond. It examines the papal interaction with the major events and ideologies over the years including its reaction to liberalism, capitalism, nationalism, imperialism, fascism, totalitarianism, internationalism, socialism, communism, modernism, Americanism, feminism, racism, Islamic extremism, and anti-Semitism.

It also traces the continuity and change in the papacy's attitude toward church-state relations. In light of the crucial role of the popes, their history is also a history of the church and of Catholicism.

The pages that follow include Rome's reaction to the revolutionary upheaval from 1789 to 1849, its attitude toward liberal Catholicism's attempted accommodation with modernization, as well as its response to Italian and German unifications and the ensuing Roman Question and *Kulturkampf*. The volume also explores the Vatican's reaction to the American Civil War, its relationship to imperialism, its role in World War I, its attitude toward the League of Nations, and its position toward the democracies and the dictatorships during the interwar period. Subsequently, it delves into Rome's stance during World War II and its alleged silence vis-à-vis the Holocaust. The remaining chapters concentrate on the papacy's attitude toward internationalism and the United Nations, communism, the Cold War, postwar reconstruction and integration, a united Europe, and the attempted accommodation with the modern world initiated by the Second Vatican Council. John Paul II's legacy is assessed and the role of Pope Benedict XVI is also included. Five of the popes during these two centuries had long pontificates: Pius VI (1775–1799), Pius VII (1800–1823), Pius IX (1846–1878), Leo XIII (1878–1903) and John Paul II (1978–2005), accounting for almost half of the twelve longest reigning popes in the institution's two thousand year history. Presently, the pope remains one of the few church officials not constrained to retire at the age of 80. The longevity of these pontificates helped to insure their impact.

Unlike many earlier studies, which concentrated upon the papacy's role within the church, this work looks at this key religious institution within a broader framework, assessing its reaction and response to a transformed world. It considers the papacy's relationship and reaction to the major secular as well as religious forces during the past two centuries. In the process, many of the questions raised by these popes remain germane, including the limits to be placed on capitalism, the rights and responsibilities of labor and the working classes, the individual's rights versus those of society, the mutual responsibility of rich and poor states and peoples, the notion of a just war versus war no more, the rights and responsibilities of the states within the international community, and the need for an equitable and stable international order.

The Papacy Between Revolutionary Upheaval and Restoration, 1789–1849

The revolutionary age at the end of the eighteenth century relied on reason and had faith in the perfectibility of humanity, while rejecting customary authority. Edmund Burke, in his *Reflections on the Revolution in France* (1790), charged it undermined all traditions, including those of the Catholic Church and its papal leadership. In the new century the old church confronted an increasingly hostile atmosphere. Internationally, this rebellious spirit posed a challenge to the papacy's privileged diplomatic position. Internally, it resented the close alliance between throne and altar that led to the summoning of the secular arm to enforce church law, while questioning the church's wealth and exemption from taxation. The determination to curb these abuses first in France and later elsewhere, contributed to a series of anticlerical measures in the six revolutionary decades from 1789 to 1848, leading the papacy to resist what it denounced as a "rebellion against the cross."

As the old regime was toppled in France, the authority of the church was brushed aside by the champions of liberty, and the National Assembly responded by unilaterally abrogating the concordat of 1516, which had regulated church-state relations for centuries. The Assembly determined not to send even one centime to the court of Rome for any purpose whatsoever, eventually nationalizing the lands of the church, and banning religious vows. Conservative Catholics condemned these measures as the latest manifestations of the apostasy of modern society flowing from the Protestant Reformation to the Enlightenment. They railed against the revolution of 1789 for its excesses, anarchy, assault on property, but above all for its persecution of the church and the violation of its "God-given mandate." The most dangerous innovation from Rome's perspective was the Civil Constitution of the Clergy of July 1790, which reorganized the church in France by creating a national and elective structure, which challenged papal control and ecclesiastical centralization.

Pius VI (1775–1799), who rejected the presumption that all men had the right to debate the status of the church in France or elsewhere, initially failed to recognize the gravity of the situation. Seeking to avoid a confrontation with the new government, and a possible schism in France, he referred the revolution's anti-ecclesiastical legislation to a commission of cardinals, hoping the problem would disappear. It did not. Continued papal silence ended following the December decree of the French Assembly constraining acceptance of the Civil Constitution by all priests holding office. In April 1791, Pius condemned the Civil Constitution in his encyclical letter *Charitas*, denouncing this legislation as destructive of papal primacy.[1] The papal rejection of the Civil Constitution of the Clergy persuaded a large number of priests and most bishops to refuse to swear allegiance to it. The government responded by a systematic persecution of these dissenters dubbed the "nonjuring clergy." At this juncture the conflict between Rome and the Revolution became painfully public.

Tension between Paris and Rome intensified after an anticlerical assembly assumed power in 1791, approving measures to curtail, if not suppress, Catholic worship in France, while conferring full civil and political rights to religious minorities. The situation deteriorated further following the French declaration of war upon Austria in 1792, as nonjuring priests were declared traitors, dechristianization proceeded rapidly in the state and the schools, and the last French monasteries were slammed shut. The wave of anti-Catholic agitation and terror led thousands of the clergy to flee abroad and many were welcomed to Rome by Pius VI, to the displeasure of church critics in Paris. They took their revenge when French forces under Napoleon stormed into Italy, and occupied and absorbed the northern tier of the papal state in 1796. To prevent the French from penetrating beyond the Legations of Bologna, Ferrara, Forli and Ravenna, which were incorporated into their newly created Cisalpine Republic, Pius agreed to the Treaty of Tolentino (1797). This did not satisfy the government of the Directory in Paris, which sought the end, not just the limitation of, the temporal power. Napoleon, who hesitated orchestrating the demolition of the papacy, predicted its demise as the modernization unleashed by the revolution proceeded.

The governing Directory in France was not reassured by Napoleon's promises. Responding to anticlerical circles in Paris that perceived the need for external pressure to hasten the papal collapse, the French government supported additional steps against the Holy See. As a consequence of this revolutionary hostility toward Rome, the papacy's problems worsened. At the end of 1797, the murder of a French general in Rome provided a convenient pretext for retaliation, constraining Napoleon to order General Alexandre Berthier to march on the city. Following Berthier's entry into the capital in February 1798, the pope was arrested and a French inspired and directed Roman Republic, proclaimed. Its constitution provided for religious equality, thus eliminating Catholicism's privileged position in the very heart of the church's territory. Here, as elsewhere, the French dismantled the Jewish ghetto and pursued principles and policies that Pius VI found objectionable and intolerable. The protesting pope was soon silenced, and dragged to Sienna and eventually to France. Before his departure, Pius VI nominated a special congregation of cardinals to supervise the governance of the church in his absence. Sensing his impending death during his captivity, Pius instructed the senior members of the sacred college to convene and select a successor upon hearing of his demise. Following his instructions, they met in Austrian-controlled Venice at the close of 1799, the last conclave convoked outside of Rome. After considerable debate, the 34 member conclave settled upon the bishop of Imola, Cardinal Luigi Barnabà Chiaramonte, who succeeded as Pius VII in 1800. Although Chiaramonte selected the name of his predecessor and like him opposed the false philosophy of the age, he was believed to be more receptive to a reasonable compromise between church and state. He found a ready and willing partner in Napoleon Bonaparte, who attained power in France at about the same time. "I don't believe in religions," he confessed, "I was Mohammedan in Egypt, I shall be Catholic here for the good of the people."[2] Nonetheless, from the first, the new French ruler appreciated the role of organized religion in the restoration and preservation of political order and social stability in France and Italy.

Pius VII, for his part, had pragmatically preached that liberty, equality, and democracy were not necessarily incompatible with Christianity and proved anxious to reconcile Rome and the revolution, imploring peace for the church in his first encyclical in 1800.[3] Assisted by his secretary of state, Cardinal Ercole Consalvi, he sought rapprochement with Paris and the new political order, and Napoleon for his part, favored the negotiations that culminated in the concordat of 1801.[4] While Napoleon was primarily inspired by political considerations, and Pius VII by religious ones, both had other motives. Nine projected drafts were discarded before the two parties found themselves willing to compromise and accept the tenth. Each side achieved some of its objectives in the two declarations and seventeen articles of the agreement. While Pius did not attain the declaration that Catholicism was the religion of state, the French Republic did recognize Catholicism as the religion of the great majority of the French people. Although the Roman faith was to enjoy full freedom of public worships, the state also assured other faiths, both liberty and legitimacy. The bishops were all to resign and their replacements named by the First Consul, while their canonical institution was reserved for the pope. Temporarily skirting the issue of the temporal power of the papacy and the loss of the Legations, the agreement secured the pope's religious power assuring him not only the right to invest bishops, but in certain circumstances to depose them. While the concordat of 1801 represented a death knell for Gallicanism, which restricted papal intervention in France, this was resurrected in the attached amendments unilaterally imposed by the French, dubbed the Organic Articles, which reimposed governmental control over various activities of the Catholic Church in France.[5] Although Pius resented and publicly protested against these Articles, he did not abrogate the concordat, fearing the loss of the advantages it provided the church.

In 1802 the church-state rapprochement led Napoleon to permit the body of Pius VI to be returned to Rome for burial. However, a number of differences between Paris and Rome, remained. The Organic Articles represented only one of many unresolved issues between the papacy and Paris, and these were not alleviated by the pope's participation in Napoleon's coronation in Notre Dame on December 2, 1804.[6] Subsequently, the pope was distressed to learn that the French civil code, with its provision for divorce would prevail in the newly created Kingdom of Italy (1805), which replaced the Cisalpine Republic and incorporated part of the papal state. Both pope and curia increasingly realized that the peace between church and state remained as precarious as that between the powers. The two conflicts would soon converge.

A dilemma confronted the papacy, which sought to avoid becoming embroiled in the European war. The need for papal independence proved contentious, as Pius refused to bow to pressure from Paris in the governance of his truncated state, or accept dictation on the diplomatic course he should chart. The pope complained that the French insistence that he exclude their enemies, and especially the English and Russians from the papal state, violated papal neutrality.[7] Small wonder, that neither he nor his advisors in the curia, favored the political treaty sought by Napoleon, which they feared would render the Holy See a virtual French satellite.[8]

Despite his reservations, Pius was pressured to place the reconstituted and truncated papal state under French protection. It was tantamount to having wolves guard the sheep and did not prevent Napoleon from having his brother Joseph occupy the papal port city of Civitavecchia, supposedly to keep the English out.

In June 1806, Pius had to accept the resignation of his Secretary of State, Consalvi, who the French found too independent and not sufficiently sensitive to their interests. Following Napoleon's defeat of Prussia and occupation of Berlin in November 1806, the Emperor imposed the "continental system" barring British ships from continental ports. The papal refusal to adhere to this boycott aroused Napoleon, who dispatched French forces into Rome in February 1808, and in April 1808 wrenched the provinces of Urbino, Ancona, Macerata, and the Camerino from the papacy, withdrawing the donation of Pepin and the confirmation of Charlemagne.[9] The papal secretary of state protested, to no avail.[10] Tension escalated during the ensuing year, and in May 1809 Napoleon incorporated what remained of the papal state into France, declaring Rome a free, imperial city. In response, in June Pius issued a bull of excommunication against the counselors and executioners of the spoliation of the dominion of St. Peter.

Resenting the continued papal resistance, early in July 1809, French forces stormed into the papal residence, the Quirinale Palace, dragging the pope into captivity, eventually placing him under house arrest in Savona, near Genoa. The French held Pius VII captive for over four years, creating difficulties for the faithful.[11] During this time the pope rejected a series of French proposals, refusing to confirm the bishops named by his captor and leading Napoleon to propose alternative methods for their confirmation. In January 1813, Napoleon met with the pope at Fontainebleu, where the two ironed out the basis for a new agreement governing church-state relations, which the Emperor announced as the *Concordat of Fontainebleu*. His proclamation was premature. After consultation with a number of cardinals, Pius rejected the tentative accord they had outlined. Only Napoleon's defeat at the battle of the nations in October 1813, and his abdication in April 1814, spared the pope from the Emperor's fury and retaliation. Pius VII's return to Rome at the end of May, while Napoleon was exiled to St. Helena, was heralded by some as the triumph of the spirit over the sword. Pius VII, appreciated for having had the moral courage to defy the overwhelming power of Napoleon, raised the prestige of the papacy at home and abroad. However, its problems were far from over as this traditional institution had to adjust to a world transformed.

The major powers were no longer predominantly Catholic following the defeat of France and the subordination of Spain. Only Catholic Austria remained in the circle of the great powers. Nonetheless, Great Britain, Prussia, and Russia along with Austria, tended to sympathize with the pope, whom they perceived as a fellow victim of French aggression as they sought the support of religion in preserving the status quo from revolutionary upheaval. This enabled Cardinal Consalvi, one of the ablest diplomats of the period, reinstalled as the papal secretary of state, to regain most of the papal territory at the Congress of Vienna (September 1814–June 1815). To preserve it, Consalvi concluded that cooperation with Austria, the sole remaining Catholic great power, was essential.[12] The arrangement came at a cost. The renewed alliance between Rome and Vienna angered both liberals and nationalists, particularly in Italy and Germany, whose national aspirations had been blatantly disregarded at the Congress.

Italian nationalists such as Giuseppe Mazzini believed that clerical dominance was an anachronism, while in Germany, liberals as well as nationalists derided the obscurantism of the retrograde papacy. On the other hand, moderate liberals appreciated that Consalvi, unlike the *zelanti*, or hard-liners in the curia who resisted all concessions and change, favored a limited reform while opposing revolution, stressing the need to humanize and illuminate the temporal government of Rome. Nonetheless, like the zelanti, who resisted any interference in church affairs by the secular authorities, Consalvi deemed constitutionalism incompatible with the papal government. "The fundamental principle of constitutional government, if applied to the government of the Church, becomes a principle of heresy," he argued. "If it were introduced in the government of the States of the Church, men would soon desire that it be extended to the government of the Church itself."[13] Thus the need to preserve absolutism in the church, required absolutism in the papal state, and contributed to the eventual collapse of the temporal power. The latter was sacrificed for the former.

Cardinal Consalvi sought to preserve both the spiritual and temporal power of the papacy, which he, like others in the curia, considered inextricably intertwined. Unlike the conservative contingent, however, Consalvi saw the need for some accommodation of the papal state with the current political and cultural reality, without compromising the church's principles and dogma. He therefore worked to mitigate, if he could not eliminate, the abuses of the papal regime, seeking some adaptation with contemporary developments. His moderate stance and sentiments were shared by Prince Klemens von Metternich, the Austrian foreign minister, and chancellor after 1821, who shunned constitutionalism in Italy, but from the beginning of the restoration called for a renovation of the administration of the papal government. Like Consalvi, Metternich was frustrated by the obstructionism of the zelanti, who regarded the revolution and its consequences as diabolical, condemned innovation of any sort, were hostile to almost all advice offered by the powers, distrusted the laity at home and the states abroad, and insisted that the canonical restrictions on the Jews be reimposed. Yearning for the return of the old order, their program called for a complete restoration of the *ancien regime* in which the church functioned as an independent corps with its own property, rights, jurisdiction, and privileged position. They were perceived to be inexorably hostile to progress and virtually immune to criticism.

Consalvi's reform proposal of 1816, which combined firmness on matters of principle but allowed for flexibility in practice, aimed to eliminate some of Rome's worst abuses. Among other things it sought to modernize the papal administration by opening it to lay men, and providing for advisory councils. However, even this limited reformism was effectively blocked by the growing reaction in the curia. The zelanti, the strongest party therein, did not share Consalvi's conviction that the papacy had to modernize and revitalize their state to allow it to survive in the postrevolutionary world. They angered the powers as well as nationalists and liberals, by insisting on ultramontism—or looking beyond the mountains to Rome and the papal curia for guidance and control of church affairs. Pius VII's fall in 1817 incapacitated him, leaving the zelanti, bitterly hostile to liberalism, free to obstruct most change and prevent all reform. Confronted with the ensuing mass dissatisfaction and increasing disturbances, Cardinal Tibero Pacca, governor of Rome, championed mass arrests to impose order and preserve Christian culture. Pacca's program presented a temporary expedient at best, providing no long-term solution to the state's problems while undermining the papacy's international image.

Consalvi proved more successful in foreign affairs, refusing to sanction the Austrian suppression of the Neapolitan revolution of 1820, and protesting the passage of Austrian troops across papal territory on their path to Naples. This did not end his cooperation with the Hapsburg State, for the papal condemnation of the Carbonari, ostensibly issued because of their sacrilegious misuse of Catholic ritual, was actually released to placate Austria.[14] It was insufficient for the zelanti, who called for greater repression in Rome to assure that the revolutions in Naples and Piedmont would not spread to their state. The zelanti prescription prevailed. Consalvi's limited reformism, stifled in the last years of Pius VII's pontificate, ended with the pope's death in 1823, and the election of the 63-year-old zelante Annibale della Gegna, as Leo XII (1823–1829). The new pope's conservative and ultramontane tendencies pleased the intransigent faction, who championed papal interests against the powers as well as the revolutionaries and radicals. What liberals championed as freedom, they condemned as anarchy that threatened both church and state, denouncing the notions of infinite progress and human perfectibility as dangerous delusions. Once pope, Leo proceeded to placate them by dismissing Consalvi, restricting the activities of the Jews in the state, imposing burdensome restrictions on the sale of wine in shops and taverns, and supervising and revising productions in theatres. Press censorship was restored while a host of judicial privileges were showered upon the higher clergy.

A decree of October 1824 purged the administrative and judicial systems of Consalvi's, innovations, while Leo's first encyclical of May 1824 denounced dechristianization, indifferentism, and toleration, tracing the contemporary degeneration to the abandonment of church teaching and decline of papal authority.[15] Thus Leo XII's *Ubi Primum* of 1824 foreshadowed the *Mirari vos* (1832) of Gregory XVI and the *Quanta cura* (1864) of Pius IX, each of which contrasted modern errors with the eternal principles of the church. Critics complained that although Leo had originally championed a spiritual revival that would garner mass support, a stance strikingly similar to the one championed by the French priest Félicité de Lamennais, he eventually bound the church and the papacy to an outmoded medieval past, relying not on the people but the conservative powers. However, the persecution of his godless opponents was sporadic rather than systematic, and proved insufficient to quell the growing dissatisfaction and disorder in the papal states.

In foreign affairs Leo pursued a more pragmatic, less ideological course. Renouncing the ultramontism and excessive papal centralization advocated by the zelanti, he eventually recognized the need for good relations with the powers—and above all Austria. Consequently, he returned to Consalvi's cooperation with Metternich to frustrate insurrectionary movement in the Italian peninsula. Thus, when his secretary of state Cardinal della Somaglia retired in 1828, Leo refused to bow to the zelanti pressure that sought the nomination of the conservative and ultramontane Cardinal Giustiniani opting instead for the more moderate Cardinal Tommaso Bernetti, who followed in the footsteps of Consalvi. Despite the opposition of the Madrid government, echoed by many conservatives in the curia, Leo did not abandon Pius VII's plan to dispatch an apostolic delegation to Latin America. Subsequently, he proceeded to fill Latin American bishoprics, providing a de facto recognition for the breakaway republics in the new world. His moderation in foreign affairs, as well as his overriding concern for the welfare of the church, combined to win the praise of the archbishop of Spoleto and future Pope Pius IX, following Leo's death in 1829.[16] He was also praised and mourned by Metternich, who feared the election of a more fanatical and ultramontane pope, who would threaten the close collaboration between Rome and Vienna, thereby undermining the stability of Italy.

Metternich's fears did not materialize as the cardinals in conclave, confronted by the prospect of another revolutionary outburst, belatedly recognized that they could not simultaneously combat the sects and the thrones, and therefore opted for a candidate who would collaborate with the powers against the revolutionaries. In fact, the election of the 68-year-old bishop of Frascati, Francesco Saverio Castiglioni, who became Pius VIII, was supported both by the Austrians and the French. Devoted to Pius VII, and a disciple of Consalvi, he also recognized the need for some reformism to avert revolution. A commission of cardinals was created to propose reforms but the pressure of European events, the outbreak of revolution, and the shortness of his pontificate conspired to prevent the implementation of these changes. He lived long enough to observe passage of the Emancipation Act of April 1829, which granted political rights to British Catholics, which had hitherto been denied them. He also witnessed the July 1830 revolution in France, followed by one in Belgium, and responded by pragmatically recognizing the government of Louis Philippe and urging the French clergy to do likewise. Refusing to bind the fortune of the church and the policy of the papal state to the legitimate but unpopular bourbon regime of Charles X, he revealed both a flexibility and willingness to compromise in his quest to preserve Rome's political and spiritual independence. The Romans were not impressed and following his death sang, "the eight Pius was pope, lived and died, and no one took note."[17]

This was not entirely true, for Vienna worried about the course of a new pope amidst the revolutionary upheaval of 1830–1831. Metternich knew that among the clergy there were competing views on the role the church should assume in the restoration world. In France Father Félicité de Lamennais claimed that the revolution had broken the nexus between throne and altar, which had in fact bound and restricted the church, and called for the church to ally with the masses to protect its primacy and principles. By the mid 1820s Lamennais vehemently attacked all forms of Gallicanism or French attempts to restrict or control the church, insisting that to fulfill its mission the church needed complete independence from the state. After the July revolution this position was presented in the newspaper L'Avenir. Its motto "God and Liberty" frightened conservatives, who doggedly defended traditional principles and papal prerogatives, vehemently rejecting any collaboration with the masses. Although conservative ultramontanes also favored greater freedom for the church and the primacy of the papacy, they found Lamennais's program dangerously liberal, and sought to revive the union of throne and altar with the papacy supporting the conservative powers, and in turn being supported by them. These views found resonance in the conclave at the end of 1830, which on February 2, 1831 selected the ascetic and zealous Bartolomeo Alberto Cappellari, who donned the papal tiara as Gregory XVI, the only pope since the eleventh century not of aristocratic background. A monk since his eighteenth year, he was shielded from, and suspicious of, the modern world. His concerns about the course of contemporary developments were confirmed by another outbreak of revolution in Europe.

Soon after Gregory's election the long-feared and predicted revolution erupted in his state, overrunning the Romagna and spreading to the Marches and Emilia. Bernetti, who was retained as secretary of state, sought to avoid the nationalist condemnation certain to follow an Austrian intervention, and therefore called upon France and Naples to rescue the pope. He was disappointed by their reluctance to do so. Bernetti's attempt to create a popular counterrevolutionary force from the loyal peasantry, likewise failed. Meanwhile, matters quickly deteriorated from the papal perspective, as a revolutionary provisional government was established in Bologna, which issued a declaration proclaiming the end of the temporal power. The danger escalated as the revolutionaries marched southwards, threatening Rome itself. Indeed, the young Prince Louis Napoleon, nephew of Napoleon I and future French emperor, who participated in the rebellion, brazenly warned Gregory that the forces advancing towards the capital were invincible.[18] While he exaggerated, the threat to Rome was real, finally constraining Bernetti to appeal for Austrian intervention to liberate Bologna and the northern provinces. Once again Metternich complied, restoring papal control in the northern provinces. The cardinal secretary of state appreciated the Austrian effort, but understood that some other mechanism to protect the papal state was urgently needed.[19] Metternich concurred, and suggested reforms to reconcile its population to the papacy and stabilize the Roman administration.

The French, disturbed by the unilateral Austrian intervention in Italy, also sought to address the source of the revolutionary movement in the papal state, suggesting a conference of the major powers (France, Austria, Great Britain, Prussia, and Russia) to propose reforms that would avert future revolutionary outbursts. Metternich agreed, noting that the Vienna government had long argued that the reform of Rome's provincial administration was absolutely essential for peace and tranquility, proposing that the 1816 decree of Pius VII and Consalvi provide the basis for these necessary changes. In May 1831, the Conference of Ambassadors meeting in Rome issued a memorandum to Gregory listing the reforms required to begin the modernization of the papal administration and avert a future revolution therein. Among other things it called for uniformity of treatment of the provinces, the admission of lay people into its administrative and judicial functions, the public supervision of finance, as well as greater self-government for the municipalities. Finally, it proposed the creation of a national consultative assembly to advise the pope on state affairs.

These modest proposals were not welcomed at Rome, especially the call for a consultative assembly, which was seen to violate the special nature of the pontifical regime by potentially challenging clerical control. In fact, Pope Gregory found most innovations inopportune, fearing that such reform in the state would inevitably provoke the call for similar changes in the governance of the church. Although Bernetti promised to consider and implement those measures that were not in conflict with the essence of the papal state, few reforms were introduced by the ascetic and zealous Gregory, who responded to political and diplomatic questions in an intransigent and uncompromising manner. "Here they are so convinced of the indestructibility and infallibility of this government," the frustrated Austrian ambassador to Rome, complained, "that its rulers often abandon themselves calmly to inaction, counting upon the aid of God and the miracles He will work to support the state against its enemies."[20]

Divine protection did not materialize. After the Austrians withdrew from the papal state in 1831, a series of disturbances erupted, prompting Vienna to dispatch a military force to the Legations in 1832. To protect Gallic interests and preserve the balance of power in the Italian peninsula, the French occupied Ancona. This dual occupation, which persisted until 1838, pinpointed the Holy See's inability to effectively govern the oldest state in Europe and compromised the future of the temporal power. Gregory, who had earlier published "The Triumph of the Holy See and Church against the Assaults of Innovators" (1799), continued to shun reform and relied on the support of the conservative powers to protect church interests. His sentiments were reflected in the *Catechism on Revolution* of 1832, which emphasized the incompatibility of revolution and Catholicism. "Does the Holy Law of God permit rebellion against the legitimate temporal sovereign?" the Catechism asked, and responded "No never, because the temporal power comes from God."[21] Following this mandate, in June 1832, in a letter to the bishops of Poland, Gregory urged Catholic Poles to be submissive to legitimate authority in the form of Russian domination, avoiding revolutionary agitation.[22]

At home, he excommunicated those who incited rebellion against his government in Ancona, using spiritual weapons to protect temporal interests.[23] Fearful of contact with and possible contamination by the outside world, he opposed the introduction of railroads in his realm because this would facilitate the infiltration of liberal ideas and subversive doctrines. He likewise resisted the illumination of streets in urban areas, perhaps because he feared this would serve to encourage nocturnal gatherings and the concoction of plots. This reclusive pontiff was alarmed by the disturbing depictions of liberal license and criminal changes drawn by zelanti clerical circles. To make matters worse, Gregory was distressed to learn that some within the bosom of the church advocated the right of revolution, freedom of religion, and the separation of church and state, as had been established in France and Belgium following the revolutions of 1830.

In the daily newspaper *L'Avenir* founded by Lamennais, these liberal Catholics presented a program calling for the regeneration of the church, an alliance of Christianity with liberty, and the promotion of the primacy of the papacy by supporting a separation between church and state such as existed in the United States, and recently introduced in France and Belgium. They contended that such a separation would prevent the enemies of the prevailing political, economic, and social orders from becoming enemies of the church and papacy. The *Avenir* movement aroused a storm of opposition. The conservative upper clergy in France deemed these ideas heretical, as part of the Catholic press proclaimed one could not be Catholic and liberal.[24] The legitimist press in France, and most of the country's hierarchy, were hostile to Lamennais, heralded by liberals as an "intellectual giant," "the greatest talent of the century" and "a man chosen by God to reinvigorate church and society." Seeking to suppress the newspaper, the bishops banned *L'Avenir*'s circulation in their dioceses, while refusing absolution and ordination to those found guilty of reading the heretical journal. Finally, they appealed to Pope Gregory, who shared many of their sentiments, to intervene in their campaign against the *Avenir*. Paradoxically, at the end of 1831, Lamennais also decided to take his case to Rome.

Liberal Catholics who favored the separation of church and state, proved unrealistic in assuming that the pope who had invoked Austrian intervention against the insurrection in his state, while denouncing revolutionary movements in Poland, Belgium, and even Ireland, would miraculously bless democracy and the liberal and revolutionary ideals they championed. They soon learned otherwise, receiving a frosty reception in the Eternal City, where Lamennais waited for two months before being granted an audience on March 13, 1832. During the course of this encounter, Lamennais was distressed that Gregory studiously avoided discussing the liberal Catholicism of his movement, or the controversy engendered by his newspaper. Instead, Gregory quietly commissioned a congregation to study both and report back to him. Its findings were cataloged in the encyclical letter

Mirari vos of August 15, 1832, the first comprehensive and explicit condemnation of liberal principles.[25] Without mentioning Lamennais or his followers, the papal encyclical condemned the central ideas of the liberal movement including religious liberty denounced as "indifferentism," the "impudence of science," and the corrosive culture of criticism, along with the separation of church and state.[26] Continuing his campaign against contemporary developments, that same year he denounced the conspiracies of secret societies and prevailing indifferentism, exposing the "idols worshipped by modern civilization."[27]

Originally submitting to the papal condemnations, in September 1832 Lamennais and his collaborators announced the closing of the *Avenir*. Lamennais later recanted and in his *Words of a Believer* (1834), denounced the papal stance as totally out of step with contemporary reality. Gregory quickly responded in June 1834 in his *Singolari nos*, which condemned the errors put forward by Lamennais in his *Words of a Believer*.[28] At the same time, Gregory did not hesitate to denounce beliefs and practices espoused by some conservatives. In December 1839, his apostolic letter (*In Supremo Apostolatus*) condemned slavery and the slave trade as unworthy of Christians, forbidding Christians from participating in, or defending, this "peculiar institution."[29] Denouncing enslavement, he defended the work of missionaries and martyrs in China,[30] especially praising the efforts of the Society for the Propagation of the Faith.[31] At the same time he challenged the dogmas of bourgeois liberalism, decrying the evils of an economic system that misused power and exploited resources for selfish use. Gregory was convinced that the papacy and the church were constrained to combat the political, economic, social as well as religious evils prevalent in many modern states, contemporary societies, and the international order.

In his crusade against the errors of the modern age, and the revolutionary agitation he believed they spawned, Gregory made some minor compromises in the political arena, if not the religious sphere. Following the pragmatic precedent established by Pope Leo XII, which had allowed the Holy See to make appointments in Latin America and India, he indicated that where there were changes of government, the Roman Pontiff would open diplomatic relations with those who exercised de facto power. He made it clear, however, that by doing so the Holy See did not intend to legitimize such regimes—a practice and policy that the papacy would continue well into the twentieth century. This distinction between de facto and de jure governments enabled Rome to condemn the revolutions, while accepting their results. No such flexibility was displayed by the church in its own state, where Gregory's siege mentality prevailed.

He found the neo-Guelph program, which looked to the papacy to foster national unification in Italy, little better and perhaps more unrealistic than Giuseppe Mazzini's revolutionary organization, Young Italy. His intransigent antinational stance contributed to the unrest in the Italian peninsula and particularly in his own state. In 1837 Viterbo was stricken;[32] in 1843–1844 the Legations were affected. Almost everywhere there was talk of an impending revolution that could not be checked by Gregory's recourse to prayer. Consequently, there was real concern in June 1846, when the monkish Gregory died at age 81, the sixteenth of his pontificate.[33]

Concern for the future of the temporal power was reflected in the 50-member conclave that opened on June 14, 1846. Apparently the cardinals sought a candidate who was neither intransigent nor permissive on reformism, while enjoying the support of the powers. This led to the rejection of the darling of the conservatives, Gregory's secretary of state Luigi Lambruschini as well as the Capuchin Cardinal Luigi Micara, who it was believed would make the broadest and most radical concessions to the so-called party of progress. Eventually Cardinal Giovanni Maria Mastai-Ferretti, Bishop of Imola, emerged as a compromise candidate for the majority that sought a moderate candidate. Elected June 16, 1846, he assumed the name Pius IX, in honor of Pius VII, who had made possible his ordination, despite his epilepsy.

Mastai-Ferretti deplored the sad condition of the papal state, and had long called for a more temperate government, better attuned to the needs of its people and the modern world.[34] He believed that common sense and Christian justice could initiate the administrative transformation that would make the papal states viable. Aware that repression had not brought tranquility, he concurred with the moderate liberals that a limited reformism might bring the stability sought. He outlined his agenda in a work entitled "Thoughts on the Public Administration of the Papal State" (1845) in which he invoked a collegiate institution or council to advise and coordinate the state's administration, failing to understand Gregory's government's opposition to science, scientific congresses, suspension bridges, the lighting of streets, and even railroads.[35] In his view the Holy Father had to concede in his state many of the amenities granted elsewhere, and once pope sought to do so. The new pope had friends in the liberal camp and upon becoming pope reportedly sent his blessing to Lamennais. Although neither a political figure nor a diplomat, he was soon heralded as the pope-liberator of the peninsula envisioned by the patriot-priest Vincenzo Gioberti, in his work *Del Primato Morale e Civile degli Italiani* [On the Moral and Civil Primacy of the Italians] (1843).

From the first the new pope's actions aroused popular expectations. The day of his coronation in St. Peter's Basilica, June 21, 1846, when he was crowned with the Tiara, the new pope distributed some 6,000 Roman *scudi* to the poor, releasing those who had been cast into prison for debt.[36] Such generosity on the part of a new pope was customary, but much of what subsequently ensued was not.

Petitioned by the people of his state to initiate a series of reforms, Pius IX was inclined to comply.[37] However, he wanted to be certain that his innovations were in keeping with the ecclesiastical nature of the papal regime.[38] To assure himself of their orthodoxy, Pius IX appointed a special congregation to screen his proposals and projects; it was this body that approved the pope's general amnesty, which aimed to demonstrate the goodwill of the new regime and garner support for it.[39] In July the amnesty was proclaimed, pardoning all subjects who were imprisoned for political crimes.[40] It created a sensation, arousing the enthusiasm of liberals and nationalists in Italy as Pius was prematurely proclaimed "father of his people" and "savior of the peninsula." His program inspired and provided hope for Giuseppe Garibaldi who was in Latin America as well as Gioberti in Turin, who proclaimed that Pio Nono had opened a new age for Italy and the World.

In many of the Italian and European capitals, the reformism of Pius IX was praised, and even public opinion in the largely Protestant United States was impressed. At this juncture the church in the United States was a mission church, the clergy and religious orders of which were largely European and remained under the supervision of the Congregation for the Propagation of the Faith. American Catholics and non-Catholics alike were moved by events in Rome. Unquestionably, the exchange of ministers between the largely Protestant United States and the center of Catholicism flowed from the goodwill enjoyed by Pius IX at the beginning of his reign. Former President Martin van Buren proclaimed that the new pope had "won the admiration and respect of the world in so brief a period," adding that his position was of "greater interest to mankind than that of any other human being."[41] President James Polk shared his enthusiasm, and opened formal diplomatic relations with the papal states by sending Jacob Martin to Rome the summer of 1848. Despite some bitter opposition, the American Congress, which was overwhelming Protestant, supported President Polk's recommendation for a *chargé d'affaires* to Rome. This post was elevated to that of Resident Minister in 1854, and maintained until 1868.[42]

What pleased Washington, and a number of other capitals, distressed Metternich, who likened the amnesty to an invitation to thieves to enter one's home. In fact, under its terms hundreds of political prisoners were released while scores of exiles were granted the right of return. The Austrian chancellor considered this generosity excessive, deeming it both unwise and unnecessary to grant an amnesty to the disturbers of the peace in the Legations.[43] God pardons, but does not grant amnesties, Metternich reminded the pope, who had expressed sympathy for youthful indiscretions.[44] In turn, Pius countered that he did intend to plunge into utopias, but favored those reforms suggested by the powers, including Austria, in the Memorandum of 1831. These intentions were subverted by those who wanted more, and had recourse to orchestrated demonstrations and staged marches to press their point. In 1847 they formed a committee to urge the pope to transcend administrative changes and grant political reforms. Pius promised to pursue the "path of progress," adding that patience was needed to bring this to fruition.[45]

Since the pope had not formulated a concrete program or set a definite timetable, only outlining generalities, he allowed himself to be pressured by the public demonstrations, to the dismay of the Austrians. Conservatives complained that a virtual revolution was being unleashed in the name of an unsuspecting pope.[46] Early in the spring of 1847, an edict was issued approving the national consultative assembly that Consalvi earlier had opposed, followed by one in June creating a council of ministers, an even more radical decision.[47] These measures only whetted the appetite of those demanding a more thorough transformation, provoking the Cardinal Secretary of State, Pasquale Gizzi, to announce that there were limits to what the papal government could concede, given the special nature of the regime. Privately, Gizzi asserted that if things spiraled further out of hand, he would have to appeal for Austrian intervention, alerting the Vienna government to the possible need for assistance.[48] Metternich, in turn, was exasperated by the spectacle of an Italian ruler, even if unwittingly, exciting the national aspirations of the people of the peninsula. He warned that if Pius continued along this path, and allowed the excitable masses to roam unrestrained, he would eventually be forced out of Rome.[49] In July 1847, when the pope agreed to putting arms in the hands of his people by sanctioning the formation of a civic guard, Metternich concluded that the pope had sealed his fate—a sentiment shared by Cardinal Gizzi, who retired as secretary of state following its authorization.

The year 1848 saw the publication of Karl Marx's *Communist Manifesto* and the birth of scientific socialism. It also witnessed revolutions in Palermo and Paris and much of Central Europe, bringing to fever pitch the clamor for constitutionalism in Rome, which all of Pio Nono's predecessors had consistently and vehemently opposed. In a spirit of accommodation, Pius promised to grant everything compatible with the special nature of his state.[50] Hoping to avert revolution by timely reforms, Pius created a special commission to determine whether he, too, could grant his people a constitution. The commission reported that the granting of a *Statuto* or constitution to restore order was preferable to the two other alternatives: revolution or foreign intervention. The pope, convinced that this further concession would allow him to preserve the temporal power seconded their decision, but was scandalized by the popular pressure to expel the Jesuits from Rome.[51] Furthermore, alongside the new institutions the older ones persisted in the guise of ecclesiastical tribunals, clerical privileges, and the dominant position of the curia. These championed authority over liberty, and invoked the support of the conservative international order. Liberals were dismayed that article 25 of the newly minted Roman Constitution (March 1848), stipulated that only Catholics would enjoy political rights in the state.

From the first the constitutional regime in Rome confronted problems, having to limit the political power of the pontiff, while leaving his spiritual authority, undiminished. No small task. The contradictions became readily apparent when Pius was pressured to join the national crusade to expel Catholic Austria from Lombardy and Venetia and liberate Italy, a step that he resisted. Waging a war of national liberation was entirely possible for a political leader, but difficult if not impossible, for the head of the universal church. In fact, it was his April 1848 allocution, which ruled out papal participation in a war against Austria that put the pope on a collision course with liberal and nationalist sentiment in his state. Pius rejected the contention that the enemies of Italy were the enemies of God. As common father of all Catholics, he could not declare war upon Catholic Austria the Pius IX proclaimed, but added he could not prevent his subjects from entering the conflict as volunteers.[52] This concession, along with the abolition of the ghetto that same month, did not mollify national sentiment in the peninsula or his state.

Pius sought to regain support at home by writing the Habsburg Emperor early in May 1848, urging an Austrian withdrawal from Italy. His pleas proved counterproductive by antagonizing the Austrians while failing to satisfy national sentiment in the papal state. Further conciliatory efforts could not contain the torrent of discontent that led to the revolution of November 16–17, 1848 in Rome, and the pope's flight from his capital and state, the evening of November 24, with the aid of the French, Spanish, and Bavarian ambassadors.[53] Convinced that Rome had become "a den of wild beasts" of "apostates" and "heretics," who threatened his temporal and spiritual power, Pius felt constrained to leave.[54] Pius explained his decision as early as November 27, citing "the need to enjoy full liberty in the exercise of the supreme power of the Holy See, which in the existing situation was impossible."[55] Ordering both the Roman chambers closed, Pius created a commission to govern in his absence, asserting that there could be no legitimate authority that did not flow from papal power. His contentions did not sway the revolutionaries in Rome, who ignored his commands and at the end of December 1848 convoked a general assembly of the papal state to reorganize its political life. Soon thereafter, in early February 1849, the second Roman Republic was proclaimed,[56] and subsequently fell under the direction of Giuseppe Mazzini, who Pius deemed a false prophet, if not an Antichrist.

The conflict between Rome and the revolution from Pius VI to Pius IX was religious as well as political for these popes sought to preserve the traditional values of the faith, as well as their own independence and political power. In Rome's view the two were intimately intertwined, for the nineteenth-century popes like their predecessors, had concluded that without a state they would be subject to the will and whim of the various princes and the vagaries of political power. This led to their conviction that their spiritual authority could only be guaranteed by the possession and exercise of their own political or temporal power. Thus, the conservative, antinational and illiberal policies of the papacy in the first half of the nineteenth century must be seen within the context of the battle with the revolutionary upheaval of the age and the threat it posed to the papacy's political power and therefore its spiritual authority. These considerations certainly guided the policies of Pius IX from the restoration of 1849 to his death in 1878. In this fashion, the Roman revolution and papal flight set the stage for the restoration that ensued.

From his exile in the Kingdom of Naples, Pius denounced the Roman Republic as "an iniquity," contrasting it to his temporal power, which he proclaimed "legitimate" and "absolutely essential."[57] Unwilling to negotiate with the heretics who declared the papacy fallen and the temporal power terminated, like his conservative predecessors he counted on the support of the friendly Catholic powers to suppress the sacrilegious republic and restore his regime. On February 18, his acting secretary of state Cardinal Giacomo Antonelli, dispatched a note imploring the armed intervention of Austria, France, Spain, and the Kingdom of Naples to restore peace and papal power in the states of the church and restore tranquility to Christianity. The Kingdom of Piedmont-Sardinia, which had spearheaded the war of liberation in Italy, was noticeably excluded. Pius was convinced that this ambitious power was dominated by antireligious as well as antipapal sentiments, threatening both the spiritual and political power of the papacy.

During a conference at Gaeta in the Neapolitan Kingdom in March, the four powers agreed to move against the Roman Republic and restore the temporal power. Austria and France assumed the major role in this intervention, albeit for different reasons. Austria regarded it as part and parcel of the overall antinational restoration in Italy, which would return Lombardy and Venetia to Austrian control, while members of the Habsburg family would be restored to Tuscany and Modena. A friendly papal regime in Rome was deemed essential for this overall restoration. France, for its part, was concerned with the balance of power in the peninsula, hoping that its participation in the restoration might preserve constitutionalism in the peninsula and avoid the conservatism and absolutism of the earlier restoration. Thus, the Austrians focused on the Legations and Tuscany, the French moved into Civitavecchia and Rome, while the Spanish and Neapolitans moved into the papal state from the south. The collapse of the Roman Republic by July 1849, and the subsequent restoration of pontifical control, resolved some problems but created others for the papacy. It arrayed Rome against nationalism as well as the liberalism and constitutionalism of the age, and would color events during the second stage of Pio Nono's pontificate, 1849–1878.

Rome Grapples with Liberalism, Nationalism, and Sectionalism, 1849–1878

A torrent of political, ideological, and technological innovations propelled the transformation of the nineteenth century. Religious traditionalism, no less than the political and economic establishment, was challenged, to the dismay of pope and curia alike. Rome resented both the canonization of liberal capitalism, which stressed individual maximization and the amassing of private wealth, as well as the countervailing dogmas of socialism and communism, which invoked a crusade against both church and state in their conflict with capitalism. The papacy found these socialist cures worse than the capitalist disease, for they too seemed to undermine the church's role in public affairs, fostering the secularization and dechristianization of society. Pius IX, who had earlier accepted aspects of the liberal and constitutional program, following the revolutionary upheaval of 1848–1849, and his flight from Rome, abandoned his earlier roseate optimism. Subsequently he rejected the greater part of the liberal agenda as destructive of traditional religious values and incompatible with Catholic precepts as well as subversive of the papal regime.

"In light of the immorality of men," Pius IX wrote the archbishop of Bourges, "the representative system is not suitable for the governance of the states of the Church, nor suitable for the independence of the Pope, because it is impossible to draw a line separating the two powers."[1] Nationalism, which posed a threat to the papal state, deemed essential for the preservation of the pope's spiritual authority, was also deemed suspect and dangerous. Not surprisingly, the pope restored to Rome by foreign bayonets, by 1849 was not the innovator of 1846. He now obstinately opposed the movement for Italian national unification or *Risorgimento*, sparking a papal resistance to it known as the counter-*Risorgimento*.

During his exile, Pius IX came to regret the reformist course he had pursued the first two years of his pontificate, believing it had led to the revolutionary upheaval threatening the papacy's political and spiritual authority. Following the restoration, he determined to avoid past errors, rejecting the call for reform by the French and Piedmontese, as well as various groups in the papal state and the Italian peninsula, who invoked national, social, economic, political, and even religious concessions. The French president, Louis Napoleon, was particularly determined to preserve constitutional government in Rome. His foreign minister catalogued the changes Paris deemed essential for the restored regime, including: a generous amnesty, a secular law code, abolition of the tribunal of the Holy Office, restricting the role of ecclesiastical tribunals in civilian jurisdiction, and the creation of a *Consulta* or Council to advise the pope on fiscal and administrative matters. This reformist course was rejected by the papal secretary of state, Cardinal Giacomo Antonelli, who revealed the Holy Father would make no concession compromising his temporal power. Consequently, the Vatican resented the French Memorandum, which outlined the reforms required of Rome.[2]

To prevent the passage of these and other dangerous innovations in Rome and its provinces, Pius IX, who postponed his return home, appointed a commission of conservative cardinals to govern in his absence.[3] Dubbed the Red Triumvirate"—because of their red robes—the commission shared the papal horror of the innovations of the Roman Republican regime. Not surprisingly it immediately annulled all that had transpired in the capital since November 16, 1848 declaring all the Republican initiatives and actions null and void. Alarmed by the papal reaction and the negative image it projected, Louis Napoleon complained that he had not dispatched the French army to snuff out Italian liberty, but to preserve it. His words, like those of the Piedmontese, who seconded the call for change, fell on deaf ears as Rome resisted granting a general amnesty, rejected the restoration of the Code Napoleon, and opposed any hint of secularization, adhering to a conservative course. Nonetheless, the French and Piedmontese reformist proposals created consternation in the pope's entourage, while encouraging opponents of papal absolutism.[4] Even the Vienna government, which felt the need to preserve the papal state, decried the reaction, abuse of power, and the recourse to exceptional tribunals in Rome.[5]

The chorus of criticism had some impact, alerting Rome to the dangers inherent in pursuing an extremist course. Thus in September 1849, Pius proposed more moderate measures for the papal regime, providing for a degree of administrative autonomy, some judicial reform, a council of state for administrative matters, and a *Consulta* for financial affairs. He rejected the call for additional changes, refusing to make any concession to nationalism, which he described as absurd and criminal as socialism. Small wonder that his regime found itself in conflict with frustrated nationalists in Italy and Germany, while liberal circles in Turin complained that Pius conspired with the Austrians to annul their constitutional regime. The pope, in turn, distrusted Piedmont, charging that it sought to undermine religion in its realm and throughout the peninsula. The Piedmontese emissary, Count Giuseppe Siccardi, who met with the pope at Portici in 1849, found him suspicious of the Turin government's projected reforms, which he denounced as a vicious attack upon the faith. This papal conviction was confirmed by the Piedmontese passage of the Siccardi Laws of March 1850, which abrogated the ecclesiastical jurisdiction enjoyed by the clergy, eliminated the church's ancient right of asylum, provided for the suppression of *mortmain*, restricted the official observance of Catholic holidays in Piedmont, while threatening to transform marriage into a civil contract.

Frustrated by the turn of political events, upon his return to Rome in April 1850, Pius focused on the spiritual needs of the universal church, placing responsibility for most political and diplomatic matters in the hands of Giacomo Antonelli, who was confirmed as secretary of state. This shift was reflected in his decision to reside in the Vatican palace rather than the Quirinale, where he had the unfortunate experience of being besieged. Disillusioned by consequences of his earlier political initiatives that he believed had led to riot and revolution, he focused on the religious realm following his return to Rome in 1850. Pius now immersed himself in a series of beatifications, naming more saints than any other pope to date, the reestablishment of the hierarchy in England in September 1850, and the elevation of the Sees of New York, New Orleans, St. Louis, and Cincinnati to the rank of archbishoprics. In 1853, he restored the hierarchy in Holland, and the following year issued the Proclamation of the Immaculate Conception of Mary, asserting that from the moment of her conception she was free from the stain of original sin. Missionary efforts were broadly supported and this pope commenced the process of the globalization of the college of cardinals even as he favored the centralization of liturgy and pressed for the adoption of the Roman rite. In 1867 he canonized Pedro d'Arbues, the fifteenth-century inquisitor of Aragon who had zealously persecuted religious dissenters, offending Jews, Protestants, and Liberals worldwide. Pius ignored their protests, which he believed confirmed the righteousness of his actions.

Despite his refuge in the religious realm, Pius IX could not ignore the political changes and the emerging ideological climate, which he perceived as anticlerical and anti-Catholic. He vehemently dismissed the numerous theoretical formulations that challenged the church's traditionalism and frequently denounced the prevailing materialism of the age. While some posited the initial triumph of economic liberalism, followed by the inevitable collapse of capitalism, Pius IX rejected both contentions. He was quick to condemn the rival faith of economic liberalism that preached unrestrained freedom to assure the personal satisfaction and maximization of some, but led to the enslavement in poverty for many others. He sought a religious solution to the social question. Thus, while Socialists such as Karl Marx demanded radical political and social changes to improve the lot of humanity in the name of historical materialism, Pius relied on the faith to provide consolation for a stricken humanity. In the process, he provided the theoretical formulation for a rival and Christian formulation of social justice, later elaborated by his successors from Leo XIII (1878–1903) to Benedict XVI (2005–). To spread this gospel, he called for a clergy trained in piety and imbued with an ecclesiastical spirit, encouraging seminarians to study in Rome. As part of his process of centralization, Pius rewarded priests loyal to Rome, creating more *monsignori* in his pontificate than his predecessors had produced in the last two centuries. He relied on concordats or agreements with the powers to protect traditional church interests, such as the one concluded with the Grand Duchy of Tuscany in 1851, again establishing a precedent later followed by popes Pius XI (1922–1939) and Pius XII (1939–1958). However, Pius IX proved unable to conclude a new agreement with Piedmont, whose liberal, social, and national policies the pope found objectionable and whose government refused to grant the concessions sought by Rome.

Suspicious of the national and political aspirations of the Piedmontese, he was not insensitive to the social problems unleashed by industrialization and fueled by an unrestrained capitalism. Early in the 1850s, Pius sought opinions on the issues troubling state and society, having recourse to Donoso Cortes, a Christian positivist who endeavored to save Europe by a renewal of Christian life and socioeconomic reforms. The pope concurred with Cortes that Catholicism provided a source of valid principles for social progress, thus serving as a precursor of sorts for the social reformism of his successor, Leo XIII (1878–1903). At the same time, Pius confessed that his primary mission was religious and remained the propagation of the faith. His task was not an easy one, when he perceived so many false philosophies and dubious political principles prevailing. During the course of 1855, the pope had to confront personal as well as political crises. During his visit to what was believed to be the recently excavated tomb of Pope Alexander I (105–115) in April, Pius stopped at the convent of Sant Agnese for lunch. When an enthusiastic crowd surged to greet him, they were startled by the sound of sagging beams as the entire group, including the pope and Antonelli, were hurled into the room below. Miraculously, not one of the hundred and thirty who fell suffered any physical harm, even though the fall had profound psychological repercussions with some predicting it represented a prophecy of the impending fall of the papacy. Within a matter of months, in June 1855, his secretary of state, Antonelli once again escaped death by foiling an assassination attempt on his life.

Napoleon III expressed his condolences, but neither regretted nor abandoned his plan to reorganize Italy and reduce and restructure the papal state. The conduct and course pursued by the pope spurred the French emperor's determination to effect change in Rome. He was especially angered by Pio Nono's obstinate refusal to return the Jewish child, Edgardo Mortara, to his parents. The boy, who had been secretly baptized by a Christian domestic in Bologna during a serious childhood illness, was now considered a Christian by some. In June of 1858, when word of the baptism reached papal authorities, the seven-year-old was forcibly taken from his parents—a move sanctioned and supported by the pope. The seizure, branded a kidnapping in liberal circles, created a worldwide sensation and aroused the tribunal of European public opinion, casting a shadow on the papal government and its French protector. Pius IX was unmoved by the adverse public reaction to the kidnapping and resented the pleas of the French and other members of the international community to return the child to his parents. In fact, the loud criticism of papal action only firmed his resolve, leading him to conclude that the course he pursued was righteous.

Napoleon III strongly disagreed, and soon had his revenge. At a clandestine conference at Plombieres, in late July 1858, the frustrated French emperor and the wily Count Cavour plotted a war against Austria as well as a substantial diminution of the papal state. Although Napoleon approved the Piedmontese plan for the reconstruction of Northern Italy, he advised treating the pope with circumspection, determined not to repeat the frontal attack on the papacy launched by his uncle. Pius was to retain Rome and its environs and compensated for his loss of the Legations with the presidency of the Italian confederation Louis Napoleon envisioned. Rome was not consulted. Suspecting the worst, Pius regretted the dire sound of war between Catholic nations, resorting to prayer to avoid the catastrophe. His prayers remained unanswered, as Austria found herself at war with Piedmont and France by early May 1859. Although the French Emperor promised to champion the cause of the Holy See and preserve the sovereignty of the Holy Father, he determined to do so on his own terms. His promises, like those of King Victor Emmanuel's to resolve the problems of the church in his state, remained largely unfulfilled.

Following the French victory at Magenta on June 4, 1859 during the Franco-Piedmontese war against Austria, Habsburg garrisons were withdrawn from north central Italy, enabling revolutionaries in Bologna to form a provisional government. Napoleon temporarily prevented the Piedmontese annexation of the Romagna, but his commitment to preserve it for the papacy proved problematic. Pius was therefore constrained to resort to his spiritual arsenal, warning Victor Emmanuel that he would fall under censure should new attacks be launched against the church. The admonition did not avert the further dismantling of the papal state, leading the pope to excommunicate those who had provoked the rebellion and seizure of a good part of his state. Pius resolutely rejected Napoleon's and Victor Emmanuel's suggestions that the Romagna be placed under Piedmontese protection or any solution that diminished or compromised his temporal power in any manner.[6] His intransigence did not prevent the usurpation and further seizure of papal territory. These losses hardened the pope's heart against the *Risorgimento,* the movement for Italian unification, which he condemned not only for the theft of his state but also for its rebellion against the church. Convinced that a concerted campaign was being waged against the papacy, Pio Nono issued more than a dozen condemnations of Count Camillo Benso di Cavour and his colleagues who fostered Italian unification, rebuking every project that might be construed as approval of Piedmontese activity in papal territory. He also refused to reconcile himself with the progress, liberalism, and nationalism of contemporary civilization, which he believed not only sanctioned but encouraged the rebellion and seizure of his state.[7]

Following the incorporation of the greater part of the papal states into the Kingdom of Italy in 1861, the papacy lost many of the rural estates from which it derived the bulk of its income and faced fiscal ruin as well as political collapse. Only the revival and reorganization of Peter's Pence undertaken by the Papal Secretary of State, Cardinal Giacomo Antonelli, and his financially astute brother Filippo Antonelli, saved the day by calling upon the faithful worldwide to ease the financial burdens of the papacy. Despite this miraculous fiscal rescue, the future of the papacy remained precarious, contributing to Pio Nono's intransigent stance and determination to bolster his spiritual authority as his temporal power was progressively undermined.

Rejecting the call of those who counseled reconciliation with progress and liberalism, Pius cited his need and responsibility to preserve intact the immovable and indestructible principles of eternal justice, attacking the modern philosophies and those who championed them. However, his admonitions and excommunications did not restrain or deter the Piedmontese, who in February 1861 abrogated the Neapolitan concordat, once the Kingdom had been absorbed into the new Italy. In March 1861, Count Cavour proclaimed Rome, preserved for the papacy by French military forces, the future Italian capital. "Holy Father, the temporal power is no longer a guarantee of independence for you," Cavour announced in parliament, "Renounce it and . . . we are ready to proclaim throughout Italy . . . this great principle: a free church in a free state."[8] Pius distrusted the program and promises of Cavour and his colleagues, and the nationalist banner that sought to justify the seizure of his state and future acquisition of his capital. Not surprisingly, relations between the Vatican and the newly proclaimed Kingdom of Italy remained strained, provoking the Roman Question—the papal refusal to recognize the loss of its territory. Rumors of a negotiated settlement between Rome and Italy proved unfounded. Pius protested that there could be no conciliation between truth and error, between the forces of light and darkness.[9] From his perspective the present offered a dual spectacle of pain and bitterness. His prediction that things would further deteriorate for the papacy and the church, before they got better, proved prophetic as a series of other problems plagued the papacy.

The 1860s proved troublesome for the papacy as well as a number of the powers. Across the Atlantic in the United States, the prospect of civil war loomed large as both North and South pondered the prospect of European intervention in the impending conflict. "The Church of Rome, notwithstanding its difficulties, wields, as you are aware, an immense power in Europe and the British Empire," the Resident Minister in Rome, Alexander W. Randall, informed the American Secretary of State, William H. Seward.[10] While Lincoln and Seward recognized the primacy of developments in London and Paris, they did not neglect Rome, which might influence the decisions made by these and other capitals. Seward sought to win the goodwill of the papacy by informing the Holy See that both the American state and the papal state found themselves in difficult situations, and thus shared a special relationship. He implored Rome not to interfere in their conflict, promising that they, in turn, would not interfere in the states of the church. Cardinal Antonelli reassured Seward by responding that Catholics in the United States individually and collectively would not interfere in their civil war adding that "the government of his Holiness concerns itself mainly in spiritual matters."[11] Antonelli adhered to this stance not only for ideological reasons but also for political considerations, having to contend with problems closer to home that threatened to undermine the last rump of the papal state.

At the beginning of January 1862, the papal secretary of state received the newly appointed minister to Rome, William J. Stillman. Burdened by a host of problems as he struggled to retain the last remnant of the temporal power, Antonelli sympathized and empathized with the problems faced by the American Union, which faced a large scale rebellion that degenerated into a civil war. His state, like the American one, had to be sensitive to the steps taken by outside powers whose actions might adversely influence the course of events. Assessing the American situation, Antonelli contemplated the positions that London and Paris might assume in their civil war. Obviously upset by the English approval of Italian unification and their recognition of the Kingdom of Italy, Antonelli warned the Americans of the English readiness to take advantage of the misery of others. They had to be closely watched in the Americas, in Europe, and elsewhere and discouraged from meddling worldwide.

Nor did the Cardinal have any kind words for Napoleon III, or reveal any gratitude toward the figure whose troops kept the Italians out of Rome and in papal hands. Antonelli's distrust of Napoleon was fueled by the part he had played in promoting Piedmont's national ambitions to the detriment of the temporal patrimony. His distrust was shared by others, who warned the Americans to watch his movements closely, and these warnings worked to influence American diplomacy. "As to the part of the Emperor of the French in American affairs," Stillman wrote Seward, Antonelli told him "that he was a man of opportunity and that his strength was in taking advantage of the blunders of other governments, and that he would avail himself of any we should make as of those which England made."[12] Dr. Evans, the French Emperor's American dentist as well as others, reported that Napoleon was surrounded by those sympathetic to the South, and bribes were offered to those who might influence the French to recognize the confederacy.[13] While personally favoring the South and invoking a joint Anglo-French intervention in the American Civil War, Napoleon shied from a unilateral recognition of the Confederacy and the prospect of war this might engender. France, the French emperor felt, was already overcommitted in its diplomatic and military missions and bogged down in Italian affairs.

Although Napoleon III felt constrained to cater to Gallic pride and sense of grandeur by pursuing a dynamic foreign policy, on numerous occasions he regretted having plunged into Italian and papal politics. He confided to the English representative at Rome, Odo Russell, that he committed his greatest political blunder when he sanctioned the French expedition of 1849 that toppled Mazzini's Republic, restored the papal regime, and embroiled him in the politics of Rome and the *Risorgimento*. Desirous, indeed anxious to withdraw his garrison from the Eternal City and its environs, a series of circumstances conspired to keep it there. His foreign minister, Edouard Thouvenel, likewise wished to withdraw French forces from Rome and find some solution to the Roman Question, but noted "It would be an absurd and a dishonest policy to protect the pope during 12 years and withdraw that protection when he was most in need of it."[14] Thus France, burdened with the task of preserving the remnant of the papal state, found its range of political and military activities limited by these Italian and papal commitments. This worked for the benefit of the Washington government, which sought to prevent French intervention in its Civil War.

In the summer of 1862, when there were increasingly loud and persistent calls for French intervention in the American conflict, Napoleon III found himself under verbal assault by Giuseppe Garibaldi, who called upon Italians to push the French out of Rome. Indeed, in August 1862, with the complicity of the Italian government and under the slogan of "Rome or Death," his forces marched from Calabria toward Rome, posing a serious problem for the French forces that protected the pope. Alarmed by the prospect of having to subdue the popular Garibaldi, Napoleon pressured the Italian government to stop his volunteers at Aspromonte, in southern Calabria. Victor Emmanuel II, who had secretly encouraged the venture, privately complained about the French intervention. This, too, worked to the advantage of the Union. The American Resident Minister at Rome wrote Seward that the French emperor was in trouble at home and abroad. "The Catholic nations, outside of France, watch him and the Catholic Cardinals, Bishops, and Priests in France watch him," he reported, adding "He will not interfere in our affairs."[15] His assessment proved accurate.

In 1862, Edouard Thouvenel, who had assumed a hard line toward the Union blockade and the Northern government, was forced to leave the foreign office over disagreements concerning French policy in Italy and Rome. According to Odo Russell, who represented England at the court of Rome, he was removed from office to satisfy the demands of the papal government.[16] Napoleon acknowledged that the volatile and serious situation in Italy required his close, if not constant attention, and therefore he could not unilaterally recognize the Confederacy. Such a step would have embroiled him with the United States at a time when he had major responsibilities elsewhere, particularly in the papal states. Hoping to extricate himself from the Roman cauldron, which limited his freedom of action, Napoleon asked Pius IX to renounce the territory incorporated into the Kingdom of Italy and limit himself to those territories the French safeguarded. The pope once again refused the request, which he found offensive, making Napoleon's position all the more difficult. For supporting such a compromise, the French ruler had aroused the suspicion of Catholics in France—thereby weakening his political power. Napoleon belatedly recognized that Rome's diplomatic course was difficult to chart, and even more difficult to control. The confederacy would learn this firsthand.

In the fall of 1862, Pius IX dispatched letters to the archbishops of New York and New Orleans, urging them to make every effort to bring about peace in North America and end the civil conflict. Taking advantage of this opening and hoping to use it to attain papal recognition of their independent status, Jefferson Davis, President of the Confederate States, sent Dudley Mann with a letter dated September 23, 1863, thanking the pope for his efforts to achieve reconciliation. "The letters which your Holiness addressed to the venerable chiefs of the Catholic clergy in New Orleans and New York have been brought to my attention," wrote Davis, noting that he like the pope decried "the devastation consequent on the war now being waged . . . against the people over which I have been chosen to preside."[17] Mann arrived in Rome on November 10, 1863, obtained an interview with Cardinal Antonelli the following day and on November 13 met with the pope who told him that he would do what he could "in putting an end to this most terrible war. . . ."[18] In December Pius responded to the letter of Jefferson Davis, deploring the cruel and internecine war and hoping for its speedy conclusion. Since it was addressed to the "Illustrious and Honorable Jefferson Davis, President of the Confederate States of America," the Southern commissioner was ecstatic, deeming the papal letter a positive recognition of the Confederacy.[19] Antonelli, who heard the assertion, quickly cleared the confederate representative of that illusion, observing that the papal use of the term President of the Confederate States was purely descriptive, without political implications.[20] The embattled secretary of state noted that Rome confronted considerable problems at home, and therefore could not and would not become embroiled in the American Civil War.

Despite this supportive stance and friendly attitude of the Vatican to the federal government, in 1867 the American mission to Rome came to an end when the Congress refused to fund the appropriation for its continued existence. The pretext for the congressional action was that the papal government had ordered the American Protestant Church outside the walls of Rome. Unquestionably, other factors influenced the closing of this mission including: anti-Catholicism and religious bigotry in many states of the Union, the conflict between the President and Congress, as well as American support for the Italian acquisition of Rome as the Italian capital. Legally, the congressional action left the mission in existence but unable to function without funding; no explanation was ever provided the papal government. The papal consulate in the United States was likewise never officially terminated. This would play a positive role in the latter part of the twentieth century when relations were finally restored. For some 70 years, however, there were no formal diplomatic relations between the Vatican and Washington.

Confederate diplomacy, having obtained little from Rome, looked once again to Napoleon III, whose forces had occupied Mexico City in June 1863, and who had signed the convention of Miramar, with Maximilian, the brother of the Austrian Emperor, who he had placed on the Mexican throne. The Confederate agents promised to accept Napoleon's establishment of a virtual satellite in Mexico—which the Union was known to oppose—in return for French recognition of the Confederacy. Napoleon was sorely tempted, but was still troubled by events in Italy and what remained of the papal state, which continued to cast a shadow over his freedom of action. To liberate himself from these obligations and burdens, he sought a negotiated solution of the Roman Question with the Turin government. Thus, in mid-September 1864 the Italian government concluded the September Convention with the French Empire to settle the Roman Question and from the French perspective enhance its freedom of action elsewhere. In return for a French withdrawal from the Eternal City within two years, the Italians pledged not to attack Rome and its immediate environs and to prevent others from doing so from its territory. Fortunately for the Americans its implementation would take some time. Napoleon's ability to intervene in their civil war was compromised by French involvement in Mexican and Italian affairs for the next several years. Although no formal commitment was made in the September Convention to renounce their quest for Rome, the Italians promised to move their capital from Turin to Florence—a signal for some that they had abandoned their determination to make the Eternal City their capital.

Suspicious of the men and the mentality that had sanctioned the seizure of his state in the formation of the Italian Kingdom, Pius IX discounted their written promises and commitments almost as much as their verbal assurances. Distrusting the liberal and national doctrines of the French and Italians who had signed the accord, he determined to formally denounce the prevailing values and underlying philosophies that he believed sought to undermine the spiritual and temporal power of the church. This condemnation was cataloged in the encyclical *Quanta cura* of December 8, 1864, to which was appended a Syllabus of Errors, listing 80 errors drawn from previous papal documents. *Quanta cura* at once denounced these modern heretical movements and beliefs while reaffirming papal authority and ecclesiastical independence vis-à-vis the civil authority.

In 10 categories the Syllabus railed against indifferentism, or the conviction that religious differences were of no significance and that all religions were equally acceptable, and the related latitudinarianism, which disregarded differences of doctrine in the various Christian churches: materialism, naturalism, pantheism, as well as rationalism. They were all rejected as incompatible with Catholicism. Socialism and communism were likewise censured for their conflict with the faith, as were the mistaken notions concerning the papacy's temporal power. However, the Syllabus transcended the religious sphere to plunge into the most controversial problems of political thought and practices of the day especially in the sections cataloging the "Errors of Civil Society" and the "Errors Having Reference to Modern Liberalism."[21] Pius rejected the notion that the national state be accorded the highest priority in the hierarchy of values. His refusal to seek reconciliation with "progress, liberalism, and civilization as lately introduced" critics charged, revealed the absurdity of the papal position. Napoleon III, aware that much of the Syllabus was directed against his Italian policy, proclaimed it "contrary to the Principles of the Constitution of the Empire." Although Pius IX had inspired both the encyclical and the attached Syllabus, Antonelli was burdened with the responsibility of pacifying the outraged French protector of the Papal States and the European-wide protests provoked by the papal documents. Pius IX was not restrained nor silenced by the whirlwind of criticism directed against his encyclical and appended Syllabus and in the following year condemned and damned the Masonic sects.

While the pope worried about the dangers threatening the church, his secretary of state dreaded the prospect of an impending war between Austria and Prussia for control of Germany, fearing the Italians would embroil themselves therein to make a move against either Venice or Rome—both excluded from the Kingdom of Italy proclaimed in 1861. Fortunately for Antonelli, the Italians opted for Venice in the treaty promising to enter the war on Prussia's side, and did so in June 1866. Although the Italians were defeated by the Austrians both on land (Custozza) and on sea (Lissa), the Prussians decisively defeated the Austrians in the battle of Sadowa (July 3, 1866)—which undermined the Habsburg position both in Germany and Italy. Antonelli was distraught that this Catholic power, which had hitherto helped curb Italian expansion and aggression, had been defeated and pushed out of the peninsula. Recognizing the unfortunate consequences of the Habsbug defeat for the Papal State, Antonelli cried out "Casca il mondo" (the world is collapsing).

The papal dilemma was compounded by the impending withdrawal of French troops from Rome under the terms of the September Convention. Distrusting the Italian promises to protect the remaining papal territory from intruders, Pius claimed this was tantamount to having the wolves guard the sheep. Informed by the French Ministry of Foreign Affairs that he should not worry because Napoleon was there, Pius responded "And I am here . . . and everyone knows that Paris is quite far from Rome."[22] Antonelli, who relied on the goodwill of the French, proved less acerbic and more accommodating than his master. It was his diplomacy that brought French forces back to the Papal State in October–November 1867, when the Italian government failed to honor the September Convention and stop another of Garibaldi's incursions into papal territory, at Mentana on the outskirts of Rome. Thus the French forces that had only departed from the peninsula in 1866, returned to Rome in 1867.

The conciliatory stance and diplomatic pragmatism of Antonelli that sought to preserve the rump of the papal state was constantly undermined by the pope's intransigence and determination to pursue his crusade against the modern errors of the age. He continued to rail against the seizure of his territory, the atrocities of the irreligious and subversive press, the license accorded men of ill will, and especially the restrictions imposed upon the church by state and society. Unwilling to consider any solution to the Roman Question that did provide for the unconditional and complete restitution of the provinces and property of the Holy See, the pope concentrated upon religious issues where he could more readily impose his will. Conservatives such as Cardinal Luigi Lambruschini had earlier advised Pius to convoke a council to confront the problems burdening the church in a secular age, and Pius had seriously considered the prospect since his exile at Gaeta in 1849. He postponed but never abandoned the project. On December 6, 1864, days before issuing the Syllabus of Errors, Pius consulted the cardinals in curia on the subject. While two opposed the notion, and half a dozen more expressed reservations, most favored the proposal.[23] On June 29, 1868, the papal bull *Aeterni patris* fixed the opening of the church council for December 8, 1869, the feast of the Immaculate Conception, in the Basilica of Saint Peter. News of its impending convocation caused consternation among some of the powers who feared the resulting political consequences.

The pope considered the council necessary to strengthen the church, rendering it better able to cope with the perceived onslaughts against it.[24] His apostolic letter cited the need to unmask the enemies of Christian society, and release it from the grasp of satanic forces. The bull of convocation repeated that the main purpose of the council was to save the church and society from the threatening calamities, correct if not extirpate modern errors, revising ecclesiastical legislation to do so.[25] This focus was reflected in the papal decision not to invite the Catholic powers to participate in the council as they had in the past, arousing suspicion in the excluded European courts. Pius IX, distressed by the political developments of the age, determined to prevent the interjection and interference of diplomats in church affairs.[26] This aroused suspicion in the European courts, whose concerns were aggravated when the Jesuit journal *La Civiltà Cattolica*, with close ties to the Vatican, cited the prospect that the council would proclaim papal infallibility, asserting that when the pope spoke from his chair, he was infallible. Reportedly, Pius supported infallibility, claiming that before becoming pope he believed in it, but once pope, felt it.[27] To make matters worse for the powers, the Jesuit journal hinted that the council would also approve by acclamation the admonitions of the Syllabus of Errors, rebuking state policies and denouncing a series of contemporary principles and practices.

News of the impending council and its possible proclamation of papal infallibility created consternation among the European states. The prospect of papal infallibility especially alarmed the Italians, who feared it would prove detrimental to their national interests by provoking further religious conflict and encouraging internal dissent and division. In Germany, which had witnessed an emergence of a scientific party in the Catholic Church under the leadership of Johann von Döllinger, grave doubts and reservations were also expressed about the consequences of the projected papal infallibility. In France, liberal Catholics and champions of Gallicanism united in an extraordinary alliance to oppose such a proclamation. The chancelleries of Europe shared their apprehension, especially after word spread that an infallible pope would even claim the right to depose sovereigns and overturn governments popes had in the middle ages.

In Catholic Bavaria, the minister-president called upon the courts to take joint action to preclude a proclamation of papal infallibility, which he deemed dangerous and an unwarranted intrusion into the political arena. These steps distressed the pope, who made it clear that he favored the proclamation. When the French Cardinal Henri Marie Gaston de Bonnechose expressed his reservations about infallibility, an irritated pope supposedly responded, "Your Eminence has always been in opposition," adding, "I remember . . . you were opposed to raising the doctrine of the

Immaculate Conception to a dogma, but thank God, we willed that it should be so, and it was so; and we will that the infallibility of the Pope shall be made a dogma, and it shall become one through the influence of the Council of 1869."[28] To those within the church who opposed infallibility on the basis of tradition, Pius supposedly responded "I am tradition."[29] Neither was the pope deterred by the reservations of the Paris and Vienna governments, nor the political concerns of his own secretary of state, who feared it would further isolate Rome. "I have the Blessed Virgin on my side," Pius retorted, "I will go ahead."[30]

The five committees of the Council devised 51 categories for consideration, and eventually two were discussed *Dei Filius* (on God, Revelation, Faith, and Reason) and *De ecclesia* (on the church). The former, adopted by a unanimous vote on April 24, 1870, condemned various aspects of modern civilization including: atheism, materialism, naturalism, pantheism, and rationalism, elaborating the doctrines that these errors violated. *De ecclesia Christi,* contained three chapters on the pope's primacy, and one on his infallibility. Pius was increasingly disturbed by the opponents of infallibility and resented the obstacles placed in the path of the definition he desired. Few were surprised when Pius agreed to give precedence to consideration of the powers of the pope, removing it from its sequence in the face of the opposition of the minority, and the reservations of many in the majority, but to the delight of the infallibilists. From May 13 to July 4, when the debate ended, there were over 160 speeches for and against the proposed dogma. On the final vote of July 18, 1870, 535 assented to infallibility, while only two voted against it: the Bishop of Little Rock, Edward Fitzgerald, and the Bishop of Caizzo, Luigi Riccio. The dogma proclaimed that the Roman pontiff, when he speaks *ex cathedra,* that is, in discharge of the office and doctor of all Christians, by virtue of his supreme Apostolic authority, is possessed of the infallibility that the divine Redeemer willed to his church.[31]

Critics in the church, Protestant circles, and the powers deplored the prospect of papal abuse provided by infallibility that they likened to a Pandora's box, which they charged enthroned clerical absolutism, retarded progress, and weakened the sovereignty of the states and the influence of the bishops. Pius denied these and other allegations, while his secretary of state, Antonelli insisted that the proclamation had not introduced anything new and threatened neither the authority of the bishops nor that of the civil power. These reassurances did not quiet the outcry that continued even following the outbreak of the Franco-Prussian War, July 19, 1870, and the evacuation of French forces from Rome, following the French defeat at Sedan, September 1–2, 1870. A host of grave problems faced the pope following the defeat of a great Catholic empire at the hands of a Protestant power. The capture of Napoleon and fall of the empire, the unification of Germany by Protestant Prussia, the withdrawal of Austria from German as well as Italian affairs, the internal crisis in Spain, and the Italian determination to seize Rome and make it their capital, all represented impending or potential dangers for the papacy. The Vatican found itself defenseless against the nationalist claims and territorial aspirations of the Kingdom of Italy, finding no power willing to preserve Rome for the papacy by stepping into the vacuum left by the departing French forces.

The Italians were quick to take advantage of the vulnerable position of the pope dispatching an "army of observation" to central Italy under General Raffaele Cadorna, with the obvious intention of seizing Rome and making it their capital. Early in September, Italian forces crossed the frontier while Victor Emanuel's envoy to the pope, Count Ponza di San Martino, brought a letter from the king justifying the occupation and annexation of what remained of his state. Pius could not concur that Victor Emmanuel's words reflected the affection of a son, the loyalty of a king, or the faith of a Catholic, rejecting his claim that he needed to act to secure Italy and the Holy See. "Nice words, but ugly deeds" the pope muttered as he rejected the king's explanation and rationalization.[32] "I bless God, who has permitted that Your Majesty should fill the last years of my life with bitterness," Pius wrote Victor Emmanuel, adding "I cannot admit the requests contained in your letter nor support the principles contained therein."[33] This rejection did not prevent the Italians from bursting into the Eternal City on September 20, 1870, nor from incorporating Rome and its nearby provinces into the Kingdom of Italy on October 9, 1870. In response Pius suspended the meeting of the Ecumenical Council and locked himself in the Vatican, proclaiming himself a prisoner therein, adamantly refusing to recognize the Kingdom of Italy that at this juncture had absorbed his entire state. He was convinced that the war was being waged not only against him but against Christ, and though the church had lost a battle, it would eventually emerge triumphant.[34]

The Italian occupation and annexation of Rome did arouse worldwide concern for the position of the papacy, even though no state was then prepared to intervene and restore the status quo. To allay the fears of the international community, the Italian government in 1871 brought forward the Law of Papal Guarantees that proclaimed the inviolability of the pope, investing him with all the attributes of sovereignty—save the temporal power. In fine, the principle adopted, though not fully implemented, was the Cavourian notion of a separation of church and state.[35] The authors of this legislation were disciples of Cavour, who died in June 1861, but they proved unable to completely effect the separation he had championed. Article 16 of the law did abolish the *exequatur* or governmental permission to publish papal documents in their state and the *placet* that provided permission to implement them, eliminating governmental authorization for the execution of most ecclesiastical decisions.[36] However, the abolition of the *exequatur* for the allocation of benefices required legislation that did not follow, so bishops could not assume the temporalities of their See until they secured royal approval. Pius resented this and other features of the Law of Guarantees, deriding the financial compensation of 3,225,000 lire annually for the loss of his territory, as a bribe for his silence. Consequently, what the Italian government presented to the powers as positive protection for the papacy, Pius denounced as a "monument of barbarous ignorance."

Pius rejected this legislation in a letter of May 15, 1871, and in his speech to the College of Cardinals on October 27, 1871.[37] He insisted that events had painfully shown that the sole guarantee for the papacy was the possession of its own civil power, free from the control of all states; any other alleged guarantee or promise of security was simply an illusion he would not and could not accept. As head of a universal church, he was unwilling to serve as the chaplain to the House of Savoy, fearing that without his own state, he would be subject, or appear to be subject, to the Italian government. Pius explained the basis of his intransigent opposition to Cardinal Costantino Patrizi, his vicar general in Rome, and to his Secretary of State, Cardinal Giacomo Antonelli. Any concession, he told Patrizi, implied power over the person to whom it is granted, and the pope could not tolerate this subordinate status. "It is not enough that he (the pope) is for the moment materially free," he informed Antonelli, "he must be and appear free and independent in the exercise of his supreme authority."[38] His appeals to the powers to assist him in his struggle with the Italians went unanswered, to the consternation of pope and curia. Unwilling to compromise his rights and status, Pius finally relied on divine intervention to come to the aid of his Vicar. "It is useless to talk of conciliation," he told a group of visitors at the end of November 1871 "for the Church can never conciliate itself with error, and the Pope cannot separate himself from the Church."[39]

Neither the prayers of the pope nor the diplomatic maneuvers of Antonelli brought the intervention of the European powers to restore the temporal power as they had in 1849, for the diplomatic situation had changed dramatically. Pius blamed the powers, who he believed had for selfish reasons abandoned the papacy and the church. Once again Pius failed to understand the present political realities, unwilling or unable to recognize that their failure to intervene was due in part to the difficult internal conditions of these states, as well as the new international configuration. The Kingdom of Naples no longer existed, having been absorbed by the Italian Kingdom; Spain continued to confront crises and chaos at home, which prevented any diplomatic or military initiative; the hastily formed Republic in France was plagued by serious internal difficulties and political strife following the defeat at the hands of the Germans; while the recently defeated Austrians were adjusting to their newly instituted dual monarchy and Austro-Hungarian organization. Otto von Bismarck's largely Protestant German Empire, in turn, was determined to preserve the friendship of the Italian Kingdom and was not prepared to jeopardize it by assisting the papacy. Furthermore, Bismarck feared that the Catholic Center Party and the largely Catholic and separatist South German states represented potential threats to the integrity of the newly constituted state. To make matters worse for Pius IX, widespread suspicion of the proclamation of papal infallibility prevailed in Europe and abroad and was particularly strong in Austria-Hungary, Switzerland, and Germany. Following the proclamation of the German Empire, the German Chancellor Bismarck, accustomed to having his own way, found the pope difficult if not impossible to deal with, and warned his representatives abroad of the problems he presented.[40]

Pius, for his part, was less than pleased by Protestant Prussia, which had defeated Catholic Austria and France, and had unified Germany. As usual the outspoken pope did not hide his sentiments. Addressing a group of visitors from Alsace, Pius revealed his displeasure at their incorporation into largely Protestant Germany and hoped that their new masters would leave them alone—particularly as regards religion. "It is better to be grieved by Catholic King," he blurted out, "than by an Emperor of another religion." He advised them to resign themselves for the time "and await the day of His mercy."[41] He urged a delegation of Catholic women from the Reich to pray for him, the church, and Europe, which was in the midst of a terrible convulsion.[42] While such talk was welcomed in Paris, it angered and aroused Berlin. Furthermore, the re-formation of the Center Party of 51 Catholic deputies in the Landtag, or lower house of the Prussian parliament, in January 1871, and the appearance of 61 of its members in the Imperial Reichstag, ignited suspicion of the church in Berlin.

The German regime retaliated by showing itself sympathetic to Döllinger and the old Catholic movement, which broke with Rome on the question of papal infallibility. Pius was upset by the favoritism shown to these apostates as well as to a number of priests and teachers in Germany who had refused to subscribe to infallibility, and were not dismissed from their posts by the government. He also deplored the government's unilateral decision to abolish the Catholic section of the Prussian Ministry of Public Worship. The campaign against the church continued in Germany and towards the close of 1871, the "pulpit paragraph" was passed, imposing penalties, including imprisonment, upon the clergy for criticism of the Reich and its constitution from the pulpit. There was also imperial legislation against the Society of Jesus. A bill was passed banning non-German Jesuits from the Empire while it curtailed the activities of German members of the order. Together these measures virtually eliminated the Jesuits from Germany.

The differences and difficulties between the Vatican and Berlin became public when Cardinal Gustav Adolf zu Hohenlohe, who had been friendly to Döllinger at the Council, was named Berlin's representative to the Holy See. The pope refused to accept this appointment, deeming it detrimental to the church, the Holy See, the pope, as well as the Cardinal himself. Disturbed by the papal rejection and Vatican pretensions, an angry Bismarck denounced their arrogance in the Reichstag on May 14, 1872, threatening to wage war against the Jesuits, the Ultramontanes, and even the church if necessary. Bismarck's call to conflict was quickly supported by the National Liberals, who noted the chasm that existed between their liberal and national culture and the outmoded traditionalism of the church, which had produced the Syllabus of Errors and papal infallibility. This clash of cultures was dubbed the *Kulturkampf,* pitting the modern culture of the German empire against the medieval mentality of the Catholic church. Pius now faced grave problems in Germany as well as Italy as the "iron chancellor" and his National Liberal allies prepared for battle. In fact, Germany was only second to Italy in creating problems for the Vatican during the last years of Pio Nono's long and troubled papacy.

After the liberal Adalbert Falk, became the Prussian minister of ecclesiastical affairs and education in 1872, legislation was passed in Prussia in May 1873 limiting the role of religion in education. These restrictive measures, which seemed to be directed against the Catholic Church, were quickly dubbed the May Laws or Falk Laws. Among other things this legislation required state control over the education of the clergy, according the state the right to approve all candidates for the priesthood. Rejecting the Holy See's centralization, the laws mandated that Catholics could not acknowledge any ecclesiastical disciplinary power outside of Prussia. Even seminaries were to fall under state scrutiny and their curricula subject to state supervision.[43] Another of the May Laws forbade Catholics in Prussia from having recourse to any court outside their state, while two other measures restricted publication of church decrees, facilitating the task of those who sought to leave the church.

Pius was outraged by this German "persecution" instructing visitors from the Reich that God wanted truth to prevail and false teaching to be combated.[44] In an address at the end of 1872, he condemned not only the abominations perpetrated by Catholic Italy but also those devised in the largely Protestant German empire. "Men who not only do not profess our holy religion but who do not even know it," Pius bitterly complained, "dare to arrogate to themselves the power to determine her dogmas and rights."[45] The pope encouraged German Catholics to resist these unwarranted, intrusive measures and wrote the German emperor, imploring his intervention.[46] William's response was less than conciliatory, insisting that the ecclesiastical legislation was rendered necessary by the action of his Catholic subjects, who with the support of the bishops, had assumed a defiant position vis-à-vis the state. An oblique reference to the Center Party, which the Emperor Bismarck and the Liberals initially opposed. William's rejoinder called upon Pius to end the controversy, presumably by accepting and adhering to these measures.[47] Pius, who had refused to compromise with the liberals and nationalists in Italy, proved equally unwilling to compromise with the German harassment. The German bishops, with papal support, refused to adhere to the obnoxious legislation, sacrilegious laws, and blatant repression launched against the church and its clergy—provoking the arrest and banishment of priests and bishops throughout the Reich.

In November 1873, the pope bewailed the closing of monasteries in Rome and the oppression of the faith in Germany.[48] Decrying the arrest and banishment of hundreds of priests and many of Germany's bishops, the closing of churches, the confiscation of their property, and the crippling of Catholic education in the Reich, Pius did not despair. He was heartened by the resistance of the faithful, the clergy, and the Center Party to the assault upon the church in Prussia and the German Empire. The pope scornfully rejected Berlin's overtures that he moderate the opposition of the Center Party to Bismarck's government, whose policies he deplored. This led the exasperated chancellor to attempt to influence the election of a more moderate successor, without much success for the pope, now in his eighties, proved robust as well as contentious.[49] In retaliation the persecution of the Catholic Church and clergy in Germany was increased. In 1874 the Prussian embassy to the Vatican was closed, most religious orders were suppressed, and church property placed under lay control. Pio Nono responded to the persecution in the Reich by urging German Catholics to stand firm against it, as he stood firm against the Italian revolution, promising that eventually the church would triumph over these new enemies as it had over others in the past.[50]

Convinced that a war was being waged against the church and her clergy under the mantle of modernization, Pius condemned the heretical liberal and nationalist doctrines, and those who preached them, refusing compromise and conciliation. Following the loss of his trusted ally, Antonelli, in November 1876—he abandoned diplomacy more completely. In naming his successor Cardinal Giovanni Simeoni, he indicated that a new type of secretary of state was needed, one who would focus on pastoral rather than political matters and concern himself primarily with religious issues. This had a negative impact across the Atlantic where there was some discussion in the last years of Pio Nono's pontificate on the need for some papal representative in the United States. In light of the anti-Catholic sentiment, which remained widespread, it was deemed best to appoint an Apostolic Delegate, who was the pope's personal representative to the faithful, clergy and laity alike, rather than a representative to the civil or national government. Such an appointment was discussed by the Congregation for the Propagation of the Faith in January 1877, and supported by Bishop George Conroy of Ireland, dispatched to North America in 1878. However, the proposal was not then implemented.

The old pope felt betrayed by the politics of the present, warning that the lay state posed a danger to the salvation of its subjects, refusing to sacrifice principle to expediency. He continued to adhere to the vision of a confessional state, which would protect the "one true faith" and combat indifferentism and religious equality. However, by 1876 even Catholic Spain had abandoned this traditionalist quest. Pius especially decried the deplorable consequences flowing from the triumph of the modern doctrines in Italy and Germany, and the harm inflicted on the faith in Central Europe. Nonetheless, Pius did not despair, finding consolation in the fact that the persecution had not weakened but reinvigorated the faith of believers. Although Pius deplored the current state of affairs and the injury sustained by the church, he remained confident that eventually God would set matters straight by punishing the wicked and aiding the just.[51] He, himself, perceived no possible compromise between the liberal and national notions of the so-called modern world and the traditional faith, between Christ and Satan, light with darkness, the claims of science and the dogmas of religion. Pius remained intransigent to the end, so that following his death the chasm between the church and the modern world remained wide. His successors would have to provide some sort of reconciliation.

The Papacy Confronts Social Issues, Modernism, and International Relations, 1878–1914

Throughout much of the latter half of the nineteenth century, the Holy See's involvement in international affairs remained rather limited, with its diplomatic role largely restricted to the futile attempt first to preserve, and later to regain, the temporal power. The Vatican steadfastly refused to recognize the Italian seizure of the papal state or abandon its "lost cause," giving rise to the Roman Question. Pius IX, who came into conflict with the modern world by his Syllabus of Errors (1864), and Proclamation of Papal Infallibility (1870), and finally shut himself in the Vatican as a self-proclaimed prisoner, did little to enhance the global presence of the papacy, whose relations with a number of states was troubled. In fact, in 1878, the year of Pius IX's death, the Vatican preserved relations with only 15 countries: seven were western European and the remaining eight were in South America.[1] Many perceived the church as enclosed in a self-imposed ghetto, as the international posture of the papacy reached its nadir.

In Italy Pio Nono's *non expedit*, eventually converted into a prohibition or *non licit* forbidding the faithful from voting or running in national elections, challenged the legitimacy of the Liberal State but also isolated Catholics. Papal support for the lost monarchical cause in the third French Republic, fueled the anticlericalism of the republicans, and likewise proved detrimental to the church. In Belgium, part of the clergy continued to oppose the separation of church and state provided by their constitution, while in Prussia and Germany the *Kulturkampf*, which had prevailed for some seven years, continued to burden the Catholic minority. Papal relations with Austria and Switzerland remained far from cordial. The news from across the Atlantic was little better as the Vatican received reports of enormous debts accumulated by the church in the United States and warnings of the independence claimed by part of its clergy.[2] In 1867 the American diplomatic mission to Rome officially ended, when the American Congress refused to renew the appropriation for its continuation. In Canada, the French Canadian clergy aroused opposition by their anticonstitutional stance, while in much of Latin America anticlericalism still prevailed. Contemporaries concluded that the new pope would be confronted with major challenges.[3] A sentiment shared by a good part of the 60 member conclave of 1878, the first following the papacy's loss of Rome.

The conclave, which opened February 18, 1878, found its members divided, with a majority rejecting the call to convene outside Rome. Most cardinals apparently sensed the gravity and urgency of the situation, recognizing the need to restore tranquility after the stormy pontificate of Pius IX. After two days and three votes, the 68-year-old Giacchino Vincenzo Pecci, the sixth son of Count Lodovico Pecci, was elected pope on February 20, 1878. Some speculated the relative haste was prompted by the fear of a possible Italian or German intervention, others quickly rallied to his cause because they were convinced that he would have a short and transitional pontificate, others suspected his rapid election reflected the attempt to thwart the exercise of the veto power wielded by Austria, France, and Spain—while still others pointed to the pressing problems facing the Vatican.

Pecci was judged well-suited for mending the papacy's relations with the powers and peoples of the modern world. He had studied at the Academy of Noble Ecclesiastics in preparation for a career in the Roman diplomatic service as well as at the Roman University. Ordained a priest in 1837, he served as Apostolic Delegate to Benevento before being dispatched to serve as governor of Perugia in 1841, and sent to Belgium as nuncio to Belgium in 1843. Three years later he returned to Perugia as its bishop, remaining there for over 30 years and named a cardinal in 1853. Pecci refused to join the reformist current within the church, but also shunned its reactionary circles. Although he had voted with the majority in favor of infallibility at the Vatican Council, and supported many of Pius IX's denunciations, he specified that these did not necessarily condemn the modern world, insisting that the church was not against "proper progress," and sought rather than spurned conciliation. "My eyes are not blind to the spirit of the age," he said, adding, "I do not reject the progress of our age where it is certainly useful."[4] In 1877, following the death of Cardinal

Giacomo Antonelli, who allegedly had kept him away from Rome, Pius IX appointed Pecci to head the apostolic chamber when the papal office of Camerlengo or papal chamberlain became vacant.

The first steps of the newly elected pope, including his decision not to reconvene the Vatican Council, provided hope that Leo would pursue a more moderate course than his predecessor and seek some reconciliation with the contemporary world. In his revised and reinvigorated neo-Thomism and scholasticism, Leo sought to harmonize revelation and reason, seeing no conflict between the two. Some saw his election as a watershed in modern papal history. Among other things, Leo XIII (1878–1903) had to redress the Vatican's diplomatic isolation by mending the Holy See's relations with a number of nations, while increasing its international presence and impact. To do so, he sent notices of his election to all heads of state, even those who were not Catholic. He especially reached out to Brussels, Paris, St. Petersburg, Berlin, Madrid, and Lisbon as well as a number of capitals outside Europe, seeking to forge good relations with almost all the powers. On the very day of his election, he wrote William I of Germany and Alexander II of Russia, invoking the reestablishment of relations with their respective empires. Subsequently the German Chancellor Bismarck, who feared the spreading specter of socialism, had an informal talk with the papal nuncio, foreshadowing the empire's improved relationship with the Vatican.

Leo's selection of the moderate Cardinal Alessandro Franchi, deemed by many the most liberal member of the College of Cardinals, as his secretary of state, provided a promising beginning, mitigating the prior policy of resistance and rejection.[5] Among the secretary's initial actions was to dispatch an apostolic delegate to Canada, instructing him to remind that country's conservative clerics that while condemning aspects of the liberal program, the Holy Father did not condemn all liberal parties.[6] Despite considerable opposition, Pope Leo recognized the Spanish Constitution of 1876, paving the way for improved relations with the Madrid government. In 1881, he opened the Secret Vatican Archives to scholars of all confessions, asserting the church had no fear of history. Later in 1882, the Vatican appointed an apostolic commissioner to Canada with instructions to the Canadian clergy to cease their campaign against the liberal regime that governed that North American country.

A similar message was transmitted to Belgian Catholics by the pope, who urged them to sustain the system of liberty established in their country, which had proved beneficial to the church. Acknowledging that the separation of church and state was not the ideal desired by the Holy See, he made it clear that oftentimes the church accepted what it could not prevent to avoid greater evils.[7] Later, in his encyclical *Immortale dei* of 1885, Leo reached out to liberals by reiterating that "the right to rule is not necessarily . . . bound up with any mode of government."[8] By 1884 Catholics secured a majority in the Belgian assembly while the papal conciliatory course led to improved relations with Catholic Spain and Austria. Subsequently, in his letter on the Civil Constitution of States in 1885, Leo pronounced that while his two immediate predecessors Gregory XVI and Pius IX had condemned governmental theories, neither had denounced any form of government or favored one over another.[9] The papal position did not influence the stance of conservative Catholics in Canada who openly championed the conservative course in the elections of 1896, leading moderates to invoke papal intervention.[10] In 1899, even after a permanent apostolic delegate had been sent with instructions to seek a reconciliation between the Canadian hierarchy and the Liberal Canadian regime, part of the clergy remained recalcitrant, adhering to its conservative, antigovernmental course.

Leo counseled moderation to the French faithful as well as the Belgians, seeking to curb the activities of the conservative clergy in France, whose alliance with the monarchist cause enraged the republicans and encouraged their anticlerical campaign. In 1880 the Jesuit order was disbanded in France. Rather than responding with excommunications that would only aggravate division between the church and state, Leo had recourse to conciliation, replacing the outspoken nuncio Monsignor Meglia with the more diplomatic Monsignor Vladimir Czacki. The new nuncio distanced the Vatican from the conservative clergy allied to the monarchist coterie by explaining that the Holy See was not bound to any particular party. Leo continued his diplomatic campaign by commending three French societies: the Society for the Propagation of the Faith, the Association of Holy Childhood, and the Society of the Schools of the East—praising them for their missionary efforts in spreading the gospel.[11] Vatican appreciation of French missionary activity was followed by the appointment of two new French cardinals, bringing their number up to seven, perceived by some as part of Leo's attempt to achieve a rapprochement with France. In 1881, Pope Leo reassured the leaders of the Republic of France that the Holy See did not prefer one form of government over another. Indeed, Leo revealed his admiration and affection for France—the eldest daughter of the church. Unfortunately, this papal effort did not strike a responsive chord in the anticlerical president of France, July Grévy (1879–1887) or his Republican allies.

Leo was not discouraged and later his initiatives developed into a major Vatican policy of attaining a rapprochement (the *Ralliement*) between French Catholics and the Third French Republic, opposing the use and abuse of religion for partisan political purposes. Leo was supported in this endeavor by his new secretary of state, Cardinal Mariano Rompolla del Tindaro and the primate of Africa, Cardinal Charles Martial Lavigerie, who was selected to appeal to French Catholics for the good of their faith. He did so during the visit of French naval officers, largely of a conservative Catholic bent, to Algiers in November 1890. His appeal was spurned by the officers and by royalist Catholic circles in France. Catholic opponents of a rapprochement with the Republic claimed that Lavigerie spoke on his own, rather than on behalf of the Vatican, and when the papal secretary of state indicated otherwise, they argued that Rompolla also expressed his own opinion.

The 1892 Declaration of the five cardinals resident in France, which invoked acceptance of the prevailing political institutions in the country, likewise failed to rupture the close alliance between monarchists and diehard conservative Catholics. Even when Leo himself called for reconciliation, his plea was not answered.[12] Critics charged that Pope Leo did not follow his own advice and made no effort to achieve a rapprochement with the liberal regime in Italy. Consequently, during the course of the tribulations of the Panama Canal Scandal and the Dreyfus Affair at the turn of the century, conservative Catholics in France remained allied to the rightist and anti-Republican camp to the detriment of the church. This conservative intransigence in France contributed to the Republican Bloc's decision to pass the Law of Associations of 1901, which placed Catholic religious orders and institutions under governmental control and threatened their very existence.

Relations between the Kingdom of Italy and the Vatican proved even worse than with the French Republic, for Leo XIII, as conservative critics observed, was no more inclined than his predecessor to achieve a reconciliation between the papacy and the *Risorgimento* and resolve the Roman Question at the expense of the temporal power. He, too, refused to recognize the papacy's loss of Rome or accept the Italian Law of Guarantees, calling upon Italian Catholics to shun participation in the national political arena. In his first of over 50 encyclicals (April 1878), issued during his long pontificate, the pope catalogued the evils of the age, while reasserting the papal need for the temporal power to assure its spiritual authority.[13] Similar sentiments were expressed in his first talk to the cardinals, warning that the pope was no longer free since his temporal power had been seized. Leo, no less than Pius IX, insisted on the need for a territorial base to protect the papacy's spiritual authority—but unlike his predecessor eventually limited his claim to the city of Rome. Nonetheless, critics charged that Leo, like his predecessor, schemed to resume the role of pope king, which they vehemently opposed.

For a host of reasons, papal relations with the Kingdom of Italy did not improve and reached a low point in July 1881, when the body of Pius IX was being transported for final burial in San Lorenzo, and disrupted by angry demonstrators who attempted to dump his casket into the Tiber River. Enraged by the threat and the belated response of the Italian authorities, Leo called upon the powers to intervene, pointing to the dangers confronting the papacy in the Vatican, and the church in Italy. None responded. During the course of 1881–1882, some believe that Leo secretly considered seeking refuge in Austrian territory. Supposedly, this pope also considered fleeing Rome in 1889. In fact, there is no solid evidence that Leo truly contemplated abandoning Rome. The vague threats to do so were likely inspired by his desire to energize the powers to assume a more prompt and protective policy toward the papacy. In 1892, he catalogued his complaints about Italian developments, citing: the interference with church activities, the expulsion of Religious from convents, and the sanction of civil matrimony along with the elimination of Catholic influence in education. To combat this campaign, he invoked a Catholic journalism to fight these "iniquities" and expose the lies launched against the church and its ministers.[14] The celebration of the Sicilian Vespers in Rome and the glorification of Giordano Bruno (1548–1600), burned at the stake for heresy, dismayed the pope who protested these anticlerical measures in Rome, where he remained.

Leo also embraced Pio Nono's critique of the doctrinal evils of the age, railing against the perverted social civilization and the modern malaise it generated. Like Pius IX, Leo XIII denounced the positivism that rejected metaphysics and relied only on facts, as well as the secularism that sought to exclude God from life. He cataloged these contemporary ills in his first encyclical in April 1878. Soon, thereafter, he followed his predecessor in condemning socialism, communism, and nihilism, presenting Christian principles as their cure. Like Pius IX he also rejected the Marxist dogma of class struggle. Critical of all secret societies, Leo determined to combat freemasonry, which he believed inspired the Italian excesses, repeating the condemnations of some nine of his predecessors in his encyclical of 1884.

Leo contributed his own negative assessment of the "pernicious sect" he believed aimed to destroy religious values and moral laws and sought the dechristianization of state and society. In their "insane and wicked endeavors" the pope perceived the "implacable hatred" and the "spirit of revenge" of Satan.[15] Later in 1890, Pope Leo tied the activity of the mason's movement to Italian developments pointing to their warfare against the church in the peninsula, the overthrow of the civil power of the papacy and other evils such as the confiscation of ecclesiastical property, proclamation of civil matrimony, and the state control of education.[16] In 1892, Pope Leo XIII issued two other encyclicals on the unfortunate role and impact of Freemasonry in Italy.[17] In 1894 he warned all rulers and nations of the world of the dangers the movement represented.[18] He did so again in 1902, in his 25 year review of his pontificate.[19]

The Vatican also perceived danger in the movement termed Americanism, which allegedly sought to bring aspects of American life and democracy into the Catholic church. Critics complained that Americanism extolled the natural virtues over the supernatural, emphasized the active virtues to the exclusion of charity and obedience, rejected religious vows, and invoked a new methodology to replace the old. They further charged that a liberal faction had emerged in the American church led by John Ireland, Archbishop of Saint Paul, Cardinal James Gibbons, Archbishop of Baltimore, and Denis O'Connell, Rector of the American College in Rome. Among other things their movement was said to favor a separation of church and state rather than the union championed by traditionalists, and sought to democratize the structure of the universal church. American openness and democracy were to replace Spanish intrigue and Italian domination, while its adherents posited that the people of God were the ultimate source of power. Conservatives complained that many of the ideas espoused by Americanism were the very same that Pope Gregory XVI had condemned in 1832 and Pope Pius IX in 1864, and called upon Pope Leo to act. The pope did so in his apostolic letter of January 22, 1899, to Cardinal Gibbons rejecting the notions that the church ought to adapt to modern civilization, relax its rigor, and show greater indulgence toward modern theories and methods. It concluded that there could not be an American church whose ideas and leadership was in conflict with the one Holy Roman Church.[20]

Leo not only criticized the democratization and Americanization of the church, but the ultra conservative right as well, refusing to bow to conservative pressure to condemn the Knights of Labor in America. He also cautioned the Spanish clergy to display moderation and not transcend the limits imposed by their office.[21] The response was mixed, as were the results following his warning to the Portuguese clergy to stay out of the political arena. In dealing with Orthodox Russia, he could not speak as leader of the faith as in the case of Catholic countries such as Italy, France, Spain, and Portugal and therefore had recourse to more diplomatic maneuvers. To win the Tsar's goodwill, assurances were given to Russia, who feared that the Vatican would champion the cause of Polish Catholics at its expense. Leo informed Alexander II that Catholicism aimed to promote peace internally and internationally.[22] Following the visit of the Russian chancellor Nikolai Giers to the Vatican in 1882, an agreement was concluded between the Holy See and Russia ameliorating the position of the church in Poland and suppressing the prosecutorial degree of 1865. As a gesture of papal goodwill, one of its representatives attended the coronation of Tsar Alexander III (1881–1894). In 1895 a permanent representative from Russia to the Holy See was established, and a Ukase issued by Nicholas II (1894–1917) in 1906 permitted a measure of religious toleration, offering Roman Catholics greater liberty than they had hitherto enjoyed. Leo continued on his diplomatic course.

Relations were improved with Protestant Germany through the efforts of Leo XIII's secretary of state, Cardinal Luigi Jacobini (1880–1887), former nuncio in Vienna, who had good relations with the Reich. In 1880 the Iron Chancellor introduced legislation in the Prussian Landtag restricting or mitigating the May or Falk Laws and abandoning the government's claim to depose ecclesiastics. Bismarck subsequently dispatched a Minister Plenipotentiary to the Vatican. In 1882, diplomatic relations were reestablished with Germany, and later the German Emperor visited Pope Leo during the course of his visit to Italy. By 1883 bishops began to be appointed to vacant Sees and a number of exiled ecclesiastics were allowed to return. By the opening of 1886 all the German dioceses had bishops. Meanwhile, Bismarck invited Pope Leo to mediate the dispute between Germany and Spain over the Caroline Islands in the South Seas, and the judicious papal solution, which recognized Spanish sovereignty but accorded Germany economic rights therein, eased international tension.[23] In 1887 a *modus vivendi* between church and state was concluded with the German empire. Relations steadily improved as Leo named Bismarck a Knight of the Order of Christ, while legislation was submitted to the Reichstag compensating the church for the clerical salaries lost during the *Kulturkampf*. Leo also managed to secure the termination of anticlerical legislation in Mexico, Chile, and Spain while resuming diplomatic relations with Brazil and Colombia in South America, and Russia in Europe.

Relations were also improved with Great Britain, toward whom Leo maintained a friendly attitude, despite the fact that in 1896 he condemned Anglican Orders as absolutely null and utterly void. The coincident celebration of Leo's jubilee and that of Queen Victoria in 1888, furthered the friendly interchange. Most monarchs of Europe sent congratulations to Leo on his fiftieth anniversary as a priest, save the rulers of Italy and Sweden. The Protestant President of the United States Grover Cleveland conveyed a copy of the American Constitution to the pope on the occasion of his priestly jubilee. At Victoria's death in 1901, Leo dispatched a diplomatic mission to London to offer condolences to King Edward VII.

Anglo-Vatican relations were facilitated by the fact that the pope urged the Irish to shun secret societies in seeking to redress legitimate grievances. While he expressed sympathy for the plight of the Irish, he rejected the policy and practice of boycotting as contrary to Christian morality.[24]

Leo did not neglect the problems of the church beyond Europe, providing for eight ecclesiastical provinces as well as an Indian hierarchy in 1886. He reestablished the hierarchy in North Africa while regulating the jurisdiction of the archbishop of Goa. In 1889 a concordat was concluded with Colombia, and that same year witnessed the convocation of a National Council of South American Bishops in Rome. The pope also opened talks for the establishment of nunciatures in Peking and Tokyo, while supporting the move to abolish slavery in Brazil. To expedite the abolition of African slavery he issued two encyclicals: *In Plurimis* of 1888 and *Catholicae Ecclesiae* of 1890. In the first the bishops of Brazil were commended for helping to rid their country of the scourge of slavery; in the second Leo called upon the missions to work for the termination of this pernicious institution. "How horrible it is to recall that almost four hundred thousand Africans of every age and sex are forcibly taken away each year from their villages," Leo wrote, revealing his "desire to help these wretched men and to alleviate their lamentable condition."[25]

He was gratified by the constitution proclaimed by the Mikado in 1891, which assured religious liberty for his subjects, including Catholics. Nor did the Vatican ignore developments in the United States and Canada. In 1878, when Bishop George Conroy of Ireland was dispatched as provisional apostolic delegate to Canada, his assignment included an assessment of developments in the United States. In his report to Rome, Conroy suggested the appointment of a permanent apostolic delegate to the United States, despite the opposition in the country and even among the clergy. The proposal was not then implemented, although some years later in 1883 Pope Leo authorized Bishop Luigi Sepiacci to preside over the third plenary Council of Baltimore. Three years later in 1886, the pope dispatched Monsignor Germano Straniero to the United States to deliver the Cardinal's hat to James Gibbons of Baltimore and tour the country. In his report to Rome, Straniero likewise urged the pope to send an apostolic delegate to the United States.[26] This was taken under consideration but again no action immediately followed. In 1889 Monsignor Francesco Satolli represented Pope Leo at the ceremonies marking the opening of the Catholic University of America in Washington, D.C. During the course of his visit, he was assured by officials of the United States government that they had no opposition to the creation of a permanent apostolic delegation, and in 1893 this was established with Satolli's appointment.

Although Satolli was not accorded any rank or status within the diplomatic corps assigned to the country, at Cardinal Rampolla's direction he engaged in correspondence between Mexico, Guatemala, and the Holy See, and in many ways acted as a virtual nuncio and diplomatic emissary rather than simply the pope's representative to the faithful—clergy and laity alike. The success of this usage led to the establishment of similar delegations in Canada, Guatemala, and Mexico over the next decade. When it seemed that war might break out between the United States and Spain over Cuba in the late 1890s, the Spanish ambassador appealed for Vatican mediation. The papal secretary of state, Cardinal Mariano Rompolla del Tindaro (1887–1903) commissioned Archbishop John Ireland of St. Paul to intercede with the McKinley government as Washington prepared for war. Washington's conditions were that Spain must grant an armistice to the insurgents and negotiate with them—and if no solution were found within six months, permit the United States to arbitrate a solution. Pressed by Pope Leo, the Spanish cabinet proclaimed a suspension of hostilities, but this was not sufficient for the American Congress, which called upon the president to intervene at once by supporting an independent government in Cuba. Leo was disappointed that the Vatican intervention, which led to the Spanish concession of an armistice, failed to satisfy the Americans who declared war in 1898.

Pope Leo XIII had greater success in dealing with the social problems troubling society, transcending the older critique of capitalism and papal condemnations of socialism and communism and proposing an alternative. From the first, he demanded justice for the mistreated workers exploited by those who sought excessive and lawless profits. In two of his earliest encyclicals, during the first year of his pontificate, Leo denounced materialism as well as the proposed Socialist, nihilist, and Communist remedies—hinting at the prospect of a Christian solution.[27] Three years later, in 1881 he established a commission to assess the economic conditions in the rapidly industrializing west and sought the opinion of Catholic social reformers on possible solutions. He returned to this theme in a letter to the bishops of Italy in 1882, insisting that the church had a social as well as a religious mission and served as the guarantor of social justice."[28] The state, he insisted in his 1885 letter "On the Christian Constitution of States" had to cooperate with the church for the social well-being of its members.[29] After having issued instructions "On Human Liberty," "On Political Power," and "On the Christian Constitution of States" among others, in 1891 Pope Leo XIII issued one "On the Condition of Workers," *Rerum novarum*. It emerged as Leo XIII's most important encyclical, and one of the most essential of the nineteenth century, which assured Leo's distinctive place among modern popes.

Acknowledging the difficulty of fixing the rights and duties of capital and labor, the papal encyclical nonetheless concluded that the defenseless workers could not be abandoned to the greed of unscrupulous employers. Discounting the solutions proposed by the Socialists and Communists as irresponsible, the encyclical defended private property and defined the role of the church, the state, and employer and employee in seeking redress of labor's grievances. Among other things, it recognized the need for state intervention to secure social justice as well as the workers' right to organize.

The church's role was to counsel justice, insisting on moral values in the solution of problems, and avoiding the creation of new difficulties while attempting to resolve the old. The state, in turn, had to provide for private as well as the public well-being, and when necessary regulating the relations between employers and employees and intervening to protect the workers when they could not defend themselves. Employers, for their part, had to be just and reasonable in their pursuit of profit respecting the human personality, adjusting work to individual capacity, and above all, avoiding direct and indirect exploitation. Finally, the workers had to perform the labor agreed upon, utilizing only just means to achieve their objectives. In this regard, Pope Leo recognized the need of the workers to form organizations to obtain their rights, but thought in terms of mutual aid groups and benevolent societies rather than confrontational labor unions that resorted to strikes.[30] Acknowledging that such associations had to provide its members an increase in the goods of body and soul, Leo insisted that moral and religious perfection had to be regarded as the principal good.

Rerum novarum was hardly a radical pronouncement, but its defense of the working class's right to organize was acclaimed by the masses throughout most of the industrial world. Dubbed the "Social Magna Carta of Catholicism," it provoked widespread discussion and prompted a series of worker visits to Rome to thank the "workingman's pope." Appreciative of the positive response his encyclical had evoked, Leo cautioned restraint and continued to insist that while the social question involved material matters, it was primarily concerned with religion and morals, urging cooperation rather than confrontation between the classes. Since God had created the different classes, Leo stipulated, these should work together to achieve the common good with workers trusting their employers and the latter treating their workers with "just kindness and prudent care."[31] Social problems, Leo pronounced, required Catholic rather than Socialist solutions. Since social conflict and crises continued, the pope returned to them at the dawn of the new century.

Early in 1901, Leo's encyclical on Christian Democracy, *Graves de Communi Re*, further elaborated the papal position on social issues, preferring the term Christian Democracy over Social Democracy in describing Catholic social movements. Here, Leo reiterated that the social question was primarily a moral and religious one, emphasizing the need for charity in the organization and activity of worker organizations. Consequently, he could not concur with the conclusions of Social Democracy, which he claimed saw little beyond the material order, mistakenly convinced that these externals were sufficient for human happiness. He disagreed with the means as well as the ends sought by this social democracy, decrying the call for class conflict, abrogating the rights of private property, and seeking to establish a community of goods. Christian Democracy, as he conceived it, was neither divisive nor political, did not turn one class or group against another, and was concerned with the salvation of souls as well as providing for worldly needs.[32] Despite Leo's protestations, it would prove difficult if not impossible to restrict Christian Democracy to these parameters.

Leo sought cooperation and conciliation between states as well as within them, convinced that international peace as well as class harmony could be promoted by Catholic principles. His last secretary of state, Cardinal Rompolla, explained that the pope, as head of the universal church, had a special obligation to seek world peace. Thus, despite differences with the Kingdom of Italy, Leo intervened to implore mercy for the Italian prisoners held by Menelik of Ethiopia following the 1896 military disaster at Adowa. Pope Leo considered mediation and arbitration better than force or great power diplomacy in providing solutions for international disputes. Invoking international arbitration for the solution of disputes, Leo and Rampolla proved supportive of the International Peace Conference convoked at the Hague in May 1899, at Tsar Nicholas's initiative. The Russian ruler and the host, Queen Wilhelmina of Holland, both invited Leo to participate, and the pope agreed to do so. However, the Italian foreign minister, Admiral Felice Napoleone Canevaro, fearful that the Vatican would bring up the Roman Question, prevailed upon the Russians and Dutch to withdraw the invitation. Although disinvited, Pope Leo promised Queen Wilhelmina he would continue to press for peace, arguing that to assure compliance and permanence, peace treaties and conferences had to be anchored in Christian principles. When nations repudiated Christian principles, the prospect of war escalated. Leo pointed to the power of prayer, calling upon the faithful in March 1900 to invoke closure for the war in South Africa.[33]

Leo died on July 20, 1903, after a pontificate of over 25 years (305 months) and was buried in the Lateran Basilica—the last pope buried outside St. Peter's Basilica. His pontificate, along with that of Pius IX, was one of the most important of the nineteenth century. Although he remained a nineteenth-century figure, his innovations paved the path for the church's

"deep-rooted malady dragging it to destruction." He concluded there could be no peace without God, and mankind could only be brought back to God through Jesus Christ—hence his program to restore all things in Christ. Not surprisingly, he preached that one reached Christ through the church, calling for a return to Catholic teaching not only in doctrine but in economic and social life, in the family, in school, in the use of private property as well as in government.[36]

Pius X stressed priestly and papal power, bolstered by a standardized catechism, a uniform code of canon law, and a centralized curial government. In the first year of his pontificate he insisted on the need for the Church's independence from those who exercised political power.[37] To protect papal independence, early in 1904 he abolished the *jus exclusive* in papal elections or veto exercised by a number of the powers, prohibiting any lay intervention in the papal election, providing for the automatic excommunication for anyone seeking to veto a candidate for the papacy.[38] To assure the implementation of this prohibition, non-cardinals were excluded from the conclave and absolute secrecy imposed on its members. At the end of 1904, he established new and more precise procedures during the vacancy of the Holy See and the election of a new pope.[39] He also established that all European bishops had to visit Rome (*ad lumina* visits) every five years, and non-Europeans every ten. His determined effort to bolster the clerical establishment led some to label him the "Second Founder of the Roman Curia."

This pope vehemently opposed those who desired to modernize or decentralize the church by adapting Catholicism to the intellectual, moral, and social needs of the time, seeking to emancipate the faithful from ecclesiastical authority, science from dogma, and the state from the church. He resented the neo-reformist call to the young clergy to abandon the sacristy and enter the real world, eliminating the chasm between laity and clergy as well as the divide between modern science and religion. He was also appalled by those who perceived scripture as one of many historical sources rather than the *fount of faith,* and sought to subject it to historical-critical scrutiny. These modernist notions he denounced as a dangerous flirtation with pseudo-science, and an attempt to undermine revelation and the supernatural. He was suspicious of the critical approach to biblical studies, and the rejection of scholastic and Thomistic theology, which both he and his predecessor favored. As early as the end of 1903 the Holy Office condemned the works of Alfred Loisy who had penned revisionist studies of both the Old and New Testaments. For his efforts, Pius was Canonized in 1954, the only pope since Pius V (1566–1572) to be declared a saint.

Acknowledging that the times had changed, Pius X retorted that "nothing is changed in the life of the church," emphasizing its role in providing "for the spiritual welfare of souls."[40] He also criticized those Christian Democrats who favored the cause of the lower classes but ignored their spiritual welfare, convinced that the church could supply everything required for the well-being of souls. For this and other reasons, he opposed the creation of independent Catholic political parties, and even distrusted the Center Party in Germany, which had played a key role in combating the *Kulturkampf*. From the first, he invoked respect for authority and peaceful social relations. Soon thereafter, he repeated his call for harmony in the social sphere.[41] He warned the faithful against the hasty acceptance of novelties, calling for Catholic associations (Catholic Action) in Italy, to be nonpolitical and subordinate to the bishops. In a circular letter to Italian episcopacy, he condemned those Christian Democrats who had a political agenda, contrary to the Church's position.[42] To clarify the lines of authority and other matters, Pius relied on the new codification of canon law he commissioned. The *Codex Juris Canonici* that appeared in 1917, three years after his death, was a remarkable achievement that made church law readily available to clergy and laity.

In the interim, in July 1907, the Holy Office with papal encouragement issued the decree *Lamentabili,* which like Pio Nono's Syllabus, cataloged the erroneous propositions being paraded as progress. It listed 65 propositions earlier condemned, denouncing the revisionist theories of authority, revelation, and dogma. The first 38 errors focused on the false interpretation of scripture, while the remaining 37 catalogued errors in interpreting dogma, and modern misconceptions concerning the authority of the church, holy scripture, revelations, the faith, dogma, the person of Christ, the sacraments, and the principles of evolution.[43] Two months later, in September 1907, Pius released *Pascendi* on the modernists, one of the longest encyclicals of the Roman pontificate, containing more than 21,000 words. Here he condemned the attempt to bring the church into harmony with the false doctrines of the age, citing the errors of modernism, which he defined as the "synthesis of all heresies." Rejecting these false doctrines, he warned that partisans of these errors were lodged not only among the church's enemies, but in her own clergy, exposing the modernist philosopher, believer, theologian, historian, critic, apologist, and reformer—noting how each undermined religion. The modernists, he charged, rendered the religious experience virtually free of dogma, describing in detail their philosophical, theological, and historical misconceptions.

To curb their abuses he created a "Council of Vigilance" to "watch most carefully for every trace and sign of Modernism both in publication and in teaching."[44] Continuing his antimodernist campaign, Pius X supported the efforts of Monsignor Umberto Benigni, the Italian priest, who formed the League of St. Pius V, also known as the Sodalitum Pianum or the Sapiniere, a secret organization and network of informers to implement the papal condemnations against modernism. Although Pius X never granted his formal approval to Benigni's society, he endorsed its general aims and exploited it to intimidate suspected heretics. In 1909 he pleased the French right by beatifying Joan of Arc. He also pleased this faction in 1910, when he condemned the lay movement known as Le Sillon, which sought to reconcile Catholicism with the French Republic. Pius X resented its desire to be free of hierarchical control and alleged modernist principles and practices.

Benigni's ecclesiastical secret police curtailed the church's dialogue with modernity, contributing to the deterioration of relations between the Vatican and France—the church's eldest daughter. Following the papal protest of the Republic's suppression of the religious orders, and President Emile Loubet's visit to Victor Emmanuel III in Rome, which the *Osservatore Romano* denounced as a grave offense against the pope, Paris recalled its ambassador from the Vatican, and in July 1904 terminated diplomatic relations. That same day the Nuncio Monsignor Lorenzelli left the French capital. At this juncture the French chamber drafted legislation for a separation of church and state in France, which secured approval in 1905. Pius denounced the Law of Separation as disastrous both for society and the church, a violation of the law of nations, and a "pernicious error."[45] Early in 1906, Pius protested the Republic's unilateral renunciation of the concordat and subsequently rejected the French Assembly's regulations for the administration of church property.[46] Relations with Spain and Portugal were little better. From the start of his pontificate Pius X complained about the violence launched against the religious orders and the situation only deteriorated following the flight of King Manoel of Portugal to England and proclamation of the Republic in 1910. The estrangement culminated in the law of separation, which Pius X condemned in May 1911. Diplomatic relations with Spain were also severed in 1910.

Although Pius X witnessed a deterioration of relations with France, Spain, and Portugal, he had a measure of success in international affairs. In 1905, the Holy See successfully acted as arbitrator in the boundary dispute between Brazil, Peru, and Bolivia. At the same time, the pope improved relations with Tsarist Russia by calling upon the bishops of Russian Poland to stand on the side of peace and forbidding Polish Catholics from belonging to "factional groups, which run counter to the law of God."[47] He was effusive in his praise and supportive of the efforts of the Carnegie

Endowment for International Peace formed in the United States in 1911. "To compose differences, to restrain the outbreak of hostilities, to prevent the dangers of war, to remove even the anxieties of so-called armed peace, is indeed most praiseworthy." He added, "We most gladly lend the weight of Our authority to those who are striving to realize this most beneficent purpose."[48] Pius X likewise lent his encouragement and support to the three South American conferences for peace.

During the prewar decade Pius X also spearheaded a drive to improve relations with Italy and moderate the animosity that had prevailed during the pontificates of Pius IX and Leo XIII, working to render the counter-*Risorgimento* against the Kingdom of Italy obsolete. The ground for this had been paved while Sarto was patriarch of Venice, for during his tenure there he received the Italian royal family when they visited his city. Furthermore, he had quietly questioned the wisdom of continuing the *non-expedit*, favoring the cooperation of Catholics and moderate liberals in local elections to defeat radical and Socialist candidates. "It will be necessary to have the courage to abolish the *non expedit*," he proclaimed before becoming pope, adding "I feel that I would have the courage."[49] Keeping Catholics from the polls, he believed, worked to the advantage of their enemies, who in their absence were able to carry on their mischief unopposed. The mechanism for their participation aroused considerable debate.

In Italy Pius showed himself more sympathetic to the moderate thought of Filippo Meda than the radical program of Romolo Murri, concurring with the former in opposition to the latter, that it was possible for church and state to subsist in harmony, opposing the creation of a Catholic party to replace the liberal regime in Italy. In fact, Pius X did not support Murri's vision of a militant Christian Democracy, opting instead to work with Giovanni Giolitti, who dominated Italy's political life during the first decade of the twentieth century. Unlike his predecessors Francesco Crispi and Antonio Di Rudinì, Giolitti sought accommodation rather than confrontation with the Catholics who remained outside of the national political arena.[50] Personally opposed to anticlericalism, his prefects discouraged it during the years of his ascendancy and encouraged toleration on religious issues. He confided to the German Chancellor Bernhard von Bulow that the religious storm brewing in France could not be duplicated in the peninsula, whose people and government shunned religious conflict.[51]

For his part, the pope appreciated the ministry's refusal to embroil itself in religious questions, assuring that it would not create further problems for the church in light of the diplomatic difficulties it had with the French Republic or the internal problems posed by the modernist threat. Giolitti, to the pope's relief, preserved neutrality, observing that in religious matters the government lacked competence. The Italian prime minister elaborated his position on church-state relations in 1904, following the ruckus provoked by the papal protest of the French president's visit to Victor Emmanuel in Rome. "Our principle is this," Giolitti proclaimed, "the State and Church are two parallels which must never meet."[52] It represented his equivalent to Cavour's "free Church in a free State." Giolitti considered anticlericalism counterproductive and sought to draw Catholics into the political life of the country and like the pope, he opposed the formation of an Italian Catholic Party.

Soon after his election, Pius revealed his opposition not only to the scriptural liberalism of Alfred Loisy and George Tyrrell but also the Christian Democracy of Romolo Murri. He rejected the formation of a democratic Christian party independent of the Opera dei Congressi, and when some in the Catholic Action movement disagreed, he dissolved the Opera in 1904, replacing it with three national unions: the *Unione Popolare,* the *Unione Economic-Sociale,* and the *Unione Elettorale,* which encompassed the various Catholic organizations in the country. The latter served as an umbrella group for Catholics in Italian political life, directing them to focus on issues important for the church and its members. Although obedient to the pope's strictures on the formation of a separate Catholic party, the *Unione Elettorale* proved more flexible on the entry of Catholics into Italian political affairs, paving the way for wider Catholic participation in the national elections of 1904 and increasing cooperation between church and state. The conciliation between Rome and the Vatican continued, and in his letter of 1905 (*Il fermo proposito*), Pius lifted the ban on Catholic participation in Italian national life.

In 1907, when a number of journalists allegedly citing government sources revealed that the government was disposed to dissolve the teaching religious orders, Giolitti quickly and openly denied the rumor. On the issue of religious instruction in the public schools, Giolitti assumed a conciliatory course aimed to placate rather than arouse the pope and curia but always preserving the separation of church and state. Despite Giolitti's moderation, the debate over religious instruction in the Italian public schools resurfaced in 1908, on the eve of elections for the twenty-first legislature. In February of that year, Leonida Bissolati, the reformist Socialist, proposed a complete secularization of the primary schools, prohibiting religious instruction in any form. Giolitti responded that those who favored the legislation did so on political grounds and sought to divide Italian politics along clerical and anticlerical lines,[53] a move that both he and the pope opposed.

Discussing religious instruction in the schools, Giolitti noted there were three possibilities: prohibit it, impose it, or provide freedom of choice, offering such instruction for those who requested it. While Bissolati favored the first choice, and Pope Pius X, the second, Giolitti supported the third alternative, which he felt was in keeping with past practice and the Cavourian ideal.[54] Giolitti's supporters defeated the Bissolati proposal by a majority of 347 against and only 60 voting for it, and the Prime Minister's compromise solution was adopted. By its terms religious instruction would be offered upon the request of heads of household at communal expense, when the provincial scholastic councils approved it; at family expense when the councils did not. While the compromise did not please the teacher organizations who wanted education to be both lay and democratic, it won grudging support from the pope, who recognized this was the best solution he could expect under the existing circumstances in liberal Italy.

Not surprisingly, in 1909 the Italian bishops authorized Catholics in their care to go to the polls to defeat opposition candidates who pursued a hostile policy towards the church. The relationship between the Catholic Church and the liberal state became closer during the Libyan War of 1911, which some saw as a Christian crusade. Although theoretically still in effect, the *non-expedit* was increasingly ignored. The broad Catholic participation in the parliamentary elections of 1913 provoked the bogus charge that Giolitti signed a secret agreement—the Gentiloni Pact—with Count Ottorino Gentiloni, president of the Catholic Electoral Union.[55] In fact, the Catholic Electoral Union offered its support to any candidate who agreed with their program, printed in the October 1913 issue of the journal *L'Italia*. Understandably, Catholics supported candidates who adhered to their seven point program but opponents of the church and government claimed that an unholy alliance had been concluded between the two. Although Gentiloni gave an interview, explaining that there was neither a pact nor an accord, his denials were either ignored or distorted by opposition liberals who were scandalized by the widespread Catholic participation in the election, as were those Catholics who favored the Christian democratic course outlined by the priest, Luigi Sturzo.[56] This Sicilian cleric opposed Catholic support of liberal candidates, arguing that it reinforced a government fundamentally antagonistic to Catholic interests, while calling for the formation of an independent national Catholic party. The pastoral pope opposed the formation of such a political party.

Papal efforts on behalf of the poor and downtrodden, and especially the Indians of North and South America whose treatment Pius deplored, engendered less controversy. He commended the work of the Society for the Propagation of the Faith for their work among Indian children in North America,[57] decrying the pernicious customs, which relegated a substantial part of the native population of Latin America to virtual servitude and genocide. He insisted that Christianity required all men, regardless of nation or color, be treated as brothers both in words and deeds. To counter the prevailing abuses, he recommended the combined efforts of church and state to eliminate the criminal degradation of Indians, calling upon the bishops to support institutions working for this oppressed population.[58] He also sympathized with the plight of the Jews, and at the end of January 1904 granted an audience to Theodor Herzl, who invoked papal support for a Jewish return to Palestine. Pius responded that while the papacy could not present the Jews from returning to Jerusalem, it could not sanction the return. Nonetheless, he was not hostile to the Jews recognizing that "the Jewish faith was the foundation of our own."[59] In 1914, Italy's leading Jewish periodical, *Il Vessillo Israeletico*, noted that Pius X was the only European sovereign to protest against the pogroms in Russia.[60]

The mistreatment of Jews and other peoples, as well as the ethnic and national rivalry that had erupted in Europe and the world beyond, distressed the pope who predicted it would lead to a war of horrendous consequences. This prophecy materialized at the end of July 1914, following the assassination of the Archduke Franz Ferdinand and his wife, when Austria-Hungary declared war on Serbia. Although Pius X's offer of mediation was rejected, he urged Catholics to pray for peace[61] and died soon after on August 20, 1914. Unable to prevent the outbreak of the war; the cardinals in conclave hoped that a more diplomatic successor might be able to hasten its conclusion.

Benedict XV, the World War, and the League of Nations, 1914–1922

The conclave of August 1914, which opened as a disastrous war, divided Europe, and sought a pope who could respond to the threats confronting the peoples of the continent and the church—a diplomatic figure such as Leo XIII, rather than a pastoral one like Pius X, who had focused on theological and ecclesiastical issues. Both belligerent camps desired a successor to Pius X who would be sympathetic to their cause. Although deprived of the temporal power, the papacy continued to play a role in the international arena, exchanging representatives and communicating with a number of governments. Some hoped, while others feared, that it might influence the course of events. A dynamic Vatican role was rendered difficult the summer of 1914 because of the restricted diplomatic reach of the Holy See. At this juncture the Vatican did not have a representative in London or Paris and while it had an apostolic delegate in Washington, he was often ignored.[1] Nonetheless, it still wielded a moral influence that could not, and was not, ignored by the powers.

The Italians were particularly concerned about the plans and schemes of the Holy See, resorting to a series of spies to keep them informed. Although relations with Italy remained strained, the government of Antonio Salandra honored article XI of the Law of Guarantees, assuring entry to Rome of cardinals from throughout the world to elect the new pope. Recognizing the need to move quickly, the conclave did not await the arrival of a number of eminences from across the Atlantic, and on September 3, after a three-day conclave, on the tenth ballot, selected the 60-year-old Giacomo Giambattista Della Chiesa, of an aristocratic

Genoese family, who had only recently been made a cardinal. He assumed the name Benedict XV, in deference to Cardinal Prospero Lorenzo Lambertini (Benedict XIV, 1749–1758), the last archbishop of Bologna to become pope, and because of his special devotion to Saint Benedict. His election followed that of Woodrow Wilson, professor of political science at Princeton University, as President of the United States (1913–1921). The paths of these two figures would cross in the following decade, with important consequences for both.

Trained as a papal diplomat in the College for Noble Ecclesiastics in Rome, the new pope was fluent in French, German, and Spanish as well as his native Italian. He had sharpened his diplomatic mettle under Leo XIII and Cardinal Rampolla, serving as undersecretary of state after 1901, and as such exhibited a great interest as well as a genuine talent for diplomacy. Subsequently, in 1907 he was named archbishop of Bologna. In 1914 he was named a cardinal, three months before his election as pope. As pope he assumed an awesome responsibility during a perilous period for the papacy, the church, and the world. This diminutive and frail figure known as "Il Picoletto," or little one, who some derisively dubbed "the midget," had to confront the plague of war, which he decried as the "scourge of the wrath of God."

Preoccupied by the war from the opening days of his pontificate, Benedict sought to restore the peace by pursuing a policy of pacifism, while scrupulously preserving Vatican impartiality. His task was complicated by the fact that neither camp was totally pleased by his election. Nonetheless, his wit and learning, if not his physique, inspired confidence and the British Ambassador to Italy was convinced that Benedict would pursue a vigorous course.[2] His assessment proved accurate, for soon after his election he called upon the faithful to pray for peace.[3] He also moved quietly to establish de facto relations with the Kingdom of Italy, which he hoped would stay out of the war, recognizing Victor Emmanuel III as His Majesty rather than the Duke of Savoy, and raising no objections to Catholic rulers visiting the Italian King in Rome. He determined to do more.

Benedict's diplomatic activity was exercised directly and officially through his nuncios and internuncios, who represented the holy father and his secretary of state before the civilian authorities, sometimes indirectly through his apostolic delegates, who represented the Vatican before ecclesiastical authorities, as well as by means of encyclicals and other papal messages. In a series of exhortations to the powers, including those of September 8 and December 6, 1914; May 25, July 28, and December 6, 1915; March 4 and July 30, 1916; January 10 and May 5, 1917, he questioned the pursuit of military victory, opting instead for the negotiation of a just peace. In his first message to the church on September 8, 1914, the distressed pope pledged to do all within his means to hasten the end of the calamity and proved true to his promise.

After the premature death of Cardinal Domenico Ferrata, who had served as nuncio to Paris and Brussels and was initially appointed secretary of state, Benedict selected another disciple of Rampolla, Pietro Gasparri to the post. Gasparri emerged as Benedict's friend as well as collaborator, and had an important impact on the secretariat of state and the pontificate. In November 1914, on the feast of All Saints Day, Benedict issued an appeal for peace within the church and in Europe. In this, the first of his 12 encyclicals, he revealed his deep distress at the carnage and ruin of the calamitous war. Benedict believed the murderous struggle was prompted by (1) the absence of mutual love, (2) contempt for authority, (3) class strife, and finally (4) the unbridled thirst for material objects.[4] He also deplored the increasing social strife and lust for money, the root of all evil. Transcending the war's origins, Benedict stressed the need to contain and mitigate its consequences, fearful that a protracted conflict would unleash political disorder, economic ruin and social upheaval, with unfortunate consequences for both belligerent and neutral countries. The papal effort to limit the struggle was criticized in both camps as the opposing camps complained of Benedict's impartiality and failure to name those responsible for the calamity.

Despite the mounting criticism, Benedict steadfastly refused to assume a partisan stance. Instead, he had his secretary of state call upon the belligerents to suspend hostilities on Christmas, 1914. This proposal, tentatively approved by Great Britain, Belgium, and Germany, was torpedoed by France and Russia. Moved by the suffering of the Belgians, Benedict prayed for the end of their misfortunes, but did not condemn the German invasion. Although he censured the violators of international law, Benedict's refusal to cite specific abuses earned him the enmity of all of the belligerents. His general denunciations did not satisfy the Allied countries, which believed Benedict should have condemned the invasion of Belgium and the occupation of Brussels. Conversely, the Central Powers felt the pope should say nothing about Belgium, focusing instead on the need to protect Catholic Austria against Orthodox Russia. The prospect of this diplomatic pope doing either was slim. In fact, on the eve of the conclave that elected him, Della Chiesa had indicated "I would regret if any parish priest [let alone the pope] should take sides for one or the other belligerents." He added that he prayed for God to end the war "without dictating to the almighty the way in which this terrible scourge might cease."[5] Once pope, he and his secretary of state refused to allot responsibility, insisting that the church and papacy not take sides. Benedict explained that the Holy See did not wish to be neutral in the European war, but had the duty to remain impartial—a distinction understood by neither the Allies nor the Central Powers.[6]

Distressed by the inability of the existing international configuration to peacefully resolve conflicts, Benedict urged the nations to find some other means of resolving their differences. Denouncing all injustice and deeming the war an unnecessary evil, Benedict would not become embroiled in national rivalry, refusing to judge the motives of the various belligerents or choose sides.[7] He also proved unwilling to apply the just-war theory, unconvinced that either side fought from a position of justice, adhering to his self-proclaimed impartiality in his search for peace. This silence on responsibility from the first antagonized both sides. The Central Powers (Germany, Austria-Hungary, and the Ottoman Empire) perceived the Vatican as a tool of the allies, while the Entente (Great Britain, France, and Russia) viewed the curia's attitude with concern, charging the papacy favored the Central Powers.[8] The Entente, seeking assistance, strongly resented the Vatican's efforts to keep Italy and the United States out of the conflict, and Italian nationalists denounced the illegal papal intervention in their internal affairs. Meanwhile, the press and other publications of a number of countries criticized the Vatican's stance, including the 1916 pamphlet "The Silence of Benedict XV," which claimed papal silence compromised the church. Even Benedict's directive to the clergy to provide for the spiritual and material welfare of prisoners of war, aroused suspicion and provoked widespread criticism. The Allies, without regular French or Italian representation at the papal court, complained of the pervasive German and Austrian influence on the Holy See. Tsarist Russia did have a representative at the Vatican, but Demitri Nelidov's influence was limited by papal opposition to orthodoxy and the Russian treatment of Catholic Poland. Belgium, likewise had a minister at the Vatican but suffering from poor health, he proved no more effective in securing Allied interests than his Russian counterpart.

The newly minted English Cardinal Francis Neil Gasquet, one of the few in the curia to counter the pro-Austrian and pro-German sentiments in the Vatican, pressed his fellow countrymen to establish diplomatic relations with the Holy See. "On Cardinal Gasquet, as the resident cardinal fell the task of countering the anti-English and anti-Allies propaganda of the Central Powers," wrote Abbot Butler in the *Dictionary of National Biography,* adding "He took a leading part in negotiating the appointment of a British minister to the Vatican in December 1914."[9] That December the British dispatched Sir Henry Howard, heir of an established Catholic family, to the Vatican, to counter the alleged influence of the Central Powers over the Vatican. He was the first British chargé d'affaires since the seventeenth century. To allay Italian fears, the English promised not to negotiate or even discuss the Roman Question with Benedict, promising they would not strike a bargain with the pope at their expense.[10] During the turmoil afflicting Europe, the Netherlands also found it expedient to establish relations with the Vatican.

As the war continued so did criticism of the Vatican's policy and position. Berlin and Vienna, no more than Paris, London, and St. Petersburg, appreciated the papal efforts on behalf of peace, resenting outside interference while nourishing hopes of winning the war. Their concern was not alleviated by Benedict's Christmas address of December 24, 1914, which called upon the powers to submit to arbitration and a peaceful settlement of the dispute. Searching for a common ground among the combatants, Pope Benedict reiterated that he would not condemn one side while favoring another, and had Cardinal Pietro Gasparri write as much to the archbishop of Lyon. His letter reiterated that the Holy See embraced all the faithful of the Universal Church requiring "the strictest and most absolute impartiality toward the different belligerent nations."[11]

Impartiality did not impede or restrict the Vatican's efforts to assist the victims of the conflict. In the new year, Benedict renewed his efforts to alleviate the suffering, if he could not end the war, expanding his extensive charitable efforts, aiding prisoners of war and refugees, and providing money, material, and food across the continent from France to Lithuania. Under his auspices, numerous Catholic agencies were established to minister to the sick, wounded and destitute, assigning priests to visit the unfortunate victims of the conflict. He also established a Papal Office for Prisoners of War, which worked for the liberation and exchange of prisoners; decent burial and marked graves for the fallen; insistence on Sunday as a feast day for the interned and providing provision for the visitation of prisoners. These efforts were supplemented by the Papal Office for Notifying Families of the whereabouts of missing members, seeking to put them in contact with the interned. This extensive charitable program of the papacy created a virtual "Second Red Cross," alleviating the suffering of combatants and civilians. Both Benedict's "apostolate of charity" and his insistence on "papal impartiality" set examples that Pope Pius XII later would emulate during the course of World War II.

In January 1915, Benedict, in an allocution or address to the cardinals, appealed to belligerents who had crossed frontiers, not to create any more damage than absolutely necessary—and it was assumed that the pope had reference to German atrocities in Belgium. The Germans protested, but the papal invocation did not satisfy the Entente, which sought an explicit denunciation of German war crimes. That same January, Cardinal Gasparri revealed that the pope, had composed a special prayer for peace, to be read worldwide. The secretary of state also reported that Benedict decreed a day of exposition of the blessed sacrament to beseech God's mercy, recommending the public recitation of his own prayer and the rosary. To quiet the continuing charges of papal partisanship, Benedict proclaimed that the Vatican embraced all the combatants in the same sense of charity. This pronouncement, like the earlier ones did not indict one side or the other, and therefore produced censure from both camps.

In June 1915, the correspondent Louis Latopié of the French newspaper *Liberté,* claimed that during an interview, the pope blamed England for the war while exonerating Germany—a contention Benedict quickly and publicly denied. Benedict complained that M. Latapié's article "reproduced neither Our thought nor Our words."[12] Not surprisingly, he was the last journalist received by Pope Benedict during the conflict. Nonetheless, this did not end the matter, nor curtail the antagonism and anger of the Allies. The French, convinced of the animosity of the Vatican provoked by the Republic's 1905 separation of church and state, were prepared to believe the most lurid accusations hurled against it. To detect the schemes allegedly being hatched by the curia, the French dispatched a number of figures to spy on the Holy See, including the writer Charles Loiseau entrusted with a semi-official mission. Among other things, Paris was convinced that the former minister Joseph Caillaux and his wife were embroiled in a Vatican conspiracy to realign France with Germany—a story eventually exposed as a complete fabrication.

The American view of the Vatican was equally skewed as the anti-Catholic ambassador to Italy, Thomas Nelson Page denounced "the nefarious influence of the 'Catholic Conspiracy' in international affairs." In Washington ignorance combined with prejudice to produce a mixture of misinformation about papal positions and policies. Page was misinformed on Vatican developments and little inclined to allay Wilson's suspicions of the alleged pro-German sentiments of the Holy See. Since Washington was also convinced that the apostolic delegate Monsignor Giovanni Bonzano was pro-German, it sought an alternative channel to the Holy See and Cardinal James Gibbons of Baltimore suggested dispatching his assistant Father Cyril Fay, supposedly to assist the Red Cross in Rome, but in reality to advise the Vatican on American issues. Although Fay endeavored to disabuse Washington of some of its misconceptions about the Holy See's stance, it did little to promote the flow of information from the Vatican to Washington.[13] The American suspicions remained and Washington ignored Benedict's advice to remain neutral in the conflict between Francisco "Pancho" Villa and Venustiano Carranza during the Mexican revolution in 1915. Instead, Wilson, son of a Presbyterian minister, recognized the latter, who persecuted the church.

The British likewise questioned papal activity as the war of maneuver was converted into one of stalemate. "As to the Pope and peace, I feel sure that the Germans, through Cardinal Hartmann and others, are bringing great pressure on His Holiness to propose some sort of intervention," Henry Howard wrote home on December 1, 1915. He went on to report that the pope had indicated this was not the right moment to do so, but commented that "all the same one can never tell what His Holiness may not do or say."[14] Some Italians were even more suspicious, convinced that the Vatican was scheming with the Central Powers to partition Italy, or at the very least to resolve the Roman Question in a manner detrimental for the Kingdom. Meanwhile, the Allied press was almost unanimous in denouncing Benedict's failure to indict the Central Powers as war criminals.

Nor were the pope's humanitarian desire and prayers to keep Italy out of the war well received in the Allied capitals, which hoped that Italian intervention would break the stalemate on the western front, assuring an Allied victory. Their resentment increased upon learning of the Vatican pressure on Austria to offer the Italians territorial compensation to keep them out of the conflict. Allied concerns were compounded when they learned that German Catholic groups were providing funds to the depleted Vatican treasury. To make matters worse, the Bavarian Monsignor Rudolf Gerlach, papal chamberlain and virtual private secretary of the pope, was denounced as a German spy by the Italians. Only after the Italians presented evidence of his espionage activity, including his scheme to destroy the Italian navy, was he turned over to the Italian authorities who conducted him to the Swiss border. Although a court inquiry exonerated the Vatican of any complicity in the Monsignor's schemes and spying, the "Gerlach affair" rocked the Vatican, sent Pope Benedict into a spiral of depression, and seriously compromised the papal image of strict impartiality. The honors bestowed on Gerlach by the German, Austrian, and Turkish governments, appeared to reveal their complicity in his espionage. It compounded Allied paranoia as some in the Entente concluded that Benedict's support of Italian neutrality flowed from German pressure and espionage. This conclusion encouraged the Salandra government in April 1915 to sign the Treaty of London, which called for Italian intervention against Austria, and whose article XV prohibited Vatican participation in the peace conference.[15] Benito Mussolini, who ardently and vociferously championed entry into the war, objected to Benedict's peace efforts, which he considered both intrusive and profoundly anti-Italian. Nationalists in the peninsula supported his accusations, and likewise railed against the pope's peace efforts.

Benedict believed that his efforts to spare Italy the trials of war was in the best interests of the Italian people and sought to preserve good relations with their government. He resolved not to embarrass it by recourse to international diplomacy to resolve the Roman Question, indicating his affection for Italy and the Italians. Departing from past Vatican practice, he recognized Victor Emmanuel as King of Italy, rather than simply as Duke of Savoy, as had his predecessors. In turn, after Italy entered the World War on May 24, 1915, the Italians allowed the Austrian, Prussian, and Bavarian envoys to relocate in the Vatican, but they preferred to withdraw first to Lugano, Switzerland and later to Bern. Benedict, however, declined the suggestion that the papacy temporarily move to Switzerland or Spain, clinging tenaciously both to Rome and his impartiality. Following the sinking of the British liner, the Lusitania, by a German submarine on May 7, 1915, Cardinal Gasquet urged Benedict XV to issue a condemnation of this atrocity. The pope responded that he planned to condemn "all methods of barbarism, which alas, we see have been introduced into the war and which among other sad conditions have caused the deaths of so many victims, such as the barbarous sinking of the Lusitania."[16] He would say no more, and continued to shun partisanship.

As the war's devastation mounted, Pope Benedict increased his efforts to seek its termination. In his exhortation of July 28, 1915, to the belligerents on the first anniversary of its outbreak, he urged the powers to end the slaughter and conclude a just peace. "Blessed be he who will first raise the olive branch, and hold out his right hand to the enemy with an offer of reasonable terms of peace," the pope pleaded, adding with prophetic insight that "the equilibrium of the world, and the prosperity and assured tranquility of nations rest upon mutual benevolence and respect for the rights and dignity of others, much more than upon hosts of armed men and the ring of formidable fortresses."[17] In September, Benedict encouraged Woodrow Wilson to launch a peace appeal, but the American President would only act if all the warring parties welcomed his intervention. Nonetheless, Benedict hoped that President Wilson might nudge the belligerents to accept a negotiated peace. Calling for an exchange of ideas and a willingness to make concessions, Benedict sought solace in prayer as he lamented the "barbaric war."[18]

Although his appeals were not answered, the pope continued his crusade to alleviate suffering, offering whatever assistance he could muster, providing aid to Serbia, Lithuania, Belgium, Poland, Luxembourg, Armenia, Syria, and Lebanon without distinction of race or religion in his charitable donations. Among other things, Benedict pleaded for the liberation or exchange of prisoners of war, decent burial for those who had fallen in battle, as well as financial and medical aid to those rendered destitute by the scourge of war. His efforts to provide such assistance virtually exhausted the papal treasury. Indeed, the entire Peter's Pence collection of 1914 was earmarked for Belgian relief as financial, material, and spiritual assistance was provided for the devastated and displaced populations of both camps. In 1915, he called for a collection from the Catholic world to provide assistance for the people of Poland. He also continued his extensive prisoner of war services. To aid families locate lost civilian and military members, a missing bureau was created in the Vatican, which helped establish a permanent mission in Bern to negotiate on behalf of soldiers and civilians. It represented the first international effort to place prisoners of war in touch with their families and proved so successful that the various national hierarchies established branch offices in their jurisdictions. The pope proved supportive of these local efforts.

Benedict also responded positively to the request that he use his moral authority to aid the Jews caught in the conflict. "The Supreme Pontiff . . . considers all men brothers and teaches them to love one another," Cardinal Gasparri responded to their appeal. "This law must be observed and respected in the case of the children of Israel, as well as of others, because it would not be conformable to justice or to religion itself to derogate from it solely on account of divergence of religious confessions."[19] Despite the Vatican's moral commitment to peace and its massive aid program, criticism of its policies did not diminish. Even its call for the humane treatment of prisoners of war by both camps, led some to charge that the Holy See was aiding the enemy.

Cardinal Gasparri responded that the Holy Father served as mediator between peoples, and had to defend law and morality for all.[20] Despite considerable pressure from the belligerents to name the aggressors, Benedict refused to assign responsibility, claiming a condemnation would provoke animosity rather than promote harmony.[21] The Germans, in turn, resented that the pope would not sanction any peace overture that did not provide for the full restoration of Belgium. On December 12, 1916, the Central Powers—Germany, Austria-Hungary, Turkey, and Bulgaria—dispatched a note to a number of governments urging the Entente Powers of Great Britain, France, Russia, and Italy to commence peace negotiations. When the Central Powers called upon the Vatican to press those in the Entente to negotiate, it did not do so recognizing that such an intervention would be ill received by England and France.[22] It might even be miscon-strued as a Vatican endorsement of the German proposal. Consequently, the pope's Christmas appeal for peace of December 24, 1916, like earlier ones, was nonpartisan, and served as the prelude for a new major papal peace effort.

In April 1917, the pope appointed Eugenio Pacelli, a member of the black or papal aristocracy, as Nuncio to Bavaria and also accredited him to the Imperial Court at Berlin. In May, this diplomatic figure who taught international relations at the school for papal diplomats in Rome, presented his credentials to Ludwig III, King of Bavaria. The following month, Pacelli met the German Chancellor Theobald von Bethmann-Hollweg, and discussed the essential conditions for a peaceful resolution of the conflict. These included: (1) the limitation of armaments, (2) the establishment of international tribunals, (3) Belgian independence, but (4) leaving contentious issues such as Alsace-Lorraine to be settled by the contending parties. Because of these talks, it was suggested in the Allied capitals that the pope's peace plan was inspired by the Central Powers. Paradoxically, the Germans were also critical of papal activities. When the Kaiser received Pacelli at the end of June 1917, he complained that the pope had not used his prerogative of papal infallibility to condemn the "atrocities of the Allies."[23]

The Allies, in turn, were distressed by the Russian Revolution of March 1917, which was welcomed by the Vatican. The Holy See's reaction was governed by religious rather than political principles, appreciative of the conciliatory attitude expressed by the provisional government towards the Catholic Church in Russia and the papacy in Rome. In fact, the new Russian government initially granted the church control of their religious buildings, while allowing it to open seminaries and religious schools. The relief proved temporary, undermined by the Bolshevik Revolution that ensued. While claiming to guarantee freedom of religion, Lenin's regime soon initiated a persecution of the church reminiscent of the French revolutionary period and its reign of terror. Nonetheless, this did not deter the Vatican from appealing to the Soviet government for the establishment of religious freedom in their revolutionary realm.[24] Despite its fulminations against Bolshevism and Communism, Benedict's Vatican continued to quietly negotiate with the Soviet Union, later sending a mission there to feed and clothe its war-torn population. The Allies and the Vatican also did not see eye to eye on Washington's intervention in the World War. The Allies proved much more enthusiastic about the American entry into the conflict, than the Vatican, whose reaction was mixed. On the one hand Benedict tended to oppose any extension of the destructive war, but on the other hand nourished the hope that American intervention might bring the war and suffering to a more speedy conclusion.

On August 1, 1917, in the third year of the catastrophic conflict, Benedict dispatched his peace note to the belligerents. The British representative at the Vatican, John Francis de Salis, was asked to transmit the papal proposal to France, Italy, and the United States, whose governments were not officially represented at the Vatican. Benedict's note reiterated the three overriding aims of his pontificate toward the war: determination to maintain absolute impartiality, to do the utmost good without distinction of persons, nationality, or religion, and finally to omit nothing to hasten the end of the calamity. To achieve these goals, Benedict outlined general terms on which a peace might be concluded proposing arbitration, the reduction of armaments, freedom of the seas, no punitive indemnities, evacuation of occupied territories, and the consultation of the inhabitants of disputed areas before redrawing frontiers. More specifically, the note called for: (1) a simultaneous and reciprocal decrease in armaments, (2) international arbitration and an international court to substitute for armies, (3) free intercourse of peoples and liberty of the seas, (4) the reciprocal renunciation of war indemnities, (5) evacuation and restoration of all occupied territories and finally, (6) the resolution of political and territorial claims between Italy and Austria and France and Germany to be determined in a spirit of equity and justice, (7) a similar spirit of equity and justice to determine other territorial and political disputes and particularly those that concern Armenia, the Balkan states, and Poland. These could be realized sequentially: first the suspension of the fighting, second the reduction of armaments, and finally the institution of arbitration to resolve differences.[25] Later, Benedict expressed the wish that Poland be restored to full independence, resuming its place in the family of nations.[26]

The initial response was positive, at least as regards a part of the press in the Allied countries. *The Evening Post* of New York proclaimed the papal initiative "a diplomatic and international event of the first rank,"[27] while Italy's *Giornale d'Italia* praised the outline of the peace proposal. On August 14, 1917, The *Evening Post* announced that Benedict's peace proposal deserved a respectful and close reading, observing that this papal mediation might provide the path to a just and lasting peace. It noted:

> For the first time, the Pope, in his approaches to the belligerents, is concrete. He goes into details. He states terms. He mentions Belgium, he mentions Servia, he mentions Rumania. And his flat proposal is that these conquered and trampled lands be

"restored." Nor is he unaware of other and subsidiary questions. His Holiness knows of Polish national aspirations, of the Italian ambitions in the Trentino and Trieste, of the French longing for the recovery of the lost provinces. These matters, too, he refers to explicitly, and urges that they be settled by peaceful negotiation. The main thing, however, is his precise definition of the minimum terms of peace. Belgium, Servia, Rumania, evacuated and restored—here is at once the greater part of what the Allies have been fighting for.[28]

Despite this early approval by part of the press, the belligerent governments, responding to poisonous rumors that fueled hatred, did not react positively to the Vatican peace proposal. While the London government courteously received Benedict's suggestions, the British cabinet spent less time on assessing its contents than the discussion on if, and how, to respond. Following considerable procrastination, the Foreign Secretary Lord Arthur James Balfour made it plain that until they and their Allies had decided on the level of reparations they required and the nature of projected restoration they deemed essential, they could not, and would not, consider the present peace proposal. This stance reflected English public opinion, influenced by the increasingly lurid war propaganda, and therefore outraged by the moderate nature of the papal proposal. Not surprisingly, most of the English press also proved less than enthusiastic about Benedict's suggestions, with the *Westminister Gazette* one of the few newspapers that perceived some merit in his outline. By and large, however, the English public found it ill-timed and unfocused, especially denouncing the papacy's impartiality and failure to condemn the Huns.

The anticlerical Italian Foreign Minister Sidney Sonnino concurred, charging that the papal note lacked precision and balance, and was at once unrealistic and dangerous. Furthermore, the Italian government, fearing the danger presented by the "Black Menace" or Holy See, considered it an unfriendly move, which warranted no response. This view was shared by the French minister to Italy from 1898 to 1924, Camille Barrère, who believed the Allies should consult, but not respond. In France, the Prime Minister Georges Clemenceau, bent on revenge, criticized the Vatican's effort as "a peace against France" and one geared to profit "the violators of justice." President Wilson was no more pleased by the papal intervention than the European Allies and supposedly complained, "What does he want to butt in for?"[29] The American president was all too prone to suspect and accept the worst calumnies launched against the Vatican and the anti-German propaganda. In fact, Wilson increasingly saw Germany as an aggressive militaristic power that had to be contained and converted. Some Europeans as well as Americans complained of papal arrogance in attempting to restore the status quo, which they considered unrealistic and unacceptable.

The American Secretary of State Robert Lansing responded more diplomatically, but like the Italians, found the Vatican plan unrealistic, supporting the British call for the need to assign culpability and moral responsibility. In late August 1917, Woodrow Wilson responded to Benedict's proposal. Despite the humanitarian impulse of the Pontiff, the American president noted that terms he suggested simply brought matters back to the *status quo ante bellum* and failed to tackle the serious issues of Prussian and German militarism and aggression. Paris, London, and Rome concurred and were pleased with Wilson's rejection. The German reply proved equally problematic. The new Chancellor Georg Michaelis promised his government would support those efforts of His Holiness, which could be reconciled with the interests of the German people, making no commitment to restore the full sovereignty of Belgium.[30]

Benedict was deeply disappointed that his mediation had been rejected by the principal powers in both camps, distressed to see the death and desolation continue. Despite repeated efforts, the papal initiative for making and preserving the peace went largely unrecognized so that the 1917 Nobel Peace Prize was awarded to the Red Cross rather than the pope. The failure of his mediation was one of the most bitter moments in Benedict's pontificate. Meanwhile, American suspicion of the Holy See contributed to its opposition to the Vatican's attempt to appoint a nuncio to Peking and Washington's reluctance to persuade Mexico to cease its persecution of the church. Depressed by these developments, Benedict found some solace in the liberation of Jerusalem at the end of 1917 by General Edmund Allenby, and Cardinal Gasparri sent congratulations to the British for this achievement. This message evoked protests from the Central Powers, who complained that this violated Vatican neutrality. Gasparri retorted that the Vatican had perforce to take sides on issues such as the recovery of the Holy Places, motivated by religious rather than political considerations. Similar religious concerns led the Vatican to worry about the British promises made to the Zionists. Early in November 1917, the British Foreign Secretary Lord Arthur James Balfour issued the "British Declaration of Sympathy with Zionist Aspirations" or "Balfour Declaration" promising support for the establishment in Palestine of a national home for the Jewish people,[31] which the Vatican found troubling. Benedict favored a Jewish return to Palestine as providential and miraculous, but like his predecessor Pius X opposed giving the Jews economic and political preferences over the other nationalities and religions, to the detriment of Christian interests. At the same time the Vatican deemed an Arab administration of Palestine as unreliable and unacceptable, veering towards an internationalization of Jerusalem. To assure the Catholic position in the Holy Land, in October 1918, Benedict confirmed the rights and privileges of the Franciscans there, providing the funding for the maintenance of the shrines and other holy places.

In the interim, the gist of the papal peace proposal was not lost and reappeared in President Wilson's "fourteen points" of January 1918, which some believe borrowed from and elaborated upon the pope's suggestions and emerged as the clarion call for the creation of an international organization for the preservation of peace. Wilson's proposal called for: (1) renunciation of secret diplomacy, (2) freedom of the seas, (3) removal of economic barriers between nations, (4) reduction of armaments, (5) impartial adjustment of colonial claims, (6) evacuation and restoration of Russian territory, (7) restoration of Belgian sovereignty, (8) evacuation of France and the return of Alsace-Lorraine, (9) redrawing the Italian frontier along national lines, (10) autonomy for the peoples of Austria-Hungary, (11) evacuation of Montenegro, Rumania and Serbia, (12) self-determination for the peoples of the Ottoman Empire and freedom of navigation through the Dardenelles, (13) establishment of an independent Poland with access to the sea, and finally (14) creation of an association of nations to govern international relations.[32] Benedict approved of Wilson's Fourteen Points seeing in them an accentuation and development of the principles he had outlined six months earlier. He also concurred with Wilson's earlier call for a peace without victory, convinced this would help assure a permanent settlement.

The peace was also to be preserved by the projected League of Nations, whose covenant formed the first part (articles 1–24) of the Treaties of Versailles with Germany, Saint Germain with Austria, Trianon with Hungary, and Neuilly with Bulgaria. Wilson, like Benedict, invoked a new diplomacy and collaborated with the English in drafting the League's structure, which was to spearhead the new era of diplomatic cooperation. The Holy See, generally described in international law as a power, was not admitted to the League whose membership was restricted to states, dominions, and colonies.[33] There were those who concluded that as a consequence the Vatican opposed the League, which allegedly usurped the papal prerogative of mediation in international disputes. Indeed, the American president blamed it for much of the opposition in the United States, claiming to have documents and correspondence pointing to its obstructionism.[34] These alleged proofs of Vatican opposition to the League never materialized, but nonetheless many in America and Europe remain convinced that the Vatican opposed the League of Nations. The charge was mistaken.

The pope and curia did have reservations about the League's restricted membership, the distribution of power within the organization, and the initial exclusion of the vanquished states. Despite these concerns, from the first Pope Benedict embraced the president's efforts on behalf of an international organization, which in large measure reflected his own thoughts and sentiments. Both he and Cardinal Gasparri hoped it would end the costly and destructive war, while providing for a just and lasting peace. Nourishing that hope, the pope called upon the clergy to celebrate mass on behalf of peace. He also authorized the publication of a "Papal White Book" to demonstrate the impartiality of the Holy See, revealing its attempts to lessen the suffering, while hastening its conclusion, all in the interest of humanity. In an Easter message to the United States, Pope Benedict invoked a lasting peace and the emergence of a new organization of peoples and nations aspiring to a "nobler, purer, and kinder civilization."[35] Shortly thereafter, the pope rejoiced to hear of the Austrian-Italian peace negotiations, pleading for a solution in conformity with the just aspirations of their peoples. He categorically denied the circulating insinuations that the Holy See was displeased by the Italian victory. In April 1918, Benedict sent Achille Ratti, the future Pope Pius XI, to Poland as Apostolic Visitor, to help in their religious and material reconstruction.

At the opening of December 1918, Benedict responded enthusiastically to the general armistice of November 11, which brought to an end the universal madness and suicide of nations. He invoked divine assistance for the participants in the peace conference, enabling them to produce a peace based on Christian principles. This invocation was repeated in his Christmas Eve message, calling for justice and charity to be the hallmark of the Versailles Peace Conference.[36] His prayerful efforts were bolstered by his recourse to diplomatic initiatives. Early in January 1919, Benedict XV met with Wilson, the first president of the United States received by a pontiff, and the first to travel to Europe while in office. Since Wilson only spoke English, and Benedict did not, an interpreter was necessary.

The two discussed prospects for a lasting peace, with the Holy Father expressing the hope that prisoners of war would soon be returned to their respective countries. The pope asserted that a punitive settlement would assure neither peace nor tranquility—a theme repeated in the columns of the Vatican's *L'Osservatore Romano* and the Jesuit-run *Civiltà Cattolica*. Among other things both Benedict and Wilson opposed the secret treaties and the selfish acquisition of additional colonies by the victors. The Roman Question was not raised, nor was there any effort on the pope's part to be included in the impending negotiations. In 1919, President Wilson, rather than Pope Benedict XV, was awarded the Nobel Peace Prize. The British representative at the Vatican confirmed that Cardinal Gasparri did not try to embroil himself in their talks.[37] Rumors of an alleged attempt of the Vatican to force itself into the peace process resurfaced when Benedict dispatched Monsignor Bonaventura Cerretti to Versailles. However, this papal envoy was sent to safeguard the missions in the former German colonies, not to interject the Vatican into the broader deliberations of the Congress.

The same papal interest in evangelization inspired Benedict's missionary pronouncement of 1919, *Maximum Illud*, the charter of the church's modern missionary movement. In his message Benedict emphasized: (1) the missionary duty of all members of the church, (2) the promotion of the native clergy, (3) renunciation on the part of the missionaries of nationalism and condescension, and (4) an appreciation of the culture of the missionary territories.[38] By its terms, Benedict explicitly disassociated the Catholic Church from European imperialism, as he prohibited nationalism among the missionaries while insisting they respect the native culture. Calling for the establishment of native clergies and episcopacies, he reorganized the Society for the Propagation of the Faith and created the Missionary Union of the Clergy. Distressed by the lack of native vocations, he ordered the Congregation for the Propagation of the Faith to determine the causes—and fix them. For his efforts he was dubbed the "pope of the missions." At the same time Benedict abandoned Pius X's attempts to Romanize the Eastern Uniate churches, establishing a special Congregation to protect the interests of Eastern Catholics, over which he personally presided. The pope and his secretary of state worried about the future of the holy places in Jerusalem that the statesmen at Versailles did not resolve. This was left for a future conference of the Allies that met at San Remo in April 1920, and granted Protestant Britain the sole mandate for Palestine, while Catholic France was accorded mandates over Syria and Lebanon. Sir Herbert Samuel, the Jewish first high commissioner, who was received by the pope prior to assuming his assignment, sought to reassure the Vatican that its interests in Holy Land would be preserved. Benedict remained concerned.

Disillusioned by the orgy of death and destruction of the past four years, Benedict confronted a continent decimated by hunger, disease, and disorder. Determined to render impossible the renewal of crimes from which the world still bled, the pope favored a reorganization of international relations. He regretted the inability of the prevailing international configuration to peacefully resolve conflicts, and as early as 1914 appealed to the nations of the world to find some other means of resolving their differences. Deploring the violation of international law, Benedict believed this contributed to the carnage and sought a new code to assure a more tranquil future. Cardinal Gasparri had said as much when he elaborated upon the pope's peace proposal, focusing on Benedict's call for restrictions on state sovereignty and a new world order, which included the suppression, by common accord of compulsory military service; the constitution of a court of arbitration for the solution of international questions, and lastly, for the prevention of infractions, the establishment of a universal boycott.[39]

In his encyclical "On Peace and Christian Reconciliation" of May 1920, the pope pleaded for nations to put aside mutual suspicion and unite in a league to prevent the outbreak of future disasters.

> Things being thus restored, the order required by justice and charity re-established and the nations reconciled, it is much to be desired Venerable Brethren, that all States putting aside suspicion, should unite in one league, or rather a sort of family of peoples, calculated both to maintain their own independence and safeguard the order of human society. What specially, amongst other reasons, calls for such an association of nations, is the need generally recognized of making every effort to abolish or reduce the enormous burden of the military expenditures which States can no longer bear, in order to prevent these disastrous wars or at least to remove the danger of them as far as possible. So would each nation be assured not only of its independence but also of the integrity of its territory within its just frontiers.[40]

Appreciative of President Wilson's efforts on behalf of a League of Nations, the Vatican neither engineered nor gloated over the American failure to enter the institution the American president had inspired, regretting this turn of events.[41] Despite its limitations and imperfections, the League of Nations, which emerged was judged the sole organized effort to realize the Vatican's pacific goals. On the other hand, the pope was displeased with the results of the peacemaking process and found the powers unwilling to forget or forgive. They ignored his call to resume cordial relations by clearing their hearts of bitterness and opening them to mutual love, concord, and Christian charity. The Gospel, Benedict preached in vain, did not have one law of charity for individuals, and another for states and nations. His advice was politically sound as well as morally ethical, as he warned there could be neither a stable peace nor lasting treaties, unless there was a return to mutual charity and the banishment of enmity. His was a voice crying in the wilderness.

The Vatican, like the Germans, expected the peace would be based on Wilson's Fourteen Points, and both were disappointed when these provisions and promises were largely disregarded. The vindictive provisions of the treaties emanating from Paris distressed Benedict, as the *Civiltà Cattolica*, close to the Vatican, branded its 440 "articles of peace" as "articles of war."[42] The pope particularly decried the consequences for Catholic Austria, lamenting that this nation, which had valiantly defended Christian civilization, had been reduced to a fragment of its former self, lacking the elements for a continued existence. He urged those who signed the treaty to provide for the people of this unhappy land, while complaining that the treaties had not provided adequate protection for the Catholic missions.[43] Finally, Benedict expressed concern about the situation in Palestine declaring, "We do not wish to deprive the Jews of their rights; we want, nevertheless, that they be not in any way preferred to the just rights of Christians."[44]

Benedict could not elude the pessimism of the postwar period, concluding that humanity would have to look to Christ for justice. "Mankind needs not the sort of peace that is built up on the laborious deliberations of worldly prudence, but that peace which was brought to us by Christ when He declared, 'My Peace I give unto you; not as the world gives, do I give unto you.'" Observing the work of the statesmen at Versailles, the Holy Father concluded that "A man-made treaty, whether of states or of classes among themselves, can neither endure nor have at all the value of a peace, unless it rests upon a peaceful disposition."[45] In the summer of 1919, Pope Benedict called upon President Wilson to use his influence to block the proposed trial of the Kaiser and his military officers, which the *Osservatore Romano* found unprecedented and impractical. The Vatican journal denounced the notion that the accusers should constitute the tribunal of justice, asserting that this procedure would create rancor rather than reconciliation. Wilson concurred, and eventually the Allies abandoned plans for such a trial.

Although disillusioned by the treaties, Benedict continued to champion charity and peace worldwide and under his leadership the Vatican became increasingly engaged in international affairs. In January 1920, after the conclusion of peace, the Prussian and Bavarian legations returned to Rome and subsequently the nuncio at Munich was transferred to Berlin. Soon, thereafter, relations were restored with France. By this time some 30 countries had ambassadors or ministers at the Holy See. Benedict even made overtures to Lenin and the Soviets as he sought to improve the international climate.

Social concerns, as well as religious and political ones, occupied Pope Benedict. In an encyclical of November 1919, he deplored the lack of sufficient aid for Europe after the war, making a specific appeal on behalf of its forlorn children. He returned to this theme December of the following year calling for continued relief assistance. He also sympathized with the suffering endured by the people of Russia, invoking aid on their behalf. Despite disagreement with the Bolshevik government, he sought to relieve the plague and famine prevalent among its suffering population. "We feel the duty laid on Us to do all that Our poverty makes possible to help Our far-off children," he wrote his secretary of state, urging him "to use all the means at your disposal to bring home to the governments of the different nations the need for prompt and efficacious common action."[46] Soon thereafter, the pope personally intervened by sending a telegram to the League of Nations, exhorting the organization and its members to help the Russian people.[47] In January 1922, toward the end of his pontificate, he planned to dispatch a secret papal mission to the Soviet Union. These conciliatory efforts were neither appreciated nor reciprocated by the Soviet leaders, disappointing pope and curia.

Benedict was also distressed by the political disorder and social upheaval that rocked post-war Italy, where there was a broad dissatisfaction with the treatment they had received at Versailles as critics charged they had "won the war but lost the peace." Sympathizing with the plight of Italians, Benedict composed and presented a special prayer for peace in Italy, deploring the fact that the "land most famed for Christian piety, cradle of civil kindness, is becoming once again a bloodstained field of civil war."[48] The Vatican's appreciation of the gravity of the Italian situation led the pope to reverse the course of his predecessor and permit the establishment of an independent Catholic political party, under the Priest Don Luigi Sturzo. In another gesture of goodwill, Benedict formally ended the *non-expedit,* which Pius X had largely ignored.

Benedict realized that his efforts could mitigate but not eliminate the problems besetting Italy, the continent, and the world beyond. Noting with sorrow and anxiety that the treaty had not produced either peace or tranquility, the pope cited the need for God's intervention to remedy the social, political, economic, and religious evils burdening mankind. He did not imply that rulers and governments should not have recourse to the available political remedies to ensure the common good, but stressed it was mistaken to rely solely on human effort.[49] He personally continued to support international reconciliation, relying on the powers to do so. His efforts met some success for during his tenure the number of countries with diplomatic ties to the Vatican doubled. In November 1921, he telegraphed President Warren Harding of the United States (1921–1923) at the opening of the Arms Conference in Washington, which addressed the thorny issue of naval disarmament, while in December the pontiff blessed the work of the First International Democratic Congress in Paris.[50]

Pope Benedict was disturbed and surprised, by the distortion of his efforts on behalf of peace, being denounced as *der franzosiche Papst* by some Germans and *le Pape boche* by some in France, and *Maledetto XV* by Italian ultra-nationalists. Benedict noted:

After the outbreak of this conflagration, which for the good of all We wished could have been averted, so far as was in Our power We missed no opportunity of doing or attempting anything that might mitigate the terrible consequences. More than once . . . , We reproved, as again now We reprove, every violation of right wherever it may be perpetrated. In addition to that, with exhortations, public prayers, expiatory functions, with proposals for a just and lasting peace, We studied to bring nearer the end of this awful slaughter. In spite of that, Beloved Son and Venerable Brothers, you know well the crazy and absurd calumnies which, under many and varied forms, publicly and secretly, by word of mouth and in writing, are being spread everywhere. In the country and the villages, where sorrow is deepest, and on that account most deserving of regard and respect, it is being said that We desired the war; in the cities, on the other hand, it is spread about that We desire peace, but an unjust peace which would be an advantage only to one of the belligerent groups. And Our word are so twisted, Our thoughts and intentions so suspected, Our silence with regard to this or that misdeed is so scandalously misinterpreted.[51]

Although Benedict XV's pontificate witnessed an increased diplomatic representation at the Vatican—including the British who dispatched a chargé d'affaires in 1915, the resumption of relations with France in 1921, and the opening of secret talks with the new Mussolini government in 1922—the views of the Holy See were often ignored or distorted. Confronted by the flagrant misrepresentation of papal thought and action, the devastation of the war in Europe, the fall of empires, and the destruction of dynasties, pessimism prevailed in the Vatican, which Benedict shared. Benedict had done his best, carefully guiding the church through the perilous conflict, preserving its neutrality or impartiality, but regretted being unable to bring the war to a more speedy conclusion and the misunderstanding and misstating of his mission. Dismayed by the treaties and the prospect that they would not assure permanent peace, the discouraged pontiff neglected the cold he caught at the end of December 1921, which contributed to a bronchial infection, influenza, and his death by pneumonia on January 22, 1922, at the age of 67. His charitable work so depleted the papal treasury that Cardinal Gasparri was constrained to borrow to pay for Benedict's funeral and the conclave that followed.

Eventually Benedict's charitable work and peace efforts secured recognition and earned Benedict the title "Pope of Peace." In fact, as early as 1920 the Muslin Turks erected a statue in Istanbul to "the great Pope of the World Tragedy." Despite considerable criticism, Benedict's cautious diplomacy had elevated the international status of the papacy. Even Benito Mussolini, who had bitterly criticized the pope's efforts on behalf of peace during the conflict, later grudgingly acknowledged that Benedict XV "was a great pope."[52]

The Vatican in an Age of Dictatorship, Totalitarianism, and Anti-Semitism, 1922–1939

In the conclave of February 2–6, 1922, after 5 days and 14 ballots, the Archbishop of Milan, Cardinal Achille Ratti, who in 1914 had been named Prefect of the Vatican Library, emerged as a compromise candidate for the Italian cardinals, who dominated the conclave. Ratti assumed the name Pius XI in honor of Pius IX, during whose pontificate he had been born and baptized, and whose outspoken manner and willingness to champion church principles, he admired. Like Pius IX he proved willing to confront challenges and tackle problems, without always considering the consequences. One of his first actions was to extend the time between a pope's death and the opening of the conclave from 10 to 18 days, to broaden participation in the papal election by allowing more cardinals from overseas to participate in the process thus rendering the papal office more truly international.

Pragmatic as well as scholarly, Ratti had been constrained to leave his serene, and somewhat secluded, existence in 1918 when he was appointed Apostolic Visitor to Poland. Almost immediately it was clear that despite his original instructions, his mission to Warsaw transcended the religious sphere, assuming an important diplomatic dimension. Following the creation of the Polish state in 1919, Ratti was named nuncio to the resurrected state, and met often with Joseph Pilsudski (1867–1935), its provisional head, whom he admired. Some believe that this figure colored Ratti's positive notions of dictators and dictatorships during the course of his pontificate and later influenced his stance toward Mussolini and Fascist Italy. In 1921, he was transferred to Milan, and made a cardinal, and the following year the 65-year-old Ratti was elected pope. Like his predecessor Benedict XV, Pius XI considered the Great War catastrophic, sharing his reservations about the justice and efficacy of the treaties as well as his concerns about the ability of the League of Nations to preserve the peace.

Following in the footsteps of Pope Benedict XV, Pius invoked international reconciliation, begging the powers to cooperate in the search for permanent remedies for the host of problems troubling Europe. "The people which have suffered so much in the past conflict and its recent unhappy consequences justly desire that the work of the Conference may result in the removal, so far as is possible, of the danger of fresh wars, and as soon as may be, in the economic restoration of Europe," he wrote Cardinal Gasparri, who he trusted and retained as secretary of state.[1] He was disappointed by the lame diplomatic efforts and lack of economic programs made to preserve the peace, repeating that peace could not be reestablished simply by silencing the guns. Having witnessed first hand Soviet militancy while stationed in Poland, Pius XI was sensitive to the peril of communism and the prospect of future Soviet expansion.

Distressed by developments from 1919 to 1922, he praised the agenda of the Genoa Peace Conference on economic reconstruction of April 1922, convinced that the alleviation of the burdens of the vanquished would redound to the advantage of the victors as well. During the Genoa Conference, which Bolshevik Russia attended, Pius regretted the hatred among nations, calling the attention of the delegates to the dismal world situation. He hoped that the victors would facilitate the alleviation of the world's burdens, imploring prayers for peace and commending the conference as a step toward international harmony. Peace, he proclaimed, required reconciliation, while his representative to the conference, Monsignor Giuseppe Pizzardo, of the secretariat of state, urged that religious liberty be included in any agreement with Russia.[2] Although the Bolsheviks proved noncommittal, Pius, like Benedict, continued to provide relief for the Russian people. Pointing to the hardships in Russia and other parts of the world, the pope urged remedies for these disasters as he aimed to bring Christian peace into the hearts of men, proclaiming "The Peace of Christ in the Reign of Christ."[3]

Determined to provide as much assistance as his treasury would allow, Pius pledged substantial Vatican resources for relief and reconstruction in the stricken European continent, with his Relief Mission to Moscow alone assisting more than one hundred fifty thousand souls during the critical period of famine in 1922. The mission to Moscow continued to provide vital aid until it was peremptorily closed by the Soviets who were suspicious of the papacy as well as the powers. Responding to those who questioned providing relief and assistance to one's ideological opponents, the pope emphasized that Christian charity had to be extended to all, and had his secretary of state provide further elaboration. "The ultimate principles of the Church imply no objection on its part against a Communist form of government," Cardinal Gasparri proclaimed in 1922, "in matters of economics the Church is agnostic."[4] Pius XI pragmatically relied on a number of German diplomats assigned to the newly formed Soviet Union to help establish a modus vivendi between the Vatican and the Bolshevik leaders. It appears that in 1922–1923, the latter sought de jure recognition from the Vatican without the acceptance of a permanent papal representative in Moscow. In the interim, at the end of 1922, the Holy See issued another plea on behalf of the persecuted Armenians, invoking immediate remedies to assist this cruelly persecuted population. The plea was ignored by the international community.

Pius was disheartened that his initial diplomatic and pastoral efforts had only a limited impact on a troubled continent, whose social, fiscal, and economic turmoil he feared would lead to unfortunate political consequences. In June 1923, he complained to his secretary of state that since donning the papal tiara, international relations had deteriorated rather than improved, threatening the peace of Europe and the world. To help relieve the tension, the pope urged a resolution of the reparations issue in the Christian spirit of reconciliation. He also prayed that the League would be imbued with this Christian spirit, which alone could render its mission successful. His message was one of guidance rather than of condemnation. In the summer of 1923, when John Eppstein, an officer of the League proposed that diplomatic relations be established between the Council of the League and the Holy See, Cardinal Gasparri outlined the papal position and conditions. "The project could be accepted only in the sense that the Holy See would be at the disposal of the League for matters coming within its competence: that is to say, for the elucidation of questions or principle in regard to morality and public international law, and also to give help to the League's relief work where its [the Holy See's] intervention would be of value to suffering people." Gasparri added, "I feel that I must tell you how much the Holy Father appreciates the zeal with which, as an officer of the League of Nations Union, you uphold Catholic principles in all circumstances."[5]

The promise of the League was not fulfilled by its performance, leading Pius XI to regret that the international order had shown neither the vision nor produced the means to fulfill its humanitarian mission. In fact, during the troubled inter-war period, the Vatican found the League's projected antislavery convention too weak and in need of material and spiritual guidance. Political as well as spiritual issues were addressed in the 37 encyclicals penned by this pope and in the 18 concordats he concluded. Determined to preserve its freedom of action, the Holy See did not seek admission to the League, despite the spate of rumors that it planned to do so. Increasingly suspicious of the efficacy of international organizations and the sincerity of party politics in the various nations, Pius preferred to have church interests safeguarded by Catholic societies under clerical control rather than independent Catholic political parties, favoring Concordats that defined the position of the church in a particular state. Through the latter, Rome sought to safeguard the presence of the church by allowing recognition of Catholic groups, assuring legal status for sacramental marriages, and providing the pope with the exclusive right to appoint bishops, without any *placet* (consent) from the various governments. In return, the Vatican recognized the states that emerged from the peace treaties, altering the religious districts to coincide with the revised boundaries. From the perspective of the postwar regimes, such agreements provided recognition, while depriving protesting Catholic minorities of cause for complaint.

While Leo XIII (1878–1903) and Pius X (1903–1914) initiated only a few such agreements, the pontificate of Pius XI (1922–1939) was an age of concordats. This pope negotiated with Authoritarian, Democratic, Socialist, and Fascist regimes as he sought to wring concessions for church principles and ecclesiastical entities in particular countries. In 1924, a Concordat was signed with Bavaria; in 1925 with Latvia and Poland; in 1927 with Lithuania and Rumania; while in 1928 accords were concluded with Czechoslovakia and Portugal. In 1929, in addition to the concordat with Fascist Italy, one was signed with the state of Prussia. Another was negotiated with Baden in 1932, the year before the controversial concordat with Nazi Germany was concluded in 1933. Efforts to iron out an agreement with the Soviet Union continued for almost a decade right up until 1927, when the attempt was abandoned by the Bolsheviks. In 1934, a concordat was approved by the conservative, Catholic and authoritarian regime of Engelbert Dollfuss in Austria. This was followed by one with the Kingdom of Yugoslavia in 1935, but the latter agreement was never ratified by its parliament. In 1938 Pius opened negotiations with Francisco Franco's emissaries for yet another concordat. The concordatarian policy pursued by Pius XI was enthusiastically supported by his secretary of state until 1930, Cardinal Gasparri, as well as his disciple and successor as secretary of state, Cardinal Eugenio Pacelli.

Pius XI, appreciative of the decisive American intervention in World War I, also reached out to the largely Protestant United States and found a willing partner in President Franklin Delano Roosevelt, who had established ad hoc contacts with Rome following his inauguration in 1933. Since anti-Catholicism still prevailed in the Republic, a concordat with Washington was then out of the question. Nonetheless, in 1936, the pope sent his Secretary of State Eugenio Pacelli (1930–1939), who replaced Gasparri, to North America to discuss the prospect of some form of renewed diplomatic relations between the Vatican and Washington, which would materialize in the subsequent pontificate. Pius XI, like Leo XIII, stressed that the church did not seek to determine which governmental form was best, and was prepared to collaborate with every system willing to uphold religion, preserve morality, and guarantee the rights of the church.

Following this directive, the Vatican, under Gasparri's guidance, even opened unofficial talks with the Soviet leaders about a possible recognition of their Communist regime. It did not materialize because Moscow refused to concede the conditions posed by the Holy See: (1) the release of Catholics imprisoned or exiled in Siberia, (2) the restoration of confiscated church property, (3) the right to teach the catechism in the churches if not the schools, and finally (4) the liberty of the pope's representative to communicate freely with the Catholic Clergy.[6] The failure of reconciliation did not preclude Pius from sending alms to the starving masses in Russia or continuing unofficial talks with the regime. It was only following Stalin's ascendancy after 1927 and upon the dictator's insistence that all negotiation between Moscow and the Vatican ceased.

Pius XI was not only pope of concordats, he was also pope of the missions. During the first year of his pontificate he reorganized missionary work, transferring their direction from Paris to Rome. Rejecting the French claims to protect religion in the Far East, he appointed an apostolic delegate to China and was the first pope to consecrate Chinese, Japanese, and Indian bishops in his effort to make the church less Euro-centric and universal in fact as well as theory. In 1925 he put together a missionary exhibition in Rome, revealing their achievements in the Eastern and Southern regions. The following year, Pius consecrated the first six Chinese bishops in Rome. Later, in 1929 he established the Russicum in Rome, which aimed to train missionaries to minister to the souls of Russia's vast and troubled population. Conscious of the need to resist identification with western imperialism, he opposed the Italian invasion of Ethiopia in 1936, fearing this would have a negative impact on the native's attitude toward the church. Withdrawing Catholics from political life, Pius focused on the role of the church in the religious and missionary spheres.

Although the Holy See relied on its own mechanisms to secure its rights and spiritual ends, it did not abandon its support for the League, and certainly did not plot against it as some alleged. Nonetheless, when Catholic Brazil withdrew from it, the English press clamored this was precipitated by Vatican resentment of its exclusion from the organization. The papal secretary of state discounted these accusations, letting it be known that the Vatican neither plotted against nor planned to join the League, once again revealing the Vatican's stance toward this international organization. When requested, it would place itself at the League's disposal in assisting those suffering worldwide. The Vatican desired neither to obstruct nor discourage the League's beneficent efforts for peace and charity, which it applauded but would contribute its official and open support only when asked. In August 1926, the *L'Osservatore Romano* published a long article commending the work of the League, suggesting it would violate the church's principles to deny support to an institution that upheld the banner of peace amid the mania of national egoism.[7] Pius XI shared this sentiment, warning against the excesses of state sovereignty and nationalism.

Seeking an alternative to the chaotic system of radical state independence in international affairs, the Vatican followed the League's activities with interest, providing its moral support. The *L'Osservatore Romano* paid particular attention to its attempts to promote disarmament and its efforts to restore peace in China and South America. It applauded the League's adoption of the Geneva Protocol for the peaceful settlement of international disputes, while branding aggressive warfare an international crime. The Protocol paralleled the papal position favoring negotiation and arbitration to resolve disputes rather than the recourse to arms, which often led to disastrous consequences. Invoking solidarity and collective action, Pius XI condemned isolationism, while his secretary of state stressed the universal obligation to promote the international common good. Like Benedict XV, his successor understood both the promise and limitations of the League, considering many of its actions motivated by Christian and Catholic principles. Pius XI's sympathetic view of the League prevailed throughout the 1920s, convinced that it espoused principles long held by the Holy See.[8] Not surprisingly, the *L'Osservatore Romano* hailed the English declaration in the Council that they sought no alliance other than the world alliance provided by the League. The Vatican newspaper deeming the English pronouncement against military alliances a vindication of the teachings of Popes Leo XIII and Benedict XV, which had been long ignored. Despite this supportive stance, rumors about Vatican hostility toward the League continued to circulate. Among other things, the Holy See was accused of orchestrating a uniform Catholic response to political and international issues. This was contradicted by the English representatives at the Vatican, who observed

Vatican activities first hand. His direct observations led him to conclude that Pius XI tended to withdraw Catholics from association with this or that political party, concentrating upon religious concerns.[9] It was the gradual realization of the limitations of the League and its inability to resolve a series of disputes that led the Vatican to seek other alternatives.

The Holy See confronted its own particular problems, including the disintegration of Austria-Hungary, and other territorial changes in Central Europe and the Balkans, which dispersed the Catholic population in the successor states of Austria, Hungary, Czechoslovakia, Rumania, Yugoslavia, and Poland. Fortunately, these states sought improved relations with the Holy See and Pius proved accommodating. Negotiations with Bucharest led to the elaboration of a concordat with Rumania, concluded in 1927 but not ratified until 1929. Church-state relations in Catholic Poland were regularized by the concordat ratified in June 1925. Catholic Hungary remained friendly to the Holy See even though differences emerged regarding ecclesiastical appointments. Austria, likewise, sought good relations with the Vatican under its prime minister, Monsignor Ignaz Seipel, a Catholic priest and leader of the Christian Socialists. In Italy, Cardinal Gasparri, the papal secretary of state, distressed by the political scene, described the "Catholic" Popular Party as "the least bad of all the parties."[10] Unhappy with the chaotic situation in Italy, the Vatican later appreciated Mussolini's restoration of order in the peninsula following his accession to power in 1922.

Disappointed by the social, political, and diplomatic developments in much of Europe, in his first encyclical letter, Pius decried the morbid restlessness and general spirit of insubordination of the postwar period, proposing the Peace of Christ as a remedy, achieved through Catholic organizations (Catholic Action) rather than political parties. Pius XI deplored the hatred between nations internationally, and class warfare and partisan political strife internally, which spawned tensions that threatened the continent's tranquility and stability. Although Pius pronounced that the church could reconcile itself with any just system of government, he warned that popular democratic governments were most in danger of being overthrown by one faction or another.[11] Some interpreted these words as papal support for the Mussolini government in Italy, which courted the church and the Vatican by invoking the name of God and restoring the crucifix to the schools. The Fascists made additional overtures to the Holy See, including a series of concessions made to Catholic schools in the peninsula as a result of the Gentile Educational Reform of 1923. This cordial climate encouraged the Vatican to open talks with Mussolini that eventually culminated in a resolution of the Roman Question. Although

Gasparri believed the Mussolini regime would not last for more than two decades, he was prepared to take advantage of the concessions the Duce was prepared to make that liberal Italy had flatly and consistently rejected.[12]

Pius recognized the price to be paid for the resolution of the Roman Question was the dissolution of the Catholic Popular Party, sought by Mussolini and the Fascists. The Vatican was not adverse to the suggestion, having little faith that the Popular Party could provide the church the protection and reconciliation it sought, while doubting it had the will or means of resolving the conflict with the Italian state. On the other hand, both the pope and his secretary of state were convinced that the Mussolini regime wielded sufficient power to negotiate a solution acceptable to the Vatican. Thus, when *Il Popolo*, the journal of the Popular Party showed itself hostile to the Acerbo Electoral Law, which accorded the party that had the greatest number of votes, two-thirds of the seats in the Chamber—a preliminary step in the establishment of the Fascist dictatorship—the *L'Osservatore Romano*, the journal of the Holy See, proved supportive. The Vatican journal went further, indicating that the *Partito Popolare* had lost its raison d'etre,[13] revealing that the party could not expect Vatican support against the regime.

The fate of the *Partito Popolare* was sealed when sources from the Holy See reported that Don Luigi Sturzo (1871–1959) created difficulties between the church and the regime. Responding to the obvious message, the Sicilian priest resigned as secretary of the party, and subsequently left the country. In turn, Pius sought to withdraw Catholicism from the political arena, protecting and expanding the six major branches of Catholic Action in Italy, placing them under ecclesiastical control. Supposedly he also approved the 1923 coup orchestrated by Primo de Rivera in Spain. Papal approval of King Alphonso XIII's visit to Rome seemed to reflect not only the Vatican's support for the Spanish dictatorial regime but also signaled the improvement in church-state relations in Italy. Liberals, and other critics of the increasingly dictatorial Mussolini regime, deplored the fact that following the December 1924 assassination attempt on the life of the Duce, Pius praised the "divine intervention" that spared his life.[14] Some prematurely envisioned a complete meeting of minds between the infallible and authoritarian pope and the dictatorial Duce who claimed never to be wrong.

While the Vatican enjoyed cordial relations with the two Mediterranean dictators, relations with the French Republic remained far less harmonious. In Paris, segments of the right and left resented the Vatican's sympathy for the plight of Germany and support for a reduction of its reparations burden. Tension heightened in the wake of the 1924 elections, in which the anticlerical bloc of the left, the Cartel des Gauches, triumphed, and Edouard Herriot prepared to pursue a policy of laicization to the Vatican's dismay. At the beginning of 1924, Pius issued an encyclical to the bishops, clergy, and people of France, cataloging the events provoking the present difficulties including the Law of Separation and the papal condemnation of the so-called Associations Cultuelles, leading to the present Diocesan Associations. Pius was prepared to accept the last on a conditional basis, provided they conformed to the laws of the church, and their rights were guaranteed against those who might prove hostile to the Faith.[15] The Paris government proved recalcitrant and rupture with the Republic was only avoided when the Herriot government collapsed in the spring of 1925.

Pius XI deplored the troubled relations with France and sought a remedy and some accommodation with the government of the democratic French Republic. Unlike Pius X, who seemed supportive of the anti-Republican and allegedly Catholic *Action Française,* in 1926 Pius XI denounced the organization's abuse and misuse of Catholicism to achieve essentially political rather than religious ends. Responding to a request from the pope, the Archbishop of Bordeaux condemned the fascist-like movement in August 1926. Pius publicly supported the cardinal's condemnation of the *Action Française* and its newspaper, affirming that those who heard the voice of their bishop also heard his voice. The French cardinals and archbishops followed the papal directive, paving the way for improved relations between Paris and the Vatican. Two years later, Pius XI had anti-Semitism condemned when the Holy Office, with his approval, suppressed the Friends of Israel.[16] By this and other actions, Pius XI won some support in French liberal circles.

Pius displayed the same mixture of principal and pragmatism in dealing with the Spanish Republic, which replaced the dictatorial regime in 1931. Critical of the closing of churches and the dissolution of religious orders, in 1933 the pope was careful not to condemn the Republic that permitted these abuses. "Nor can it be believed that Our words are inspired by sentiments of aversion to the new form of government or other purely political changes which recently have transpired in Spain," he wrote. As proof, Pius pointed to "the numerous concordats and agreement concluded in late years, and in the diplomatic relations the Holy See has established with different states in which, following the Great War, Monarchic governments were succeeded by republican forms."[17] The pope's words were not simple rhetoric but reflected the postwar reality and policy pursued by the Vatican. Skeptics remained unconvinced, complaining that this authoritarian pope's disposition to negotiate and conclude concordats with dictatorial regimes legitimized them. Perhaps this was a consequence of some of his concordats, but certainly was not the papal intention. In fact, Pius XI's agreements with Fascist Italy (1929) and Nazi Germany (1933) have to be seen within the broader concordat and political policy of the pontificate that sanctioned and concluded agreements with all sorts of states and governments.

The Vatican's negotiations with the Italian government commenced in 1923 and continued through 1927. Considerable disagreement emerged during the private exchanges between Francesco Pacelli, brother of Monsignor Eugenio Pacelli, nuncio to Berlin and the future Pius XII, and Domenico Barone, councilor of state of the Fascist government. Father Pietro Tacchi-Venturi, who termed himself "a good Jesuit and a good Fascist," sought a compromise between the Holy See and the regime, playing an active role in the negotiations. The ups and downs of the still secret negotiations followed the prevailing relations between church and state in Italy. Thus, while the Vatican was pleased by the restoration of the cross in the Coliseum, Pius looked unfavorably on the Balilla, the Fascist national youth organization, which interfered with the activities of the Catholic Boy Scouts. Nonetheless, by the end of 1927 a draft agreement with Mussolini's Italy had been ironed out, so that in 1928 Cardinal Gasparri felt sufficiently confident to publicly authorize official negotiations.

On February 11, 1929, after some 20 preliminary drafts, an agreement was finally signed by Rome and the Vatican in the Lateran Palace. The Lateran Accords would prove to be a mixed blessing for both parties. Included were: a treaty, resolving the Roman Question; a concordat, regulating church-state relations in Italy; and a financial convention, providing the papacy partial compensation for its losses during unification.[18] In many respects the treaty establishing the Holy See as the world's smallest sovereign state, according it some 44 hectares (108.7 acres) and a population of 500, was most important for the Vatican. First and foremost, it assured the Vatican's sovereignty, including its right to send and receive diplomats thereby according it international recognition. The Holy See, in turn, promised in article 24, to remain aloof from temporal disputes and international congresses for their solution, unless invited to do so. Nor would Vatican City enter the League of Nations. In March 1929, Pius XI received the entire diplomatic corps accredited to the Holy See, consisting of some 70 diplomats from 35 countries, to inform them of the settlement. Later, in June, the fundamental law or constitution of Vatican City was published in the *Acta Apostolicae*, its official gazette. That year Italy, along with the Irish Free State and Panama, was added to the countries having diplomatic relations with the Vatican.

The concordat with Fascist Italy abandoned Cavour's separation of church and state, which had prevailed throughout the liberal age of the Kingdom and the first years of the Fascist regime. Among other things it recognized Catholicism as the state religion in the peninsula, honored the Catholic calendar, made religious instruction in the primary and secondary schools compulsory, accepted the church position that marriage was a sacrament, while seeking to harmonize public policy with church teaching. Critics complained these terms contributed to the clericalization of Italian public and private life. Committed Fascists resented the fact that article 43 provided for the immunity of Catholic associations, which included various lay organizations, from the Regime's control, so long as they refrained from political activity. Others grumbled that the financial settlement, which included some one billion lire in state bonds along with 750 million lire in cash, gave the Holy See an unhealthy stake in the Fascist Regime. Actually, the funds that fell to the Vatican were dispersed and invested worldwide by Bernardino Nogara, who the pope selected as his financial manager.[19] Meanwhile, Pius XI focused on the positive aspects of the agreement, which he believed restored God to Italy and Italy to God. Despite papal approval, the concordat did not resolve all tensions, and controversy soon erupted over the Regime's attempt to monopolize education contrary to a number of provisions of the concordat. At the end of 1929, the pope released an encyclical reasserting the church's right to supervise instruction, stressing its duty to protect the young from the danger of doctrinal and moral evils.

This church stance conflicted with the all-embracing vision of Mussolini and Fascist ideologues who sought to consolidate their totalitarian regime by restricting nonstate organizations and especially those under Catholic Action, claiming they harbored political ambitions. Pius denied these accusations and in April 1931, denounced the Fascists attacks on Catholic organizations, protected by article 43 of the 1929 concordat. In June, he issued a critical letter, written in Italian *Non abbiamo bisogno,* which rejected the Fascist claim to monopolize youth activities and organizations. His encyclical on Christian marriage at the end of the year, denounced birth control while chastising the advocates of neo-Paganism, who attacked the sacrament of marriage. The conflict continued until the beginning of September 1931, when a truce was declared. Under this agreement, Catholic Action activities of an educational, recreational, and religious nature under diocesan control were permitted, but all political action was prohibited. This compromise upset some in the Catholic camp as well as the Fascist party. For most others, however, the advantages offered by the agreement outweighed the difficulties it created and therefore were hesitant to provoke its collapse.

Church-state relations temporarily improved in 1932 as Pius bestowed a papal decoration on the Duce in January and on February 11, the anniversary of the Lateran Accords, received Mussolini in private audience. This did not hinder the Holy Office from placing all the works of Giovanni Gentile, the theorist of Italian Fascism, on the Index, nor prevent the *L'Osservatore Romano* from condemning Fascist Italy's Pact of Friendship and Non-Aggression with the Soviet Union in 1933. Meanwhile, the pope continued to openly denounce totalitarianism as incompatible with Catholicism. Differences remained until the end of Pius XI's pontificate, and the Vatican never became subservient to the Fascist regime, nor did it admire or copy, Fascist corporativism.

It is true that in May 1931, Pius had recourse to corporativism in his longest encyclical *Quadragesimo Anno* (On the Reconstruction of the Social Order), issued on the fortieth anniversary of Leo's *Rerum novarum*. However this corporativism reflected Catholic thought rather than fascist ideology. The pope acknowledged that the system of corporations created by Fascist Italy offered some advantages, especially in calling the classes to work together peacefully. However, he quickly noted the shortcomings of Mussolini's program, including the papal concern that the state transcended its appropriate role by substituting itself for free activity, adding that the fascist corporative order emphasized political ends, rather than focusing on the improvement of the social order.[20] His encyclical continued the social program of the papacy, denounced the inhumanity of employers and the greed of competitors, concurring with Leo XIII that both liberalism and socialism had failed to resolve the social question. Furthermore, Pius found the totalitarian alternative equally fallacious, rejecting the state idolatry, excessive nationalism and racism, put forward by the Fascists and Nazis. At the same time he denounced the attempt to purge Christianity of its Jewish roots, deeming blasphemous the notion that Jesus was an Aryan.

Pius XI found Nazism even more deplorable than Fascism, denouncing it as uncompromising, intolerant, racist, and totalitarian. Racism he found particularly reprehensible, repeating that God had no preference for any specific nation and totally rejected race as a road to redemption. These sentiments were shared by the bishops of Prussia and Bavaria, who at the end of March 1931 issued pastoral letters, condemning the party program declaring all creeds subordinate to racial considerations. Six bishops of the Cologne Church Province in March 1931 deemed the errors of National Socialism similar to those of the *Action Française,* condemned by Pius XI, while the three bishops of the Paderborn Province ruled that membership in the Nazi part was impermissible for Catholics. Equally odious, in their eyes, was the exaltation of nationalism over religion, the recognition of violence as a legitimate political weapon, the agitation for nondenominational education, the furtherance of artificial birth control, and the blatant anticlericalism of Nazi leaders.

The Vatican responded more diplomatically as Cardinal Eugenio Pacelli, who became secretary of state in 1930 replacing Gasparri, revealed that Catholic critics of the party in Germany acted on their own initiative. Although Pius XI was troubled by the Nazi movement, and received the news of Hitler's appointment on January 30, 1933 with considerable misgiving, the Vatican issued no public statement. In mid-March 1933, it simply noted that Hitler had assumed police powers following his electoral victory.[21] Pius XI initially was little inclined to conclude a concordat with the Hitler regime. Once the Nazis commenced their reign of terror in 1933, including the harassment of the organizational church, the Vatican confronted with the impending dissolution of the Catholic Center and the Bavarian's People's Party, reassessed the Nazi offer to conclude a concordat and sanctioned negotiations. The pope was encouraged to do so by his secretary of state, Pacelli, who sought to protect the Catholic faith and population in the Reich. Pius XI followed Pacelli's advice despite his personal doubts and reservations and rejection of the conclusion of his nuncio to Germany Cesare Orsenigo that the Nazi government had shown toleration toward religious groups and organizations.[22] Thus, while the pope reluctantly approved the negotiations that resulted in the Reich concordat, he remained cautious about the prospect of a real rapprochement with Nazi Germany.

Many of the papal concerns were shared by the Jesuits of the *Civiltà Cattolica,* who took pains to explain that the agreement neither legitimized the Nazi regime nor indicated Vatican approval of its policies. The Vatican journal reported that the pope had signed the accord to preserve the Catholic Church in Germany.[23] Their assessment was corroborated by Pacelli, who revealed to the English Chargé that he deplored the Nazi reign of terror and had agreed to the concordat solely to protect church interests. Apparently Pacelli had fewer reservations than the pope in accepting the consequentialism, which argued that the moral value of an action must be weighed in light of the consequences it produces. In simple terms the concordat proved helpful for the church and therefore was justified. Pius, who was prepared to negotiate with the devil on behalf of the church, recognized that the issue was morally and practically far more complex. Despite papal protestations and reservations, the concordat helped the Nazi regime as well as the church and was unquestionably a diplomatic victory for Hitler. In Mussolini's words it accorded the German government "credit in foreign affairs, which it had lacked heretofore."[24] In fact, the concordat had negative as well as positive consequences for both church and Reich.

Pius XI would not tolerate the subservience of the Catholic Church in Germany to the Nazis, nor subscribe to the slogan of those evangelists who proclaimed "One people, One Reich, One Fuehrer, One Church." The pope, for his part, sought to shield the organization and activity of Catholic groups in the Reich, while instructing the nuncio in Berlin to intervene on behalf of the persecuted Jews.[25] Papal pleas on these and other sensitive issues were not answered, and Pius did not hesitate to denounce the Nazi sterilization legislation as contrary to divine law. He soon complained that German affairs caused him the gravest consternation. The American Myron Taylor, who later served as President Roosevelt's personal representative to Pius XII, met Pope Pius XI and was impressed by his "earnestness."[26] During these troubled times, Pius XI sought the support of the United States, dispatching his secretary of state to North America. In his month long visit Pacelli traveled some 8,000 miles of United States territory. Unquestionably the political highlight of the trip was Pacelli's meeting in November 1936 with President Roosevelt at Hyde Park, and the discussion of renewed diplomatic relations. Although American public opinion was still not prepared for such a step, the Roosevelt government revealed its appreciation of Vatican policies and actions. Indeed William E. Dodd, the American ambassador to Germany, wrote Roosevelt that during the Ethiopian crisis, Pius XI lent support to the opposition to Mussolini. Washington also appreciated the clear and forthright papal condemnation of anti-Semitism.

It was well known that Pius XI was scandalized by the Nazi regime's racism, and flatly rejected their contentions that clerical anti-Judaism served as a precursor to their anti-Semitism or that the Jewish question was an internal political issue, rather than a religious one. Like the American Jesuit John La Farge, who had served for years in predominantly African American parishes in Maryland, where he witnesses firsthand the evil of racism, the pope considered racism, sinful. Pius XI concurred with La Farge, who had established himself as a leading Catholic opponent of racism, arguing that racism was immoral,[27] and the Christian could not remain silent in the presence of this unmitigated evil. Antagonized by the neo-paganism of the regime, Pius XI promised visiting German students that he would defend the faith. There was ample opportunity to fulfill the promise, for the regime's racism, persecution of the church in Germany, and harassment of Catholic youth organizations continued throughout 1934. Papal concern was expressed in the pastoral letter Pius XI sent to the youth of Germany in April 1934.[28] The Nazi actions led the nuncio in Bavaria to warn Pacelli that after the purge of Ernst Roehm, Catholics might well be Hitler's next victims. To strengthen the Vatican's diplomatic position in Europe Pope Pius dispatched his secretary of state to France in 1935, and again in 1937, as well as across the Atlantic in 1936. Pacelli established a cordial, if off the record, relationship with Breckenridge Long, the American ambassador to Italy.

Nazi threats did not deter the pope from denouncing their racism and persecution, and during Pacelli's month long absence from Rome in 1936, complained to the German ambassador Diego von Bergen about their policies and actions. Distressed by the level of papal anger, von Bergen wrote home that in Pacelli's absence, and without his moderating influence, the prospect increased that the pope will take disastrous decisions. In fact, Pius XI increasingly questioned the usefulness of the Reich concordat and considered renouncing it, but was restrained by his secretary of state, who feared the consequences for German Catholics. However, Pacelli could not prevent the Holy Office from placing Alfred Rosenberg's anti-Christian and racist *Myth of the Twentieth Century* on the Index of Prohibited Books, nor prevent the *L'Osservatore Romano* from denouncing it not only as anti-Christian, but antihuman. Papal opposition to the Nazi doctrine of blood and race also found reflection in the critical articles that appeared in the Jesuit-run *Civiltà Cattolica*. Early in 1936, when the Fuehrer sent the pope a congratulatory message on the anniversary of his coronation, Pius XI responded by complaining of developments in the Reich, as he sought to disrupt the Rome-Berlin Axis.

Pius XI was also responsible for the three major encyclicals launched against the totalitarian regimes that threatened Christianity: *Non abbiamo bisogno* of 1931 against the abuses of Fascist Italy, *Mit brennender sorge* of 1937 against those of Nazi Germany, and *Divini redemptoris* likewise of 1937, against the evils of communism, which he denounced as a satanic scourge. In 1938, eight months before his death the pope who suffered from diabetes and heart trouble, commissioned a fourth encyclical to denounce racism and issue an explicit condemnation of anti-Semitism. The Vatican's opposition to the Nazi doctrine of blood and race was also reflected in the critical articles in *L'Osservatore Romano* and *La Civiltà Cattolica*, which did not escape the notice of the Nazis, who throughout 1937–1938 denounced the church for its rejection of their racial teaching. Pius XI was particularly vilified. Chastised for his efforts on behalf of the Jews, he was branded "The Chief Rabbi of all Christians."[29] *Civiltà Cattolica* responded by claiming that the church had always opposed persecution.[30] Meanwhile, *L'Osservatore* warned that a new *Kulturkampf* was not a future prospect but a present reality. This sentiment was echoed by the German bishops, who met at Fulda in 1936, and issued a pastoral letter reaffirming the church's hostility to neo-paganism and sterilization. In a series of articles the *Civiltà Cattolica,* charged that Nazism elaborated a theory of racism in conflict with the doctrines of the faith and therefore in fundamental opposition to the church.

The pope concurred with this assessment.[31] As a result, by 1937–1938, Pius XI was perceived as one of the few world leaders defending human rights against both Fascism and Nazism. Pius XI resented Nazi laws that violated church teachings and basic human rights, complaining to the German ambassador that he was "deeply grieved and gravely displeased." Diego Von Bergen reported that Pacelli was upset by the pope's outburst, and sought to pacify the German government, but was not prepared to contradict his chief. Following the remilitarization of the Rhineland (1936), Pius XI confided to the French ambassador, "If you [French] had called forward 200,000 men you would have done an immense service to the entire world."[32] By this juncture Pius XI's initial distrust of the Nazis had deepened and he found the promises of the Fuehrer virtually worthless.

Continued attacks on church doctrines and its clergy led Pius XI to speak out despite the restraining influence of his secretary of state. Rejecting the National Socialist claim to the whole of man, on Palm Sunday in March 1937, he issued the encyclical *Mit brennender Sorge* (With Deep Anxiety) to the Catholics in Germany, the sole papal encyclical against the Third Reich in its 12-year existence. Read in all the parishes in Germany, it launched the Vatican's harshest criticism of any political regime to date. "With deep anxiety and increasing dismay," Pius revealed his increasing outrage at witnessing the "progressive oppression of the faithful." Condemning the regime's racism, he protested that "none but superficial minds could stumble into the concept of a national God, of a national religion, an attempt to lock within the frontiers of a single people, within the narrow limits of a single race, God the creator of the Universe." The pope also catalogued the other articles of faith abused by the Nazis, as he harped upon the differences between Catholicism and Nazism and the anti-Christian tendencies of the movement. He concluded by urging the clergy to unmask and refute Nazism's errors, whatever their form or disguise.[33] Pacelli believed the encyclical represented a compromise between the Holy See's conviction that it could not remain silent and its fears that too strong a condemnation would endanger the concordat. In reality the pope represented the first position, and Pacelli the latter. As Pius asserted the superiority of divine law over the man-made dogmas of nation and race, the Nazis viewed the church as an enemy they had to combat, and Hitler moved from a conspicuous indifference to Catholicism to increasing hostility. The growing rift between the Reich and Rome disturbed Pacelli and his allies in the curia, who feared Nazi retribution and worried about the future of the church in Germany.

Pacelli's fears materialized as Himmler's *Das Schwarze Korps* denounced the papal encyclical as a propaganda pamphlet against the Reich and Berlin prohibited the printing in Germany of all future encyclicals. A furious Hitler withdrew into virtual isolation for three days and upon his return to social intercourse, vowed revenge. On the other hand, this encyclical, which enraged the Nazis, pleased the western democracies, who applauded the actions of Pius XI. The pope determined to do more. In June 1937, he presided over a special meeting of the Congregation for Extraordinary Ecclesiastical Affairs to discuss the Nazi menace, deploring the anti-Christian developments in Germany no less than those in the Soviet Union. When Cardinal George William Mundelein of Chicago depicted Hitler as "an Austrian paperhanger," Pius expressed his admiration for the cardinal, further provoking the enmity of Hitler. In September 1937, Mussolini made a state visit to Germany—much to the distress of the pope. Soon after the Duce's return on September 29, 1937, Pius issued an encyclical denouncing "men who endeavor to revive the errors of the pagans and their way of life" and exalt "the power of the state," and in a talk on Christmas Eve, 1937, he impugned the "brutal, cunning and violent" Nazi persecution.[34] These denunciations widened the rift between the Holy See and the fascist dictatorships.

Despite the growing tension between the Vatican and the Reich, Pacelli assured the German ambassador that friendly relations would be restored.[35] He, like many others in the secretariat of state, judged the position of Catholics in the Reich precarious, and therefore urged caution and restraint in opposing Nazi doctrines and policies. The pope did not make reconciliation with the Reich easy for his secretary of state, condemning the nationalism championed by the Hitler regime as a veritable curse. He felt constrained to rebuke the Reich's racism and exaggerated nationalism, which posed barriers between men and men, people and people, populations and populations. The secretary of state's efforts to mitigate the pope's opposition were recognized by the German ambassador who reported to Berlin that "Cardinal Pacelli constantly strives to pacify, and to exert a moderating influence on the Pope, who is difficult to manage and influence."[36] Indeed, Pacelli later confided that Pius, outraged by Nazi policies and actions, had contemplated withdrawing the Nuncio from Berlin and only with great difficulty had he persuaded the pope not to do so. The secretary of state opposed all actions that jeopardized the concordat, which he considered the sole remaining shield for the church in Germany. The pope, however, was not easily intimidated and determined to undertake a number of other steps to display his displeasure of Nazi antics and abuses.

In April 1938, the Sacred Congregation of Seminaries, under papal direction, condemned the pernicious racism pursued by the Reich, hailed in the Catholic press as an encyclical against racism! That same month Pius XI issued instructions to the heads of Catholic universities and seminars to reject Nazism's ridiculous racial dogmas and errors.[37] In July, Pius XI noted the complete incompatibility between Catholicism and Nazi ideology, which flagrantly violated the teachings of the faith. For this among other reasons he deplored the *Anschluss* of 1938, which saddened him as Pontiff and as an Italian. Viewing the Nazi takeover of Austria as a disaster, Pius XI repudiated Cardinal Theodore Innitzer and the Austrian bishops, who rejoiced at the union and sought an accommodation with the Nazis.[38] The *L'Osservatore Romano* made it clear that the bishop's statement did not have the Holy See's approval, while Gustav Gundlach on Vatican Radio denounced their pro-Nazi pastoral letter as inspired by a false political Catholicism. In fact, in April 1938, Cardinal Innitzer was summoned to Rome, lectured by an angry pope and constrained to sign a retraction. In 1938, when the Holy See granted diplomatic recognition to the Franco regime, the pope revealed his opposition to Nazism and the threat its pernicious doctrines posed to the spirit of Catholic Spain. His strong and public hostility towards Nazism undermined efforts to reconcile the church and Nazi Germany.

Pacelli, who more than anyone else sought to prevent a break with the Nazis, found the task increasingly difficult.[39] Pius XI was outraged by Mussolini's Italy's close relationship to Hitler's Germany, and found it difficult to conceal his anger and disgust. In May 1938, when the Fuehrer visited Rome, Pius left for Castel Gandolfo and closed the Vatican Museum, which Hitler had hoped to visit. From Castel Gandolfo, the pope expressed his displeasure at the glorification in Rome of the "cross that was the enemy of Christianity."[40] Aware that Pacelli opposed his contentious course, Pius XI planned to issue an encyclical condemning the racism and anti-Semitism of Hitler's Germany without involving him. Gustav Gundlach, one of the collaborators on the projected encyclical, was convinced that the secretary of state had been purposely kept in the dark, which Pacelli—the future Pius XII—corroborated once he was selected as Pius XI's successor. Thus Pacelli was not included in the pope's discussion with John La Farge when he commissioned the encyclical against racism, even though he had been with the pope moments before. Perhaps the pope recognized that Pacelli would oppose the project? Or having made up his mind to forge ahead, he did not want to hear arguments against the action he was determined to pursue.

The specter of a closer relationship between Fascist Italy and Nazi Germany spurred the pope to action. On May 2, 1938, Hitler began an official seven-day visit to Rome, marking a decisive turn in Fascist Italy's policy on race, to the consternation of Pius XI. Shortly thereafter, a Nazi commission ventured to Milan to assist the Italians in drafting their racist legislation. On June 22, 1938, the pope asked to see the American Jesuit John La Farge, the author of numerous books and articles condemning racism, calling upon him to write an encyclical against this erroneous ideology. The pope had read and liked La Farge's *Interracial Justice,* published in 1937, in which La Farge had denounced the notion of pure race as a myth, the church had to oppose. Since Christian social philosophy looked upon the deliberate fostering of racial prejudices as a sin. it could not be ignored by the faith.[41] Pius XI approved of La Farge's ideas, which reflected his own thought. The pope, who deemed the enterprise of the utmost importance and the burning issue of the day, and fearful of attempts to subvert the project, swore La Farge to secrecy.[42]

Meanwhile the pope continued his condemnation of racism, and those regimes that flaunted it. "If there is anything worse than the various theories of racialism and nationalism," Pius complained, "it is the spirit that dictates them."[43] Like La Farge, the pope saw the need for a spiritual and moral defense of human rights. Pius XI outlined the topic and its treatment, while discussing its underlying principles with La Farge. "Simply say what you would say to the entire world if you were Pope," Pius confided to La Farge.[44] The pope acknowledged that he should have spoken to Father Vladimir Ledochowski, the Polish General of the Jesuits, before assigning La Farge the responsibility, but added, "I imagine it will be all right." To this, La Farge added, in a July 3 memo, "After all, a Pope is Pope."[45] When La Farge informed Ledochowski of the pope's pressing assignment, the latter suggested that he collaborate with two other Jesuits: the Frenchman Gustave Desbuquois of Action Populaire (a social action center in Paris) and the German Gustav Gundlach, a social theorist and professor at the Gregorian University in Rome. The three worked throughout the summer of 1938, and in late September submitted the draft of the encyclical commissioned by Pius XI, *Humani Generis Unitas* (The Unity of the Human Race) to Ledochowski for transmission to the pope.

While La Farge and his collaborators had met the papal deadline for the condemnation of racism, delay ensued afterwards. Acting on his own initiative, Ledochowski did not transmit the draft directly to Pius XI, but to a fellow Jesuit, Enrico Rosa, who scrutinized it slowly and was commissioned by the general to mitigate its message. The extraordinary and unauthorized procrastination in its presentation to Pius XI led Gundlach to fear that their draft of the encyclical would not be presented to the pope, while he still preserved the energy and initiative to release it. Without knowing of the unwarranted tampering with the document, he warned La Farge in mid-October 1938 of possible subversion. "An outsider might well see in all this an attempt to sabotage by dilatoriness and for tactical and diplomatic reasons the mission entrusted to you by [the Pope]," Gundlach wrote La Farge, who had returned to the United States.[46] He was not far from the mark, for Father Heinrich Bacht, the German Jesuit who translated the encyclical into Latin, reported that Ledochowski found the La Farge draft too strong and provoking. The general agreed with Pacelli that it would be unwise to have a head-on confrontation with the Hitler government and transcending his rights and competence, instructed Rosa to tone it down.[47]

The draft encyclical defended human rights, condemned anti-Semitism and "did not permit the Catholic to remain silent in the presence of racism."[48] Aware that Pius XI deplored anti-Semitism in both Italy and Germany, the authors reported that such persecution had been censured by the Holy See in the past. "It is the task and duty of the Church, the dignity and responsibility of the Chief Shepherd and of his brother Shepherds, whom the Holy Ghost has placed to rule the Church of God, that they should point out to mankind the true course to be followed, the eternal divine order in the changing circumstances of the times."[49] "The Redemption opened the doors of salvation to the entire human race," the encyclical continued, establishing "a universal Kingdom, in which there would be no distinction of Jew or Gentile, Greek or barbarian."[50]

Although deemed provocative and therefore unwise by Ledochowski and his allies in the secretariat of state, the document drawn by La Farge and his collaborators clearly reflected papal sentiments and determination to openly challenge the racism that violated Catholic beliefs and principles. Upset by the racist and anti-Semitic policies, which Fascist Italy adopted as it moved closer to Nazi Germany, Pius XI branded the Fascist Aryan Manifesto of July 14, 1938 a "true form of apostasy," initiating a chorus of opposition to the racism of the totalitarian regimes.[51] Nor did the pope hesitate to have his nuncio to Italy, Monsignor Borgongini Duca, denounce Italy's racist legislation. Human dignity, he repeated, rested in a unified humanity.[52] When Pius XI visited the College of the Propaganda Fide in August 1938, he warned its students to shun "exaggerated nationalism," which he branded a real curse.[53] These talks and their publication provoked criticism in Fascist Italy, whose press accused the pope of transcending the realm of religion and intruding into the political arena. Pius responded that he did not wish to provoke polemics, but could not remain silent in the face of grave errors.[54] Italy's racist legislation represented an attack on the church's teachings. "No, it's not possible for we Christians to participate in anti-Semitism," the pope told a group of visiting Belgians on September 6, 1938. "Spiritually, we are Semites."[55] He repeated his opposition two days later on September 8, denouncing the Manifesto on Race as contrary to Catholic doctrine.

In November 1938, when Mussolini published a decree forbidding marriage between Italian Aryans with persons of another race, Pius complained to the King and Mussolini that this was contrary to Catholic teaching and hence a violation of the concordat.[56] He made public his displeasure of the racist course being pursued by Fascist Italy in his Christmas allocution, once again attacking these measures as a violation of the Lateran Accords.[57] In January 1939, the Franco regime concluded an "Agreement between the German Reich and Spain for Intellectual and Cultural Cooperation," which angered and displeased the pope. He instructed Pacelli to transmit his disapproval to Franco. While the more cautious members of the curia and the secretariat of state quietly questioned the old pope's confrontational course, liberal observers in Europe and across the Atlantic praised Pius XI for his outspoken opposition to all forms of racism. This papal stance was echoed in the original and still secret La Farge encyclical, which had not been transmitted to Pius XI.

The three Jesuits who drafted the encyclical knew that the pope was seriously ill and therefore did not expect a long letter of thanks for their effort, but were surprised that they had not even received word of its receipt—leading them to suspect that it had not been delivered to Pius XI. Their assessment proved accurate, but they had little opportunity to communicate with the pope, who was suffering from cardiac weakness and asthma, and whose schedule was closely controlled and severely curtailed, especially after his two heart attacks on Thursday, November 25, 1938.[58] Political considerations as well as medical reasons led to the pope's increasing isolation. Even public audiences with diplomats were now limited to five minutes supposedly necessitated by his poor health and grave condition. "The papal court was filled with competing voices," one observer noted, "which Pius XI sought to orchestrate, but could not dominate."[59] Those who opposed his contentious course vis-à-vis the Nazi and Fascist regimes, hoped that a more conciliatory approach would be followed by his successor and sought to subvert any additional steps that would further widen the rift with the totalitarian regimes. Wedded to the preservation of the concordats with Nazi Germany and Fascist Italy, they were alarmed by Pius XI's determination to combat the Reich's racism and its imitation by Mussolini's Italy. In mid-August 1938 this faction secretly concluded a pact with Fascist Italy, without the pope's knowledge or approval, promising not to interfere with the regime's treatment of Jewish matters and racial legislation in return for certain guarantees regarding Catholic organizations.[60]

While some in the curia and secretariat of state continued to contest the papal policy, others on the outside applauded the pope's outspoken opposition to Fascist and Nazi racism. In Paris, Edouard Herriot, president of the chamber, praised the pope's spiritual gallantry as protector of outraged weakness. Illness and intrigue combined to keep the pope from doing more. The realization that the pope's days were numbered encouraged opponents of his policies in the curia, who could not silence him, but could and did limit access to his person. Thus the authors of the encyclical against racism and anti-Semitism could not easily reach the Holy Father, alerting him to the fact that they had met his deadline and delivered it. Given the hierarchical structure of the church, and the quasimilitary discipline of their order, and their vows of obedience, an appeal to the pope over the heads of their superior was no trivial matter. Nonetheless, Father Gundlach urged La Farge to write directly to Pius XI, who had assigned him the task of writing the encyclical, and La Farge, whose suspicion was aroused, complied. Clearly, Ledochowski only transmitted the La Farge draft to Pius XI after the American Jesuit had written the pope. The charge launched by Cardinal Eugene Tisserant, prefect of the Vatican Library, that Mussolini had Pius XI murdered to prevent the publication of his encyclical against anti-Semitism, remains conjecture, very likely inspired by the known opposition of many in the curia to Pius XI's confrontational course.

Reportedly Pius received a draft of the document on January 21, 1939, but is not known if the gravely ill pope saw or read it before his death on February 9–10. The draft of the La Farge encyclical was later found on Pius XI's desk together with an attached note from Monsignor Domenico Tardini, indicating that Pius XI wanted the encyclical without delay![61] Gundlach was not surprised when the draft of their encyclical condemning racism and anti-Semitism was returned to its authors, with an indication that they might wish to release it under their own names. They chose not to do so, hoping that eventually church officials would change their minds and publish it. They never did, and the encyclical remained hidden during the course of the next three pontificates.

The Vatican's "Impartiality," "Silence," and "Internationalism" During World War II and Beyond

The March 1939 conclave, which opened as Europe was on the brink of another war, sought a diplomatic pope to deal with the impending crisis and serve as a mediator to preserve the peace. The European cardinals, who still constituted a majority, quickly concluded that if anyone could prevent the conflict, or mitigate its consequences, it was Eugenio Pacelli, descendant of a family of lawyers. Eugenio, whose grandfather had founded the *L'Osservatore Romano*, the Vatican journal, had an extensive diplomatic background, serving as nuncio to Germany in the 1920s, and papal secretary of state throughout the 1930s. Some believe that Pacelli was the figure Pius XI had groomed to succeed to the papal throne, while others favored him because they were convinced he would abandon the confrontational course Pius XI pursued against Fascist Italy and Nazi Germany. On March 2, 1939, on the third ballot of a short conclave, the aristocratic and ascetic Pacelli was elected pope on his sixty-third birthday—the first Roman elected since Innocent XIII (1721–1724) and the first papal secretary of state to immediately don the tiara since Clement IX (1667–1669). When Pacelli became pope early in 1939, President Franklin D. Roosevelt, seeking a closer relationship with the Vatican, dispatched Joseph Kennedy, American ambassador to Great Britain, as the United States special representative to the papal coronation. It was a bold step in light of the prevailing anti-Catholicism in the United States and in fact Roosevelt's action prompted protests from the United Lutheran Church in America and the Southern Baptist Convention. Despite their outcry, the American president, appreciating the importance of the papacy in world affairs, determined to open some form of representation with the Vatican.

The Nazis, on the other hand, were less pleased by Pacelli's election and did not send a representative to his coronation. The selection of the name Pius XII, as well as his long association with the former outspoken pope, led the Hitler regime to assume he would continue his predecessor's combative policies, explaining Berlin's initial reservations about his election. These concerns proved premature, for the new pope was convinced that his predecessor's confrontational course had been counterproductive and determined to change direction. German doubts were soon dispelled as the bespectacled pontiff made a sustained effort to improve relations with the Nazi state, confiding to the Italian Foreign Minister Count Galeazzo Ciano his intention to pursue a more conciliatory policy towards the Reich.[1] He proved true to his promise, which dictated discretion and a degree of silence, even though the Hitler regime showed itself increasingly anti-Christian, anti-Catholic, anti-Semitic, and brazenly aggressive.

One of Pacelli's first actions as pope was to gather the German cardinals, revealing his intention of sending a personal letter to Hitler to announce his accession. In an audience of April 23, 1939, speaking to a group of German pilgrims, Pacelli avoided the condemnations of his predecessor, substituting protestations of sympathy for Germany, whose people and culture he admired, and among whom he found his own penchant for precision and perseverance. He did not attempt to hide his pro-German proclivities, reflected in the fact that his housekeeper, private secretary, and confessor all hailed from the Reich. "We have always loved Germany, where We were able to spend many years of Our life, and We love Germany even more today," he told the pilgrims.[2] He also assured the German Ambassador Diego von Bergen that friendly relations would be restored between the Reich and the Vatican. In fact, the ambassador immediately sensed a relaxation of the tension that had accelerated during the last year of the pontificate of Pius XI, and his visit of March 5, 1939, with the new pope might be considered among the first in a series of steps leading to détente.[3] The fascist regimes appreciated that Pius XII did not protest the virtual Nazi annexation of Bohemia and Moravia in March, nor the Italian invasion and annexation of Albania, the following month.

Trained as a diplomat, Pius XII followed the cautious path paved by Benedict XV rather than the confrontational one of Pius XI. Although Papa Ratti (Pius XI) and Papa Pacelli (Pius XII) shared a determination to safeguard the rights of the church by concordats, they differed in physical attributes and temperament. In comparison to the loquacious and robust mountain climber Ratti, Pacelli was aloof and frail. Furthermore, in contrast to Pius XI, Pius XII was indecisive according to Angelo Roncalli, the future Pope John XXIII. While Ratti was easily agitated and given to angry outbursts, Pacelli remained calm and diplomatic, seeming to prefer contemplation to action. He scrupulously avoided partisanship and shunned public condemnations. By nature shy, reserved, and gentle, with a mild constitution, he lacked the fighting spirit of his predecessor. He also disagreed with his predecessor on how much the church could and should endure to preserve the Reich concordat, and the best means of securing Nazi compliance with the agreement. In light of this divergence, it is not surprising that when Pacelli succeeded as Pius XII, Pius XI's projected encyclical against racism and anti-Semitism was scuttled, as was the former pope's last critique of the Fascist violations of the Lateran Accords.

Papa Pacelli, seeking to preserve the peace, the primary objective of his early pontificate, shunned all steps that might compromise his diplomatic efforts. Following in the footsteps of Benedict XV, Pius XII, invoked peace among families, rulers, and nations based on justice and charity repeating this invocation in his Easter message of April 9, 1939. Almost immediately critics complained that this pope sought conciliation at any cost, charging he was not doing enough to condemn the contemplated aggression by the Reich against Poland.[4] In June 1939, when Nazi Germany's expansionist demands and blatant racism rendered the outbreak of a new cataclysm inevitable, the French Ambassador to the Holy See, François Charles-Roux lamented the cautious and neutral position of the new pope. The French Ambassador respected Pius XII's desire to preserve the peace, but resented his refusal to pass judgment or assign responsibility, treating aggrieved and aggressor alike, considering this an unfortunate departure from the course of his predecessor. "Without doubt all expected a change because each has his own temperament and own methods," the Frenchman explained, adding "to many, however, the differences seemed excessive."[5]

Pius XII did denounce the violation of treaties and the preparation for war in his Easter message of April 1939 and his radio appeal of August 24, 1939, but without assigning responsibility. Seconding President Roosevelt's initiatives for peace, in May the Holy Father invited Britain, Germany, France, Italy, and Poland to a Vatican conference to consider the Polish-German dispute and Franco-Italian friction, calling for concessions from both camps to avert war. Neither the Western Powers nor the Axis states proved amenable, and on May 22, 1939, Italy and Germany solidified the loose alliance of the Axis by signing the military alliance Mussolini dubbed the "Pact of Steel." Confronted with this aggressive agreement, which increased the likelihood of war, Pius invoked divine intervention, urging the faithful to commence a crusade of prayer. These prayers were not answered and on August 23, Pius learned of the Nazi-Soviet Pact, which was widely perceived as the prelude for war. Still, Pius did not lose hope and the next day issued a radio appeal to the heads of nations, politicians, writers, and public leaders to help prevent another catastrophe, proclaiming "Nothing is lost with peace; all may be lost with war."[6] Like his model, Benedict XV, this pope showed patience and persistence in continuing his peace efforts in the face of apparent failure.

The French, convinced that war was now inevitable, implored the pope to make a pronouncement in favor of Poland to console that country's Catholic population. Pius refused, fearing the retribution the Nazis would impose upon German Catholics in retaliation.[7] When German forces invaded Poland on September 1, 1939, he did not condemn this aggression. After Britain and France declared war on Germany on September 3, Pius revealed his determination to remain neutral to a group of visiting German pilgrims telling them "For a priest, it is now more than ever before, imperative to be wholly above all political and national passion; to console, to comfort, to prayer and to penance, and himself to pray and do penance."[8] He steadfastly adhered to this public posture.

In October 1939 Pius XII issued his first encyclical *Summi Pontificatus* (On the Limitations of the Authority of the State), which borrowed from Pius XI's unreleased encyclical against racism while condemning the claims of absolute state authority.[9] However, he ignored its explicit condemnation of anti-Semitism. Wishing to improve the Vatican's relations with the Berlin government, he had reason to shunt the encyclical aside. While La Farge's encyclical with its references to the Jew's obstinate refusal to recognize Christ as redeemer and their spiritual blindness, displayed an insensitivity toward the Jews and the prevailing anti-Judaism in the church, Papa Pacelli worried that its critique of racism would antagonize the Hitler regime, leading to a further deterioration of its relations with the Holy See and unfortunate consequences for the church and Catholics in Germany.

Pius XII frankly acknowledged his determination to preserve the concordat, contrasting his approach and that of his predecessor, explaining that Pius XI had sought to terminate relations with the Reich, but he had restrained him.

> Yes, Pius XI was so indignant about what was happening in Germany that he once said to me, "How can the Holy See continue to keep a Nuncio there? It conflicts with our honor." The Holy Father feared that the world would not understand how we could continue diplomatic relations with a regime which treated the Church in such a manner. So I replied to him, "Your Holiness, what good would that do us? If we withdraw the Nuncio how can we maintain contact with the German bishops?" The Holy Father understood and became quieter.[10]

As pope, Pacelli continued this conciliatory course to the satisfaction of those Nazis who were not rabid anticlericals. The German Foreign Minister Joachim von Ribbentrop, comparing Pius XI and Pius XII, declared of the latter, "here is a true Pope." Von Ribbentrop concluded that "the Pope has always had his heart in Germany," claiming that he sought a lasting understanding with Hitler. Heinrich Himmler likewise revealed his appreciation of Pius XII's tact and prudence.[11] Ciano, also, concluded that Fascist Italy could get along with this pope. The Allies, who considered themselves the victims of Nazi aggression, proved less appreciative of this pope and his policies.

While Pius refused to condemn the belligerents in the conflict, preserving a rigorous public neutrality, he denounced aggression in general in November 1939, calling for the renunciation of the cult of might against right, and the acceptance of the supreme authority of the Creator as the basis of individual and collective morality. It represented an indirect criticism of the policies of the fascist regimes as well as an indictment of the present international order. Early on, the pope spoke of the need to fashion a new organization to assure the independence of small and large nations, while safeguarding the liberty, human dignity, and prosperity of all. Pius XII returned to the theme of a reorganization of international life and the construction of new juridical institutions, in his Christmas message of December 24, 1939. Here he lamented the "calculated act of aggression against a small, industrious, and peaceful nation."[12] However, when von Ribbentrop complained, the pope responded that the small nation he had referred to was Finland, the victim of Soviet aggression.[13]

Pius was disappointed though not discouraged by the failure of his mediation. During the first months of the war he worked to keep Italy from entering the conflict as Benedict had in 1914, indicating to the new Italian ambassador to the Holy See, Dino Alfieri, that the wisdom of its rulers and the instinctive inclinations of the Italian people had spared the peninsula from the catastrophe of war. A message the pope repeated during the visit of King Victor Emmanuel III and Queen Elena to the Vatican on December 21, 1939, and reiterated the following week when he returned the visit by going to see the Italian royal family. President Franklin Delano Roosevelt, appreciating papal efforts to contain the conflict, continued to ponder the prospect of closer relations with the Vatican. He was encouraged to do so by Archbishop Francis J. Spellman of New York (1889–1967), who had long served as an intermediary between Washington and the papacy.

To coordinate American and papal efforts to limit the dimension of the war, President Roosevelt decided to dispatch the businessman Myron C. Taylor to Pius XII, as his personal representative at the end of December

1939. To avoid the outbreak of bigotry and opposition a formal confirmation might provoke, the status of the Episcopalian Taylor was not specified nor funding for his mission requested. Aware of the intricate network of international representation that had the Vatican at its focus, Roosevelt hoped it might be used to reinforce peace efforts. For its part, the Vatican was pleased, and responded to the American initiative with unprecedented speed. "This is a Christmas Message which could not have been more welcome to Us," wrote the pope, "since it represents on the part of the eminent head of a great and powerful nation, a strong and promising contribution to Our desire for the attainment of a just and honorable peace and for a more effective and wider effort to alleviate the sufferings of the victims of war."[14] During these calamitous times when both Nazi Germany and the Soviet Union threatened the future of the church, Pius was reassured by the presence of Roosevelt's representative, whose mission to the Vatican lasted from 1940 to 1950.

Soon after Taylor arrived in Rome in February 1940, the Vatican expressed its fear that Mussolini was preparing to plunge Italy into the war alongside Germany, rendering the position of the Vatican precarious. The United States and the Vatican sought to dissuade Mussolini from doing so. While publicly preserving the strictest neutrality, Pius XII's Vatican secretly informed the British government early in 1940 that a group of German generals were prepared to overthrow the Nazi regime, if they could be assured a just and honorable peace. On January 11, 1940, Pius XII sent for Francis D'Arcy Osborne, the British representative to the Vatican, to acquaint him with the scheme of part of the German military to oust the Fuehrer and seek a peace settlement that would include a restoration of Poland and Czechoslovakia, but would not challenge the *Anschluss*. The message was transmitted to the war cabinet in London, which in mid-January 1940 decided it could not proceed on this "nebulous proposition."[15]

Later, the Vatican again revealed a pro-Allied bias, when it quietly alerted them to the impending Nazi invasion of the Low Countries. However, Pius XII was not prepared to publicly reveal his inner sentiments. Thus, when German troops pushed into Belgium, the Netherlands, and Luxemburg in May 1940, he dispatched messages of sympathy to the victims, but did not condemn the aggressor. Some defended, while others deplored, this cautious diplomatic course. Charles-Roux appreciated the telegrams of sympathy the pope directed to the leaders of the Low Countries, who were the latest victims of Nazi aggression in 1940, adding that sympathy was one thing but the condemnation of crime another. Furthermore, Catholic circles in France charged that even these expressions of sympathy were virtually wrenched from a reluctant pope. Pius, apparently aligned himself with the more cautious elements in the curia, chose not to send the stronger message of his secretary of state, which decried the violations of international law and natural rights.[16] The pope supposedly also ignored the condemnation of the aggression drafted by Monsignor Domenico Tardini.

Father Gustav Gundlach, who had collaborated with John La Farge in drafting the encyclical against racism and anti-Semitism for Pius XI, appreciated the difficult position of Pius XII, surrounded by a faction in the Vatican and Curia who called for caution and silence. He wrote La Farge on May 30, 1940.

> His [Pius XII's] three telegrams are well-known; they were good and beneficent. But now the . . . opportunists and idolaters of success are back, and they are exhorting him to remain silent. Here come those who, never learning anything, say: the dictator, after having imposed a victorious peace, will reign with good will and wisdom, and will come to terms with the Church. These eternal stupidities have already done so much damage and caused so much confusion among Catholics in all countries! Everything we know concretely about the dictator's intentions points to the contrary: *he wants to destroy Christianity and the Church, or at least let them die out!* All the same, the Holy Father has to reckon with the possibility that the dictator will win, for millions and millions of Catholics live in his future empire, in G[ermany] itself, in Czech territory, in Poland, in Austria, in Switzerland[?], in Belgium, in Holland, and also in Denmark and Norway, not to mention the flourishing missions in the Congo.[17]

The Vatican found itself in a quandary and its plight was soon compounded. Toward the end of May, when Belgium had surrendered, Calais had fallen, and the evacuation of Dunkirk had commenced, Mussolini revealed his intention of entering the war and did so on June 10, 1940, shortly before the French agreed to an armistice. Although Pius was disappointed, the *L'Osservatore Romano* published news of the declaration of war without comment. In June and July, diplomatic, military, and political circles were nearly unanimous in their conviction that the war would soon be over, but the Vatican had doubts. However, the Vatican rejected Allied suggestions that the pope excommunicate Mussolini or Hitler. It considered the advantages of such excommunications problematic at best, but the disadvantages very predictable. Nonetheless, critics complained that rather than seeing the struggle as one between the forces of good versus evil, Pius XII seemed to perceive it as conflict between brothers of the same faith. This public stance did not necessarily reflect his personal convictions and inner sentiments.

Confronted with the calamity of war, and unwilling to abandon his diplomatic impartiality, Pius called upon God to calm the tempest raging over a stricken humanity. In his sermons he prayed for the return of order, tranquility, liberty, and security for all the nations of the world, themes he reiterated in his Christmas message of December 24, 1940. On the eve of the Nativity, Pius prescribed universal prayer for a victory over the hatred that divide the nations of the world, the restoration of peace, and the creation of a lasting and equitable order. Like Benedict during World War I, Pius scrupulously preserved papal neutrality or impartiality during World War II.

In 1940 and 1941, despite repeated reports of Nazi atrocities, he adhered to this diplomatic course. He did lament the evils afflicting not only fighters but entire populations: the old, innocent, peace-loving, and those bereft of all defense. "To the powers occupying territories during the war, We say with all due consideration: let your conscience guide in dealing justly, humanely . . . with the peoples of occupied territories, the pope noted in his Easter message of 1941. "Do not impose upon them burdens which you, in similar circumstances, have felt or would feel to be unjust."[18] The allies and the Americans hoped that Pius would say more, and denounce the notorious Nazi violations of the moral and natural law, but he did not heed their advice. He also adhered to this neutrality following the German invasion of the Soviet Union in June 1941, refusing to provide moral support for the venture.

President Roosevelt pressed the Vatican to support Great Britain and the Soviet Union against the Nazi menace, urging the Vatican to moderate its anti-Communist stance. On the other hand, Bernardo Attolico, Mussolini's representative to the Holy See, described the war against Russia as a crusade that warranted the Vatican's moral support. Pope and curia questioned both contentions. On September 9, 1941, Pius received a letter from the American president, which claimed the Soviets were preparing to introduce religious freedom in their territories, while asserting that the survival of Russia would prove less dangerous to religious life than that of the Nazi dictatorship.[19] The pope remained skeptical of the alleged Soviet conversion and both he and the curia feared the specter and spread of Communism. In turn, the Soviets unfairly depicted the Germanophile Pius XII as a crypto-Nazi and Hitler's pope. Despite the prevailing suspicion of Communism by the Vatican, pope and curia sought to accommodate the Americans regarding the Soviet Union, drawing a distinction between Communism, which

Pius XI had condemned in *Divini redemptoris* (On Atheistic Communism) and the suffering people of Russia. The Vatican perceived Nazism and Bolshevism as two devils in conflict and hoped they would destroy one another. Pius XII, preoccupied by the Communist menace, told the Spanish ambassador that he had nothing against Germany, which he "loved and admired" nor against the Hitler regime, although he acknowledged that some of its measures caused him profound sadness.[20] The pope proved unwilling to say more to the representative of a potential ally of the Fascist regimes.

Following the Japanese attack on Pearl Harbor on December 7, 1941, as Italy and Germany joined Japan in waging war on the United States, disturbing reports reached the Vatican of Hitler's genocidal practices and executions of the feeble minded and inmates of insane asylums and hospitals. The Allies hoped that the pope would denounce these atrocities, but Pius XII's long awaited Christmas message of December 1942 provided only vague statements and indirect criticism, without citing the gross Nazi violations of human rights and persecutions. It did express Vatican concern for those "who without fault on their part, sometimes only because of race or nationality, have been consigned to death or to a slow decline."[21] By this time the Metropolitan Andrey Sheptytsky had warned the pope that the German regime, perhaps to a higher degree than the Bolshevik one, was evil and diabolical, committing the most horrible crimes against the Jews and others, falling upon the helpless like a band of rabid wolves. In May of 1942 Pius was told of the mass extermination (*uccisioni in massa*) of Jews from Germany, Poland, and the Ukraine. By this time the Undersecretary of State Giovanni Battista Montini, who later became Paul VI, concluded that the massacre of Jews had assumed atrocious and frightening proportions. Meanwhile, the military chaplain Father Pirro Scavizzi personally reported to Pius XII that the elimination of Jews through mass murder was almost total, without regard for children or even infants.[22] The bewildered Pontiff pondered what he should do. Some believe he was influenced by the fact that his earlier diplomatic plea to the Vichy government on behalf of Jewish expatriates was ignored, and foreign Jews were arrested and deported as the Germans demanded.[23]

Pius did not publicly condemn the Nazi genocide, fearing the consequences of such denunciations for those subject to their occupation and the existence of the organizational church in Germany and the conquered territories, a stance he shared with a majority in the curia. Vatican officials defended this papal posture avoiding a more partisan and direct intervention in international affairs.

There is constant pressure on the Holy See from the Axis powers to denounce alleged Allied atrocities and, because of its silence, the Holy See is very often accused of being pro-ally. The
Holy See could not very well, therefore, condemn Nazi atrocities on the one hand without saying something, for instance,
about Russian cruelties on the other.[24]

Despite his relative public silence, Pius XII was not indifferent to the
plight of the persecuted, establishing the Vatican Information Service in
1939, putting relatives in touch with prisoners of war, missing persons,
and refugees while monitoring and mitigating the suffering and separa-
tions provoked by the Second World War. This service was asked to learn
the fate of millions of these displaced and incarcerated people and report
back to their families—and did so with considerable efficiency.[25] In addition, the Pontifical Relief Commission provided material assistance to
the needy in those countries where it was allowed to function, and some
believe that Pius quietly instructed the church and clergy to provide dis-
creet aid to the Jews—which saved many lives. Although the Vatican effort was the sole avenue of information and assistance for many, others
complained that the Holy See could and should have done more.

Some in the diplomatic community and the church pressed the pope to
follow in the footsteps of Pius XI and denounce the Nazi persecution, citing
the danger his continued "silence" posed to papal moral leadership. Even
Sister Pasqualina, the pope's housekeeper, cook, and closest thing to a com-
panion and confidant, claims she advised the pope to take a stronger stance
against Nazi inhumanities. "The Holy See must aid the Jewish people to the
best of our ability," Pius XII supposedly responded, "but everything we do
must be done with caution. Otherwise the Church and the Jews themselves
will suffer great retaliation."[26] "They deplore the fact that the Pope does not
speak," he told Paolo Dezza, the Jesuit rector of the Gregorian University
in December 1942, adding "But the Pope cannot speak. If he spoke, things
would be worse."[27] Undoubtedly, Pius was aware that the July 1942 protest of the Dutch bishops against the deportation and genocide of the Jews
had provoked a devastating Nazi retaliation. In addition, Vatican officials
argued: that the Holy See could not condemn Nazi atrocities without criticizing Soviet ones; that the charges would have to be investigated, and
the difficulties in assembling impartial and accurate evidence would be
enormous; that the pope had already condemned major offenses against
morality in wartime, to which was added the voice of the hierarchy, who
spoke on his behalf; and finally, that a condemnation of Nazi abuses would
further undermine the position of Catholics in these areas.

Papal caution was also dictated by the fact that the Vatican's principal preoccupation remained the bolshevization of Europe, fearing that the task of defending the continent against this danger would exceed German resources. This is why Monsignor Domenico Tardini suggested to Roosevelt and Churchill that they help the Russians—but only within limits, hoping that a stalemate between the Nazis and the Soviets would weaken both. Consequently, Pius hesitated to condemn the first, lest it redound to the advantage of the latter. For this among other reasons, he was reluctant to speak out against Germany's brutal conduct in Poland even though its president in exile pleaded "may the voice of the Holy Father . . . finally break [through] the silence of death."[28]

In April 1943, Pius responded to the Bishop of Berlin's plea on behalf of the persecuted Jews, claiming his Christmas message of December 1942 referred to what was being done to the non-Aryans under German occupation. "We have spoken briefly but we have been well understood," wrote the pope. He appreciated the difficulties confronting the Jews but added, "as the situation is at present we are unfortunately not able to help them effectively in other ways than our prayers." He promised to do more on their behalf, if it were necessary and circumstances permitted.[29] That he did not speak more openly and frankly was due to his desire to prevent greater evil—*Ad maiora mala vitanda*. There was disagreement by a minority in the Vatican with this cautious and conservative approach. "I am afraid history will reproach the Holy See for following a policy of convenience for itself, and not much more," complained Cardinal Eugene Tisserant, Prefect of the Congregation of the Eastern Church, adding that this was "extremely sad, above all for those who lived under Pius XI."[30] On the other hand, others appreciated the papacy's diplomatic course while providing refuge for the dispossessed within a number of Catholic institutions and thereby quietly rescuing many.

The course of the war also caused concern at the Vatican, which quietly opposed the unconditional surrender policy that Churchill and Roosevelt had agreed upon during the Casablanca conference of January 1943. The pope reflected this sentiment opposing unconditional surrender. He deemed this Allied policy neither prudent nor practical, fearing it would prolong the war and benefit the Soviet Union, which would push its way into Eastern Europe. In May 1943, Taylor informed the Vatican that the United States was prepared to negotiate with a successor government to Mussolini's regime, suggesting that this message be transmitted to those in a position to depose the Duce. This prospect apparently struck a response chord in the Vatican, which once again secretly abandoned its public neutrality by conveying the message to King Victor Emmanuel III, who proved cautious and noncommittal. However, the Vatican later learned that the king was involved in the conspiracy to replace Mussolini.[31]

The Allied invasion of Sicily in July 1943, paved the way for the dismissal of the Duce on July 25, 1943, followed by Italy's surrender in September. This prompted a German drive into the peninsula from the north, leading to the occupation of Rome on September 10. The Vatican was now more vulnerable and subject to increased Nazi pressure. "I'll go into the Vatican when I like, Hitler allegedly threatened. "You think the Vatican worries me? We'll just grab it. . . . After the war there won't be any more concordats. The time is coming when I will settle my accounts with the Church."[32] Rumor circulated of a Nazi plot to seize the Vatican and kidnap the pope. Hitler did not do so, and Pius remained in the Vatican throughout the German occupation. Nonetheless, on October 16, 1943, the Germans arrested over one thousand Jews in occupied Rome and commenced transporting them to concentration camps, where more than eight hundred were slaughtered. In response to the arrest and deportation of Rome's Jews, Bishop Alois Hudal, the Rector of Santa Maria dell' Anima, complained to the German Commander General Rainer Stahel, while the papal secretary of state, Cardinal Luigi Maglione protested to the German ambassador, quietly securing the release of some two hundred baptized Jews. Pius XII preserved his diplomatic approach even when the Germans rounded up the Jews of Rome in October 1943, "under his very windows." During this unfortunate incident, the Germans commented on the differences between the approaches of Pius XI and Pius XII.[33] Nor did Pius protest the massacre of 335 Italians in the Ardeantine Caves on March 24, 1944.

Despite the pope's moderation and prudence, tensions increased between the Vatican and the German occupiers, and veiled threats of a possible papal deportation continued to circulate. Pius let it be known that he would not leave Rome under any circumstances, privately protesting against any violence contemplated against the Vicar of Christ. However, the precarious position of the papacy improved, and that of the Germans deteriorated, as Allied forces pushed toward Rome. The commander of German forces in Italy, General Albert Kesselring, proposed that Rome be considered an open city and withdrew his troops from the Eternal City, as Pius issued an address to the cardinals reviewing the afflictions of the church and the city. On June 4, 1944 the allies entered Rome. "Today we rejoice," Pius told the assembled Romans, "because, thanks to the mutual collaboration of both contending parties, the Eternal City has been preserved."[34] Some concluded that Pius XII had been right in adhering to his strict neutrality; others assumed a more critical attitude.

The papacy paid a price for its neutrality and "silence," which Pius XII himself suspected might occur. As early as 1940, he privately acknowledged his doubts about his conciliatory approach, fearing his caution would be perceived as anti-Semitism. These doubts were also expressed to the Italian Ambassador Dino Alfieri in May 1940, according to notes taken by Monsignor Giovanni Montini, later Pope Paul VI, who records that Pius XII said

> The Pope at times cannot remain silent. Governments only consider political and military issues, intentionally disregarding moral and legal issue in which, on the other hand, the Pope is primarily interested and cannot ignore. His Holiness, said regarding this point, that he had occasion of late to read St. Catherine's letters, who writing to the Pope, admonishes him that God would subject him to the most stringent judgment if he did not react to evil or did not do what he thought was his duty. How could the Pope, in the present circumstances, be guilty of such a serious omission as that of remaining a disinterested spectator of such heinous acts, while all the world was waiting for his word?[35]

Later, in March 1944, Pius confided to the Archbishop of Cologne that it was "painfully difficult to decide whether reticence and cautious silence are called for, or frank speech and strong action."[36] The record reveals that Pius XI was more prone to resort to frank speech and strong action while Pius XII more often relied on reticence and cautious silence, pursuing a policy of "prudent delay" and "enlightened reserve." Critics proved more judgmental, charging that the ethical course pursued by Pius XI was abandoned in favor of the more expedient one of Pius XII. This policy shift does not substantiate nor indicate that Pius XII was indifferent to the plight of the Jews. His concern is revealed by his formation of the Vatican Information Office and the Pontifical Relief Commission and the fact that this pope permitted Catholic Religious to rescue Jews, and utilize ecclesiastical institutions, including Vatican properties, to shelter them, initiating a virtual "crusade of charity."[37] Furthermore, his nuncios in Slovakia, Bulgaria, Rumania, and Hungary made strenuous and repeated efforts to stop the deportation of Jews to the death camps. In his encyclical of April 15, 1945, appealing for prayers for peace, Pius called upon the faithful to pray for those who have been banished from their homeland and those in captivity still awaiting liberation.[38] He revealed his sentiments and his strategy to a group of visiting Jewish refugees (*La vostra presenza*) in November 1945, after the war, confiding that the ideal of brotherhood did not permit racial distinctions.

From the collapse of Nazi German until 1963, there was considerable praise and little public criticism of Pius XII's conduct during World War II and his stance during the Holocaust. At his death Jewish leaders joined Catholics in praising this pope for his wartime efforts in favor of the Jews and other persecuted populations. Gratitude was often expressed in the form of donations, including one by the World Jewish Congress, which contributed $20,000 to Vatican charities in recognition of the work of the Holy See in rescuing Jews from Fascist and Nazi persecution.[39] This positive perception of Pius was challenged as the magnitude of Hitler's genocide became manifest in the early 1960s, and the pope's measured words, indirect accusations, and limited actions were weighed against the gravity of the crimes. The latent critique was given expression by Rolf Hochhuth's play "The Deputy," which presented a negative and far from objective portrayal of this pope. In this drama, translated into more than 20 languages, Pius XII emerged as a selfish, cold, and calculating figure, preoccupied by church welfare to the detriment of the Nazi victims. Apologists, in opposition, pointed to the historical inaccuracies of Hochhuth's play and its failure to consider Pius XII's enduring and extensive humanitarian efforts on behalf of the Jews. In fact, some Jews remain among the staunchest defenders of Pius XII.[40] In this atmosphere, polemical attacks and defensive discourse prevailed over historical inquiry as opposing camps emerged to either defend or denigrate this pontiff and his policies.

Critics charge that Pius did not respond to the plight of the Jews with a sense of urgency and moral outrage, failing to raise an authoritative voice on behalf of the persecuted, with some even suggesting a latent anti-Semitism. His defenders respond that the "silence" of Pius XII on Nazi war crimes was not provoked by anti-Semitism but flowed from his diplomatic training and conviction that public protests would have made matters worse, and proven detrimental to all. The plethora of publications continues. We do not know, and cannot know, what impact more spirited papal protests of the Holocaust would have had on the Nazi genocide. Many believe it would have preserved the moral integrity of the papacy, disregarding the cost and unfortunate consequences of this interventionist course. Furthermore, the emphasis on this pope's "silence" has led some to ignore or downplay his religious vision, the Vatican's response to the formation of the United Nations, and Pius XII's part in the opening of the Cold War.

Pius XII assumed an active and far from silent role in internal church affairs. Among other things he named 33 new saints while his *Divino afflante Spiritu* (With the Help of the Divine Spirit) of 1943 sanctioned a limited use of critical historicism in religious studies, inspiring a biblical revival among Catholics. This was reinforced by the reform of the Psalter, the liturgical book used in divine services, with a new translation appearing in 1945. His other 1943 encyclical *Mystici corporis* (Mystical Body of Christ) defined the church as the mystical body of Christ while promoting a more positive relationship between the church and nonbelievers. There, and in his 1946 address to the College of Cardinals, he stressed the fundamental role of the laity in the church. Some have seen his encyclicals on the church, the laity, and the revival of biblical studies as preparing the path for the reforms of the Second Vatican Council and John XXIII's *aggiornamento.*

Others depict Pius XII in a more conservative light, pointing to his encyclical on the liturgy *Mediator Dei* (Mediator of God) of 1947, which defined his position on the liturgical movement seeing it as the worship the faithful render to its founder. Adhering to the motto *Non nova sed noviter* (not new things, but in a new form) his encyclical called for adherence to tradition and discouraged innovation in the liturgy. This traditionalism was also reflected in ecumenical matters in the 1948 admonition of the Holy Office against Catholic participation in interfaith activities and in his encyclical *Humani generis* (Of the Human Race) of 1950, which condemned the new theology, related dangerous theological tendencies, and the French worker priest movement. He also proved to be a traditionalist regarding marital relations and birth control. Thus, though he approved of the rhythm method of contraception, he adhered to church teaching that sexual union must remain open to the conception of new life.

His encyclical on the missions (*Evangelis praecones* of 1951) and that on radio, the cinema, and television (*Miranda prorsus* of 1957) struck a more positive note, and sanctioned some change. In 1953 this pope regularized the innovations introduced during the war for fast requirements for the Eucharist, and the holding of evening masses.[41] Devoted to Mary, as was Pius IX, in November 1950 he proclaimed the dogma of the Assumption, that at the end of her life, she was taken body and soul, into heaven. To date, this is the sole infallible papal declaration made after the First Vatican Council defined infallibility in 1870. Some complained that this posed yet another barrier to ecumenism and Christian unity. Both liberals and conservatives have wondered what path Pius would have pursued had he convoked the church council that he contemplated, made preparations for, but ultimately did not call.

Suspicious of elements of ecumenism, Pius XII nonetheless embraced aspects of internationalism and looked forward to a new order to supersede the selfish nationalism that had provoked the worldwide conflagration. Thus, during his pontificate the papacy further abandoned the political and diplomatic isolationism of Pius IX (1846–1878) and Pius X (1903–1914) to assume an increasingly interventionist stance that led to the Permanent Observer Mission of the Holy See to the United Nations. To be sure, he was not the first twentieth-century pope to invoke a universal order and international institutions. Pope Benedict XV (1914–1922), pinpointing the inability of the prevailing international configuration to peacefully resolve conflicts, as early as 1914 proposed an alternative. In his encyclical *Ad Beatissimi* (On World War I) of early November 1914, he appealed to the nations of the world to find some other means of resolving their differences. Later, in an encyclical of May 1920, "On Peace and Christian Reconciliation," the pope forcefully expressed his support for the League of Nations President Woodrow Wilson had proposed, the forerunner of the United Nations.[42]

Although many of the solemn principles advocated first by the League of Nations and later adopted by the United Nations mirrored positions of the Catholic Church, and centuries-old Christian traditions, there were obstacles to papal participation in an international organization structured on the basis of independent sovereign states. It is true that the creation of Vatican City in 1929 provided the Holy See with the claim to enter the concert of powers, altering in the eyes of some the chief obstacle it had confronted at the time of the formation of the League of Nations. The papacy, however, pointed out that some confused the Holy See with Vatican City, attributing to Vatican City recognition as a sovereign entity juridically equal to other states, despite its small territory and population, and the peculiarities of its organization and action. The church, on the other hand, insisted on the attribution of sovereignty to the Holy See, as the supreme organ of government of the Catholic Church. This difference in perception has influenced the Holy See's attitude toward the League of Nations, the United Nations, and international conferences.

Pius XII, who assumed the papal tiara on the eve of World War II, like his predecessors favored negotiation and arbitration to resolve international tensions. In his first encyclical letter *Summi Pontificatus* (On the Limitations of the Authority of the State) in October 1939, the pope decried the lack of morality in international relations. In a letter to the Haitian minister, Pius called for an international organization, which would secure the reciprocal independence of small and large nations alike, while safeguarding the liberty of all.[43] He returned to this theme in his Christmas message of 1939, invoking international institutions for preserving the peace, a call he repeated in his Christmas message of 1941, and those that followed. Meanwhile, in 1942 President Roosevelt coined the term United Nations to refer to the 26 nations at war with the Axis, suggesting the name for the new international organization to replace the moribund League. From

August to October 1944, when delegates from the United States, Great Britain, the Soviet Union, and China met in Washington to outline plans for the new organization, Pius proved supportive.

In his Christmas message of 1944, Pius XII concluded that "an essential point in any future international arrangement would be the formation of an organ for the maintenance of peace, of an organ invested by common consent with supreme power . . . to smother in its germinal state any threat of isolated or collective aggression."[44] Convinced that war was no longer an appropriate means of settling disputes, Pius indicated that no one would hail the establishment of an alternative mechanism more than he. The pope proved true to his promise to support a global peacekeeping mechanism, invoking such an international organization to enforce "universal respect for a people's frontiers and wealth without recourse to war."[45]

When the United Nations officially came into existence in October 1945, Pius approved of its general aims as Benedict had earlier approved those of the League. In fact, the Vatican urged the newly formed organization to resolve the problem of Palestine in a manner that respected the rights of Christians, Jews, and Arabs.[46] It is true that the pope had some reservations about the United Nations two-tier organization, which differentiated the great powers of the Security Council from the general membership in its Assembly—as well as the veto power accorded the Soviet Union. Nonetheless, in his Christmas message of 1948, Pius revealed the doctrinal basis for papal support of the United Nations, asserting that the universal church had long maintained that the nations of the world constituted a community, once more rejecting the notion of absolute state sovereignty. In 1951, following the suggestion of Giovanni Montini, Pius appointed Angelo Roncalli, the future Pope John XXIII, as Vatican observer to UNESCO in Paris, but did not then accept permanent observer status that was accorded to any state that belonged to one or more of the United Nations agencies. This hesitation stemmed from the question of the nature of papal participation. This was resolved in September 1957, when it was agreed that the papacy would be represented at the United Nations as the Holy See.

In postwar Europe, Pius XII championed economic and political integration as a means of easing the suffering of its people, effecting a reconciliation between victors and vanquished, while serving to stop Soviet expansion into Western Europe. His vision was shared by the Christian Democratic leaders who emerged including Robert Schuman of France, Konrad Adenauer of West Germany, and Alcide de Gasperi of Italy. These men, and the parties they led, seconded the papal commitment of defending Western Europe against the Soviet Union and the free capitalist economy against the Communist alternative. Economic realities, the emergence of the Cold War, American advice, and papal pressure all contributed to the call for some form of supranational and intergovernmental European union. The first step followed the American insistence in 1947 on the need for a European organization to distribute United States aid under the European Recovery Program or Marshall Plan. This led to the formation of the Organization for European Economic Cooperation (OEEC) by 17 western European nations. Two years later in 1949 a Council of Europe was established to advance European integration. Its task proved difficult as the Eastern European states, pressured by Stalin, refused to participate and a number of Western European states, particularly Great Britain, fearing infringement of their sovereignty, offered only a limited commitment. Pope Pius XII was not upset by Stalin's refusal to join, but citing the supranational nature of the church, regretted the obstacles placed in the path of European union in Western Europe. In his Christmas message of December 1948, he again rejected absolute state sovereignty and invoked an alternative.

The resistance to political integration and the determination of a number of states to protect their national sovereignty led Europeanists such as the French Foreign Minister Robert Schuman and the economist Jean Monnet to call for a pooling of the continent's coal and steel resources and production. In May 1950 they proposed to place Franco-German coal and steel production under a common authority, while making provision to have other European states join this economic entity. Following their suggestion, the Treaty of Paris was signed in April 1951, and in 1952 six countries: France, Germany, Italy, and the Benelux countries (Belgium, the Netherlands, and Luxemburg) established the European Coal and Steel Community (ECSC). Britain, still concerned about the infringement of its sovereignty, refused to then join—but did so later. The French continued to call for further economic integration, proposing the establishment of a European Economic Community (EEC). This was created by the Rome Treaties of 1957, which abolished tariffs between members and made provision for a common tariff upon goods entering from non-EEC countries. The objectives of the EEC were applauded by Pius XII the summer of 1957, who cataloged the advantages provide by the European organization the fall of that same year and called for closer political union as well—citing the importance of Christian inspiration and values in their effort.

While some appreciated Pius XII's support for the new international order and European integration; his traditionalism and "silence" during the Holocaust disturbed others. There is a general consensus that Eugenio Maria Giuseppe Giovanni Pacelli, pope from March 2, 1939, to October 11, 1958, confronted innumerable challenges during the course of his troubled pontificate including: the destructive Second World War, the abuses of the Fascist, Nazi, and Soviet regimes, and the Holocaust; and in the postwar period: European reconstruction, the spread of Communism, the Cold War, and the threat of nuclear annihilation. Disagreement and debate flows from conflicting interpretation of his responses to these challenges. Praised by some for his tact and diplomacy, he has been denounced by others for his alleged silence during the Holocaust. The debate continues.

Other actions undertaken during the postwar period of his pontificate also generated controversy. Pius XII persevered in his neutrality of the World War II period, by scrupulously abstaining from taking sides in the fighting between Jews and Arabs in Palestine, despite repeated attempts by both sides to enlist his support.[47] In the early 1950s Pius pleased conservatives and displeased liberals by his role in the Cold War and the suppression of the priest-worker movement in France. On the other hand, he pleased liberals and angered conservatives by changing the rules for the period of fasting before Communion and his revision of the liturgy, which made evening masses possible. There was a mixed reaction from the right and left to his denunciation of atomic weapons and his establishment of a Latin American Episcopal Council in 1956. Few doubted his commitment to social justice, revealed in his motto *Opus justitiae pax*—Peace is the Work of Justice. His emphasis on the importance of the laity in the church, and need to reform the curia, dismayed some conservatives, who questioned his commitment to tradition. Finally, though Pius did not abandon the conclusion of concordats with repressive regimes such as that with Franco's Spain in 1953, and with Trujillo's Dominican Republic in 1954, he did not allow the church, much less the Vatican, to become subordinate to these dictators. Among other things, he resisted Juan Peron's pressure to beatify his wife Evita and in 1955 had him excommunicated.

Following the death of Pius XII in 1958, Pope Paul VI in 1965 proposed that he be considered for sainthood—at the same time that the controversy over his alleged silence was at its peak. The prospect of declaring this pope a saint energized both his defenders and denigrators, generating another cycle of publications. Unfortunately, most of these works tended to be more partisan than historical. In fact, much of the polemical literature on Pius XII and the Holocaust has not been produced by historians but dramatists, novelists, journalists, and lawyers. From Hochhuth's 1963 influential play to the study of the journalist John Cornwell, with the inflammatory title *Hitler's Pope: The Secret History of Pope Pius XII* (1999), nonhistorians have driven much of the discourse, whose sweeping generalizations have clouded rather than clarified matters.

Bestowing sainthood always has political implications and consequences, and this certainly was the case with the cause of Pius XII. Only three popes have been declared saints in the past 900 years, and only one, Pius X, in the twentieth century. In fact, a renewed controversy erupted following the announcement of Pius XII's beatification alongside that of John XXIII at the dawn of the twenty-first century, as a virtual publishing war emerged between those seeking to besmirch or restore the memory of Pius XII. Some believe that this competition contributed to the postponement of Pius XII's beatification in 2000, as Pius IX was beatified along with John XXIII. Despite the increasingly bitter controversy, in May 2007, the Congregation for the Causes of the Saints, recognizing Pius XII's "heroic virtues" recommended that Pope Benedict XVI recognize him as venerable—a step towards his eventual canonization.[48] The announcement did not end the debate.

The Papacy and the Cold War: The Confrontation Between Catholicism and Communism

Study of the role of religion in the Cold War has been neglected, as has the crucial intervention of the Catholic Church. While some historians have belatedly scrutinized the part played by the United States in provoking the conflict, the papal contribution has not been adequately recognized or recorded. Pius XII's religious and ideological opposition to bolshevism has been explored, but this pope and his predecessors also understood the political danger posed by the Soviet Union in Europe and the world beyond, which has been largely ignored. Both the religious and political aspects of Pius XI's and Pius XII's anti-Communist policies, and the Vatican's role in the emergence and termination of the Cold War, need to be explored and assessed.

Rome's concern about the threat of communism was long-standing. Nineteenth-century popes from Gregory XVI (1831–1846) to Leo XIII (1878–1903) vehemently and frequently denounced this ideology. Following the revolutionary upheaval in Russia and the first formation of a Bolshevik regime in 1917, papal opposition intensified. Before the United States acknowledged the threat of Soviet expansion, before Churchill's Iron Curtain speech (1946), the Truman Doctrine (1947), and the formation of the North Atlantic Treaty Organization (NATO) (1949), the papacy had decried communism, which it perceived as an assault upon church doctrine, institutions, and community. The Holy See feared both the militant atheism of the soviet state, and its subversion of the social and political orders elsewhere. It perceived this ideology and the state, which championed it as a threat to traditionalism, at once dangerous to Christian civilization and detrimental to the Catholic Church. These concerns were revealed early on in the apparitions of Fatima, Portugal, in 1917, where Mary was said to have invoked prayers for the conversion of Russia, and by the confrontation of Eugenio Pacelli, the papal nuncio and future Pius XII, with Communist insurgents during the Sparticist revolt in Bavaria in 1919.

Pacelli's fears were shared by Achille Ratti, the future Pius XI, who was the papal representative in Warsaw the summer of 1920, when the Polish capital was threatened by a Soviet invasion. Ratti, who showed his mettle by refusing to flee the capital along with most other diplomats, was influenced by the panic produced in the Polish capital by the advancing Bolsheviks. Once pope, he lamented the aggressive attitude and the anticlerical measures adopted by Moscow, and sought redress. When none was forthcoming, at the end of 1924, Pius XI renewed his protests against the Soviet attacks upon the individual, family, and religion, again stressing the grave danger presented by communism.[1] The pope hoped that divine providence would intervene, provoking the collapse of what he perceived as a spurious ideology and pseudo religion. When this did not occur, he invoked prayers of atonement for the outrages against divine law and religion perpetrated in the Soviet Union, and bemoaned its refusal to negotiate a settlement. His opposition to Communist abuses was cataloged in his 1937 encyclical *Divini Redemptoris* (On Atheistic Communism), which condemned this movement as subversive of Christian culture.[2]

His successor Pius XII (1939–1958), continued and intensified his predecessor's battle against communism, mobilizing Catholic forces and others to combat it after the Second World War. His pontificate initiated a global campaign against bolshevism in general, and the Soviet Union in particular, thus contributing to the opening of the Cold War. In fact, in October 1939, his first encyclical letter *Summi Pontificatus* (On the limits of the authority of the state), condemned the claims of absolute state authority.[3] Its denunciation of totalitarianism was applicable to the Soviet Union as well as Nazi Germany, for Pius abhorred the ideologies and political practices of both. Indeed, he judged the frontal assault by communism upon organized religion and the church more serious than the indirect Nazi attacks. His suspicion of communism and the Soviet Union increased following the reign of terror introduced by Joseph Stalin after 1926, during his creation of a totalitarian state in Russia.

Despite Stalin's flagrantly oppressive internal policies, President Franklin Delano Roosevelt pragmatically established formal diplomatic relations with the Soviet Union, and during the Second World War appreciated its crucial role in combating Nazi aggression. He sought to convince

Pius XII that the road to peace rested in supporting Great Britain and the Soviet Union against the Nazi menace, urging the Vatican to moderate its anti-Communist stance. Meanwhile, Mussolini's Italy sought to convince the pope that the war against Russia warranted the Vatican's moral support. Politically skeptical, Pius XII rejected both suggestions. "I see the crusade, but I don't see the crusaders," his Undersecretary of State Domenico Tardini noted, responding to the request for Vatican support of the Nazi invasion of Bolshevik Russia. The pope personally repeated this position to the Italian representative to the Vatican, Bernardo Attolico. "If I should speak of Bolshevism—and I am quite prepared to do so—why should I therefore say nothing about Nazism?" He concluded by warning, "if I 'have' to speak one day, I shall do so, but I shall say everything."[4] He did not do so during the course of the war—leading to the charge of silence.

Preserving a cautious neutrality throughout the conflict, Pius XII was pleased by Roosevelt's appointment of Myron Taylor as his personal representative to the Vatican in December 1939. Troubled by the Anglo-American support of Stalin, this did not prevent the Vatican from making an accommodation of sorts by not condemning American lend lease aid to Moscow, while remaining silent on Soviet as well as Nazi atrocities during hostilities. Still, there were limits to what Pius XII would tolerate to placate the western allies, who were tied to the Russian regime that systematically persecuted the Catholic Church.

In September 1941, Pius received a letter from the American president proclaiming the Soviets were on the brink of introducing religious toleration in their territories, concluding that the survival of Russia would prove less dangerous to religious life in Europe than the survival of the Nazi dictatorship.[5] The pope privately questioned Washington's account of the alleged Soviet conversion, which was contradicted by all of the reports he received from a series of informants. While the Vatican's relations with Hitler's Germany were troublesome, and becoming increasingly worse, they were nonexistent with the Soviet regime. The Vatican also noted that the Nazi persecution, unlike the Bolshevik one, had not completely outlawed religion and suppressed the churches. Furthermore, if Stalin found it prudent to make some concessions to the Russian Orthodox Church to curry favor with his suffering masses, these were not extended to the Catholic Church, which was persecuted, as the Soviets moved to liquidate the Ukrainian Catholic Church (Uniate) and forcefully reunite it with the Orthodox Church. Members of the hierarchy who resisted were imprisoned, along with clergy or lay faithful who opposed the Soviet scheme. Few priests remained in Russia so that Father Leopold Braun, chaplain to the American embassy in Moscow, was a rare exception.[6] To make matters worse, seminaries, schools, publishing houses, along with charitable foundations and institutions were confiscated and closed, or turned over to the Russian Orthodox Church. For these and other reasons, the pope and the curia feared the specter of communism, placing little credence in the positive American assessment and unrealistic assurances.

Pius XII deplored Stalin's unrelenting harassment of the Catholic Church, which saw its property nationalized and its hierarchy shattered by deportations, arrests, and executions. The repression had been thorough, so that by the end of the 1930s the Catholic Church had been virtually eliminated from the Soviet Union. Conditions were particularly deplorable in the western Ukraine, a hotbed of anti-Soviet agitation, where the Uniate Church was closely linked to national identity. In fact, the Ukrainian Catholic Church of Eastern Rite, was the sole church the Soviets outlawed outright. Furthermore, once Soviet forces occupied eastern Poland and the Baltic states, the persecution was extended. Catholic schools were shut and religious instruction in the schools terminated, church property confiscated, monasteries suppressed, and an aggressive program introduced to impose atheism. In Catholic Lithuania the church was likewise persecuted during the Soviet occupation. Despite these hostile actions and developments, which contradicted Roosevelt's optimistic appraisal of Communist policies, the Vatican did not denounce the American collaboration with the Soviet Union, drawing a distinction between communism, which Pius XI had earlier condemned, and the suffering people of the Soviet Union. Vatican silence on Soviet atrocities was justified to avoid further suffering for the Russian population as well as the need to preserve papal neutrality.

Nonetheless, Pius, dreaded the prospect of the extension of Stalin's system, and hoped that a stalemate between the Nazis and the Soviets would undermine both. He perceived the unconditional surrender policy that Churchill and Roosevelt had sanctioned during the Casablanca Conference (January 1943), as dangerous, fearing it would prolong the conflict, and benefit the Soviet Union and its subversive ideology. Pius worried not only about the future of Germany and Italy, but feared the consequences of a Soviet victory upon Poland, the Baltic states,[7] and the whole of Eastern Europe. Finally, he expressed concern about the spread of communism over the entire war-torn continent, which was deemed unlikely by the Allies and initially dismissed by them as a reflection of Vatican paranoia. Other differences developed as the Vatican rigidly adhered to the Polish government in exile, whereas Washington and London were eventually constrained by political and military realities to accept the Soviet-sponsored Polish government, with minimal representation by the democratic London group. To make matters worse for Rome, which championed a restoration of the old Polish boundaries, Washington was constrained to accept the Russian expansion of their frontier at the expense of Poland, which was to be compensated with the eastern territory wrenched from Germany.

The Holy Father and the American president also disagreed on the Soviet Union's role in the reconstruction of Europe at war's end. The Americans, appreciative of the Soviet military effort, justified the prominent participation of the Soviet Union in the peacemaking process and the postwar settlement. "Russia, when final victory comes for the United Nations, will have earned the right to participate in arrangements for peace," Harold H. Tittmann, Jr. advised the pope. More ominously for the Vatican, he added, "At the peace table and in the many adjustments that will inevitably have to be made in international matters after the war, Russia will have an important voice." Dismissing the papal fear of communism, Tittmann concluded that "Communism is . . . an essentially internal problem," and deemed it unrealistic for any state to "overcome a possible Communist menace within its borders by attacking Russia publicly."[8] Pius was appalled by the American assessment. "Communism is materialistic, totalitarian, militarist, and anti-religious," Tardini wrote on Pius XII's behalf in 1944, adding, "there is no concrete and notable fact to show that Communism has now really changed its theories and its practical way of action." Pius concurred, placing little confidence in the promise allegedly made by Stalin to the Polish-American Priest Stanislas Orlemanski in 1944 that he wanted to collaborate with the Vatican and combat the Nazi persecution of the church. The Vatican responded that Stalin's actions belied these promises. For this and other reasons the Holy See adopted "an attitude of prudent reserve toward the Soviets and their allies."[9]

The pope brooded about the fate of Europe following the collapse of Nazi Germany, alarmed by the expansionism of the Soviet Union and the spread of its dangerous and destructive ideology. The curia was likewise concerned. Before his death, Cardinal Luigi Maglione, the papal secretary of state, warned of the grave danger of Russian hegemony in Europe. His apprehension was shared by Monsignor Tardini, who predicted the war would end with a predominant Russian victory in Europe, leading to the spread of communism, to the detriment of European civilization and Christian culture.[10] Even if the allied armies remained in Europe, Tardini foresaw the onset of the Cold War, predicting that the ensuing peace would only rest on mutual fear. Within the next decade, the Vatican's criticism proved even more explicit, contributing both to the campaign against communism, and the waging of the Cold War.

Pius XII and the Vatican were not surprised that the Soviets sought to reap the harvest of the protracted conflict and uneasy peace by imposing their imperium and ideology on Eastern Europe. The pope believed that Marx had denounced religion as the opium of the people, Lenin had preached a crusade against it on the basis of class struggle and dialectical materialism, and during his years in power, Stalin had brutally exploited their goals. Pope and curia trembled at the prospect of a Russian hegemony in Europe, leading to a rapid diffusion of communism and atheism throughout the greater part of the continent. The Vatican acknowledged that during the summer of 1944, Stalin had momentarily suspended his atheistic propaganda, permitting the clergy and faithful to gather in the few churches remaining open. Monsignor Tardini observed that this limited concession flowed from the political and military exigencies of the war, and the desire to quiet Catholic Poland, which the Soviets were poised to occupy. Under these circumstances, Stalin pragmatically sought improved relations with the Holy See. Nonetheless, the Vatican deemed this thaw a temporary expedient, noting that the Communist program remained profoundly anti-religious.[11] There was talk of a rapprochement between Rome and Moscow, but none occurred. At the beginning of August 1944, Monsignor Giovanni Montini denied the reports circulating that Russia had offered to open diplomatic relations with the Holy See, which had rejected the offer.[12] No offer was made, and the alleged papal rejection was myth rather than reality.

Pius clarified the papal position toward communism in a radio address of September 1, 1944, insisting that Christians could not admit a social order, which opposed the possession of private property.[13] The pope continued to challenge American optimism regarding Stalin, questioning not only the Allied call for unconditional surrender, but the Yalta agreements as well. His skepticism was well-founded, and indirectly acknowledged by the Americans themselves. Regarding the issue of some Soviet assurance on the religious question, the Americans advised Pius that it would be unwise to raise the question openly.[14] Citing Russian sensitivity, Taylor proposed relying on American goodwill and influence rather than seeking a formal commitment from the Soviets. The pope placed no more credence in this American approach toward the Soviets than earlier ones made by Washington. On the other hand, Pius was pleased by Washington's support for a new international organization to preserve the peace.

Although the Vatican approved of the general aims of the United Nations as constituted at San Francisco in June 1945, the emerging organization did not fulfill all of Pius XII's expectations. The pope harbored reservations about its structure, and especially the veto exercised by the Soviet Union in the Security Council. The *L'Osservatore Romano* complained that it continued the distinction between great and small, victor and vanquished, perpetuating the errors and discriminations of the League of Nations. The Vatican also deplored the key role assumed by the Soviet Union in postwar Europe. Stalin discounted papal opposition. "The Pope! The Pope! How many divisions has he got?" the Soviet dictator repeated at the Yalta Conference of 1945.[15] He realized that Pius nourished serious reservations about the proposed postwar settlement, and challenged the contention that the Russian occupation was benign. The pope said as much in his Christmas message of 1946, wherein he lamented the compromises made at war's end by the western Allies toward the Soviets.

Rejecting the Roosevelt administration's continued optimism regarding the Soviet Union, the Vatican informed the Americans at the close of 1944, and the beginning of 1945, that over 400 priests were deported from the Lublin district into the interior of Russia, a dozen priest-professors of Lublin University were executed, and the Bolsheviks were systematically closing church and parochial schools.[16] Early in 1946, a Vatican pronouncement denounced the forced assimilation of the Catholic United Church into the Russian Orthodox one. Even as pope and curia catalogued the perils of what would eventually be labeled the Cold War, they differentiated the danger stemming from the Communist ideology and the state that adopted it. A 1947 editorial in the Vatican journal *L'Osservatore Romano* reported that in Stalin's Russia, state interests prevailed over Marxist convictions, concluding that so long as Stalin did not deem war profitable, he would not wage it.[17] Although Rome had reservations about containment, it was deemed preferable to Soviet expansion. Pius warned that unless the West championed and upheld democratic regimes in Eastern Europe, the Russians would impose Soviet ones there and beyond.

In combating communism, the Catholic Church and its papal leadership introduced much of the early ideological rhetoric of the Cold War, which resounded abroad. However, initially, Washington provided the Holy See with little sympathy or support, so the papacy was left to its own devices.[18] Immediately following the death of President Roosevelt in April 1945, the new American president seemed determined to follow Roosevelt's policy of cooperation with the Soviet Union in Europe and was somewhat suspicious of the strident anticommunism of the Vatican, which continued its anti-Soviet campaign. Charging that the totalitarian, anti-religious state demanded the silence and acquiescence of the church, the pope at this juncture refused to remain silent. "What was in the opinion of many a duty of the church, and what they demanded of her in an unseemly[!] way," Pius protested, "is today . . . a crime in their eyes and a forbidden interference in domestic affairs of the state: namely resistance against unjust restraint of conscience by totalitarian systems and their condemnation all over the world."[19] Repeatedly setting forth the tenets of the faith contradicted by Communist doctrines and policies, he fought Soviet political designs in Europe and abroad.

During these postwar years, Pius called for the banishment of atheism and the defense and promotion of spiritual values in the struggle against communism and the Soviet Union. Pius determined to play an important part in this campaign, which had religious as well as political implications. "Can, may the Pope be silent?" Pius asked the assembled crowd in St. Peter's Square, adding "Can you imagine a successor to Peter who would bow to such demands?" The crowd shouted an unequivocal "No!"[20] The response pleased the pope, who utilized the support of the faithful for his diplomacy of condemnation and containment of the Soviet Union. This papal position was eventually endorsed by the United States, when Truman adopted the anti-Communist stance of Pius XII, Churchill, and George Kennan.[21] In 1947, there was an exchange of letters between the Vatican and Washington in which the two concurred in seeing communism as a threat both to religion and Western civilization. This concurrence was accelerated by Russia's heavy-handed actions, which prompted the American response to contain the threat of Communist expansion.

Adhering to the containment course of the United States, the pope welcomed the 1947 European Recovery Program (Marshall Plan), which George C. Marshall announced at Harvard in June 1947 to reconstruct the faltering European economies. Pius enthusiastically supported the proposal, relieved that the Americans had finally perceived "the extreme gravity of the hour."[22] In fact, Washington increasingly adopted the view of the world emanating from the Vatican. Meanwhile, the pope also approved the initial steps toward European economic and political integration, deemed another means of curtailing social unrest and thus blocking the unfortunate consequences of Soviet expansion. In 1949 and 1950 Pius veered further away from papal neutrality by approving NATO, designed to thwart Moscow's diplomatic coercion and military threats. This papal position enabled Alcide De Gasperi and his Christian Democrats to overcome left-wing opposition and secure Italian ratification of the NATO treaty in April 1949, and also helped the Christian Democrats under Konrad Adenauer to secure West Germany's adherence to NATO in 1955.

Throughout most of the 13 years of his pontificate following the close of World War II (1945–1958), Pius generally pursued a conservative, anti-Communist course. He supported conciliatory measures towards Italy and Germany to diminish the appeal of Communism there and stop its spread

into Central and Western Europe. Some have seen his entire postwar pontificate as defensive, attempting to preserve Catholic civilization in a world
shaken by militant Bolshevism. Whatever the motivation, Pius did range
the church against the Union of Soviet Socialist Republics (USSR), moving
it closer to the West. Indeed, the common interests of the United States and
Vatican multiplied following Roosevelt's death, during the increasingly
hostile reaction of the Truman administration toward the Soviet Union.[23]
As early as 1946 Myron Taylor suggested to President Truman that communism could be defeated in Italy and Western Europe with papal support. "The Pope has openly challenged Communism from the beginning,"
Taylor wrote, adding "The leadership of the Pope in this field is as important to the Western democracies as to Italy as to the Catholic Church itself
in Europe." Churchill shared Taylor's conviction, declaring "I am for the
Pope . . . I join him in combating Communism. . . . He has been outspoken
against it very consistently . . . I have great admiration for the Pope."[24]
Across the Atlantic the television priest, Bishop Fulton Sheen, branded communism the Antichrist, as many American Catholics pressed Washington to
join the war against Satan and his Soviet allies.

Despite the increasing confluence of Washington and the Vatican on
the Communist threat, the United States Division of Southern European
Affairs recommended the termination of the presidential personal representation to the Vatican, arguing it was no longer possible to justify the mission
in terms of its original aims. Taylor's assistant, Harold H. Tittmann, disagreed, convinced that though the mission had changed, it was still useful
to have an American at the Vatican in the postwar period, citing the importance of exchanging ideas and information with the 40 or so states with
representation to the Vatican. He also noted the favorable impact of this
diplomatic mission on Latin America, adding that now both Washington
and the Vatican shared a similar concern about the march of communism
and the fate of Eastern Europe. President Truman, who now appreciated
the Vatican connection, reappointed Taylor as his personal representative
to the pope. Toward the end of 1949, when Taylor informed Truman of
his impending resignation as of January 1950, the president, convinced
of the importance of preserving an American presence at the Vatican,
sought to transform the personal representative into a regular diplomatic
appointment.

In October 1951 Truman announced the appointment of General Mark
W. Clark as American ambassador to Vatican City. The nomination of a
representative to the pope of the Atlantic alliance had to be withdrawn
in 1952 following the widespread criticism and outburst of indignation
in the American heartland whose anti-Catholicism was still stronger

than anti-Communism. Nonetheless, the failure to open full diplomatic relations, did not end the cooperation between Washington and the Vatican. Despite this rebuff, the pope continued to preach against godless communism and to provide moral support for the American efforts in Europe and the Far East. In 1956, he denounced the Soviet violation of human rights and invasion of Hungary. Two years later, Pius XII issued yet another condemnation of Chinese persecution of the church.[25]

Once Stalin dominated Eastern Europe, and especially after 1948, when he forged a bloc of compliant satellites from the Baltic to the Black Sea, the dictator's allies initiated a brutal repression against the church and clergy of the region. Following the Communist putsch in Czechoslovakia, the Communists proposed a new constitution and commenced their domination. Among other things, they introduced obligatory civil marriage, followed by legislation, which extended the prohibition against reading Episcopal messages and papal messages from church pulpits. In response, Pius called the Czech bishops to Rome, inspiring them to take a firm stance against their state's violations of the fundamental rights of the church. Despite this increased tension, early in 1949 the Vatican and the Czech church sought to negotiate with the Communist controlled government, and talks were opened but failed. This provoked a swift retaliation by the regime, which under the auspices of the Cominform (Communist Information Bureau) sought to create a catholic church free of papal control. Subsequently, under the prodding of the Soviet Foreign Minister Andrei Vishinsky, the government proclaimed a "Karlsbad Protocol," which provided for the eventual liquidation of the traditional Catholic Church in Czechoslovakia. In turn, the Vatican excommunicated the Communists and their allies, prohibiting marriages between Catholics and Communists. In Bulgaria the Communist regime, with Soviet support, pressed Bishop Eugene Bossilkov to enter the Orthodox Church or form a National Catholic Church without ties to the Vatican. His refusal to follow either of the Communist directives led to his execution by a firing squad in 1952.

The Vatican's relations with Tito's Yugoslavia were not much better. During the Second World War, Archbishop Alojzije Viktor Stepinac, of Zagreb, had been arrested by Communist partisans, who considered him a symbol of Croat oppression of the Serbs, and though released, he remained persona non grata, in the eyes of the Communist regime. Deemed a divisive and disruptive figure, Tito requested he be recalled to Rome, but Pius proved unwilling to comply. In retaliation, the Archbishop was put on trial in October 1946, and found guilty of unlawful collaboration with the fascist Ustasha regime, and admitting forcibly converted Orthodox Serbs into the Catholic Church. The Vatican responded with spiritual

strictures, excommunicating all who had participated in, or even contributed to, the trial! Tito's government responded by encouraging the
formation of professional organizations of priests, free from Episcopal and
Vatican control. These organizations were immediately condemned by the
Yugoslav bishops, who appealed to Pius XII for support. The pope upheld
their stance, encouraging them to oppose "the heavy threat represented
by the priests' organizations." His message was accidentally leaked,
leading the Tito government to complain early in November 1952 of the
Vatican's unwarrantable interference in Yugoslavia's internal affairs. To
make matters worse, Pius honored Archbishop Stepinac by naming him a
cardinal, and adding insult to injury, did so on November 29, Yugoslavia's
national holiday. This dual insult prompted Tito's government to sever
diplomatic relations with the Vatican in mid-December 1952.[26]

Similar problems developed elsewhere in Communist controlled Eastern
Europe, where churches and other ecclesiastical properties were nationalized, schools taken over by the state, religion eliminated from the curricu-
lum, monasteries and seminaries slammed shut, and the Catholic clergy
either arrested or deported. In Hungary, the persecution led to the condemnation of its Primate, Cardinal Jozsef Mindszenty in 1949. In response, Pius
launched a counterattack on those who harassed and sought to subvert
the Faith. During these years, the pontiff who had consistently avoided
confrontation during the war period, minced no words in his postwar
condemnation of communism. In 1949 the Holy Office published a decree
that attacked the totalitarianism Stalin had imposed on Eastern Europe,
prescribing excommunication for those who voted for, joined, collaborated
with, or even read the newspapers of the Communists and their allies. This
Vatican hard line conflicted with the stance of some of the national hierarchies, which called for conciliation rather than confrontation with the
Communist regimes in Eastern Europe. In fact, the Polish hierarchy secretly
negotiated an agreement with the Communist government in April 1950,
in defiance of papal directives. Soon, thereafter, the Hungarian hierarchy
did likewise. The year 1950, which witnessed the celebration of the Holy
Year in Rome, found the pope almost alone in his intransigent opposition
to communism. Things began to change in the west, which increasingly
followed the Vatican's anti-Soviet stance following the outbreak of the war
in Korea.

In 1951, the year after the Cold War flared red hot in Korea, Pius urged
Catholics in Czechoslovakia to stand firm in their faith, praising them for
their constancy in the face of persecution. Pius also deplored Peking's
disruption of relations between Rome and the Chinese hierarchy, and its
attempt to foster an alternative to the traditional faith. During the courses

of 1952, he continued his denunciation of the Chinese attacks upon the church with his letter of January 18, 1952, "To the Bishops, Priests, and People of China," urging Chinese Catholics to stand firm in their faith and trust in Christ.[27] That same year he assured the clergy and faithful of Rumania of ultimate victory.[28] The pope also reached out to the people of Russia in his address *Carissimis Russiae populis* of July 1952, regretting the tribulations they endured while predicting that the Communists could not undo the thousand year history of the church in Russia, whom he consecrated to the Immaculate Heart of Mary.

At the end of 1952, a papal letter to the Catholic Churches of the East *Orientales Ecclesias,* reaffirmed Rome's desire for unity and deplored the attempts to exclude God from their lives. In combating persecution in the East, Pius increasingly looked to the states of the West, and particularly their leader, the United States, whom he finally found a willing collaborator. On January 7, 1953, in his State of the Union message, President Truman reported that the United States had developed a hydrogen bomb, which proved a double-edged sword for the Vatican. On the one hand this would hopefully restrain the Russians; on the other hand, the potential for global destruction and human annihilation was exponentially increased. Pius XII, who was in the forefront of preaching against the development and use of weapons of mass destruction, worried about the devastating consequences of a third world war, and thus preferred negotiation to confrontation.[29] Seeking the collapse of communism without the recourse to war, the summer of 1953 he called upon the Poles to remain united in resisting dechristianization and dishonor.

In June 1953, Pius XII dispatched a pastoral letter to the three imprisoned archbishops of Eastern Europe: Stepinac of Zagreb, Mindszenty of Budapest, and Beran of Prague, inspiring them and their followers to persevere, predicting they too, would eventually prevail. Meanwhile, Pius vigorously refuted the scurrilous charges made against Chinese Catholics following the expulsion of the papal nuncio from Communist China and Rome's recognition of Taiwan in 1951. Addressing the clergy and people of China, whose conditions he deplored, the pope protested the false accusations against the Holy See, the propaganda campaign against the church, and the arbitrary expulsion of the Nuncio and again rejected attempts of the Communist regime in China to establish an Catholic Church independent of the Holy See.[30] Most missionaries were expelled from China in the early 1950s but it was not until the fall of 1955 that there were sweeping arrests of Chinese bishops, priests, and religious, prompting another papal protest. In 1957 the Chinese Communist regime created the long threatened Chinese Catholic Patriotic Association, which was constructed to

sever all political and economic ties with the Vatican and to obey the pope
only in matters of faith and church law. Pius issued yet another protest in
June 1958—the final year of his pontificate. The animosity between Peking
and the Vatican has fluctuated over the years, but to date the rupture has
not been resolved.

While the pope once more preached against the march of communism in
his Christmas message of December 24, 1954, he was not an unrepentant
"cold warrior," recognizing the danger of the "coexistence of fear," which
prevailed. He was not only in the forefront of focusing upon the Communist threat, but subsequently among the first to warn of the dangers
posed by the launching of a nuclear war. "There will be no song of victory
flowing from a future world conflict," he warned, "only the inconsolable
weeping of humanity, which will gaze upon the catastrophe brought on by
its own folly."[31] Here and elsewhere, the pope, emphasized the opposition
of the church to wars, except those of a strictly defensive nature, and relied
on prayer and the intercession of Mary—to whom he was devoted—to
overcome the dilemma facing the church in Eastern Europe and the Far
East.

Pius XII also expressed concern about the Middle East, and especially
Jerusalem, which became embroiled in the Cold War, the Arab-Jewish
struggle, great power diplomacy, as well as the religious rivalry of various
groups. Like his predecessors, harking back to Pius X, Pius XII did not
favor the creation of a Jewish state in Palestine, which he felt would prove
detrimental to Catholic interests, arousing the enmity of the Arab population and very likely sparking a catastrophic conflict. Early in 1947, the British turned the thorny problem over to the United Nations whose Special
Committee on Palestine recommended its partition and the internationalization of Jerusalem. While the Vatican had reservations about the partition,
it supported internationalization—but both were called into question by
the Arab-Israeli war, which erupted in May 1948. During the hostilities the
Jordanians occupied most of biblical Jerusalem, while the Israeli's pushed
their boundaries beyond those outlined in the United Nation's partition
plan. In May 1948, October 1948, and April 1949, Pius XII issued encyclicals on the Palestinian issue, insisting on the internationalization of Jerusalem. At the end of 1949 the United Nations General Assembly adopted a
resolution for such an internationalization, but it was never implemented.
Instead, the Israelis proposed a limited international or functional supervision over the holy places and towards the end of his pontificate Pius XII
pragmatically moved to support this "functional internationalization" of
the Holy Places.[32] Some believe that this failure to obtain a broader internationalization led the pope to reassess the importance of gaining political

support internally in the various states, as well as allies in the international arena.

Following the path projected by all popes in the twentieth century, Pius XII remained suspicious of partisan politics even though he relied on the Christian Democratic parties of Belgium, France, the Netherlands, and Italy to confront and combat communism. Fearful of a Communist conquest of Italy, the Vatican journal, *L'Osservatore Romano,* warned the faithful that one could not be a Catholic and Communist simultaneously.[33] "Communism is a very grave and imminent danger for the Italian people," the pope reported, complaining that it would jeopardize the Holy See "if it were surrounded by a restless, agitated and extremist population."[34] Once members of the Italian Communist Party entered the government following the liberation of Rome, Pius, convinced that the papacy and church were under siege in postwar Europe, became increasingly alarmed.[35] The Vatican even expressed concern about who would distribute American aid in the peninsula, calling for committees composed of Catholic and honest citizens to spread the largesse, rather than Socialists or Communists.

Seeking allied assistance to spare Italy from the Communist menace, Pius embroiled himself in the peninsula's affairs, by means of organized Catholic groups (Catholic Action), under the leadership of Professor Luigi Gedda, and supervised by the bishops. In March 1946, in a first salvo, the pope alerted the Italian clergy that it was their duty to instruct the faithful to combat anti-Christian forces in politics and society, sharing the American concern that the Communists not triumph in the parliamentary elections of April 1948. To prevent such a development, Pius encouraged Gedda's civic committees to support conservative parties and policies in Italy, opposing those of the Left. Although the Vatican continued to disdain partisan politics, it encouraged Catholic groups, whose members numbered some three million, to support the Christian Democrats, to keep the Communists out of power. Indeed, Amleto Cicognani, the Apostolic delegate to the United States, urged the American bishops to have Italian-Americans write their relatives in the old country, pressing them to reject Communist candidates.

The Vatican policy played a major role in assuring the Christian Democrats almost half of the vote, and over half the seats in the Italian Chamber of Deputies. In Italy it relied not only on the varied Catholic organizations but also on its own religious authority. In mid-July 1949 the Holy See made public a decree issued earlier by the Congregation of the Holy Office, initially formed as the Sacred Congregation of the Universal Inquisition, and today known as the Congregation for the Doctrine of the Faith, on the relationship between Catholics and Communism. A series of questions were posed in the decree including: (1) was it legitimate to become a member of the Communist Party or to support it? (2) was it permissible for Catholics to publish, disseminate, or read periodicals or other literature that upheld the Doctrine of Communism, or collaborate in their writing or publication? (3) could the faithful who professed the materialist, anti-Christian Doctrine of Communism, and especially those who knowingly and willingly engaged in the activities listed above, be admitted to the sacraments? Finally, (4) it asked whether those faithful who professed the materialist, anti-Christian Doctrine of Communism, and especially those who became its proponents, did not automatically fall under excommunication as apostates of the Catholic Faith?

The Holy Office responded no to the first query, reporting it was not permissible for the faithful to join or support the Communist Party, because it was materialistic and anti-Christian while its directors, both in theory and practice, proved hostile to God, religion, and the Church of Christ. Secondly, Catholics could not publish, disseminate, or even read books, periodicals, or other literature that upheld this pernicious doctrine. Those who violated these first two prohibitions should not be admitted to the sacraments. Finally, the decree proclaimed that those who affirmed such doctrines and practices automatically fell under excommunication as apostates of the Catholic faith. On July 1, 1949, the decree *Responsa ad dubia de communismo* was promulgated in the *Acta Apostolicae Sedis*, providing papal support for an excommunication of those who supported communism, a condemnation that had never been launched by the Vatican against the adherents of Nazism or Fascism.[36]

The Vatican's political activism and alliance with the western bloc contributed to the triumph of Christian Democracy in Italy and Germany, as well as the containment of the Soviet Union, but compromised the long flaunted papal neutrality. Pius, who had foreseen the opening of the Cold War, looked forward to its conclusion following the death of Stalin. To be sure, the dictator's death in March 1953, did not immediately end the East-West tension, but initiated the movement from Cold War to "cold peace." Pius, for his part, contributed to this development by offering hints that an accord with the Soviet Union might be possible. Indeed, in his Christmas message of December 1954, he called for a "coexistence in truth" to replace the climate of fear.[37] During the course of 1955, the year that Konrad Adenauer visited Moscow, Pius—distressed by the proliferation of the nuclear arsenal in a bipolar world—further elaborated his call for coexistence between east and west. "The true Christian westerner nourishes thoughts of love and peace toward the peoples of the east, who live within the sphere of influence of a materialistic *Weltanschaunng* supported by state power," the pope proclaimed. "If the question of co-existence continues to move the spirit: faithful westerners pray together with those on the other side of the iron curtain who are still stretching out their hands to God."[38]

Pius XII's anti-Communism though fervent was never unconditional, tempered in part by the more conciliatory course assumed by the hierarchies in the Communist countries and his own fear of a nuclear holocaust. At the end of 1955, the pope who continued to condemn communism as a social system, warned the West of the inherent danger of an indiscriminate opposition to any sort of coexistence and the peril inherent in the use of weapons of mass destruction. Pius thus offered the Soviet regimes of Eastern Europe a cease fire in the Cold War. The signals from the Vatican were received by Moscow, which recognized that despite ideological differences there might be useful and perhaps even official relations between their party and the papacy. In December 1956, in his Christmas message, Pius revealed that though he abhorred communism, he refused to launch a Christian crusade against the Soviet regime.[39] He also invoked European solidarity and union as well as the acceptance of the authority of the United Nations as means of preserving the peace. At the same time, a new understanding was elaborated between the Communist regime in Poland and the Catholic Church. The following year Auxiliary Bishop Josip Lach of Zagreb was allowed to venture to Rome, and facilitated an agreement between the Vatican and Yugoslavia, allowing their bishops to travel to Rome for the obligatory *ad limina* visits to the Holy See every five years. At the beginning of 1958, Soviet Foreign Minister Gromyko, acknowledging the deep ideological differences between Moscow and Rome, still believed that agreement was possible with the Vatican on "various questions of peace."[40]

In March of 1957, Pius XII commended and encouraged the American government for seeking peace, citing the need for collective agreements. That same year he condemned the destructive use of nuclear energy and called for its peaceful use. He continued to support the efforts of the United Nations. "One would expect . . . that an association that aims at fostering understanding and concord between peoples will command the church's sympathy," he told the American ambassador to Italy in February 1958. Later in May of that year, the ailing pontiff emphasized the opposition of the church to war except in a strictly defined defensive sense.[41] Toward the end of Pius XII's pontificate, the Vatican was slowly moving to reach some accommodation with the Soviet system, as it sought to shift from de facto alliance with the West to nonalignment. Paradoxically, the pope who had assumed a leading role in the opening of the Cold War, now joined forces with those who called for its conclusion. This process would reach fruition with his successors, John XXIII's *aggiornamento*, or updating of the church and Paul VI's eastern politics or *Ostpolitik*, with the Cold War finally ending during the pontificate of the Polish pope, John Paul II.

Concerned with the needs of the persecuted church in Eastern Europe, Pope John XXIII (1958–1963), who succeeded Pius XII, encouraged an opening to the eastern bloc, and particularly Moscow. Adversaries had to talk to one another, he explained. He initiated this policy of accommodation with the eastern bloc, despite the grave reservations of the conservative Tardini, distinguishing between communism as an atheistic creed, with which the church could not compromise, and communism as a social, political, and economic theory, which he deemed a reality that could not be ignored. Further abandoning the papacy's earlier anti-Communist course, he revealed that the Vatican sought better relations with Moscow. Early in November 1958, he invoked a just and fraternal peace among all nations, and shortly thereafter he confided to Cardinal Stefan Wyszynski and a group of Poles, that he prayed for the peace and prosperity of all peoples. John sought to strengthen the local churches across eastern Europe, avoiding philosophical debate with the Communists, while focusing upon pragmatic issues and specific measures such as the appointment of bishops. He thus changed the atmosphere of Vatican-Soviet relations by moving from Pius XII's earlier containment, to his own limited engagement.

Later, Pope John utilized Monsignor Agostino Casaroli, who succeeded as secretary of state, to reach informal accords with a series of Communist governments, securing the liberation of incarcerated ecclesiastics from Eastern Europe, while filling a number of vacant bishoprics. In 1963, he dispatched his secretary of state to Budapest and Prague to initiate conversations with their Communist regimes. Casaroli stressed the practical nature of their policy, assuring nervous conservatives that these talks did not dilute the church's ideological opposition to communism, while pointing to the specific successes attained by this conciliatory course. In this atmosphere, the Yugoslav government, allowed the public funeral of Cardinal Alojzije Viktor Stepinac. Meanwhile, the pope seemed to support the "opening to the left" in Italy, and possible cooperation with Communist regimes, when he wrote that one had to distinguish between error as such, and one who falls into error—repeating that a man who has fallen into error does not cease to be a man. Likewise, John differentiated between "a false philosophy of the nature, origin and purpose of men and the world," and the practical "political and socio-economic changes, which might have drawn inspiration from that philosophy."[42]

In September 1961, Nikita Khrushchev paid tribute to Pope John's reasonableness. "One thing struck me in my meetings in Prague and Budapest," Cardinal Casaroli noted upon his return from Hungary and Czechoslovakia, "it was quite evident that these Communist leaders were convinced that the pope was sincere, trustworthy, and loved them as well."[43] Relations were further improved in November 1961, following Khrushchev's telegram congratulating John on his eightieth birthday, which also expressed support for his efforts to solve international problems by negotiation. The pope responded warmly, thanking the Soviet leader for his greetings, and promising to pray for the people of his vast state. Dividends were soon forthcoming, as the Vatican utilized the Soviet ambassador to Turkey to facilitate the participation of the bishops from Eastern Europe to the Second Vatican Council (1962–1965). Assured that the council would not condemn communism, Khrushchev, secretary general of the Communist Party, allowed Russian Orthodox observers to attend. Both the failure of the council to explicitly condemn communism, and the participation of bishops from Eastern Europe, represented crucial developments in the church's détente with communism, facilitating the Vatican's *Ostpolitik*.

Despite John's efforts for reconciliation, the Cold War continued during the first years of his pontificate, as the superpowers remained locked over the issue of Berlin, and confronted one another over Cuba. Nonetheless, relations between the Vatican and Moscow improved on the eve of the Cuban Missile Crisis of October 1962, which threatened to unleash a nuclear confrontation. Urged to intervene by the Americans, on October 25, 1962, the pope appealed to the superpowers to answer humanity's cry for peace. The papal peace message was given front page coverage in *Pravda*, representing the first signal that the Soviets were prepared to negotiate a peaceful resolution to the Cuban Missile Crisis. Subsequently, Moscow encouraged regular, if private, contracts with the Vatican, releasing Cardinal Josyf Slipyj, primate of Ukranian Catholics, from prison. In December 1962, John received a Christmas message from Khrushchev, thanking him for his efforts on behalf of the whole of humanity, and the following year the pope received Alexis Adzhubei, the editor of *Izvestia*, and his wife, Rada, Khrushchev's daughter. In March 1963, John was awarded the Balzan Prize for fostering brotherhood and peace.

Pope John's policy of reconciliation was continued and extended by Paul VI (1963–1978), who stressed that the global social and economic problems burdening humanity flowed not from the division between east and west, but by the north-south divide. In fact, he chastised the prosperous capitalist countries of the North for their exploitation of the poor third world countries of the South. His message was welcomed and found resonance not only in the impoverished parts of the globe but also the Communist countries of Eastern Europe, as well as the Soviet Union. In September 1964, his conciliatory course contributed to the written agreement concluded with Communist Hungary. Two years later, in April 1966, Pope Paul was visited by the Soviet Foreign Minister Andrei Gromyko, and the following year he met with the president of the Soviet Union, Nikolai Podgorny. This spirit of détente in June 1966 led to an agreement between the Vatican and Yugoslavia.

The Vatican's "opening to the east" was continued by Paul's successor, the Archbishop of Krakow, who became John Paul II in 1978. The election of the first Polish pope, influenced his compatriots who welcomed him home in June 1979. The papal visit—the first of eight to his homeland—is believed to have influenced the Gdansk shipyard workers to strike and encouraged the formation of the Solidarity Labor Organization. These developments frightened the Kremlin, which according to an Italian parliamentary report, commissioned the assassination attempt of Mehmet Ali Agca on the life of John Paul II in 1981. It did not succeed, and in collaboration with President Ronald Reagan in the United States, and the reformism of Mikhail Gorbachev in the Soviet Union, John Paul II contributed to the revolutionary outburst in Eastern Europe, the destruction of the Berlin Wall, the reunification of Germany, the collapse of communism in Eastern Europe and the Soviet Union, and the end of the Cold War by 1990. Thus the papacy, which had played an important role in the opening of the Cold War, played an equally important one in its demise.

The Second Vatican Council, *Aggiornamento*, and Papal Accommodation with the Modern World, 1958–1978

The death of Pius XII on October 9, 1958 led to the conclave of October 24, to elect his successor. Although the College of Cardinals officially numbered 70, only 53 wore the red hat at Pacelli's death, and since two died prior to the conclave, their number was reduced to 51. The Europeans still constituted a majority representing 65 percent of the members, with the Italians still forming the largest bloc, followed by the French. Speculators expected a conservative pontiff, for Pius XII had named all but two of the cardinals in the college. This was not only expected but desired by the conservative contingent in the conclave. On the other hand, its more progressive members invoked a more moderate figure, who would address the need for some change in the church. After 11 inconclusive ballots (October 26–27), fueled by the division between "reformers" and "traditionalists," on October 28, during the course of the twelfth ballot and the fourth day, the 77-year-old Angelo Giuseppe Roncalli, primate of Venice, was elected as a compromise candidate, receiving the 38 votes needed for election. The advanced age of the 259th pope was deemed an advantage for those seeking a transitional figure or caretaker pope who would not change the papacy or challenge the church. In fact, the election of this smiling, sincere, and unassuming figure would prove decisive for the institution and its leadership, ushering in far-reaching changes for both.

The new pope chose to be called John, a name no pope had borne for hundreds of years. He favored John because it was his father's name, as well as the church in which he was baptized. Some later concluded that Roncalli envisioned himself another John the Baptist for the church.[1]

The warm and gregarious new pope was dramatically different from his ascetic and aloof predecessor, lacking the regalism of the prior pope, reflecting instead the soul of "the servant of the servants of God." Whereas Pius kept personal communication to a minimum, Roncalli acknowledged his tendency to talk too much.[2]

The third of 13 children, Angelo Giuseppe Roncalli was born on November 25, 1881 to a family of sharecroppers from Sotto il Monte, 10 miles outside Bergamo and baptized the day he was born. In 1888, he made his first communion at the age of seven and received his elementary education in town. In 1892 he entered the minor seminary of Bergamo and the major seminary in 1895. That same year, he received the clerical habit and commenced keeping a diary. In 1900, he took a pilgrimage to Rome for the Holy Year, and visited Loreto and Assisi. In 1901, Roncalli enrolled in the Roman Seminary of the Apolinare, where he studied under the antimodernist church historian, Umberto Benigni, receiving a degree in theology. Shortly thereafter, he reported to the Umberto I military barracks in Bergamo for a year of compulsory military service in the 73rd Infantry Regiment, the Lombardy Brigade, attaining the rank of sergeant and at the close of 1902, Angelo returned to the seminary.

A deacon in 1903, he received a doctorate in sacred theology and ordained a priest in 1904. In 1905, when Giacomo Radini-Tedeschi was suspected of modernist tendencies and assigned to Bergamo as its bishop, Angelo was named the secretary of this socially minded prelate, following him to Lourdes and Palestine, and collaborating with him for the better part of a decade (1905–1914). He also continued to travel widely, revisiting Lourdes in 1908 as well as Marseilles, Toulouse and Nimes, Switzerland in 1911, and Vienna, Krakow, and Budapest in 1912. In 1915, following Italy's entry into World War I, he was recalled to the military, serving first as a hospital orderly and later as a chaplain until the end of 1918. Near the close of 1920, he was summoned to Rome to preside over the Italian section of Propaganda Fide, where he remained until 1925. Although not formally trained in diplomacy, he spent almost three decades in the foreign service of the Holy See. From 1925 to 1953 Roncalli was dispatched abroad to serve in a series of diplomatic posts. In 1925 he was nominated apostolic visitor to Bulgaria, confronting numerous problems, provoked by the central organs of ecclesiastical administration, and in 1931 named the first apostolic delegate to Bulgaria. Transferred to Turkey and Greece as apostolic delegate in 1934, during World War II he established an office in Istanbul for finding prisoners of war, and assisting Jewish refugees. During the Fascist and Nazi occupation of Greece (1941–1944), Roncalli worked diligently to prevent the deportation of Jews. His genial personality and the fact that he spoke seven languages proved useful in his various diplomatic missions.

At the end of 1944, when General De Gaulle branded Valerio Valeri, who has served as nuncio since 1936 both in Paris and Vichy, persona non grata, Pius XII dispatched the 63-year-old Roncalli to Paris as apostolic nuncio, to resolve differences with the French. Roncalli proved successful during the course of his eight-year tenure there (1944–1953), resisting the Gallic attempt to expel some 30 bishops from their Sees as Vichy collaborators. Appointed Vatican observer to United Nations Educational, Scientific, and Cultural Organization (UNESCO) in 1951, in 1953 the 71-year-old prelate was made a cardinal and named patriarch of Venice, where he served from 1953 to 1958. In his later 70s, Roncalli expected to spend his remaining time there in pastoral pursuits, but in October 1958 left to take part in the conclave which elected him pope. He immediately generated excitement not only because of the name he chose, but because of his decision to preach a homily at his coronation mass on November 4, 1958, an innovation. He also broke with tradition in creating 23 new cardinals, exceeding the number of 70 set at the end of the sixteenth century, selecting the first ever cardinals from the Philippines, Japan, Mexico, and Africa, increasing the internationalization of the college. Among the new cardinals was the African Monsignor Laurean Rugambwa, the Filipino Monsignor Santos, and the Japanese Monsignor Peter Tatsuo Doi. John's visit to the Queen of Heaven prison in Rome revealed his compassionate nature, contributing to his broad, popular appeal.

John quickly developed a three-fold program that included plans for a diocesan synod for Rome, an Ecumenical Council for the Universal Church, and the revision of Canon Law. These measures were means to his long-range goal—the need for an *aggiornamento,* or updating of the church, as well as its *aperturismo* or opening up toward the world. To win support for this program he recognized the need to balance conservative and liberal forces in the church and curia. Thus, both the conservative Domenico Tardini, and the more liberal Giovanni Battista Montini, were granted the red hat that had eluded them during the pontificate of his predecessor. Tardini's selection as secretary of state served to reassure conservatives in the curia, while John's promise not to remain a recluse in the apostolic palace but look toward the world beyond, pleased liberals. Early on he considered calling a council to effect the ecclesiastical *aggiornamento* and the church's reconciliation with the modern world he believed long overdue and absolutely necessary. Initially his call for a church council was seconded by conservatives, who believed it was needed to reaffirm the traditionalism in the church, which they perceived as threatened by the clamor for innovation and the restlessness of the postwar period. Thus when John discussed the prospect with Tardini, his conservative secretary of state readily endorsed the project. Pope John's decision of January 25, 1959, to convoke a council, shocked some and surprised others. Montini, the Archbishop of Milan, who seconded the call for change, proved one of its most enthusiastic supporters.

At this juncture there was no clear indication whether it would be the council of renewal that reformers invoked, whose emphasis would be positive rather than negative, or one like the first Vatican Council called to refute contemporary errors, as some conservatives desired. John's early generalizations did not clarify its specific mission or provide an agenda. To further confuse matters John sent mixed signals, pleasing conservatives by appointing the conservative Domenico Tardini president of the Preparatory Commission for the Council and the traditionalist Archbishop Pericle Felici as its secretary, even as he spoke of transforming the church. Although the council's scope, mission, and program remained undefined, a vast administrative machinery was devised for its operation. Only after Giovanni Montini's Lenten pastoral of 1962 entitled *Pensiamo al Concilio* (Let Us Think About the Council) and John's September 1962 broadcast on Vatican Radio, did it become clear what direction the pope wanted the council to take. Although aiming for a renewal of the inner life of the church, the council was also considered crucial for redefining its relationship to the modern world.

Whether these goals could be attained remained uncertain. John appreciated the gravity of the task before him. "When on 28 October, 1958, the Cardinals of the Holy Roman Church chose me to assume the supreme responsibility of ruling the universal flock of Jesus Christ, at seventy seven years of age, everyone was convinced that I would be a provisional and transitional Pope," he wrote in his diary in August 1961. "Yet here I am, already on the eve of the fourth year of my pontificate, with an immense program of work in front of me to be carried out before the eyes of the whole world, which is watching and waiting."[3] In fact, the eyes of much of the world focused on Rome. Even Moscow took note, moving Nikita Khrushchev to dispatch a congratulatory telegram for the pope's eightieth birthday. John responded warmly to the message from Moscow, confiding to his secretary that the message was "better than a slap in the face."[4]

Prior to the council's opening, Pope John undertook a pilgrimage to Loreto and Assisi to pray for its success—the first visit of a sitting pope outside of Rome for almost a century. Although as Pope Roncalli did not venture outside of Italy, John inaugurated a new age for papal travel that would be adapted and extended by his successors as he struggled to transform the papacy from a Roman to a universal institution. Once the council was convoked on October 11, 1962, Pope John and Archbishop Giovanni Montini of Milan collaborated to outline its sessions. Session one would focus on the nature of the church; the second would explore its mission and what it does; while the third session would examine the church's relationships with other groups. From the first, Montini envisioned a positive role for the council, leading to renewal and *aggiormamento* and predicting it would embrace civil society worldwide.[5]

Cardinal Montini like Pope John sought to reconcile the church with the contemporary age and the ongoing global transformation, viewing the council as the means to this end. In his very first public address on October 29, 1958, John called for social justice, urging the industrialized world to assist the underdeveloped third world while deploring the squandering of wealth on arms rather than uplifting the downtrodden at home and abroad.[6] His vision was universal as he proclaimed the unity of the human race. He returned to the theme of the unity of humanity in his June 1959 letter to the president of Turkey, and in his 1958 Christmas message, summarizing the 19 Christmas messages of Pius XII in two words: unity and peace. Regarding the whole world as his family, he foresaw the need for welfare to assume a global dimension, applauding the United Nations' work in assisting refugees.[7]

Favoring ecumenism, the call for unity of all Christian churches, John named the Jesuit Cardinal Augustin Bea head of a new Secretariat for Promoting Christian Unity. It sought to facilitate the participation of the "separated brethren" in the council as observers, as well as proposing a statement against the traditional anti-Judaism in the church. John personally met with the observers representing the non-Catholic communities, while mandating a change in the Easter liturgy that made reference to the "perfidious Jews." His attitude initiated the increased sensitivity of Catholics toward Jews, even before critics were to accuse his predecessor Pius XII of silence in the face of the Holocaust. In 1960, John XXIII met with Geoffrey Fisher, the Archbishop of Canterbury, deploring the more than 400 years of separation between the Catholic and Anglican churches. Greetings were also exchanged with the Orthodox Patriarch Athenagoras and the Patriarch Alexis of Moscow. With papal approval Catholic observers attended the World Council of Churches meeting in New Dehli.

Convinced that in the long run conciliation would prove more productive than the confrontation introduced by the Cold War, Pope John initiated a policy of accommodation with the eastern bloc, placing relations with their Communist governments on a new footing. This opening toward the east or *Ostpolitik* was questioned by some, especially conservatives in the curia. Despite these reservations, John forged ahead. On March 7, 1962, Pope John received Khrushchev's daughter and son-in-law as relations improved between Moscow and the Vatican. John's rapprochement with the eastern bloc and the Soviet Union on behalf of the church of Silence, and papal mediation between Washington and Moscow during the Cuban Missile Crisis in October 1962, contributed to the release of Cardinal Josef Slipyj, Metropolitan of Lemberg, early in 1963. In May 1963, as Pope John was dying, he dispatched his undersecretary of state, Monsignor Agostino Casaroli to Budapest where he secured the freedom of four bishops from enforced residence and then proceeded to Prague and opened talks with its Communist government. Improving relations with the Warsaw Pact powers was integral to John's policy of opening the church to the realities of the contemporary world.

John's focus on the Council and reconciliation with the eastern bloc did not lead him to neglect the social question. In his first of eight encyclicals "On Truth, Unity and Peace" of June 29, 1959, he stressed that all were to share the fruits of the earth and the necessities of life, deploring the great and growing disparity in the possession of material goods. Expressing sympathy for the poor and underprivileged, he proclaimed that the church recognized their needs. "She preaches and inculcates a social doctrine and social norms, which would eliminate every sort of injustice and produce a better and more equitable distribution of goods, if they were put into practice as they should be," John wrote.[8] The pope encouraged cooperation and mutual assistance among the various classes and states, hoping that humanity would become one family, in fact as well as in name. He returned to the questions of social justice and fraternal union in his third encyclical, *Grata Recordatio* of September 26, 1959, and in his address to a delegation of The National Convention on the Dignity of Labor. Christian principles, he explained, did not call for the acceptance of stagnation nor did they require that one abandon efforts to achieve progress. On the contrary, he noted the church encouraged efforts to improve humanity's living standards and assure universal temporal prosperity. John sympathized with those who suffered because of their race or economic conditions, defining work as "the intelligent and effective collaboration of man with God" and offering St. Joseph as an example to those conditioned and constrained by the laws of labor. Meanwhile, John praised the United Nations Food and Agricultural Organization's worldwide "Campaign against Hunger," and for providing aid and assistance for those in the migration provoked by poverty.[9]

Pope John further elaborated his social program in two other encyclicals: *Mater et Magistra* and *Pacem in Terris*. *Mater et Magistra*, on the church as mother and teacher of all nations (1961), his fifth encyclical, was issued on the seventieth anniversary of *Rerum novarum* (1891), which he believed commenced the process by which the church and papacy made themselves the champions and restorers of the rights of the working class. This encyclical, which endorsed aspects of the welfare state, seconded Pope Leo XIII's judgment that labor was not another commodity as some liberal theorists and champions of unfettered capitalism proclaimed, but a crucial human activity. Like Leo, John insisted that private property entailed social obligations, adding that the state had the responsibility of insuring that employers fulfilled their responsibilities toward their labor force, thus safeguarding the dignity of workers.

John also concurred with the conclusions of Pius XI's *Quadragesimo Anno* (1931), issued 40 years after the publication of *Rerum Novarum*, and likewise sought to assure social justice. Like Pius, John believed it was mistaken to ascribe to property alone or to work alone, what had been produced through their joint effort, insisting that the relationship between wages and profits had to be regulated with the common good in mind. While John like Pius XII would not accept a communism whose objectives were fixed solely on material considerations, he did not reject the notion of public ownership of some means of production, especially when these carried great power. In *Mater et Magistra*, he repeated the call for governmental intervention and the state's safeguarding the common good. Deploring the glaring social imbalances internally and internationally, he preached that those who had the means should help the less fortunate.[10] Assisting the less fortunate and down trodden was not only a responsibility of wealthy individuals but also the obligation of prosperous nations. For John such international aid and internal assistance represented nothing less than a Christian duty.

These calls for social and international justice and peace were repeated in his eighth and final encyclical, *Pacem in Terris* (1963), which was addressed to people of goodwill, worldwide. It applauded many contemporary developments and sought to reconcile the church to liberalism and individualism within a Christian context. In it John elaborated what was needed to preserve domestic tranquility and international order, while accepting the hitherto condemned doctrine termed "indifferentism" that man had a right to worship God as his conscience dictated, professing his faith both in public as in private.[11] *Pacem in Terris* also reconciled the papacy with democracy, recognizing the need for a broad participation in public life. Foreign domination, like class and gender subordination, John stressed, were in decline as the conviction grew that all were equal in natural dignity. Foreign relations, in John's vision had to be governed by truth and justice with the understanding that all states are by nature equal in dignity if not in power. Differences between states, he argued, should be resolved by negotiation not armed conflict, which required some form of world organization. In this regard Pope John followed Pius XII in supporting the role of the United Nations with its "special aim of maintaining and strengthening peace between nations, and . . . important international functions in the economic, social, cultural, educational, and health fields."[12] This last encyclical represented the spiritual testament John wished to bestow upon the church and the whole of humanity, and it struck a responsive chord, worldwide.

John's world view led him to encourage the work of the missions. From the time of his appointment to Rome in the service of the Congregation for the Propagation of the Faith, at the end of 1920, John was devoted to its efforts. He pledged his commitment to it in January 1924, writing that "the Association for the Propagation of the Faith is the breath of my soul, and my life."[13] As pope, John continued his ardent support of the missionary work of the Propagation of the Faith, exhorting aid for its efforts. He frequently praised the missionary contributions of various orders and nationalities, now praising the spirit of the Belgians, then that of the Irish. In his first encyclical, he praised "these heralds of the gospel who dedicate and consecrate theirs lives to . . . enlighten every man who comes into the world . . . There is, perhaps, no undertaking that pleases God more than this one; it is an integral part of the duty all men have to spread the kingdom of God."[14] In October 1959, he presented crucifixes to over four hundred Catholic missionaries in St. Peter's, as they ventured to bring the faith to distant peoples, and expanding the universal embrace of the church.

On the fortieth anniversary of Benedict XV's encyclical *Maximum illud* of 1919, Pope John issued *Princeps Pastorum* (1959), his own mission encyclical. Noting that in the 40 years following Benedict's pronouncement the missions flourished, bringing the church to the entire world, with the first bishop of East Asian origins consecrated in 1923, and the first vicars apostolic of African Negro descent, named in 1939. John announced that by 1959 there were 68 Asian and 25 African bishops, observing that while the church had historically been closely linked to Western civilization, it did not belong to any one culture. Following Benedict, John asserted that the missionary effort had to consider local needs, supporting the emergence of a local clergy.[15] Delighted by the establishment of hierarchies in several African and Asian countries, he cautioned that evangelization was incomplete. In *Mater et Magistra* (1961), Pope John applauded the collapse of imperialism and the attainment of independence of the peoples of Asia and Africa, addressing the unity of the human family in *Pacem in Terris* of 1963. In this and other matters, John's papacy was in the forefront of foreseeing the emergence of a new world order. Like many other major transitions, John's program confronted difficulties.

When the first session of the Second Vatican Council closed in December 1962, its promise remained largely unfulfilled, both because of its brevity and the deep divide between *progressisti* or progressives from the United States, France, German, and the Benelux countries and the *conservatori* or traditionalists from Italy and the curia. Nonetheless, John's five-year pontificate did much to reinvigorate the social and diplomatic role of the church, paving the way for profound reforms. His pontificate, which captured the imagination of the world, had closed an epoch and era, and opened another. It is true that during the course of the two crowded months of the first session of the council, which aroused worldwide interest, no decrees had been approved. John, whose cancer was advanced and inoperable, was dying and had barely six more months to live, and proved unable to preside over the second session of the council, which was to reconvene on September 8, 1963. When he died in a coma on June 3, 1963, he was mourned in both the Western and the Communist worlds by those who regretted that the pope had not been able to complete his reformist agenda, leaving much still to be done. In 1965, the Vatican opened the process for his beatification, the next to the last step towards sainthood, which was proclaimed in 2000 along with that of Pius IX. The legacy of "Good Pope John" remains important, explaining why alongside Gregory the Great, he has been named one of the two greatest popes of all time.[16] The conclave to name his successor recognized that following him would not be easy.

The June 1963 conclave was more diversified than earlier ones, but the Europeans still remained dominant. Of the 81 cardinals eligible to vote: 57 were Europeans, including 29 Italians; there were 12 from Latin America; 7 from North America; 3 Asians; 2 Oceanians; and 1 African. Word circulated that the contest was between the liberal Giovanni Battista Maria Montini, Archbishop of Milan, and the conservative Cardinal Giuseppe Siri, Archbishop of Genoa. In fact Cardinal Ildebrando Atononiutti, champion of the traditionalist *Opus Dei*, emerged as the conservative favorite. Montini's main advantage was a double-edged sword, proving to be his greatest disadvantage as well, once the story spread Montini was the cardinal the liberal prior pope sought to succeed him. Thus, the election represented an assessment of John's *aggiornamento* and the council, as much as the figures competing for the office. The first ballots proved inconclusive, but on June 21, the 65-year-old Montini was elected, assuming the name Paul.[17]

The new pope, born on September 26, 1897, the second of three sons of a family active in Catholic political circles was well known in Italy and abroad, and had access to important figures in the Vatican. In 1907, when the family visited Rome, they were received by Pope Pius X in private audience. During their visits to Giorgio's sister Elisabetta in Milan, the family mingled socially with the librarian and mountain climbing priest, Achille Ratti, who in 1922 became Pope Pius XI. Giovanni was profoundly influenced by his family's liberal and Christian democratic sentiments, progressive leanings, support of the Catholic Popular Party and a strong devotion to the papacy. Although Montini entered the diocesan seminary in Brescia in 1916, the frail seminarian, who had suffered a heart attack at the age of 10, and whose health remained precarious, spent considerable time at home. During these years, he collaborated with his friend Gian Andrea Trebeschi in the publication of a journal called *La Fionda* (The Sling) for Catholic Students.[18] Appointed to the Nunciature in Warsaw in 1923, he returned to Rome within a year, unable to endure the harsh Polish climate. Assigned to the secretariat of state, and serving as Ecclesiastical Assistant or chaplain to the Italian Association of Catholic University students in Rome (Federazione Universitaria Cattolica Italiana or FUCI), Cardinal Eugenio Pacelli made him undersecretary for ordinary affairs.

Once Pacelli became pope in 1939, this collaboration continued, and while Montini recognized the need for the pope to preserve his neutrality, he remained staunchly anti-Fascist. Following the death of the secretary of state, Cardinal Luigi Maglione in 1944, Pius XII made Montini, pro-secretary of state for Internal Church Affairs. Throughout World War II, Montini presided over the Vatican Information Office created by Pius XII in 1939 to search for prisoners of war, displaced persons, and other missing individuals. Devoted to this pope, some believed that Pius XII championed Montini as his successor. This assessment proved mistaken.

Pius XII never named him a cardinal, and some suspected that the pope had become disenchanted with Montini, who was closely identified with the condemned priest-worker movement in France and supposedly found the pope's *Humani generis* of 1950 too critical of the new theology. Montini was also criticized by conservatives for his close association with French liberal theologians such as Jacques Maritain, and berated for his alleged attempt to encourage Italian Christian Democrats to ally with the Socialists. We do not know how the conservative Pius perceived Montini during the anti-Communist postwar period. We do know that in 1953, when Pius named a number of new cardinals, Montini, who had served him loyally for years, was not on the list. Following the death of Cardinal Ildefonso Schuster in 1954, Montini was appointed Archbishop of Milan, where he was soon dubbed the "workers archbishop." Despite the fact that the Archbishop of Milan is normally named a cardinal, Montini was excluded from the college, and therefore ineligible for the papal throne in 1958. Some believed, on the basis of hints leaked from Vatican sources, that Montini had been offered the honor and rejected it. The subsequent course of events seemed to challenge that contention.

The new pope, John XXIII, immediately placed Montini at the top of the list of the 23 new cardinals created in 1958, and Montini readily accepted the offer. In fact, John counted on the collaboration of his friend and confidant, reserving special rooms for him in the Vatican during the Vatican Council.[19] Montini rose to the occasion and was appointed to the Council's Preparatory Commission assigned the task of elaborating the agenda for the body. In that capacity he suggested that the council include at least three sessions, instead of the one originally proposed by Pope John, and outlined its tentative goals. In June 1960 Montini visited the United States and Brazil, revealing his conviction that the church had to transcend Italy and Europe and assume a truly universal posture. This would be one of the guiding principles during the course of the council.

Following the death of Pope John in 1963, after a momentous but short pontificate of less than five years, rumor again surfaced that the former pope wanted Montini as his successor. This time the speculation proved accurate, and Montini was elected as a compromise candidate between the conservative and progressive forces in the still divided college, on the third day of the conclave, June 21, 1963. His pontificate opened during a tumultuous age when the Cold War continued, the competition between the United States and the Union of Soviet Socialist Republics sparked global tension, terrorism stalked the Western World and burdened Italy, and profound differences persisted in the council on the need for, and the wisdom of, change in the church. Paul's broad diplomatic background, which led some to label him "The Perfect Diplomat," prepared him for the many challenges ahead and the obstacles confronting the council. The divisions in the council were so formidable that some feared they would disrupt the unity of the church.

The emergence of these problems served to intensify Paul's usual caution, but did not alter his commitment to peaceful and orderly change. Despite the divisions in the council, he determined on its resumption in September 1963, making it clear, in his first radio address that the main task of his pontificate would be the completion and the implementation of the council's decisions. "As far as understanding the modern world and drawing close to it," wrote Paul, "I think I am on the same lines as Pope John."[20] Indeed he claimed that John was more conservative than he. He fully shared John's conviction that ultimately peace depended on justice, love, and liberty and sought to avoid persecutions, admonitions, and suppressions, appointing bishops who were champions of the poor and downtrodden. To reassure traditionalists, who questioned his liberal and open attitude toward the modern world, Paul confirmed the cautious Amleto Cicognani as his secretary of state.

The assumption of the name Paul revealed Montini's determination to have the Vatican reach out to the entire world. Thus when he received President John Kennedy in early July, he discussed Vietnam, elaborating the Vatican's stance towards the countries of Eastern Europe, and praising the pacific and universal mission of the United Nations. Paul brought these same sentiments to the second session of the council, which he convoked in September, outlining new directives including: collegiality, the admission of lay Catholics, ecumenism, Christian unity, and dialogue with the modern world. The second session, which met from September 29 to December 4, 1963, included more than 40 working meetings with over 600 speeches. During its course Paul sought to accommodate the liberal majority without alienating the conservative minority. It proved a difficult task. Nonetheless, this second session introduced innovations on Episcopal collegiality and liturgical matters pleasing liberals but alienating conservatives. Assessing the accomplishments, Paul expressed gratitude for the results achieved citing the proclamation of the constitution on the liturgy and the decree on the means of social communication.[21] In discussing these documents Paul stressed that the church was open to the new avenues of communication and particularly the press, cinema, radio, and television that influence not only single individuals, but the whole of human society.

As 1963 drew to a close, Paul proposed an agenda for the council's third session, while announcing his intention of visiting the Holy Land at the opening of the new year. In undertaking this historic pilgrimage, Paul was not only the first pope to fly in an airplane but also the first to visit the Holy Land. The papal objective during the January 4–6 trip, which included Jordan and Israel, was peace and unity. Hoping that his pilgrimage would foster harmony, he urged prayers for its realization. Paul considered the Jerusalem meeting between pope and patriarch, the first since the schism of 1054, the start of a new relationship between the Holy See and the Ecumenical Patriarchate.[22] In August 1964, Paul published his first encyclical *Ecclesiam Suam,* which envisioned and encouraged dialogue within the church, with non-Catholic Christians, with non-Christians, and even nonbelievers, seeking to engage the church with the entire contemporary world. It represented a departure from the course pursued by a number of his predecessors and most notably Pius IX, who locked himself in the Vatican in 1870 and continued his condemnations of contemporary developments until his death in 1878. The vision of Paul differed as can be seen by this first encyclical on "His Church." "The aim of this encyclical," Paul wrote, was "to demonstrate with increasing clarity how vital it is for the world, and how greatly desired by the Catholic Church, that the two should meet together, and get to know and love one another."[23] Some deemed this a dangerous innovation; others derided the endeavor as too little, too late.

While the pope pleaded for unity, divisions continued in the third session of the council that convened in mid-September 1964. At this juncture the conservatives led by Archbishop Marcel Lefebvre (1905–1991), of the French Holy Ghost Missionary Order, launched a counterattack against the emerging notions of collegiality and modernization, identifying them with the modernism condemned by Pius X. They were also shocked by the call to have John XXIII canonized by an act of acclamation, skirting the regular procedure. Paul rejected the proposal, and in 1964 sought to please both conservatives and liberals by announcing that the Congregation for Saints would examine the causes of both Pius XII and John XXIII! Despite divisions in the Council, with Paul's support three important decrees were approved: *Lumen Gentium*, explaining the relationship of the pope, the bishops, the priests, and the laity within the church; *Orientalium Ecclesiaum*, the decree on the Catholic eastern churches; and *Unitatis redintegratio*, the decree on ecumenism.[24] In early December 1964, Pope Paul, continuing his campaign to reach out to the world beyond Rome, ventured to Bombay, India, where he expressed the church's love and respect for the people of Asia, whom he included in its universal mission. Continuing the dialogue with all the people of the globe, in February 1965, he named 27 new cardinals, including the four major Eastern patriarchs.

Upon returning to Rome, Paul prepared for the fourth and final session of the council. The session which opened September 14, 1965, included bishops from countries where the church had been persecuted. However, despite Paul's efforts to conciliate the major factions, the council remained divided on a number of issues including birth control, which had engendered considerable dissension during John's pontificate. Besides birth control, other problems included the implementation of collegiality, the reform of canon law, how to respond to mixed or interfaith marriages, and how best to implement world peace. Invoking divine intervention, the pope proposed that the opening of the fourth session would be marked by a penitential procession, and a call for prayer for its success. Shortly after its opening, Paul, convoked a special advisory conference of bishops to collaborate with him in the governance of the church, a first step in implementing his notion of collegiality.

The following month Paul addressed the United Nations on its 20th anniversary, the first pope to do so. As he left for New York in early October 1965, he sought to encourage, strengthen, and bless the efforts that people of good will were making worldwide to safeguard, guarantee, and promote peace. He repeated this message when he arrived in New York, and in his address to the General Assembly of the United Nations. In his view the world organization had to do even more to facilitate coexistence among nations as it sought to "organize the brotherly collaboration of the world's people."[25] Paul continued to place great faith in the organization whose aims he believed mirrored those of the papacy. His program on behalf of all peoples was "no more war, war never again." He prayed that relations between states would be governed by reason, justice, law, and negotiation rather than by fear, violence, deceit, or war, as he called for a greater effort on behalf of the poor and disinherited suffering from hunger and thirsting for justice. The funds to feed the hungry and clothe the naked would be available if disarmament was pursued and the recourse to war, rejected. The money saved by ending the arms race, Paul preached, could and should be diverted to assisting the developing nations and tackling the plight of global poverty. This goal represented a universal responsibility. In New York, he invoked not only the protection of fundamental human rights, freedom, and the fulfillment of physical needs but also the religious liberty advocated by Vatican II.

In his note to Secretary General U Thant, of the United Nations, Paul revealed that he had come across the ocean as a messenger of peace, repeating the Vatican's support for the United Nation's pacific and humanitarian efforts. Similar assurances were given by the pope to the various religious organizations maintaining relations with the United Nations. During the course of the first papal mass celebrated in the United States during his 36 hour stay, Paul proclaimed that peace ultimately relied on moral and religious principles. He echoed this message upon his return to Rome on October 5, proclaiming the church's commitment to the cause of peace. The warm reception he received from President Lyndon Johnson, the American people, and the United Nations, made his American visit a public relations triumph, confirming the Vatican's position as a key transnational force.

At the opening of the new century in 2001, the American State Department released a number of documents on American-Vatican relations with reference to Vietnam in the years from 1965 to 1968 at the height of the war there. In a series of letters, meetings, and memoranda, President Johnson repeatedly sought papal mediation in the conflict even though at this juncture the Vatican and the United States did not have any formal diplomatic relations. To press his initiative during these difficult days, Johnson personally met with the pope twice and wrote him three letters that largely focused on the war in Vietnam. Paul VI also met with Vice President Hubert Humphrey, Henry Cabot Lodge, the United States Ambassador to South Vietnam, and James Rowe, a personal friend of the American president and in their talks also addressed the war issue. These documents reveal that President Johnson sought papal help in persuading North Vietnam to negotiate and to provide a more humane treatment of American prisoners of war. At the same time Johnson urged the pope to encourage the Catholic President of South Vietnam Nguyen Van Thieu to commence talks with the Communist National Liberation Front.

Paul reacted favorably to the American requests indicating that he would do "whatever is possible" to restore the peace. However, Paul added that he would have to preserve a degree of neutrality to serve as a credible mediator, and revealed a willingness to undertake a peace mission to Vietnam by visiting both North and South Vietnam and talking to both parties. However, Ho Chi Minh responded that "because of the war, the conditions necessary to receive (the Pontiff) are lacking." In effect, he and the other North Vietnamese Communist leaders made it clear that at that moment the pope would not be welcomed in Hanoi. Hoping to draw upon the moral influence of the pope, the Americans suggested a visit to the South. Paul rejected the notion of simply visiting Saigon, noting that such a visit would not advance the cause of peace but "might even aggravate the situation." At the same time the pope diplomatically urged the American president to reconsider its bombing campaign in the North, which he judged detrimental to America's moral credibility and international image. He also suggested that the Americans play down their role and allow the South Vietnamese to speak on behalf of a free Vietnam.[26]

Paul faced problems at home as well as abroad for upon his return to Rome from America, he found the council discussing the final chapter of *Gaudium et Spes*, on war and peace. Its passage pleased liberals, but they resented Paul's decision to withdraw the issue of clerical celibacy from conciliar debate. Alongside contraception, celibacy was another subject removed from the council's agenda. Critics complained that this final session of the council was more notable for problems ignored than those addressed! Nonetheless, on October 28, 1965, Paul promulgated five important council documents including *Nostra aetate* on the church's attitude toward non-Christian religions.[27] It stipulated that the church reproved every form of persecution and deplored "all hatreds, persecutions, displays of anti-Semitism leveled at any time or from any source against the Jews."[28] Repudiating the centuries old anti-Judaism in the church as well as the racist anti-Semitism of the nineteenth century, it inaugurated a new relationship between Catholics and Jews. As the council ground to a close on December 7, 1965, a joint declaration issued by Pope Paul VI and Partiarch Athenogoras I, nullified the Catholic-Orthodox exchange of excommunications of 1054, proclaiming those sentences were directed at persons rather than at churches, and did not seek to sever the ecclesiastical communion between the Sees of Rome and Constantinople. December 7 also saw the promulgation of the Declaration on Religious Liberty, the decree on the church's missionary activity, and the Pastoral Constitution on the Church in the Modern World. The next day Pope Paul declared the Council officially closed.[29]

Not all members of the church and its hierarchy supported the modernization attempted by the council, engendering a disconcerting polarization within Catholicism. Consequently, the *dopoconcilio,* or post-conciliar age was dominated by continuing debates over issues raised by council and the persistent rift between conservatives and liberals. Neither group was satisfied as conservatives perceived the council a "betrayal of the church" and liberals complained of "a betrayal of the council." Distressed by this ideological conflict, Paul moved cautiously during the remaining 13 years of his pontificate. He issued directives to the Post-conciliar Central Commission alluding to the unfinished tasks to be tackled. In January 1967 he established a Council on the Laity, which attempted to integrate them into the church's official organizations and activities, as well as a Pontifical Commission for Justice and Peace. The following month Paul provided canonical form to the deaconate, implementing this ministry called for by the council. Restoring the order of permanent deacons in the western church, Paul made it clear that its implementation depended on the decision of competent national or regional conferences of bishops, with the consent of the pope.[30] This reform was providential in light of the shortage of priests that burdened the church in the subsequent decades.

During his pontificate, Paul VI issued five encyclical letters from 1964 to 1968. The social encyclical *Populorm Progressio* (1967), established Paul's progressive social position by pleading for the world's impoverished masses, insisting that when private gain and human needs were in conflict, the public authorities had to find an equitable solution. "You are not making a gift of what is yours to the poor man," he wrote, quoting St. Ambrose, "but you are giving back what is his."[31] Some deemed this a papal endorsement of liberation theology, which called for the emancipation of those oppressed by political, economic or social subjugation. This stance pleased liberals but alarmed conservatives. The opposite reaction followed Paul's reaffirmation of the church's traditional position of priestly celibacy and rigid opposition to physical and chemical methods of contraception provided in *Humane vitae* (On the Regulation of Birth, 1968). Despite his adherence to traditionalism on priestly celibacy and birth control, Paul shared the council's conviction that the church had to draw closer to the world. However, he insisted that there was a wrong and right way to do so. In his words, the church was in the world, not of the world, but for the world.[32] This distinction confused some, who condemned Paul VI's reactionary position on celibacy and contraception.

Paul's *Humane vitae* was not well received in a year of cultural turmoil, student rebellion, social turbulence, war protests, and the beginnings of the sexual revolution and feminine militancy. Indeed, the media and the public ignored its more balanced passages and concentrate primarily on its banning of artificial birth control, unleashing a torrent of criticism, particularly in the secular circles of North America and Western Europe. Across the Atlantic Father Charles Curran of the theology department of the Catholic University of America, deemed it a mistaken and unfortunate policy and one not binding on the Catholic faithful because it was not issued as an infallible dogma. His critique found resonance in a good part of the Catholic community in the United States and in liberal circles in SWestern Europe. Despite Curran's and other criticisms of his policy on birth control, Paul adhered to his position, although he never claimed it represented an infallible pronouncement. Still, Paul was stung by the strong reaction his encyclical provoked, and did not issue another during the remaining 10 years of his pontificate. Even in acknowledging the eightieth anniversary of Leo XIII's *Rerum Novarum* in 1971, he did not issue an encyclical, dispatching a simple letter to the head of the Commission on Justice and Peace instead. In it, he condemned the excesses and abuses of capitalism as well as communism, deploring the continued exploitation of workers in an increasingly global economy.

One positive development in Paul's pontificate was the growth of the church in the third world countries of Latin America and Africa. In August 1968, Pope Paul traveled to Colombia, the first visit of a pope to Latin America, to preside over the opening of the Latin American Bishops Conference, and to close the Eucharistic Congress in Bogota. In Latin America Paul's *Populorum Progressio* was applauded, as was his condemnation of the unequal distribution of the world's goods cataloged in *Humanae Vitae*. At the Madellin Conference in 1968, the Latin American bishops pledged to preach the gospel to the poor and neglected, stressing liberation not only from individual sins but the sinful structures of society, anticipating the liberation theology preached and popularized by the Peruvian Priest Gustavo Gutierrez. Critics of the class-oriented structure of much of Latin America charged that governments that supported repressive economic systems were guilty of violence, and applauded the pope's address that stressed human rights and social justice, considering his words a confirmation of their liberation theology. Paul quickly responded that while he considered social justice a Christian responsibility, he did not favor all aspects of liberation theology. Supporting its peaceful mission to assist the poor, Paul rejected the recourse to Marxism and Communist ideology to do so. Papal critics perceived Paul's attempts to balance the extremes in the church, a sign of indecisiveness, branding him the "Hamlet of the papacy." Paul, who distinguished reform from revolution, believed his efforts to achieve social justice had been misunderstood and mischaracterized.[33]

Stung by the criticism emerging from the liberal and progressive western countries, Paul more than ever sought the support of the non-European world that applauded his social reformism and call for justice for the poverty-stricken. His vision remained decidedly global. In 1969, he made Jean Villot his secretary of state, the first non-Italian to hold the post since the Spanish Rafael Cardinal Merry del Val, who had served Pius X. Furthermore, many of the new cardinals he named in 1969 were non-Italians, making the College of Cardinals far more international. That same year he visited Africa—again the first pope to do so—while in 1970 he visited the Philippines where he escaped the attempt to take his life. In 1971 Pope Paul established the pontifical council *Cor Unum* (One Heart), as the agency of the Holy See responsible for coordinating the organizational and charitable activities promoted by the Catholic Church worldwide.

Pope Paul continued, and indeed accelerated, John's *Ostpolitik* of seeking reconciliation with the Communist regimes of Eastern Europe. In 1964, he named Karol Wojtyla as Archbishop of Krakow, and this Polish prelate following papal directives, revealed both realism and political agility in negotiating with Poland's Communist regime. Subsequently, the Holy See established diplomatic relations with Yugoslavia in 1971, and improved relations with Communist controlled Hungary to the point that Cardinal Mindszenty was released that same year. He did not hesitate to inject the Vatican in international affairs, encouraging negotiations on Vietnam, and supporting the peace efforts of the United Nations. In July 1972, the Holy See was invited to participate in the Conference on Security and Co-operation in Europe (CSCE) at Helsinki, the Holy See's first participation in an international conference since the Congress of Vienna of 1814–1815. Casaroli visited Moscow in 1972, the first to travel there in an official capacity, and subsequently he ventured to Castro's Cuba. By the spring of 1974, Pope Paul had more or less pragmatically abandoned the earlier Vatican demand drafted by Pius XII for the internationalization of Jerusalem, setting the stage for an eventual agreement with Israel.

Paul VI determined to transcend the Roman and Italian atmosphere permeating the papacy and deliver the Christian message to the world beyond, relying on innovations in transportation and communication to do so. Following in the footsteps of the Apostle Paul, this pope insisted that Catholic meant universal so that its message and responsibility should not be confined. During the course of eight visits he ventured to all the inhabited continents including: his pilgrimage to the Holy Land (January 4–6, 1964); the voyage to Bombay, India (December 2–5, 1964); the visit to the United Nations in New York (October 4–5, 1965); the pilgrimage to Portugal on the 50th anniversary of the apparition at Fatima (May 13, 1967); the trip to Turkey (July 25–26, 1967); his venture to Bogata, Colombia (August 22–25, 1968); the visit to Geneva (June 10, 1969); the trip to Uganda in Africa (July 31–August 2, 1969); and finally the trip to the Far East, Polonesia, and Australia (November 26–December 4, 1970). Although all were religiously inspired, these trips had important social and political implications for both the church and the modern world. In many respects Paul VI's decision to travel abroad was both revolutionary and transformative, contributing to his reputation as the first modern pope. Paul thus brought the papacy outside its habitual ambience and sought rapport and reconciliation with the outside world as both he and Pope John favored. Paul even proposed the admission of Red China to the United Nations in the interest of peace and withdrew the church's long standing opposition to the construction of a Muslim Grand Mosque in Rome. The reaction to this and his other initiatives was mixed.

Paul's progressive inclinations and policies, combined with his respect for the conservative opposition and willingness to listen to their objections, was perceived by some as a vain attempt to pursue a via media or middle path regarding reform. It aroused criticism on both the right and left. This pope's personality, likewise, provoked polemic. His reflective mind, which grasped the complexity of issues and problems, resulted in a certain caution in making decisions—which led some to charge he was both uncertain and indecisive. The sensitive pontiff was disheartened by this criticism of his personality and policies as well as the course of world events in general, and the turbulent situation in Italy. Following the kidnapping and murder of his friend and former Christian Democratic leader Aldo Moro by the terrorists of the Red Brigade in 1978, some suggested that the frail, and weak pontiff lost the will to live.

In March 1978, he caught a cold that contributed to his death at Castel Gandolfo on August 6, 1978, after a massive heart attack. He requested a simple funeral, imploring that no monument adorn his grave. An attempt to assess his pontificate followed. Conservatives complained that he and John had opened the floodgate of revolution, holding him and his predecessor responsible for encouraging revolution and Liberation Theology in Latin America, while claiming his *Ostpolitik* bolstered the Communist regimes in Eastern Europe. On the other hand, liberals resented his position on celibacy, birth control, his stance on the position of women in the church, and the slow pace of implementing Vatican II's collegiality. Both conservatives and liberals failed to appreciate Paul's contribution in bringing the council to a successful conclusion, and his efforts to achieve the church's internationalization and reconciliation with the modern world. Ironically, conservatives charged he had gone too far, while liberals complained that his reformism remained incomplete.[34] History will judge whether his pontificate was the "Bridge to the Modern World" or one that thrust the church into upheaval.

The Contemporary Papacy, Shuttle Diplomacy, and the Collapse of Communism, 1978–2005

Following Pope Paul's death in 1978, the church remained divided between the adherents of *progressismo* and those of *conservatismo,* with some claiming it confronted the most serious crisis since the French Revolution. Conservatives opposed the reforms of the council, regretted the replacement of the Latin mass and the enhanced role of the laity, while invoking the traditionalism and integralism of the pre-Vatican period that opposed ecumenism and blocked modern biblical studies. Liberals, on the other hand, complained that the reformism of the council had not been brought to its logical conclusion. These ideological divisions were reflected in the conclave to name Paul's successor, and this chasm was compounded and complicated by national rivalries. The Italians, though diminished in numbers, remained the largest bloc, constituting almost a quarter of the voting cardinals. They expected the tradition of almost half a millennium to continue, and called for another Italian pope. Others disagreed, convinced that the time had come to smash the centuries old Italian hold on the papacy.

The first several ballots on August 26, proved inconclusive but in the fourth, on August 28, Cardinal Albino Luciani, the patriarch of Venice, was elected—almost by acclamation—as the 261st successor to Peter. This compromise candidate was the first to choose a double name, John Paul, thereby indicating his intention of continuing the work of his two predecessors and the council over which they presided. In his inaugural message, he revealed his desire to continue the pastoral plan of Paul, whose pontificate drew from his predecessor, "the great-hearted pastor, Pope John XXIII." At the same time, he pledged his commitment to the teaching of the Second Vatican Council, championing a more just social order. He had attended all the council's sessions, but never spoke publicly in any of them. In 1969, Paul made him patriarch of Venice, naming him a cardinal in 1973.

As bishop and patriarch, Luciano was liked by his clergy, whom he consulted before making major decisions, while the public appreciated his simplicity, humility, and goodness. He chose the motto *humilitas,* revealing much about the man and his mission. The real treasure of the church, he proclaimed, were the poor, the disinherited, and the weak. While at Venice his numerous projects on behalf of the downtrodden revealed his commitment to social justice and he was acclaimed the "bishop of the poor." Lacking curial experience, and having spent most of his time in pastoral work, he was virtually unknown to the public, unlike Montini who had an Italian and international reputation. Few knew that Luciani had written a book *Illustrissimi,* containing a series of letters to fictional and historical characters presenting church principles within an accessible—critics said childish—literary format. However, this volume was little read in Italy, and less so abroad.[1]

Once pope, John Paul sought to implement the guidelines of the Vatican Council, pledging his ministry to its heritage.[2] Recognizing that he had neither the "wisdom of heart" of John, nor the "preparation and learning" of Paul, John Paul shared their vision to serve the church.[3] Although assisted by Cardinal Jean Villot, whom he confirmed as secretary of state, the new pope's pastoral experience did not prepare him for the enormous papal burdens and the church's global responsibilities, constraining him to rely on the curial cardinals to administer the departments of the Vatican. He urged the faithful to pray for the success of the Camp David talks, calling for a just solution to the Israeli-Arab conflict,[4] noting that the poor suffered most in times of unrest and war. He did more than catalog the prevailing difficulties, urging his listeners to propose solutions to alleviate the suffering. Defying convention, he sent greetings to the first child conceived through in vitro fertilization.[5]

The numerous responsibilities imposed on the new pope took their toll. The church, he explained, could never do too much to help solve the problems of freedom, justice, peace, and development worldwide, and had to promote friendship between individuals and peoples. Not violence, but love could do everything.[6] Nonetheless, there were limits to what he could personally accomplish. John Paul's health had never been good. He was afflicted by a tubercular condition early in life, complicated by several heart ailments and phlebitis, a painful circulatory disease aggravated by the series of heart attacks he had earlier endured. Not one to complain, he reluctantly acknowledged his ailments and difficulties.[7] When he died on September 28, 1978, after only 33 days in office, one of the shortest pontificates in modern times, some refused to hold coronary occlusion, heart fibrillation or myocardial arrest responsible, convinced that foul play was responsible for his untimely death. These suspicions were fueled by the curia's refusal to sanction an autopsy. As more than half a million mourners passed his coffin in St. Peter's the rainy day of his wake, journalists dramatically wrote that even the heavens cried. His funeral followed on October 4; like Paul VI he was buried in a simple wooden coffin in the crypt of St. Peter's Basilica.

The ensuing conclave in October once more divided on ideological lines. The Italian and European cardinals split between the ultraconservative Giuseppe Siri, and the more progressive Giovanni Benelli, diverging on a number of issues but especially on the innovations introduced by Vatican II. On October 16, the 58-year-old Cardinal Karol Wojtyla, Archbishop of Krakow, like his predecessor was elected as a compromise candidate— the first Slav and Polish pope, and first non-Italian, since Hadrian VI of Utrecht in 1522–1923. Only 58, he was the youngest pope since the election of Pius IX in 1846, 132 years ago. In Poland, church bells were rung in celebration of his election. The Soviet Union as well as the Poles dispatched a delegation to his inauguration. His youth, nationality, and the fact that he came from a Communist country, surprised many. Liberals hoped his decision to be called John Paul II, revealed a commitment to his predecessors' efforts on behalf of the Second Vatican Council. Conservatives believed that his appreciation of Pius XII revealed his commitment to traditionalism. Both studied his background in the hope of forecasting his future action.

Born in Wadowice, outside Krakow, on May 18, 1920, this son of a retired army lieutenant witnessed his mother and brother die while he was young, leaving him an only child.[8] His stint at the University of Krakow ended when the Nazi invasion closed the school and in 1942 Wojtyla found refuge in the palace of Cardinal Adam Sapiha, the Archbishop of Krakow, where he prepared for the priesthood. Ordained in November 1946, he later ventured to Rome where he received a doctorate in theology. In 1958, he was appointed auxiliary bishop of Krakow, one of the last appointments of Pius XII. In 1964, Paul VI named him Archbishop of Krakow, and in that capacity he revealed both realism and political agility in negotiating with Poland's communist regime. For his efforts, in 1967 Paul bestowed the red hat, making him Poland's youngest cardinal. Wojtyla participated in the sessions of the Second Vatican Council (1962–1965), and the meetings of the Synod of Bishops between 1969 and 1977. During the council, he called for a more biblical, less clerical tone to the church, pleading that it must never again appear as an authoritarian institution. He was credited with affecting the compromise that produced the pastoral constitution on the Church in the Modern World, of December 1965, quoting from it at length in his later volume *Crossing the Threshold of Hope.*[9] At home, he supported the strikes of 1976, and maintained cordial contacts with Krakow's Jewish community. During these years he traveled widely, broadening his mind and perspective.

Wojtyla, became the 264th pope on October 16, and took the name John Paul II on October 22. He immediately declared his support for the Second Vatican Council, promising to implement its reforms.[10] He shared Paul VI's interest in the world outside the Vatican, viewing the papacy as a player in international affairs and was personally committed to the restoration of European unity on a Christian foundation. At the same time he recognized the church's role and responsibility in the world beyond Europe, revealing his intention of continuing and expanding the global apostolic visits initiated by Paul VI. Like Paul, the new pope appreciated the importance of travel in spreading the message of Christ and the church. Neither Roman nor Italian, he determined to make the world his parish, transcending geographical boundaries and his presence and presentations soon electrified vast numbers in the continents and countries he visited. In rapid secession he visited Assisi and Siena, and the shrines of the patron saints of Italy, inspected the papal residence at Castel Gandolfo, and quickly planned a series of visits outside the peninsula. A brilliant communicator, who spoke 12 languages, the new pope also revealed his intention of utilizing modern communications as well as improved transportation to reach the masses worldwide. Subsequently he pioneered the Vatican website and was the first pope to use e-mail.

Following his election, John Paul held a press conference for journalists, and later in the day addressed the members of the diplomatic corps. The pope pleased the diplomats by talking privately with most of them, revealing his universal vision and international goals. From the first he proved to be a brilliant communicator. Recognizing that the pope could not do everything, he assumed as his first task to gather the people of God in unity. His claim of contemporary universality for the papacy was repeated in his talk of December 8, 1978. From the beginning, John Paul II assumed a dynamic diplomatic and political posture, transcending that taken by most of his modern predecessors. He also revealed that the Christian concept of human relations did not succumb to the liberal logic of profit, but sought to put into practice the teaching of the Second Vatican Council, which intended that the earth be utilized for a universal well-being. In his homily following his investiture, this pope revealed his intention of serving humanity, invoking the opening of frontiers, along with political and economic systems.[11] Some in Moscow found this mission ominous.

Although John Paul II retained Villot as his secretary of state, from the first he intended to personally initiate and supervise the Vatican agenda. Deeming communism a spent force, he predicted its collapse, opening a dialogue with Warsaw and making preparations to visit his native land. Meanwhile, he announced an impending visit to Mexico, which had long shunned relations with the Vatican. He also discussed the prospects for a broader peace and the ending of the Cold War with the Soviet Foreign Minister Andrei Gromyko. At the end of January 1979, the pope left for Mexico, and after meeting with its President Lopez Portillo, formally opened the Latin American Bishops Conference at Puebla, cautioning its members to be wary of a Marxist inspired Liberation Theology. Sympathetic with the plight of the poor, and supporting their call for social justice, he would not sanction any liberation, which ignored liberation from sin.[12] True liberation, he insisted, called for changes in the materialism of the age,[13] citing the stance outlined by the nineteenth-century papacy. His traditionalism was also reflected in his order to the Jesuit Father Robert Drinan to surrender his seat in the American congress, and the decree of the Congregation for the Doctrine of the Faith that Hans Kung could no longer teach as a Catholic theologian. At the same time John Paul denounced conservative critics, ordering Marcel Lefebvre, the archbishop who challenged the innovations of the Second Vatican Council and papal authority, to cease his public attacks on Vatican innovations or face excommunication.

Following Villot's death, John Paul named Agostino Casaroli, the architect of Paul's opening to the East or *Ostpolitik*, secretary of state, sending a signal to Moscow and the Warsaw Pact countries that he would continue the policy of conciliation with the communist regimes of the East. The improvement of the Vatican's relations with the regimes of eastern Europe, enabled John Paul to return to his homeland in 1979, the first of eight trips to his native Poland. The initial papal visit, June 2–11, was religious but had profound political implications, altering the mentality of fear that prevailed in Poland and much of the Eastern bloc, as he spoke of a united Christian Europe. The return to his fatherland was immensely important for a number of reasons: it was the first visit of a pope to Poland, an unprecedented papal trip to a Communist country, and the first time a pope said mass in a Communist country. Calling for evolutionary change, John Paul's message produced shock waves, which reverberated throughout Central and Eastern Europe, arousing hope and expectation in the Polish people while instilling fear and consternation in the communist authorities, whose rule was questioned if not challenged.

At Auschwitz his critique of Nazi totalitarian abuses was seen by some as an indirect condemnation of Communist crimes as well. There, and elsewhere, John Paul indirectly challenged the Communists regimes on the issue of human rights, proposing an ethical alternative to the status quo in Poland and Eastern Europe. For this among other reasons the Polish regime sought to limit public participation in the open air meetings, without much success. Likewise, the regime's "escorts," who followed the pope everywhere, proved unable to curb the popular enthusiasm. Despite Communist efforts to curtail the impact of the visit, the pope planted the seeds of change in Poland. Some suspect that the papal visit inspired the strike in the Gdansk Shipyards in August 1980 and the formation of the Solidarity Labor Organization, inspired by Catholic social teaching. John Paul returned to Poland in June 1983 and four years later in June 1987. The subsequent victory of Solidarity in the Polish elections of June 1989, signaled the collapse of communism in Poland and beyond.

John Paul called for change in the West as well as the East, distressed by the increasing secularization that prevailed in the prosperous countries of the world. This critique was expanded during the course of his October 1979 visit to the United States. In Boston, he invoked obedience on issues such as birth control, abortion, and women's role in the church, reiterating and reinforcing his orthodox positions. Similar sentiments were expressed in New York, where he addressed the United Nations, and in Washington, D.C., where he met with church officials at the Catholic University of America. Here, Sister Theresa Kane, president of the Leadership Conference of Women Religious, asked him to reconsider the role of women in the church.[14] The pope refused to do so. Acknowledging the importance of women in the church and society, the pope continued to oppose their ordination. John Paul adhered to the position of Pius XII that each of the sexes had to play a part in society according to its nature, character, and physical, intellectual, and moral aptitude. He agreed with the former pontiff "that if men are by temperament more apt to deal with matters outside the home, in the public domain, women have, generally speaking, more understanding and tact for comprehending and resolving the delicate problems of domestic life, which is the foundation of social life."[15]

These remarks, as well as his selection of the traditionalist Cardinal Silvio Oddi as the prefect of the Sacred Congregation for the Clergy, assured there would be no ordination of women during his pontificate. This was later confirmed in his apostolic letter of 1995, asserting that the church could not ordain women. Critics decried his opposition to female ordination, determination to keep priests out of the political arena, reluctance to sanction the laicization of the clergy, and his insistence on obedience. Not all concurred with the conservative courses he outlined during his visits to Turkey in 1979, and France, Germany, Brazil, and Africa in 1980.

Pope John Paul II's vision of the role of the church in the contemporary world was also revealed in "The Redeemer of Man" (1979), the first of his 14 encyclicals. In this programmatic letter, the pope insisted that human dignity was best preserved in the church.[16] The problems burdening humanity including economic oppression and political persecution, John Paul explained, could be resolved by the implementation of Christ's revelation, a call he repeated in his second encyclical of December 1980. When liberals challenged his suspension of Hans Küng, John Paul responded by reaffirming the dogma of papal infallibility, presenting the Vatican's justification for the suspension. The summer of 1980, when the pope heard that the Russians ordered the Polish regime to purge Solidarity or face invasion, he cautioned President Leonid Brezhnev against the projected aggression. Some believe the papal intervention contributed to the compromise between Solidarity and the Polish regime. Others are convinced that it inspired the assassination attempt on his life in May 1981 by a Turkish radical. In fact, Italian authorities later determined that the Soviets were behind this assassination attempt.[17] While in the hospital, the pope grieved to hear that Italy had voted to approve abortion. The pontiff survived the news, as well as the six and a half hour operation. Hospitalized for 70 days, it was only after five months that he was able to resume his full schedule and his travels. John Paul II forgave his would-be assassin and visited him in prison in December 1983. Pursuing peace in the Middle East, he met with Yasser Arafat of the Palestine Liberation Organization (PLO) in 1982, and despite criticism by some, eight more times during the course of the next two decades. Later, a basic agreement was signed between the Holy See and the PLO.

In September 1981, the pope released the first of his three social encyclicals "By Means of Labor," defending labor's right to organize and shunning the evils of capitalism and Marxism. Tied to the thinking of Poland's Solidarity Movement, it accepted participatory Socialism while rejecting Marxism. Following the banning of Solidarity in Poland, he opened a dialogue with Warsaw and the Kremlin. In June 1982, he met with the American President Ronald Reagan, who had also survived an assassination attempt the year before, discussing the Soviet domination of Eastern Europe. Richard Allen, Reagan's National Security advisor, claimed the two plotted to "hasten the dissolution of the communist empire."[18] The Vatican and the United States did exchange information on the Eastern bloc as well as assessments of the prevailing political situation. It has been suggested that the United States and the Vatican collaborated—some would say plotted—to support the outlawed Solidarity movement after December 1981. We know that Central Intelligence Agency (CIA) Director William Casey, an architect of the American-Vatican cooperation on Solidarity and Poland, met with various Vatican officials including Archbishop Achille Silvestrini, the Vatican's deputy secretary of state, and the Vatican's apostolic delegate in Washington, Archbishop Pio Laghi. These, among other factors, encouraged Allen's successor, William Clark, to propose opening diplomatic relations with the Holy See. In 1984, President Reagan appointed William A. Wilson of California, ambassador to the Holy See, reestablishing full diplomatic relations between the Vatican and the United States.

The Vatican also sought to improve relations with Italy and to that end in 1984 John Paul II agreed to replace the concordat of the Lateran Accords of 1929. Under article one of the new agreement, "The Italian Republic and the Holy See reaffirm that the State and the Catholic Church, each in its own order, are independent and sovereign, and . . . to mutually cooperate for the promotion of mankind and the welfare of the Nation."[19] As part of its mission of promoting welfare worldwide, the Vatican continued to interject itself in international affairs undertaking a number of diplomatic initiatives.

In 1982, during the Falkland War, John Paul visited both Great Britain and Argentina, in an attempt to stop the conflict. His failure to do so did not discourage further papal international efforts on behalf of peace and social justice. In fact, 1982 was one of John Paul II's busiest travel years that included visits to Benin, Equatorial Guinea, Gabon, and Nigeria, a well as Portugal, Spain, Switzerland, San Marino, and Brazil in addition to Great Britain and Argentina. In 1983 the "pilgrim of peace" resumed his voyages, venturing to Lourdes, Austria, Poland, and Central America, continuing his global outreach. In 1984 he visited Spain, Switzerland, Korea, Santo Domingo, Latin America, and Canada, while in 1985 he traveled to Holland, Belgium, Liechtenstein, and Africa. The voyages were at once both pastoral and political.

John Paul II also pursued the *Ostpolitik* initiated by John XXIII and followed by Paul VI, but Moscow remained suspicious of closer relations with the papacy, fearing it would undermine its control of Eastern Europe, However, Mikhail Gorbachev's election as general secretary of the Central Committee of the Communist Party of the Soviet Union in 1885 led to new Soviet policies including *glasnost* or "openness" and *perestroika*, the restructuring of Soviet society, facilitating Warsaw's pledge to negotiate with the Catholic Church. In 1988, to commemorate the millennium of the birth of Christianity in the Ukraine, Gorbachev invited religious leaders to Moscow. John Paul, made his acceptance conditional on being allowed to visit the Catholics of Lithuania. His request denied, the pope dispatched a delegation of cardinals led by Secretary of State Cardinal Casaroli, who carried a catalog of complaints. Russia and China were the two major countries that John Paul II did not visit in his more than one hundred trips abroad.

The summer of 1988, Gorbachev ventured to Warsaw, aware that the government could not rule without the cooperation of Solidarity, and some understanding with the Catholic Church. For his part, the pope provided approval to have Polish bishops participate in a joint committee with communist delegates to outline a new church-state relationship. In April, the government promised to legalize Solidarity, called for open parliamentary elections in June of 1989, and agreed to establish diplomatic relations with the Vatican. Poland, the key Soviet satellite in Europe, was the first Communist bloc nation to do so, contributing to the dramatic changes there and throughout Eastern Europe.

As change reverberated throughout much of Europe the summer of 1989, President Bush's new ambassador to the Vatican, Thomas Patrick Melady, arrived in Rome. In December 1989, Gorbachev in a historic visit, met with the pope in Rome, discussing among other things, the position of Catholics in the western Ukraine. Melady's first assignment was to obtain the pope's evaluation of Gorbachev following their historic December meeting—prior to Bush's and Secretary of State Baker's encounter with the Soviet leader off the island of Malta. John Paul's positive evaluation was shared by the American president.[20] Lech Walesa, with crucial Vatican's support, became president of Poland at the end of 1990, undermining communism there and throughout Eastern Europe. Moscow was also affected so that by 1991, the Communist system in the Soviet Union itself collapsed.[21] The dissolution of the Soviet empire without recourse to violence has been deemed nothing short of miraculous. At the end of that year, President Boris N. Yelstin of Russia visited the pope in Rome. Gorbachev, the ousted Soviet leader readily acknowledged that Pope John Paul II had played "a major political role" in crippling communism in Eastern Europe.[22] Certainly, it was with the Vatican's support in the early fall of 1991 that the Soviet Union sanctioned the independence of the Baltic republics of Latvia, Lithuania, and Estonia, whose incorporation into the Soviet Union the Holy See had never recognized. Without any military divisions, the Vatican had emerged as an important, not to say crucial, factor in diplomatic relations. In 1993 John Paul II visited the former Soviet Baltic states of Lithuania, Latvia, and Estonia as well as Albania. In 1994, the peripatetic pope ventured to an independent Croatia following the disintegration of Yugloslavia.

John Paul's political activism and sweeping diplomatic initiatives did not inhibit his social activism, which likewise had global implications. On the centenary of Leo XIII's *Rerum Novarum*, he released the third of his social encyclicals "The Hundredth Year" (1991), following his second "On the Social Concern of the Church" in 1988. Although he continued to reject any alliance between Marxism and Christianity as championed by some followers of Liberation Theology, he deplored and chastised the exploitation of the poor. "The Marxist solution has failed, but the realities of marginalization and exploitation remain in the world, especially the third world," the pope wrote. "Against these phenomena the Church strongly raises her voice."[23] Consequently John Paul criticized militant priests as well as conservative authorities during the course of his 10-day visit to Brazil, in October 1991, pressing President Fernando Collor de Mello to resolve the enormous social and economic problems of the country and stark disparities, which persisted in its society. He apologized to Brazil's Indian population for any missionary abuse during the centuries of conversion, calling for a recognition of their rights. The church, he insisted, belonged to the poor, reminding the slum dwellers of the poorest quarter of Rio de Janeiro, that those in poverty are particularly close to God's Kingdom.

Addressing the themes of poverty and inequality, the pope appeared to accept aspects of the Liberation Theology of the Brazilian bishops, who combined the Marxist notion of class struggle with the Christian conception of championing the defenseless. However, John Paul complained of "Marxist messianism" within the movement, insisting that the interests of the poor were to be championed by Christian conscience, uncontaminated by Marxist class struggle. He reminded his fellow clergy that the church's kingdom was not of this world and that politics was not the end of her mission. The role of the church was to bare witness to the truth, counseling cooperation rather than confrontation.[24] In doing so, this pope was prepared to have recourse to politics and diplomacy to achieve his ecclesiastical objectives. Thus his protracted negotiations with Mexico ended more than 70 years of governmental hostility towards the Roman Catholic Church, and in 1992 led to the establishment of diplomatic relations. Some were convinced that John Paul's ultimate aim was to reunify the Christian world under papal leadership.

The pope did not ignore the turmoil in Yugoslavia and called for Christian charity and negotiation in good faith in this country's disintegration, which was marked by brutal ethnic and religious warfare. During the course of his August 1991 five day visit to Hungary , the pope received a group of Croatian pilgrims. Supportive of the legitimate aspirations of this Catholic population vis-à-vis the Orthodox Serbs, John

Paul proposed they achieve their goals through international mediation rather than warfare, promising to use his office to appeal to the world community on their behalf. This proved difficult in light of the fact that federal army tanks crossed the border into Croatian territory, while their air force bombed Stara Gradiska on their border with the republic of Bosnia-Herzegovina.[25] In response, in January 1992 the Vatican formally recognized the independence of Croatia and Slovenia. Learning of a series of atrocities committed in Bosnia-Herzegovina, the Vatican pressed for the intervention of the United Nations. The European states and the United Nations had both the right and duty to intervene to disarm one who wants to kill, reported Cardinal Angelo Sodano, the papal secretary of state. Although working with the United States against Soviet policy in Eastern Europe, and favoring its intervention in the Balkans, the Vatican charted its own policy in international affairs.

Relations between Rome and Washington were solidified during the course of President George Herbert Walker Bush's hour-long talk with Pope John Paul II in November 1991. To be sure, differences remained—including the fact that the Vatican in the early 1990s still did not officially recognize Israel, a key American ally in the middle east. The stumbling block to the Vatican's recognition of the Jewish state remained political rather than religious, as the Holy See played a major role in the campaign against racism and anti-Semitism. The pope, who had helped protect Jews in his native Poland during the Nazi occupation and the Holocaust, continued to denounce the outbursts of xenophobia in Europe, expressing his solidarity with the Jews. Following the Madrid Conference, which promised an improvement in Arab-Israeli relations, the Holy See announced the opening of complete diplomatic relations with the Jewish state, which were established at the end of 1993. Early in 2000, the church issued a document condemning the prior anti-Judaism in the church,[26] paving the way for the pope's historic pilgrimage to the Holy Land at the dawn of the new millennium. This reconciliation with Judaism and other faiths was temporarily jeopardized the summer of 2000 when the Congregation for the Doctrine of the Faith (CDF) issued *Dominus Jesus,* which focused on the role of salvation within the church and found other churches and religions deficient in this regard. Despite the difficulties created by this document, the dialogue with the other faiths continued.

During the last years of the old millennium, Pope John Paul II resumed his journeys abroad, logging more miles and visiting more countries than all of his predecessors combined, projecting the Vatican's universal outreach. In 1992, he ventured twice to Africa visiting Senegal in February, and Angola in June. In May, he pleaded for peace in the Sudan, decrying the conflict between the Muslim and Arab dominated government in the north, and the black, Christian south. The pope warned Sudan's military leader that his Muslim fundamentalist government had the duty to protect the right of Christians to practice their faith.[27] Under John Paul's leadership the Vatican assumed a global presence intervening in a series of domestic and international issues. In 1992, the pope visited Santo Domingo for the opening of the Fourth Latin American Bishops Conference. While restating the church's preferential option for the poor, liberation theologians such as Enrique Dussel were not invited to the conference, and the pope cautioned the Latin American clergy not to lose sight of their primary spiritual mission while combating economic, social, and political injustices.[28] Later, the Vatican imposed a year's silence on Leonardo Boff, a leading liberation theologian, who taught that the Second Vatican Council provided the theoretical justification for liberation theology. Following his censure, Boff eventually abandoned the priesthood, distressed by the conservative signals he perceived emanating from the Vatican. John Paul's campaign against liberation theology succeeded, but in the regions where it lost influence it was followed by the striking success of Protestant evangelic groups.

Liberal critics complained of Rome's conservative course under John Paul II. In March 1992, the German Catholic theologian Eugen Drewerman was suspended for challenging the Vatican's stance on clerical celibacy and contraception, while questioning whether Jesus physically rose from the dead, and whether Mary was a virgin. It should have provided an example for dissenting clergy, but did not deter the Bishop of Evreux, Jacques Gaillot, from advancing similar views. The bishop, who endorsed the controversial French-made abortion pill, advocated the use of condoms, and favored the marriage of priests, was allowed to retain his title, but all churches were removed from his jurisdiction. In 1985 Joseph Ratzinger, head of the Congregation for the Doctrine of the Faith sent the American Father Charles Curran a set of observations on his departure from church teaching. This was followed by a formal notification, approved by the pope, prohibiting him from teaching theology at the Catholic University of America in Washington, D.C., and eventually suspended him from his post. The Vatican also refused permission to publish the proceedings of an Episcopal Conference of 1988, which challenged the church's ban on artificial contraception. Archbishop Raymond G. Gunthausn of Seattle, chastised by the Vatican for his liberal policies involving marriage annulments, liturgy, sterilizations at Catholic hospitals, matters involving homosexual groups, and clerical education, found his authority in these areas transferred to his auxiliary, Bishop Wuerl. John Paul ordered the four Nicaraguan priests who participated in the Marxist

Sandinista government to withdraw after a transition period, and had them defrocked when they refused to do so.

In 1990 John Paul II issued directives in *Ex Corde Ecclesiae*, to assure the orthodoxy of Catholic universities, and was supported in this course by Cardinal Ratzinger, and the equally traditional Jean Jerome Hamer, head of the Congregation for Religious. Both shared the pope's contention that the reforms following Vatican II transcended what the council fathers had envisioned and determined to return to a more moderate course. To gain approval for his stance, and the support of the younger generation, the pope instituted World Youth Days. The summer of 1993, John Paul traveled to Denver, Colorado, for World Youth Day, where he refused to temporize on what he deemed absolute. In September 1993, the pope returned to the issue of moral relativism, in his letter on "The Splendor of Truth." In this long document, he rejected the idea that human reason could create values, rather than discover them in the order of the universe created by God. Arguing that good is distinct from evil and morality cannot be situational, he again rejected abortion and euthanasia, as well as a series of current sexual errors including premarital sex. The church, he insisted, could not court popularity at the expense of teaching what humanity must do to gain eternal life. This message caused considerable controversy among those American Catholics, who adhered to more liberal positions.

The pope also condemned certain television programs as a threat to family life, denouncing their glorification of sex and violence and the spreading of false and degrading values. During his weeklong trip to the Baltic region in September 1993, he denounced atheism's immoral successors including prostitution and pornography. In Riga, John Paul II presented church doctrine as a middle path between discredited communism and capitalism's excesses, citing the inability of both to fulfill the needs of the weak and downtrodden. Accepting the legitimacy of private property, he also spoke of the rights of labor, referring to "the dignity of the human subject who performs it, who can never be reduced to a commodity or a mere cog in the machinery of production."[29] His words and admonitions were not received kindly in parts of the capitalist and increasingly secular, west.

Although appreciative of American efforts on behalf of peace, the Vatican disagreed with many of the policies adopted by the Clinton administration especially on issues such as abortion and birth control. These differences were not resolved in June 1994, when John Paul II met with the American president in Washington, to discuss the agenda for the International Conference on Population and Development to be held in Cairo in September. Upset that the original draft seemed to support contraception, the Vatican responded by criticizing the cultural imperialism of the west vis-à-vis the third world. Some saw the impending clash between the Vatican and the United States at the Cairo Conference as the greatest since the dropping of the atomic bomb on Japan, which the Vatican had opposed. The pope expressed his concern that the world community in general, and the United States in particular, were not sufficiently sensitive to the value of life and the unfortunate ensuing consequences.

Despite the pope's traditional stance on birth control, abortion, and divorce, in December 1994, John Paul II was selected as *Time* magazine's "Man of the Year." The pope did not rest on his laurels, but continued to press his convictions, hoping to impose his authority through public pronouncements and personal presence. Contraception he held manifestly wrong, while insisting that the church did not have the authority to permit priestly ordination for women. During his talk to the Synod on religious life, he specified that the Synod should not discuss the issue of female ordination. Abortion he branded a grave sin, holding that even rape did not justify what was intrinsically evil. Sex outside of marriage he deemed wrong, and pledged that the church would continue to uphold that prohibition despite deviations among couples. John Paul planned to visit New York in October 1994, during the International Year of the Family, to address the General Assembly. A fall led to the cancellation of the trip for one year. In October 1995, he made it to New York to speak before the United Nations, again expressing his esteem for this international institution, seeing in it "the hope of a better future for human society" and an important "moral center."[30]

Meanwhile, the pope praised Africa's people love of life and seconded their cry for an end to the slaughter in Rwanda. On African ecclesiastical issues, he favored acculturation, blending traditional African values with Vatican's dogma, so long as these local practices did not violate church principles. Determined to make the church a universal reality as well as theoretical transnational force, John Paul indicated that Catholicism had to become de-westernized and global. This aim was reflected in the consistory of 1994, which appointed 30 new cardinals from 24 countries, reducing the Italians to 20 out of 120 in the college.[31] However, this opening to the non-western world was not accompanied by any abandonment of traditional beliefs and practices, and in 1994 John Paul again rejected the ordination of women.

By the end of the twentieth century the pope's health had clearly deteriorated as he suffered bouts of shaking and trembling, later diagnosed as Parkinson's disease. Despite his growing frailty, John Paul II continued his global outreach and travel; in 1995 visiting the Philippines, Papua-New Guinea, Australia, Sri Lanka, Cameroon, South Africa, Kenya, the United States, and in Europe, Belgium, and Poland. The pope visited the Philippines for the International Youth Forum, followed by an Asian tour that brought him to New Guinea, Australia, and Sri Lanka. In his final Mass in the Philippines, more than four million Filipinos gathered to greet John Paul II, who was joined in prayer by members of China's state sponsored supervised church, the Chinese Patriotic Association, which since 1949 has elected its own bishops without the approval of the Vatican. The pope in a mid-January message, broadcast to the estimated ten million Roman Catholics in China, called for reconciliation and unity in the Chinese Catholic Church. Leaving the Philippines, the pope ventured to New Guinea for the beatification of the Catechist Peter ToRot, one of the many personages named as blessed—the second step in the process of proclaiming a saint.

To conciliate feminists, among other factors, in Australia the pope presided over the beatification ceremonies for Mother Mary MacKillop, the nineteenth-century foundress of the Josephite Order of Nuns, who fought the male dominated Australian hierarchy to do so. Some suspected that a similar motivation later led to his announcement of the sainthood of Mother Katharine Drexel, who founded the Sisters of the Blessed Sacrament for Indians and Colored People in 1891. John Paul also repeated that "the Church stands firmly against every form of discrimination, which in any way compromises the equal dignity of women and men," but did not budge from his ban on the ordination of women. He proved more conciliatory in Sri Lanka, where angry Buddhists were livid about his remarks about their faith made in his volume *Crossing the Threshold of Hope*, in which he described Buddhism as an "atheistic system," while he criticized its indifference to the world.[32] In 1996 John Paul focused on Latin America going to Venezuela, Nicaragua, Guatemala, and El Salvador, as well as Muslim Tunisia in North Africa and Slovenia, Hungary, Germany, and France in Europe. The following year he returned to Brazil, Poland, France, and such troubled spots as Lebanon and Bosnia-Herzegovina, as well as the Czech Republic.

Continuing his global outreach, in 1998 he ventured to Nigeria, Austria, Croatia, and Cuba. During his historic visit to Communist Cuba, the pope met with Fidel Castro. In 1999, he returned to Mexico and the United States in North America; Poland and Slovenia in Europe, making his first visits to Rumania and India. He is also the only pope to visit the five Nordic and largely secular countries of Norway, Iceland, Denmark, Finland, and Sweden. In Sweden less than five percent of the population attended weekly church services, so the papal visit had a missionary dimension. More pastoral were his pilgrimages to the Holy Land and Fatima in 2000, as his health became increasingly fragile. At this juncture in March 2000,

John Paul revealed his gratitude for the gifts he had received during his lifetime listing among these: Vatican II, the end of communism, the failure of the assassination attempt on his life, and his long pontificate. He also introduced a jubilee day of memory and reconciliation, during which a number of high prelates asked forgiveness for offenses against other Christians, Jews, native peoples, women, as well as against truth. The pope also invited the cardinals to Rome to discuss and assess the future of the church.

In the interim, the spring of 1995, John Paul II issued his eleventh encyclical letter *The Gospel of Life,* in which he denounced the culture of death in which he included abortion, euthanasia, and even cloning. In its passages he restated and reaffirmed the church's opposition to contraception, abortion, euthanasia, and capital punishment. His opposition to euthanasia did not deter the Dutch from forging ahead to provide for its legalization, to the distress of the pontiff. Noting that the passing of unjust laws created problems of conscience for morally upright people who have a right not to be implicated in evil actions, John Paul warned that "each individual in fact has moral responsibility for the acts, which he personally performs; no one can be exempted from this responsibility, and on the basis of it everyone will be judged by God himself."[33] Addressed to the whole of humanity, its reception was mixed. Conservatives, appreciating the message on sexual ethics, were less comfortable with his critique of capitalism.

Others, who concurred with his social pronouncements, found fault with his teaching on moral and doctrinal issues, while still others criticized what they perceived as the Vatican's belated and inadequate response to the sex abuse scandal that rocked the church and its hierarchy in the United States. Eventually, in 2002 the pope summoned the cardinals of the United States to the Vatican to discuss the sexual scandal and reluctantly accepted the resignation of Cardinal Bernard Law, the Archbishop of Boston, who the attorney general of Massachusetts accused of participating in a massive cover-up. The following year, 2003, the pope urged world leaders, and especially President Bush, not to go to war in Iraq. Although his call was not heeded, the pope continued to assert that "Christ's peace could not be achieved through war.[34]

In 1998 John Paul II issued his thirteenth encyclical letter *Fides et ratio,* which explored the relationship between faith and reason and reiterated the critique of relativism earlier annunciated by Gregory XVI (1831–1846) and Pius IX (1846–1878). At this juncture, John Paul had become the longest reigning pope of the twentieth century, and by the end of his pontificate in 2005, the fourth longest reigning pope: 26 years, 5 months, and 17 days for a total of 9,665 days. The pope's health had visibly deteriorated, and rumors circulated that he would resign. These stories were denied by the Vatican, but confirmed following John Paul's death by his personal secretary Stanislaw Dziwisz, who revealed that the pope was on the brink of resigning in the year 2000 because of his deteriorating health.[35] He did not do so and continued to preside over the church. Perhaps he was influenced by the fact that no pope had retired since Gregory XII (1406–1415) in the fifteenth century.

Not only did John Paul remain in office, but to the surprise of many, he continued his travels. In 2002 the pope made three trips abroad including a final return to his Polish homeland. The summer of 2004 John Paul made his last foreign trip to Lourdes, following in the footsteps of so many of the faithful who sought a miraculous cure. None was forthcoming for the pope. In January of 2005 he contacted the flu and was taken to the Gemelli Hospital in Rome; in late February a tracheotomy was preformed. At the end of March 2005, John Paul II received the last rites and thousands of Catholics and non-Catholics alike crowded into St. Peter's Square to pray for the dying pope. He died of septic shock and heart failure on April 2, 2005, and his death was confirmed by the Cardinal Camerlengo or Papal Chamberlain, Eduardo Cardinal Martinez Somolo. Reportedly, his last words were "Let me go to the house of the Father" uttered in Polish.[36]

News, and especially television and radio coverage of his last days, was panoramic and contributed to the millions of faithful who flocked to Rome for his funeral. On April 4, the pope's body was transferred from the Apostolic Palace to St. Peter's Basilica. The participation of the diplomatic community and presence of leading political figures attested to his international role and reputation. Among those attending were President George W. Bush and his wife, from the United States; Prime Minister Tony Blair from Great Britain; President Jacques Chirac of France; Chancellor Gerhard Schröder of Germany and President Bashar al-Assad of Syria, among others. The American delegation included Secretary of State Condoleezza Rice, as well as former presidents Bill Clinton and George H. W. Bush. Despite his differences with Communist China, John Paul II was praised in a memorial mass held at Southern Cathedral in Beijing by the state controlled Catholic Church, which described him as "a man of peace."[37]

Almost immediately there commenced an assessment of this most traveled and photographed figure of his age, who appeared on the cover of *Time* magazine 15 times and made 104 voyages outside of Italy, which brought him to 129 countries as he traveled more than 725,000 miles. Only 4 countries barred him from visiting: North Korea, Vietnam, China, and post-Communist Russia. His trips and the more than 700 meetings and audiences he had with heads of state, as well as his meetings with a good number of monarchs, extended the diplomatic reach of the Holy See and made the papacy an international presence that could not be ignored. In 1980 Queen Elizabeth II visited John Paul II, the first British monarch to visit a pope at the Vatican. Two years later the British appointed their first ambassador to the Holy See since the reign of Henry VIII (1509–1547). Their example was followed by Protestant Denmark, Norway, and Sweden. In 1984 the United States established full diplomatic relations with the Holy See and in 1993 the Vatican established diplomatic relations with Israel. At the close of his pontificate the Holy See had diplomatic relations with over 170 countries, three times the number during the course of World War II. This diplomatic outreach enabled him to influence the course of events worldwide.

Among the many documents he issued there were 14 encyclicals, 15 apostolic exhortations, 11 apostolic constitutions and 45 apostolic letters,[38] addressing issues within the church and the broader society and culture and the international community. He named 231 cardinals during his pontificate, more than any other modern pope. It was not forgotten that he was the first pope to visit a Synagogue and a Mosque, the first to preach in a Lutheran church, and was deemed largely responsible for the reconciliation between Catholics and Jews. In recognition of his efforts, the Simon Wiesenthal Center gave its 2003 Humanitarian Award to John Paul II "for his lifelong friendship with the Jewish people and efforts to promote Jewish-Catholic understanding."[39] "In the 25 years of my pontificate, I have striven to promote Jewish Catholic dialogue," he told the chief rabbis of Israel, on their first trip to the Vatican, "and to foster even greater understanding, respect and cooperation between us."[40] He was seen to advance ecumenism by his sponsorship of interfaith prayer at Assisi in 1986 and again in 2002. The first pope to meet with a leader of the Soviet Union (Gorbachev), John Paul II has been seen as an important factor in the collapse of Communism in Eastern Europe and the Soviet Union.

Although a poor administrator, who proved indifferent to the operations of the Vatican bureaucracy and some charged barely capable of keeping it on track, he remained immensely popular with the masses. Thus, many attending his funeral shouted "Santo subito" or sainthood immediately. The shouts were apparently heard by his close collaborator and successor Cardinal Ratzinger, who as Pope Benedict XVI waived the usual five year waiting period for consideration of his canonization. Over 70 percent of United States Catholics polled shortly after this pope's death expressed confidence that he would soon be proclaimed a saint and would easily meet the Vatican requirement that a miracle be attributed to his intercession. Indeed, the Rome Diocese produced tens of thousands of pages on behalf of his cause including a series of miracles such as his curing of an American Jew of terminal cancer. Furthermore, a Mexican teenager has claimed the pope cured his leukemia after meeting him in 1990, and Cardinal Francesco Marchisano of Italy reports that John Paul II restored his ability to speak—lost during surgery. Interestingly and ironically, Sister Marie Simon Pierre has claimed that she was cured of Parkinson's disease—which afflicted the pope—after she prayed to him.

In 2007 Catholic officials concluded the first phase of the process for his sainthood, which was expected shortly. Cardinal George Pell, Archbishop of Sydney, Australia, was among the first to refer to this pope as John Paul, the Great. Subsequently, some 90 percent of those polled deemed John Paul II a "great pope."[41] This sentiment was shared by Michael Novak, the 1994 recipient of the Templeton Prize for Progress in Religion, who ranked John Paul II among the greatest in the long history of the papacy. In recognition of his contribution to the church and society, the square in front of Notre Dame Cathedral in Paris was christened the "John Paul Square"[42] and the Caritas Soup Kitchen in Rome was likewise given his name.

Unquestionably, he was one of the most active popes naming more saints than all of his predecessors combined. During his long pontificate he beatified over 1,300 individuals and proclaimed more than 480 new saints and named Thomas More the patron saint of politicians. He intervened in political affairs not only in Eastern Europe but also in the Americas and the Middle East, seeking to dissuade the United States from waging a preventive war against Iraq. Although he proved unsuccessful in this endeavor, many appreciated his efforts to preserve the peace. Liberals also appreciated his ecumenical measures, visit to the synagogue of Rome, pilgrimage to Jerusalem's Western Wall and his prayer services with other religions at Assisi. While some have maintained that John Paul modernized the papacy making it better attuned to the contemporary world, ironically others complained that he bound it to the past.

Clearly, not all have been pleased by this pope or his pontificate, and John Paul had a number of critics as well as admirers. In evaluating his pontificate the *National Catholic Reporter* noted both the positive achievements and negative features of his pontificate. Among the negative aspects catalogued were: the suppression of theological dialogue, the muting of academic freedom, the muzzling of liberation theology, the return to Vatican I concepts, the re-clericalization of the church, and the shoddy and second class treatment accorded the laity and women in the church. A less than positive evaluation was also provided by the more than 400 Catholic theologians who signed the "Cologne Declaration" of 1989, which charged that in denying the church's historical practice of constructive questioning, this pope overstepped papal competence. There was also dissatisfaction with his restriction of the authority of the Bishop's Conference and the suspension of the constitution of the Jesuits for two years. Meanwhile, others questioned his support of the Legion of Christ, a conservative international religious order founded in Mexico in 1941, and the ultra-conservative Opus Dei, which originated in Spain in 1928 and John Paul established as a personal prelature, in 1982, with its own statutes and pre-sided over by its own prelate.

Critics also complained that his 1990 letter "On the Permanent Validity of the Church's Missionary Movement" condemning the notion that one religion was as good as another, resurrecting the doctrine of indiffer-entism. This notion was reinforced by his *Dominus Jesus* of 2000, which seemed to suggest that Christ and the church provided the only hope of salvation and was seen to jeopardize ecumenism. Likewise, counterpro-ductive in the eyes of some, was the pope's critical assessment of Islam as well as Hinduism in his 1994 volume, *Crossing the Threshold of Faith*. It was also charged that while John Paul II talked constantly about fulfilling the strictures of Vatican II, this was more rhetoric than reality for those who accused him of backtracking. Others have criticized him for appointing conservative, unimaginative, and generally docile bishops. For these and other reasons, some critics have depicted John Paul II as a rigid ideologue who assumed an uncompromising stance and quashed public debate in the name of doctrine and tradition, polarizing the church.[43] Finally, his insistence on abstinence rather than condoms as the sole solution for the Acquired Immune Deficiency Syndrome (AIDS) crisis in Africa raised a storm of protest. The controversy continued after his death.[44] In Rome, the leftist opposition, which opposed much of what John Paul II stood for and did, blocked the renaming of the Termini Central Railroad Station in his honor.[45]

Some have commented that most of the millions who cheered this pope during his lifetime, and mourned him after his death, did not follow his rigid directives! Nonetheless, they did cheer and had reason to do so. The *National Catholic Reporter* has listed some his John Paul II's achievements including his role in ending the Cold War, his many broad public utter-ances on behalf of the poor and third world countries, his engaging and evangelizing personality, his personal relations with the leaders of other faiths and his cordiality toward the Jews and the establishment of dip-lomatic relations with Israel. One might also cite his worldwide travels and efforts to make the church truly universal as well as his numerous diplomatic initiatives on behalf of peace. By word and deed he favored social justice while he opposed Marxist means of attaining it. His efforts had an impact on the church whose membership increased during the course of his 26 year pontificate by 342 million so that its members who numbered 756 million at his accession were just under 1.1 billion at his death in 2005,[46] even if the number of its clergy declined. To be sure he did not resolve all the problems confronting the church but few would deny he worked tirelessly to prepare it for the Third Millennium—although not all shared his vision.

Quo Vadis Benedict XVI?

As Pope John Paul II was mourned worldwide, and praised effusively by his close collaborator Joseph Ratzinger, many wondered who would be selected to preside over the 1.1 billion members of the church. In speculating about a successor, some pointed to the ideological divide between conservative and liberal Catholics, others to the north-south division of the faithful, and still others to the differences among the Italian cardinals—who though diminished, still constituted the largest, single national bloc in the College of Cardinals. Furthermore, while some saw the need for a pastoral pope to address internal ecclesiastical issues, others called for a more diplomatic pontiff to deal with the international concerns of the universal church. Voting members of the conclave, 115 from 52 different countries, ventured to Rome for the papal election, the most diverse gathering to date. Nonetheless, the Europeans still controlled some 50 percent of the membership—of which the Italians constituted 17 percent—followed by the South Americans and North Americans who respectively accounted for 18 percent and 12 percent of the voters, while the Asians and Africans each constituted 9 percent of the conclave. The shadow of John Paul II loomed large over the proceedings, for during his long pontificate he had appointed all but three of the cardinals who would name his successor.

The conclave opened April 18, 2005, and among many Vatican watchers, Cardinal Joseph Ratzinger, whose ecclesiastical pronouncements had proven influential though often controversial, emerged as first among the *papabili*—those deemed serious contenders for the papacy. Observers listed his advantages. First, he had worked closely with the previous pope, whom he had helped to elect;[1] second, he was perceived as conservative and orthodox in doctrinal matters, hallmarks of John Paul II's pontificate; third, he was a European, and thus potentially controlled half of the conclave votes; fourth, he was favored by the conservative and influential members of the curia; fifth and finally, he was 78 years old and appealed to those who sought a transitional pope, after the very long pontificate of John Paul II. His primacy was confirmed during the *Sede Vacante,* when the papal throne remained empty, and as dean of the College of Cardinals, he delivered the homily at the pope's funeral mass, eulogizing John Paul II and his policies. He also opened the conclave to choose the new pope, presenting the electoral guidelines and delivering a discourse denouncing moral relativism. Some saw it as a campaign speech for the papal office that Ratzinger insisted he did not want, but whatever its motivation, it played a part in his selection in the conclave that followed.

On April 19, during the fourth ballot on the second day of a short session, Ratzinger was elected pope, receiving more than 80 votes out of 115—thus meeting the two-thirds plus one needed for election. Since one of the cardinals broke his vow of secrecy, we now know that the moderate Cardinal Jorge Mario Bergoglio, Archbishop of Argentina of Italian descent, was his major competitor.[2] Cardinal Jorge Medina Estevez of Chile, the senior cardinal, alerted the crowd in Saint Peter's Square, *Habemus papam*—we have a pope. They soon learned that Ratzinger was the first German pope since Victor II (1055–1057), the second non-Italian since Hadrian VI (1522–1523), and the oldest since Clement XII (1730–1740). A theologian rather than a diplomat as his actions would soon reveal, he was the first prominent theologian to occupy the chair of Peter since Clement XI (1700–1721) at the opening of the eighteenth century The fact that he was a European, who had long called for a re-Christianization of the West, led some to conclude that the conclave was concerned about the materialism and secularism prevailing in the "first world," convinced that the European world had to be re-evangelized. His selection of the name Benedict was seen to reflect both his devotion to the founder of Western Monasticism and patron saint of Europe, and his appreciation of Pope Benedict XV (1914–1922), who strove tirelessly to mediate the destructive European Conflict of 1914–1918. Critics complained that his election represented the conclave's conservative bent and Eurocentric bias, despite the greater growth of the church in Africa and Latin America. Ratzinger was invested as pope in a grand mass outside St. Peter's on April 24, 2005, in a ceremony attended by some 500,000 including such dignitaries as the president of the United States and the chancellor of Germany, attesting to the key role of the Vatican in international affairs.

The new pope, who is said to speak 10 languages and supposedly fluent in Italian, French, Spanish, English, as well as his native German, reportedly assumed the post with trepidation. This concern was shared by his 81-year-old brother, George Ratzinger, also a priest, who believed that the responsibilities of the job were too great for Joseph. In fact, Ratzinger later confided that he had hoped to retire a decade earlier and spend the rest of his life on research and writing—his first love.[3] He did not do so. Although Ratzinger enjoyed reasonable health at his election, he had been hospitalized twice in the early 1990s: once in September 1991 for a cerebral stroke that affected his left field of vision, followed by a fall in August 1992, which inflicted a cut to his head. Perhaps this influenced Benedict's conclusion that working too hard is never a good thing, even for those involved in the governance of the church.[4] His advanced age and disinclination to overdo did not prevent the new pope from planning trips to Germany, Poland, and Brazil nor others from assuming that his pontificate would be a short one. As congratulations flooded the new pope's e-mail, Benedict, seeking assistance and continuity, reappointed senior officials, including Cardinal Angelo Sodano, the previous pope's secretary of state for 14 years. Although he admired his predecessor, Benedict soon made it clear that some of his opinions differed. Among other things, he suggested that the church should be more selective in choosing candidates for sainthood,[5] and approved stricter guidelines for selecting saints to be honored with mandatory feast days. In the new norms, approved by the pope, special consideration would be accorded to saints from continents without representation in the general calendar and from underrepresented categories such as lay people and married couples.[6] He also showed himself more willing than John Paul II to openly challenge Islam's potential for extremism, without carefully considering the diplomatic and political ramifications of pursuing such a course.[7]

Unlike some who assumed the papacy as virtual unknowns, much was known about Ratzinger, who had played a prominent part in the previous pontificate. Born in Marktl am Inn in the diocese of Passau in Bavaria on April 16, 1927, to Josef and Maria Ratzinger, his father was a local policeman who quietly opposed the Nazi regime. The youngest of three children, Joseph and his brother George sought refuge in the church, but this did not prevent them from being brought into the Nazi Youth Movement. Joseph spent his childhood and adolescence in Traunstein, a small village near the Austrian border. In 1943, when he was 16 years old, he was summoned for duty and drafted into an anti-aircraft unit in which he served from August 1943 until September 1944. This was followed by a stint in the Reich's War Service, and then the infantry. At the beginning of May 1945, following Hitler's suicide, he deserted and was briefly interned in an American prisoner of war camp in June 1945. Apparently the brutality of the Nazi years fueled his decision to enter the priesthood.[8] Upon his release, he actively prepared for his vocation and was ordained in 1951. He earned a doctorate in theology from the University of Munich, six years later, writing a dissertation on Saint Augustine.[9] Subsequently he taught theology at a number of universities including Freising, Bonn, Münster, and Tübingen. During the early 1960s he joined liberal theologians such as Karl Rahner, Yves Congar, and Hans Küng in their campaign against conservative Roman theologians.

During the course of the Second Vatican Council, 1962–1965, Ratzinger served as an advisor to Cardinal Joseph Frings, Archbishop of Cologne, working to align him with those bishops who favored reform and sought a renewed vision for the church. At this juncture he remained a theological liberal influenced by French thought, and critical of the Holy Office, the forerunner of the Congregation for the Doctrine of the Faith, over which he would later preside. He was a founding member of the progressive theological journal *Concilium* and as late as 1968 signed a declaration supporting the right of theologians to seek and speak the truth.[10] Shortly, thereafter, he commenced his departure from the reformist camp, a turning point apparently prodded by the student uprisings of 1968 and his mounting concern and disturbing guilt that the liberalization he had supported during the council might lead to chaos in church and society. For this among other reasons, Ratzinger left the University of Tübingen in 1969 for the recently founded conservative university at Regensburg, where he taught the history of dogma. Increasingly he perceived the *aggiornamento*, which flowed from Vatican II as an accommodation with the modern world, which might weaken the faith without improving the world.[11] That year (1969), Pope Paul VI appointed Ratzinger a member of the International Theological Commission of the Holy See, a position he held until 1980.

Ratzinger's drift from the progressive to the conservative camp brought rewards from Rome: in 1977 Pope Paul VI made him Archbishop of Munich and named him a cardinal. John Paul II brought him to Rome in 1981, appointing him Prefect of the Congregation for the Doctrine of the Faith, and enforcer of traditional doctrine, earning him such unflattering nicknames as the vicar of orthodoxy, heresy hunter, grand inquisitor, the enforcer, the Hitler Youth Cardinal, the Vatican's Rasputin, Rome's Darth Vader, God's Rottweiler, and *panzerkardinal* among others. As head of the oldest of the curia's congregations, founded in 1542 as the Sacred Congregation of the Universal Inquisition, Ratzinger diligently sought to purge the church of error and heresy and to curtail if not eliminate western secularization. He worked methodically during more than two decades of theological collaboration with John Paul II, serving as a loyal doctrinal watchdog. In 1985 he published the Ratzinger Report, criticizing those Catholics who displayed an uncritical openness to the world. Some deemed this nothing less than an insidious assault upon the *Aggiornamento* of John XXIII, Paul VI, and the Second Vatican Council. He also aroused opposition when he summoned Leonardo Boff, who had earlier studied under Ratzinger in Germany, and was one the founders of liberation theology, to Rome. Ratzinger challenged the movement's Marxist inspired political activism on behalf of the poor, and silenced Boff—who eventually left the priesthood. In 1985, he also warned Father Charles Curran—of the faculty of theology at the Catholic University of America—that he departed from church teaching, and the following year notified him he could no longer function as a professor of Catholic theology. In his traditionalist crusade, Ratzinger denounced rock music as a vehicle of anti-religion and decried the consequences of the sexual revolution. From 1986 to 1992 he presided over the commission for the preparation of the new Catechism of the Catholic Church, which he hoped would solidify traditionalism, clarify church principles and practices for the faithful, and help contain the hedonism afflicting western society.

Ratzinger continued his defense of established ecclesiastical principles and displayed a degree of doctrinal rigidity in the decade that followed, repeatedly denouncing religious pluralism and relativism. "We have moved from a Christian culture to aggressive and sometimes intolerant secularism," he complained in 2004, warning that "a society from which God is completely absent self-destructs."[12] Some even blamed him for the attempt to fuse the church's definitive teaching and infallible dogma. He was also held responsible for the marginalization of progressive bishops and their replacement by figures denounced by some critics as conservative cronies. His hand was seen behind John Paul II's *Redemptoris Missio* of 1990, which denounced the belief that one religion was as good as another, as well as the apostolic constitution on higher education *Ex Corde Ecclesiae* (From the Heart of the Church) 1990, which called for restrictive norms for Catholic colleges and universities. Ratzinger was also seen to influence John Paul II's *Evangelium vitae* of 1995, which proclaimed abortion and euthanasia as crimes. Ratzinger later drafted directives for denying the sacraments to politicians and public figures who upheld abortion legislation.

While cardinal, he consistently condemned the notion of same sex marriage and the secularism and hedonism that he believed nourished it. At the opening of the new millennium Ratzinger authored *Dominus Iesus: On the Unicity and Salvific Univrsality of Jesus Christ and the Church*, which seemed to assert that salvation could only be found in the Roman

Catholic Church and some felt dismissed non-Christian faiths as gravely deficient while branding Protestant churches as not churches in the proper sense. "The one Christ is the mediator and the way of salvation," it proclaimed, adding "he is present to us in his body, which is the church."[13] This notion was reinforced in a note Ratzinger dispatched to the world's bishops that same year, ordering them to cease referring to the Orthodox, Anglican, and Protestant churches as sister churches. These measures did not facilitate interfaith dialogue.

In 2002 Ratzinger issued a Doctrinal Note to bishops on Catholic participation in political life, asserting that Catholics in lawmaking had an unmistakable obligation to oppose any law that attacked human life.[14] He issued specific guidelines for the American bishops advising them to have their priests deny communion to politicians who supported abortion. Following these general directions Archbishop Alfred C. Hughes of New Orleans refused to attend the graduation at Loyola in May 2005 because its law school honored the Landrieu family, some of whose member had voted to uphold abortion.[15] Likewise, Cardinal William Keeler of Baltimore refused to attend the graduation ceremony at Loyola College of Maryland, because the keynote speaker, Rudolph Giuliani, was known to support abortion. During his tenure as head of the Congregation for the Doctrine of the Faith, Ratzinger paid a number of visits to the United States: Dallas, St. Paul, and Minneapolis in 1984; New York in 1988; Philadelphia and Washington, D.C., in 1990; Dallas in 1991; and San Francisco in 1999.

When the sex abuse scandal erupted in the new millennium, critics charged that Ratzinger initially minimized its scope and consequences. "In the United States, there is constant news on this topic, but less than one percent of priests are guilty of acts of this type," he reportedly complained during a trip to Spain in November 2002. Defensively, the dean of the College of Cardinals argued that "one comes to the conclusion it is intentional, manipulated—that there is a desire to discredit the church." Subsequently, albeit belatedly, he appreciated the gravity of the situation,[16] and as pope reopened the Vatican investigation of the allegations against the Reverend Marcial Degollado, the Mexican founder of the Legionaires of Christ. Deeming the priestly sexual abuse of minors a heart rendering tragedy, he called bishops to prevent future crimes and to provide measures to bring healing to its victims.[17] Instructions were also transmitted to the bishops worldwide to bar men with homosexual tendencies from being rectors or teachers at seminaries. He proved willing to change course on this issue by confronting the sex abuse scandal, but on many other issues remained on his traditionalist track.

Ratzinger's conservative convictions were expressed in his call for the Crucifix to be displayed in public as well as private places and his doubts on having Muslim Turkey admitted into the Christian European Union. He also perceived radical feminism as an ideology that obscured the natural differences between the sexes and endangered the family and like his predecessor deemed impossible the ordination of women. The day before he was elected pope he once more warned the cardinals of succumbing to current trends and fashions claiming: "We are moving toward a dictatorship of relativism which does not recognize anything as for certain and which has as its highest goal one's own ego and one's own desires."[18] Some liberal elements in the church were dismayed by his words, actions, and his election to succeed John Paul II.

Liberal concerns were confirmed by the events that followed, and above all the resignation of the Reverend Thomas Reese as editor-in-chief of the liberal Jesuit journal, *America*. Reese had been questioned and challenged by Ratzinger before his election, and once he became pope, Reese thought it prudent to resign.[19] Some deemed his ouster a chilling sign of Benedict's conservative course. Others feared that the Vatican scapegoated homosexuals for the sex abuse scandal and stereotyped them, while doing precious little to deal with the hierarchy's cover-up.[20] In November 2005, the Vatican issued a nine page document against the ordination of gays. Earlier, in August, during the course of World Youth Day in Cologne, Germany, Benedict returned to a theme he had addressed many times before: the peril of consumer convictions or Cafeteria Catholicism, whereby members of the faith arbitrarily choose what to believe and follow, and what to ignore. Catholics, Benedict insisted, had to adhere to all church doctrines, not only those they found personally convenient or acceptable.

He maintained his firm stance against abortion and scientific research on embryos, insisting that they were full and complete human beings, discounting those scientific opinions that said otherwise. Furthermore, he warned that science alone could not combat AIDS or other social ills.[21] Benedict also denounced genetic engineering and related scientific practices that permitted parents to select designer babies as well as artificial insemination and medical tests to determine hereditary disorders in embryos.[22] He has continued to thunder against the notion of gay marriage, insisting that married couples had nourished the church.[23] Benedict denounced social and cultural trends as well as what he perceived as mistaken religious beliefs, denouncing the Harry Potter works, which he claimed distorted Christianity. At the same time he joined those who decried the commercialization of Christmas.[24] The following year Benedict rejected the message of the newly discovered gospel of Judas, which claimed that Jesus commissioned Judas to betray him to the Roman authorities, contesting the traditional interpretation of Judas as a betrayer.[25] He also continued to rail against the "inane apologies of evil," the "senseless cult of Satan," the "dishonest and frivolous freedom," and the prevailing "immorality and selfishness."[26] He blamed the media for portraying and thus encouraging anti-social behavior and vulgar sexual action.[27]

During the course of his visit to Spain the summer of 2006, his third outside Italy, Benedict harped upon the need for family values, insisting that they could only flow from a marriage between a man and a woman. Benedict's stance created consternation in certain liberal church circles. Later en route to Brazil—his sixth trip outside Italy—he again stirred controversy by telling the journalists who accompanied him that Catholic politicians who supported abortion, such as those that legalized the procedure in Mexico, were automatically excommunicated.[28] In Brazil (May 9–13, 2007) he addressed the bishops of Latin America and the Caribbean, and continued the campaign against liberation theology that John Paul II had commenced during the Santo Domingo meeting of 1992, and some believe even then was inspired by Ratzinger. Benedict told the bishops that they should never forget that the Catholic faith had molded the region rather than any political ideology, social movement, or economic system. These words, and his claim that the Europeans did not impose Catholicism on the native Americans, disturbed a number of Indian leaders and public figures in Latin America, including Hugo Charvez, President of Venezuela, who demanded an apology.[29] Subsequently the pope acknowledged that injustices were committed in the colonization of the continent but did not apologize for his earlier statement.

Benedict's traditionalist bent was also seen in his decision to allow Catholics worldwide to celebrate the Latin Mass of the Tridentine Rite, parts of which date from the time of Saint Gregory in the sixth century and had been restricted by the reforms of the Second Vatican Council.[30] In fact, Pope Paul VI questioned the motives of those seeking its restoration as did a number of bishops past and present who shared his reservations. Benedict, on the other hand, perceived the Tridentine Mass as an important bridge to tradition and an instrument of "liturgical reconciliation" in the modern church.[31] The same argument can, and has been made, for his call for the return of the Gregorian Chant in the music of the liturgy, but critics perceived this too as Benedict's attempt to turn back the clock.[32] In a 131-page document on the Eucharist, Benedict insisted that Catholics had to believe in the real presence of Jesus in the Eucharist.[33] In this and other matters Benedict XVI appeared to indicate that the church was not in need of reform but renewal. His assessment was challenged by some both inside and outside the church.

Not all were critical of the new pope, urging a wait and see attitude—a sentiment expressed by Cardinal Edward Egan of New York and others. After celebrating his first Mass, Pope Benedict offered some clues regarding the course of his pontificate, pledging to continue the work begun by Pope John Paul II, with the Second Vatican Council as a guide. Critics complained that this was pure rhetoric that did not reflect reality. Nonetheless, in some ways Pope Benedict XVI proved to be more complex and somewhat more liberal and tolerant than many had predicted.[34] Defying the expectations of a number of pessimistic pundits, the new pope promised to work for unity among Christians seeking to preserve dialogue and reconciliation with other faiths, promoting rather than discouraging ecumenism, and revealing his intention of meeting with the Archbishop of Canterbury, and did so November 23, 2006.[35] Within the church, he proved supportive of an enhanced role for the laity and encouraged lay movements.

Indeed, during the first week of his pontificate, Benedict did much to soften the image he had earned as a hard-liner imposing church orthodoxy, and once pope he promised not to abandon either the strictures or the spirit of the Second Vatican Council.[36] While some questioned his commitment, his later call to the international community to combat discrimination against those inflicted by AIDS, regardless of their sexual orientation, surprised both liberals and conservatives.[37] Subsequently he offered prayers for the families of the more than two million men and women who had succumbed to AIDS worldwide, urging the faithful not to scorn those afflicted with the dreaded disease but provide comfort, understanding, and compassion.[38]

Benedict's words were followed by actions, revealing that he was compassionate and not always consistent in his conservatism. His Vatican rebuked "design theory," which asserted that the complexity of universe reveals that it must have been created by a higher power, as not belonging to the realm of science. In November 2005, the Vatican hosted an international conference on "Science, Technology, and the Ontological Quest" that called for dialogue between scientists and theologians.[39] To the surprise of many, Benedict proved personally amenable to much of the new technology, and despite his age very much appreciated and put to immediate use the iPod presented to him by the staff members of Vatican radio.[40] This startled some while others were surprised by his appointment of the moderate and pragmatic Archbishop of San Francisco William Levada, to succeeded him as prefect for the Congregation for the Doctrine of the Faith. Meanwhile, Benedict revealed his humanity and humility in asserting that divorced and civilly remarried Catholics should be welcomed in the parishes, confessing that he could not provide all the answers regarding their treatment.

Although Benedict XVI adhered to the prohibition of the ordination of women, he was prepared to discuss their increased role in the church.[41] Perhaps, most surprising, the pope asked the Vatican's Pontifical Council for the Pastoral Care of the Health Care Apostolate, whether condom use in restricted cases might be a lesser evil than the spread of AIDS. "The Pope is not a prophet," he confessed, "He is infallible in very rare circumstances, as we all know."[42] Despite his authoritarian image, Benedict revealed a fairly restricted conception of the power of the papacy. Although this authority was far from absolute, Benedict determined to use it to bolster church doctrine and return the west to its Christian roots.[43] Concerned about the environment and the abuse of natural resources, Benedict was ranked as one of the leading "green" religious figures by the online environmental magazine *Grist*.[44] In fact, in a series of speeches, Benedict called for industrial nations to share their clean technologies with developing nations to avoid the proliferation of pollution.[45]

Pope Benedict revealed his humility by inviting his former colleague but now chief critic, Hans Küng to spend a day with him at Castel Gandolfo, listening attentively to what Küng had to say. Rather than harping upon the doctrinal divisions between Küng and the teaching of the church, the two discussed "humanity's essential moral values through a dialogue of religions and through an encounter with secular reason." Benedict's willingness to listen impressed Küng. Others concurred with his assessment, finding the first months of the new pontificate more collegial and ecumenical than that of his predecessor.[46] Benedict again emphasized the importance of listening during the course of his pastoral visit to Bari in May 2005. "We must open our hearts to the magnanimity of listening to others," he said in his homily, "open our hearts to understanding them, eventually accepting their apologies, to generously offering our own."[47]

Throughout the remaining months of 2005, the new pope revealed his deep commitment to social as well as moral issues, but never forgetting that the major aim of Catholicism remained religious. He viewed Social justice as an aspect of Christian charity. This was one of the themes of his book on *Jesus of Nazareth* published in 2007, which emphasized that Jesus was on a divine mission rather than a social one.[48] In a sense it continued his campaign against liberation theology, while strengthening the case for Christian charity. In September 2005, he dispatched his top humanitarian aid official of "Cor Unum," responsible for coordinating Catholic charitable projects worldwide, to New Orleans to assist in the reconstruction.[49] That same month Benedict dispatched his Secretary of State Cardinal Angelo

Sodano to attend the United Nations World Summit in New York, urging the members to fulfill their previous commitments to help the poor, sick, and hungry.[50] This social message was reinforced by Archbishop Silvano Tomasi, Benedict's representative to the sixth ministerial conference of the World Trade Organization meeting in Hong Kong. "The goal of free trade should be to help spread the world's riches fairly to all people and not to defend already privileged economic powers," the Vatican representative declared.[51]

In his peace day message Pope Benedict called for a commitment to justice and peace, insisting that international humanitarian law was "binding on all peoples" even in times of war.[52] An overemphasis on profit, he warned would lead to global poverty and an ecological crisis.[53] On Palm Sunday the pope called for a crusade against poverty. The need for charity was also emphasized in his first encyclical, which stated that state social policy could never replace the personal commitment of individuals. During his visit to Vienna in early September 2000—his seventh abroad—he returned to this theme noting that "Christian charity shatters the rules of a market economy."[54] In the words of one observer, God's Rottweiler didn't bite."[55] Even skeptics were constrained to concede that the new pope did not pursue the ultraconservative agenda they had feared and expected, nor did he seek to undermine the work of Vatican II. His first encyclical was on God's love rather than his wrath and vengeance.[56] His second, issued at the end of 2007, focused on humanity's hope, which flowed from belief in God.[57]

Confounding critics who were convinced that he would abandon the Second Vatican Council's call for ecumenism, Benedict proved supportive of interreligious dialogue and reconciliation. Indeed, he urged the faithful to reread the Vatican documents and especially *Nostra Aetate* on relations with Jews and Muslims, finding their teachings to be of great relevance. *Nostra Aetate* not only deplored anti-Semitism and repudiated the charge that the Jews were responsible for Christ's death, but indicated that the church regarded Muslims "with esteem."[58] When he met with Israeli President Moshe Katsay in November, he gave him an autographed copy of *Nostra Aetate*, which launched a new era in Catholic-Jewish relations. In a letter to the president of the Commission for Religious Relations with the Jews, on the occasion of the 40th anniversary of *Nostra Aetate,* Benedict invoked continued dialogue and further improvement in Catholic-Jewish relations. He repeated his pledge to continue to see reconciliation to the representatives of the Anti-Defamation League and those of the World Jewish Congress. At the same time he invited Archbishop Christodoulos of Athens, head of the Orthodox Church of Greece, to visit Rome, marking a new stage in their dialogue.[59] Benedict has made closer ties to all the orthodox churches one of the priorities of his papacy.[60] During his visit to Turkey he met with the Ecumenical Patriarch Bartholomew I, the head of the Orthodox community of some three hundred million souls.

He reached out to non-Christians as well. In his birthday message to the retired rabbi of Rome, Elio Toaff, Benedict cited the importance of continuing and extending the Catholic-Jewish dialogue. For one thing, the pope's historic visit to the rebuilt Roonstrasse Synagogue in Cologne during World Youth Day the summer of 2005, was emotionally and symbolically crucial. Although his visit was far more low-key than the trips of his predecessor, it was equally important. On August 19 Pope Benedict XVI addressed 500 Jewish representatives in the synagogue destroyed during Kristallnacht and rebuilt in 1959. The second pope to visit a synagogue, he denounced the Nazi persecution of the Jews as "the darkest period of German and European history."[61] There he reaffirmed his intention of continuing to seek improved relations and friendship with the Jewish people, following the path paved by John Paul II.

He later voiced his concerns about the resurgence of anti-Semitism in Europe and the world to Riccardo Di Segni, the chief rabbi of Rome. In light of the shared Judeo-Christian heritage and mission, Benedict called for joint action to fight the hatred, incomprehension, injustice, and violence that flowed from this bigotry. During the last day of his trip to Poland in May 2006, Pope Benedict visited Auschwitz, following the path of John Paul II who visited the camp in 1979. Walking past the ruins of the gas chambers, he was profoundly and visibly moved by the horrors of the Holocaust, asking why the Lord remained silent and permitted this grave injustice.[62] Supportive of John Paul II's reconciliation with the Jews, some even suggesting he provided some of the inspiration for it, Pope Benedict welcomed the formal invitation to visit Israel. The pope responded that he would love to go and despite his tight schedule, considered it a priority as he prayed for peace in the Holy Land. Benedict believed the media could support the crusade for peace, convinced that the tools of communication could favor reciprocal knowledge and dialogue or could fuel prejudice. During the course of World Media Day, May 8, 2005, he urged the media to tear down the walls of hostility dividing the world's peoples, while respecting their common human dignity.[63]

Under Benedict's auspices, Vatican and Anglican Communion officials resumed the work of the International Anglican-Roman Catholic Commission for Unity and Mission, seeking "a foundation for continued dialogue and ecumenical cooperation."[64] In mid-May 2005, the commission released a statement of agreement on the nature and role of Mary.[65] These negotiations facilitated the conversion of Tony Blair from Anglicanism to Catholicism at the end of 2007—six months after stepping down as Britain's prime minister. Pope Benedict reached out to non-Christians as well, urging the bishops of Sri Lanka to continue to build upon the interreligious and interethnic cooperation that emerged following the destructive tsunamis that struck the region. "I am confident that you will find ways of building further on the fruits of this cooperation," the pope told the bishops, "especially by ensuring that aid is offered freely to all those who are in need."[66] Despite the fact that an Italian missionary priest was murdered in Turkey on February 6, 2006, four days later the pope accepted the invitation of the Turkish government to visit their country in November 2006.

Not all were surprised that Benedict's first encyclical *Deus Caritas Est* (God is Love), issued December 25, 2005, and released in January 2006, struck a positive rather than a negative note, and focused on Christian love and its role in the church and world.[67] In it Benedict announced that the church had no desire to govern or control the state, but added it could not remain silent in political matters because its charity was needed to ease suffering. Continuing to discuss church-state relations, Benedict added that while the state should not impose religion upon its public, it had a responsibility to promote the religious freedom that some earlier popes had condemned. In Benedict's view, the church had to transcend the confines of national communities, broadening its scope and mission to encompass the entire world. Some considered it symbolic that Benedict XVI ordered a new and fifth gate in the centuries-old walls of the Vatican.

Benedict was convinced that cooperation, led to reconciliation, while the recourse to terror led to destruction and division, citing terrorism, nihilism, and fanatic fundamentalism as the most insidious threats to peace.[68] He deemed the terrorism unleashed in London as an attack upon the whole of humanity, and resolutely condemned the suicide bombing in Tel Aviv in mid-April 2006.[69] Following the publication of the caricatures of Mohammed in the European press, Benedict worried about the violence unleashed in Beirut, Damascus, and elsewhere in the Muslim world. He urged the bishops from the four West African countries of Senegal, Mauritania, Guinea-Bissau, and Cape Verde to work with the Muslims for harmony.[70] Unfortunately, the pope did not always follow his own advice.

When he returned to Germany in September 2006, and spoke before his old university, his words ignited a firestorm in the Muslim world. During his September 12 lecture, "Faith, Reason and the University," delivered at the University of Regensburg, he quoted the fourteenth-century Byzantine Emperor Manuel II Paleologus, who reportedly said, "Show me just what

Mohammed brought that was new, and there you will find things only evil and inhuman, such as his command to spread by the sword the faith he preached."[71] Benedict's use of the quote provoked worldwide protests against the pope, the Catholic Church, and Christianity—all accused of being anti-Muslim and Eurocentric. The foreign ministers of the 56-member organization of the Islamic Conference urged Pope Benedict XVI to apologize for his unfortunate linking of Islam and violence.[72] Muslim leaders in Gaza, Iraq, Syria, and Pakistan issued protests, the parliament in Pakistan passed a resolution denouncing the papal statement, while churches were burned in the West Bank. In Basra, in the south of Iraq, the pope was burned in effigy, while in Mosul an orthodox priest was kidnapped and killed for his failure to condemn the pope's comments. In Kashmir protesters called for vengeance against the pope and his church, and extremist elements called for the bombing of the Vatican.

The King of Morocco recalled his ambassador to the Vatican, while Yemen's president denounced the pontiff. In Turkey the deputy leader of the country's governing party perceived the pope's speech as an effort to revive the crusades, and as inflammatory as the rhetoric of Hitler and Mussolini. In Lebanon the top Shiite cleric demanded an apology, while in Somalia a nun was murdered in an apparent act of retaliation. Public protests also erupted in India and Indonesia, while in Cairo Egyptians shouted "down with the pope." In London and New York Muslims joined the chorus demanding an apology for the pope's offensive remarks, while religious leaders in Iran denounced the pope's words and actions.

Surprised by the breadth and vehemence of the protests, Federico Lombardi, speaking on behalf of the Vatican, explained that Benedict meant no disrespect and did not intend to offend Muslim sensibilities. The governor of Vatican City, speaking before the United Nations General Assembly, revealed that the pope was saddened that his use of the quote had been misunderstood, not that he was sorry he said it. These explanations as well as that of the new papal secretary of state, Cardinal Tarcisio Bertone, were deemed apologies by proxy and though necessary were considered insufficient. Finally, the pope himself stated that he was deeply sorry about the reaction to some of his words, adding that the text quoted did not reflect his personal opinion. Benedict personally assured some 22 foreign diplomats and representatives of Italian Muslim organizations that he had a profound respect for Islam.[73]

In fact, a footnote to clarify the pope's intent was belatedly added to the text of his talk. Although not the full and forthright apology demanded by his extreme critics, the more moderate elements accepted it as a step in the right direction.[74] Meanwhile, Benedict responded to a letter signed by 138 Muslim scholars by inviting a group of them to meet with him and the Pontifical Council for Inter-Religious Dialogue to explore means of improving understanding between their two faiths. Furthermore, in a historical and unprecedented encounter, Abdullah, the King of Saudi Arabia, met with the pope in November 2007 and the two exchanged gifts and invoked an improved dialogue between their two faiths. Some saw this historical meeting as the first step in the establishment of diplomatic relations between Saudi Arabia and the Vatican. Papal supporters applauded the pope for mending relations with the Muslim world while critics complained about Benedict's lack of finesse and diplomatic deficiencies.

Some in the church and Curia hoped that in the future the pope would chose his words more carefully and ponder the diplomatic consequences of his discourse rather than giving professorial lectures as he had while a university professor. Stung by the chorus of criticism, Benedict was more careful in drafting his extraordinary apology that reflected his determination to preserve the papacy as supranational force for peace and harmony, serving the universal mission of the church.

This global vision was also reflected in his nomination of 15 new cardinals from 5 continents and 11 countries in February 2006. To be sure, eight of these were Europeans, but the other seven hailed from the United States (2), Latin America (1), Asia (3), and Africa (1).[75] At the end of 2007, in his second consistory, Benedict named another 23 cardinals from throughout the world. The inclusion in the first consistory of Bishop Joseph Zen Ze-kiun of Hong Kong, a key figure in Vatican-Beijing negotiations, was considered indicative of Holy See's desire to open formal diplomatic negotiations with China. There has even been speculation that the Vatican would be willing to switch its diplomatic recognition from Taiwan to China to do so.[76] Benedict did not hide the fact that he would very much like to unite the four million Catholics who attend the state-sponsored churches with those underground Chinese Catholics who have remained loyal to Rome. The ordination of two Chinese bishops in communion with Rome was welcomed by the Vatican, which hoped it would lead to an improvement in their relations with Beijing.

Benedict also sought to further mend relations with the 1.2 billion followers of Islam, the second largest religion in the world, calling for Catholic–Muslim dialogue rather than confrontation. For this among other reasons he did not cancel his visit to Turkey at the end of November 2006, despite the threats made against his life should he venture there, and the loud and long protests of some 20,000 Turks in Istanbul.[77] The pope was not prepared to abandon his first visit to a predominantly Muslim country. Once there he watched his words and actions carefully. He did not attempt to pray at the Hagia Sophia, an Eastern Orthodox Church until the fifteenth century when it was converted into a mosque, as some Turks feared. Instead, he prayed alongside the Grand Mufti in Istanbul's Sultanhamet or Blue Mosque, facing Mecca as Muslims prescribe, undoing some of the damage of his much criticized earlier speech.

This pope was prepared to make political as well as religious concessions and during the course of his trip to Muslim Turkey, Benedict offered an olive branch to the Turks and the Muslim world beyond by altering his stance on the entry of Islamic Turkey into the European Union. As late as 2004, the year before he became pope, Ratzinger had opposed Turkish membership in the Union claiming that a predominantly Muslim country would not fit into a Christian Europe.[78] As part of his fence mending operation, he now supported their entry, a move that was much appreciated in Ankara and a number of Muslim countries and populations. The papal trip was deemed a success by many western observers, some of whom claimed that Benedict started the journey as a theologian but ended it as a diplomat and a man of dialogue.[79] The claims were exaggerated and the assessment premature. To be sure he had learned some lessons in diplomacy, but still lacked the diplomatic agility and universal image of John Paul II. An acknowledged expert in the theological realm of certainty, he remained a relative novice in the shifting sands of politics and diplomacy. Unlike the popes from John XXIII to John Paul II, Benedict was not a public figure. "His problem," reported the Reverend Thomas Reese of the Woodstock Theological Center at Georgetown University, "is that he's a German academician who hasn't realized he's a pope."[80] In fact, while Pope Ratzinger has continued to write and publish and in 2007 two of his works were number one (*Jesus of Nazareth*) and two (*The Apostles*) on the Catholic Best Sellers List outselling *The Catechism of the Catholic Church*, which was number three in September 2007.

Despite Benedict XVI's lack of experience and expertise in diplomacy, he has come to understand the need for papal input in international affairs where he has generally followed the path paved by John Paul II. In his Christmas message of 2006 Benedict followed his predecessor in calling for an end to violence worldwide and warning of the global consequences of the escalating violence in the middle east.[81] The pope personally related his fears to the President of Israel Shimon Peres during the course of their meeting at Castel Gandolfo, the papal summer residence, on September 6, 2007. Benedict welcomed the prospect of an international conference to settle Israeli-Palestinian issues that have troubled the people of the region for more than half a century.[82] This pope has also pointed to the danger of the proliferation of weapons of mass destruction, and especially the prospect of nuclear weapons falling into the hands of terrorists. Like all his predecessors in the post–World War II period, from Pius XII to John Paul II, he has also questioned the option of nuclear deterrence exercised by a number of states.

Opposition to the option of nuclear deterrence has been supported by the Vatican's new nuncio to the United States, Archbishop Pietro Sambi as well as the Vatican's Nuncio to the United Nations, Cardinal Celestino Migliore. The latter called for a re-examination of this deterrence policy on the occasion of the organization's review of the Nuclear Non-Proliferation Treaty signed in 1968 and implemented in 1970. The nuncio explained that the Vatican had accepted deterrence during the Cold War as a necessary evil and transitional phase toward progressive disarmament, but never envisioned it as a permanent solution or feature of international life.[83] Precisely the stance of Pius XII a half century earlier.

Assisted by his secretariat of state, the pope outlined the Vatican's position when he met with President George W. Bush in June 2007, reportedly rejecting the decision by the United States and a number of other nuclear powers to rely on deterrence, which included the possible use of atomic "weapons, as permanent part of their defense mechanism. While the Vatican expressed approval of the American president's stance on abortion and his defense of life, it was less pleased with his interventionist foreign policy, recourse to war, and continued reliance on atomic weapons of mass destruction.[84] Many of these sentiments were repeated in his telegram to Mohamed El Baradei, the 2005 winner of the Nobel Peace Prize, in which the pope expressed his concern "that the peace of the world continues to be at risk from the spread of nuclear weapons."[85] On the nuclear issue and other global problems, Pope Benedict XVI has generally followed his predecessors in outlining the papacy's diplomatic position and ecclesiastical policies—what he will do to implement them remains to be seen.

Conclusion: Continuity and Change in Papal Policy

The Holy See or papacy, also known as the Vatican after the loss of Rome in 1870, has long exercised a dual role in the public perception, with some seeing it as a fulcrum of world politics, while others have stressed its religious mission, proclaiming it "pastor of the world." It remains unlike any other religious institution in the contemporary age, functioning both as a church and an organization exchanging political representation. As head of a global faith it possesses its own website, and another for its leadership of the smallest country in the world. The papal contribution to the church, and world beyond, has been assessed by both those inside and outside its confines. Citing the importance of the pope, Napoleon warned his representative to Rome to treat him as if he had two hundred thousand troops at his disposal! Pope Paul VI wrote that without the pope the Catholic Church would no longer be Catholic, for its unity would totally collapse. On the other hand, this same pope considered the papacy the greatest obstacle in the path of Christian unity. Despite this dichotomy, it is widely recognized that under the nine popes who have occupied the Chair of Peter in the twentieth century, from Leo XIII to John Paul II, the papal voice has been crucial not only in the religious realm but in diplomatic affairs as it adjusted to a "world transformed." Since Pius XII (1939–1958), all popes have been international public figures.

During the Iran hostage crisis the Holy See's pro-nuncio was able to act as an important intermediary between the Americans and Iranians, having had continuous diplomatic relations with this Islamic nation since the 1950s. More recently, Pope Benedict XVI has intervened in the Sudanese crisis, calling upon its government to cease the military campaign against the war-ravaged region of Dafur, insisting that it respect the rights of the country's regions and minorities.[1] He has also interjected the papacy in the Middle East peace process, cautioned against the use of embryos for stem cell research in various countries, and championed social issues, worldwide—deploring the materialism and greed of the age.[2] He was not the first pope to do so. The social critique of liberal capitalism and the need for some sort of corrective and restriction upon unbridled capitalism, has long been part of the papal agenda. A call for social reform was proclaimed by Leo XIII in his *Rerum novarum* of 1891; by Pius XI in his *Quadragesimo anno* of 1931; by John XXIII in *Mater et Magistra* of 1961 and *Pacem in terries* of 1963; by Paul VI in *Populorum progressio* of 1967; and John Paul II's trilogy of social encyclicals, which include *Laborem exercens* of 1981, *Sollicitudo rei socialis* of 1987, and *Centesimus annus* of 1991. Benedict XVI addressed the social issue in 2005 his first encyclical, *Deus caritas est.* Each of these social letters received worldwide publicity, if not universal approbation. Pope Benedict XVI, like his predecessors, has deplored the famine and malnutrition worldwide and denounced the funneling of global resources and wealth to a select few at the expense of many others.[3] The Vatican has been more than a spectator of the social injustice prevailing between nations as well as within the various states. Over the course of the last 13 years the Holy See has sponsored a series of conferences on social issues in a global age including one on "Charity and Justice in the Relations Among Peoples and Nations."[4]

In its campaign against hunger and its other social crusades, the post–Vatican II papacy has been skillful in the use of the media, attracting the attention of a global audience by using the press, radio, television, and film to deliver its message. It has also utilized its website to communicate with both clergy and laity. These technological means of communication have been complemented by the papal use of modern transportation to visit the faithful worldwide. John Paul II's globe-trotting proved helpful in presenting the Holy See's stance and messages as he logged over a million miles and ventured to every continent except Antarctica. In the process this pope helped transform the papacy into an international presence, as attested by the record setting crowds drawn to Rome and the Vatican during and after his pontificate. Some have perceived a contradiction in the contemporary papacy exemplified by John Paul II, who has clung tenaciously to traditional values but utilized modern means to broadcast his message. No one contests that John Paul II did much to further the cult of the papacy. At his death in 2005, the Vatican received over 150 pages of condolence messages and testimonials from political and religious leaders worldwide, as millions flocked to Rome. In Paris, the center of the Enlightenment and perhaps the most secular city in Europe, the esplanade in front of Notre Dame was renamed in his honor.

The papal installation of Benedict XVI on April 25, 2005, brought thousands of dignitaries from over 130 countries to Rome. Representatives from Communist China did not attend, in part to protest the Vatican's relations with Taiwan, but the government dispatched congratulations to the new pope. Those who earlier had predicted the papacy's demise were wrong, as the world witnessed a renaissance rather than the nadir of its power. It was not the first time predictions of its collapse or emasculation failed to materialize. To be sure, Rome was challenged by the march of modernization and secularization, but following the Industrial and French revolutions at the end of the eighteenth century, its role in the modern world expanded. In terms of diplomatic recognition the Vatican proved eminently successful, witnessing the tripling of its formal diplomatic representation during the course of the long pontificate of John Paul II (1978–2005). Promising "to offer its collaboration to safeguard human dignity and the common good," Pope Benedict XVI urged those remaining countries without formal ties to the Vatican to initiate such representation soon.[5] Vatican watchers perceived the visit of King Abdullah to Benedict XVI in 2007 as the preliminary step to the opening of diplomatic relations between the Holy See and Saudi Arabia.

Presently, some 170 countries exchange diplomatic relations with the Holy See, whose influence extends beyond the one billion Catholic faithful, with some heralding the oldest transnational organization second in importance only to the United Nations. Observers note that during the past two centuries, it has assumed a global dimension and impact transcending Europe,[6] whose voice is heard within the industrial world and the third world, in capitalist countries as well as in the remaining Communist ones. While the policy of *Ostpolitik,* which contributed to the collapse of communism in Eastern Europe and the Soviet Union, was initiated by the Vatican, sometimes the collaboration between the higher clergy and governments has occurred without the Holy See's sanction and provoked its opposition. Thus the collaboration between the Communist Secret Police in Poland and the Reverend Stanislaw Wielgus, which Rome did not approve, led to the resignation of this archbishop of Warsaw following the disclosure.[7]

Assessments of the Vatican's relations with the outside world vary, as do those exploring its response to modernization.[8] At times its religious and diplomatic roles have been seen to clash. For example some believe that Pius XII's diplomatic silence during the Nazi genocide during World

War II was pursued at the expense of the papacy's moral mission charging that political expediency triumphed over ethical responsibility. At other times the religious and diplomatic roles of the papacy have been seen to reinforce one another as in the fall of 2000, when the Vatican canonized 120 Christians killed in China from 1648 to 1930. Some contend that these canonizations aimed in part to provide inspiration for the persecuted church and clergy there, and thus had political overtones for the Chinese Communists, who denounced them as an insulting reminder of colonial imperialism.

Since the Communist takeover of China in 1949, Chinese Catholics have been constrained to join the Chinese Patriotic Catholic Association (CPCA) or state-controlled church, which includes some four million members. It is estimated that twice that number are members of the secret underground church, loyal to the Vatican, arousing the suspicion of the Beijing government. Tensions between Beijing and Rome erupted in 2006 when the CPCA ordained two new bishops without Vatican consent—provoking their subsequent excommunication by Rome. This escalation of tension and conflict rendered problematic the détente that Rome sought with China, despite the opening of a renovated Catholic cathedral in South China. The prospect of the Vatican breaking relations with Taiwan and formally opening them with Communist China has been postponed, if not eliminated. The Vatican's relations with Vietnam have been even more strained.

Despite the setbacks in its relations with mainland China and Vietnam, the Vatican has become increasingly international in its outlook, relations and policies, sponsoring conferences on such international issues as global warming. During the course of the twentieth century it was propelled out of its "first world ghetto" to reach the world beyond and the "Bishop of Rome" was transformed into the "Pastor of the World." Today the four countries with the largest Catholic populations include: Brazil (149,329,000); Mexico (92,220,269); the United States (67,259,768); and the Philippines (65,063,000). Not one European country is included among these top four.[9] At the opening of 2006, Catholics constituted 17.2 percent of the total global population, with Africa and Asia showing the greatest growth.[10] Furthermore, since Vatican II the papacy has had an ambitious agenda and increasingly emerged as an international institution with global concerns and problems.

Among these problems one might cite a shortage of priests, a questioning of papal policies and practices among young Catholics in the West, the issue of centralization versus local control, and the call by some for Rome to share greater authority with the bishops.[11] In Africa, Catholic bishops have invoked a structure that would enable them to speak and act as a unit and have a greater voice in church affairs.[12] In Latin America the proliferation of Pentecostal churches has posed a threat to a Catholic community confronting a severe shortage of clergy. Although priestly celibacy is a disciplinary norm and not a church dogma, and therefore subject to change, the papacy to date has refused to alter its insistence on its continuation. This, among other considerations, has precipitated the steep decline of vocations in the West and has led the church to increasingly look to the non-European, third world, to recruit its priests—reversing the trend that prevailed in the age of imperialism from 1870 to 1914. In the half decade between 1999 and 2004, priests from North America and Europe declined respectively by 5 percent and 6 percent. This has created consternation in some Catholic circles and had led the Dominicans in the Netherlands to propose that lay people be allowed to celebrate mass when no ordained priests are available, a suggestion rejected and denounced by the Vatican.[13] Other less radical proposals have been approved, In the United States, for example, many dioceses have created parish councils whose lay members are selected to administer church programs, relieving the clergy of many nonecclesiastical responsibilities.

During these same years Asia's priesthood increased by 13 percent and Africa's by 18 percent.[14] In light of these changed demographics, some have questioned whether the same principles should, or indeed could, be applied to widely divergent populations such as those of the modern consumer societies of Western Europe, the United States, Japan, and the societies of underdeveloped reaches of Africa, Latin America, and Asia. Presently, the church in Africa, Latin America and other developing lands account for two-thirds of the world's Roman Catholics with Latin America alone accounting for 43 percent of the Catholic population and Europe only 25 percent. This European decline has been reflected to some extent in the College of Cardinals. Thus Europe, which in 1903 accounted for 98 percent of the College of Cardinals, by 2005 had been reduced to 25 percent.[15]

Numerous changes in the church and among its clergy flowed from the increased globalization witnessed in the twentieth century. It affected the actions of Benedict XV (1914–1922), who intervened to propose a negotiated peace during the course of the First World War. The Vatican's global diplomatic outreach was continued by Pius XII (1939–1958), who actively recruited non-Italians to the curia, and continued by his successors, John XXIII (1958–1963) and Paul VI (1963–1978), contributing to the election of John Paul II (1978–2005), the first non-Italian pope in centuries. In 2005 he was followed by Benedict XVI, another non-Italian. Following the unsuccessful attempts of the papacy to prevent the outbreak of the two world wars, and its exclusion from the League of Nations, its importance was belatedly reflected in the observer status it was granted to UNESCO in 1951, and Permanent Observer status in the United Nations as the Holy See in 1957.

All six postwar popes from Pius XII to Benedict XVI have opposed the death penalty while favoring the efforts of the United Nations to avert war, just as Benedict XV and Pius XI supported the League of Nations. During the course of his 1995 visit to the United Nations, John Paul II reaffirmed his support for this transnational organization. In turn, Pope Benedict XVI has urged the nations of the world to fulfill the programs and initiatives of the United Nations on behalf of the poor, sick, and hungry.[16] Applauding the international relief efforts of the United Nations, its contributions have been supplemented by Caritas Internationalis, the Vatican's own confederation of Catholic relief and development agencies. Pope Benedict has also championed a global and cooperative approach to ecology and conservation, praising the work of the United Nations in the endeavor. Not surprisingly, the campaign of a small minority to terminate the Vatican's Permanent Observer Status in the United Nations has found neither sympathy nor support among the 180 members.

The papacy and the United Nations not only share similar humanitarian and pacific goals, but have confronted similar problems. Like the United Nations, the papacy has been plagued by financial problems, for its charitable efforts and other expenses have continuously exceeded its income.[17] Despite a deficit of $20.2 million, which jumped to $28 million in 1980, and escalated to some $460 million by 1987,[18] the papacy did not curtail its voice, activities, or travel. Gradually the papacy's fiscal situation improved, and despite the extraordinary expenses entailed in the funeral services for John Paul II and the election and installation of Benedict XVI, the Vatican closed the 2005 budget with a surplus of more than twelve million dollars.[19] This surplus at the end of 2006 declined to 3.2 million.[20] To make matters worse, the Vatican's financial stability and viability has been potentially threatened by the decision of a United States Federal Court that ruled that the Holy See could be held liable for damages inflicted by abusive clergy in the United States.[21] The decision has been appealed and to date has not curtailed the papacy's international charitable efforts nor papal participation in world affairs.

Among other things the Vatican assumed a key role during the Cold War and its aftermath. In 1988, Cardinal Agostino Casaroli had a long meeting with Mikhail Gorbachev, transmitting a three page letter from the pope. Papal intervention has been seen as crucial in the collapse of Communism in Eastern Europe, and contributed to its collapse in the Soviet Union.

Perhaps this is why Communist China has remained wary of improved relations with the papacy, which it has perceived as Eurocentric. Generally allied with the West during the course of the Cold War, the Vatican has not seconded every aspect of Western and American policy and has frequently decried the increasing secularization of the western world. It was distressed by the actions of the Spanish government in 2006 that ended the state subsidy of the church, restricted religious education in the schools, and legalized gay marriages in this former Catholic stronghold.[22] It found some comfort the summer of 2007 when the statue of Christ the Redeemer in Rio de Janeiro, was named one of the seven modern day wonders of the world by the vote of over one hundred million on-line voters. Skeptics in the Vatican wondered if this vote reflected piety or simply artistic merit and national pride.

While the modern papacy has railed against communism, at the same time it has invoked social justice and condemned the glaring inequalities fostered by the capitalistic system. Indeed, it has been in the forefront of those insisting on the moral urgency of debt relief for under developed areas, most of which are in Africa, indirectly criticizing the parsimony of the Group of Seven developed countries (United States, Japan, Great Britain, France, Germany, Italy, and Canada) and their financial leaders. Insisting that fundamental ethical principles must be reflected in international relations, the Vatican has renewed its calls for a reduction or outright cancellation of the enormous debt burdens on poor countries, liberating them from the financial burdens that hinder their development and keep their populations in squalor and poverty. It also disagreed with some of the west's and Washington's political and military decisions. Favoring the American intervention in the Balkans, it had reservations about its position toward Haiti and the government of Reverend Jean Bertrand Aristide, who was elected in December of 1990, and overthrown by the military in September 1991. Notwithstanding the anti-papal rhetoric of the ousted Aristide, the Vatican promised not to oppose his peaceful return to the Haitian presidency, despite its disinclination of having clerics serve in secular offices.[23]

Washington and Rome also diverged on how to respond to Iraq's movement into Kuwait, with the pope favoring the convocation of a conference and the United States pushing for a military confrontation, which John Paul II believed would represent a decline for the whole of humanity and might trigger a broader regional conflict. The papal stance reflected its consistent anti-war position.[24] These doubts about the efficacy of war were expressed in the *Civiltà Cattolica* and the *L'Osservatore Romano*, which openly criticized the American led war. Only at its conclusion, when the United States and the Soviet Union cosponsored the Madrid Middle East Peace

Initiative, were relations improved between Rome and Washington.[25] The Vatican under both John Paul II and Benedict XVI has also questioned the continuing need, validity, and results of the American deterrence policy.[26] In fact, the Vatican envoy later dispatched to Washington to discourage the second Bush administration from acting unilaterally against Iraq asserted that a war against Iraq without United Nations approval would be "immoral," "illegal," and "unjust."[27] Following the invasion and the occupation of Iraq the Vatican complained that Iraqi Christians were safer under Saddam than the present regime.[28]

The bishops of Australia have followed the lead of the Holy See and likewise concluded that the war in Iraq was not justified. Indeed, as the threat of war was launched against Iran for its alleged determination to possess atomic weapons, the Australian bishops went beyond Benedict and warned their government not to participate in another preemptive strike alongside the United States, doubting that the doctrine of preemption was consistent with the Catholic teaching on a just war.[29] The summer of 2006, when the United States backed the Israeli invasion of Lebanon, Pope Benedict described the incursion as unfortunate and counterproductive.[30] The differences between Washington and Rome were clearly evident during the course of President Bush's June 2007 visit to the Vatican.

The papacy has been distressed by events elsewhere including Africa, Asia, and the Middle East. During his pontificate John Paul II appealed to the Burundi government to permit displaced persons to return to their homes, while invoking religious toleration in places like the Sudan, Ethiopia, and Algeria. At the same time, he has pleaded for greater religious liberty and especially religious freedom for the Cubans. Addressing Christians, Muslims, and Jews, John Paul II denounced violence in the name of religion as nothing less than an offense against God. During the course of the papal visit to the Holy Land in the spring of 2000, this pope used his moral authority not only to seek interfaith reconciliation but to promote the quest for peace in the region. More recently, the Vatican Secretariat of State has intervened on behalf of Iranian Jews arrested for spying and has pleaded with authorities in the United States to commute the death sentences of prisoners.[31] In fact, the pro-life Vatican has opposed Washington's positions on the death penalty, contraception, and abortion. There are those who believe that the conservative course charted by John Paul II influenced American bishops and played a part in the American presidential election of 2004.[32]

In its participation in international conferences as well as its messages to the various national states, the Vatican has invoked social justice while denouncing the "culture of death" it has associated with birth control, abortion, the application of the death penalty, and the recourse to war to resolve differences. It has consistently called for the ban of destructive weapons such as cluster bombs and atomic weapons. During the 1994 Cairo Conference, the Vatican found itself in accord with conservative Muslims in opposing the United Nations plan to slow population growth by contraceptive means. Vatican diplomacy shifted the conference's focus from controlling population through birth control, to an emphasis on increasing education, job opportunities, and full civil rights for women, criticizing the globalization driven by profit. Some believe that the strong position and moral dimension assumed by the papacy at the conference, marked a turning point in the role of religious groups in such international gatherings. "The Vatican has been a consistent voice for the poor and a critic of a callous capitalistic economic system," reported the Lutheran Minister James B. Martub-Schramm, who nonetheless disagreed with its position on women's issues.[33] In a shrewd, new tack in international diplomacy, the Vatican for the first time selected a woman to head its delegation to a major world conference, the Fourth World Conference on Women held in Beijing in 1995.[34] Convinced of the impact and importance of religion in world affairs, John Paul II's broad conception of papal authority has led to one of the most active pontificates in papal history.

John XXIII and Paul VI set the stage for this new papal internationalism, which was in part implemented by the Second Vatican Council (1962–1965) and the work of the commissions that followed. The Council launched a series of changes that brought the church into a closer relationship with the modern world, prompting the Vatican to adjust to the industrial world and even the postindustrial age by modernizing its use of the media, while preserving its mission and message. After Vatican II, the papacy continued to adhere to aspects of John's *aggiornamento* or updating of the church and its reconciliation with the contemporary world. Some believed it provided the groundwork for a reappraisal of Catholicism, even though a minority in the church found its innovations disruptive. Despite this minority opposition, all the popes who followed the closing of the council have adhered to its mandates. "I will make every effort and dedicate myself to pursuing the promising dialogue that my predecessors began with various civilizations," Pope Benedict XVI proclaimed in his homily at the first mass for the College of Cardinals, adding "it is mutual understanding that gives rise to conditions for a better future for everyone."[35]

John Paul II, the first pope to visit a Synagogue (1986), furthered the papacy's reconciliation with the Jews. At the end of 1993 a "Fundamental Agreement Between the Holy See and the State of Israel" was signed and went into effect in March of 1994. This was followed by a "Basic Agreement

Between the Holy See and Palestine Liberation Organization" at the opening of the new millennium. In 2003 the Simon Wiesenthal Center presented its 2003 Humanitarian Award to John Paul II, for his lifelong friendship with the Jewish people and his promotion of Jewish-Catholic harmony.[36] The following year the chief Rabbis of Israel made their first ever visit to the Vatican as the papacy continued to promote reconciliation with Judaism. John Paul's successor Benedict XVI has continued along this course and has often stressed the importance of the Old Testament to improve the dialogue with Jews and assure them that biblical texts will not be used to foster anti-Judaism.[37]

John Paul II was also the first pope (1989), to meet a leader of the Soviet Union (Mikhail Gorbachev), continuing John XXIII's and Paul VI's policy of a dialogue with the regimes of Eastern Europe that was instrumental in bringing them out of the Communist orbit and into a closer relationship with Western Europe. Like all the postwar popes, he and his successor have supported a united, Christian Europe.[38] In a series of speeches Pope Benedict XVI has backed the expansion of the European Union, embracing its mission of transcending narrow nationalism, bridging economic and ideological divisions, and increasing cooperation among the former competing states of the continent.

The papacy has also sought an accommodation with science, technology, and reason, which has defined the contemporary age. In doing so, John Paul II referred his listeners to his 1998 encyclical *Fides et Ratio* (Faith and Reason), which stressed that philosophy and theology, reason and faith, have a natural rapport and cannot be separated, returning to the Thomistic notion that reason and scientific inquiry help rather than hinder faith, a stance strongly supported by his successor. At the end of 1999, as the notion of Intelligent Design circulated, John Paul II revealed that the papacy accepted evolution as a solidly researched theory, finding no essential conflict between Darwinism and Catholicism. Acknowledging past errors, as the millennium came to a close, John Paul II asked forgiveness for past infractions. In apologizing for these historical transgressions committed by Catholics in the name of the church, this pope went beyond all of his predecessors in seeking forgiveness. Benedict XVI's Vatican has also found evolution to be compatible with Catholicism.[39]

While some focused on the papacy's reconciliation with modernization and the present world, others have concentrated on the conflict between the two and the resistance of the Vatican to many current developments and the moral values of the modern generation. Liberal Catholics complained of papal support for the Legion of Christ (founded in Mexico in 1941), a conservative international religious order that operates outside the traditional church structure, and Opus Dei, another group of ultraconservative Catholics. Meanwhile, Leonardo Boff, one of the founders of Liberation Theology, was silenced. More recently the Vatican has criticized the scholarship of Jesuit Father Jon Sabrino, a leading proponent of liberation theology. In response, Father Sobrino has charged that curial officials were "trying to put an end to liberation theology."[40] Earlier, Father Charles Curran who had challenged a number of the Vatican's pronouncements was notified he could no longer teach Catholic theology and suspended from his position at the Catholic University of America. The support of his ouster by the hierarchy led critics to grumble that John Paul II appointed conservative and docile bishops.[41]

Some had hoped that under papal leadership there would be a relaxation of church policy on contraception, sexuality, celibacy of the clergy, and female ordination. This did not occur as Pope Paul VI, followed by John Paul II, confirmed the traditional teaching on these issues, stemming the tide of innovation. Benedict XVI to date has done likewise.

Furthermore, John Paul II's encyclical of 1990, *Redemptoris Missio,* appeared to denounce the notion that one religion was as good as another.[42] This was reinforced by the Congregation for the Doctrine of the Faith, which under Cardinal Ratzinger had issued traditional position papers on papal primacy, women's ordination, Catholic higher education, and the limits placed on dissent, and in *Dominus Iesus* seemed to reject the notion that the church is only one path to salvation alongside those constituted by other religions. Its assertion that Jesus Christ represented the only path to salvation represented a setback for prior efforts towards ecumenism. Papal efforts to achieve Christian unity have confronted numerous obstacles, some of its own making.[43]

A number of papal pronouncements have angered Asian and European religious leaders, while temporarily impeding Jewish-Christian Dialogue.[44] In Italy, the disquiet created by the Vatican's messages was compounded by the stance of Cardinal Giacomo Biffi of Bologna, who indiscreetly suggested that Italy favor Roman Catholic immigrants over Muslims to protect its identity. Furthermore, liberals in the western church have decried the fact that Rome has increased its control over the more than 100 bishop conferences worldwide and expressed concern over Benedict XVI's widespread restoration of the Tridentine or Latin Mass. While some have applauded this restoration as a response to the yearning and reverence for the ancient rite, critics have seen it as a step in the erosion of the reforms of Vatican II. Paradoxically, the return of the Latin Mass, which has alarmed some liberals, has not satisfied the excommunicated members of the Society of St. Pius X, founded by the late Archbishop Marcel Lefebvre. This

Swiss-based society, which has long led the campaign against the Mass liturgy of Vatican II, has rejected other teachings of the council including its call for interreligious dialogue, ecumenism and religious liberty. Thus, while the society has welcomed the return to liturgical tradition, it has insisted that this is only the first step necessary for an eventual reconciliation with Rome.[45]

The dissent on the legacy of the Second Vatican Council has continued unabated with some perceiving it as providing the groundwork for a reappraisal and reorganization of Catholicism, with others complaining it has allowed Satan into the temple. This division was apparent in the beatification (the last step prior to canonization) of the conservative Pius IX (1846–1878), who condemned the modern world (Syllabus of Errors) and the liberal John XXIII (1958–1963), who sought reconciliation with it (aggiornamento) in September 2000. The beatification of these very different popes was widely interpreted as an attempt to satisfy these divergent groups within the church. Considerable controversy has also surrounded the projected beatification of Pope Pius XII who has been criticized by some for his silence during the Holocaust and praised by others for his saintly persona, his crusade of charity, and diplomatic measures that spared both Catholics and Jews further pain and suffering.

The projected beatification of Pius XII, following that of Pius IX and John XXIII, brought to the surface the division between conservatives and liberals in the church. In an attempt to conciliate the conflict, John Paul II noted that "Beatifying a son of the church does not celebrate particular historic choices that he has made," adding "but rather points him out for imitation and for veneration for his virtue, praising the divine grace that shines in him."[46] These words did not end either the controversy or the divisions within the church. In fact, some have questioned the role of the papacy in the contemporary age with progressives pushing for decentralization in decision making and traditionalists insisting on the preservation of the primacy of Rome. The debate continues.

Notes

CHAPTER 1

1. Cindy Wooden, "Two Americans Among the 23 New Cardinals," *The Tablet* (Brooklyn), October 27, 2007, p. 3.

2. Francesca Coppa, "Joan or Joanna, Alleged Pope," in *Encyclopedia of the Vatican and Papacy,* ed. Frank J. Coppa (Westport, CT: Greenwood Press, 1999), pp. 230–31.

3. Interest in the papacy and the popes had led to the compilation of a series of general studies including P. G. Maxwell-Stuart, *Chronicles of the Popes: The Reign by Reign Record of the Papacy From Saint Peter to the Present* (London: Thames and Hudson, 1997); Frank J. Coppa (ed.), *Encyclopedia of the Vatican and the Papacy* (1999) and his later 2 volume edited work, *The Great Popes Through History* (2002); Richard P. McBrien, *Lives of the Popes* (1999); Eamon Duffy, *Saint and Sinners: A History of the Popes* (1997); and William J. La Due, *The Chair of Saint Peter: A History of the Papacy* (Maryknoll, N.Y. Orbis Books, 1999), among others.

4. For a detailed description of espionage activity at the Vatican (1815–1945), see David Alvarez, *Spies in the Vatican: Espionage and Intrigue from Napoleon to the Holocaust* (Lawrence: University Press of Kansas, 2002).

5. "Pope: Put an End to War," *The Tablet* (Brooklyn), July 28, 2007, p. 2.

6. "The Legacy of the Knights Templar," *US News & World Report,* October 22, 2007, p. 28.

7. "Pope: Church Was Wrong on Galileo," *New York Newsday,* November 1, 1992, p. 67.

8. John Thavis, "Benedict Reverses Rule for Electing a Pope," *The Tablet* (Brooklyn), June 30, 2007, p. 10.

9. Avro Manhattan, *The Vatican in World Politics* (New York: Gaer Associates, 1949), p. 14.

10. *Bullarii Romani Continuatio* (Rome: 1835–1855), XV, pp. 446–48.

11. The Syllabus of Errors, December 8, 1864," in G. A. Kertesz, in *Documents in the Political History of the European Continent, 1815–1939* (Oxford: Clarendon Press, 1968), p. 241.

12. These concordats are discussed in Frank J. Coppa, ed., *Controversial Concordats: The Vatican's Relations with Napoleon, Mussolini, and Hitler* (Washington, DC: Catholic University of America Press, 1999).

13. Jerry Filteau, "Paul VI Directed Council and its Implementation," *The Tablet* (Brooklyn), October 29, 2005, p. 10.

14. Anthony Grafton, "Reading Ratzinger: Benedict XVI, the Theologian," *The New Yorker,* July 25, 2005, p. 47.

15. In this regard, see Bernard J. O'Connor, *Papal Diplomacy: John Paul II and the Culture of Peace* (South Bend, Ind.: St Augustine's Press, 2005) and Chester Gillis, ed., *The Political Papacy: John Paul II, Benedict XVI and their Influence* (Boulder, Colo.: Paradigm Press, 2006).

16. "Ten Driving Commandments," or "Guidelines for the Pastoral Care of the Road," issued by the Pontifical Council for Migrants and Travelers (2007).

17. "Israel President asks Pope to be More Vocal on Terrorism," *The Tablet* (Brooklyn), November 19, 2005, p. 6.

18. For a dated though balanced assessment, see Eric O. Hanson, *The Catholic Church in World Politics* (Princeton, NJ: Princeton University Press, 1987).

19. In this regard, see: José M. Sànchez, *Pius XII and the Holocaust: Understanding the Controversy* (Washington, DC: Catholic University of America Press, 2002) and Joseph Bottum and David G. Dalin, eds., *The Pius Wars: Responses to the Critics of Pius XII* (Lanham, MD: Lexington Books, 2004).

20. For an overview of papal diplomacy over the years, see: Robert A. Graham, *Vatican Diplomacy* (Princeton, NJ: Princeton University Press, 1959) and Vincent Viaene, ed., *The Papacy and the New World Order* (Brussels: Belgian Historical Institute of Rome, 2005).

21. "Pope Hopes for More Diplomatic Ties with Vatican," *The Tablet* (Brooklyn), May 21, 2005, p. 6.

22. "Muslims Attend Course on Diplomacy at the Vatican," *The Tablet* (Brooklyn), May 12, 2007, p. 9.

23. "Vatican Considers UN Membership," *Conscience,* vol. XXIV, n. 3, Autumn, 2003, p. 9.

CHAPTER 2

1. *Magnum Bullarium Romanum Continuatio* (Graz, Austria, 1964), IX, pp. 11–19; Anne Fremantle ed., *The Papal Encyclicals in their Historical Context* (New York: G.P. Putnam's Sons, 1956), p. 117; Owen Chadwick, *A History of the Popes, 1830–1914* (Oxford: Clarendon Press, 1998), p. 448.

2. Robert B. Holtman, *The Napoleonic Revolution* (New York: Lippincott, 1967), p. 121.

3. See his first encyclical letter *Diu Satis* of May 15, 1800 in *The Papal Encyclicals 1740–1878,* ed. Claudia Carlen (Ann Arbor MI: Pierian Press, 1981), I, pp. 189–93.

4. "Convention between French Government and Pius VII," in *The Encyclopedia of Religion & Ethics,* ed. J. Hastings (New York: Scribner, 1911), III, pp. 191–93.

5. These 77 articles, under 4 headings, were approved by the French legislature on April 8, 1802, at the same time it approved the concordat.

6. Cardinals Pacca and Gabrielli discuss the details of the papal visit to Paris and participation in the coronation of Napoleon in their correspondence found in the *Archivio Segreto Vaticano, Archivio Particolare Pio IX, oggetti vari,* n. 909, fascicolo 3.

7. On the exclusion from Rome of the English and other enemies of France requested by Napoleon, *ASV, Archivio Particolare Pio IX, oggetti vari,* n. 909, fascicolo 6.

8. Project for a political treaty between the Emperor Napoleon and the Holy See, *ASV, Archivio Particolare Pio IX, oggetti vari,* n. 909, fascicoli 4 and 5.

9. Napoleonic decree of April 2, 1808, *ASV, Archivio Particolare Pio IX, oggetti vari,* n. 909, fascicolo 1.

10. *ASV, Archivio Particolare Pio IX, oggetti vari,* n. 909, fascicoli 8 and 11.

11. *ASV, Archivio Particolare Pio IX, oggetti vari,* n. 909, fascicolo 16.

12. Consalvi to Cardinal Spina, *ASV, Archivio de Propaganda Fede, fondo Consalvi,* busta 34.

13. Joseph H. Brady, *Rome and the Neapolitan Revolution of 1820–1821: A Study in Papal Neutrality* (New York: Octagon Books, 1976), p. 15.

14. Alan J. Reinerman, "Metternich and the Papal Condemnation of the Carbonari," *Catholic Historical Review,* vol. LIV, n. 1, (1968), p. 56.

15. Claudia Carlen, ed., *Papal Pronouncements. A Guide: 1740–1978* (Ann Arbor, MI: Pierian Press, 1990), I, p. 21.

16. Giovanni Maria Mastai-Ferretti's Funeral Oration for Leo XII at Spoleto, February 21, 1829, *ASV, Fondo Particolare Pio IX,* cassetta 9, fascicolo 46.

17. Fiorella Bartocinni, *Roma nel Ottocento* (Bologna, It.: Cappelli Editore, 1985), p. 26.

18. Antonio Monti, *Pio IX nel Risorgimento Italiano con documenti inediti* (Bari, It.: Laterza, 1928), p. 38.

19. "Bernetti to Spinola, March 30, 1831," *ASV, Segretaria di Stato Esteri,* Rubrica 247.

20. Alan J. Reinerman, *Austria and the Papacy in the Age of Metternich: Revolution and Reaction 1830–1838* (Washington, D.C.: Catholic University of America Press, 1989), II, 47.

21. "Catechismo sulle rivoluzioni (1832)," *ASV, Fondo Particolare Pio IX,* cassetta 5, busta 4.

22. "Cum Primum (To the Bishops of Poland: On Civil Obedience)," June 9, 1832, in *Papal Pronouncements,* I, p. 25.

23. *Magnum Bullarium Romanum Continuatio,* Gregory XVI, XIX, pp. 117–19.

24. M. Patricia Dougherty, "The Rise and Fall of *L'Ami de la Réligion:* History, Purpose, and Readership of a French Catholic Newspaper," *The Catholic Historical Review,* LXXXVII, 2 (January 1991), p. 31.

25. "Mirar vos," August 15, 1832 in *Acta Sanctae Sedis* (Rome, 1865–1908), III, pp. 336–45.

26. Carlen, *The Papal Encyclicals,* I, pp. 235–38.

27. Carlen, *Papal Pronouncements,* I, p. 26.

28. "Singolari nos," June 25, 1834, in *Papal Pronouncements,* I, p. 26.

29. "In Supremo Apostolatus," December 3, 1839, in *Papal Pronouncements,* I, p. 27.

30. "Afflictas in Tunquino," April 27, 1840, in *Papal Pronouncements,* I, p. 27.

31. "Probe Nostis," September 18, 1840, in *Papal Pronouncements,* I, p. 28.

32. Giacomo Antonelli to Filippo Antonelli, September 7, 1837, *Archivio di Stato di Roma, Fondo Famiglia Antonelli,* busta 1, fascicolo 15.

33. Klemens von Metternich, *Mémoires, documents et écrits divers laissés par le Prince de Metternich,* ed. M. A. Klinkowstroem (Paris: Plon, 1883), VII, p. 246; Great Britain, *British and Foreign State Papers,* XXXVI (1847–1848), p. 1195.

34. Giovanni Maioli, ed., *Pio IX da Vescovo a Pontifice. Lettere al Card Luigi Amat, Agosto 1839–Luglio 1848* (Modena, It.: Società Tipografico Modenese, 1943), pp. 16, 46.

35. Giovanni Maria Mastai-Ferretti, "Pensieri relative alla Amministrazione pubblica dello Stato Pontificio," in Alberto Serafini, *Pio IX, Giovanni Maria Mastai-Ferretti dalla giovinezza alla morte nei suoi scritti e discorsi editi e inediti* (Città del Vaticano, It.: Tipografia Poliglotta Vaticano, 1958), I, pp. 1397–1406.

36. "Pubbliche beneficenze dispensate della Santità di Nostro Signore alla occasione di sua solenne coronazione," in *Atti del Sommo Pontefice Pio IX Felicemente Regnante. Parte seconda* (Rome: Tipografia delle Belle Arti, 1857), I, pp. 3–4.

37. Report on Central Italy, *ASV, Archivio Particolare Pio IX, oggetti vari,* n. 412.

38. Breve racconto degli avvenimenti succcessi in Roma dall' esaltazione al trono del gliorioso Pontefice Papa Pio IX fino all' epoca in cui ebbe luogo l' intervento delle quattro potenze cattoliche: Austria, Francia, Spagna, Napoli, fatto da un suddito Pontifice Romano, *ASV, Archivio Particolare Pio IX, oggetti vari,* n. 515.

39. Report of Monsignor Corboli-Bussi to Pius IX on the first session of the congregation of state, July 1, 1846, *ASV, Archivio Particolare Pio IX, Stato Pontificio,* n. 1.

40. "Amnistia accordata dalla Santità di Nostro Signore nella Sua esaltazioin al pontificato," July 16, 1846, in *Atti del Sommo Pontefice Pio IX,* I, pp. 4–6.

41. *Proceedings of the Public Demonstration of Sympathy with Pope Pius IX and with Italy, in the City of New York, on Monday, November 29, A.D. 1847* (New York: William van Norden, 1847), pp. 13–14.

42. Frank J. Coppa, "Italy, the Papal States, and the American Civil War," in *La Parola del Popolo, November–December 1976,* p. 364; *Consular Relations between the United States and the Papal States,* ed. Leo F. Stock (Washington, DC: Catholic University of America Press, 1945), pp. 92, 114.

43. *British and Foreign State Papers,* XXXVI (1847–1848), p. 1195.

44. Metternich's report on Central Italy, *ASV, Archivio Particolare Pio IX, oggetti vari,* n. 412; Metternich, *Mémoires,* VII, p. 255.

45. Marco Minghetti, *Miei Ricordi* (Turin. It.: Roux, 1888), I, p. 214.

46. Giacomo Martina, *Pio IX (1846–1850)* (Rome: Università Gregoriana Editrice, 1974), pp. 109–10.

47. *Atti del Sommo Pontefice Pio IX,* I, pp. 47–48; 52–54.

48. Romolo Quazza, *Pio IX e Massimo D'Azeglio nelle vicende romane del 1847* (Modena, It.: Società Tipografica Modenese, 1954), I, p. 168; II, p. 5.

49. Metternich, *Mémoires,* VII, p. 572.

50. Pius IX to Cardinal Fieschi, February 26, 1848, *ASV, Archivio Particolare Pio IX, Stato Pontifico,* n. 6.

51. *British and Foreign State Papers,* XXXVII (1848–1849), p. 918.

52. *British and Foreign State Papers,* XXXVII (1848–1849), p. 1065.

53. "Breve racconto degli avvenimenti successi in Roma," *ASV, Archivio Particolare Pio IX, oggetti vari,* n. 515.

54. Pius IX to Monsignor Corboli-Bussi, December 28, 1848, *ASV, Archivio Particolare Pio IX, Stato Pontifico.*

55. "Allontanamento temporaneo del S. Padre dai suoi stati, protesta per le violenze usate e creazione di una commissione governativa," *Atti del Sommo Pontefice Pio IX,* I, p. 252.

56. *ASV, Archivio Particolare Pio IX, oggetti vari,* n. 515.

57. "Protesta fatta in Gaeta da Sua Santità Pio PP. IX," *Atti del Sommo Pontefice Pio IX,* I, pp. 262–63.

CHAPTER 3

1. Pius to Archbishop Dupont of Bourges, June 10, 1849, *ASV, Archivio Particolare Pio IX, Francia, Particolari,* n. 48.

2. French Memorandum on Reforms the pope should concede to his subjects, July 30, 1849, *ASV, Archivio Particolare Pio IX, Francia, Sovrani,* n. 24.

3. Pius IX to his Subjects, July 17, 1849, *Atti del Sommo Pontefice Pio IX,* I, pp. 269–70.

4. Consul General in Marseille to Apostolic Nuncio in Paris, September 9, 1849, *ASV, Archivio Nunziatura Parigi,* 1849, busta 4, n. 77.

5. Apostolic Nuncio in Vienna to Antonelli, August 26, 1849, *ASV, Archivio Particolare Pio IX, Segreteria di Stato,* 1849, *Rubrica* 242.

6. Victor Emmanuel to Pius IX, February 7, 1860, *ASV, Archivio Particolare Pio IX, Sovrani, Sardegna,* n. 57.

7. Allocution of March 18, 1861, *Acta Sancta Sedis,* VI, pp. 175–76.

8. *Discorsi parlamentari di Camillo Benso di Cavour,* ed. A. Omodeo and Luigi Russo (Florence: Ente Nazionale di Cultura, 1932), XI, p. 337.

9. "Allocuzione di N.S. Papa Pio IX nel concistorio segreto del 18 Marzo 1861," *Civiltà Cattolica* (1861), series 4, X, pp. 5–12.

10. *United States Ministers to the Papal States: Instructions and Despatches, 1848–1868,* ed. Leo Francis Stock (Washington, DC: Catholic University Press, 1933), I, p. 248.

11. Ibid., I, p. 236.

12. *Consular Relations between the United States and the Papal States: Instructions and Despatches,* ed. Leo Francis Stock (Washington, DC: Catholic University Press, 1945), II, p. 226.

13. *The Memoirs of Dr. Thomas W. Evans: Recollections of the Second French Empire,* ed. Edward A. Crane (London: Fisher Unwin, 1905), I, p. 145.

14. Noel Blakiston, ed., *The Roman Question: Extracts from the Despatches of Odo Russell from Rome, 1858–1870* (London: Chapman and Hall, 1962), p. 185.

15. *United States Ministers to the Papal States,* I, p. 255.

16. Blakiston, p. 244.

17. Robert L. Rogers, *"Jeff" Davis and the Pope: A Sketch of Confederate History* (Aurora, Mo.: Parker Publishing Co., 1925), p. 77.

18. Ibid., p. 83.

19. Ibid., p. 87.

20. *United States Ministers to the Papal States,* I, p. 288.

21. "The Syllabus of the Principal Errors of Our Time . . . ," in *Documents in the Political History of the European Continent,* ed. C. A. Kertesz (Oxford: Oxford University Press, 1968), pp. 233–41.

22. Pius to Archbishop Bonnechose of Rouen, November 10, 1866, *ASV, Archivio Particolare Pio IX, Francia, Particolari*, n. 183.

23. Eugenio Cecconi, *Storia del Concilio Ecumenico Vaticano Scritta sui Documenti Originali* (Rome: Tipografia Vaticana, 1872), I, pp. 3–8.

24. Michele Maccarone, *Il Concilio Vaticano I e il "Giornale" di Mons. Arigoni* (Padua, It.: Antenore, 1966), I, pp. 267–68.

25. Cuthbert Butler, *The Vatican Council: The Story Told from Inside in Bishop Ullathorne's Letters* (New York: Longmans, Green, and Co., 1930), I, p. 88.

26. Monsignor Mermillod to Pius IX, October 12, 1870, *ASV, Archivio Particolare Pio IX, Stato Pontifico*, n. 181.

27. Fernand Mourret, *Le concile du Vatican d'après des Documents inédits* (Paris: Bloud & Gay, 1919), pp. 312–13.

28. Rev. Thomas Mozley, *Letters from Rome on the Occasion of the Oecumenical Council, 1869–1870* (London: Longmans, Green, and Co., 1891), I, pp. 43–44.

29. Raffaele De Cesare, *Roma e lo stato del Papa. Dal ritorno di Pio IX al XX settembre* (Milan: Longanesi, 1970), p. 695.

30. Mourret, *A History of the Catholic Church*, VIII, p. 658.

31. Butler, II, p. 295.

32. Antonio Monti, *La politica degli Stati Italiani durante il Risorgimento* (Milan: Vallardi, 1948), p. 226.

33. Pius IX to Victor Emmanuel II, September 11, 1870, *ASV, Archivio Particolare Pio IX, Sovrani, Sardegna*, n. 82.

34. Pius IX to an Austrian Delegation, May 16, 1871, De Franciscis, I, p. 89.

35. Great Britain, *British and Foreign State Papers*, LXV (1873–74), pp. 638–42.

36. *Raccolta Ufficiale delle Leggi e dei Decreti del Regno d'Italia*, 2nd series (1871), pp. 1012–22.

37. "Allocution to the College of Cardinals, October 27, 1871" in Pasquale De Franciscis, *Discorsi del Sommo Pontefice Pio IX Pronciati in Vaticano ai Fedeli di Roma e dell' Orbe dal principio della sua prigionia fino al presente* (Rome: Aurelj, 1872), I, p. 248.

38. Hubert Bastgen, *Die Romische Fräge: Dokumente und Stimmen* (Freiburg, Ger.: Herder, 1917–1919), III, p. 98.

39. De Franciscis, I, pp. 283–84.

40. "Bismarck's confidential diplomatic circular to the German representatives abroad, May 14, 1872" in *Bismarck*, ed. Frederic B. M. Hollyday (Englewood Cliffs, NJ: Prentice Hall, 1970), p. 43.

41. Speech of Pius IX to a deputation from Alsace, June 20, 1871, De Franciscis, I, p. 146.

42. Pius IX to a delegation of Catholic women from Germany, February 10, 1871, De Franciscis, I, p. 53.

43. "Law Concerning the Education and Appointment of Priests," May 11, 1873 in *Documents in the Political History of the European Continent, 1815–1939*, p. 247.

44. Papal address to German Club of Catholic Literature, June 24, 1872, De Franciscis, I, p. 457.

45. Allocution of Pius IX to the Cardinals of the Church, December 23, 1872 in De Franciscis, II, p. 130.

46. Pius to William of Prussia, August 7, 1873 in De Franciscis, III, p. 573.

47. William of Prussia to Pius IX, September 3, 1873 in De Franciscis, III, p. 574.

48. Encyclical letter of Pius IX in De Franciscis, III, pp. 543–56.

49. "Bismarck's confidential diplomatic circular to German representatives abroad," May 14, 1872, in *Bismarck,* ed. Frederic B.M. Hollyday (Englewood Cliffs, NJ: Prentice Hall, 1970), p. 43.

50. Encyclical of Pius IX to the archbishops and bishops of Prussia, February 5, 1875 in De Franciscis, III, pp. 562–65.

51. Pius IX to De Corcelles, December 17, 1876, *ASV, Archivio Particolare Pio IX, Francia, Particolari.*

CHAPTER 4

1. David Alvarez, *Spies in the Vatican: Espionage & Intrigue from Napoleon to the Holocaust* (Lawrence: University Press of Kansas, 2002), p. 58.

2. "Relazioni sul progetto di stabilire una Delegazione Apostolica nell' America del Nord," *Archivio de Propaganda Fide* (Rome: *Acta,* 1877), v. 245, f. 39.

3. Foreign Correspondent, "The Death of Pius IX: The Conclave and the Election," *The Catholic World* XXVII (April 1878), p. 129.

4. Owen Chadwick, *A History of the Popes, 1830–1914* (Oxford: Clarendon Press, 1998), p. 294.

5. "What's Going On At the Vatican? A Voice from Rome," *Littell's Living Age* CXXXIX (December 14, 1878), p. 650.

6. "Sulla nomina di un nuovo delegate apostolico per Canada sulle speciali istruzioni di darsi al medesimo," *Archivio de Propaganda Fide,* (Rome: *Acta,* 1879), v. 247, ff. 351–79.

7. "Licet Multa," Carlen, ed., *The Papal Encyclicals, 1878–1903* (Ann Arbor, MI: The Pierian Press, 1981), II, pp. 59–61.

8. Harry C. Koenig, ed., Principles for Peace: Selections from Papal Documents from Leo XIII to Pius XII, p. 25.

9. "Immortale Dei," November 1, 1885, in Carlen, PE, II, p. 117.

10. Calls for an Apostolic Delegate in Canada, *ASV, Delegazione Apostolica del Canada,* scatola 76.

11. "Sancta Dei Civitas," December 3, 1880, Carlen, ed., *The Papal Encyclicals,* II, p. 44.

12. "Au Milieu des Sollictues," February 16, 1892 in *The Papal Encyclicals,* II, pp. 277–83.

13. "Inscrutabili Dei Consilio," in *The Papal Encyclicals,* II, pp. 5–10; Koenig, *Principles for Peace,* pp. 3–6.

14. "Etsi nos" On Conditions in Italy, in *The Papal Encyclicals,* II, pp. 63–68.

15. "Humanum Genus," On Freemasonry, April 20, 1884, in *Papal Pronouncements* I, p. 46.

16. "Dall' alto dell' Apstolico seggio," On the Destructive Work of the Freemasons in Italy," in *The Papal Encyclicals,* I, p. 51.

17. "Custodi di quella fede" and "Inimica vis" in *Papal Pronouncements,* I, p. 53.

18. "Praeclara," June 20, 1894, in *Papal Pronouncements,* I, p. 55.

19. "Annum ingressi," March 19, 1902,in *Papal Pronouncements,* I, pp. 62–63.

20. "Testem Benevolentiae," January 22, 1899 in *Papal Pronouncements,* I, p. 60.

21. "Cum Multa" on Conditions in Spain, December 8, 1882," in Koenig, ed., pp. 18–21.

22. Koenig, ed. pp. 11–12.

23. "Cum de Carolinis Insulis," December 31, 1885, ibid., pp. 68–69.

24. "*Saepe nos,*" To the Bishops of Ireland, June 24, 1888, in Carlen, *The Papal Encyclicals*, II, pp. 183–85.

25. "*Catholicae Ecclesiae*", November 20, 1890, in *Acta Sancte Sedis*, XXIII, 257 and *American Ecclesiastical Review* IV (February 1891), p. 410.

26. "Rapporto sulle condizioni della Chiesa Cattolica negli Stati Uniti d'America umiliato alla Santità di Nostro Signore Leone XIII da Monsignor Germano Straniero," *Archivio Segreto del Vaticano, Segreteria di Stato,* 1902, rubrica 280, fascicolo 10.

27. "Inscrutabili Dei consilio, April 21, 1878" and "Quod Apostolici muneris," of December 28, 1878" in *Papal Pronouncements,* I, p. 43.

28. "Etsi nos," February 15, 1882, in Carlen, *Papal Encyclical,* II, pp. 63–68.

29. "Immortale Dei," November 1, 1885, in Carlen, *Papal Pronouncements,* I, p. 47.

30. "Rerum novarum," May 15, 1891, in Carlen, *Papal Encyclical,* II, pp. 241–61.

31. "Permotti nos," July 10, 1895 in Carlen, *Papal Encyclical,* II, pp. 371–73.

32. "Graves de communi re," January 18, 1901, in Carlen, *Papal Encyclical,* II, pp. 479–86.

33. Koenig, *Principles for Peace,* pp. 91–100.

34. The conclave consisted of 62 cardinals, 98 percent of whom were from Europe and 61 percent from Italy.

35. "Search for Peace Marked his Reign," *The New York Times,* October 9, 1958, p. 23.

36. "E Supremi," October 4, 1903,in Carlen, *Papal Encyclical,* III, p. 8.

37. "Primum vos," November 9, 1903, in Carlen, *Papal Pronouncements,* II, p. 65.

38. "Commissum Nobis," January 4, 1904, in Carlen, *Papal Pronouncements,* II, p. 67.

39. "Vacante Sede Apostolica," December 25, 1904, in Carlen, *Papal Pronouncements,* II, p. 68.

40. Carlen, *Papal Encyclicals,* III, p. 27.

41. "Instaurandum in Christo," in Carlen, *Papal Pronouncements,* II, p. 65.

42. "La lettera cicrolare," March 1, 1905, in Carlen, *Papal Pronouncements,* II, 69.

43. Giuseppe Hergenrother, *Storia universale della Chiesa,* trans. P. Enrico Rosa, ed. G. P. Kirsch (Florence: Libreria Fiorentina, 1911), p. 767; Igino Giordani, *Pius X: A Country Priest,* trans. Thomas J. Tobin (Milwaukee, WI: Bruce Publishing, 1954), p. 154.

44. "Pascendi Dominici Gregis": On the Modernists, in Frank J. Coppa, *The Papacy Confronts the Modern World* (Malabar, FL: Krieger Publishing, 2003), p. 148.

45. Giordani, *Pius X: A Country Priest,* p. 105; "Vehementer Nos," February 11, 1906, in Carlen, *Papal Pronouncements,* II, p. 70.

46. "Gravissimo officii munere" of August 10, 1906 and "Une Fois Encore" of January 6, 1907 in Carlen, *Papal Encyclical,* III, pp. 63–65, 67–70.

47. "*Polonie Populum,*" December 3, 1905, in Koenig, *Principles for Peace,* p. 116.

48. Letter *Libenter abs Te,* June 11, 1911, in Koenig, *Principles for Peace,* p. 122.

49. Ernesto Vercesi, *Il movimento cattolico in Italia (1820–1922)* (Florence: La Voce, 1923), pp. 121–22.

50. Frank J. Coppa, "Giolitti e I Cattolici nell' Italia Liberale, 1904–1914," *Rassegna Storica del Risorgimento*, LXIV (July–September 1977), p. 309.

51. Giovanni Spadolini, *Giolitti e I Cattolici, 1901–1914* (Florence: Felice Le Monnier, 1960), p. 82; Prince von Bulow, *Memoirs*, trans. F. A. Veight (London: Putnam, 1931), II, pp. 68–69.

52. Giovanni Giolitti, *Discorsi parlamentari* (Rome: Tipografia della Camera, 1954), II, p. 820.

53. Ibid., II, p. 1018.

54. Ibid., II, pp. 1019–20.

55. Frank J. Coppa, "Giolitti and the Gentiloni Pact between Myth and Reality," *The Catholic Historical Review*, LIII n. 2 (July 1967):pp. 217–28.

56. "Gli insegnamenti delle elezioni generali a suffragio allargato," *Civiltà Cattolica*, anno 64 (1913) vol. IV, pp. 532–36; *Il Giornale d'Italia*, November 8, 1913.

57. To James Cardinal Gibbons of Baltimore, April 3, 1908," in Carlen, *Papal Pronouncements*, II, p. 73.

58. "Lacrimabili statu," June 7, 1912 in Carlen, *Papal Encyclical*, III, pp. 131–33.

59. *The Diaries of Theodor Herzl*, ed. and trans. Marvin Lowenthal (New York: Dial Press, 1956), pp. 428–30.

60. Andrew M. Canepa, "Pius X and the Jews: A Reappraisal," *Church History*, vol. 61, n. 3 (1992), p. 369.

61. "Dum Europa fere," August 2, 1914, in Carlen, *Papal Pronouncements*, II, p. 78.

CHAPTER 5

1. David Alvarez, *Spies in the Vatican: Espionage & Intrigue from Napoleon to the Holocaust* (Lawrence: University of Kansas Press, 2002), p. 127.

2. William A. Renzi, "The Entente and the Vatican during the Period of Italian Neutrality," *The Historical Journal*, XIII (1970), p. 491.

3. "Ubi primum," September 8, 1914, in Claudia Carlen, ed., *Papal Pronouncements. A Guide: 1740–1978* (Ann Arbor, MI: Pierian Press, 1990), II, p. 79.

4. "Ad Beatissimi," November 1, 1914, *Acta Apostolicae Sedis* (Rome, 1909–), VI, pp. 585–99.

5. "The Pope and the War," *The London Times*, September 6, 1914, p. 1.

6. "Pope Eager to Convince the World at Large of His 'Absolute Impartiality' in the War," *The New York Times*, July 24, 1916.

7. "*Ad Beatissimi*," November 1, 1914, in Harry C. Koenig, ed, *Principles for Peace: Selections From Papal Documents, Leo III to Pius XII* (Washington, DC: National Catholic Welfare Conference, 1943), p. 132.

8. Thomas E. Hachey, ed., *Anglo-Vatican Relations 1914–1939: Confidential Reports of the British Minister to the Holy See* (Boston: G.K. Hall, 1972), p. 9.

9. Shane Leslie, *Cardinal Gasquet: A Memoir* (New York: Kenedy and Sons, 1952), pp. 212–13.

10. Sidney Sonnino, *Diario, 1914–1916,* ed. Pietro Pastorelli (Bari: Laterza, 1972), p. 40.

11. Koenig, *Principles for Peace*, pp. 145–48.

12. Ibid., p. 177.

13. Alvarez, *Spies in the Vatican*, pp. 119–26.

14. Leslie, *Cardinal Gasquet*, p. 214.

15. Hachey, ed., *Anglo-Vatican Relations 1914–1939*, p. 19.

16. Leslie, *Cardinal Gasquet*, p. 242.

17. "Allorché Fummo," July 28, 1915 in Koenig, *Principles for Peace*, p. 181.

18. "E pur troppo vero," in Koenig, *Principles for Peace*, pp. 193–97.

19. Reply of Cardinal Gasparri to Petition of American Jewish Committee of New York, in Koenig, *Principles for Peace*, p. 199.

20. Koenig, *Principles for Peace*, pp. 197–210.

21. Hachey, *Anglo-Vatican Relations 1914–1939*, p. 6.

22. Walter H. Peters, *The Life of Benedict XV* (Saint Paul, MN: Bruce Publishing Co., 1959), pp. 140–45.

23. Ibid., p. 143.

24. "Telegram of Cardinal Gasparri to Lenin, March 12, 1919," in Koenig, *Principles for Peace*, p. 269.

25. "Dès le Début" (To the Belligerent Peoples and to their Leaders), August 1, 1917, ibid., pp. 229–32.

26. Benedict XV to Archbishop Kakowski of Poland, October 15, 1918, ibid., pp. 255–56.

27. "The Pope Acts," *The Evening Post*, August 14, 1917.

28. Ibid.

29. Peters, *The Life of Benedict XV*, p. 149.

30. *New York Times*, August 29, 1917, p. 1; September 23, 1917, p. 2.

31. Andrej Kreutz, *Vatican Policy on the Palestinian-Israeli Conflict* (Westport, CT: Greenwood Press, 1990), pp. 36–37.

32. "The fourteen points," January 8, 1918, in Kertesz, *Documents in the Political History of the European Continent, 1815–1939*, (Oxford: Clarendon Press, 1968), pp. 347–49.

33. Joseph Thomas Delos, *International Relations from a Catholic Standpoint* (Dublin: Brown and Nolan, 1932), pp. 137, 143.

34. *The Papers of Woodrow Wilson: June 1–17, 1919*, ed. Arthur S. Link (Princeton: Princeton University Press, 1989), vol. 60, p. 389.

35. "Papal Peace Message is Sent to America," *The New York Times* , March 23, 1918.

36. "E la Quinta Volta," December 24, 1918, in Koenig, *Principles for Peace*, pp. 261–65.

37. Peters, *The Life of Benedict XV*, p. 167; Report on Mission to Holy See, Count de Salis to Marquis Curzon, October 25, 1922, in Hachey, *Anglo-Vatican Relations 1914–1939*, p. 12.

38. "Maximum illud," November 30, 1919 in Carlen, *Papal Pronouncements*, II, p. 83.

39. Koenig, *Principles for Peace*, pp. 238–39.

40. "Pacem Dei Munus Pulcherrimum," May 23, 1920, in Koenig, *Principles for Peace*, p. 290; Carlen, *Papal Pronouncements*, I, p. 174.

41. Anne O'Hare McCormick, *Vatican Journal 1921–1954* (New York: Ferrar, Straces and Cudahy, 1957), pp. 20–21.

42. *La Civiltà Cattolica*, August 30, 1919.

43. On these matters see his allocution of December 16, 1920 to the College of Cardinals and his letter of January 24, 1921 to Cardinal Gasparri on conditions in Austria, in Koenig, *Principles for Peace*, pp. 301–2; 304–6.

44. James H. Ryan, "The Vatican's World Policy," *Current History, New York Times Magazine,* December 1922, p. 437; *Tablet,* June 24, 1921.

45. Encyclical *"Sacra Propediem,"* January 6, 1921, in Koenig, *Principles for Peace,* pp, 303–4.

46. "Le Notizie," August 5, 1921, ibid., p. 314.

47. Benedict XV's Telegram to League of Nations, September 1921, ibid., p. 314.

48. *"O Dio di Bontà,"* ibid., p. 312.

49. Allocution *"In Hac Quidem,"*November 21, 1921, ibid., p. 316.

50. Benedict XV to President Harding, November 10, 1921 and "Telegram of Cardinal Gasparri to the Congrès Démocratique International, December 4, 1921," ibid., pp. 315–16, 317.

51. "Maximas inter Horum," May 22, 1918, ibid., p. 252.

52. Emil Ludwig, *Talks with Mussolini* (Boston: Little, Brown, and Co., 1933), p. 181.

CHAPTER 6

1. "Pius XI to Cardinal Gasparri, April 29, 1922," in Harry C. Koenig, ed., *Principles for Peace: Selections from Papal Documents from Leo XIII to Pius XII* (Washington, DC: Nation Catholic Welfare Conference, 1943), pp. 321–22.

2. "Memorandum sent by Cardinal Gasparri to the Diplomatic Representatives at the Genoa Peace Conference," ibid., pp. 323–24; Edmund A. Walsh, *Why Pope Pius XI Asked Prayers for Russia on March 19, 1930* (New York: Catholic Near East Welfare Association, 1930), pp. 23–24.

3. "Annus fere iam est," July 10, 1922 and "Ubi Arcano Dei Consilio," December 23, 1922 in Claudia Carlen, *Papal Pronouncements. A Guide: 1740–1978.* (Ann Arbor, MI: Pierian Press, 1990), I, pp. 88, 90.

4. Wilfred Daim, *The Vatican and Eastern Europe,* trans. Alexander Gode (New York: F. Ungar, 1970), p. 56.

5. "Gasparri to Eppstein," August 11, 1923, in Koenig, *Principles for Peace,* p. 365.

6. Thomas E. Hachey, ed., *Anglo-Vatican Relations 1914–1939: Confidential Reports of the British Minister to the Holy See* (Boston: G.K. Hall, 1972), p. 68.

7. Ibid., p. 111.

8. Ibid., p. 192.

9. Ibid., p. 96.

10. John F. Pollard, *The Vatican and Italian Fascism, 1929–1932: A Study in Conflict* (Cambridge: Cambridge University Press, 1985), p. 21.

11. "Ubi Arcano Dei," December 23, 1922, in Koenig, *Principles for Peace,* pp. 334–35.

12. Francois Charles-Roux, *Huit ans au Vatican, 1932–1940* (Paris: Flammarion, 1947), pp. 46–48.

13. "Fascismo e Sindicalismo," *Civiltà Cattolica,* March 3, 1923; *L'Osservatore Romano,* March 17, 1923; March 28, 1923; November 1, 1923.

14. Antonio Pellicani, *Il Papa di Tutti. La Chiesa Cattolica, il Fascismo, e il Razzismo, 1929–1945* (Milan: Sugar Editore, 1964), p. 10.

15. "Maximam Gravissimamque," January 18, 1924, in Carlen, *The Papal Encyclicals, 1903–1939,* (Ann Arbor, MI: 1981), pp. 265–69.

16. Decretum De Consociatione Vulgo, "Amici Israel" Abolenda, March 25, 1928, *Acta Apostolicae Sedis,* Series XX, pp. 103–4.

17. Koenig, *Principles for Peace,* p. 474.

18. The text of the Lateran Accords can be found in Nino Tripodi, *Patti lateranese e il fascismo* (Bologna: Capelli, 1960), pp. 267–79; and in Wilfrid Parsons, *The Pope and Italy* (New York: The America Press, 1929), pp. 81–114. For an analysis of the three documents see Ernesto Rossi, *Il Managnello e l'aspersorio* (Florence: Parenti, 1958), pp. 227–36.

19. A good account of Vatican finances during this and earlier pontificates is provided in John F. Pollard, *Money and the Rise of the Modern Papacy: Financing the Vatican, 1850–1950* (New York: Cambridge University Press, 2005).

20. "Quadragesimo anno," May 15, 1931, in Koenig, *Principles for Peace,* pp. 426–27.

21. "Cronoca Contemporanea," March 10–13, 1933, *Civiltà Cattolica, anno* 84 (1933), II, p. 301.

22. "Orsenigo to Pacellli, March 22, 1933 and June 18, 1933," *ASV, Segreteria di Stato, Rapporti con gli Stati, Archivio Storico, Affari Ecclesiastiche Straordinari, Germania, 1922–1939,* posizione 641–643, fascicolo 157, nn. 6736, 7461.

23. E. Rosa, "Il Concordato della Santa Sede con la Germania," *Civiltà Cattolica,* anno 84 (1933), IV, p. 345; Mr. Kirkpatrick (the Vatican) to Sir R. Vansittart, August 19, 1933, *Documents on British Foreign Policy,* n. 342, pp. 524–25.

24. George O. Kent, "Pope Pius XII and Germany: Some Aspects of German-Vatican Relations, 1933–1943," *American Historical Review,* LXX (October, 1964), p. 60.

25. "Pacelli to Orsenigo, April 4, 1933," *ASV, Segreteria di Stato, Rapporti con gli Stati, Archivio Storico, Affari Ecclesiastiche Straordinari, Germania, 1922–1939,* posizione 643, fascicolo 158.

26. Edgar B. Nixon, *Franklin D. Roosevelt and Foreign Affairs: II—March 1934–August 1935* (Cambridge: Harvard University Press, 1969), p. 143.

27. Robert A. Hecht, *An Unordinary Man: A Life of Father John La Farge, S.J.* (Lanham, Md.: Scarecrow Press, 1996), pp. 103, 107.

28. "Una lettera del Papa alla gioventù cattolica," *La Tribuna,* April 4, 1934, *ASV, Segreteria di Stato, Rapporti con gli Stati, Archivio Storico, Affari Ecclesiastiche Straordinari, Germania, 1922–1939,* posizione 650, fascicolo 199.

29. *The Persecution of the Catholic Church in the Third Reich: Facts and Documents* (London: Burns and Oates, 1940), pp. 423–27.

30. "La Questione Giudaica," *La Civiltà Cattolica* (1936), anno 87, volume IV, p. 45.

31. "Ai Giovani Cattolici Tedeschi," October 8, 1934, *Discorsi di Pio XI,* III, p. 218.

32. Francois Charles-Roux, *Huit ans au Vatican* (Paris: Flammarion, 1947), p. 106.

33. "Lettera enciclica sulla situazione della Chiesa Cattolica nel Reich Germanico," *Acta Apostolicae Sedis,* 1937, XXIX, pp. 168, 182, 185–86.

34. Koenig, *Principles for Peace,* pp. 538–39.

35. George O. Kent, "Pope Pius XII and Germany: Some Aspects of German-Vatican Relations, 1933–1943," *American Historical Review,* LXX (October, 1964), p. 62.

36. *Documents on German Foreign Policy,* Series C, IV, n. 482.

37. Pius XI's Instructions to the Rectors of Catholic Universities and Seminars to Refute 'Ridiculous Dogmas'," in Peter Godman, *Hitler and the Vatican: Inside the Secret Archives that Reveal the New Story of the Nazis and the Church* (New York: Free Press, 2004), appendix IV, pp. 222–25.

38. Hachey, *Anglo-Vatican Relations 1914–1939: Confidential Reports of the British Minister to the Holy See,* p. 387; *Tablet* (of London), March 26, 1938.

39. William M. Harrigan, "Pius XII's Efforts to Effect a Detente in German-Vatican Relations, 1939," *The Catholic Historical Review,* XLIX (July, 1963), p. 177.

40. Camille Cianfarra, *The War and the Vatican* (London: Oates and Washbourne, 1945), p. 122; Hachey, *Anglo-Vatican Relations 1914–1939,* pp. 389–94.

41. John La Farge, S.J., *Interracial Justice: A Study of the Catholic Doctrine of Race Relations* (New York: America Press, 1937), pp. 12–15, 59–61, 75, 172–73.

42. Robert A. Hecht, *An Unordinary Man: A life of Father John La Farge, S.J.,* (Lanham, MD: The Scarecrow Press, Inc., 1996), pp. 114–15.

43. Charles F. Delzell, "Pius XII, Italy, and the Outbreak of War," *Journal of Contemporary History,* II, n.4 (October 1967), p. 138.

44. Hecht, *An Unordinary Man,* p. 115.

45. Castelli, *National Catholic Reporter,* December 15, 1972, p. 8.

46. Frederick Brown, "The Hidden Encyclical," *The New Republic,* April 15, 1996, p. 30.

47. "Jesuit Says Pius XI asked for Draft," *National Catholic Reporter,* December 22, 1972, p. 4.

48. Galleys of La Farge's copy of the encyclical *Humani Generis Unitas,* which was to be published in *Catholic Mind,* preserved in the offices of *America* and uncovered by Professor Robert A. Hecht. The encyclical was supposed to appear in *Catholic Mind* of 1973 but somehow was never published. In 1996 a copy of the hidden encyclical was published by Georges Passelecq and Bernard Suchecky in their volume called *L'Encyclique Cachée de Pie XI. Une occasion manquée de l'Eglise face a l'antisémitisme* (Paris: La Decouverte, 1995). My reference is to the galleys of the encyclical for the *Catholic Mind,* p. 31, paragraph 123.

49. Galleys of La Farge's copy of the encyclical *Humani Generis Unitas,* p. 38b, paragraph 154; Passelecq and Suchecky, *L'Encyclique Cachée de Pie XI,* p. 296.

50. Galleys of La Farge's copy of the encyclical *Humani Generis Unitas* I, p. 34, paragraph 135; Passelecq and Suchecky, *L'Encyclique Cachée de Pie XI,* p. 286.

51. *La Civiltà Cattolica,* July 29, 1938; Cianfarra, *The War and the Vatican,* pp. 133–34.

52. *Discorsi di Pio XI,* III, pp. 782–83.

53. "Agli Alunni di 'Propaganda Fide,' August, 21, 1938," *Discorsi di Pio XI,* III, pp. 784–86.

54. "Ad Insegnanti di Azione Cattolica," September 6, 1938, *Discorsi di Pio XI,* III, p. 796.

55. Passelecq and Suchecky, *L'Encyclique Cachée de Pie XI,* p. 180.

56. *L'Osservatore Romano,* November 14–15, 1938.

57. "Con grande," December 24, 1938, in Koenig, *Principles for Peace,* pp. 549–51; Carlen, *Papal Pronouncements. A Guide: 1740–1978,* II, p. 114; *The New York Times,* December 25, 1938.

58. Desmond O' Grady, "Pius XI—Complex and Imperious," *National Catholic Reporter,* December 15, 1972, p. 15.

59. Godman, *Hitler and the Vatican*, p. 29.

60. Angelo Martini, S. J., "L'Ultima battaglia di Pio XI," in *Studi sulla questione romana e la conciliazione* (Rome: Cinque Lune, 1963), pp. 186–87.

61. "Jesuit Says Pius XI Asked for Draft," *National Catholic Reporter*, December 22, 1972, pp. 3–4.

CHAPTER 7

1. Galeazzo Ciano, *The Ciano Diaries, 1939–1943*, ed. Hugh Gibson (Garden City, NY: Doubleday, 1946), pp. 45–47.

2. George O. Kent, "Pope Pius XII and Germany: Some Aspects of German-Vatican Relations, 1933–1943," *American Historical Review* LXX (October 1964), p. 65.

3. *Documents on German Foreign Policy*, Series D, nn. 473, 475.

4. *Records and Documents of the Holy See Relating to the Second World War, The Holy See and the War in Europe, March 1939–August 1940*, ed. Pierre Blet et al., trans. Gerard Noel (Washington, DC: Corpus Books, 1968), I, p. 211.

5. Ibid., I, p. 169.

6. Harry C. Koenig, ed., *Principles for Peace: Selections from Papal Documents, Leo XIII to Pius XII* (Washington DC: National Catholic Welfare Conference, 1943), pp. 584–86.

7. *Records and Documents of the Holy See Relating to the Second World War*, I, p. 39.

8. *Records and Documents of the Holy See Relating to the Second World War*, I, p. 293.

9. *Acta Apostolicae Sedis* (hereafter referred to as *AAS*), XXXI (1939), pp. 413–53.

10. Anthony Rhodes, *The Vatican in an Age of Dictators, 1922–1945* (New York: Holt, Rinehart, and Winston, 1973), p. 228.

11. *Records and Documents of the Holy See Relating to the Second World War*, I, pp. 166, 358–59.

12. Koenig, *Principles for Peace*, p. 634.

13. *Records and Documents of the Holy See Relating to the Second World War*, I, p. 356; Hansjakob Stehle, *Eastern Politics of the Vatican*, trans. Sandra Smith (Athens: Ohio University Press, 1981), p. 197.

14. Koenig, *Principles for Peace*, p. 640.

15. John S. Conway, "The Vatican, Britain and Relations with Germany, 1938–1940," *The Historical Journal* XVI (1973), pp. 162–63.

16. *Records and Documents of the Holy See Relating to the Second World War*, I, pp. 415, 421, 431.

17. Georges Passelecq and Bernard Suchecky, *The Hidden Encyclical of Pius XI*, trans. Steven Rendall (New York: Harcourt Brace & Company, 1997), p. 91.

18. Koenig, *Principles for Peace*, p. 714.

19. Myron C. Taylor, ed., *Wartime Correspondence between President Roosevelt and Pope Pius XII* (New York: Macmillan, 1947), p. 61.

20. José M. Sànchez, "The Popes and Nazi Germany: The View from Madrid," *Journal of Church and State*, XXXVIII (Spring 1996), p. 374.

21. Koenig, *Principles for Peace*, p. 804.

22. Hansjakob Stehle, *Eastern Politics of the Vatican*, trans. Sandra Smith (Athens: Ohio University Press, 1981), pp. 214–20.

23. "Vichy France Rounds up Foreign Jews," *The Washington Post*, August 27, 1942.

24. Kent, *American Historical Review* LXX (October 1964), p. 71.

25. The files of this Vatican Information Service are now open in the Vatican Archives. Its holdings are catalogued in the two volume *Inter Arma Caritas: Uffizio Informazioni Vaticano per I prigionieri di guerra istituito da Pio XII (1939–1947)* (Vatican City: Archivio Segreto Vaticano, 2004).

26. Paul L. Murphy with Rene Arlington, *La Popessa* (New York: Warner Books, 1983), p. 197.

27. José M. Sànchez, *Pius XII and the Holocaust: Understanding the Controversy* (Washington, DC: Catholic University Press, 2002), p. 115.

28. John Lukacs, "The Diplomacy of the Holy See During World War II," *The Catholic Historical Review* LX (July 1974), p. 277.

29. Karl Otmar von Aretin, *The Papacy and the Modern World,* trans. Roland Hill (New York: McGraw-Hill, 1970), p. 213.

30. Stehle, *Eastern Politics of the Vatican*, p. 215.

31. George J. Gill, "The Myron C. Taylor Mission, the Holy See, and 'Parallel Endeavors For Peace,' 1939–1945," *Honorus: A Journal of Research,* I, n. 1 (1986), p. 3.

32. Peter Hebblethwaite, *Paul VI: The First Modern Pope* (New York: Paulist Press, 1993), p. 187.

33. John F. Morley, *Vatican Diplomacy and the Jews During the Holocaust, 1939–1943* (New York: KTAV Publishing House, Inc., 1980); Raul Hilberg, *The Destruction of the European Jews* (Chicago: Quadrangle Books, 1961), p. 430.

34. Oscar Halecki, *Eugenio Pacelli: Pope of Peace* (New York: Farrar, Strauss and Young, Inc., 1951), pp. 205–6.

35. *Records and Documents of the Holy See Relating to the Second World War,* I, p. 423.

36. Stehle, *Eastern Politics of the Vatican,* p. 213.

37. In this regard see the works of Margherita Marchione, particularly her *Crusade of Charity: Pius XII and POW's* (New York: Paulist Press, 2006).

38. *AAS*, XXXVII (1945), pp. 97–100.

39. "World Jewish Congress Hails Holy See's Work in Europe," *New York Times*, October 11, 1945, p. 12.

40. In this regard see Rabbi David G. Dalin, *The Myth of Hitler's Pope: How Pope Pius XII Rescued Jews from the Nazis* (New York: Regnery Publishing, 2005).

41. Battisa Mondin, *The Popes of the Modern Ages: From Pius IX to John Paul II* (Vatican City: Urbaniana University Press, 2004), pp. 104–12.

42. "*Pacem, Dei Munus Pulcherrimum,*" May 23, 1920, in Claudia Carlen, ed., *The Papal Encyclicals* (Ann Arbor, MI: Pierian Press, 1981) III, p. 174.

43. *AAS*, XXXI, pp. 454–80, 674–76.

44. "1944 Christmas Message of His Holiness Pope Pius XII," in *Selected Documents of His Holiness, Pope Pius XII, 1939–1958* (Washington, DC: National Catholic Welfare Conference, 1959), p. 10.

45. "Pope Asks Rulers to Prevent War," *New York Times*, November 7, 1955, p. 2.

46. "New Palestine Peace Efforts Urged by Pope," *The Washington Post*, November 11, 1949, p. 4.

47. "Pope is Troubled by Palestine War," *New York Times*, May 16, 1948, p. 6.

48. "Congregation Recommends Pope Pius XII Be Venerable," *The Tablet* (Brooklyn), May 19, 2007, p. 10.

CHAPTER 8

1. Harry C. Koenig, ed., *Principles for Peace: Selections from Papal Documents from Leo XIII to Pius XII* (Washington, DC: National Catholic Welfare Conference, 1943), pp. 371–72.

2. "*Divini Redemptoris* on Atheistic Communism," in Koenig, *Principles for Peace*, pp. 510–34.

3. *Acta Apostolicae Sedis*, [*AAS*], XXXI (1939), pp. 413–53.

4. Italo Garzia, "Pope Pius XII, Italy and the Second World War," in *Papal Diplomacy in the Modern Age, ed.* Peter C. Kent and John F. Pollard (Westport, CT: Praeger, 1994), p. 129.

5. Myron C. Taylor, ed., *Wartime Correspondence between President Roosevelt and Pope Pius XII* (New York: Macmillan and Co., 1947), p. 61.

6. Dennis J. Dunn, "Stalinism and the Catholic Church during the Era of World War II." *The Catholic Historical Review* LIX n. 3 (October 1973), p. 406.

7. "The Papal Secretary of State to the Minister if Great Britain Osborne and the Representative of the United States," July 27, 1944, in *Actes et documents du Saint Siège relatifs à la Second Guerre Mondiale* [*ADSS*], XI, ed. Pierre Blett, Robert A. Graham, Angelo Martini, and Burkhard Schneider. (Rome: Libreria Editrice Vaticana), p. 469.

8. "U.S. Representative to Pius XII," February 5, 1944, *ADSS*, XI, p. 125.

9. "Notes of points drafted by the Secretariat of State for Pope to discuss with Churchill during his visit," August 23, 1944, *ADSS*, XI, p. 511.

10. "Notes of Monsignor Tardini on German peace proposal," February 20, 1945, *ADSS*, XI, p. 692.

11. "Notes of Monsignor Tardini on the Holy See's Relations with the Soviet Union," July 14, 1944, *ADSS*, XI, pp. 462–63.

12. "Note of Monsignor Montini," August 3, 1944, *ADSS*, XI, p. 483.

13. "Oggi, al compiersi," in Sister M. Claudia Carlen, ed., *Papal Pronouncements. A Guide: 1740–1978* (Ann Arbor, MI: The Pierian Press, 1990), I, p. 121.

14. "Myron Taylor to Pius XII," September 21, 1944, *ADSS*, XI, p. 552.

15. Hansjakob Stehle, *Eastern Politics of the Vatican, 1917–1979* (Athens: Ohio University Press, 1981), p. 225.

16. "Monsignor Tardini's note to Taylor on the religious situation in Poland," April 5, 1945, *ADSS*, XI, p. 727.

17. Giuseppe della Torre, "Is War Inevitable?" *L'Osservatore Romano* [*OR*], June 14, 1947.

18. Peter C. Kent, "The Lonely Cold War of Pope Pius XII," in *Religion and the Cold War*, ed. Dianne Kirby (London: Palgrave Macmillan, 2003), p. 68.

19. Stehle, *Eastern Politics of the Vatican, 1917–1979*, p. 268.

20. Ibid., pp. 270–71.

21. George Kennan, *Memoirs, 1925–1950* (Boston: Little, Brown, and Co., 1967), pp. 90–91.

22. Letter of Pius XII to President Truman, July 19, 1948, in Ennio di Nolfo, *Vaticano e Stati Uniti, 1939–1952. Dalle Carte di Myron C. Taylor* (Milan: Agneli Editore, 1978), pp. 582–85.

23. John S. Conway, "Myron C. Taylor's Mission to the Vatican 1940–1950," *Church History*, vol. 44, n. 1 (March 1975) p. 98.

24. Dianne Kirby, "Harry Truman's Religious Legacy: The Holy Alliance, Containment and the Cold War," in *Religion and the Cold War* (New York: Palgrave/Macmillan, 2003), pp. 79–80, 84.

25. "Ad Apostolarum Principis," June 29, 1958, *AAS*, 50 (1958), pp. 601–4.

26. Stella Alexander, "Yugoslavia and the Vatican, 1919–1970," in Kent and Pollard, *Papal Diplomacy in the Modern Age, ed.* Peter C. Kent and John F. Pollard (Westport, CT: Praeger, 1994), pp. 158–61.

27. *AAS*, 44 (1952), pp. 153ff.

28. "Veritatem," March 27, 1952, in Carlen, *Papal Pronouncements*, I, p. 145.

29. Monsignor Harry Koenig, "The Pope and the Peace in the Twentieth Century," in Waldemar Gurian and M.A. Fitzsimons, eds., *The Catholic Church in World Affairs* (Notre Dame: University of Notre Dame, 1954), p. 67.

30. "Ad Sinarum gentum," *AAS*, 47 (1955), p. 5ff.

31. "Pope Pius Arrayed Catholicism's Spiritual Strength Against Materialistic Forces," *New York Times*, October 9, 1958, p. 22.

32. Richard P. Stevens, "The Vatican, the Catholic Church and Jerusalem," *Journal of Palestine Studies*, vol. 10, n. 3 (Spring 1981), pp. 104–7.

33. *L'Osservatore Romano*, July 23, 1944.

34. "Notes of points drafted by the Secretariat of State for Pope to discuss with Churchill during his visit," August 23, 1944, *ADSS*, XI, pp. 505–6.

35. Elisa A. Carrillo, "Italy, the Holy See and the United States," in *Papal Diplomacy in the Modern Age, ed.* Peter C. Kent and John F. Pollard (Westport, CT: Praeger, 1994), p. 148.

36. Sandro Magister, *La politica vaticana e l'Italia, 1943–1978* (Rome: Reuniti, 1979), pp. 132–33.

37. *L'Osservatore Romano*, January 3, 1955.

38. Stehle, *Eastern Politics of the Vatican, 1917–1979*, p. 287.

39. Émile Poulat, *Une Église Ébranlée. Chagement, conflit et continuité de Pie XII à Jean Paul II* (Paris: Casterman, 1980), p. 27.

40. Stehle, *Eastern Politics of the Vatican, 1917–1979*, p. 299.

41. Carlen, *Papal Pronouncements*, I, pp. 197, 201.

42. Claudia Carlen, ed., *The Papal Encyclicals, 1958–1981* (Ann Arbor, MI: The Pierian Press, 1990), V, p. 125.

43. Peter Hebblethwaite, *Pope John XXIII: Shepherd of the Modern World* (Garden City, NY: Doubleday and Co., Inc., 1985), p. 496.

CHAPTER 9

1. Peter Hebblethwaite, *Pope John XXIII: Shepherd of the Modern World* (Garden City, NY: Doubleday and Co., Inc., 1985), p. 286; Claudia Carlen, ed., *Papal Pronouncements. A Guide : 1740–1978. Volume I : Benedict XIV to Paul VI,* (Ann Arbor, MI: The Pierian Press, 1990), p. 211.

2. Pope John XXIII, *Journal of a Soul,* trans. Dorothy White (New York: McGraw-Hill, 1965), p. 43.

3. Ibid., p. 303.

4. Hansjakob Stehle, *Eastern Politics of the Vatican, 1917–1979,* trans. Sandra Smith (Athens: Ohio University Press, 1981), p. 300.

5. Hebblethwaite, *Pope John XXIII,* pp. 326, 373, 409, 422, 442–443; Hebblethwaite, *Paul VI: The First Modern Pope* (New York, Paulist Press, 1993), p. 284.

6. Claudia Carlen, ed., *Papal Pronouncements,* I, p. 211; Hebblethwaite, *Pope John XXIII,* p. 292.

7. Carlen, *Papal Pronouncements,* I, pp. 212, 214, 225, 230, 243, 251; Pope John XXIII, *Journal of a Soul,* p. 299.

8. Claudia Carlen, ed., *The Papal Encyclicals, 1958–1981* (Ann Arbor, MI: Pierian Press, 1981) V, p. 17.

9. Carlen, *Papal Pronouncements,* I, pp. 229, 237–39.

10. Carlen, *The Papal Encyclicals, 1958–1981* (Raleigh: The Pierian Press, 1981), V, pp. 59–90.

11. "Pacem in Terris," April 11, 1963, in Carlen, *The Papal Encyclicals, 1958–1981,* V, p. 108.

12. Ibid., V, p. 123.

13. Pope John XXIII, *Journal of a Soul,* p. 199.

14. Carlen, "Ad Petri Cathedram," June 29, 1959, in *The Papal Encyclicals, 1958–1981,* V, p. 15.

15. "Princeps Pastorum," in Carlen, *The Papal Encyclicals, 1958–1981,* V, pp. 43–57; Peter Nichols, *The Politics of the Vatican* (New York: Praeger, 1968), p. 212; Carlen, *Papal Pronouncements,* I, p. 219.

16. "Who Is the Greatest Pope of All time," *The Tablet* (Brooklyn), April 17, 1999, vol. 92, n. 3.

17. Hebblethwaite, *Paul VI,* pp. 319, 326–31.

18. Antonio Fapani and Franco Molinari, eds., "Giovanni Battista Monti giovane, 1897–1944," in *Documenti inediti e testimonianze* (Turin, 1979), pp. 116–18.

19. Hebblethwaite, *Pope John XXIII,* p. 345; Carlen, *Papal Pronouncements,* I, p. 211.

20. Hebblethwaite, *Paul VI,* p. 12.

21. Austin Flannery, ed., *Vatican Council II: The Conciliar and Post Conciliar Documents* (Grand Rapids, MI: Eerdmans, 1992), I, pp. 1–40, 283–49.

22. Carlen, *Papal Pronouncements,* I, pp. 308–11, 317.

23. "Ecclesiam Suam," August 6, 1964, Carlen, *The Papal Encyclicals* V, p. 135.

24. Flannery, *Vatican Council II,* pp. 350–426, 441–51, 452–70.

25. John Dietzen, "U.N. Offers a Reason for Hope, Dialogue? *Tablet* (Brooklyn), May 13, 2006, p. 20.

26. John Norton, "Paul VI's Wish to Visit Vietnam was Unwelcomed," *The Tablet* (Brooklyn), April 28, 2001, p. 1.

27. Flannery, *Vatican Council II,* I, pp. 707–43.

28. Ibid., I, p. 741.

29. Carlen, *Papal Pronouncements,* I, p. 355.

30. Ibid., I, pp. 380, 386, 390, 401.

31. "Populorum Progressio," March 26, 1967, in Carlen, *The Papal Encyclicals,* V, p. 187.

32. "Uno dei risultati," of July 12, 1967 and "Noi divevamo," of July 19, 1967, in Carlen, *Papal Pronouncements,* I, p. 404.

33. Hebblethwaite, *Paul VI,* p. 7.

34. Ibid., pp. 9, 13, Wilton Wynn, *Keepers of the Keys: John XXIII, Paul VI, and John Paul II: Three Who Changed the Church* (New York: Random House, 1988), pp. 243–244.

CHAPTER 10

1. Albino Luciani, *Illustrisimi: Letters from Pope John Paul I,* trans. William Weaver (Boston: Little, Brown and Co., 1976).

2. "John Paul I to the cardinals and the world," August 27, 1978, in Albino Luciani, *The Message of John Paul I* (Boston: Daughters of St. Paul, 1978), pp. 25–40.

3. Claudia Carlen, ed., *Papal Pronouncements. A Guide: 1740–1978* (Ann Arbor, MI: The Pierian Press, 1990), II, p. 843.

4. "John Paul's talk to a general audience on September 6, 1978," in Luciani, *The Message of John Paul I,* pp. 89–90.

5. Paul Elie, "The Year of Two Popes," *The Atlantic Monthly* (January–February 2006): p. 91.

6. Carlen, *Papal Pronouncements* II, pp. 845–48.

7. "John Paul I to a general audience, September 13, 1978," in Luciani, *The Message of John Paul I,* p. 105.

8. Andre Frossard, *Be Not Afraid: Pope John Paul Speaks Out on his Life, his beliefs, and his Inspiring Vision for Humanity,* trans. J. R. Foster (New York: St. Martin's Press, 1984), pp. 13–14, 23.

9. Pope John Paul II, *Crossing the Threshold of Hope,* ed. Vittorio Messori (New York: Alfred A. Knopf, 1994), pp 29–31.

10. Mieczyslaw Malinski, *Pope John Paul II: The Life of Karol Wojtyla,* trans. P. S. Fall (New York: Seabury Press, 1979), p. 23.

11. Daughters of St. Paul, ed., *Messages of John Paul II,* (Boston: St. Paul Editions, 1979), II, pp. 15–16; "The Pope: A See Change," *The Economist,* April 29, 1995; Malinski, pp. 82, 118; Frossard, p. 28.

12. *Messages of John Paul II,* II, pp. 274–281; Malinski, p. 241.

13. Frossard, p. 207.

14. Annie Lally Milhaven, *The Inside Story: 13 Valiant Women Challenging the Church* (Mystic, Conn.: Twenty-Third Publications, 1987), pp. 5–6; *National Catholic Reporter,* October 19, 1979; *New York Times,* October 8, 1979; *Newsweek,* October 15, 1979.

15. "Pope: Women, Men Equal, But Each Role Differs," *The Tablet* (Brooklyn), May 3, 1979.

16. Pope John Paul II, *Crossing the Threshold of Hope,* p. 48.

17. Corky Siemaszko, "Soviets led Pope hit, says Italy," *Daily News,* March 3, 2006, p. 7.

18. Carl Bernstein, "The Holy Alliance," *Time,* February 24, 1992, p. 28.

19. Maria Elisabetta de Franciscis, *Italy and the Vatican: The 1984 Concordat Between Church and State, Studies in Modern European History,* ed. Frank J. Coppa (New York: Peter Lang, 1989) volume II, p. 225.

20. Thomas Patrick Melady, *The Ambassador's Story: The United States and the Vatican in World Affairs* (Huntington, IN: Our Sunday Visitor, 1994), pp. 17–18.

21. Michael Mandelbaum, "Coup de Grace: The End of the Soviet Union," *Foreign Affairs* 71 (spring 1992): pp. 164–82; Eduard Shevardnadze, *The Future Belongs to Freedom* (New York: Free Press, 1991), pp. 25–27.

22. Shevardnadze, p. 25.

23. "Excerpts from the Pope's Encyclical: On Giving Capitalism a Human Face," *The New York Times,* May 3, 1991.

24. Alan Cowell, "Pope Challenges Brazil Leaders on Behalf of the Poor," *The New York Times,* October 15, 1991; Cowell, "Pope's Law: Less Politics," ibid., October 16, 1991; Cowell, "Protect Children, Pope tells Brazil," ibid., October 21, 1991; Alan Cowell, "Pope Asks Amends of Brazil's Indians," ibid., October 17, 1991; Frossard, pp. 152, 154.

25. Stephen Kinzer, "Pope Tells Croats He Supports Them," *The New York Times,* August 18, 1991.

26. "Memory and Reconciliation: The Church and the Mistakes of the Past," *The New York Times,* March 2, 2000.

27. Alan Cowell, "Pope Visits Angola, Urging Amity After Long War," *The New York Times,* June 5, 1992; ibid., February 21, 1992; Agostino Bono, "At Beatification, the Pope's Mind in On Africa," *The Tablet,* May 23, 1992; "Pope Scolds Sudan," *New York Newsday,* February 11, 1993.

28. Laurie Hansen, "Pope tells Latin American Bishops: Put Church at Center of all Life," *The Tablet* (Brooklyn), October 24, 1992; Ron Howard, "Pope: Spread Faith," *New York Newsday,* October 12, 1992; Howard W. French, "Dissent Shadows Pope on his Visit," *The New York Times,* October 14, 1992.

29. Alan Cowell, "The Pope's Struggle Against Marxism and Its Successors," *The New York Times,* September 26, 1993.

30. John Dietzen, "U.N. Offers a Reason for Hope, Dialogue," *The Tablet* (Brooklyn), May 1, 2006, p. 20.

31. Alan Cowell, "Pope Appoints 30 Cardinals, 2 from U.S.," *The New York Times,* October 31, 1994.

32. Pope John Paul II, *Crossing the Threshold of Hope,* p. 86.

33. "Pope's Letter: A Sinister World Has Led to Crimes Against Life." *The New York Times,* March 31, 1995.

34. "Pope: Christ's Peace Will Not Be Achieved Through War," *The Tablet* (Brooklyn), January 31, 2004, p. 13.

35. *The Telegraph* (United Kingdom), January 23, 2007.

36. *The Tablet* (Brooklyn), October 1, 2005, p. 33; "John Paul's last days & words on the record," *Daily News,* September 18, 2005, p. 16.

37. Jim Yardley, "China's State Catholic Church Honors John Paul," *The New York Times,* April 5, 2005, p. A10.

38. Matthew E. Bunson, *We Have a Pope! Benedict XVI* (Huntington, Ind.: Sunday Visitor, 2005), p. 46.

39. "Menorah for the Pope," *The Tablet* (Brooklyn), December 6, 2003, p. 12.

40. Cindy Wooden, "The Chief Rabbis of Israel Make First Visit to Vatican," *The Tablet* (Brooklyn), June 24, 2004, p. 7.

41. "Great Pope," *The Tablet* (Brooklyn), April 23, 2005, p. 3.

42. "John Paul Square in Paris," *The Tablet* (Brooklyn), September 9, 2006, p. 8.

43. A hostile evaluation of John Paul II's pontificate is found in Paul Collins, *God's New Man: The Election of Benedict XVI and the Legacy of John Paul II* (New York: Continuum, 2005).

44. "The Pope: A See Change," *The Economist,* April 29, 1995, pp. 23–24.

45. John Thavis, "Rome Train Station Will Not be Named for Late Pope," *The Tablet* (Brooklyn), January 27, 2007, p. 22.

46. John Thavis, "Church Grew under JP II," *The Tablet* (Brooklyn), June 10, 2006, p. 1.

CHAPTER 11

1. John L. Allen, Jr., *Pope Benedict XVI: A Biography of Joseph Ratzinger* (New York: Continuum, 2005), p. 121.

2. "Anonymous cardinal breaks vow of conclave secrecy," *Daily News* (New York), September 24, 2005, p. 12.

3. "Pope Says He Had Hoped to Retire," *The Tablet* (Brooklyn), June 30, 2007, p. 21.

4. "Pope Benedict: Working Too Much is Never a Good Thing," *The Tablet* (Brooklyn), August 26, 2006, p. 7.

5. "Church May Be More Selective in Choosing Saints," *The Tablet* (Brooklyn), May 26, 2006, p. 27.

6. "Stricter Norms for Mandatory Feast Days in Church," *The Tablet* (Brooklyn), May 26, 2007, p. 6.

7. John L. Allen, Jr., "A Challenge, Not a Crusade," *The New York Times,* September 19, 2006, p. A5.

8. Cindy Wooden, "Pope: Nazi Violence Fueled his Vocation," *The Tablet* (Brooklyn), April 15, 2006, p. 8.

9. Anthony Grafton, "Reading Ratzinger: Benedict XVI, the Theologian," *The New Yorker,* July 25, 2005, pp. 42–49.

10. Allen, *Pope Benedict XVI: A Biography of Joseph Ratzinger,* p. 67.

11. Peter J. Boyer, "A Hard Faith: How the new Pope and his predecessor redefined Vatican II," *The New Yorker,* May 16, 2005, p. 57.

12. "On the Issues," *New York Times,* April 20, 2005, p. A10.

13. "Dominus Iesus: On the Unicity and Salvific Univrsality of Jesus Christ and the Church," *The Tablet* (Brooklyn), September 30, 2000, p. 3A.

14. Boyer, "A Hard Faith," p. 64.

15. Peter Finney, "Archbishop Skips Graduation to Protest Award," *The Tablet* (Brooklyn), May 14, 2005, p. 15.

16. Laurie Goodstein, "Pope Has Gained the Insight to Address Abuse, Aides Say," *New York Times,* April 23, 2005, p. A1.

17. "Pope Says Truth Will Combat Priestly Abuse," *The Tablet* (Brooklyn), November 4, 2006, p. 7.

18. Joseph Bottum, "A Pope for the Grown-Ups," *New York Post,* April 20, 2005, p. 31.

19. John Thavis, "Jesuit Editor Resigns as Vatican Applied Pressure," *The Tablet* (Brooklyn), May 14, 2004, p. 2.

20. Ian Fisher, "Vatican Officially Releases Documents on Banning New Gay Priests," *New York Times,* November 30, 2005, p. A6; "Vatican: No gay seminary

teachers," *Newsday,* December 4, 2005, p. A22; Andrew Sullivan, "The Vatican's new Stereotype," *Time,* December 12, 2005, p. 92.

21. "Science alone could not control AIDS or other social ills: Pope," *Daily News,* September 11, 2006, p. 21.

22. "Pope slams genetic tech," *Daily News,* February 25, 2007, p, 21.

23. Cindy Wooden, "Pope Says Married Couples Helped the Early Church to Grow," *The Tablet* (Brooklyn), February 17, 2007, p. 3.

24. John Thavis, "Pope: Commercialism is Polluting Christmas," *The Tablet* (Brooklyn), December 17, 2005, p. 2.

25. Cindy Wooden, "Judas Becomes Papal Topic in Holy Week," *The Tablet* (Brooklyn), April 22, 2006, p. 1.

26. *Newsweek,* April 24, 2006, p. 25.

27. "Pope: Violence in Media is Aimed at Young People," *The Tablet* (Brooklyn), May 26, 2007, p. 7.

28. "The Pope's Warning to the Politicians," *U.S. News & World Report,* May 21, 2007, p. 27.

29. "Venezuelan President Wants Apology from Pope," *The Tablet* (Brooklyn), May 26, 2007, p. 1.

30. "Pope pushes Latin Mass," *New York Post,* May 14, 2007, p. 7.

31. "Pope Sees Tridentine Mass As a Bridge to Tradition," *The Tablet* (Brooklyn), April 7, 2007, p. 6.

32. "Pope seeks a return to the good, old chants," *Daily News,* March 14, 2997, p. 31.

33. Cindy Wooden, "Pope Issues Document on Eucharist," *The Tablet* (Brooklyn), March 17, 2007, p. 1.

34. George Weigel, "A Pope of Quiet Surprises," *Newsweek,* November 7, 2005, p. 60.

35. "Pope, Anglican Leader 'Journey of Friendship,'" *The Tablet* (Brooklyn), December 2, 2006, p. 9.

36. " 'Hard-liner' will work to promote unity," *New York Post,* April 21, 2005, p. 10; Helen Kennedy, "Now he's seeking harmony," *Daily News,* April 21, 2005, p. 6; "Benedict Promises Dialogue and Reconciliation," *New York Times,* April 21, 2005, pp. A1, A13.

37. "Pope Urges International Efforts to Cure AIDS," *The Tablet* (Brooklyn), December 2, 2006, p. 9.

38. "Pope Prays for Families of Those Who Died of AIDS," *The Tablet* (Brooklyn), December 8, 2007, p. 9.

39. Cindy Wooden, "Vatican Hosts Dialogue Between Scientists and Theologians," *The Tablet* (Brooklyn), November 12, 2005, p. 22.

40. Marsha Kranes, "Pope grooves with new iPod," *New York Post,* March 9, 2006, p. 4.

41. Cindy Wooden, "Pope: Role of Women Open for Discussion," *The Tablet* (Brooklyn), March 11, 2006, pp. 1, 9.

42. Cindy Wooden, "Pope: Divorced Should Be Welcomed in Parish," *The Tablet* (Brooklyn), August 6, 2005, p. 2.

43. "Benedict XVI says Pope's Power not Absolute," *The Tablet* (Brooklyn), May 14, 2005; "Pope: The West Must Return To Its Christian Roots," *The Tablet* (Brooklyn), October 28, 2006, p. 8.

44. Joshua Garner, "The 'Green' Pope," *The Tablet* (Brooklyn), August 18, 2007, p. 2.

45. "Clean Technologies Will Clean the Earth, Says Pope," *The Tablet* (Brooklyn), September 15, 2007, p. 7.

46. Beth Griffin, "Panelists Assess First 100 Days of Benedict XVI," *The Tablet* (Brooklyn), August 13, 2005, p. 4.

47. Homily of His Holiness Benedict XVI, May 29, 2005 in http://www.vati can.va/holy_father/benedict_xvi/homilies/2005/documents/hf_ben-xvi_ho. . . (accessed March 14, 2006), p. 4.

48. John Thavis, "Pope's New Book Says Jesus Was More Than a Social Reformer," *The Tablet* (Brooklyn), April 21, 2007, p. 3.

49. "Pope Sending Vatican Envoy to New Orleans," *The Tablet* (Brooklyn), September 10, 2005, p. 3.

50. "Pope Challenges Nations to Keep U.N. Program for Poor," *The Tablet* (Brooklyn), September 17, 2005, p. 5.

51. "Wealth Should Be Spread Fairly, Says Vatican Official," *The Tablet* (Brooklyn), December 31, 2005, p. 6.

52. Cindy Wooden, "In Peace Day Message, Pope Defends Human Rights," *The Tablet* (Brooklyn), December 17, 2005.

53. "Pope: Logic of Profit Can Lead to Disaster," *The Tablet* (Brooklyn), September 29, 2007, p. 3.

54. John Thavis, "Pope Emphasizes Europe's Christian Roots," *The Tablet* (Brooklyn), September 15, 2007, p. 3.

55. Jay Tolson, "A Pontiff's First Year," *U.S. News & World Report*, May 1, 2006, p. 38.

56. Andrew Greeley, "A Pope's Progress," *Daily News*, April 2, 2006, p. 29.

57. John Thavis, "In Second Encyclical Pope Benedict Says People Need God To Have Hope," *The Tablet* (Brooklyn), December 8, 2007, pp. 1, 3.

58. "Pope: Church lessons on Jews, Muslims key," *The Tablet* (Brooklyn), October 31, 2005, p. 1.

59. "After Meeting, Pope, Israeli President exchange Gifts," and "Pope Invites Greek Orthodox Head to Visit the Vatican," *The Tablet* (Brooklyn), November 26, 2005, p. 10.

60. "Orthodox Ties to Catholics Seen as Vital," *New York Times*, February 21, 2006, p. A6.

61. Linda Bussetti, "Teacher Institute Focuses on Catholic-Jewish Relations," *The Tablet* (Brooklyn), September 3, 2005, p. 3.

62. Newsletter of Association of Contemporary Church Historians, July/ August 2006, Vol. XII, n. 7/8, p. 1.

63. "Pope asks media to spread peace," *New York Post*, May 9, 2005; Eleni E. Dimmler, "Tear Down Hostile Walls," *The Tablet* (Brooklyn), May 14, 2005, p. 16.

64. "Vatican, Anglicans Resume Work of Mission Panel," *The Tablet* (Brooklyn), May 14, 2005, p. 18.

65. Cindy Wooden, "Catholics, Anglicans Reach Agreement on Mary," *The Tablet* (Brooklyn), May 21, 2005, p. 8.

66. "Sri Lankan Bishops Urged to Cooperate After Tsunamis," *The Tablet* (Brooklyn), May 14, 2005, p. 18.

67. Cindy Wooden, "Benedict's First Encyclical Is About Love," *The Tablet* (Brooklyn), January 28, 2006, p. 4.

68. "Pope: We must unite vs. terror," *New York Post*, January 2, 2006, p. 14.

69. "Pope Benedict Calls Terrorism in London 'Barbaric Acts Against Humanity,' " *The Tablet* (Brooklyn), July 16, 2005; "Pope Condemns Latest Suicide Bombing in Tel Aviv," *The Tablet* (Brooklyn), April 17, 2006, p. 13.

70. "African Bishops Told to Work With Muslims for Harmony," *The Tablet* (Brooklyn), February 25, 2006, p. 11.

71. Lecture of the Holy Father, Aula Magna of the University of Regensburg, September 12, 2006, http://www.vatican.va/holy_father/benedict_xvi/speeches/2006,september/documents/hf_b. . . (accessed 9/19/2006).

72. "Push for pope penance," *New York Post*, September 9, 2006, p. 25.

73. "Pope to Muslims: Let's united and end violence," *Daily News*, September 26, 2006, p. 14.

74. Ian Fisher, "In a Rare Step, Pope Expresses Personal Regret," *The New York Times*, September 18, 2006, pp. A1, A10.

75. "Chinese Ordinations with Papal OK Raises Hopes," *The Tablet* (Brooklyn), September 29, 2007, p. 1.

76. John Thavis, "Pope Names 15 New Cardinals, Including Two from U.S.," *The Tablet* (Brooklyn), February 25, 2006, p .5; Ian Fisher and Keith Bradsher, "Pope Picks 15 Cardinals, One a China Critic," *New York Times*, February 23, 2006, p. A24.

77. "20,000 Turks protest pope," *New York Post*, November 27, 2006, p. 19.

78. "Benedict Goes to Turkey," *New York Times*, November 29, 2006, p. A28; "The Pope in Istanbul," *N.Y. Post*, November 29, 2006, p. 30.

79. "Papal Trip a Success," *The Tablet* (Brooklyn), December 9, 2006, p. 15.

80. Liz F. Kay, "Pope needs to refocus, critics say," http://www.baltimoresun.com, September 20, 2006 (accessed September 21, 2006).

81. "Praise God, end violence, pleads Pope," *Daily News*, December 26, 2006, p. 10.

82. "Pope Benedict Meets Israeli President, Hopes for Peace," *The Tablet* (Brooklyn), September 15, 2007, p. 7.

83. Tracy Early, "Vatican Wants Deterrence Policy Revisited," *The Tablet* (Brooklyn), May 14, 2005, p. 10.

84. John Thavis, "Bush Meets Pope," *The Tablet* (Brooklyn), June 16, 2007, pp. 1–2.

85. "Pope Tells Nobel Winner Nuclear Threat Continues," *The Tablet* (Brooklyn), December 17, 2005, p. 6.

CHAPTER 12

1. Carol Glatz, "Pope Urges Sudan to End Dafur Military Campaign," *The Tablet* (Brooklyn), June 9, 2007, p. 11.

2. John Thavis, "On Palm Sunday, Pope Preaches About Poverty," *The Tablet* (Brooklyn), April 15, 2006, p. 2.

3. "Pope Cites Hunger Around the World," *The Tablet* (Brooklyn), November 25, 2006, p. 6.

4. "Kissinger to Participate in Vatican Meeting on Charity," *The Tablet* (Brooklyn), May 5, 2007, p. 6.

5. "Pope Hopes for More Diplomatic Ties with Vatican," *The Tablet* (Brooklyn), May 21, 2005, p. 6.

6. In the volume edited by Tom Buchanan and Martin Conway, *Political Catholicism in Europe, 1918–1965* (Oxford: Clarendon Press; New York: Oxford University Press, 1996) the nine essays included examining political Catholicism in Europe—largely Western Europe—from the post-World War I period to the mid-1960s. The contributors concur that political Catholicism has played a key role in the historical landscape of Continental Europe, even though it has not received the same attention lavished on Liberal, Socialist, and Communist parties there. There are, however, at least two other two general accounts of political Catholicsm in Europe—that of J. M. Mayeur in French and Karl-Egon Lonne in German. Further-more, there are volumes that examine political Catholicism in particular countries such as John Neylon Molony, *The Emergence of Political Catholicism in Italy: Partito Popolare, 1919–1926* (London, 1977); Ellen Lovell Evans, *The German Center Party, 1870–1933: A Study in Political Catholicism* (Carbondale, IL, 1981); Aline Coutrot and Francois Dreyfus, *Les forces religieuses dan la societe francaise* (Paris, 1965); and F. Lannon, *Privilege, Persecution, and Prophecy: The Catholic Church in Spain, 1875–1975* (Oxford, 1987) to cite only four.

7. Jonathan Luxmore, "Polish Prelate Denies He Withheld Information," *The Tablet* (Brooklyn), January 20, 2007, p. 7.

8. Some studies of the papacy are scholarly, others more journalistic. A few such as Luigi Marinelli's *Via col vento in Vaticano* (Rome, 1999), which has delved into the dark side of the Vatican, supposedly exposing the intrigues and plots therein, has seen its author summoned before the Roman Rota. Likwise critical is the recent study by Gary Wills whose title *Papal Sin: Structures of Deceit* (New York: Doubleday, 2000), reveals its message. Others such as Richard P. McBrien's *Lives of the Popes: The Pontiffs from St. Peter to John Paul II* (1997); Eamon Duffy's *A History of the Popes* (1997); and P. G. Maxwell-Stuart's *Chronicle of the Popes: A Reign-by-Reign Record of the Papacy from St. Peter to the Present* (New York, 1997) have not caused as much controversy. While these three latter studies have concentrated more on the popes than the papacy, that of Thomas J. Reese, S.J. *Inside the Vatican: The Politics and Organization of the Catholic Church* (Cambridge, MA, 1996) focuses on "The Politics and Organization of the Catholic Church," as its subtitle indicates.

9. Matthew E. Bunson, *We Have a Pope! Benedict XVI* (Huntington, IN: Sunday Visitor, 2005), p. 80.

10. John Thavis, "Vatican Stats Confirm Growth of Church in Asia and Africa," *The Tablet* (Brooklyn), February 17, 2007, p. 7.

11. Agostino Bono, "New Pope Challenged by Global Church," *The Tablet* (Brooklyn), April 23, 2005, p. 3.

12. "Nigerian Archbishop Calls for New Bishop's Structure," *The Tablet* (Brooklyn), January 27, 2007, p. 9.

13. Carol Glatz, "Dominicans Surprised by Dutch Proposal for Priestless Masses," *The Tablet* (Brooklyn), September 29, 2007, p. 5.

14. Adam L. Freeman, "Vatican Forced To Turn to Third World for New Priests," *The New York Sun*, August 11–13, 2006, p. 5.

15. "A Century of Conclaves," *New York Times*, April 10, 2005, p. 14.

16. "Pope Challenges Nations to Keep U.N. Programs for Poor," *The Tablet* (Brooklyn), September 17, 2005, p. 5.

17. In this regard see John F. Pollard, *Money and the Rise of the Modern Papacy: Financing the Vatican, 1850–1950* (New York: Cambridge University Press, 2005).

18. At the end of 1993 the dire situation continued as the Vatican revealed it would have to ask dioceses worldwide to increase their contributions to cope with the projected 1994 deficit of more than 26 million dollars. However in 1994 under the careful supervision of the pope, the Vatican had a surplus of $412,000. "Vatican Appeals for Funds," *New York Times,* November 7, 1993; "Vatican Paid All Its Bills in 1994," *The Tablet* (Brooklyn), July 1, 1994.

19. "Despite Papal Transition, Vatican has 12 Million Surplus," *The Tablet* (Brooklyn), July 22, 2006, p. 7.

20. "Vatican's 2006 Budget Finishes in the Black," *The Tablet* (Brooklyn), July 28, 2007, p. 6.

21. "Judge Says Abuse Lawsuit versus Vatican Can Go Abroad," *The Tablet* (Brooklyn), January 20, 2007, p. 12.

22. "Spain Ends Church Money," *Daily News,* September 24, 2006, p. 46.

23. Thomas Patrick Melady, *The Ambassador's Story: The United States and the Vatican in World Affairs* (Huntington, IN: Our Sunday Visitor, 1994), p. 81.

24. "Pope: Christ's Peace Will Not Be Achieved Through War," *The Tablet* (Brooklyn), January 31, 2004, p. 13.

25. Melady, *The Ambassador's Story,* pp. 95–96, 113–24.

26. Tracy Early, "Vatican Wants Deterrence Policy Revisited," *The Tablet* (Brooklyn), May 14, 2005, p. 14.

27. "Vatican Denies Brokering Deal to Exile Saddam," *The Tablet* (Brooklyn), March 15, 2003, p. 1.

28. "Vatican Official: Iraqi Christians were Safer Under Saddam," *The Tablet* (Brooklyn), August 11, 2007, p. 3.

29. "Australian Bishops Warn Against Pre-Emptive Strike," *The Tablet* (Brooklyn), October 13, 2007, p. 9.

30. John Thavis, "Mideast War Brings Pope's Foreign Policy into Focus," *The Tablet* (Brooklyn), August 12, 2006, p. 3.

31. "Vatican Appealed for Just Treatment of Iranian Jews," *The Tablet,* September 30, 2000; "Papal Appeals for Clemency Sent to Two Governors," ibid., November 13, 1999.

32. Peter J. Boyer, "A Hard Faith: How the new Pope and his predecessor redefined Vatican II," *The New Yorker,* May 16, 2005, p. 65.

33. Nancy Frazier O'Brien, "Role Played by Vatican in Cairo Foreshadows Beijing," *The Tablet* (Brooklyn), June 24, 1995.

34. Barbara Brossette, "Vatican Picks U.S. Women As Delegate to U.N. Parley," *The New York Times,* August 25, 1995.

35. "In Benedict's Own Words: Praise for Predecessors Pleas for Ecumenism," *The New York Times,* April 21, 2005, p. A13.

36. "Menorah for the Pope," *The Tablet* (Brooklyn), December 6, 2003.

37. "Vatican Tackles Anti-Semitism," *New York Post,* April 28, 2007, p. 4.

38. "Vatican Foreign Minister: Pope Seeks United Europe," *The Tablet* (Brooklyn), May 21, 2005, p. 6.

39. "Evolution Is Seen as Compatible with Catholicism," *The Tablet* (Brooklyn), August 13, 2005, p. 9.

40. "Vatican Criticizes Jesuit Liberation Theologian," *The Tablet* (Brooklyn), March 24, 2007, p. 7.

41. Boyer, "A Hard Faith," p. 63.

42. Boyer, "A Hard Faith," p. 54.

43. "Pope Says Christian Unity Faces New Challenges," *The Tablet* (Brooklyn), November 25, 2006, p. 9.

44. John Thavis, "Vatican Document on Salvation Sets a Theological Boundary, *The Tablet* (Brooklyn), September 16, 2000; Cindy Wooden, "Jews Walk Out on Dialogue," ibid., September 30, 2000.

45. John Thavis, "Latin Mass Will Not Be Enough for Lefebvrites," *The Tablet* (Brooklyn), July 14, 2007.

46. "Two Popes Advance Toward Sainthood, to Mixed Reviews," *The New York Times*, September 4, 2000, p. A7.

Select Bibliography

The major source for the study of the papacy's ecclesiastical, political, and diplomatic policies remains the *Archivio Segreto Vatican (ASV)*, the central repository for the correspondence and the acts promulgated by the Holy See, opened to scholars by Pope Leo XIII in 1880. The documents therein are accessible for all popes through Benedict XV (1914–1922). The controversy over the Holocaust and the papal reaction to the genocide has led to the selective opening of the papers of Pius XI and those of the Munich and Berlin nunciatures from 1922 to 1939. Microfilm copies of much of this material (some 95 reels) is now housed in the United States Holocaust Memorial Museum in Washington, DC. In 2006 Pope Benedict XVI opened additional papers of the secretariat of state including Pacelli's personal notes on meetings and audiences with Pius XI and other figures from 1930 to 1939, and their publication is pending. Earlier, a more limited access was provided to the papers of Pius XII (1939–1958) when Pope Paul VI in 1964 allowed four Jesuits to examine part of his papers that resulted in the publication of 12 volumes of documents of the Holy See during the onset and course of the Second World War: *Actes et documents du Saint Siège relatifs à la seconde guerre mondiale, [ADSS]*, ed. Pierre Blet, et. al. (Rome: Libreria Editrice Vaticana, 1965–1981). The first of these volumes has been translated into English as *Records and Documents of the Holy See Relating to the Second World War. I: The Holy See and the War in Europe, March 1939–August 1940. [RDHSWW]*, trans. Gerard Noel. Washington, DC: Corpus Books, 1968.

Other useful printed primary sources include

Abbott, Walter M., ed. *The Documents of Vatican II.* New York: America Press, 1966.

Acta Apostolicae Sedis (Acts of the Apostolic See): 1909–present [AAS].

Acta Nuniature Polanae: Achilles Ratti (1918–1921). Rome Institum Historicum Polonicum, 1995.

Acta Pio IX. Pontificis Maximi. Pars prima acta exhibens quae ad Ecclesiam universam spectant (1846–1854). Rome: Artium, 1855.

Acta Sanctae Sedis (Compendium of Documents of Holy See): 1865–1908 [ASS].

Acta Summi Pontificis Joannis XXIII. Vatican City: Typis Polyglottis, 1960, 1964.

Actes de Benoit XV: Encycliques, motu proprio, brefs, allocutions, actes des dicastres. Paris: Bonne Presse, 1926–1934.

Actes de Leon XIII: Encycliques, motu proprio, brefs, allocutions, actes des dicastres. Paris: Bonne Presse, 1931–1937.

Actes di S.S. Pie XI: Encycliques, motu proprio, brefs, allocutions, actes des dicastres. Paris: Bonne Presse, 1932–1936.

Appeals for Peace of Pope Benedict XV and Pope Pius XI. Washington, DC: Catholic Association for International Peace, 1931.

Atti del Sommo Pontefice Pio IX, Felicemente Regnante. Parte seconda che comprende I Motu-proprii, chirografi editti, notificazioni, ec. per lo stato pontificio. Rome: Tipografia delle Belle Arti, 1857.

Barberi, Andreas, ed. *Bullarii Romani Continuatio.* Rome: Camerae Apostolicae, 1835–1857. *[BullRomCont]*

Bertone, Domenico, ed. *Discorsi di Pio XI.* Turin: Società Editrice Internazionale, 1959.

Blakiston, Noel, ed. *The Roman Question: Extracts from the Despatches of Odo Russell from Rome, 1858–1870.* London: Chapman and Hall, 1962.

Blet, Pierre. *Pius XII and the Second World War according to the Archives of the Vatican.* New York: Paulist Press, 1999.

Brady, W. Maziere, ed. *Anglo-Roman Papers. Volume III—Memoirs of Cardinal Erskine, Papal Envoy to the Court of George III.* London: Alexander Gardner, 1890.

Butler, Cuthbert. *The Vatican Council: The Story Told from Inside in Bishop Ullathorne's Letters.* New York: Longmans, Green, and Co., 1930.

Capovila, Loris F., ed. *Giovanni XXIII. Quindici Letture.* Rome: Edizioni di Storia e Letteratura, 1970.

Caprara, Jean. *Concordat, et recueil des bulles et bres de N.S.P., le Pape Pie VII, sur les affaires actuelles de l'Eglise de France.* Liege: Lemarie, 1802.

Caprile, Giovanni, ed. *Il Concilio Vaticano II.* 5 vols. Civiltà Cattolica, 1965.

Caprile, Giovanni, ed. *(Paul VI) Il Sinodo dei vescovi. Interventi e documentazione.* Rome: Edizione Studium, 1992.

Carlen, Claudia, Sister M, ed. *A Guide to the Encyclicals of Roman Pontiffs from Leo XIII to the Present Day, 1878–1937.* New York: H.W. Wilson Co., 1939.

———, ed. *The Papal Encyclical. I: 1740–1878; II: 1878–1903; III: 1903–1939; IV: 1939–1958; V: 1958–1981.* Ann Arbor, MI: The Pierian Press, 1981. [PE]

———, ed. *Papal Pronouncements. A Guide: 1740–1978. I: Benedict XIV to Paul VI; II: Paul VI to John Paul I.* Ann Arbor, MI: The Pierian Press, 1990. [PP]

Cavalleri, Ottavio, and Germano Gualdo, eds. *L'Archivio de Mons. Achille Ratti visitatore apostolico e nunzio a Varsavia (1918–1921).* Vatican City: Archivio Vaticano, 1990.

Cerio, F. Diaz de, and M. F. Nunex y Monez, eds. *Instrucciones secretas a los nuncios de Espana en el siglio XIX (1847–1907).* Rome: Editrice Pontificia Università Gregoriana, 1989.

Charles-Roux, Francois. *Huit ans au Vatican.* Paris: Flammarion, 1947.

Cianfarra, Camille M. *The War and the Vatican.* London: Oates and Wasbourne, 1945.

Ciano, Galeazzo. *Diario.* Milan: Rizzoli, 1950.

Civiltà Cattolica, La. 1850 to Present. [CC]

Colapietra, Raffaele. "Il Diario Brunelli del Conclave del 1823." *Archivio Storico Italiano* CXX (1962): 76–146.

———. "Il Diario del Conclave del 1829." *Critica Storica* I (1962): 517–41.

Collecion de Enciclicas y Otras Cartas de los Papas Gregory XVI, Leon XIII, Pio X, Bededicto XV y Pio XI. Madrid: Saes Hermanos, 1935.

Collins, Joseph B., ed. *Catechetical Documents of Pope Pius X.* New York: Saint Anthony Guild Press, 1946.

Crispolti, Filippo. Pio IX, Leone XIII, Pio X, Benedetto XV. Ricordi personali. Milan: Treves, 1932.

Dalla Torre, Paolo. *Pio IX e Vittorio Emanuele II. Dal loro carteggio privato negli anni del licaceramento (1865–1878).* Rome: Istituto di Studino Romani Editore, 1972.

Di Nolfo, Ennio. *Vaticano e Stati Uniti, 1939–1952. Dalle Carte di Myron C. Taylor.* Milan: Agneli Editore, 1978.

Discorsi e Radio Messagi di Sua Santità Pio XII. 2 vols. Milan: Società Editrice "Vita e Pensiero," 1941.

Discorsi, messaggi, colloqui del Santo Padre Giovanni XXIII. 5 vols. Vatican City: Tipografia Poliglotta, 1961–1967.

Discourses of the Popes from Pius XI to John Paul II to the Pontifical academy of Sciences, 1936–1986. Vatican City: Pontificia Academia Scientiarum, 1986.

Duerm, Charles van, ed. *Correspondence du Cardinal Hercule Consalvi avec le Prince Clement de Metternich.* Louvain: Polleunlis & Ceuterick, 1899.

———. *Un peu plus de lumiere sur le conclave de Venise et sur le commencements du pontificat de Pie VII, 1799–1800.* Louvain: University Press, 1896.

Flannery, Austin, ed. *Vatican Council II: The Conciliar and Post Conciliar Documents.* Grand Rapids, MI: Eerdmans, 1992.

Franciscis, Pasquale de, ed. *Discorsi del Sommo Pontefice Pio IX Pronunziati in Vaticano ai fedeli di Roma e dell'orbe dal principio della sua prigionia fino al presente.* Rome: G. Aurelj, 1872.

Fremantle, Anne, ed. *The Papal Encyclicals in their Historical Context.* New York: G.P. Putnam's Sons, 1956.

Frossard, Andre. *"Be Not Afraid: Pope John Paul Speaks Out on his Life, his Beliefs, and his Inspiring Vision for Humanity.* Translated by J. R. Foster. New York: St. Martin's Press, 1984.

Gabriele, Mariano, ed. *Il Carteggio Antonelli-Sacconi (1868–1860).* Rome: Istituto per la Storia del Risorgimento Italiano, 1962.

Gasquet, Cardial. *A Memoir.* New York: P.J. Kenedy and Sons, 1953.

Great Britain Foreign Office. *British Documents on the Origins of the War, 1898–1914.* Edited by George P. Gooch and Harold Temperly. London: H.M. Stationery Office, 1926.

Grissell, Hartwell de La Garde. *Sede Vacante, Being a Diary Written During the Conclave of 1903.* London: James Parker and Co., 1903.

Guitton, Jean. *Dialogues avec Paul VI.* Paris: Fayard, 1967.

Hachey, Thomas E., ed. *Anglo-Vatican Relations 1914–1939: Confidential Reports of the British Minister to the Holy See.* Boston: G.K. Hall, 1972.

Insegnamenti di Paolo VI. 16 vols. Vatican City: Libreria Editrice Vaticana, 1963–1977.

John Paul II. *Crossing the Threshold of Hope.* Edited by Vittorio Messori. New York: Alfred A. Knopf, 1994.

John Paul II. *Pilgrim of Peace: Homilies and Addresses.* New York: Harmony Books, 1987.

Kennan, George. *Memoirs, 1925–1950.* Boston: Little, Brown and Co., 1967.

Klinkowstroem, M. A., ed. *Memoires, Documents et Écrits Divers laissés par le Prince de Metternich.* Paris: Plon, 1883.

Koenig, Harry C., ed. *Principles for Peace: Selections from Papal Documents from Leo XIII to Pius XII.* Washington, DC: National Catholic Welfare Conference, 1943.

La Briere, Yves de. *La Patrie et la Paix: Textes pontificaux traduits et commentes.* Paris: Desclee, 1938.

Lehnert, Pascalina. *Pio XII. Il prilegio di servivlo.* Milan: Rusconi, 1984.

Leonis XIII Pontificis Maximi Acta. 23 vols. Rome: Ex typographia Vaticana, 1881–1905.

Lettres apostoliques de S.S. Pie X. Encycliques, motu proprio, brefs, allocutions, actes des dicastres. 8. vols. Paris: Bonne Press, 1930–1936.

L' Opera della Santa Sede nella Guerra Europea. Raccolta dei documenti (Agoston 1914–Luglio 1916). Rome: Tipografia Poliglotta Vaticana, 1916.

Luciani, Albino. *Illustrisimi: Letters from Pope John Paul I.* Translated by William Weaver. Boston: Little, Brown and Co., 1976.

———. *The Message of John Paul I.* Boston: Daughters of St. Paul, 1978.

Lukacs, Lajos. *The Vatican and Hungary 1846–1878: Reports and Correspondence on Hungary of the Apstolic Nuncios in Vienna.* Translated by Zsofia Kormos. Budapest: Akademiai Kiado, 1981.

Maiolo, Giovanni, ed. *Pio IX da Vescovo a Pontifice. Lettere al Card Luigi Amat, Agosto 1839–Luglio 1848.* Modena, It.: Società Tipografico Modonese, 1943.

Martina, Giacomo. *Pio IX e Leopold II.* Miscellanea Historiae Pontificiae, Rome: Pontificia Università Gregoriana, 1967.

Mazzini, Joseph. *Italy, Austria, and the Pope.* London: Albonesi, 1845.

McCormick, Anne O'Hare. *Vatican Journal, 1921–1954.* New York: Farrar, Straces and Cudahy, 1957.

Melady, Thomas Patrick. *The Ambassador's Story: The United States and the Vatican in World Affairs.* Huntington, IN: Our Sunday Visitor, 1994.

Messages of John Paul II. Boston: St. Paul Editions, 1979.

Meurthe, A. Boulay de la, ed. *Documents sur la négociation du concordat et sur les autres rapports de la France avec le Saint-Siège en 1800 et a1801.* Paris: E. Leroux, 1891–1905.

Miller, J. Michael, ed. *The Encyclicals of John Paul II.* Huntington, IN: Our Sunday Visitor, 1999.

Momigliano, Eucardio, ed. *Tutte le encicliche dei sommi Pontefici.* Milan: dall'Oglio, editore, 1959.

Monti, Antonio. *Pio IX nel Risorgimento Italiano con documenti inediti.* Bari: Laterza, 1928.

Montini, Giovanni Battista. *Pensiamo al Concilio.* Milan: Archdiosesen Press, 1962.

Morgan, Thomas B. *A Reporter at the Papal Court: A Narrative of the Reign of Pope Pius XI.* New York: Longmans, Green, and Co., 1937.

————. *The Listening Post: Eighteen Years on Vatican Hill.* New York: Putnam, 1944.

Mourret, Fernand. *Le Concile du Vatican d'après des Documents inédits.* Paris: Bloud & Gay, 1919.

O'Gorman, Mother E., ed. *Papal Teachings: The Church.* Boston: Daughters of St. Paul, 1962.

O'Reilly, Bernard. *Life of Leo XIII. From an Authentic Memoir Furnished by his Order.* New York: John Winston Co, 1903.

Osservatore Romano, L'. 1861-present. [OR]

Pacca, Bartolomeo. *Historical Memoirs.* 2 vols. Translated by George Head. London: Longman, 1850.

Pacelli, Eugenio. *Discorsi e Panegirici.* Milan: Società editrice "Vita e Pensiero," 1939.

Pacelli, Francesco. *Diario della Conciliazione.* Città del Vaticana: Libreria Editrice Vaticana, 1959.

The Persecution of the Catholic Church in the Third Reich: Facts and Documents. London: Burns and Oates, 1940.

Pii X Pontificis Maximi Acta or Acta Pio X. 5 vols. Rome: Typographia Vaticana, 1905–1914.

Pirri, Pietro, ed. *Pio IX e Vittorio emanuele II dal loro carteggio privato. I. La laicizzazione dello Stato Sardo, 1848–1856.* Rome Università Gregoriana, 1944; II, *La questione romana, 1856–1864.* Rome: Università Gregoriana, 1951.

Pius XII and Peace, 1939–1940. Washington, DC: National Catholic Welfare Conference, 1940.

The Pope and the People: Select Letters and Addresses on Social Questions by Pope Leo XIII, Pope Pius X, Pope Benedict XV, and Pope Pius XI. London: Catholic Truth Society, 1932.

Pope John XXIII, *Journal of a Soul.* Translated by Dorothy White. New York: McGraw-Hill, 1965.

The Pope Speaks: The Words of Pius XII. New York: Harcourt, Brace, and Co., 1940.

Ratti, Achille. *Essays in History.* Freeport, NY: Books for Libraries, 1967.

Ratzinger, Joseph Cardinal. *Ratzinger Report.* With Vittorio Messori. San Francisco: Ignatius Press, 1985.

Roncalli, Angelo. *Scritti e discorsi, 1953–1958.* 4 vols. Rome: Paoline, 1959–1962.

Rosmini, Antonio. *Della misssione a Rome.* Turin: Paravia, 1854.

Schaefer, Mary C. *A Papal Peace Mosaic, 1878–1936. Excerpts from the Messages of Popes Leo XIII, Pius X, Benedict XV, and Pius XI.* Washington, DC: Catholic Association for International Peace, 1936.

Selected Documents of His Holiness Pope Pius XII: 1939–1958. Washington, DC: National Catholic Welfare Conference, n.d.

Selected Papal Encyclicals and Letters, 1928–1931. London: Catholic Truth Society, 1932.

Stock, Leo F., ed. *Consular Relations between the United States and the Papal States: Instructions and Despatches.* Washington, DC: Catholic University of America Press, 1945.

Talks of Paul VI, John Paul I, and John Paul II to the Hierarchy of the United States. Boston: St. Paul Editions, 1979.

Tardini, Domenico, ed. *Memories of Pius XII*. Westminister, Md.: Newman Press, 1961.

Taylor, Myron C., ed. *Wartime Correspondence between President Roosevelt and Pope Pius XII*. New York: Macmillan, 1947.

Val, Cardinal Merry del. *Memories of Pope Pius X*. Westminster, MD: The Newman Press, 1951.

Wiseman, Cardinal Nicholas Patrick. *Recollections of the last four Popes and of Rome in their Times*. New York: Wagner, 1958.

Wycislo, Aloysius J. *Vatican II Revisited: By One Who Was There*. New York: Alba House, 1987.

Wynne, John J., ed. *The Great Encyclical Letters of Pope Leo XIII*. New York: Benziger Brothers, 1903.

Yzermans, Vincent A., ed. *All Things in Christ: Encyclicals and Selected Documents of Saint Pius X*. New York: Newman Press, 1954.

SECONDARY SOURCES

Anderson, Robin. *Between Two Wars: The Story of Pope Pius XI (Achille Ratti) 1922– 1939*. Chicago: Franciscan Herald Press, 1977.

Angelucci, G. A. *Il grande secretario della Santa Sede. Sunto della vita di Ercole Consalvi*. Rome: Scuola Tipogrofia, Pio X, 1924.

Aradi, Zsolt. *Pius XI: The Pope and the Man*. Garden City, NY: Hanover House, 1958.

Aretin, Karl Otmar von. *The Papacy and the Modern World*. Translated by Roland Hill. New York: McGraw-Hill, 1970.

Ascoli, Max. "The Roman Church and Political Action." *Foreign Affairs* 13 (April 1935): 441–51.

Aubert, Roger. *The Church in a Secularized Society*. New York: Paulist Press, 1978.

———. *Le Pontificat de Pie IX*. Paris: Bloud and Gay, 1952.

Barth, Markus. *Israel and the Church: Contribution to Dialogue Viatal for Peace*. Richmond: John Knox Press, 1969.

Barthel, Manfred. *The Jesuits: History and Legend of the Society of Jesus*. Translated by Mark. Howson. New York: William Morrow and Co., 1984.

Bartlett, J. V. *The Popes: A Papal History*. Scottsdale, AZ: Sim Ridge Publisher, 1990.

Bea, Augustin Cardinal. *The Church and the Jewish People*. New York: Harper and Row, 1966.

Bernardini, Gene. "The Origins and Development of Racial Anti-Semitism in Fascist Italy." *Journal of Modern History* 49 (March 1977): 431–53.

Binchy, D. A. *Church and State in Fascist Italy*. New York: Oxford University Press, 1941.

Blanshard, Paul. *Paul Blanshard on Vatican II*. Boston: Beacon Press, 1966.

Brennan, Anthony. *Pope Benedict XV and the War*. London: King, 1917.

Brennan, James F. *The Reflection of the Dreyfus Affair in the European Press, 1897– 1899*. Studies in Modern European History. edited by Frank J. Coppa. New York: Peter Lang, 1998.

Brennan, Richard. *A Popular Life of our Holy Father Pope Pius IX*. New York: Benziger Brothers, 1877.

Bressan, Edoardo. "L'Osservatore Romano e le relazioni interazionali della Santa Sede (1917–1922)." In *Benedetto XV e la Pace—1918*, edited by G. Rumi. 233– 53. Brescia: Morcelliana, 1990.

Burton, Katerine. *The Great Mantle: The Life of Giuseppe Melchiore Sarto, Pope Pius X.* New York: Longmans, Green, and Co., 1950.

———. *Leo the Thirteenth: The First Modern Pope.* New York: David McKay Co., 1962.

Canepa, Andrew M. "Pius X and the Jews: A Reappraisal." *Church History* 61, no. 3 (1992): 362–72.

Carpi, Daniel. "The Catholic Church and Italian Jewry under the Fascists." In *Yad Washem Studies on the European Jewish Catastrope and Resistance,* edited by Shaul Esh. 43–56. IV. New York: KATV Publishing House, 1975.

Carroll, James. *Constantine's Sword: The Church and the Jews.* Boston: Houghton Mifflin, 2001.

Chadwick, Owen. *Britain and the Vatican during the Second World War.* Cambridge: Cambridge University Press, 1986.

———. *A History of the Popes, 1830–1914.* Oxford: Clarendon Press, 1998.

Cicognani, Amleto Giovanni. *A Symposium on the Life and Work of Pope Pius X.* Washington, DC: Confraternity of Christian Doctrine, 1946.

Collins, Joseph B., ed. *Chatechetical Documents of Pope Pius X.* New York: Saint Anthony Guild Press, 1946.

Conway, J. S. (Myron C. Taylor's Mission to the Vatican 1940–1950), *Church History,* vol. 44, no. 1 (March 1975): 85–99.

———. *The Nazi Persecution of the Churches, 1933–1945.* London: Weidenfeld and Nicolson, 1968.

Coppa, Frank J. "Cardinal Giacomo Antonelli: An Accommodating Personality in the Politics of Confrontation." *Biography* II no. 2 (Fall 1979): 283–302.

———. *Cardinal Giacomo Antonelli and Papal Politics in European Affairs.* Albany: State University of New York Press, 1990.

———. "Cardinal Antonelli, the Papal States and the Counter-Risorgimento." *The Journal of Church and State* XVI (Autumn 1974): 453–71.

——— ed. *Controversial Concordats: The Vatican's Relations with Napoleon, Mussolini and Hitler.* Washington, DC: The Catholic University of America Press, 1999.

———. "Giolitti and the Gentiloni Pact between Myth and Reality." *The Catholic Historical Review* LIII no. 2 (July 1967): 217–28.

——— ed. *The Great Popes Through History.* 2 vols. Westport, CT: Greenwood Press, 2002.

———. *The Modern Papacy Since 1789.* Longman History of the Papacy, London and New York: Longman, 1998.

———. *The Papacy, the Jews and the Holocaust.* Washington, DC: Catholic University Press, 2006.

———. *Pope Pius IX: Crusader in a Secular Age.* Boston: Twayne Publishers, 1979.

———. "Pope Pius XI's 'Encyclical' *Humani Generis Unitas* against Racism and Anti-Semitism and the 'Silence' of Pope Pius XII." *Journal of Church and State* 40 no. 4 (Autumn 1998): 775–95.

———. "Realpolitik and Conviction in the Conflict between Piedmont and the Papacy during the Risorgimento." *The Catholic Historical Review* LIV no. 4 (January 1969).

Cornwell, John. *Hitler's Pope: The Secret History of Pius XII.* New York: Viking, 1999.

Corrigan, Raymond. *The Church and the Nineteenth Century.* Milwaukee: Bruce Publishing Company, 1938.

Daniel-Rops, Henri. *The Church in an Age of Revolution 1789–1870.* Translated by John Warrington. Garden City, NY: Image Books, 1967.

Delzell, Charles F., ed. *The Papacy and Totalitarianism between the Two World Wars.* New York: John Wiley and Sons, 1974.

Duffy, Eamon. *Saints and Sinners: A History of the Popes.* New Haven: Yale University Press, 1997.

Dunn, Dennis J. "Stalinism and the Catholic Church during the Era of World War II," *The Catholic Historical Review* LIX n. 3 (October 1973), 404–28.

Falconi, Carlo. *The Popes in the Twentieth Century: From Pius X to John XXIII.* Translated by Muriel Grindrod. Boston: Little, Brown, and Co., 1967.

———. *The Silence of Pius XII.* Translated by Bernard Wall. Boston: Little, Brown, and Co., 1970.

Fattorini, Emma. *Germania e Santa Sede. La Nunziature di Pacelli tra la Grande Guerra e la Repubblica di Weimar.* Annali dell' Istituto storico italo-germanico, Milan: Il Mulino, 1992.

Fesquet, Henri. *The Drama of Vatican II: The Ecumenical Council, June 1962–December 1965.* New York: Random House, 1967.

Fogarty, Gerald P. *The Vatican and the Americanist Crisis: Denis J. O'Connell, American Agent in Rome, 1885–1903.* Pontificia Università Gregoriana, Rome: Università Gregoriana Editrice, 1974.

Forbes, F. A. *Life of Pius X.* London: Burns, Oates & Westminister, 1918.

Giordani, Igino. *Pius X: A Country Priest.* Translated by Thomas J. Tobin. Milwaukee: Bruce Publishing Co., 1954.

Giovanetti, Alberto. *El Vaticano y la guerra 1939–1940.* Translated by Felice Ximenez de Sanoval. Madrid: Sposa-Calpe, S.A., 1961.

Gorresio, Vittorio. *The New Mission of Pope John XXIII.* Translated by Charles Lam Markmann. New York: Funk and Wagnalls, 1969.

Gurian, Waldemar. "Hitler's Undeclared War on the Catholic Church." *Foreign Affairs* VI (January 1938): 260–71.

Gurian, Waldemar, and M. A. Fitzsimons, eds. *The Catholic Church in World Affairs.* Notre Dame, IN: University of Notre Dame Press, 1954.

Halecki, Oscar. *Eugenio Pacelli: Pope of Peace.* New York: Farrar, Strauss and Young, Inc., 1951.

Hales, E.E.Y. *The Catholic Church in the Modern World.* Garden City, NY: Hanover House, 1958.

———. *Pio Nono: A Study in European Politics and Religion in the Nineteenth Century.* Garden City, NY: Doubleday, 1962.

———. *Revolution and Papacy, 1769–1846.* Notre Dame, IN: University of Notre Dame Press, 1966.

Hanson, Eric O. *The Catholic Church in World Politics.* Princeton, NJ: Princeton University Press, 1987.

Harrigan, William M. "Nazi Germany and the Holy See, 1933–1936." *The Catholic Historical Review* XLVII (1961): 164–98.

———. "Pius XII's Efforts to Effect a Détente in German-Vatican Relations, 1939–1940." *The Catholic Historical Review* XLIX (July 1963): 173–91.

Hebblethwaite, Peter. *Paul VI: The First Modern Pope.* New York: Paulist Press, 1993.

———. *Pope John XXIII: Shepherd of the Modern World.* Garden City, NY: Doubleday and Co., Inc., 1985.

————. *The Year of Three Popes.* New York: Collins, 1979.

Hecht, Robert A. *An Unordinary Man: A life of Father John La Farge, S.J.* Lanham, MD: The Scarecrow Press, Inc., 1996.

Hehir, J. Bryan. "Papal Foreign Policy." *Foreign Policy* (Spring 1990): 26–48.

Hitchcock, James. *Catholicism and Modernity: Confrontation or Capitulation.* New York: Seabury Press, 1979.

Holmes, J. Derek. *The Papacy in the Modern World, 1914–1978.* New York: Crossroad Publishers, 1981.

Irani, George Emile. *The Papacy and the Middle East: The Role of the Holy See in the Arab-Israeli Conflict, 1962–1984.* Notre Dame, IN: University of Notre Dame Press, 1986.

Keefe, Patricia M. "Popes Pius XI and Pius XII, the Catholic Church, and the Nazi Persecution of the Jews." *The British Journal of Holocaust Education* 2 no. 1 (Summer 1993): 26–47.

Kent, George O. "Pope Pius XII and Germany: Some Aspects of German-Vatican Relations, 1933–1943." *American Historical Review* LXX (October 1964): 59–78.

Kent, Peter C. *The Pope and the Duce.* New York: St. Martin's, 1981.

————. "A Tale of Two Popes: Pius XI, Pius XII and the Rome-Berlin Axis," *Journal of Contemporary History* 23, n. 4 (October 1988): 589–608.

Kent, Peter C., and John F. Pollard, eds. *Papal Diplomacy in the Modern Age.* Westport, CT: Praeger, 1994.

Kertzer, David I. *The Kidnapping of Edgardo Montara.* New York: Random House, 1998.

————. *The Popes Against the Jews: The Vatican's Role in the Rise of Modern Anti-Semitism.* New York: Knopf, 2001.

Kirby, Dianne. *Religion in the Cold War.* New York: Palgrave/Macmillan, 2003.

Klenicki, Rabbi Leon, and Cardinal Avery Dulles. *The Holocaust, Never to be Forgotten: Reflections on the Holy See's Document, "We Remember."* Mahwah, NJ: Paulist Press, 2001.

Kreutz, Andrej. *Vatican Policy on the Palestinian-Israeli Conflict: The Struggle for the Holy Land.* Westport, CT: Greenwood, 1990.

Kubov, Aryeh L. "The Silence of Pope Pius XII and the Beginnings of the Jewish Document." In *Yad Vashem Studies of the European Jewish Catastrophe and Resistance,* edited by Nathan Eck and Aryeh Leon. VI. 7–25. Jerusalem: Yad Vashem, 1967.

La Farge, John. *Interracial Justice: A Study of the Catholic Doctrine of Race Relations.* New York: America Press, 1937.

Lapide, Pinchas E. *Three Popes and the Jews.* New York: Hawthorne Books, Inc., 1967.

Levai, Jeno. *Hungarian Jewry and the Papacy.* London: Sands and Company, 1967.

Lewy, Guenter. *The Catholic Church and Nazi Germany.* New York: McGraw-Hill, 1965.

————. "Pius XII, the Jews, and the German Catholic Church." *Commentary* 37 (February 1964): 23–33.

Littell, Franklin H. "*Kirchenkampf* and Holocaust: The German Church Struggle and Nazi Anti-Semitism in Retrospect." *Journal of Church and State* 13 no. 1 (Winter 1971): 209–26.

Magister, Sandro. *La politica vaticana e l'Italia, 1943–1978.* Rome: Reuniti, 1979.

Malinski, Mieczyslaw. *Pope John Paul II: The Life of Karol Wojtyla.* Translated by P. S. Fall. New York: Seabury Press, 1979.

Murphy, Paul L., and Rene Arlington. *La popessa.* New York: Warner Books, 1983.

Otmar von Aretin, Karl. *The Papacy and the Modern World.* Trans. Roland Hill. New York: McGraw-Hill, 1970.

Passelecq, Georges, and Bernard Suchecky, *L'encyclique cachee de Pie XI. Une occasion manquee de l'Eglise face a l'antisemitisme. Preface "Pie XI, les Juifs et l'antisemitisme," de Emile Poulat.* Paris: Editions La Decouverte, 1995.

———. *The Hidden Encyclical of Pius XI.* New York: Harcourt, Brace, and Co., 1997.

Pellicani, Antonio. *Il Papa di tutti. La Chiesa Cattolica, il fascismo, e il razzismo, 1929–1945.* Milan: Sugar Editore, 1964.

Phayer, Michael. *The Catholic Church and the Holocaust, 1930–1965.* Bloomington: Indiana University Press, 2000.

Pollard, John F. *The Unknown Pope: Benedict XV (1914–1922) and the Persuit of Peace.* London and New York: Geoffrey Chapman, 1999.

———. *The Vatican and Italian Fascism, 1929–1932: A Study in Conflict.* Cambridge: Cambridge University Press, 1985.

Poulat, Emile. *Une Eglise Ebranlee. Chagement, conflit et continuite de Pie XII a Jean Paul II.* Paris: Casterman, 1980.

Reinerman, Alan J. *Austria and the Papacy in the Age of Metternich: Revolution and Reaction 1830–1838.* Washington, D.C.: Catholic University of America Press, 1989.

Rhodes, Anthony. *The Vatican in the Age of Dictators, 1922–1945.* New York: Holt, Rinehart, and Winston, 1973.

Rossi, Ernesto. *Il Managnello e l'aspersorio.* Florence: Parenti, 1958.

Ryan, Edwin. "Papal Concordats in Modern Times." *The Catholic Historical Review* XVI (October 1930): 302–10.

Sanchez, Jose M. *Pius XII and the Holocaust: Understanding the Controversy.* Washington, DC: Catholic University of America Press, 2002.

———. "The Popes and Nazi Germany: The View from Madrid." *Journal of Church and State* XXXVIII (Spring 1996): 365–76.

Tinnenmann, Ethel Mary (Sisters of the Holy Names of Jesus and Mary). "The Silence of Pius XII." *Journal of Church and State* 21 no. 2 (Spring 1979): 265–85.

Walker, Lawrence D. "Young Priests as Opponents: Factors Associated with Clerical Opposition to the Nazis in Bavaria." *The Catholic Historical Review* LXV (July 1933).

Wallace, Lillian Parker. *Leo XIII and the Rise of Socialism.* Durham, NC: Duke University Press, 1966.

Webster, Richard A. *The Cross and the Fasces.* Stanford: Stanford University Press, 1960.

Wills, Gary. *Papal Sin: Structures of Deceit.* New York: Doubleday, 2000.

Wynn, Wilton. *Keepers of the Keys: John XXIII, Paul VI, and John Paul II: Three Who Changed the Church.* New York: Random House, 1988.

Zahn, Gordan C. "Catholic Opposition to Hitler: The Perils of Ambiguity." *Journal of Church and State* 13 no. 3 (Autumn 1971): 413–25.

Zuccotti, Susan. *The Italians and the Holocaust: Persecution, Rescue, and Survival.* New York: Basic Books, Inc., 1987.

———. *Under his Very Windows: The Vatican and the Holocaust in Italy.* New Haven: Yale University Press, 2000.

Index

About the Author

FRANK J. COPPA is professor of history at St. John's University in New York and director of the university's doctoral program in modern world history. He is an associate editor of the New Catholic Encyclopedia. An expert in modern European, modern Italian, and papal history he has published widely in all three areas. He is the recipient of numerous grants including Fulbright and National Endowment for the Humanities as well as university grants. He has served as general editor and contributor to *The Dictionary of Modern Italian History* (1985); *The Encyclopedia of the Vatican and Papacy* (1999); *The Great Popes through History* (2002); and *The Encyclopedia of Modern Dictators* (2006) among others. Most recently he has published *The Papacy, the Jews, and the Holocaust* (2006).

This book is dedicated to the victims of the Darfur genocide and to those humanitarians and peacekeepers who gave their lives trying to protect the victims.

Contents

Appendices

Acknowledgments

Genocide in Darfur: Investigating the Atrocities in the Sudan could not have been produced without the contributions, insights, and help of a broad array of individuals and organizations. First and foremost, we wish to acknowledge the incredible support that Nina Bang-Jensen, Executive Director, Coalition for International Justice, and Stefanie Frease, Director of Programs, Coalition of International Justice, provided throughout the development of this book. In addition to co-authoring a chapter, Nina and Stefanie made countless contributions to this project, ranging from helping to persuade key Washington, D.C. "insiders" to contribute to the book to critiquing several of the chapters while in draft form. No editors could ask for more astute or hard-working colleagues. It was, indeed, an honor to work with Stefanie in the field and both Nina and Stefanie on this book.

In our estimation, what makes this book particularly unique and valuable is the expertise of each and every contributor. Thus, we sincerely thank all of the contributors to this volume. All are extremely busy individuals who work long hours in demanding jobs and gave up valuable time from immediate work at hand and family time to write their pieces.

We also wish to thank those members of the Darfur Atrocities Documentation Team (ADT) investigative team — Vanessa Allen, Debb Bodkin, Jamal Jafari, Linda Patrick, Jan Pfundheller, Brenda Sue Thornton, and Larissa Wakim — who shared their personal insights with us for inclusion in Chapter 6.

As readers may note, none of the translators, who were critical to the ADT, is mentioned by name herein. That is because it was feared that if their names became public it could result in severe repercussions for them should they return to Sudan, and/or their family members, many of whom are still in IDP camps in Darfur and/or unaccounted for. That said, we wish we could name each translator by name and provide a short account of his efforts. Our translators were committed to the success of the project, worked arduously under extremely trying conditions, and, as a result of the nature of their efforts, worked twice as hard as the interviewers. So, herein, we offer a heartfelt thanks to such diligent, caring individuals.

We also owe our editor at Routledge, Robert Tempio, a huge thank you for his enthusiasm from the start of this project and his support throughout the development of this book. We also wish to thank Charlotte Roh for her fine work as well. We greatly appreciate how she kept this book moving forward after Rob Tempio's departure from Routledge. And a special thanks to Taylor & Francis Group Project Editor Judith Simon for her expert guidance of the book through the production process.

Finally, we offer sincere thanks to the refugees themselves for agreeing to be interviewed by the ADT investigators — something we know must have been terribly difficult, as it required them to revisit the horrific experiences they suffered at the hands of the Government of Sudan and the *Janjaweed*. Some, perhaps many, of them have died since the interviews, as have their children. Others are still eking out an existence, but for how long?

Introduction

In July and August 2004, a multinational team of investigators, the Darfur Atrocities Documentation Team (ADT), traveled to various points along the Chad/Sudanese border to interview some of the two hundred thousand refugees from the Darfur region of Sudan. Government of Sudan troops and Arab militia (known as the *Janjaweed*) had attacked village after village of black Africans in retaliation against rebel attacks on government installations, but in doing so they engaged in the mass killing and raping of innocent men, women, and children who had nothing to do with the rebel groups. Approximately 1.5 million black Africans had been forcibly displaced from their homes and at least one hundred fifty thousand had died as a direct result of the ongoing violence or of malnutrition and disease (Reeves, 30 July 2004).* The investigators' purpose was to collect data that would enable the U.S. State Department to determine whether the mass violence being directed against African tribes (particularly the Fur, Massaleit, and Zaghawa) constituted genocide. The ADT conducted interviews with more than twelve hundred refugees over a five-week period. The State Department's Bureau of Intelligence and Research subsequently analyzed the data collected. Relying substantially on this data, on September 9, 2004, U.S. Secretary of State Colin Powell appeared before the Senate Foreign Relations Committee and announced that "genocide has occurred in Darfur and may still be occurring." With that announcement, the United States officially accused the Government of Sudan of perpetrating genocide.

* Eric Reeves. 2004. "Darfur Mortality Update: July 30, 2004; Current data for total mortality from violence, malnutrition, and disease." http://www.sudanreeves.org/modules.php?op=modload&name=Sections&file=index&req=viewarticle&artid=203&page=1 (accessed 4 July 2006).

The Darfur Atrocities Documentation Team, a project developed by the U.S. State Department and implemented in partnership with the U.S. Agency for International Development's Office of Transitional Initiatives (OTI) and the Coalition for International Justice (CIJ), a nongovernmental organization, was historic in several respects. First, it was the first official investigation by a sovereign nation of an ongoing case of mass violence for the express purpose of determining whether or not the violence amounted to genocide. Second, U.S. Secretary of State Powell's declaration was the first time that one government formally accused another government of ongoing genocide. Third, Secretary Powell, during his public testimony, invoked for the first time ever (by any government) Chapter VIII of the United Nations Convention on the Prevention and Punishment of the Crime of Genocide (UNCG), calling on the Security Council to take action "...appropriate for the prevention and suppression of acts of genocide... ." Fourth, on September 18, 2004, the UN Security Council passed Resolution 1564, calling for the immediate establishment of an international commission of inquiry into the situation in Darfur. The latter constituted the first time that the UN had undertaken an investigation to determine whether genocide was being committed by a member state. Fifth, after reviewing and debating the report from the Commission of Inquiry, on March 31, 2005, the Security Council voted, in Resolution 1593, to refer the situation in Darfur to the International Criminal Court — the first time such a Security Council referral had occurred.

This book is comprised of essays that present a thorough overview and critical analysis of this historic government-sponsored genocide investigation. Its contributors include U.S. Government and nongovernmental organization (NGO) officials involved in the genesis of the project as well as the analysis of the data; those who were involved in designing the project and hiring and training investigators, interpreters, and support personnel; investigators who served on the ADT; and several scholars who were not directly involved with the project but who offered critiques of the ADT as well as reflections on its significance

Goals of the Book

Our primary goal in developing this book is to present a comprehensive examination of the genesis and evolution of the Darfur Atrocities Documentation Project, along with its key findings and the ramifications of the latter. Thus, in part, it provides a detailed discussion as to why and how such a project was launched under the auspices of the U.S. Government (how the kernel of the idea made its way through the various bureaucratic hallways of government), the methodology used in the investigation, and the actual or potential significance of the ADT.

We believe that the book serves many valuable purposes. First, as previously mentioned, it provides a detailed examination of a "first" in regard to the investigatory powers taken by a sovereign nation to ascertain whether genocide was occurring in another part of the world. Second, it provides current and future genocide scholars with useful insights into both the potential value of such an investigation as well as the limitations of such (especially in regard to the timing of the investigation and its ramifications). Third, it reveals how a world power reacted to the findings of its own investigation. Fourth, it documents how the international community reacted to the findings of such an investigation. Fifth, it delineates the seemingly good intentions and hard work of a handful of individuals within the U.S. Government who were ostensibly dedicated to do something concrete to draw attention to the ongoing crisis in Darfur. Sixth, it provides unique insights into the dedication of NGOs — in particular, the Coalition for International Justice — to assist people in critical need whose very existence is threatened because of who they are and where they reside. Finally, and possibly most significant of all, it provides a unique perspective into a genocide unfolding before the very eyes of the world.

Organization and Chapters

Chapter 1, by Robert Collins (Professor Emeritus of History at the University of California, Santa Barbara), provides essential background information on Sudan in general and the Darfur conflict in particular.

In Chapter 2, Andrew Natsios, who was Chief Administrator of the U.S. Agency for International Development (USAID) at the time of the investigaton, describes how and why the U.S. Government decided to undertake a systematic investigation of atrocities that were being widely reported in Darfur. Natsios also discusses how USAID's experiences in Darfur have led to important changes in the Agency in order to make it more effective in providing humanitarian aid and supporting United States national security.

Chapter 3 describes how the ADT was created and launched as a partnership between USAID, the U.S. State Department, and several NGOs, notably the CIJ. Co-authors Nina Bang-Jensen, Executive Director and Counsel of CIJ, and Stefanie Frease, CIJ's Special Projects Director, who served as field director for the ADT, describe the process of establishing goals for the mission, securing funding, recruiting personnel, and coping with challenges in the field.

In Chapter 4, Jonathan Howard, a research analyst specializing in African public opinion for the U.S. State Department's Office of Research, discusses the development of the research methodology, including the eight-page questionnaire used by the investigators in the field, and the process of analyzing the massive amounts of data contained in the over one thousand interviews. He also summarizes the findings from the mission and discusses lessons learned from the overall experience.

The recruiting and training of the interpreters are discussed in Chapter 5 by Helge Niska, Professor of Linguistics at Stockholm University. Since it was known in advance that sexual crimes against women were widespread among the victim groups, efforts were made to recruit female interpreters. Under the circumstances, this proved impossible, so special training on how to interview and interpret with victims of sex crimes was provided to both interviewers and interpreters.

Chapter 6, by the book's co-editors, Samuel Totten and Eric Markusen, both of whom served as investigators on the ADT, details the briefings and training received by the 24 investigators prior to going into the field, challenges encountered in the field (e.g., extreme heat, flooding, vehicle breakdown, illness), and the information they obtained in their interviews with refugees. Insights and anecdotes from a number of the ADT investigators, dispersed throughout the chapter, vividly convey the human reality of suffering experienced by the refugees during the attacks on their homes and villages and the difficult conditions of their precarious existence in over-crowded refugee camps and settlements.

In Chapter 7, Steve Kostas, an attorney working with the Appeals Chamber of the International Criminal Tribunal for the former Yugoslavia, relates how the U.S. Government concluded that the atrocities being committed by the government of Sudan and its proxy Arab militias warranted being labeled "genocide." The chapter is based on interviews conducted with former U.S. Ambassador at Large for War Crimes Pierre-Richard Prosper and former U.S. Assistant Secretary of State Lorne Craner.

The implications, legal and otherwise, of the genocide determination are discussed in Chapter 8 by attorney Jerry Fowler, Director of the United States Holocaust Memorial Museum's Committee on Conscience. After reviewing the origins of the UN Genocide Convention, Fowler looks at the reasoning that led the U.S. State Department to conclude that the killings and deaths in Darfur constitute a case of genocide and the UN Commission of Inquiry to decide that they do not.

In Chapter 9, Kelly Askin, Senior Legal Officer for the Open Society Justice Initiative, who accompanied investigative teams into the field in order to focus specifically on gender crimes, discusses the widespread and systematic commission of rape and other sexual crimes against members of the targeted groups — the vast majority of whom were young girls and women — by Sudanese government soldiers and Arab militias.

Chapter 10 through Chapter 13 feature comments and criticism by individuals who were not involved with the ADT and, hence, offer "outsiders'" perspectives on the project and its significance. Taylor Seybolt, a

Senior Program Officer with the United States Institute for Peace, calls the ADT "both a great success and a disappointing failure." Gerald Caplan, an independent consultant on Africa, who wrote the report on the Rwanda genocide for the Organizations of African Unity's International Panel of Eminent Personalities, notes differences between United States and international responses to the 1994 genocide in Rwanda and the ongoing genocide in Darfur and suggests several lessons from Rwanda for Darfur. Gregory Stanton, a lawyer and former U.S. State Department official, who is currently a professor of human rights, argues in support of the geno-cide determination based on ADT data and then analyzes various reasons that help account for the fact that other relevant organizations, including the United Nations, the European Union, and human rights groups, like Amnesty International, may have been reluctant to reach a similar conclu-sion. A fourth "outsider's" perspective is offered by University of Wisconsin political scientist Scott Straus, who examines some of the singular accom-plishments of the ADT, but also considers why the international response to Darfur, notwithstanding the evidence collected by the ADT and the U.S. Government's declaration of genocide, has been so "lackluster." It should be noted that the views expressed in these essays do not necessarily reflect the opinions of the editors or other contributors to this book.

In Chapter 14, Samuel Totten examines the genesis and implementation of the Atrocities Documentation Project as well as the U.S. government's determination that genocide had been perpetrated in Darfur between late 2003 and August 2004. In doing so, he considers and analyzes the rationale for the investigation and the reasoning for the determination as given by U.S. officials. He also delineates and discusses the perceptions of various scholars *vis-a-vis* the same issues, noting that many of the latter suspect that there were ulterior motives behind the development and implementai-ton of the investigation as well as the genocide determination.

Finally, in the Afterword, Editors Markusen and Totten review some of the positive and even historic contributions of the ADT as well as some hopeful initiatives to end the violence by a variety of groups and organiza-tions. But they also note the discouraging fact that, as the book went to press in Summer 2006, the situation in Darfur remained horrific. Only time and ensuing events will determine whether the ADT's endeavors will be regarded as a milestone in the fight against impunity and the effort to establish the rule of law.

Chronology:
The Darfur Crisis

2003

February 26, 2003 — Darfur rebels attack Sudanese military garrison at the town of Golu. Nearly two hundred soldiers are killed.

March 2003 — Fighting breaks out in the Darfur region of western Sudan between Government of Sudan (GoS) forces and black African rebels with the Sudan Liberation Army (SLA) and the Justice and Equality Movement (JEM).

April 2003 — Refugees from Darfur flow into eastern Chad and tens of thousands also become internally displaced within Darfur as GoS troops and *Janjaweed* (militias from wholly and semi-nomadic Arab tribes) counterattacks against government installations by black African-led rebel groups (the SLA and JEM). The former do so by attacking rebel strongholds as well as carrying out indiscriminate attacks on the villages of black Africans.

April 25, 2003 — Darfur rebels launch attacks against Sudanese military and police forces in Nyala and El-Fashir. The El-Fashir attack results in the deaths of more than thirty government soldiers, the destruction of several military aircraft, and the capture of the commander of the Sudanese air force base.

September 4, 2003 — A cease-fire is agreed upon by the SLA and the GoS. The GoS promises to address the complaints of the rebels (e.g., that the needs of the black Africans residing in the Darfur region have been neglected by the GoS: needs such as lack of adequate representation of the government, a lack of equal justice in the courts, a lack of roads, and inadequate schooling). Soon after, though, each side makes accusations that the other has broken the cease-fire.

October 7, 2003 — The United Nation's High Commissioner for Refugees (UNHCR) calls for over $16 million to meet the needs of the Sudanese refugees who have fled to Chad.

Early December 2003 — The *Janjaweed* carry out intensive attacks against black African villages during which they murder and rape civilians and burn the villages to the ground. Some ten thousand new refugees arrive in Chad.

The GoS restricts humanitarian access to the refugees by both refusing and/or delaying travel permits to Darfur.

December 5, 2003 — UN Undersecretary-General for Humanitarian Affairs and Emergency Relief Coordinator Jan Egeland asserts that Darfur "has quickly become one of the worst humanitarian crises in the world."

December 9, 2003 — UN Secretary-General Kofi Annan states that he is alarmed by the human rights violations and lack of humanitarian access in Darfur.

It is estimated that over a half million people have been displaced from Darfur and that up to one million individuals are in need of humanitarian aid.

December 23, 2003 — The UNHCR announces plans to establish refugee camps farther inside Chad in an effort to stave off the ongoing attacks against refugees in camps along the Chad/Sudanese border. It is estimated that approximately one hundred thousand Darfurian refugees have now sought refuge in Chad.

2004

January 7, 2004 — The U.S. Holocaust Memorial Museum's Committee on Conscience issues a "Genocide Warning" for Darfur, expressing concern that the organized violence underway could result in genocide.

UN Special Envoy for Humanitarian Affairs Tom Vraalsen travels to N'Djamena, Chad, calling on the GoS and the SLA to resume peace talks. He also calls on the GoS to allow greater access for humanitarian aid.

Late January 2004 — Over the course of a single week, about eighteen thousand refugees enter Chad as the *Janjaweed* intensify their attacks in Darfur.

February 10, 2004 — Following a promise by Sudanese President Omar Al Bashir to grant aid workers greater access to internally displaced persons (IDPs), UN Undersecretary-General for Humanitarian Affairs and Emergency Relief Coordinator Jan Egeland calls for a rapid humanitarian response.

Early to Mid February 2004 — UN agencies continue to provide ever-increasing humanitarian support to the refugees based in Chad.

IDPs in Darfur complain that humanitarian aid being provided to them by the UN and various nongovernmental organizations (NGOs) is being stolen, on a regular basis, by the *Janjaweed.*

February 18, 2004 — UN Undersecretary-General Jan Egeland deploys a UN Disaster and Assessment Coordination Team (UNDAC) to Darfur.

March 19, 2004 — UN Special Envoy for Humanitarian Affairs Tom Vraalsen asserts that the crisis in Darfur is "one of the worst in the world."

March 30, 2004 — The UN Office for the Coordination of Humanitarian Affairs (OCHA) issues a report that claims attacks by the *Janjaweed* are taking place on a daily basis across Darfur.

April 2, 2004 — After briefing the UN Security Council, Undersecretary-General Jan Egeland asserts that a coordinated "scorched earth" campaign of ethnic cleansing is being carried out by the *Janjaweed* against the black Africans of Darfur.

The UN Security Council issues a presidential statement of concern in regard to the humanitarian situation in Darfur and calls for a cease-fire.

April 3, 2004 — A joint statement of "deep concern" is issued by UN Secretary-General Kofi Annan and the directors of UN agencies and programs in regard to both the critical humanitarian crisis and major human rights violations in Darfur.

April 6, 2004 — Upon the request of UN Acting High Commissioner Bertrand Ramcharan, a fact-finding team from the Office of the High Commissioner for Human Rights undertakes an investigation in the refugee camps in Chad to assess the extent of human rights violations that have been perpetrated in Darfur.

April 7, 2004 — During the course of the tenth-year commemoration of the beginning of the Rwandan genocide, UN Secretary-General Kofi Annan asserts that he fears the unfolding of a similar tragedy in Darfur and calls on the international community to act.

April 9, 2004 — The GoS and rebel groups sign a forty-five-day "humanitarian cease-fire" (beginning on April 11), which allows for the deployment of observers from the African Union (AU). The agreement allows humanitarian assistance to be provided to the hundreds of thousands of IDPs in dire need of help.

April 22, 2004 — The UN sends a second fact-finding mission to Sudan to undertake an investigation into alleged human rights violations in Darfur.

May 4, 2004 — As a result of the UN's human rights investigation in Darfur, it is reported that the GoS and *Janjaweed* are guilty of perpetrating a "reign of terror" against the region's black African population. It is further asserted that among the crimes perpetrated against the black African population are killings, rapes, pillaging, destruction of property, and ethnic displacement.

The UN estimates that over one million black Africans have been internally displaced in Darfur as a result of the attacks by the GoS and the *Janjaweed*.

May 7, 2004 — UN Acting High Commissioner for Human Rights Bertrand Ramcharan provides the UN Security Council with a report of the findings of the two UN-sponsored human rights investigations. He reports that they both found that the GoS and the *Janjaweed* have committed massive human rights violations, which is liable to "constitute war crimes and/or crimes against humanity."

May 13, 2004 — UN Secretary-General Kofi Annan calls on Sudanese President al-Bashir to rein in and disarm the *Janjaweed*, maintain the cease-fire while attempting to negotiate a final settlement to the crisis, and provide more ready and safe access for humanitarian workers.

May 14, 2004 — An estimated sixty-five thousand refugees from Darfur are currently in Chad.

May 17, 2004 — UN Secretary-General Kofi Annan has a meeting with the GoS's Permanent Representative to the United Nations in order to express his alarm over the GoS's continued interference and placement of obstacles (e.g., long visa delays and slow customs clearances) in the way of humanitarian access.

May 20, 2004 — The UN Office for the Coordination of Humanitarian Affairs (OCHA) reports that its funds have been depleted and a looming crisis mounts due to a lack of adequate water, food, and healthcare services available for the IDPs.

The GoS promises, once again, to provide more ready access to those providing humanitarian care.

May 24, 2004 — The cease-fire, which was brokered six weeks earlier between the GoS and rebel groups, is broken as the government and the rebel factions blame each other for an attack that resulted in the murder of forty-five people in a village south of Nyala.

May 25, 2004 — The UN Security Council issues another presidential statement of "deep concern" in regard to the ongoing reports of human rights abuses in Darfur and, in doing so, calls on the GoS to both rein in and disarm the *Janjaweed*.

May 26, 2004 — Undersecretary-General Jan Egeland informs the UN Security Council that the GoS continues to prevent humanitarian aid from reaching the IDPs in Darfur and that the number of IDPs has increased to two million people.

The Sudanese government and rebel groups reach an agreement that allows the first international observers into Darfur.

May 27, 2004 — UN Secretary-General Kofi Annan's office announces that the Secretary General continues to be deeply concerned over the situation in Darfur and that he is willing to mediate a settlement.

June 8, 2004 — Approximately ninety thousand refugees are relocated to safer camps inside Chad by UNHCR.

June 11, 2004 — The UN Security Council calls for an end to the violence in Darfur and calls on all involved actors to help make that a reality.

June 14, 2004 — Following a visit to Darfur, Asma Jahangir, the UN's Special Rapporteur on Extrajudicial, Summary, or Arbitrary Executions, claims that GoS forces and the *Janjaweed* have committed numerous human rights violations, including the slaughter of civilians in Darfur villages.

June 15, 2004 — UN officials report that every fifth child in Darfur suffers from severe malnutrition. Additionally, it is reported that many children suffer from dysentery, measles, and high fever, and that every day children in refugee camps are dying from starvation and exhaustion.

June 18, 2004 — UN Secretary-General Kofi Annan names former Dutch Environment Minister Jan Pronk as the UN's Special Envoy to Sudan.

The United States threatens to impose sanctions on Sudan due to the deteriorating humanitarian situation in Darfur.

June 19, 2004 — Sudanese President al-Bashir orders all "illegally armed groups" to disarm.

June 20, 2004 — Reports continue to flood out of Darfur regarding bombings by GoS-operated Antonov planes, the rape of black African women in *Janjaweed*-controlled camps, and the murder of black African men who attempt to escape from the camps.

June 24, 2004 — U.S. Ambassador-at-Large for War Crimes Pierre Prosper asserts: "I can tell you that we see indicators of genocide and there is evidence that points in that direction." Prosper further states that the U.S. Government "is actively reviewing" the possibility that genocide is taking place in the Darfur region.

The U.S. Holocaust Memorial Museum (Washington, D.C.) closes access to its main exhibitions for the first time in its history for a half-hour program on the humanitarian crisis in Darfur, Sudan, calls for immediate action.

June 25, 2004 — Prior to his departure for Sudan, UN Secretary-General Kofi Annan states that he would use his forthcoming trip to press Khartoum to meet its obligations of protecting its civilians and disarming the *Janjaweed*. Noting that the black Africans of Darfur "are suffering a catastrophe" and that "terrible crimes have been committed" against them, Annan urges the international community to maintain pressure on Sudan. Asked if what was taking place in Darfur was ethnic cleansing or genocide, Annan asserted, "We don't need a label to propel us to act."

Lorne Craner, Assistant Secretary of State for the Bureau of Democracy, Human Rights, and Labor (DRL), in a meeting with leaders of several NGOs, including the Coalition for International Justice (CIJ), announces that he wants to send a team of investigators to Chad in order to interview refugees from Darfur.

June 28, 2004 — The CIJ tells the U.S. State Department that it can recruit a team of investigators for the investigative mission to Darfur. This mission eventually becomes known as the Atrocities Documentation Project (ADP).

June 30, 2004 — Secretary-General Kofi Annan arrives in Sudan for a three-day visit to Khartoum, Darfur, and Chad. While in Khartoum, Annan meets with GoS officials and also meets with U.S. Secretary of State Colin Powell concerning the Darfur crisis.

U.S. Secretary of State Colin Powell calls on Sudanese President al-Bashir to bring the *Janjaweed* under control, to begin negotiations with the Sudan Liberation Army (SLA) and the Justice and Equality Movement

(JEM), and to allow complete and unimpeded access to humanitarian agencies.

July 2, 2004 — While visiting refugee camps in eastern Chad, refugees inform UN Secretary-General Kofi Annan about the "gross and systematic" human rights violations that have been perpetrated by the *Janjaweed* in Darfur.

Following a visit to Sudan and a tour of Khartoum, U.S. Secretary of State Colin Powell informs the GoS that the only way relations with the United States will be normalized is if the GoS makes immediate and effective efforts to rein in the *Janjaweed* in Darfur.

July 3, 2004 — The United Nations and Sudan sign a joint communiqué in which each pledges to help to halt the conflict in Darfur. The GoS asserts that it will disarm the *Janjaweed*, bring to justice those responsible for human rights abuses, protect those in IDP camps from any additional attacks, resume peace talks with the rebel groups, and remove all obstacles to providing humanitarian assistance. The United Nations asserts that it will assist the African Union (AU) to quickly deploy cease-fire monitors and carry out more humanitarian relief.

The United Nations and GoS also agree to establish a Joint Implementation Mechanism (JIM) for the purpose of monitoring the agreement.

July 5, 2004 — Upon the conclusion of his trip to Sudan and Darfur, UN Secretary-General Kofi Annan warns of "catastrophic levels" of suffering.

July 7, 2004 — The UN Security Council issues a threat to impose an arms embargo and a travel ban against Sudan unless the GoS takes serious and effective measures to bring the Darfur conflict to an end. The Security Council reports it will begin reviewing the proposal in late July.

Briefing the UN Security Council via satellite link from Kenya, Secretary-General Kofi Annan reports that the situation in the IDP camps in Darfur is grave.

The UN Security Council's President for July, Ambassador Mihnea Ioan Motoc of Romania, calls for sustained pressure on Khartoum to resolve the Darfur crisis.

Undersecretary-General Jan Egeland issues a warning that "hundreds of thousands of people may die" if the *Janjaweed* is not reined in and, ultimately, disarmed.

The Coalition for International Justice (CIJ) sends an advance team to Chad to field-test the [Darfur] Atrocities Documentation Questionnaire, hire interpreters, and evaluate the situation on the ground. In addition to CIJ personnel, the advance team includes representatives from the State Department's Bureau of Democracy, Human Rights, and Labor (DRL), the

Bureau of Intelligence and Research, the American Bar Association's Central European and Eurasian Law Initiative (CEELI), and a consultant with vast experience working in Sudan.

July 9, 2004 — The UN Commission on Human Rights reports that Arab militias, with ties to the GoS, have destroyed food and water resources in the Jabal Marrah area in West Darfur, Sudan.

The UN High Commissioner for Refugees (UNHCR) reports that humanitarian organizations continue to be denied access to "the most affected areas" in Darfur.

July 12, 2004 — The GoS sends a 1,025-strong police force to Darfur to "maintain security, law, and order," and to "uphold the sense of nationhood." The police force's primary tasks, it is reported, are to protect refugee camps, set up security checkpoints along the border with Chad, and safeguard roads for the return of refugees. Ultimately, the force will be about six thousand strong, and include medics and traffic and riot police.

July 14, 2004 — Oxfam warns of the "spectre of disease" and an outbreak of cholera and/or malaria in the refugee camps based in Chad.

The U.S. Holocaust Memorial Museum and American Jewish World Service host an emergency nongovernmental summit on Darfur, leading to the creation of the Save Darfur Coalition.

July 15, 2004 — Secretary-General's Special Representative for Sudan Jan Pronk travels to Khartoum to take part in the first meeting of the Joint Implementation Mechanism (JIM).

The World Food Programme (WFP) reaches an agreement with Libya to allow transport through Libya in order to deliver emergency supplies to refugees in Chad and the IDPs in Darfur

July 18, 2004 — The SLA and JEM break off peace talks in Addis Ababa, Ethiopia, asserting they will not take part until the GoS agrees to leave Darfur and to disarm the *Janjaweed*.

July 19, 2004 — UN agencies report that the GoS is trying to pressure Darfur's massive population of IDPs to return to their home villages, even though the latter remain fearful of attacks by the *Janjaweed* and GoS troops.

The United Nations also reports that the number of people in the IDP camps has risen by one hundred thousand over the past month.

July 21, 2004 — Secretary-General Kofi Annan reports that the United Nations has received only $145 million of the $349 million it has requested to assist the people of Darfur. He also reports that the GoS has not taken "adequate steps" to meet its promise to disarm the *Janjaweed*.

July 22, 2004 — In a unanimous vote, the U.S. House of Representatives passes H.R. Resolution 467, declaring the conflict in Darfur to be a case of genocide and urges the U.S. Government to take more robust action to intervene. The U.S. Senate, without dissent, unanimously concurs.

In a joint press conference, UN Secretary-General Kofi Annan and U.S. Secretary of State Colin Powell call on the international community to apply more pressure on the GoS to honor its promises *vis-a-vis* Darfur.

July 23, 2004 — The leaders of the SLA and JEM agree to hold peace talks with the GoS.

July 26, 2004 — The U.S. Holocaust Memorial Museum's (USHMM) Committee on Conscience (COC) declares a genocide emergency for Darfur, which is the first such declaration in the COC's nine-year history. It reflects the COC's conclusion that there is a reasonable basis to believe that genocide is occurring in Darfur. The USHMM also opens a special exhibition on Darfur in order to alert visitors to the genocide emergency.

July 29, 2004 — UN Secretary-General Kofi Annan issues a statement about continuing reports of rapes, other types of attacks, and acts of intimidation and threats against IDPs, especially in North and West Darfur.

The United States introduces a draft resolution at the United Nations threatening sanctions against Sudan if the government fails to control the militias in Darfur. (The United States later softens the wording of the resolution after some members of the UN Security Council expresses concern over the word "sanctions.")

July 30, 2004 — The UN Security Council passes Resolution 1556 13-0, with China and Pakistan abstaining, giving the GoS thirty days to disarm the *Janjaweed*, otherwise economic and military sanctions will be considered.

August 2, 2004 — Following a trip to Darfur, Francis Deng, Secretary-General Kofi Annan's Representative on IDPs, reports that Darfur remains in a state of crisis bereft of security and rife with human rights violations.

The United Nations begins dropping food by air into the Darfur region.

August 4, 2004 — UN Secretary-General Kofi Annan asserts that the United Nations will continue to pressure the GoS to honor its pledge to protect IDPs and disarm the *Janjaweed*.

The United Nations reports that IDPs in Darfur now number approximately 1.2 million.

About one hundred thousand demonstrators march through Khartoum in a protest, sponsored by the Sudanese government, against the recent United Nations resolution demanding an end to violence in Darfur.

The GoS agrees with UN Special Envoy to Sudan Jan Pronk's action plan outlining concrete steps and policy measures regarding the disarmament of the *Janjaweed*. The AU reports that it is considering the possibility of increasing its three hundred-man observer mission to a full-fledged peacekeeping mission.

August 5, 2004 — Jan Pronk and Sudanese Foreign Minister Mustafa Osman Ismail sign an agreement that commits Khartoum to undertake concrete actions over the course of the next thirty days to disarm the *Janjaweed* and improve security for the IDPs.

August 6, 2004 — A UN human rights investigator says there is "overwhelming evidence" the GoS is complicit in the killing of civilians in the Darfur region.

August 9, 2004 — The GoS rejects the AU's proposal for a peacekeeping mission, and calls the proposed plan a case of "colonialism."

August 12, 2004 — At a meeting of the Joint Implementation Mechanism (JIM), Khartoum presents United Nations officials with a plan delineating the actions that it will take to ameliorate the situation in Darfur.

August 15, 2004 — Approximately one hundred fifty Rwandan troops arrive in Darfur to protect African Union (AU) cease-fire monitors. They are to be stationed in six regions where large IDP camps are located.

August 19, 2004 — AU cease-fire monitors corroborate the fact that in the past week the GoS troops brutally mistreated IDPs at the Kalma camp in South Darfur and then looted the camp.

The Nigerian Senate approves plans to send up to fifteen hundred additional troops to join the AU cease-fire monitoring force in Darfur.

August 20, 2004 — The UN's Special Envoy to Sudan, Jan Pronk, arrives in Darfur for a three-day mission that includes trips to IDP camps (including Kalma) and talks with local officials and humanitarian workers.

August 23, 2004 — The GoS and representatives of rebel groups (SLA and JEM) conduct peace talks (which are sponsored by the AU) in Abuja, Nigeria, with the aim of bringing the conflict in Darfur to a close.

August 25, 2004 — Declaring its operations in Sudan "grossly under-funded," United Nations humanitarian agencies say they have received only $288 million of the $722 million needed to meet the needs of the IDPs.

August 29, 2004 — UN Security Council Resolution 1556 expires. It does so with no clear-cut United Nations strategy for imposing sanctions against the GoS. In light of the divisiveness over the issue in the Security Council, many speculate that it is dubious as to whether sanctions will ever be imposed.

August 30, 2004 — Darfur's IDPs are "traumatized and humiliated and remain at risk of being raped, assaulted, and/or forced to return to their homes," Dennis McNamara, Director of the UN's Internal Displacement Division, reports during a press conference in Nairobi, Kenya.

The United Nations' deadline for the Sudanese Government to both disarm militias and remove them from Darfur expires.

August 31, 2004 — The peace talks between the GoS and the rebel groups are about to resume after rebel leaders walked out on August 29 following accusations of cease-fire violations.

September 2, 2004 — The UN's Special Envoy to Sudan, Jan Pronk, informs the UN Security Council that Khartoum has neither disarmed the *Janjaweed* nor stopped their attacks against civilians. He argues in favor of an expansion of the AU mission in Darfur (both in regard to its mandate and its size) in order to provide better protection for the IDPs. He further notes that the Sudanese Government should be commended for removing obstacles to humanitarian access and for deploying extra police in the region.

September 3, 2004 — Secretary-General Kofi Annan reports to the UN Security Council that the international presence in Darfur must be increased as soon as possible due to the fact that the "vast majority of militias" have not yet been disarmed. The report concludes that a "scorched-earth policy" by the *Janjaweed* is responsible for most of the violence in Darfur.

September 4, 2004 — The SLA and the Sudanese Government reach a cease-fire agreement, but almost immediately break into acrimonious debate where each side accuses the other of violating the agreement.

September 7, 2004 — The World Food Programme (WFP) reports that it delivered food aid to more than 900,000 people during August, below its target of 1.2 million because the rainy season made many roads impassable.

September 9, 2004 — U.S. Secretary of State Colin Powell announces that the U.S. Government has concluded that the ongoing violence in Darfur constitutes genocide. It is the first time one sovereign nation has accused another sovereign nation of genocide while the conflict is still ongoing.

U.S. President George W. Bush states, "We urge the international community to work with us to prevent and suppress acts of genocide."

Note: The sole action of the U.S. government following its declaration of genocide was to refer the matter to the UN Security Council. See September 18, 2004.

September 13, 2004 — A World Health Organization (WHO) survey reports that more than two hundred IDPs are dying every day (or between six to ten thousand a month) in North and West Darfur because of *Janjaweed* attacks and unhygienic conditions in camps. Figures for South Darfur are not available because of security problems.

September 14, 2004 — Under pressure from China, the United States eases its threat of oil sanctions against Sudan, revising its motion to the Security Council to read that the United Nations "shall consider" punitive action, rather than "will take."

September 15, 2004 — Talks between the Sudanese government and SLA and JEM break down after three weeks.

United Nations agencies investigate reports saying that as many as four thousand people have fled their villages in North Darfur and another five thousand recently arrived at a town in South Darfur over the past week.

September 16, 2004 — UN Secretary-General Kofi Annan reports that he is sending High Commissioner for Human Rights Louise Arbour and Special Adviser on the Prevention of Genocide Juan Méndez to Darfur to assess the situation for the express purpose of making recommendations in regard to what can be done to protect civilians.

Annan also reports that he has informed UN Security Council members that he wants a proposed Commission of Inquiry (COI) to proceed for the express purpose of ascertaining whether genocide has occurred in Darfur.

The peace talks in Abuja, Nigeria, reach a stalemate.

September 17, 2004 — Tom Vraalsen, Secretary-General Kofi Annan's Special Envoy for Humanitarian Affairs in Sudan, undertakes the Greater Darfur Initiative, an appeal for $23 million to help those IDPs in greatest need.

September 18, 2004 — The UN Security Council passes Resolution 1564 (11-0, with Algeria, China, Pakistan, and the Russian Federation abstaining), which calls for the creation of a COI to determine whether genocide has occurred, and threatens possible sanctions against the Sudanese Government if the latter fails to comply with earlier resolutions. The resolution also supports expanding the role of multinational African Union (AU) troops in Sudan.

September 19, 2004 — Sudanese President Omar al-Bashir claims he does not fear sanctions threatened by the United Nations: "We are afraid neither of the United Nations nor of its resolution."

September 20, 2004 — High Commissioner for Human Rights Louise Arbour and Special Adviser on the Prevention of Genocide Juan Méndez begin a week-long mission to Darfur, where they visit IDP camps and meet with AU monitors.

September 21, 2004 —Arbour and Méndez report "a sense of fear pervading" the IDP camps in Darfur, and a pervasive skepticism among the IDPs that authorities can or will protect them.

September 22, 2004 — In his first speech as Canadian Prime Minister before the UN General Assembly, Paul Martin criticizes the world's slow reaction to the violence in Sudan, asserting that the United Nations has been bogged down with the legal definition of "genocide."

United Nations agencies report that the number of IDPs has increased to 1.45 million and continues to rise.

September 23, 2004 — Sudanese Foreign Minister Mustafa Osman Ismail informs the UN General Assembly that Sudan will respect human rights and work for peace in Darfur, but casts blame at the rebel groups for the conflict. He also denounces the UN Security Council resolution threatening action against Sudan.

September 24, 2004 — In a UN Security Council meeting, UN Secretary-General Kofi Annan asserts that the "terrible violence" in Darfur constitutes a global issue, and "not simply an African problem."

Nigerian President and AU Chairman Olusegun Obasanjo asserts that the AU force needs greater international funding and logistical support if it is to expand to a size of about three thousand troops and take on new responsibilities.

September 25, 2004 — UN High Commissioner for Human Rights Louise Arbour asserts that most of the IDPs are living in "prisons without walls," but Sudanese Government officials continue to deny the scale and gravity of what is happening.

September 30, 2004 — Reporting on the findings of their mission, UN High Commissioner for Human Rights Louise Arbour and Special Adviser on the Prevention of Genocide Juan Méndez tell the UN Security Council that international police officers are a must if the IDPs are to have any confidence that they will be protected if and when they leave their camps.

October 4, 2004 — UN Secretary-General Kofi Annan proposes four ways in which the United Nations can assist the AU to expand its mission, including the establishment of a Darfur regional office of the UN Advance Mission in Sudan (UNAMIS).

October 5, 2004 — UN Special Envoy to Sudan Jan Pronk informs the UN Security Council that the Sudanese Government continues to sponsor violence against innocent civilians in Darfur. More specifically, he states that the GoS has made no progress over the past month in disarming the *Janjaweed*, stopping their attacks or prosecuting those responsible for the worst atrocities. He also asserts that banditry is on the rise and both the GoS/*Janjaweed* and the rebel groups have frequently breached the cease-fire.

In his regular report to the Council, UN Secretary-General Annan asserts that the AU mission should have the power to protect IDPs and refugees, monitor the local police, and disarm the fighters, including the *Janjaweed*.

October 7, 2004 — UN Secretary-General Kofi Annan names the members of the UN Commission of Inquiry (COI) whose task is to conduct an investigation into the atrocities in Darfur.

October 15, 2004 — The World Health Organization (WHO) reports that at least seventy thousand people have perished since March 2004 as a result of poor conditions in refugee camps. It states that the refugees have died of diarrhea, fever, and respiratory disease, and that that toll *does not include* those killed in the ongoing violence.

October 28, 2004 — The first contingent of the expanded AU cease-fire observation force arrives in Darfur.

Early November 2004 — UNHCR reports that GoS-allied militias have launched at least six raids on refugees camped near Chadian–Sudanese border.

November 4, 2004 — UN Secretary-General Kofi Annan reports to the UN Security Council that there are "strong indications" that war crimes and crimes against humanity have occurred on a "large and systematic scale" in Darfur.

November 7, 2004 — The UN Office for the Coordination of Humanitarian Affairs (OCHA) warns that Darfur is facing its worst humanitarian crisis since 1988. It further states that, in certain cases, access for humanitarian workers is virtually nonexistent.

November 9, 2004 — The GoS and the Sudanese Liberation Army (SLA) and the Justice and Equity Movement (JEM) agree to a halt of all military flights over Darfur and guaranteed access for humanitarian aid to the IDP camps in the region.

November 18–19, 2004 — The UN Security Council meets in Nairobi, Kenya, to discuss the Darfur crisis, but fails to pass a resolution imposing any sanctions on the combatants.

December 14, 2004 — Two aid workers from the British charity Save the Children are killed when their convoy comes under gunfire. The United Nations suspends humanitarian operations in response to the attack. Save the Children pulls out of Darfur a week later.

December 23, 2004 — The UN High Commissioner for Refugees reveals plans to build safe camps in Chad, a good distance away from the border with Sudan, where militias continue to conduct attacks.

2005

January 9, 2005 — The Comprehensive Peace Agreement is signed by the GoS and the SPLM, bringing to an end to twenty-one years of civil war between the government and rebel forces in the south of Sudan.

January 12, 2004 — Jan Pronk, UN Special Envoy to Sudan, asserts that the crisis in Darfur has resulted in killing over one hundred thousand people. He warns that: "We may move into a period of intense violence unless swift action is taken and new approaches are considered."

January 24, 2005 — UN Secretary-General Kofi Annan, in an unprecedented meeting of the UN General Assembly to commemorate the Holocaust, issues a dire warning about the violence in Darfur.

January 25, 2005 — The UN Security Council's Commission of Inquiry (COI) releases its report to the Secretary-General. It concludes that serious violations of international law have occurred in Darfur, including "crimes against humanity." It does not, though, conclude that genocide has been perpetrated. The COI recommends that the evidence of the crimes committed be referred to the International Criminal Court (ICC).

January 26, 2005 — African Union (AU) observers accuse the Sudanese air force of bombing villagers in southern Darfur.

January 29, 2005 — UN Undersecretary for Humanitarian Affairs Jan Egeland warns that violence and insecurity in Darfur is seriously impeding the delivery of humanitarian aid to displaced persons.

February 2, 2005 — Researcher Eric Reeves releases the first of a two-part critical analysis of the UN Commission of Inquiry Report (COI) on Darfur, particularly criticizing its failure to find that genocide had been committed. The second part is posted on February 6. (Part 1 and Part 2 are available at: http://www.sudanreeves.org/modules.)

February 4, 2005 — UN Special Envoy for Sudan Jan Pronk calls for a larger international military force in Darfur. He tells the UN Security Council that it is the only way to stop the raging violence. The Council debates whether war crimes trials should be held at the International Criminal Court (ICC), or even could be, given the United States opposition to the ICC.

February 5, 2005 — The African Union (AU) warns that the security situation in Darfur has deteriorated during the past four months.

The U.S. Holocaust Memorial Museum organizes and hosts, in cooperation with Georgetown University's Students Taking Action Now on Darfur (STAND), the National Student Leaders Conference on Darfur, which is attended by four hundred students from more than ninety schools across the United States and Canada.

February 16, 2005 — UN High Commissioner for Human Rights Louise Arbour recommends that the UN Security Council refer the situation in Darfur to the International Criminal Court (ICC).

March 2, 2005 — U.S. Senator Jon S. Corzine (D-NJ), with thirty co-sponsors, introduces S. 495, the Darfur Accountability Act of 2005, calling for the President of the United States to impose sanctions against individuals named as probable perpetrators of crimes against humanity in Darfur by the UN Commission of Inquiry (COI) on Darfur. It never comes to a vote before the full Senate.

Human Rights Watch reports that a high-level member of the *Janja-weed* informed its researchers that the Sudanese Government directed and supported attacks on Africans in Darfur. The GoS, though, denies its involvement.

March 7, 2005 — *Médecins Sans Frontières* (Doctors Without Borders) issues a report stating that it has treated approximately five hundred women and girls who were raped between October 2004 and mid-February 2005. The report asserts that the five hundred treated rape victims represent only a fraction of those who have been sexually assaulted.

March 15, 2005 — A senior United Nations official reports that the number of individuals who have died from disease and malnutrition in Darfur could be as high as three hundred-fifty thousand. That estimate is approximately five times the official WHO estimate.

March 16, 2005 — Due to threats by the *Janjaweed*, the United Nations reports that it is withdrawing all its staff from part of western Sudan. In doing so, the United Nations is relocating to El-Geneina, which is in Darfur, near the Sudan/Chad border.

United Nations Human Rights experts call for urgent, effective action on Darfur.

March 17, 2005 — Jan Pronk, the UN's Special Envoy to Sudan, states that the African Union peacekeeping force (currently at about two thousand) needs as many as eight thousand troops to do an adequate job of providing security.

U.S. House of Representative Donald M. Payne (D-NJ) introduces, with 132 co-sponsors, H.R. 1424, the Darfur Accountability Act of 2005, which directs the President to block property and assets of GoS officials and calls for the use of force, including a no-fly zone, to stop the genocide in Darfur. It never comes to a vote before the full House of Representatives.

March 24, 2005 — The UN Security Council unanimously passes Resolution 1590, which authorizes the deployment of ten thousand soldiers and hundreds of police to southern Sudan to support the Comprehensive Peace Agreement between the Government of Sudan and the southern rebel groups.

March 25, 2005 — The UN Security Council fails to pass a resolution that would end the crisis in Sudan. Sanctions against the GoS, again, cannot be agreed upon.

The UN Security Council vote on the French draft resolution to bring war criminals to trial at the International Criminal Court (ICC) is delayed.

March 28, 2005 — The GoS asserts that fifteen military and security officials have been arrested on charges of murder, rape, and the burning of villages in Darfur. This is the first time arrests are made for crimes committed in Darfur. The GoS states that it wants to try the accused in a Sudanese court.

March 29, 2005 — The UN Security Council approves a travel ban and an asset freeze for individuals accused of committing crimes in Darfur. The sanctions will apply in thirty days to individuals who will be identified by a special United Nations committee comprised of representatives from all fifteen member countries of the Security Council.

March 31, 2005 — After debate and discussion of the Commission of Inquiry's Report on Darfur, Resolution 1593 is adopted by the UN Security Council, referring the situation in Darfur to the ICC. Eleven members of the Council vote in favor of the Resolution, while the United States, Algeria, Brazil, and China abstain.

April 5, 2005 — The ICC obtains more than twenty-five hundred items of evidence collected by the UN Commission of Inquiry (COI) on Darfur, as well as a secret list of fifty-one names of individuals deemed by the Commission of Inquiry as being potentially responsible for the crimes committed in Darfur.

April 21, 2005 — The CIJ announces that recently collected information suggest that nearly four hundred thousand people have died in the Darfur conflict since it began more than two years previously and that as many as five hundred people may be dying each day.

April 29, 2005 — Reporter Ken Silverstein writes in *The Los Angeles Times* that the Central Intelligence Agency (CIA) flew in a private jet, a high-ranking Sudanese official, Salah Abdallah Gosh, the head of Sudan's intelligence agency, to Washington, D.C. to discuss antiterror policies, despite the fact that Gosh is thought by some to be heavily implicated in the genocide in Darfur.

May 24, 2005 — Human Rights Watch declares that between 3.5 and 4 million people in Darfur are in need of food aid due to the conflict.

May 26, 2005 — At a fundraising conference in Addis Ababa, Ethiopia, donor nations pledge $300 million to help support (AU) forces in Darfur. The amount is several hundred million dollars less than the AU had requested.

June 1, 2005 — Chief Prosecutor of the ICC, Luis Moreno Ocampo, decides that there is sufficient evidence to start a formal investigation into the Darfur situation.

June 6, 2005 — ICC Prosecutor Ocampo publicly announces his decision to begin the official ICC investigation of crimes committed in Darfur. It is expected to be the largest investigation handled by the ICC since its establishment in June 2002. UN Secretary-General Kofi Annan has provided the ICC a list of fifty-one names, including top GoS officials, army officials, army commanders, *Janjaweed* leaders, and those suspected of murder and rape in Darfur. It is reported that Sudan is not going to cooperate with the ICC, and that it insists on prosecuting alleged perpetrators in its own courts.

June 30, 2005 — U.S. Representative Henry J. Hyde (R-IL) introduces H.R. 3127, calling for sanctions against individuals responsible for genocide and other crimes committed in Darfur.

July 6, 2005 — The International Crisis Group releases a report in which it asserts that a total peacekeeping force of between twelve and fifteen thousand is needed in Darfur, vastly more than the number currently deployed.

July 9, 2005 — John Garang, leader the southern rebels, is sworn in as First Vice President of Sudan, under terms of the January 9th Comprehensive Peace Agreement.

July 19, 2005 — The GoS signs a Declaration of Principles with leaders of the two rebel factions in Darfur. Despite the political overture toward peace, the situation on the ground remains volatile.

July 21, 2005 — U.S. Secretary of State Condoleeza Rice visits the Abu Shouk camp for IDPs in Darfur.

July 21, 2005 — U.S. Senator Sam Brownback (R-KS) introduces, with thirty-seven co-sponsors, S. 1462, a bill that calls for the President George W. Bush to impose sanctions against Sudanese Government officials and others responsible for genocide and other crimes committed in Darfur. It also authorizes the President to increase support for the African Union's mission in Sudan and places limits on the Sudanese Government's access to revenues from oil.

July 29, 2005 — The United Nations releases a report stating that widespread rapes and sexual assaults are being committed in Darfur by Sudanese soldiers and police.

July 30, 2005 — First Vice President of Sudan John Garang dies in a helicopter crash.

September 15, 2005 — Continuing insecurity in Darfur prompts the closure of roads connecting El Geneina, the capital of West Darfur, leading to serious reduction in humanitarian aid to IDPs in the region.

September 18–20, 2005 — More than twenty villages in North Darfur are attacked by GoS and *Janjaweed* fighters. Thousands of people are displaced from their homes.

September 28, 2005 — UN Undersecretary-General for Humanitarian Affairs Jan Egeland announces that the United Nations will withdraw its workers in several areas of Darfur due to increasing violence.

October 4, 2005 — UN Special Adviser on the Prevention of Genocide Juan Mendez issues a report based on his visit to Darfur between 19 and 26 September, warning of escalating violence, but noting an improvement in humanitarian access since the previous September.

October 6, 2005 — The International Crisis Group (ICG) releases a report warning that prospects for peace are very low, notwithstanding ongoing negotiations in Abuja, Nigeria, between the GoS and Darfur rebel groups.

October 9, 2005 — Thirty-eight members of an African Union team are kidnapped by rebels in Darfur.

October 10, 2005 — Juan Mendez, Special Adviser to the UN Secretary-General for the Prevention of Genocide, warns of escalating violence in Darfur.

November 18, 2005 — The U.S. Senate votes on and submits S. 1462 (see the entry under July 21, 2005) and passes it to the U.S. House of Representatives.

November 21, 2005 — In his monthly report to the Security Council on Darfur, Secretary-General Kofi Annan warns that "the looming threat of complete lawlessness and anarchy draws nearer."

December 11, 2005 — Human Rights Watch releases a report on serious international crimes being committed in Darfur. The report names President Omar al-Bashir, and other top leaders in the Sudanese Government, as individuals who should be investigated for crimes against humanity.

December 20, 2005 — The United Nations Children's Fund (UNICEF) releases a report entitled "Child Alert Darfur," asserting that as many as one million children displaced by the conflict in Darfur have not been reached by humanitarian relief efforts due to the persisting violence and insecurity in the region.

December 23, 2005 — Researcher Eric Reeves releases a report arguing that more than one million children have been "killed, raped, wounded, displaced, traumatized, or endured the loss of parents and families" in Darfur. (Available at http://www.sudanreeves.org/index.)

December 29, 2005 — UN Secretary-General Kofi Annan warns that mass killing and rapes of civilians are continuing in Darfur.

2006

January 11, 2006 — Physicians for Human Rights release a detailed report on the destruction of livelihoods in three non-Arab communities in Darfur. The report, "Darfur: Assault on Survival," further underscores the genocidal nature of the Government of Sudan's attacks against targeted groups.

January 13, 2006 — The African Union (AU) extends its peacekeeping mandate in Darfur for two months in anticipation that the AU force of nearly seven thousand troops will ultimately be handed over to the United Nations.

January 16, 2006 — Special Representative of the Secretary-General for Sudan Jan Pronk warns that the present peacekeeping force in Darfur is inadequate to end the violence.

Early-April, 2006 — Chadian rebels attack N'Djamena, the capital of Chad. Chadian President Idriss Déby accuses Sudan of supporting and harboring the rebels, and subsequently cuts diplomatic relations with Sudan.

April 25, 2006 — The UN Security Council imposes sanctions on four Sudanese accused of having committed abuses in Darfur. The sanctions are the first to be imposed against individuals vis-à-vis the Darfur crisis.

April 28, 2006 — The World Food Programme announces it will cut food rations to refugees in half.

May 1, 2006 — A day of protests is held across the globe calling for concrete and effective action in Darfur.

May 5, 2006 — The GoS and a SLA faction sign a peace agreement. JEM rejects the agreement.

May 8, 2006 — *The New York Times* reports that despite the signing of the peace agreement, violence in Darfur continues unabated.

May 11, 2006 — United States Secretary of State Condoleezza Rice addresses the UN Security Council on Darfur, and, in doing so, she references the "Responsibility to Protect" and also submits a draft resolution on Darfur under Chapter VII of the UN Charter

May 16, 2006 — In an unanimous vote, The UN Security Council passes a resolution on Darfur under Chapter VII to initiate the planning of a possible UN peacekeeping mission in Darfur.

May 25, 2006 — The GoS rejects the proposal by the UN Security Council of deploying a peacekeeping force in Darfur under Chapter VII of the UN Charter. Instead, the GoS suggests that the UN take on a "watchdog" role to monitor the implementation of the peace agreement.

May 25, 2006 — UN Special Envoy Lakhdar Brahimi announces the GoS' agreement to allow a "technical assessment team" into Sudan.

May 31, 2006 — The two rebel groups fail to meet the May 31st deadline to sign the peace agreement.

June 1, 2006 — UN Humanitarian Coordinator Jan Egeland asserts that unless security conditions quickly improve in Darfur, the UN will be forced to pull its aid staff.

June 5, 2006 — The UN Security Council travels to Sudan and applies pressure on the GoS to accept the deployment of an international force in Darfur.

June 6, 2006 — The UNHCR reports that attacks along and across the Chad/Sudan border by the *Janjaweed* have become more "systematic and deadly." It is estimated that up to 50,000 Chadian citizens have been displaced from their homes by the attacks.

June 7, 2006 — In stating why he refuses to allow a UN peacekeeping mission into Darfur, al-Bashir compares the situation in Iraq by asserting that he is not going to allow a "foreign occupation" of Sudan.

June 9, 2006 — Following tremendous international pressure, the two rebel factions holding out against a peace agreement sign an "annex" to the peace agreement.

June 13, 2006 — A Joint UN-AU team arrives in Darfur to assess the situation in preparation for an international force. UN peacekeeping coordinator Jean-Marie Guehenno reports that the soonest a UN peacekeeping mission will be deployed to Darfur is January 2007.

June 15, 2006 — Following a lengthy investigation (but not in Darfur itself due to the risky security situation), the International Criminal Court (ICC) reports evidence of large-scale massacres and rapes in Darfur to the Security Council. ICC chief prosecutor Luis Moreno-Ocampo states that, "The available information indicates that these killings include a significant number of large-scale massacres, with hundreds of victims in each incident." Continuing, Moreno-Ocampo states that, "although some of the massacres appear to have been carried out with 'genocidal intent,' the final decision will not be made what to deem the crimes until a full investigation and analysis by the prosecutor's office is completed."

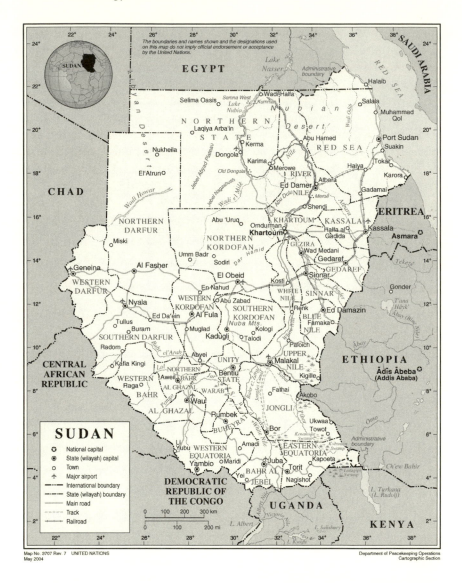

Map of Sudan, showing the three Darfur provinces and the nine nations that border Sudan: Eritrea, Ethiopia, Kenya, Uganda, Democratic Republic of Congo, Central African Republic, Chad, and Libya (upper left corner under map of Africa). (UN map of Sudan, UN Cartographic Section, no. 3707 Rev. 7 May 2004. With permission.)

PART 1

The Background on Darfur

CHAPTER 1

Disaster in Darfur: Historical Overview*

ROBERT O. COLLINS

Introduction

Darfur (Land of the Fur) is the western region of The Republic of the Sudan (*Jumhuriyat as-Sudan*). It is approximately the size of France and is divided into three administrative states — North, West, and South — that represent the three ethnic zones of Darfur. Northern Darfur State is the home of camel nomads, a small minority of whom are Meidab Arabs, but the overwhelming majority are non-Arab Zaghawa. In the Western Darfur State, on both sides of the volcanic Jabal Marra massif towering three thousand feet above the vast Sudanic plain, live non-Arab sedentary farmers, the Fur, Massalit, Daju, and Berti. Southern Darfur State is inhabited by the cattle and camel nomads, the Baqqara, who claim Arab (*Juhayna*) origins and speak Arabic, but are ethnically the result of intercourse with their surrounding African neighbors after arriving in southern Darfur in the eighteenth century. All the peoples of Darfur are Muslims. A few Africans still practice their traditional religions, whose vestiges can be found in the Darfurian symbiotic Muslim practices on this frontier of Islam.

---

* A slightly revised version of this chapter first appeared in the Summer–Fall 2004 issue, No. 15–16, *African Geopolitics/Géopolitique Africaine*. Reprinted with permission.

The rainfall and drainage from Jabal Marra onto the fertile soils of the western province support a vigorous agriculture by the African settled cultivators, and this is in stark contrast to the semidesert of the north that is dependent for water on intermittent *wadis* and wells, many of which go dry in the winter months. In the south, the summer rains produce a rolling mantle of grass and reliable sources of water from wells and excavated reservoirs, *hafri*, for the Baqqara and their cattle.

This bucolic description of cultivators and herdsmen peacefully tending to their traditional pursuits obscures the historic struggle for scarce resources by different people competing for land and water in Darfur. The past — and most certainly, the current crisis — in Darfur cannot be understood without its history, a fact often overlooked by the media and many of the non-Sudanese officials swept up in the disaster in Darfur.

Darfur in History

Historically, Darfur was transformed from a geographic to a well-defined political entity by the establishment of the sultanate in 1650. Its foundations rested on a centuries-old tradition of state formation dominated by the Fur and a ruling elite that included members of all the principal ethnic groups in Darfur. The Fur sultanate consisted mostly of non-Arab cultivators who employed the organized resources of the state and its heavy cavalry to contain the Arab nomads in their seasonal pastures well beyond Fur and Massalit agricultural lands. This equilibrium was not to last. In 1874, al-Zubayr Rahma Mansur, the Ja'ali Arab slave trader who had created a personal fiefdom in the Bahr al-Ghazal in the southern Sudan, destroyed the Fur sultanate, opening the pastures and cultivations to the Baqqara Arab nomads. When in 1898 the British had destroyed the revolutionary religious Mahdist State, which had ruled the Sudan since 1885, Ali Dinar, who had inherited the title of sultan in 1890, restored the Fur sultanate and spent most of the next eighteen years driving the Arab nomads north and south of the agricultural lands surrounding Jabal Marra, which comprised the heartland of his sultanate. A significant difference today in this historic struggle for the land is the ferocity of the killing by the Kalisnikov rather than the spear or sword.

In 1916, Ali Dinar, who had been sympathetic to the Ottoman Empire during World War I, was killed by a British expeditionary force, and Darfur was annexed to the Anglo-Egyptian Condominium (1898–1956), which had succeeded the Mahdist State in the Sudan. The British soon learned that Darfur had little to contribute to the rebuilding of the Sudan. The principal city of El Fasher lay far to the west, and to this day there is neither an all-weather road nor a railroad to this historic capital. In 1959, Sudan Railways completed a line to Nyala, capital of Southern Darfur State and 120 miles south of El Fasher, but its irregular service has never ended the region's isolation. Darfur had no exploitable resources, only subsistence cultivators and impoverished herdsmen. The administration consisted of a few resourceful British officers who kept law and order by ruthlessly enforcing gun control and little else, leaving the day-to-day governance to local African chiefs and Arab *shaykhs*.

The steady improvements in education and healthcare and the introduction of development schemes by British authorities in the greater Khartoum area along the Nile never made their way to Darfur. Peace, however, did result in the migration eastward of young men (all of whom were struggling in a stagnant subsistence economy) looking for work in the new riverain (riparian) development projects, particularly the vast Gezira cotton scheme south of Khartoum between the Blue and White Niles. Once by the river, however, they encountered discrimination by the *awlad al-bahar* (people of the river) for the *awlad al-ghareb* (people from the west).

The perceived differences between those Sudanese living along the Nile in villages, towns, and cities and those from the rural hinterland run very silent but very deep in the past and present Sudan. The *awlad al-bahar* (sometimes *awlad al-bilad*) are the descendants of the Arab migrants into the Nile valley, who were mostly *Ja'aliyyin* (pl. of *Ja'ali*) who infiltrated into the heart of the Sudan in the sixteenth and seventeenth centuries. They became a sedentary urban society with a literate elite who during the fifty years of British rule became a sophisticated, if not worldly, ruling class that reinforced the disdain and derision of their grandfathers and fathers for the rustic illiterate folk from the West, East, and South. It was among these simple farmers and coarse herdsmen in the western Sudan of Kordofan and Darfur that the Umma Party of Sayyid Abd al-Rahman could count on for the loyalty to solidify his political position in any Sudan of the future. His father, Muhammad Ahmad ibn Abdallah, the Mahdi, had recruited among the Baqqara and Fur the shock troops for his army that destroyed Egyptian rule in the Sudan and established the Mahdist State. They have remained passionately loyal to Mahdism, and after the independence of the Sudan in 1956, the Umma began to introduce selected sons of the old Darfur elite into the political life of Omdurman and Khartoum. Here they became assimilated into the ruling riverain *awlad al-bahar;* or, in the contemptuous words of the Darfurian political activist, Dr. Sharif Harir, they were corrupted by "riverization" after abandoning their traditional roots in Darfur for the political highlife of Khartoum.

The ethnic and cultural discrimination by the riverain-ruling elite in Khartoum against those Sudanese living on the periphery has historically established the pattern of governance by the *awlad al-bahar*, which constitutes a circumference of no more than a few hundred miles from the confluence of the two Niles and those lands beyond where the authority diminishes with the distance from the heartland. At no time in the past two hundred years has the central government of the Sudan — neither nineteenth century Turks nor twentieth century British and certainly not the independent Sudanese — actually governed Darfur, the southern Sudan, or even the Red Sea Hills. Officials from the central government occupied the periphery with scattered symbolic posts in the countryside and a garrison and governor in the traditional provincial capitals, but at no time have they rigorously administered, effectively controlled, or demonstrated the usual characteristics associated with governance, good or bad. Geography was much to blame, for El Fasher is some seven hundred miles from Khartoum and El Geneina, on the Chad border, another two hundred twenty miles across sandy plains and dunes, known as *goz*, stretching hundreds of miles around the mountain massif of Jabal Marra and crossed by ancient tracks whose reliability is largely determined by the weather. The fundamental reason for fragile governance in Darfur, though, remains the dearth of resources and political leadership by those in authority in the central government of Sudan who have preferred to adopt a policy of benign neglect.

Historically, ethnic tensions between farmers and herdsman, African and Arab, latent and volatile, have always been present and accepted in Darfur, but are exacerbated by long-standing competition for pasture, agricultural land, and water, the mundane matters so important in daily life in which verbal disputes can quickly erupt into violence. Quarrels over scarce resources became particularly acute during the great global drought of the 1980s that hastened the desertification of northern and central Darfur, and resulted in increasing tensions over water and grazing areas as the camel nomads moved south in search of both. The drought of the 1980s was not new, just more severe. In the past, the different ethnic groups had usually settled their disputes over land ownership and right to water wells by conferences, *ajaweed/muatamarat al-sulh*, of the traditional leaders whose rulings were invariably respected and honored. This mechanism began to break down when desertification was accompanied by the introduction of thousands of automatic weapons. By the 1990s, Darfur was short of water but awash in guns.

The Price of Impotence

When the British departed in 1956, they left behind the Sudan Defense Force, soon to become the Sudan Armed Forces (SAF). It was a disciplined, professional, mobile army, the finest in the Middle East, equal to the Arab Legion of Jordan. In the Arab–Israel War of 1967, the Sudanese battalion sent to Sinai to help the Egyptians refused to retreat, disdained to surrender, and had to be annihilated before the Israeli advance could proceed. Moreover, the British found their best soldiers from the peoples of the periphery — the Nuba and Dinka of the southern Sudan and the Fur and Baqqara from Darfur who, as the shock troops of the Mahdist armies, had established a reputation as fierce warriors during the Mahdiya and during their sporadic outbursts against the British — for the sons of the *awlad al-bahar* preferred the urban life of the riverain towns and a political or professional career to the hardships and hazards of soldiering. In 1956, the army was, in fact, the only national institution in the Sudan and in the past half-century of Sudanese independence has intervened three times — 1958, 1969, and 1989 — to seize power from incompetent, corrupt, and self-seeking political leaders who had been democratically elected. At the time of their respective coups, most Sudanese were delighted to see the politicians depart from government until later realizing the tyranny of military dictatorships that have ruled the Sudan for thirty-seven of its forty-eight years of independence.

The decline of the SAF began during the sixteen years of the rule of General Ja'far Numayri (1969 to 1985) when the senior officers of the Sudan Defense Force were succeeded by younger, less professional officers who could not resist abusing their authority for their own personal advancement while at the same time fighting a war they could not win against the southern Sudanese insurgents. Moreover, the demise of a professional Sudanese fighting force was accompanied by the creation of the People's Defense Force (PDF) after the Islamist *coup d'état* of 1989 to make the army theologically "correct," yet, as it turned out, incapable of suppressing insurgencies.

During the 1970s and 1980s, the Islamic Charter Front (later the National Islamic Front, NIF), led by Hasan al-Turabi, methodically recruited young officers at the military academy into the NIF, among them Omar Hassan Ahmad al-Bashir. When Bashir and his fellow Islamist officers seized power on June 30, 1989, the Revolutionary Command Council founded the aforementioned PDF in order to protect the June 30 Revolution and to suppress the rebellion in the South, essentially replacing the army as the instrument to enforce the Islamization of the Sudan. The soldiers for the PDF were not volunteers but conscripts by a very unpopular draft that numbered one hundred fifty thousand recruits by 1991. Instructors from the Sudan army introduced them to weaponry, but their indoctrination was more religious than military, including interminable lectures on Islam. The ideological guide for the Islamist state, Hassan al-Turabi, made clear that it would be impossible to "Islamize" the Sudanese army because its professional officers had been "secularized" and unwilling to accept an Islamist regime that required a "large popular defense force" that would create an "Islamized" society (Middle East Policy, 1992).

The PDF, though little more than a rabble in arms, was to crush the battle-hardened Nilotic veterans who constituted the bulk of the Sudan People's Liberation Army (SPLA) forces in southern Sudan. When Colonel John Garang decided to defect from the Sudanese army after the mutiny of the Fifth Battalion at Bor in May 1983, he spent that summer forging them (along with a flood of other disaffected southern troops) into the Sudan People's Liberation Movement (SPLM), whose military branch was separate from the political branch and was known as the Sudan People's Liberation Army (SPLA). The latter trained in camps across the Ethiopian border and received support from the communist regime of President Haile Miriam Mengistu. Within two years, the SPLA was ready to take the offensive against the Sudanese army and later the PDF.

Neither the demoralized remnants of the old Sudan Armed Forces nor the massive cannon fodder of the PDF were trained, equipped, or motivated to fight in the semideserts of the West or the swamps and rainforests of the South. They suffered successive defeats, failing utterly to crush the insurgencies or to establish the authority of the Sudan government in these peripheral regions.

In 1986, Prime Minister Sadiq al-Mahdi, great grandson of the Muhammad Ahmad, al Mahdi, leader of the Umma Party, and a dominant figure in Sudanese politics since the 1960s, decided to reverse the failure of the Sudanese army to defeat the SPLA by arming with automatic weapons his Baqqara supporters on the southern Sudan frontier. He gave them freedom to pillage, rape, enslave, and kill the Dinka across the Bahr al-Arab (the Kiir) River, who supported the SPLA and its Dinka leader, John Garang. Riding their horses and brandishing their Kalisnikovs, the young Baqqara commandos from the Missiriyya and Humr, known as the *murahileen*, wreaked havoc and death upon the Dinka of the Bahr al-Ghazal and the Upper Nile for the next ten years. The other large Baqqara group to the west in southern Darfur, the *Rizayqat*, also carried out raids across the Dinka frontier to the south, but at the outbreak of the insurgency in Darfur, they turned this new and powerful weaponry against their northern African neighbors — the Fur, Massalit, and Zaghawa — with whom they had many ancient quarrels over territory and water.

After the Islamist *coup d'état* of June, 30 1989, the arming of the Baqqara *murahileen* continued under the illusion that these unruly, independent militias could be integrated into the PDF. More subtle but equally divisive to any settlement on the frontier of Islam was the determination by the regime to impose its Islamist ideology on all Sudanese — with Arabic culture, language, and Islam as the foundation of Sudanese society — even though less than half the Sudanese claim Arab origins and another third were non-Muslims. The Arabo-centric enthusiasm of Bashir and his National Islamic Front (after 1998, it became known as the National Congress Party) government reopened old and deep wounds in Sudanese society. Throughout the centuries there has been (by consent, intermarriage, or forced enslavement) a mixing of African and Arab in the Nile Basin that has produced those unique individuals today known as the Sudanese. The sensible Sudanese are more concerned about their cultural heritage than their genetic purity, but the hardcore fervently seek, through manufactured Arab genealogies, their direct descent from the Prophet. Injecting an ideological and racist definition as to who is "Arab" and who are *zuruq*, black, or the more pejorative epithet *abid*, slave, to distinguish between Arab and African — and justify the killing, rape, and enslavement of these marginalized people — has been the tragic legacy of the cynical and dysfunctional Islamist government of the Sudan.

The Crisis in Darfur

On February 26, 2003, some three hundred rebels calling themselves the Darfur Liberation Front (DLF), led by Abd al-Wahid Muhammad Ahmad Nur, a member of the Communist Party and the SPLM, the political arm of the southern insurgency movement, seized the town of Gulu, capital of Jabal Marra Province in the state of western Darfur. Equipped with automatic weapons, mortars, and "technicals" — Toyota trucks with mounted machine guns made famous in the Chadian wars with Libya — they attacked scattered police and army posts before retiring to their training camps in Jabal Marra. Two weeks later the DLF changed its name to the Sudan Liberation Movement/Army (SLM/A) and then "recaptured" Gulu in a fierce fire-fight, killing one hundred ninety five government soldiers and forcing the garrison to flee. Minni Arkou Minnawi, secretary-general of the SLM, the political arm of the movement, released to the press the *Political Declaration of the SLM*. In part, it stated that since the government of Khartoum had "systematically adhered to the policies of marginalization, racial discrimination, exclusion, exploitation, and divisiveness," the objectives of the SLM are:

a united democratic Sudan ... predicated on full acknowledgment of Sudan's ethnic, cultural, social, and political diversity. Viable unity, therefore, must be ultimately based on the right of self-determination... . The fundamental imperatives of a viable unity are an economy and political system that address the uneven development and marginalization that have plagued the country since independence... . Religion and politics ... must be kept in their respective domains, with religion belonging to the personal domain and the state in the public domain... . SPLM/A firmly opposes ... the Khartoum Government's policies of using some Arab tribes ... to achieve its hegemonic devices that are detrimental both to Arabs and non-Arabs... . [Consequently], the brutal oppression, ethnic cleansing, and genocide sponsored by the Khartoum Government [have] left the people of Darfur with no other option but to resort to popular political and military resistance for the purpose of our survival (The Sudan Liberation Movement and Sudan Liberation Army 2003).

Within a few days the government security committee in western Darfur opened negotiations with the SLM, for the armed forces of the Sudan were insufficient and unprepared to fight a major insurgency in the West or isolate the insurgent's camps in the Jabal Marra massif. The SLM presented five demands — including an amnesty for the rebels and a pledge to implement development projects in Darfur — under a fragile cease-fire that soon collapsed on March 18 when Arab militias assassinated, near Geneina, a respected Massalit leader, Shaykh Saleh Dakoro. That was followed two days later by the destruction of much of the town of Karnoi by helicopter gunships.

The SLA retaliated on the 25th of March, when it seized the strategic town of Tine on the Chad frontier and captured large stocks of arms and equipment from its garrison. Thereafter, fighting raged throughout Western Darfur State in which the victories of the Sudan Liberation Army (SLA) dramatically revealed the inadequacy and incompetence of the Sudan army. The best the Government of Sudan (GoS) could do was to blame the revolt on "gangsters" and "highwaymen." On Friday, April 25, an SLA force consisting of thirty-three technicals staged a hit-and-run attack on the airport outside El Fasher, now capital of the Northern Darfur State, destroying helicopters and Antonov bombers, occupying army headquarters, and capturing Air Force Major General Ibrahim Bushra. At the same time, another SLA unit captured four tanks in clashes outside of Kutum, seventy-five miles north of El Fasher. Ten days later, the SLA captured Colonel Mubarak Muhammad al-Saraj, chief of intelligence for public security in Aynshiro, north of Jabal Marra.

In the attack on El Fasher, the SLA was joined by Darfurians from the Justice and Equality Movement (JEM), which many in Darfur have called the "Opposition Forces." There was little difference in the goals of these two resistance movements except the JEM (n.d.) "has come to rally all the peoples from the various regions of the Sudan into a broad based and inclusive Movement," not just Darfur. Fighting now raged widely throughout Darfur. In late May, the SLA, north of Kutum, destroyed a Sudanese battalion, killing five hundred and taking three hundred prisoners. In mid-July, they attacked Tine again leaving two hundred fifty soldiers dead. On August 1, they captured Kutum, inflicting heavy casualties on the garrison before retiring after four days. The response to these victories by the GoS was to continue its denials that there was a resistance movement, and to rearm and unleash their Arab militias to rescue the army. Ironically, this new war in the West provided the Islamist regime with new opportunities for its preservation. As the most unpopular regime in the history of the independent Sudan, the government was now able to weaken any potential opposition by exploiting ethnic divisions, branding the insurgency as an African attempt to rid Darfur of the "Arab race," whose dominance was the very foundation of the Islamist government and its extremists groups like the "Arab Gathering." Moreover, with the prospect of peace at Naivasha after twenty-two months of negotiations with the SPLM, which would bring to an end the violent twenty-two-year civil war between the government and the southern insurgents led by the SPLM/A, the new war in Darfur would keep the army preoccupied with fighting instead of giving its disaffected officers the opportunity to plot a *coup d'état*. It would also provide a pretext to purge the army of Darfurian officers in March 2004 by accusing them of attempting to overthrow the government.[1]

The government militias consisted of the sons of former Baqqara *murahileen* now resuscitated as the *Janjaweed,* or *peshmerga* as they are known in western Darfur. Unlike the *murahileen* of the 1990s who were Baqqara from southern Kordofan, the *Janjaweed* of 2003 came from both the cattle Baqqara of southern Darfur and the camel Baqqara of central Darfur, but among them were strangers whom the local people suspected to be Arab extremists, perhaps Afghan–Arabs, or West African Muslims. The *Janjaweed* began their ethnic cleansing as early as October 2002 from their camps in Jabal Kargu, Boni, and Idalghanam in southern Darfur, with some five thousand *Janjaweed* in each, where they were equipped and trained by the Sudanese army. The Fur, whom Salah Ali Alghali, the governor of southern Darfur, openly vowed to exterminate, were singled out as the mounted *Janjaweed* commandos, usually comprised of one hundred warriors, would sweep down on a village just before dawn.[2] The pattern of destruction was the same. The men were killed, often mutilated, the women raped, and the children sometimes abducted. The village was burnt, the livestock seized, the fields torched, and the infrastructure — wells, irrigation works, schools, clinics — methodically destroyed in a systematic scheme to drive the African population from their ancestral holdings. Ethnic cleansing to the *Janjaweed* meant clearing the land for Arab colonization. By January 2003, a few hundred Fur had been killed and hundreds wounded, but tens of thousands had fled from the wasteland left by the *Janjaweed*, more units of which were now being trained in camps in Northern Darfur State. Little did the Africans know that these early attacks were but the prelude to the firestorm that was to sweep through Darfur after the victories of the "Opposition Forces" in the spring and summer of 2003.

The *Janjaweed* killing and displacement of Fur, Massalit, and Zaghawa escalated throughout the summer and autumn of 2003 supported by helicopter gunships and Antonov bombers, while the Sudan army defeated the SLA north of Kutum in late August with heavy losses including two of its leading commanders. In September, the SLM signed a cease-fire proposed by the government of Chad that soon collapsed, and both sides returned to the fields of death and destruction. Throughout the remainder of 2003, fighting raged particularly in western Darfur with rhetorical claims of victory by both sides and occasionally a reliable report. On December 27, the JEM ambushed a *Janjaweed* column moving against the rebel-held town of Tine on the Chad border, inflicting very heavy losses, and in January 2004 the JEM repulsed another attempt to take Tine, reportedly killing over a thousand government troops and militias.

Increasingly, *Janjaweed* columns would pursue and kill those they had evicted, even crossing the Chad border to hunt down fleeing refugees. By February 2004, one year after the beginning of the insurgency, the conflict, ethnic cleansing, and displacement of Africans had conservatively claimed thirty thousand lives, forced a million people from their lands as Internally Displaced Persons (IDPs), and sent another two hundred thousand across the border into Chad. Another three hundred fifty thousand Darfurians were expected to die within the next nine months from famine and disease when the rains arrived in late spring. James Morris, the Executive Director of the World Food Program, observed, "In all my travels as the head of the World Food Program, I have never seen people who are as frightened as those displaced in Darfur" (UN News Centre, 2004).

The International Community Struggles to Respond

Although the numbers of black African IDPs and refugees steadily increased during the spring and summer of 2003 as the fighting escalated, it was not until September that the magnitude of the destruction and displacement began to be recognized by the international humanitarian agencies. In October, *Médecins Sans Frontières* (MSF) reported that thousands of IDPs had been traumatized by the violence, but when the United Nations and other humanitarian agencies sought entrance into Darfur to assess and relieve the suffering, they were met with manipulative obstruction from the Khartoum government. The UN humanitarian coordinator in the Sudan, Mukesh Kapila, "bitterly complained about slow and cumbersome travel procedures as well as permission to visit affected areas being withheld ... . [Continuing, he warned that] the situation in the Greater Darfur Region of western Sudan could result in the worst humanitarian crisis in the Sudan since 1998" (quoted in Reeves, 2004b). By the end of November, the international relief agencies were thoroughly alarmed about a looming food crisis in western Sudan, particularly when the Ministry of Agriculture refused food aid for Darfur from the U.S. Agency for International Development (USAID). In December, the UN Secretary-General's Special Envoy for Humanitarian Affairs for Sudan, Tom Vraalsen (2003), was more than blunt about the crisis situation: "Delivery of humanitarian assistance to populations in need is hampered mostly by *systematic denied access*. While [Khartoum's] authorities claim unimpeded access, they greatly restrict access to the areas under their control, while imposing blanket denial to all rebel-held areas... . [P]resent humanitarian operations have practically come to a standstill."

By New Year 2004, virtually all the respected international humanitarian organizations, including the International Crisis Group (ICG), Amnesty International, the Red Cross, MSF, and the various United Nations agencies, were reporting the enormity of the disaster, the violation of human rights, and the need for relief assistance. Also, by then, the term "ethnic cleansing" to describe the devastation in Darfur became commonplace among diplomats, aid workers, and the media. Among the many statements made by the various organizations were as follows: "*System-atic* human rights abuses against unarmed civilians have been reported including against women and children ..." (emphasis in text) (Ramcharan, 2004a) and, "Forty percent of the refugees from fighting in Sudan's western Darfur province were children under five. About 75 percent of the adult refugees were women ... . All the ingredients are in place for a rapid deterioration of the humanitarian situation" (Rafirasme, 2004). As for the emotions of the international community, the title of Amnesty International's report on Darfur of February 3, 2004, expressed them well: "Too Many People Killed for No Reason."

During this period, the United States reaffirmed its commitment to addressing the immediate protection and assistance needs of those in Darfur. Norway's Minister of Foreign Affairs, Jan Petersen, declared that

"Norway will, together with other donors, do what is necessary to provide humanitarian relief and protection…" (Government of Norway, 2004). And Canada's Foreign Minister, Bill Graham, announced that "It is imperative that agencies providing humanitarian assistance have immediate, safe and unhindered access to Darfur" (Government of Canada, 2004).

When the Centre for Humanitarian Dialogue in Geneva sought to broker an agreement for humanitarian access, both the SLM and the JEM readily agreed, but Khartoum refused, arguing disingenuously that the issue of humanitarian access had been politicized, used for military gains, and was subject to manipulations. Besides, when President Bashir announced on February 9 that the Sudan army and militias had crushed the rebellion, the proposed peace talks in Geneva were obviously irrelevant. Three days later, the rebel forces, now numbering some twenty-seven thousand men, shot down two army helicopters and in the succeeding weeks launched hit-and-run attacks near El Fasher and cut the road from Khartoum to Nyala, the capital of Southern Darfur State.

When the world commemorated the tenth anniversary of the 1994 Rwandan genocide in April 2004, the international media could not avoid comparing the two human rights disasters in Rwanda and Darfur. And UN Secretary-General Kofi Annan could hardly remain silent, for he had been the Under-Secretary-General for all United Nations peacekeeping missions in 1994 and had had ultimate responsibility for the United Nations force in Rwanda under Lt. General Roméo Dallaire. Indeed, genocide in Darfur was much on his mind. On April 7, Annan declared that "If [full humanitarian access] is denied, the international community must be prepared to take swift and appropriate action. By 'action' in such situations, I mean a continuum of steps, which may include military action … . The international community cannot stand idle" (Annan, 2004a). His UN humanitarian coordinator in Sudan, Mukesh Kapila (2004), who had also been with the United Nations in Rwanda during the genocide, argued that "the only difference between Rwanda and Darfur now is the numbers involved … . This is more than just a conflict, it is an organized attempt to do away with a group of people." The response by Foreign Minister Mustafa Ismail on behalf of the GoS was succinct and no surprise. "Some UN officials do not keep to the truth when speaking about the situation in the Sudan to the extent at which we can label some of their statements as lies and acts of deception" (quoted in Reeves, 2004a).

In late March, President Idriss Deby of Chad, who was deeply concerned about the influx of Sudanese refugees and the violence spilling into Chad, offered to mediate in N'Djamena. The Sudan government readily agreed, for its traditional ally would hardly be the neutral mediator he claimed to be. The SLM and JEM, who together represented a single delegation, wanted a different venue but reluctantly accepted N'Djamena when assured of their safety by the United States. The atmosphere was poisoned by eight days of bickering over the status of the international observers whose presence was demanded by the SLM and JEM, with the United States favoring the rebel position to permit observers and the French supporting Idriss Deby and, by proxy, the Sudan government, who wanted to disbar them. This division effectively enabled Deby to minimize the role of the western observers to only the first sessions dealing with humanitarian concerns. They were later excluded from the political talks that were to follow. Once at the table, the Chadian team promptly presented a complete draft cease-fire agreement in English, French, and Arabic that did not include several points agreed upon in earlier discussions with the SLM and JEM delegation. Deby acknowledged these oversights but insisted they would be subsequently included after the signing ceremony, but they never were. The SLM and JEM in their naiveté and inexperience foolishly agreed. The cease-fire agreement without its amendments was duly signed on April 8 to end hostilities for forty-five days (which was renewable), to free prisoners, and to facilitate humanitarian access to the victims of the war. The Sudan government committed itself to "neutralize armed militias."

After two sessions during separate political talks two weeks later, the parties signed a political agreement on April 25, 2004 that stipulated a conference of "all representatives of Darfur" to seek a comprehensive and final solution to the conflict, in which "the government of the Sudan must assure that the armed militias are neutralized and disarmed according to a program to be decided upon."[3] Before the ink was dry, both the SLM and JEM disavowed the agreement on April 26 and 27, respectively, stating its delegation had exceeded its mandate (thus, revealing internal schisms within each movement — tensions between Zaghawa and Fur/Massalit in the SLM, as well as disagreements between the political wing of the JEM led by President Khalil Ibrahim and his military commander, Jibril Abel Karim, who he accused of being in the pay of the Sudan Military Intelligence. Both the SLM and JEM would have nothing to do with an all-inclusive conference of Darfurians, insisting on direct political talks with the government to reach "a comprehensive settlement." The government announced it would continue its preparations for convening the forum at some future date.

Despite the fact that both sides agreed to continue the humanitarian cease-fire agreement of April 8, this deal was badly flawed. There were gross discrepancies between the English and Arabic versions, the scope of which could not be attributed to mistranslation. Divisions among the international observers, combined with the less than neutral mediation of President Deby and the internal tensions within the rebel movement, provided Khartoum the opportunity to exploit these divisions — a tactic expertly employed by the Islamist government in the past and throughout its infamous history of negotiations. When the African Union (AU) was asked to establish a Cease-Fire Commission, it further marginalized western representation. There were different versions of the article in the agreement pertaining to the neutralization of the militias, the Arabic text carrying an additional provision requiring the rebels to confine their forces to specific camps that was totally unacceptable to the "opposition forces."

The Sudan government clearly appeared to have gained the initiative after the negotiations at N'Djamena, despite the fact that the continued prosecution of the war in Darfur had deepened the division within the inner circle of the Islamist Movement, the name for those few thousand hard-core Islamists dedicated to preserving the Revolution of 1989. On the one hand, there were those who supported the peace talks with the SPLM to end the twenty-year-old conflict between the northern and southern Sudan while seeking to reconstitute the Islamist Movement into an effective political party; on the other hand, there were those determined to reject any peace agreement with the SPLM. The latter were more concerned with consolidating their authority in order to control the state than the prospect of having to share it with the SPLM. Indeed, the government, at least early on, adroitly employed the fragility of the peace talks with the SPLM to divert United States and European Union (EU) attention from Darfur by implying it is the price for a peace agreement at Naivasha. On May 18, Khartoum appeared to have received its reward when Secretary of State Colin Powell announced that the Sudan would be removed from the list of those not fully cooperating in the war on terrorism. Be that as it may, it is important to note that the Sudan was not removed from the State Department's list of state sponsors of terrorism because of the government's failure to close the offices of Hamas and the Palestinian Islamic Jihad in Khartoum.

Despite the public outcry, declarations from the EU and unanimous Congressional resolutions from the United States demanding "unconditional and immediate access to Darfur to humanitarian aid organizations," the Sudan government had successfully frustrated western humanitarian efforts by its wall of Byzantine bureaucratic procedures to obtain visas and proper permits to work in Darfur. The SLM/A and the JEM had not proved particularly helpful either. Indeed, the SLM/A has emphatically rejected aid coming from government-held territory on the likely assumption that it would simply give the *Janjaweed* an excuse to attack the SLA and loot relief goods given to the IDPs. Despite their dearth of political experience, they had learned not to trust Chad as a venue or as a mediator. They insisted, with little conviction, to be allowed to coordinate their positions to present a common front in any direct negotiations with the GoS as they had done at N'Djamena. Khartoum, however, continued to remain aloof, to delay, and to manipulate. Having successfully lobbied the UN Human Rights Commission not to re-institute the position of Special Rapporteur for Human Rights and convinced that the Security Council would not place ethnic cleansing in Darfur on its agenda, the GoS brazenly mobilized support in the UN Human Rights Commission not to consider the report by its own Acting High Commissioner for Human Rights, Bertrand Ramcharan (2004b), which described the "reign of terror" imposed by the government of the Sudan and government-sponsored *Janjaweed*.

Despite massive international demands to disarm the *Janjaweed*, on May 14, the Sudan's Foreign Minister, Mustafa Ismail, contemptuously refused to "disarm the militia as long as weapons remained in the hands of rebel forces .... The *Janjaweed* were a spontaneous tribal response to rebels who are predominantly Zaghawa" (quoted in *Al-Hayat*, May 14, 2004 and cited in International Crisis Group, May 23, 2004).

On May 19, President Omar Hassan Ahmad al-Bashir arrived quietly with no fanfare in Nyala to demonstrate his solidarity with the *Janjaweed*, who he reviewed as they paraded past him astride their fierce horses, shouting, and brandishing their automatic weapons. Equipped with their racist ideology and warrior culture, the government had no intention of disarming, controlling, or arresting the *Janjaweed*. A week later, the UN Security Council condemned the attacks and atrocities committed by the *Janjaweed* and called upon the Sudan government to disarm them. The government responded by easing restrictions on issuing visas and humanitarian access, but the staffs of the nongovernmental organizations (NGOs) were still required to give local Sudanese aid commissioners twenty-four-hour notice to travel beyond the three principal towns — El Fasher, El Geneina, and Nyala.

The Media, Diplomacy, and Humanitarians

Thereafter, throughout a long, hot summer of terror, flight, and survival, events in Darfur were characterized by the massive outcry in the international media demanding their governments come to the aid of the people of Darfur and asking how best to protect and aid the hundreds of thousands of IDPs and refugees. They were frustrated and angered by the prevarication and obfuscation of the GoS in its negotiations with the United Nations, the United States, and the EU, and with the representatives of the SLM and JEM at Abuja, Nigeria. The disingenuous and contradictory statements by the GoS were accompanied by repeated attacks from the armed forces and their allied *Janjaweed* militia on the people of Darfur, which provided fuel for the intensive debate then taking place as to whether the disaster in Darfur constituted genocide.

The Western media — newspapers, magazines, journals, television, and the Internet — have relentlessly featured the plight of the beleaguered civilians of Darfur. Many harsh denunciations carried the guilt of the silence or dilatory response to the Rwanda genocide in 1994 that came vividly to mind during the ten-year memorial services for that tragedy held in April 2004. The media in the Arab world, even the usually strident *Aljazeera* were more subdued. They were embarrassed by a conflict now between Arabs and Africans, not just among Africans as in Rwanda, and by the rhetorical appeals for Arab solidarity with Sudanese Islamists committed to the spread of Arabic language, culture, and religion. Reporting by the Western media was accompanied by demonstrations in Europe and the United States, countless meetings, and speeches, both provocative and practical, exhorting their governments to do something to protect the Africans of Darfur.

The political response from the West was ambiguous, their humanitarian response emphatic. With its armed forces ensnared in Afghanistan and Iraq, the United States was unwilling to commit its few remaining troops to a difficult military mission in yet another Muslim country. Although both Britain and France had regularly been involved in peacekeeping missions in Africa, neither was inclined to plunge into isolated Darfur to challenge an Arab Islamist government. Both the United States and the EU sought to resolve this dilemma militarily by urging the AU to intervene, while at the same time promising to provide the necessary logistical support, diplomatically through the UN Security Council, and humanely by drastically increasing humanitarian aid and facilitating its passage to Darfur. By August, the AU Cease-Fire Commission of one hundred twenty five monitors under the Nigerian Brigadier General Okonkwo, who had helped stabilize Liberia, was in Darfur supported by three hundred troops from Rwanda and Nigeria, which constituted the African Union Mission to Sudan (AUMIS). They had orders to protect the United Nations monitors and provide security so that IDPs could avail themselves of humanitarian assistance, but the GoS adamantly refused to accept any AU peacekeepers with a mandate to impose peace by force, thereby emasculating the AU armed presence and limiting it to solely protecting AU personnel in Darfur who were there to monitor the violence. In his report to the Security Council on August 30, Secretary-General Kofi Annan urged the rapid expansion of AUMIS.

Diplomatically, by mid-July the United Nations had established the Joint Implementation Mechanism (JIM) to monitor events in Darfur, whose report to the Security Council, combined with pressure from the United

States, resulted in Security Council Resolution 1556 demanding that the GoS cease immediately all offensive military operations, disarm the *Janjaweed*, arrest their leaders, and report back to the Security Council in thirty days. In response, the GoS convened an All Darfur conference on August 11 and 12 calling for "harmony" and "peaceful coexistence" with much rhetoric and little reality. More substantially, Olusegun Obasanjo, President of Nigeria and the African Union, arranged for direct negotiations between the GoS and the representatives of the SLM and the JEM at Abuja. Neither side was in a mood for compromise. After many days of argument over the agenda, the two sides ended up deadlocked as to whether the rebels should be disarmed along with the *Janjaweed* and then placed in cantonments (temporary quarters) where the SLM and the JEM perceived they could easily be destroyed. A constant theme running throughout the negotiations was the complete lack of credibility of the GoS — their legacy of too many agreements dishonored. On August 30, Kofi Annan dutifully submitted his report required by Resolution 1556 in which he concluded that the GoS had "not met its obligation" to stop "attacks against civilians and ensuring their protection" (United Nations, 2004a).

While the military and diplomatic initiatives remained dismal, a greater humanitarian effort began to reach many more IDPs and refugees despite the rains that made the roads impassable, requiring that food, medicines, and supplies be transported by air or special all-weather vehicles. In July some nine hundred fifty thousand IDPs, out of an estimated 1.2 million received some food assistance, and over two hundred thousand Sudanese refugees in Chad were assisted by the UN High Commission for Refugees (UNHCR), governmental agencies (USAID alone had contributed $212 million by September 2004), and the fifty-six NGOs operating in Darfur. By September there were over thirty-seven hundred international and national aid workers in Darfur who, by then, had greater access to rebel held areas, including those from which they had previously been excluded. Furthermore, a convoy of twenty trucks carrying four hundred forty tons of wheat flour arrived at Bahai on the Darfur border having crossed seventeen hundred miles (twenty-eight hundred km) of the Sahara Desert from Benghazi and, thence, over the Ennedi Plateau on the old caravan route established in 1811. Still, only half of the $531 million needed for the United Nations response for food aid had been provided.

During the summer of 2004, the GoS could no longer fail to respond to the mounting international pressure to ease its restrictions on the humanitarian NGOs. But Darfur is an isolated region and Khartoum infamous for its Byzantine regulations and bureaucracy, and that was the reality the Western humanitarian agencies had to contend with despite the rhetoric of cooperation that poured forth from the government media. In fact, the hard-liners in Khartoum frequently pointed out that only four of the fifty-six registered NGOs were Islamic, the remainder composed of crusaders determined to convert the Muslims of Darfur into Christians.

Prevarications and Genocide

Although the GoS had received a thirty-day reprieve from Resolution 1556, presumably to act on the demands from the United Nations, its response was more smoke and mirrors than constructive efforts to curb the marauding *Janjaweed*. During the spring and summer, the GoS had repeatedly denied that it had any control or even influence over the *Janjaweed*. During discussions in the JIM in August, however, the government had to accept the overwhelming evidence that the militia had been trained, armed, and supplied by the army — including those *Janjaweed* who had not been incorporated into the PDF. Moreover, the killing, raping, and pillaging had not stopped. The flood of reports from UN monitors and humanitarian personnel, NGO staffs, and Amnesty International and Human Rights Watch could not be ignored. During the latter half of August, the *Janjaweed*, operating sometimes from government camps and supported by government armed forces, continued the destruction of Darfur and its inhabitants. Villages in the Yassin area northeast of Nyala were destroyed and their inhabitants slaughtered during a week of *razzia* (raids), while further to the west, near El Geneina in the Nertiti area and at Masteri, those IDPs, of whom there were thirty thousand, who ventured from their camp were regularly assaulted as part of "the consistent and widespread pattern of atrocities (killings, rapes, burning of villages) committed by the *Janjaweed* and government forces against non-Arab villagers" (Powell, 2004).

By February 2004, the ethnic devastation by the *Janjaweed razzias* was so widespread and consistent that some commentators began to warn of genocide in Darfur (See Amnesty International, 2004; Justice Africa, 2004; Annan, 2004c). Despite the rising demands from humanitarian agencies for the U.S. government to declare genocide, particularly after the U.S. Congress passed a unanimous resolution in July declaring the carnage in Darfur "genocide," officials in the Bush administration, the United Nations, and the European Union were more restrained.

That same month, the leadership of the AU concluded there was no genocide in Darfur. Not surprisingly, the Arab League and the influential Organization of the Islamic Conference reached the same conclusion. The personal representative of Kofi Annan in the Sudan, Jan Egeland, used the more sanitary "ethnic cleansing" that soon became fashionable. The reaction of the GoS was complete denial.

Much of the dialogue about genocide became focused on the sterile and legal definitions as to what actually constitutes "genocide." The 1948 Convention on the Prevention and Punishment of the Crime of Genocide (Article 1) obliges its signatories to prevent and punish if, indeed, genocide was/is taking place.

Following U.S. Secretary of State Colin Powell's visit to Darfur at the end of June, an Atrocities Documentation Team (ADT) was, rather belatedly, being organized by the U.S. Department of State. In mid-July and early August, the ADT conducted over a thousand interviews with Sudanese refugees who had crossed the border into Chad. Having assessed the work of the ADT and other reports by a wide variety of agencies, Colin Powell, in testimony before the Senate Foreign Affairs Committee on September 9, 2004, concluded that "genocide has been committed in Darfur, and that the government of Sudan and the *Janjaweed* bear responsibility — and genocide may still be occurring." Despite the determination and declaration of genocide, Powell (2004) asserted that "no new action [by the U. S.] is dictated by this determination." This was the first time that a sovereign nation had accused another sovereign state of genocide under the 1948 Genocide Convention. Secretary Powell was careful in his declaration to invoke Article VIII of the Genocide Convention, which enables its signatories to refer the matter to the United Nations for any further action it considers appropriate "to prevent genocide." By referring the matter to the United Nations, the United States thereby had fulfilled its obligation.

The proposed draft of the U.S. resolution to the UN appeared to recognize the reality that the United States, having expended most of its diplomatic capital in Iraq, could no longer prevail in negotiations with members of the Security Council to get tough with the GoS. Its resolution benignly requested a rapid expansion of the three hundred AU troops in Darfur without raising the thorny question of defining whether they were to be simply security forces to protect monitors and IDPs or interventionist peacekeepers. Regular international surveillance flights would continue to watch the *Janjaweed* and the armed forces of the GoS, which U.S. reconnaissance flights had been flying, and it would be left to UN Secretary-General Kofi Annan to assess whether acts of genocide had been carried out in Darfur and by whom. Secretary Powell hoped for "the possibility of sanctions" particularly on petroleum that would, of course, ensure a veto by the Chinese who were dependent on imported oil and had no intention of jeopardizing their large and productive concession in the Sudan.

After a week of intense negotiations with members of the UN Security Council by U.S. Ambassador John Danforth, the United States submitted its carefully drafted second resolution on Darfur, co-sponsored by Germany, Romania, Spain, and the United Kingdom that was adopted by the

Security Council on September 18, 2004 by a vote of eleven to zero with Algeria, China, Pakistan, and Russia abstaining. The principal articles of Resolution 1564 on Darfur "declared its [UN] grave concern that the Government of the Sudan had not fully met its obligations noted in Resolution 1556" (Article 1), the first Darfur resolution of July 31, and endorsed "the African Union to enhance and augment its monitoring mission" (Article 2), but remained silent about any "peacekeepers," which the Sudan government adamantly opposed in Darfur. Article 12 of the resolution also requested the Secretary-General to "rapidly establish an international commission of inquiry … to determine … whether or not acts of genocide have occurred and to identify the perpetrators … ." It further stated that in the event that the Sudan does not comply with Resolution 1556 [July 31] "or this resolution," the Security Council "shall consider taking additional measures … such as to affect Sudan's petroleum sector" (Article 14), while still scrupulously avoiding any mention of sanctions (United Nations Security Council, 2004b). Not surprisingly, the GoS condemned the resolution, and Mutrif Siddiq, undersecretary in the Sudan Foreign Ministry, declared on state-run television, "This resolution, according to our assessment, frustrates our aims and is discreditable."

Without peacekeepers, only monitors and vague demands for accountability without any provisions for enforcement, the GoS can satisfy its critics by the customary rhetoric of obfuscation and the token easing of restrictions on the humanitarian agencies. The United States declaration of genocide in Darfur may intensify the debate of this terrible tragedy, but the Sudan will remain inviolate behind its denials and assured that the threat of international intervention has dissipated, leaving them to practice their own diplomacy of "splendid isolation." Protected by the geographical vastness of their country, secured by infusions of oil revenues, and with no viable Sudanese opposition, the Islamist regime will continue to contain its marginal ethnic groups by divide and rule and, when applicable, terror.

References

Amnesty International (2004). "Darfur: Too Many People Killed for No Reason." February 3. London: Author.

Annan, Kofi (2004a). "Action Plan to Prevent Genocide" [Press Release]. April 7. Geneva: United Nations. Available from: www.preventgenocide.org

Annan, Kofi (2004b). "Report of the Secretary-General pursuant to paragraphs 6 and 13 to 16 of Security Council resolution 1556 (2004). Draft (30/9/04), 30 August 2004. Available at: http://daccessdds.un.org/doc/UNDOC/GEN/N04/474/12/PDF/N0447412.pdf?OpenElement

Annan, Kofi (2004c). "Comments at the Stockholm International Forum 2004: Preventing Genocide: Threats and Responsibiilties." January 30. Stockholm: InterPress Service.

Government of Canada (2004). "Statement by Bill Graham, Foreign Affairs Minister." February 5. Ottawa: Foreign Affairs Ministry Office.

Government of Norway (2004). Norwegian Ministry of Foreign Affairs Press Release. February 4. Oslo: Norwegian Foreign Ministry.

Government of the United States (2004). USAID Press Release. February 3. Washington, D.C.: USAID.

Justice Africa (2004). "Prospects for Peace in the Sudan." January. London: Author.

International Crisis Group (2004). *Sudan: Now or Never in Darfur. ICG African Report No. 80* (p. 11). Nairobi/Brussels: Author.

Kapila, Mukesh (2004). "Statement of UN Humanitarian Coordinator." March 22. *UNIRIN*, (n.p.) Also quoted in Eric Reeves, "Darfur: Ongoing Genocide," in *Dissent Magazine*, Fall 2004. See: www.sudanreeves.org/modules

Middle East Policy (1992). "Islam, Democracy, the State and the West; Roundtable with Dr. Hassan Turabi," *Middle East Policy*, 1(3): 49-61.

Movement for Justice and Equality (n.d.). "The Battle for al Fashir." Press Release No. 5.

Powell, Colin L. (2004). "The Crisis in Darfur: Written Remarks Before the Senate Foreign Relations Committee." September 9, 2004. (n.p.) Available at: www.state.gov/secretary/former/powell/remarks/36032.htm

Rafirasme, Ramin (2004). "Statement by the Spokesman for the World Food Program." *UN Integrated Regional Information Networks* (IRIN). January 26. Nairobi: IRIN.

Ramcharan, Bertrand (2004a). "Statement Issued by the UN High Commissioner for Human Rights." January 29. Geneva: UN High Commissioner for Human Rights.

Ramcharan, Bertrand (2004b). "Report of the High Commission for Human Rights: Situation of Human Rights in the Darfur Region of Sudan." E/CN.4/2005/3. 7 May 2004. (n.p.) Available at: www.unhchr.ch/huridocda/huridoca

Reeves, Eric (2004a) "Day One of the Darfur Ceasefire: Khartoum Continues Aerial Assaults, Janjaweed Militia Attacks Continue, No Prospect of Full Humanitarian Access" (p. 1). Posted April 13, 2004. Available at: www.sudanreeves.org/modules

Reeves, Eric (2004b). "Genocide in Darfur: The End of Agnosticism" (p. 1). February 1, 2004. Available at: www.sudanreeves.org

The Sudan Liberation Movement and Sudan Liberation Army (SLM/SLA) (2003). *Political Declaration of the SLM*. Press release/commentary by SLM/SLA. Posted on March 14, 2003, 13:42:53, EST.

United Nations (2004). Report of the Secretary-General Pursuant to Paragraph 6 and 13 to 16 of Security Council Resolution 1556. New York: Author.

UN Commission for Human Rights (2003). "Statement from UN Humanitarian Coordinator for Sudan." November 10. Nairobi/Khartoum: Author.

UN News Centre (2004). "Sudan Humanitarian Crisis Characterized by Violence and Fear" (p. 1) *UN News Centre*, May 7.

United Nations Security Council (2004a). *UN Security Council Resolution 1556*. Adopted by the Security Council at its 5015th meeting, on July 30, 2004. S/Res/1556 (2004). Available at: http://daccessdds.un.org/doc/UNDOC/GEN/

United Nations Security Council (2004b). *UN Security Council Resolution 1564*. Adopted by the Security Council on September 19, 2004. New York: United Nations.

Vraalsen, Tom (2003). "Sudan: Humanitarian Crisis in Darfur" [Note to the Emergency Relief Coordinator]. December 8. (n.p.). Retrieved January 8, 2006 at: www.sudanreeves.org

Notes

1. After the signing of the Machakos Protocol in July 2002, which established the principles by which peace negotiations would be conducted to end the twenty-year civil war in the Sudan between the Government of Sudan (GoS) and the Sudan People's Liberation Movement/Army (SPLM/A). After the GoS and the SPLM/A had agreed to a general cease-fire in October 2002, the negotiations were opened at Naivasha in Kenya under the auspices of the Intergovernmental Authority for Development (IGAD). It involved the active participation by the international community represented by the troika of Great Britain, Norway, and the United States. The subsequent talks at Naivasha were lengthy, complex, and contentious before a Comprehensive Peace Agreement (CPA) was signed on January 9, 2005.

2. Alghali's candid comments soon made him a liability in Khartoum, which was already under increasing pressure from the international community to end the conflict in Darfur. He was, however, replaced as governor of southern Darfur by a more discrete but hard-line member of NIF, Al Masnan Idriss, who Human Rights Watch has placed on its list of Sudanese to be tried by the International Criminal Court for their role in the killings and destruction in Darfur.
3. Agreement between the Government of Sudan on one part, the Sudan Liberation Movement and the Justice and Equality Movement on the other under the auspices of H. E. Idriss Deby, President of the Republic of Chad, Chief of State, assisted by the African Union and the United Nations, N'Djamena, April 25, 2004.

CHAPTER 2

Moving Beyond the Sense of Alarm

ANDREW S. NATSIOS

The Importance of Places like Sudan

In 1956, Sudan freed itself from British rule and became one of the few independent countries in sub-Saharan Africa. This east African country with an estimated population of forty million has since then been the scene of almost incessant conflict. More than two million of its people have died from famine and war-related causes, and millions more have been displaced.

Sudan is also the largest country in Africa, about one-quarter the size the United States. It borders nine states in one of the poorest and most troubled regions of the world. Internally, Sudan endured one of the longest-running civil wars in Africa, some twenty-two years in length (which only came to an end in January 2005). Externally, over these same years, it has found itself dealing with cross-border violence in a series of wars that have erupted in virtually all the countries surrounding it. It has both contributed to the general instability that has rocked the Horn of Africa and been victimized by it.

In 1989, a coup engineered by General Omar Hassan Bashir established the Revolutionary Command Council for National Salvation, which gave Sudanese politics a decidedly more fundamentalist orientation. The coup occurred the day the Northern Government was to sign a peace agreement with the South. The National Islamic Front (NIF) took over as the leading party, led by Dr. Hassan al Turabi, who inspired and planned the change in regime. They seized the moment to reinvigorate the war effort against rebels in the South, who are divided from the Arab and Islamic North by religion and race.

The South long suffered marginalization and condescension at the hands of the North. As historian Bernard Lewis (1992) points out in *Race and Slavery in the Middle East,* the Arab perception of black Africans was formed in the experience of a trans-Saharan slave trade that goes back a millennium, predating the trans-Atlantic trade that brought West Africans to the Americas by some six hundred years. The bloody civil war that raged off and on since independence only added to the historic grievances.

In 1992, Sudan played host to Osama Bin Laden. Bin Laden used his considerable wealth and contacts to gather around him the veterans of the Afghan war against the Soviet Union. They were shocked by the ease of the American victory over Iraq in the Gulf War and the attitude of the Arab ruling elites who allowed the U.S. military to remain in the region. Six years later (in 1998), United States embassies in Tanzania and Kenya were bombed by *Al Qaeda.* This was the same year that the United States bombed a Sudanese facility suspected of fabricating weapons of mass destruction.

In summary, this was the situation in Sudan that faced President George W. Bush in 2001, and these are some of the reasons why he immediately made Sudan one of his principal foreign policy concerns. Its pathologies infected the entire Horn of Africa, the source of the humanitarian crises that periodically gripped the region. Moreover, it posed an active threat to the peace in an area of the world that had assumed great strategic importance for the United States. Thus, it made strong claims on the attention of the new administration for both moral and strategic reasons.[1]

Nine months later, on September 11, we knew that the national security of the United States was even more directly affected by what had taken place in Sudan and other failed states in the region. By best estimates, more than twenty thousand *Al Qaeda* operatives in the 1990s passed through camps in Sudan, Somalia, Afghanistan, and elsewhere.[2] It was there that they were indoctrinated and trained and became foot soldiers in a new global war.

The National Security Strategy document declares, in a succinct and a disarmingly straightforward statement, that "America is now threatened less by conquering states than by failing ones." Few, it seems, have grasped the full thrust of what is being said here. Simply put, Sudan is a test case of the challenges that the world now faces. What had transpired there and in other failed states of the region was to become the catalyst of the most fundamental reorientation in the strategic thinking of the United States since World War II and the Cold War, as well as the most sweeping reorganization of its foreign policy apparatus.

The Vision for Sudan

U.S. Deputy Secretary of State Robert Zoellick articulated the goals the Bush administration is trying to achieve in Sudan when he appeared before the House International Relations Committee on June 22, 2005: "A unified and peaceful Sudan that contributes to regional development and cooperates on counter-terrorism; a participatory and inclusive democratic government in a federal system that respects human rights and shares resources for the benefit of all Sudanese."

Substantial steps were taken in this direction upon the signing of the Comprehensive Peace Agreement (CPA) in January 2005 in Naivasha, Kenya. This historic compromise permitted the North to retain *Sharia* (Islamic) law while allowing the South to gain a large measure of autonomy. A power-sharing agreement provided that the First Vice President of a new Government of National Unity in Khartoum would be represented by the President of the Government of Southern Sudan. Moreover, after six years, the South could opt out of this arrangement and decide for independence by referendum. Protocols had also been signed on how to share oil revenues, on establishing parallel monetary systems in the North and South, and on security arrangements involving the two armies.

How certain geographic areas would be administrated was also decided. These had been flashpoints of conflict in the past and include, Abyei, the Southern Blue Nile, and the Nuba Mountains.[3] In 1992, in the Nuba Mountains, *jihad* was declared against a group associated with the Sudan People's Liberation Army (SPLA), but its attempt to establish *Sharia* law there failed. In 1998, the Northern army and the militias began a campaign of starvation in the oil field zones of the Upper Nile Province in southern Sudan. In this instance, the focus was on oil revenues, not the extension of Islamic law. This may have indicated a softening of ideology on the part of Khartoum. It was part of the evidence of a new realism, where the very survival of the regime became more urgent than Islamic ideology.

The prospects for peace and reconciliation between North and South brightened after negotiations began in Machakos, Kenya, where the overall framework for peace emerged. But peace for the country as a whole dimmed because of events that were to take place in the West of the country, in Darfur. This was the scene of the world's worst humanitarian crisis at the time — the consequence of a genocide, according to former U.S. Secretary of State Colin Powell, and the subject of this essay.[4]

Sudan is in the early stages of implementing the North/South Agreements, which is the result of complex and detailed negotiations that started in 2002. Quite simply, the tenuous peace we are witnessing in one part of the country cannot gain traction if war is raging in another part. This means first and foremost putting a definitive end to the violence in Darfur and assuring against its renewed outbreak. It means beginning the process of reconciliation among groups in the area to encourage the voluntary return of people to their homes. It means restoring pillaged property and helping to rebuild shattered lives and devastated villages. And it means, finally, calling the perpetrators of atrocious crimes to account.

A cautious optimism is warranted for at least two reasons. Leaders of both the South and North have a strong interest in working together to solve the Darfur problem and shore up the North/South peace. The North may be particularly reticent at this moment to resume the war in the South when it must contend with the Darfur whirlwind it has sown in the West. The Northern leadership may also feel the pressure of the referendum that looms in the South in 2011. Among other things, failure to reconcile differences by then will cause Khartoum to lose control of territory that contains vast stores of oil riches. Secondly, the international community has been mobilized. It is taking significant steps, through the African Union (AU), to reinforce security in the area and is assembling the carrots and sticks to move the peace forward.[5] It is now essential to keep the attention of the world community focused and engaged.

Developing a Strategy to Document the Atrocities in Darfur

This chapter presents an account of the efforts by the U.S. Government (USG) to develop a strategy to document the atrocities in Darfur and to bring its plight to the attention of the U.S. Congress and the world. It is offered as an object lesson of the changed dynamic in which the humanitarian and development mission of the U.S. Agency for International Development (USAID) now operates.[6] It is also offered to illustrate some of the new tools we are using to fulfill our mission as well as some of the changes we have initiated at the agency to bring it into better alignment with the national security imperatives of the present day.

The Historic Background to the Violence in Darfur

Khartoum traders and mercenaries carved out a state in the area of present day Sudan through conquest of the upper Nile Valley in the nineteenth century. The administration of the state fell to a very small circle of rulers principally drawn from Arab tribes in the Nile valley. Khartoum has essentially operated as an Arab metropolis, surrounded by impoverished sub-Saharan expanses. The riverine Arab-dominated center presides over a very weak political system that has tried to extend its power base by co-opting the leaders of regional tribal groups.

The face Sudan presents to the outside world is one that is culturally Arab and religiously Muslim. It has been a member of the Arab League since its independence. Its diplomats are drawn from Arab ranks and they can appear at diplomatic gatherings as readily in Western business suits as in turbans and robes. Internally, however, the country is much more complex.

While the North is the home to Arab tribes and Khartoum gives it an urban cast, the East is home to the pastoral Beja, who trace their ancestry to the ancient peoples of the Nile, the Nubians. In the South is found animism and Christian communities and traditional African tribal structures. Cleavages in the country are sharp and run along ethnic, tribal, racial, geographic, and religious lines.

The West is the location of the three provinces of Darfur. This "Land of the Fur" existed as the Independent Fur Sultanate for well over two centuries before being conquered by the British in 1916. Unlike the country as a whole, cleavages here are muted. The religion of the region is nearly entirely Muslim. Ethnically and racially, it is mixed. This is the result of a fascinating history of migration by West Africans that took place over the centuries. The search for arable land set these impoverished peoples in motion; they later were drawn along the same migratory path, out of religious obligation, to Mecca. Upon settling in Darfur, they mixed with nomadic Arab peoples from the North. Simple tribal mores prevail in Darfur, in large part because of its poverty and geographic isolation. This is not the likely tinder for a genocide. It is rather the formula for a way of life fixed in time and tradition. This is but one of the paradoxes in the extraordinarily complex history of Darfur.

The most salient cleavage for understanding the genocide could be described as an *economic* one, properly understood. It is the story of conflicting ways of life and land disputes in what is essentially a premodern setting and a very harsh environment. The land of the Fur has supported both farmers and nomads. These have imported ways of life from the West, and the North and Near East, which have persisted through the millennia. The commingling of these groups has created a very complex social network.

Both groups are heavily dependent on rainfall: the farmers in their desert-edged villages for the subsistent agriculture that sustains them and the nomadic herders for the grasses that feed their camels and flocks. The region is periodically subject to famine because of drought. (It is also subject to pests and plagues of various kinds, such as the locust infestation in 2004 and 2005.) This causes friction between the groups who are forced to compete for scarce lands and water sources, which has grown more intense because of the growth in population. Their struggle for survival can turn violent at these moments. The tenuous equilibrium that has persisted between these groups has been periodically disturbed by nature. But, arguably, political changes in the last century have had a more pronounced destabilizing effect.

Britain ruled the country (following the First World War to 1956) by designating local sheiks and chiefs they favored as paramount leaders of administrative homelands. In Darfur, this displaced some of the traditional leaders as it blocked certain nomadic groups from access to the lands they had customarily grazed. The older, fluid social system that functioned according to certain tacit understandings among indigenous groups gave way to a more rigid administrative machinery that was designed for the convenience of the British. The severe drought and famine in 1984 was a particularly severe blow to the social system that had already been rendered fragile by colonial rule and the years of civil war, following independence, which had drained the country of resources.

Racist ideology plays an important part of the story, as it has in the history of other twentieth century genocides. And the psychology of "genocide" has become familiar through the sorry repetition of genocidal acts that the last century has witnessed. In 1987, Libya used the northwest Darfur corner as a backdoor to attack Chad. It had equipped and sent out the so-called Arab Legion, an Arab supremacist militia, to pursue Arab expansion in the mineral-rich sub-Saharan regions it bordered and to drive out the African tribes. Libya was not orchestrating a simple border raid on a poor country; it was pursuing a new strategy of pan-Arabism, couched in an emotionally charged ideology.

The sharp distinctions between Arabs and Africans in the racially mixed Darfur region had not been drawn until the ideology of pan-Arabism that came out of the Libya made itself felt. Some of the nomadic sheiks of the region came to see themselves as the avatars of Arabism, the authentic representatives of their Bedouin origins. They foisted a racial label on a farming people whose way of life they simultaneously disdained and felt threatened by. Turabi's (NIF) fundamentalism was later to raise the political temperature even further in a country that now roiled with extremist ideology. When the GoS tried to impose *Sharia* law in 1983, it retriggered civil war in the South. This marked the first use of government-backed militias as part of a counterinsurgency strategy. Some of the cattle herding Arabs of Darfur were employed in a strategy of brutality, starvation, rape, and pillage that was to be visited upon Darfur two decades later.

Complaints of Arab militia harassment in Darfur surfaced in 2003, at the same time Khartoum was negotiating a cessation of hostilities in the war in the South. Rebels attacked the police station and the military airport at Al Fasher, in the province of Northern Darfur, accusing the government of neglecting their region and arming militias. This sparked a more concerted campaign of counterinsurgency that eventually enlisted the *Janjaweed* militia and covered the whole of Darfur. This resulted in nearly two million internally displaced persons, including about one hundred fifty thousand Darfurians who escaped chaos by fleeing to refugee camps across the border in Chad. The leaders in Khartoum may have been pushed to take action by certain elements in the government who could not reconcile themselves to peace and thought that too much was being given away to the Sudan People's Liberation Movement (SPLM). There are loosely two rebel groups. The larger is the Sudanese Liberation Army (SLA). The smaller group is the Justice and Equality Movement (JEM). The latter is more militantly Muslim and has ties with National Islamic Front's Turabi, who was pushed from power by the current rulers as a liability in the post-9/11 world for his terrorist links. The rebel groups operate according to separate agendas and have added to the crisis in Darfur by diverting international aid and relief for their own purposes. Negotiations between the Sudanese Government and the two Darfurian rebel groups were held in N'Djamena, Chad, and led to a cease-fire in April 2004. This allowed the U.S. Agency for International Development (USAID) to mobilize a Disaster Assistance Response Team (DART). But the agreement failed to put an end to the conflict or to eliminate violence in Darfur.

Why the Janjaweed Militia?[7]

Many Darfurians have sought service in the Sudanese armed forces as one of the only practical alternatives to the hardscrabble existence that would otherwise be their lot. Demographic pressures that pushed against an unyielding land played its part in this. So did the weakening of traditional ties of clan and tribe that extraneous social and political forces came to exert. Khartoum, for its part, also needed the Darfurians. It came to rely on them to fill the ranks of its armed forces, which assumed critical importance in guaranteeing the state after independence and because of the wars, internal and external, which threatened it. For these reasons, the mainstay of the Sudanese national army, if not its officers (which remained Arab), came to be made up of Darfurians.

The phenomenon is similar to what happened in Great Britain in the course of forming a modern armed force that could serve the purposes of national unity and Empire. The British army came to rely on a core of Scottish effectives, who found in armed service an alternative to a similar hardscrabble existence in some very remote and very severe terrain. It offered to second sons, in particular, a way to escape marginalization that was forced upon them by strict laws of primogeniture. Theirs was a hard position, for the customs and laws that made for the very possibility of the "clan" made these second sons redundant. But this also posed problems for Britain when certain clans and regions in Scotland became politically restive. In these instances, London would be forced to rely on Scottish troops to discipline their own kith and kin.

A similar dilemma faced Khartoum in the aftermath of the Darfur rebellion in 2003. Darfurian regulars in the Sudanese army could not be relied upon to fire upon their own people. This is why the *Janjaweed* was enlisted and let loose. And, once let loose, it became difficult to control. The Darfurian campaign may be coming to an end, not because sanity has prevailed, but because there is precious little left in Darfur to plunder and burn.

The risks for Khartoum at the present moment are great. It must contend with the rage of Darfurians. At the same time, the *Janjaweed* has indicated that it will not be the "fall guy" for Khartoum for actions that were licensed and abetted there. It is in the interest of the Khartoum leaders to treat the problem that they have created if they are not themselves to be victims of violent blowback. This would mark the vengeance of the Sudan periphery, long ignored and disdained, against the Arab metropolis that has culturally and politically dominated the country.

Early Warnings

USAID has long provided assistance to Darfur. I first visited Darfur in 1991 during an incipient famine where USAID was providing food aid. In 2001, I made my first trip back to Sudan as USAID Administrator. Even before this trip, Secretary Powell and I agreed to augment USG aid to more effectively respond to the drought that had gripped the region. Shortly after the violence in Darfur began, I led a United States delegation there to assess the crisis firsthand and evaluate the humanitarian needs. The USG responded with more than three quarters of a billion dollars in Fiscal Year (FY) 2003–2004 in humanitarian assistance for the Darfur emergency, and almost half a billion dollars more in FY 2004–2005. This marks a significant acceleration of aid because of an improving security situation, thanks in large part to the AU commitment of troops and peace monitors. Security, though vastly improved, remains problematic as many areas remain inaccessible to nongovernmental organizations (NGOs) and the United Nations.

USAID funds have supported a broad array of implementing partners, including CARE, the International Committee of the Red Cross (ICRC), UNICEF, and World Vision, among more than a score of others. The World

Food Program (WFP) has been the principal conduit of United States food aid, which accounts for 85 percent of all such aid reaching the region.

It was the smattering of NGOs on the spot that first reported on the presence of *Janjaweed* militia and the widening campaign of terror. In May 2004, they reported an aerial bombardment in North Darfur that killed at least twelve persons. Civilians also alluded to additional attacks and harassment in that region. That same month, in parts of South Darfur, *Janjaweed* attacks reportedly killed at least fifty-six persons. Local populations said that the *Janjaweed* continued to perpetrate rapes and assaults in the area. In West Darfur, security problems were particularly acute along the Sudan–Chad border. Large numbers fled new violence in late May, creating a new refugee outflow into Chad in early June. This followed the massive displacement that had taken place at the end of 2003. Some villagers in West Darfur reported that fear of *Janjaweed* attacks along the roads made them virtual prisoners in their own homes. Since the onset of violence, victims throughout Darfur consistently reported that government troops participated in attacks with *Janjaweed* militia and oversaw militia activity.

In early 2004, senior officials of the USG, including USAID staff, flew by helicopter over the region. Deliberate wholesale destruction was evident on the ground. One international human rights agency had reported that, in West Darfur alone, the *Janjaweed* attacked and burned fourteen villages in a single day. The USG began to document a long list of destroyed villages as well as to gather precise evidence of the scope of the violence that was being inflicted. In one village we knew about, all thirteen hundred structures were destroyed; in another village, all four hundred sixty-six structures; in yet another, out of seven hundred twenty structures, less than one hundred were left standing. The *Janjaweed* and GoS troops burned crops, killed or stole cattle, and destroyed irrigation systems, thereby devastating much of Darfur's economic base and discouraging eventual population return and complicating any future reconstruction effort.

Victims of the attacks by the *Janjaweed* and GoS military regularly described massacres, executions, and rapes committed in plain view. GoS planes were seen to bomb villages and attack them with helicopters. We received reports that some victims were buried alive and others mutilated after death. At one isolated location visited by USAID staff in Darfur, local leaders reported that attackers had raped more than four hundred local women and girls; some women reportedly were raped in front of their husbands, compounding the shame and humiliation inflicted by the attackers. We received reports of *Janjaweed* branding their rape victims, presumably to make the act of rape permanently visible and to discourage husbands from taking back their wives. A health survey in parts of West Darfur in

April 2004 found that wounds inflicted in the violence caused 60 percent of the deaths of children older than five years.[8]

Many of the estimated one million residents of Darfur who were displaced by the violence had been denied safety even in camps where they had gone to seek refuge. Armed *Janjaweed*, apparently under GoS instructions, claimed to be "protecting" camps of displaced persons who fled their attacks days earlier. Camp occupants endured additional killings, rapes, and theft of relief items. Those inside the camps had to deal with a network of informers. They said that they could not venture outside their camps or villages for fear of being assaulted by *Janjaweed*, who kept close watch, inside and out. Because many men feared death if they left, many families relied on women to venture outside of camps to forage for food, firewood, and other necessities because women need fear "only" rape, according to interviews with displaced families. Some communities refused to accept sorely needed humanitarian assistance because they feared that distributions of relief items might attract *Janjaweed* atrocities. A United Nations official reported that he had never encountered displaced populations as traumatized as the people he met in Darfur.

I can attest that they are also seething with rage. In my trip in September 2004, I was personally caught up in the violence. The intervention of the USAID team with which I was traveling prevented the stoning of a GoS official. These are the reasons why AU presence in the camps and overall peacekeeping operations are so crucial.

The Problem of Access

The Government of Sudan was slow to allow any outside presence in Darfur. International organizations and NGOs, the United Nations, and donors like USAID faced numerous obstacles in reaching victims of the conflict with humanitarian assistance. Early on, at the peak of the violence, in fact, it was necessary to wade through three levels of GoS bureaucracy before outside groups could get to their projects. First, NGO workers had to obtain visas to enter Sudan, a process that, in certain instances, took from six to eight weeks. Initially, USAID's Disaster Assistance Response Team (DART) waited over three weeks to receive less than half of the twenty-seven visas requested from the Government in Khartoum. Second, the GoS impeded the access of relief agencies *to* Darfur once they were in Sudan through the issuance of required travel permits, which are frequently delayed or denied altogether. Third, the movement of relief workers *in* Darfur was hampered by GoS requirements for daily travel permits to leave the regional capitals to visit project sites. The GoS customs office also frequently impounded vehicles and other relief items and held them for months when they were (and are) urgently needed for emergency operations in Darfur.

The denial of humanitarian access over many months had other cumulative effects. All of these tactics created an environment where many NGOs were fearful of speaking out because they were afraid of losing any access they may have had.

Building the Case for Emergency Aid

In April 2004, I requested the USAID staff to prepare an estimate of potential deaths in Darfur from starvation and disease given the existing circumstances. USAID's Office of Foreign Disaster Assistance (OFDA) issued a mortality study projecting that as many as three hundred thousand people would likely perish by early 2005 if the GoS continued to block most Darfur relief deliveries and the violence did not stop. Experts within USAID/OFDA based the mortality projection on death rates experienced during a 1998 conflict-induced famine in southern Sudan's Bahr el-Ghazal province, as well as previous famines in Ethiopia.[9] The study also arrived at its mortality projection after examining local vaccination rates and interruptions in Darfur's agricultural cycle.

Adding to our alarm was a nutrition survey conducted in Darfur that suggested that the mortality rate projected in the USAID report might be too conservative. A health survey in West Darfur concluded in late May 2004 that nearly five percent of all children under age five had died within the past three months at the surveyed locations — a mortality rate more than double emergency thresholds.

The mortality chart was the centerpiece of USAID testimony in Congressional hearings during the spring of 2004 where Roger Winter, the Assistant Administrator for the Democracy, Conflict and Humanitarian Assistance (DCHA) Bureau responsible for the humanitarian response, shared our analysis with lawmakers and the press. Its dramatic warning about the stunning number of lives immediately at risk helped galvanize public opinion. To my knowledge, such a scientifically grounded, predictive study had never been done before by the United Nations or any donor government during any previous humanitarian emergency. It placed added pressure on Sudanese officials to reduce their restrictions on emergency relief efforts in Darfur so that life-saving food, shelter, healthcare, and other aid could reach victims of the violence.

Building the Case for Genocide

Equally unprecedented was the USG's use of satellite imagery to inform the American public and the rest of the world about the extent of violence and devastation on the ground, the forced abandonment of entire villages, and the mass migration of uprooted people to vulnerable new locations. Tapping into classified as well as unclassified sources, the interagency Humanitarian Information Unit (HIU), jointly supported by the State Department and USAID, was able to distill massive amounts of data and imagery into maps, photos, and charts that enabled U.S. Government officials to visualize the vast extent of the carnage in Darfur.

In June 2004, the HIU maps and imagery proved to be powerfully persuasive documents in our discussions with Congress, at the United Nations, and with other donor governments, some of which had not fully appreciated the magnitude and urgency of the crisis in Darfur. The availability of the aforementioned satellite imagery and new technologies that are capable of synthesizing data and creating visual representations to specification have proved to be invaluable tools. Commercial use of remote-sensing imagery meant that much of our material already was unclassified and ready for public use. We subsequently secured declassification of other material that helped greatly in showing the world what was happening in Darfur despite the Sudanese Government's attempts to hide reality by blocking access on the ground.

The surveillance imagery provided conclusive evidence that, by June 2004, at least three hundred seventy-seven villages in Darfur had been destroyed or damaged — a sobering testament to the systematic scope of the attacks by the Sudanese government military and *Janjaweed* militia. In a functional village, one can observe trees, animals, and houses with cone-shaped roofs made of grass. In a destroyed village, houses look like "donuts." One sees the circular walls, without the roofs, which have been burned or otherwise destroyed. We continued to revise the maps as more information became available. By 2005, the imagery showed that the number of villages left damaged or destroyed was over eight hundred.[10]

In June 2004, I traveled to Geneva, Switzerland, to share our satellite imagery and mortality projection firsthand with some thirty-six donor nation representatives and United Nations officials attending a Darfur consultation meeting. The evidence that was presented became the basis for a formal statement condemning "grave violations of human rights and international law" in Darfur and demanding that "all acts of violence, particularly all forms of sexual violence, must stop immediately." An additional U.S. Government pledge of $188 million in humanitarian assistance for Darfur was announced, bringing the total United States contribution to nearly $300 million in response to the crisis. Other countries eventually boosted their financial commitments as well. This brought contributions overall to almost $472 million.[11]

In early July, I took an updated version of the imagery showing the destruction to UN Secretary-General Kofi Annan and then to the

"Permanent Five" representatives to the UN Security Council. The USG evidence we presented that day put to rest the lie that Darfur was something "invented" by the U.S., another "aggression" on our part, a further "insult" to an Islamic nation. It was also meant to rally the Permanent Members of the Security Council who might otherwise be tempted, for various reasons, to downplay what was allegedly happening in Darfur. This was yet another "crisis" being put on the docket of the world body that was already straining with other obligations and that would be competing for its attention and resources. It was also inconvenient for more ambiguous reasons. For some nations, "Darfur" would complicate relations with Khartoum at the very time they were being cultivated as a way of gaining access to the country's oil wealth. This is part of the reason why some diplomats from the Permanent Five members of the Security Council displayed such attentiveness during the presentation. They were being presented evidence that could not be ignored.[12]

Classified imagery has long been used in closed-door diplomacy; the innovation for Darfur was in declassifying USG aerial photographs to use as a humanitarian tool before the United Nations and elsewhere. It was put to use to pressure the GoS. It was used to inform the U.S. Congress. It was put before the UN Security Council. And it was brought to U.S. airwaves in a segment of the television news show, the News Hour with Jim Lehrer. We used both commercial satellite imagery and the declassified aerial photographs. Both types pinpoint locations and show extent of damage, but the latter has been especially useful in providing temporal evidence — pictures of what a village looked like on a certain date, and then subsequent pictures showing the destruction.

The utility of this tool in tracking gross human rights abuses should not be underestimated. Satellite imagery and spectral analysis, which measures changes in ground surface composition, were put to use recently in Iraq to find mass graves. The new methods, which do not disturb the grave, impede any efforts to keep the graves secret, such as happened in Bosnia when bodies were moved in order to cover up mass killings. This will make it much harder for perpetrators of atrocities to hide their crimes.

As important as developments in satellite imagery are, there are limits to the effective use of such tools. Imagery can be misleading. For example, in Kosovo many buildings appeared intact from the air, but on-the-ground observation showed that their sides had been heavily shelled. Also, there could be other reasons for destruction or burn patterns aside from bombardment or ground attacks, e.g., brush fires. Imagery does not show the whole picture. It does not indicate perpetrators. Nor can it show intent and motive. Imagery is not "hard evidence" until ground-truthed by testimony and on-site investigations. However, imagery can indicate the best place to start the investigative process, especially when access is not possible or negligible.

Documenting Atrocities in Darfur

In the summer of 2004, the U.S. State Department and USAID organized an Atrocities Documentation Team (ADT) to verify through firsthand testimony what satellite imagery showed in stark detail. U.S. Secretary of State Colin Powell did not make the genocide determination until after the team systematically gathered testimony from refugees in Chad and made its report.[13] The team was composed of staff from the State Department's Bureau of Intelligence and Research (INR), its Bureau of Democracy, Human Rights, and Labor (DRL), as well as from USAID, which also provided funding for the project. Experts were recruited from and by the Coalition for International Justice (CIJ) and the American Bar Association (ABA).

The ADT conducted a random-sample survey of Darfurian refugees in eastern Chad in July and August 2004. The team interviewed over eleven hundred refugees, many of whom had endured harsh journeys across the desolate Chad–Sudan border. Analysis of the refugee interviews points to a pattern of abuse against members of Darfur's non-Arab communities, including murder, rape, beatings, ethnic humiliation, and destruction of property and basic necessities. Many of the reports detailing attacks on villages refer to GoS and militia forces, preceded by aerial bombardment, acting together to commit atrocities. Respondents said government and militia forces wore khaki or brown military uniforms. Roughly one-half of the respondents noted GoS forces had joined *Janjaweed* irregulars in attacking their villages. Approximately one-quarter of the respondents said GoS forces had acted alone; another 14 percent said the *Janjaweed* had acted alone. Two-thirds of the respondents reported aerial bombings against their villages; four-fifths said they had witnessed the complete destruction of their villages. Sixty-one percent reported witnessing the killing of a family member. About one-third of the respondents reported hearing racial epithets while under attack; one-quarter witnessed beatings. Large numbers reported the looting of personal property (47 percent) and the theft of livestock (80 percent).

Numerous refugee accounts point to mass abductions, including persons driven away in GoS vehicles, but respondents usually did not know the abductees' fate. A few respondents indicated personal knowledge of mass executions and grave sites.

A subset of four hundred respondents was asked about rebel activity in or near their villages. Nearly nine in ten said there was no rebel activity before the attack. Nine percent noted rebels were in the vicinity; two percent said the rebels were present in their villages. The overwhelming majority (91 percent) said their village was not defended at all against the attack. One percent asserted their village had been successfully defended and another eight percent cited an unsuccessful defense.

The report is based on results from personal interviews conducted by the ADT between July 12 and August 18, 2004. DRL, USAID, and the CIJ jointly designed the questionnaire in conjunction with other NGOs. INR provided technical assistance on questionnaire design and survey methodology. The teams used a semistructured interviewing approach that permitted the refugees to give the broadest possible accounts of the events they had experienced. The interviews were conducted in nineteen locations in eastern Chad, including the UN High Commissioner for Refugees (UNHCR) camps and informal settlements.

The Atrocities Documentation Project was a critical part of the evidence that led the USG to conclude that a genocide had taken place. It also catalyzed United Nations action. Nine days after the State Department's release of the *Documenting Atrocities in Darfur* report, the UN Security Council responded by instructing the UN Secretary-General to establish an International Commission of Inquiry (COI) to investigate human rights violations in Darfur and identify perpetrators. The subsequent United Nations report, issued in January 2005, concluded that "the Government of Sudan and the *Janjaweed* are responsible for serious violations of international human rights and humanitarian law amounting to crimes under international law." Although the United Nations inquiry did not characterize the crimes as genocide, United Nations investigators noted that "offenses such as the crimes against humanity and war crimes that have been committed in Darfur may be no less serious and heinous than genocide."[14]

The COI announced that it had identified specific Sudanese Government officials and members of militia forces responsible for atrocities in Darfur. It urged that the International Criminal Court (ICC) break the climate of impunity by prosecuting persons implicated in the worst crimes. The evidence the USG gathered will be critical in helping prosecute Sudanese individuals guilty of planning and executing the ethnic cleansing and widespread killings. Some contend that the perpetrators have modified their behavior in Darfur due to fear of indictment.

Relief and Protection

USAID is the chief government agency charged with humanitarian relief work, a mission that regularly takes us to conflict situations. It is often the case in such "complex humanitarian emergencies" that an official government has ceased to exist or that local populations find themselves beyond the reach of its security personnel. Moreover, it is sometimes the case in such situations that government officials themselves are the perpetrators of atrocities. A "protection" role for the agency in such situations is a logical extension of its "relief" mission.

In this regard, the documentation project in Darfur was an important step toward institutionalizing USAID's role as a government tripwire for identifying and addressing protection problems and human rights violations and pushing for accountability of those responsible. Official USAID policy now explicitly states that "as a matter of priority, USAID will work where possible to ensure that basic protection and human rights for at-risk populations receive adequate attention." The policy also emphasizes that USAID will support within the U.S. Government such efforts by working "to analyze, document, and respond to the protection problems of internally displaced persons (IDPs) during all phases of displacement."

The "protection" function of the agency has been formally housed in the Office of Conflict Mitigation and Management (CMM), our Office of Transitional Initiatives (OTI), and the Office of Disaster Assistance (OFDA). In Darfur, more than $2 million has been allocated in programs designed to promote protection and monitoring, support justice mechanisms and human rights associations, increase access to balanced information, and help develop conflict resolution frameworks.

In addition to its role in documenting the atrocities in Darfur and embedding a protection advisor in USAID's DART team, OTI is canvassing Sudan diaspora groups (Sudanese humanitarian NGOs based in the United States that are not involved in the rebellion) to determine their capacity in handling information they possess regarding atrocities in Darfur. It is providing appropriate technical support to enable them to participate in transitional justice efforts in Darfur. Additionally, OTI has provided funding to double the number of human rights monitors in Darfur to sixteen and extend the duration of their mission. It also has provided training and leadership on protection issues, "know your rights" campaigns, and the strengthening of the humanitarian intervention (such as health, water/sanitation, and others) to include protective programming (e.g., dealing with issues such as firewood and rape).

OTI funded Physicians for Human Rights and the Harvard School of Public Health to produce a comprehensive report on *Rape as a Weapon of War in Darfur* (Gingerich and Leaning, 2004). The report uses a variety of perspectives (health, psychosocial, legal, societal) to analyze the problem and make recommendations for programmatic action. It is also providing funding to the CIJ for the production of two short films that document, for advocacy purposes, the atrocities being committed in Darfur.

Conclusion

The Darfur Atrocities Documentation Project is notable for a number of reasons. It was the first investigation by a sovereign nation of an ongoing case of mass violence with the aim of determining whether or not the violence amounted to genocide. It was also the first time that any signatory of the Genocide Convention took steps under its provisions to get a UN Security Council response while a genocide was occurring.[15] This represents a critical test for the world body. It speaks to the very principles, which animated the founding of the United Nations and the credibility of the Charter under which it operates. It can be an important precedent for action when other outbreaks of genocidal violence appear in the future.

References

Gingerich, Tara and Leaning, Jennifer (2004). *The Use of Rape as a Weapon of War in the Conflict in Darfur, Sudan*. Washington, D.C.: U.S. Agency for International Development/OTI.

Lewis, Bernard (1992). *Race and Slavery in the Middle East: An Historical Inquiry*. Oxford, U.K.: Oxford University Press.

Notes

1. Shortly after assuming office in 2000, President George W. Bush signaled his interest in Sudan by making former Senator John Danforth a Special Envoy to Sudan. Danforth's report encouraged a deepening of American involvement. Along with counterparts from the United Kingdom and Norway, as well as front-line African leaders, he later proved himself indispensable in shepherding the Naivasha (Kenya) Accords to its conclusion. The President also made me the Special Humanitarian Coordinator for the country early in 2000. I had been head of the Office of Disaster Assistance during his father's administration and was the newly appointed head of the United States Agency for International Development (USAID). Since then I have been to Sudan more than a dozen times.
2. Estimates ranged as high as seventy thousand.
3. The U.S. team, including USAID, negotiated an agreement with the Sudan People's Liberation Army (SPLM) and Government of Sudan (GoS) to meet directly for the first time to discuss a Nuba Mountains cease-fire and to allow an international assessment of needs. The needs assessment was completed in January 2002 and the Nuba cease-fire was signed in Switzerland January 19 with Swiss and United States facilitation. Establishing this humanitarian access was immensely important in giving peace traction.
4. The Secretary of State made this charge before the Senate Committee on Foreign Relations on September 9, 2004, and provided the Committee with the evidence he had compiled.
5. With logistical help from the United States, the African Union (AU) is now playing an essential role in guaranteeing security. According to the AU, there are approximately five thousand military and civilian police currently deployed in Darfur. Plans were to increase the force level to approximately seventy-five hundred by the end of September 2005.
6. See Note 1.
7. The translation of *Janjaweed* is "a man with a horse and a gun."
8. Hearings before the Subcommittee on Africa, U.S. Senate Committee on Foreign Relations, 109th Cong., 1st Sess. (2005), testimony of Roger Winter, Assistant Administrator, Bureau for Democracy, Conflict, and Humanitarian Assistance, U.S. Agency for International Development.
9. The 1998 famine in Bahr el Ghazal was largely the result of denial of access by the Government of Sudan to the region.

10. The destruction of villages, which this documents, does not pinpoint the exact time that it occurred.

11. In April 2005, I accompanied Deputy Secretary of State Robert Zoellick, who represented the U.S. Government in Oslo, Norway, at a Sudan Donor's Conference. This brought $4.5 billion in total pledges for the country, $853 million being the official United States pledge.

12. Later in the month, I accompanied U.S. Secretary of State Colin L. Powell on a tour of Internally Displaced Persons (IDP) camps in Darfur. UN Secretary-General Kofi Annan and the Undersecretary-General for Humanitarian Affairs, Jan Egeland, were in Sudan at the same time and made courageously strong statements on Darfur. The U.S. Government subsequently urged the UN Security Council to pass a resolution that placed additional pressure on the Government of Sudan to follow through on its assurances to facilitate humanitarian access to Darfur and to stop the violence against innocent civilians.

13. According to the 1948 Convention on the Prevention and Punishment of the Crime of Genocide, genocide occurs when the following three criteria are met:

Specified acts are committed, such as killing, causing serious bodily or mental harm, deliberately inflicting conditions of life calculated to bring about physical destruction of a group in whole or in part, imposing measures to prevent births, or forcibly transferring children to another group. These acts are committed against members of a national, ethnic, racial or religious group.

They are committed "with intent to destroy, in whole or in part, [the group] as such."

The totality of the evidence from the interviews conducted in July and August, and from the other available sources showed that:

- The *Janjaweed* and Sudanese military forces have committed large-scale acts of violence, including murders, rape, and physical assaults on non-Arab individuals.
- The *Janjaweed* and Sudanese military forces destroyed villages, foodstuffs, and other means of survival.
- The Sudan government and its military forces obstructed food, water, medicine, and other humanitarian aid from reaching affected populations, thereby leading to further deaths and suffering.
- Despite having been put on notice multiple times, Khartoum has failed to stop the violence.

In July 2005, Secretary of State Condoleezza Rice visited the sprawling Abu Shouk refugee camp, the second largest in the region. She did not retreat from the findings of her predecessor and was rather blunt in recounting what she saw. "The United States has called it by name, that is that a genocide was committed here," she said.

14. Resolutions 1556 and 1564 were issued subsequent to the U.S.'s reports to the Security Council of the United Nations. These increased international pressure for improved security and humanitarian access, held the Government of Sudan and the perpetrators of violence accountable, and expressed the Council's intention to consider further actions, including economic sanctions, in the event of noncompliance.

15. Article VIII of the Genocide Convention provides that Contracting Parties "may call upon the competent organs of the United Nations to take such action under the Charter of the United Nations as they consider appropriate for the prevention and suppression of acts of genocide or any of the other acts enumerated in Article III."

PART 2
The Investigation

CHAPTER 3

Creating the ADT:
Turning a Good Idea into Reality

NINA BANG-JENSEN AND STEFANIE FREASE

The Seeds of the Atrocities Documentation Project (ADP)

In late June 2004, the Coalition for International Justice (CIJ) was asked to attend a meeting of nongovernmental organizations (NGOs) at the U.S. State Department in Washington. We had no idea that that meeting would turn into a project of historic importance. Gathered around the table were representatives of groups with experience in working on the ground in Sudan or the region, documenting human rights abuses, and/or investigating or assisting in the prosecution of war crimes. While there were numerous reports that many crimes were being committed in Darfur, to its credit, the U.S. Government wanted to try to assess the extent and nature of the crimes. Lorne Craner, then Assistant Secretary of State for the Bureau of Democracy, Human Rights and Labor (DRL), took the lead.

In speaking to the assembled NGO representatives, Craner radiated determination. He said that the Bureau wanted to develop a survey questionnaire to help understand the nature of the crimes in Darfur in order in part to determine if they could be described as genocide under the 1948 Convention on the Prevention and Punishment of the Crime of Genocide (UNCG). He asked each group to offer suggestions about how best to embark upon such an effort in a manner that would be authoritative, rigorous, and fast. The first task was to design a questionnaire that would capture the full extent of what the refugees experienced in Darfur before fleeing into Chad.

Calling upon his background in polling and survey research as a former high-level Congressional staff member and, more recently, as head of the International Republican Institute that engages in democracy and civil society promotion activities around the world, Craner challenged the group to consider designing a project that would produce a large, credible sample of data, immune to political manipulation (see Chapter 4, "Survey Methodology and the Darfur Genocide"). He set an ambitious goal of conducting over eleven hundred random interviews, a statistically significant sample, among the two hundred thousand Darfurian refugees scattered in ten refugee camps and numerous settlements along the eastern border of Chad. The assembled group of NGO representatives worked productively and collegially around the conference table with State Department staff to design a questionnaire within two days. At the third meeting on Friday, June 25, 2004, Craner announced that his goal was to send twenty people to Chad by the following Saturday. He then turned to everyone at the table and asked each representative, one-by-one, how many people their organization could commit to lending for such a project. Some could offer one or two people at some point in the near future, but none had sufficient trained personnel to take on the task individually or even collectively.

Accepting the Challenge

As CIJ had extensive contacts with current and former personnel in the various United Nations war crimes tribunals and investigative bodies, we decided to try. Co-author Stefanie Frease called former colleagues that evening. These individuals, in turn, sent e-mails to their contacts. The response was immediate and heartening. By the end of the weekend, we had heard from many experienced criminal investigators, prosecutors, regional experts, and other specialists and believed we could quickly assemble a team of between twelve and twenty from many parts of the world. By Monday, June 28, 2004, we felt confident enough to call the State Department's DRL Bureau to say CIJ could put together a team of investigators on the ground in Chad within about ten days.

The goal was to assemble small teams composed of individuals with diverse yet complementary skills. We wanted people who had investigated or prosecuted large-scale atrocities, others who had regional expertise, and those with experience in interviewing victims of sexual assault and others suffering from trauma. So, for example, we had a male prosecutor with experience at the Yugoslav tribunal, a female French-speaking refugee and trauma worker, an experienced female detective with gender crimes experience, and a male genocide scholar, each of whom had experience working in difficult environments. This was typical of the six teams of four interviewers/investigators and four interpreters that we recruited. We were keen on getting people with solid investigative experience who knew how to take statements, ask nonleading, follow-up questions and avoid hearsay. With the assistance of Jerry Fowler of the U.S. Holocaust Memorial Museum's Committee on Conscience, we identified two social scientist genocide scholars. From the International Crisis Group, we identified some individuals with experience working in Sudan or the region.

Then a deluge of resumes from around the world started to arrive by e-mail and fax. (By the end of the summer, we had received close to one thousand inquiries.) Several applicants became energetic short-term interns in our Washington, D.C. office and helped us deal with numerous administrative and other tasks, such as arranging for visas; waiting in the airline ticket offices for tickets and then sending them to team members who lived on several different continents; hand-delivering cash to departing team members since credit cards and travelers checks were useless in Chad; tracking down mosquito nets, tents, rehydration powder; responding to applicants; communicating with worried family members, etc.

Despite the challenges, the group was buoyed by the response of talented investigators and others from around the world who were willing to take time off from their jobs and live in tents under harsh conditions. In the end, members of the team came from eight different countries. Many had worked or were working as criminal investigators and prosecutors for United Nations criminal tribunals, including the International Criminal Tribunal for the former Yugoslavia (ICTY), the International Criminal Tribunal for Rwanda (ICTR), the Special Court of Sierra Leone, and the UN's Serious Crimes Unit in East Timor.

Just as it was beginning to look like we might actually be able to get teams in the field in about a week, we started to receive briefings from various State Department bureaus and NGOs about the difficulties we could face on the ground. In particular, staff from the Bureau of Population, Refugees, and Migration and the U.S. Agency for International Development (USAID) warned of the many logistical hurdles — there was a lack of readily available food, water, and accommodation; potentially paralyzing weather conditions with the approaching rainy season; poor communication systems; extremely hazardous unpaved roads; and an already overstretched aid community. They advised it was only possible to take five to six people at most, not the sixty or so we knew we needed (including interpreters and drivers) to conduct a sample survey of this size. This stark evaluation sharpened our planning and equipment requirements.

To achieve the goal of conducting over eleven hundred interviews, CIS staff concluded that it would be best to stagger the arrivals of the teams of four investigators and accompanying interpreters by one or two days so as not to overwhelm the fragile infrastructure. That first week, at the end of June 2004, was a blur of telephone interviews, preparation of personnel contracts, gathering of information about what was and was not available on the ground, developing a field plan, writing budgets and proposals, figuring out what supplies each investigator would need, preparing planning documents and figuring out varying visa, medical, and transportation needs.

We coordinated with the State Department on the final version of the eight-page questionnaire, which they hurriedly printed and bound, along with laminated map booklets. We reached out to many NGOs with regional expertise, including Darfur Peace and Development, which provided invaluable practical advice without which we could not have succeeded. At the time, the Washington office of CIJ had a small, full-time staff and an extraordinarily resourceful and organized legal intern, Vanessa Allyn, a Peace Corp alumna, who had just arrived for the summer from Willamette Law School. Frease, who had extensive experience working in war zones and on criminal investigations, took the lead on the ADT throughout, and Nina Bang-Jensen, CIJ Executive Director, and Allyn assisted.

The Focus and Effort of the Assessment Team

Having been involved in numerous field missions, Frease knew the importance of sending an assessment team out before the investigation teams arrived. The assessment team needed to accomplish a number of goals — to interview and hire interpreters who spoke tribal languages; to make contact with Chadian and refugee authorities; to enter into negotiations with local vendors to obtain cars, food, potable water, gasoline; to get a better sense of the logistical challenges on the ground; and to test the questionnaire. Among the mundane, but essential, tasks was determining where investigators would sleep and how investigators would get from one area of Chad to another, a vast country with challenging weather and topography. There were many concerns about the timing of the mission given the impending rainy season.

The assessment team was relatively small, and included representatives from the State Department's DRL Bureau, the Bureau of Intelligence and Research, one staff member from the American Bar Association's Central European and Eurasian Law Initiative (CEELI), and a consultant, Diane de Guzman, with vast experience working in Sudan. From CIJ's side there was Frease; John Thornton, a Florida-based litigator with human rights experience who was available for the duration of the project; a masterful coordinator originally from Darfur; and a medical doctor also originally from Darfur.

CIJ staff arrived in Chad's capitol, N'Djamena, on Wednesday, July 7, with other members of the assessment team arriving the next day. Meanwhile, at CIJ headquarters in Washington, recruiting and hiring continued as logistical challenges abounded. For one, as the potential interviewers were coming from different continents and there was only one reliable airline servicing Chad and limited consular offices, much juggling ensued. Adding to the complications was the strong desire to make sure the four-person subteams were balanced in skills, backgrounds, and gender.

Arranging for and purchasing tens of thousands of dollars of airline tickets, obtaining visas, and reimbursing participants for certain supplies and equipment was, in many instances, paid for (at least temporarily) by CIJ staff members' personal credit cards and bank accounts. Bang-Jensen and CIJ's part-time Finance Manager, Shirley Long, received some odd looks from bank tellers because of the near daily withdrawals and wires from CIJ and personal accounts throughout the course of the project.

Once in Chad, the assessment team quickly set out renting vehicles and replacing communications equipment stolen from bags en route to N'Djamena. They also needed to recruit a small number of interpreters who spoke various tribal languages in addition to English and Arabic. Knowing it would be difficult to find professional interpreters, if any, CIJ recruited a talented Swedish professor and expert in field interpretation, Helge Niska, to assist in training and operations (see Chapter 5, "The Critical Link: Interpreters"). Dr. Niska and Jan Pfundheller, an experienced detective and trainer, arrived after the assessment team completed its work and just ahead of the first investigation team. Once in place, Niska and Pfundheller remained in Chad throughout the summer providing invaluable support to each of the teams.

Early Saturday morning, July 10, the assessment team and five newly recruited interpreters loaded up four rented four-by-four vehicles and headed east to Abeche, which is close to the Chad–Sudanese border. While Abeche is only about four hundred fifty miles (or seven hundred fifty km) from N'Djamena, the trip took more than thirty hours. Within minutes, the team confronted the types of challenges that would face the teams for the entire summer. Just before leaving the parking lot of the Hotel Novotel, a downpour briefly delayed departure; then ten minutes after leaving N'Djamena, the team faced its first government checkpoint and attendant delays associated with ensuring passage; within two hours one vehicle had a flat tire. A slow steady pace gradually evolved, which included periodic but necessary tea breaks, refueling, prayer time for the drivers and interpreters who were all Muslim, as virtually everyone is in the region, and bathroom breaks for all, mostly in open fields.

That night, the advance team camped on the grounds of a government guest house kindly opened up to them by the local official in the village of Ati. The team members rose at 4:30 the next morning and were on the road by 5 a.m. Not long into the second day's journey, one of the vehicles had a brake problem; by 9:30 another car was stuck in the mud; a few minutes later, one of the team's vehicles was pulling a passing pick-up overloaded with passengers and goods from the same spot. Continuing on, they drove through wadis (flash-flood river beds that fill with astonishing speed) whose water reached the hood of the cars. The team finally arrived in Abeche at 3 p.m. and, through local contacts, was quickly able to find a house that they could use as the team's base camp for the summer.

At times, being an independent NGO caused some confusion over lines of authority. One of the few differences of opinion between CIJ and State officials came as a result of a misunderstanding over the project's goals. A State Department official who had not been involved in the planning meetings in Washington, but who had traveled to the region to participate in the assessment, was focused on conducting a total of two hundred interviews rather than the broader goal of recording nearly twelve hundred statements. At a meeting Sunday evening with United Nations High Commissioner for Refugees (UNHCR) officials, it became clear that the agency was so consumed by the ongoing aid operation that they could lend little support, including guaranteed access to United Nations flights. It meant that the teams would have to be self-sufficient with respect to housing, fuel, food, water, and ground and air transportation. This was our first hint that we would have to modify fundamental aspects of our plans in order to conduct the interviews within five weeks.

That evening we discussed the possibility of hiring planes to get the teams of investigators to the remote camp locations. The next morning Bang-Jensen spoke to Leah Werchik, the talented and resourceful program officer at USAID's Office of Transition Initiatives (OTI), the project donor in Washington. (Funding for the project came from OTI, then was passed through an available funding line at the American Bar Association's CEELI, and then to the project leader, CIJ.) Contrary to what one might think in dealing with a government bureaucracy, OTI has many people with practical field experience and Werchik immediately understood the necessity of shifting resources to cover the cost of renting planes. Our request to hire aircraft on an as-needed basis was quickly approved. CIJ also quickly realized that the original plan of providing a stipend to each team member for food and water was impractical. There was very little food in remote local markets, bottled water could only be bought in Abeche, and there were no real restaurants. Before sending teams out, vehicles, therefore, were stocked with enough food and water for about one week and then resupplied halfway through their missions. Despite, or perhaps because of, these enormous challenges, team cohesiveness was strong.

On Monday morning, the assessment team headed to the Farchana camp, a two- to three-hour drive east of Abeche, to test the questionnaire and reinforce the methodology of randomly selecting refugees to interview. It also provided an opportunity to ensure all additional information vital to investigation team deployment was gathered, such as identifying the tribal composition of each camp, checking the availability of food and water in the local markets, identifying areas where the investigative teams could pitch their tents, and any other unforeseen logistical obstacles.

Over the next couple of days the assessment team split into two groups to conduct additional site surveys focusing on locations where the first three teams scheduled to arrive the next week would work. By the end of the week, Frease returned to N'Djamena to contact an airplane charter company, rent additional vehicles, and meet with the U.S. Ambassador and other officials to inform them of the team's progress and plan of activities. Unbeknownst to her at the time, violence had broken out in the Farchana camp among frustrated refugees, and when Chadian authorities intervened to restore order, two refugees were killed. Violence also erupted in the Breijing camp, near Farchana. In both instances, rumors flew about Sudanese infiltrators in the camps. More than one dozen refugees were arrested.

Concern over these events caused some in Washington to question whether the project should move forward. That next weekend was tense as UNHCR tried to clarify what precisely had happened and determine whether similar incidents were likely to happen in other camps. There was additional concern whether the project could be self-sustaining without support from UNHCR and other groups already on the ground. For a couple of days it looked like the project might be shut down before it had really begun. Indeed, at least one United States and one international official advised that the effort be abandoned.

As security concerns were being discussed, Undersecretary of State Mark Grossman's office contacted DRL representative Michael Orona, asking that fifty interviews be taken over the weekend, then analyzed and sent to Washington by Monday morning, July 19, so that Secretary of State Colin Powell could review and potentially refer to the information at the United Nations early that week. The team members in the field said they could do it, even though it would interrupt further testing of the questionnaire and logistical planning. By Sunday evening, fifty interviews had been recorded and analyzed and sent to Washington by the Monday deadline.

The Preparation and Work of the Field Investigators

Within the next few days, some members of the assessment team returned to Washington.

CIJ's John Thornton, who was responsible for operations, and also conducted interviews, remained in N'Djamena to meet the first incoming teams of investigators whose arrivals were staggered by one day, and get them registered with local authorities and onto flights for Abeche. Frease had already returned to Abeche to meet the investigators and organize training for them and to give them time to get acquainted with their interpreters. In Abeche, each team received information and training about the history of the conflict, application of the survey methodology, working with interpreters, and approaches to taking statements from victims of sexual assault. Over the course of the next five weeks, the carefully selected interviewers arrived in small groups and were sent to separate areas of Chad. By project's end, the groups had covered all ten UNHCR-sponsored refugee camps in eastern Chad and several settlement areas along the border.

Conditions in the different areas varied tremendously. It was extremely hot in the north. There, Pundheller, Niska, and Frease were enthusiastically welcomed by exausted team members during a mid-term visit. They had been living in extremely harsh conditions, without water for showers during the first few days, and they were getting low on food and bottled water. The temperature in the North, in the Sahara desert, often reached 130 degrees Fahrenheit (48 degrees Celsius) during the day.

Throughout the project, the ability to shift gears quickly was critical to its progress. In Washington, incoming team members were advised by CIJ to bring flavored rehydration powders for the water; not to bring solar showers, as buckets were faster and easier to use; and to scale back on supplies because of a fifteen kilogram (thirty-three pound) weight restriction on most of the flights. While phone service was sporadic, requests from CIJ's Frease, Thorton, Pfundheller, and, eventually, Allyn, who spent the rest of her summer in Chad, came into CIJ's Washington office for hand-held radios, batteries, and more cash, which a number of interviewers carried in by hand as there was no way to wire money to Abeche. Resumes kept flooding in, Frease kept extending her stay, and CIJ staff in Washington struggled to communicate with the teams in the field through highly erratic satellite telephone service, to be responsive to changing requests when they were reached, and to keep in touch with the families of the team members who had questions and concerns.

During the entire project, individual team members carried their own supplies — one- or two-person tents, mats, flashlights, mosquito nets, etc. On reflection, it would have been helpful to have had one large tent per field team, as well as camping chairs as interviewers found it increasingly difficult to record an average of five statements each day sitting on the ground without support. The exhausted interviewers would typically fall asleep in their tents by 7 p.m. and be up again at 4 a.m. to begin a new day.

The teams discovered that adhering to the random methodology was challenging to many of the experienced prosecutors and investigators because their professional impulse was to follow evidentiary links and to interview witnesses with the most compelling firsthand information or experiences. What each team was supposed to do was to, first, meet camp leaders and, then, once introductions had been made, begin counting off every tenth "occupied space" (whether that was a group of people standing under a tree or sitting in a tent), to identify the adults in that group, and select, based on the established protocol, the person to interview. (For a more complete description of the methodology and protocols, see Chapter 4, "Survey Methodology and the Darfur Genocide.")

As team members finished their two-week assignments, they returned to Abeche for individual and group debriefings. Among the subjects that arose were common crime patterns, such as coordinated attacks between Sudanese Government forces and *Janjaweed* militias; the widespread use of aircraft, including Antonovs and attack helicopters; the killing of civilians, in particular, men and baby boys; widespread rape of girls and women, but also men; the frequent use of racial epithets; the destruction of food stores, crops, and burning of villages; the cutting down of fruit trees, the poisoning of water sources; and the destruction of mosques. Team members also discussed the need for additional and more-specific event codes to be added to the questionnaire, challenges in coding the crimes, issues of interpretation, among other issues.

Not far into the first team's work, CIJ received word there would be two Congressional visits. Senator Bill Frist (R-TN), Senate Majority Leader, and Representative Donald Payne (D-NJ) were visiting the region because of their long-standing interest in Sudan. They wanted to meet with our teams in the field and observe or participate in interviews. Fortunately and coincidentally, the Congressional visits coincided with the visit of one of the world's experts on gender crimes and war, Dr. Kelly Askin, a senior legal adviser to the Open Society Justice Initiative, an international NGO. She was able to share with Senator Frist her analysis of how the Genocide Convention applied to what she had observed. Roger Winter, then Deputy Administrator at USAID and long-time Sudan expert, accompanied Senator Frist. He had been instrumental in ensuring USAID/OTI funds were made rapidly available to support the project.

As the media was interested in talking to the members of Congress, the issue of just what team members should or should not say to the press accompanying the Congressmen arose. Previously, team members had generally deferred to Frease in speaking with reporters encountered along the way. As an independent NGO, CIJ was, of course, not constrained from speaking to reporters, but there was concern that team security and the overall project could be compromised if its progress and locations were widely known. The fact that there was a team in the field collecting information was well known and had been confirmed July 20 by the State Department's spokesperson. At the daily press conference, Richard Boucher (Assistant Secretary of State for Public Affairs) said:

> The State Department, the United States, has sent teams out to interview people, refugees in Chad, and over the last weekend and earlier this week, we've had a team of a half dozen or so people with, you know, Land Rovers and sleeping bags and equipment starting refugee interviews in camps in Chad near the Sudanese border to talk to people in, I think, a fairly systematic way about what happened to them, what they know, what we can identify as the atrocities and the perpetrators of things that might have occurred in ... Sudan.

At the request of the U.S. State Department in Washington, CIJ agreed to respond to press questions by addressing the data collection process, but not offering conclusory or summary statements while in the field, particularly on the question of genocide. CIJ had to walk a delicate balance between maintaining its independence while respecting State Department concerns about compromising the outcome of the analysis and research.

In the last two weeks of the project, the much-anticipated rains arrived in force. As the teams struggled to drive through huge expanses of desert, dry riverbeds suddenly turned into wadis, a mixture of rushing water and mud. At almost every turn, vehicles got stuck or stranded. One team spent the night in a refugee camp, another pitched its tents next to a wadi riverbed, waiting for the waters to subside enough to cross the next day.

Fortunately the CIJ medical evacuation insurance purchased for the interviewers was not used. Team members were felled by intestinal ailments, food poisoning, bug bites, sunstroke, the odd fever, and heavy ingestions of dust during sandstorms. (Two members were hospitalized briefly upon their return home, but have recovered completely.) Given the extremely treacherous road conditions (and lack of roads through portions of the desert), the fact that there were not serious accidents is a tribute to the skill and professionalism of CIJ's Chadian drivers. Two car axles broke, many tires were blown, radiators overheated, and all vehicles required major repair and maintenance by the end of the seven weeks of hard driving.

Six team members were there throughout most of or all of the project: it was essential to continuity. Of course though, they bore the brunt of the harsh conditions, logistical crises, pressure, and overall management.

Remaining team members filtered out of Chad between August 18 and 20, and the last completed questionnaires were hand-carried to CIJ's office in Washington. It was with a great sense of achievement that CIJ delivered more than twelve hundred statements to the State Department for processing and review.

State Department analysts, after coding and processing the first two hundred witness interviews, quickly realized they would need outside help with data entry and hired a firm in Ohio to do this work.

In the intervening weeks, team members returned to their home countries, and many remained in contact by e-mail or phone, sharing photos, and their impressions and analysis of the events they had recorded. Worried family and friends were happy to have them back. There were many administrative and financial matters for CIJ to tie up in Washington. Each team member completed evaluations so that any new project would benefit from our "lessons learned" over the summer.

The Finding Based on ADT (and other) Data

Despite the fact that the interviewers were scattered in many parts of the world, they kept in close touch with each other and with CIJ, monitoring press reports about when the State Department analysis would be completed, speculating as to what the Department would conclude. During this period, CIJ was in contact with State and USAID/OTI staff engaged in the project, but did not know when the statistical and subsequent legal analysis would be completed. By the end of August, rumors circulated that there was a policy battle among various bureaus in the State Department. Common wisdom among commentators in the media and others who were closely following Darfur policy was that the Africa Bureau was resisting a genocide determination, largely on political and diplomatic grounds.

While CIJ was not a participant in the State Department's internal debate and analysis over its final genocide determination, CIJ staff was told that Secretary Powell himself was engaged in the review and had taken statements and the statistical analysis home over the first weekend in September 2004. There was growing anxiety among participants on the CIJ team over how the data would be interpreted. Those concerns were heightened by two newspaper articles — an August 25, 2004 article in *The New York Times* by Marc Lacey, in which it appeared he had a draft copy of an August 5 State Department analysis of the first two hundred fifty statements, and then a September 8, 2004 *Washington Post* article by Emily

Wax, quoting an anonymous, high-ranking State Department source as saying, "Use of the word genocide is 'a political question now' … 'not a legal one.'" To some on the scattered CIJ team, the latter was an affirmative sign that the threshold had been met for a genocide determination while others saw it as a worrisome indication that insufficient political will existed to follow through on what the facts supported.

State Department officials invited CIJ staff to a late-afternoon meeting on September 8, 2004, one day prior to Secretary Powell testifying on Darfur before the Senate Foreign Relations Committee. During that meeting and during a previous phone call with a high-level State Department official, it was hinted that Secretary Powell would make a strong, possibly unprecedented statement. No one revealed, however, what precisely he would conclude.

At 9 a.m. on September 9, the Senate Foreign Relations Committee convened in the largest hearing room in the Dirksen Building in Washington, D.C. Minutes before the hearing was to begin, Reuters Washington correspondent, Saul Hudson, provided CIJ's Bang-Jensen and Frease a copy of Powell's testimony, in which he stated that:

> When we reviewed the evidence compiled by our team, we concluded — I concluded — that genocide has been committed in Darfur and that the government of Sudan and the *Janjaweed* bear responsibility, and that genocide may still be occurring.

Powell's historic testimony represented several firsts. It was the first time the United States had ever publicly and formally documented and concluded that a series of crimes likely amounted to genocide, while those crimes were unfolding. It was the first time that the United States had ever announced its intention to formally invoke Article VIII of the Genocide Convention calling upon the United Nations to take action under its Charter to prevent and suppress "acts of genocide," as well as to request a full United Nations investigation of all violations of international humanitarian law and human rights law that have occurred.

Team members around the world got in touch to discuss the finding. CIJ had already made it clear to everyone that as an independent NGO, it would not hesitate to disagree publicly, were the report not a good reflection of the information collected on the ground. It was gratifying instead to be able to endorse Secretary Powell's non-judicial finding wholeheartedly. Indeed, team members with whom we spoke concurred with Secretary Powell's assertion that the "specific intent of the perpetrators to destroy 'a group in whole or in part,' … may be inferred from their deliberate conduct." For those who heard firsthand from over twelve hundred refugees about their similarly harrowing accounts of attacks, murder, rape, racial epithets, and destruction of their way of life, it was gratifying to know their voices had been heard, at least by some.

Note

1. Nina Bang-Jensen is CIJ's Executive Director/Counsel and Stefanie Frease is CIJ's Director of Programs (currently on leave) and was the leader of ADT on the ground in Chad.

CHAPTER 4

Survey Methodology and the Darfur Genocide

JONATHAN P. HOWARD

Introduction

I arrived in my office the morning of June 24, 2004 to find a brief e-mail from my office director outlining a possible survey project involving Darfur — "about two hundred interviews, about ten days." Three months later, U.S. Secretary of State Colin Powell testified before Congress, holding the results of what began as a small documentation project, but evolved into a body of survey data representing the unique stories of over eleven hundred randomly selected Darfuri refugees. The data, Powell testified, supported his conclusion that genocide was being perpetrated in Darfur.

Conducting public opinion research in Africa presents significant challenges to the survey methodologist.[2] Out of date and unreliable census data, populations unreachable through customary modes of transportation, and the thousands of languages spoken across the continent must all be taken into account when designing and fielding a survey. The Darfur Atrocities Documentation Team's (ADT) mandate to conduct a large-scale, random sample survey in the refugee camps of Chad was perhaps one of the most methodologically and logistically challenging projects of its kind in recent history.

The views presented in his chapter are solely those of the author and in no way represent the views or opinions of the U.S. Government or the U.S. Department of State.

This chapter traces the story of how that challenge was met, from inception through final data analysis. Though the history and development of the Darfur Atrocities Documentation Team mission is chronicled in greater detail in other chapters, this chapter's narrative relates the development of the project through the lens of the survey methodology applied by the team. The first section reviews how the project was designed prior to deployment, from questionnaire development to sampling methodology.[3] The second section examines the experiences of the team that implemented the survey in the field. The data processing and analysis stage is the subject of the third section, followed by the statistical results of the analysis. Finally, the strengths and deficits of the methodology as applied are evaluated in retrospect.

The Decision to Apply Survey Methodology in Documenting the Darfur Crisis

Reports of atrocities perpetrated along ethnic lines and rooted in decades of political grievance had been trickling out of Darfur since 2003. By early 2004, the media began to focus increasing attention on the conflict. While it was clear that violence and displacement were increasing across Darfur, the precise nature and extent of the events remained unknown. Sudanese authorities denied reports as rumors, or isolated worst-case scenarios. As the U.S. State Department sought to stay abreast of the growing problem, a sound understanding of the scope of the conflict and its impact on the civilian population became increasingly important.

The three Sudanese states comprising Darfur — North, West, and South — cover an area the size of Texas and are sparsely populated by roughly seven to ten million people, mostly seminomadic pastoralists (herdsmen). The area has few paved roads, little telecommunications, and what transport exists is intermittently cut off by rains that fill *wadis* — dry sand river beds — in minutes. The State Department's knowledge about the unfolding crisis in Darfur was limited to information from nongovernmental organization (NGO) workers, media on the ground, and limited reporting from embassy and U.S. Agency for International Development (USAID) cables. By late June 2004, when this survey project began, the latest map from a series based on satellite imagery and compiled by the Humanitarian Information Unit (HIU)[4] revealed three hundred and one completely destroyed villages in the Darfur region, with another seventy-six significantly damaged. These two primary sources for information — field reporting and imagery — fell short, however, in two regards. The ad-hoc nature of field reporting, while consistently pointing to an ethnic dimension of the conflict, could not provide a reliable accounting of the scale of the conflict; thus, it was impossible to determine to what degree the wrenching stories trickling out were representative of the Darfuri population at large. Analysis of the satellite imagery provided evidence that destruction was extensive, but could not establish the ethnicity of destroyed villages or the identity of the perpetrators. While it was possible to photograph destroyed villages, it was impossible from imagery alone to determine whether the villages were destroyed because of their ethnic composition.

Initially working independently, two bureaus within the Department of State, Intelligence and Research (INR) and Democracy, Rights, and Labor (DRL), concluded that a survey of refugees would provide the most accurate account of past and ongoing events in Darfur. INR conceived of a small team conducting two hundred interviews — a number that could be achieved by a team of three officers working over the course of ten days — while DRL Assistant Secretary Lorne Craner suggested that the Department set a goal of interviewing twelve hundred refugees. A sample of twelve hundred, while posing significant logistical challenges, could provide a more broadly representative sample of the Darfuri refugees residing in Chad. The decision to base the survey in Chad was necessitated by the ongoing conflict in Darfur, which would have presented significant security risks to the interview team.

When INR and DRL began coordinating their efforts in late June 2004, it quickly became apparent that conducting a full-scale survey among Darfuri refugees would present significant logistical and methodological challenges, and these were all taken into account as the planning of the project continued apace.

The questionnaire used to gather each refugee's testimony, the survey design as developed by the Office of Research, and the capabilities of the survey team recruited by the Coalition for International Justice (CIJ) all evolved rapidly as the project scaled up from two hundred to over eleven hundred interviews and adapted to continuously changing humanitarian and logistical realities on the ground.

Questionnaire Design

Prior to deploying to the field, representatives from INR, DRL, CIJ, and the Office of Research began developing the questionnaire. In order to adequately address the needs of both the State Department and CIJ, the questionnaire needed to collect data for three distinct purposes. The State Department needed quantitative data — statistics that captured the type and extent of the events taking place in Darfur. These included geographic data sought by the HIU that would allow analysts to connect the experiences of the refugees to specific locales. The NGO partners, specifically CIJ and the American

Bar Association (ABA), were interested in gathering narratives from each refugee that could provide a detailed picture of the conflict and possibly be used as the basis for future legal prosecution of the perpetrators.

The questionnaire drafting process began with a collaborative meeting between State Department and NGO representatives, which fleshed out the essential information the questionnaire needed to gather. A rough draft of questions was developed: "What happened to you? Were you physically harmed? Where did this happen? Can you identify who did this to you?" Since the issue of intent is key in ascertaining whether a situation constitutes genocide or not, several questions were included whose aim was to identify the nature and intent of the perpetrators' actions. These questions included, "Did those who harmed or attacked you say anything to you?" and "Were there any particular groups or types of people who were singled out for harm?"

The next task was to take the first rough draft of questions and create a clear, logically ordered questionnaire that would effectively capture the narrative, quantitative, and spatial data the State Department and NGOs required. As most of the questions were open-ended, capturing the narrative of each refugee's experience would be relatively simple, consisting of the interviewer's transcription of the responses.

Even under the best survey conditions, generating quantitative data from qualitative responses is difficult. The process of coding open-ended responses[5] inherently involves human evaluation of the information and judgment calls when trying to fit responses into a finite set of codes. Creating a quantitative dataset from the refugee's responses — many filled with emotion or, from the perspective of the researcher, incomplete — would present unique challenges.

Considering these challenges, the Office of Research took two steps to overcome them. As the coding process is subjective and essentially a series of judgment calls, it was decided that the interviewer and translator (the two people closest to the refugee) would initially code the narrative immediately following the interview for specific types of events,[6] the perpetrator(s) involved in each event, the date of the event, number of victims, and location. The decision to have interviewers perform initial coding in the field also allowed for clarification with the respondent if there was any ambiguity in the narrative. Subsequent to the field coding, during the data entry stage, an analyst in the United States reviewed the narrative and assigned codes, providing a cross-check for accuracy and ensuring that no relevant codes were missed.

Customary practice in coding open-ended survey questions involves collecting all survey responses, and then deriving response categories[7] from a randomly selected sample of the total responses. Defining response categories, and their correspondent codes, usually occurs after the survey is completed. Our decision to have the interviewers conduct the initial coding in the field meant that the team designing the questionnaire had to generate a set of response categories, or event codes, in advance of the administration of the survey. A small group of individuals spent a grim afternoon writing a list of the types of experiences they anticipated the refugees might relate. The events list reflected both contemporary reports on the Darfur conflict, as well as human rights abuses that typically occur in large-scale conflicts. In the end, the group generated thirty-five event codes and ten perpetrator codes. The event and perpetrator codes, along with a blank grid, were printed on the back of each questionnaire as a "Preliminary Field Coding" form to be used by the interviewers.[8]

Our final challenge in the questionnaire design stage was creating an instrument to gather spatial data — information which would be used to locate each refugee's village of origin. With reliable spatial data, we would be able to map or geo-reference reported destroyed villages and events, possibly identifying patterns in the attacks. Collecting such data for a region like Darfur is difficult, particularly when using a survey instrument. No reliable maps of Darfur were available down to the village level; the best maps available showed rivers, large towns, and what few roads existed in the three states. The Darfur team was also aware that most respondents would be illiterate, not necessarily understanding compass directions or metric distances.

Taking these challenges into account, the HIU created an atlas of Darfur that detailed the major natural features of the area, state boundaries, and the known towns and roads with their Arabic place names. An overall map was broken down into nine more detailed maps, each overlaid with grid quadrants. A series of questions asked the respondents to identify the state their village was located in, the name of the village, and the latter's proximity to large towns and roads. Using this information, it was hoped that the interviewer and translators would work together to identify which grid quadrant the respondent was from.

The next step was to lay out the questionnaire on paper. Under customary survey conditions, questionnaires are pre-tested with a small group of respondents before the wording and order are finalized. Given the constraints posed by administering a survey in the midst of a humanitarian emergency, pre-testing and questionnaire editing would be limited to hand-written corrections in the field; it was thus imperative that the questionnaire be clear, concise, easy for the interviewers to use, and understandable to the respondents.

The first page of the questionnaire requested information from the interviewer about the time, date, location of the interview, and the name of the interviewer. A random-number grid provided the survey parameters for sampling and respondent selection, a process that will be discussed later. Finally, the purpose of the interview is explained to the refugee and their consent for participation in the interview is requested. The second page recorded the demographic details of the respondent, as well as the geo-referenced information. Pages three through six were the core of the questionnaire; a series of open-ended questions intended to document the refugees' stories without prompting or leading the refugees' responses. The questions progress through four levels. Questions first pertain to the individual, then the family, village, and conclude with those about the refugee's journey to the refugee camp and observations of other villages along the way. In addition to providing space for the narrative response to each question, the questionnaire included spaces to record victim names, ages, dates of incidents, perpetrator descriptions, and other information useful to reconstructing the event after the fact.

Page seven contained questions for the interviewer, intended to assess the utility of the questionnaire, the comprehension level of the respondent, and some questions concerning the environment in which the survey was administered, such as whether the interview took place in private, the reactions of other refugees to the interview team, and whether or not the interview team was threatened in any way. The grid for field coding, as well as the lists of event and perpetrator codes, comprised the back page.

Once the layout was complete, the questionnaire was printed in a stapled booklet format, designed to withstand the field conditions in Chad. Fifteen hundred copies were checked as excess baggage and carried to the field by the initial survey team. As successive waves of interviews were completed, they were couriered back to Washington by some of the returning interviewers.

Sampling Methodology: Design and Implementation

Most random sampling methodologies utilize demographic data such as that obtained by a census of the total population to define the process by which the sample is drawn. From census statistics, a sampling frame[9] is drawn and a sampling method is applied in an effort to draw respondents whose overall demographic characteristics reflect that of the broader population. From a methodologist's perspective, the complete absence of demographic data about the Darfuri refugees was perhaps the most fundamental dilemma facing the Office of Research in developing the sampling plan. While we had a rough idea of the total size of the refugee population in Chad — around two hundred thousand — we did not have complete information about the size of all the refugee camps, the ethnic variations in the refugee population, or the percentage of refugees in UNHCR camps as compared to those in informal settlements. Demographic information of this type is necessary to draw a stratified random sample[10] of the kind most commonly used in survey research today.

Given the lack of demographic data, a sampling methodology was developed that randomized respondent selection at two stages. While the approach utilized was not a truly random scientific sample, it did follow accepted practices of respondent selection in less developed areas of the world by using a random route method. Furthermore, the methodology was robust in preventing individuals, politically interested or not, from influencing respondent selection.

When the advance team reached the field, we found that the UNHCR camps were administered through a system of lettered grids or sectors. Sectors were added as new refugees arrived, and were generally ethnically homogenous. Using information supplied by camp administrators about the number and ethnic composition of the grids in each camp, teams attempted to distribute the number of interviews in each camp in a manner proportionate to the ethnic composition, increasing the representativeness of the results.

Between the methodology devised in Washington and the camp information gathered in the field, the following respondent selection process was applied in UNHCR camps. Interview teams, generally composed of four interviewers and four translators (two exceptions were in Goz Beida and Goz Amer where the distance between the two refugee camps, along with a swollen wadi, made it more practical to divide the teams into two interviewers and two translators each) first met with camp administrators to gather information on the camp sectors and their demographics. A list of the sectors and the ethnicity of their residents was drawn. The total number of interviews to be conducted in the camp was divided so as to be approximately proportionate to ethnicity, and then sectors were randomly selected for each ethnic group. Once ten interviews were conducted in a sector, another was chosen, until the number of interviews specified per ethnic group was reached.

Once a sector was selected for sampling, the interview team drove to the sector and identified the tent belonging to the sheikh for that sector. Each sector had one recognized sheikh, who served as both a religious leader and liaison between the refugee population and the camp management. The sheikh's tent served as the starting point for the interviewers, who set out along a random route in opposite directions from the tent. Every tenth occupied space was chosen for inclusion in the survey.

Once an occupied space was selected, the interviewers assigned numbers to the adults present, from left to right. Using a standard Kish grid,[11] printed on the front cover of the questionnaire and keyed to the first letter of the questionnaire serial number, the interviewer selected one of the refugees present to be interviewed. Consent for the interview was obtained, and the interview was conducted in a private location, others being asked to leave the vicinity for the duration of the interview.

The interview teams applied a similar methodology for informal settlements. In the absence of the United Nation's sector structure, interviewers scouted the settlements for natural divisions and points of reference, such as *wadis*, trees, and rock formations. These divisions served as sampling sectors, with interviews equally distributed, and major landmarks as the starting point for random walks. The interview teams described the divisions and landmarks on the front of the questionnaire should their work need to be reconstructed.

The Achieved Sample

The two stages of randomization — through the random walk to select tents or other occupied spaces and use of the Kish grid to select individual respondents — worked well in the field. Interviewers found that people were very willing to be included in the survey; for the refugees selected, the interview was usually the first chance they had to tell their story from beginning to end. Though no overtly political motivations were apparent, people did ask to be included in the survey who were not selected, and sheikhs tried to steer interviewers to people with particularly egregious stories. Interviewers attributed this to an eagerness to be able to report the events witnessed, rather than intentional manipulation of the sample. The selection methodology enabled interviewers to gently decline such offers and assistance, and ensured that the sample broadly reflected the refugees' experience as a whole.

At the conclusion of the interview process, the Office of Research was able to evaluate the representativeness of the achieved sample. While unable to compare the sample against demographic data, as such information about the refugees was still unavailable, the evaluation confirmed that the applied methodology and oversight on the ground had yielded a sample that geographically captured the entire scope of Darfuri refugees in Chad. Interviews had been conducted in all UNHCR camps open at the time, as well as nine informal settlements. 58 percent of respondents were women and 42 percent were men, in keeping with the interviewers' observation that few fighting-age men were present in the camps (Table 4.1).

Geo-referencing Events

Heading into the field, the Darfur team had its doubts that it would be able to successfully map the events reported using the geo-referencing questions

Table 4.1 Achieved Sample

Location	Number of Interviews
UNHCR Camps	
Breidjing	129
Djabal	109
Farchana	35
Goz Amer	79
Iridimi	126
Kounoungo	164
Mille	152
Touloum	70
Other Refugee Clusters	
Adre	2
Am Nabak	81
Atshana	47
Baggi	1
Bahai	10
Birak	14
Cariari	58
Duwas	7
Gabbina	33
Seneit	2
Tine	15
Unknown Location	2

developed by the HIU. Given the paucity of accurate map information and the largely illiterate population we intended to survey, the chances of gathering spatial data for a significant number of cases seemed unlikely.

The team's eventual success in this regard — the interviewers were able to designate a location for 90 percent of the reported events — was a testimony to the INR cartographers and the translators working on the Darfur project. During field training for the interviewers and translators, both were briefed on the spatial referencing questions and the atlas folio. The translators, many English students originally from the Darfur region, spent hours scrutinizing the maps and discussing amongst themselves the landmarks, cities, and roads depicted. From their collective knowledge of the region, they were then able to question the respondents using place names previously unavailable to us and, in an overwhelming majority of cases, successfully identify the origin of the refugee and the locations of reported events.

Data Entry and Analysis

The final dataset used for the "Documenting Atrocities in Darfur" report represented three successive waves of data entry. The first dataset was created in the field by the Atrocities Documentation Team (ADT), and comprised the first fifty interviews conducted by the advance team that deployed to the field in mid-July. The questionnaires and field codes were reviewed by the advance team, entered into an Excel® database, and transmitted through satellite modem back to Washington from the Darfur team's base in Abeche, Chad.

Once the first team of interviewers was established in the field, some of the members of the advance team returned to Washington carrying a set of two hundred questionnaires — the original fifty, plus an additional one hundred fifty newly completed interviews. These were again coded by State Department officers in Washington, D.C. and the first-round Excel database expanded. As successive teams of interviewers rotated through Chad, the Office of Research hired an international public opinion research company to create a dataset from the remaining questionnaires.

After a briefing by a State Department official on the background of the conflict and the nature of the survey, the company's team of professional coders read each questionnaire thoroughly, verifying and correcting if necessary the interviewer's field codes. In all three rounds of data entry, a fifth of the questionnaires were randomly selected and recoded by an additional analyst to ensure accuracy in the coding process. Each questionnaire's demographic information, event codes, and attendant information were entered into the dataset. Every questionnaire was entered by two different data entry specialists, or double-punched, to verify that the correct information had been entered. Once the two data entry specialists separately entered the data from a questionnaire, a computer compared the two and flagged any discrepancies.

From the final dataset, two databases were created. The first was the respondent database, in which each line of data represents an individual refugee with all related demographics and event codes for that refugee. Eleven hundred thirty-six refugees are represented in the refugee database. The respondent data set was used to generate the atrocity percentages in the final report, which reflect the percent of refugees who reported witnessing or directly experiencing each type of event (e.g., bombing, looting, village destruction, killings, etc.).

Because each respondent may have experienced the same event multiple times — numerous refugees had experienced several attacks during their journey to Chad — during the analysis stage it was necessary to write a syntax[12] to prevent the statistical software from counting multiple events towards the total for the survey population. The Office of Research devised a short string of code that analyzed each refugee's twenty separate possible event codes in the database, and then assigned a value of 1 (experienced the event) or 0 (did not experience the event) for each type of event. This enabled accurate reporting of the percentage of refugees who had experienced each type of event.

A second event database was also created in which the multiple events from each refugee's story were separated so that each line of data in the event database represented a single event. Over ten thousand events are represented in the event database. The reported perpetrator percentages were generated using this database; perpetrator percents reflect the percentage of events in which specific perpetrators were implicated.

From the outset, the team decided to adopt a conservative approach to reporting data collected during the documentation mission. To this end, during all three stages of data entry, events were coded as either eyewitness or hearsay. Eyewitness events were those reported to have been directly witnessed by the respondent, while hearsay events took place outside the respondent's presence. The atrocity statistics that were eventually reported reflected only events reported as eyewitnessed by the refugees. The inclusion of hearsay reports — some of which, such as death of family members, were verified by respondents after the fact — increased the percentage of refugees experiencing each event, but the decision to conservatively report what we had gathered precluded our including them.

As the first wave of interviewers carried out their work in Chad, it soon became clear that the code list of events generated in Washington and printed on the questionnaire was insufficient to cover the range of human rights violations occurring in Darfur. Additional codes were developed at two points in the project; first by the advance team upon conclusion of the first fifty interviews, and second by the public opinion research company that carried out the third wave of data entry. In all, twenty additional event codes were developed. Several refined previously existing categories, four referred to specific groups targeted for violence, and the rest covered a range of acts from the burning of mosques to the disembowelment of pregnant women — acts the drafters of the questionnaire had not foreseen or could not imagine taking place.

Quantitative Findings

The analysis of the data set confirmed the impression of the interviewers in the field — that killing, property destruction, and other human rights violations were epidemic in Darfur (Figure 4.1). Six in ten refugees witnessed the death of one or more family members, while two-thirds were present as members of their community were killed by members of the

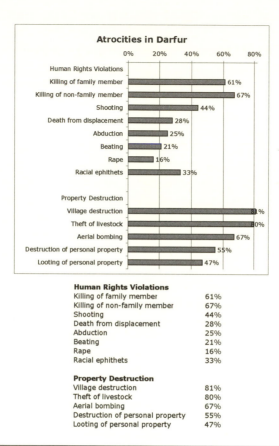

Human Rights Violations
Killing of family member   61%
Killing of non-family member   67%
Shooting   44%
Death from displacement   28%
Abduction   25%
Beating   21%
Rape   16%
Racial ephithets   33%

Property Destruction
Village destruction   81%
Theft of livestock   80%
Aerial bombing   67%
Destruction of personal property 55%
Looting of personal property   47%

Figure 4.1 Atrocities in Darfur.

Janjaweed militia or Sudanese military. Abduction of community members, beatings, racial slurs, and rape were commonplace. Extreme forms of torture, sadism, and desecration of mosques were also reported by a small minority of refugees.

Village and property destruction were experienced by eight in ten refugees, and were the most commonly experienced atrocity. Two-thirds of refugees experienced aerial bombing of their village. Living on the fringes of the Sahara desert, such deprivations were not trivial; more than a quarter of refugees reported the death of a family or community member due to displacement.

The analysis of perpetrator responsibility for the atrocities yielded surprising results (Figure 4.2). Rather than demonstrating that the *Janjaweed* were acting independently in attacking villages, nearly half of atrocities

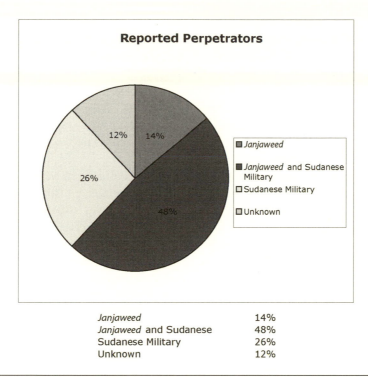

Reported Perpetrators

12%   14%

26%

48%

- Janjaweed
- Janjaweed and Sudanese Military
- Sudanese Military
- Unknown

Janjaweed	14%
Janjaweed and Sudanese	48%
Sudanese Military	26%
Unknown	12%

Figure 4.2 Reported Perpetrators.

were committed by the *Janjaweed* militia and Sudanese military working in coordination. Another quarter of atrocities were committed by Sudanese troops, clearly implicating Khartoum in the events unfolding in Darfur.

The Statistics in Narrative Context

Although the quantitative statistics generated by the Darfur ADT supported Secretary of State Powell's assertion that genocide was unfolding in Sudan, an assessment based only upon the summary statistics risks losing sight of the complexity of each refugee's story. The team's use of open-ended questions and documentation of the narrative recounted by each respondent preserved valuable details that contextualized each event.

Though each refugee's experience was unique, a pattern emerged, which pointed to a consistent method of attack being perpetrated upon the civilian population of Darfur by the *Janjaweed* militia and Sudanese military. The broad contours of the pattern are described below.

Prior to any ground attack, villages were often subjected to aerial bombing, which was perceived by some as a warning to leave the village and to signal an imminent ground attack. Within days or even hours of the bombing, villages would be surrounded by *Janjaweed* militia and/or Sudanese soldiers, who formed a perimeter around the village. Light arms fire began from the perimeter and then the attackers would ride through the villages, targeting young men. Males were at times rounded up and executed or abducted, while women were raped. The latter act reflected a cultural logic of genocide; given that Darfuri culture regards ethnicity to be determined by the paternal bloodline — any women inseminated by *Janjaweed* attackers would bear offspring perceived to be Arab.

Villages frequently suffered multiple waves of attacks; in each successive wave, the militia and soldiers would loot livestock and transportable items of material value, often using Sudanese military vehicles to carry them away. Once a village was looted of all items of value, the houses were burned. In isolated cases, the attacks were accompanied by extreme acts of cruelty, such as the killing of children by burning and desecration of mosques.

Victims were not safe once they had fled their village; many respondents fled to neighboring villages, which were subsequently subject to attack. Sudanese aircraft also appeared to target escape corridors used by internally displaced persons (IDPs).

Applied Methodology in Retrospect

In evaluating the methodology and findings of the survey conducted by the Darfur ADT, what lessons learned might inform future survey research into humanitarian crises? There are several notable limitations to the Darfur dataset that highlight the constraints of conducting surveys in extreme environments.

The problem of underestimation of mortality is well known to methodologists researching human rights violations, and applies to the Darfur survey as well. Put crudely, individuals killed in any conflict do not survive to tell the tale, or to be selected as a respondent in any survey. Thus, there is an inverse relationship between the percentage of people killed in a community and the likelihood that that attack will be documented in the survey. The proximity of the location of attack to the survey sampling point — the size of the village, and the disposition of survivors — can also impact the probability that a survivor will be sampled. The results obtained by the Darfur Atrocities Documentation Team thus should not be utilized as the basis for mortality estimates; alternative forms of mortality documentation would be necessary to verify the mortality rate within Darfur.

The decision to sample refugees residing in Chad, while a necessity for the security of the survey team, limited the dataset in several ways. Most notably, while broadly representative of refugees in Chad, the data cannot be considered representative of the IDPs still in Darfur. While there are no indications that the Chadian refugees differ in any significant way from the IDPs, it is still not scientifically acceptable to project their exact experience to the broader IDP population. The respondents were primarily from the region of Darfur immediately bordering Chad, reflective of the fact that such individuals were able to cross the border with greater ease than those further inside the region. In addition, the refugees may represent better-off Darfuris who possessed the resources and means to reach and cross an international border. Finally, reports of events by Chadian refugees were dated because most of them fled the region a year or more prior to the survey.

Compared to other reported atrocities, rape — at 16 percent — was less common, though still alarmingly high. Nevertheless, the actual incidence of rape is likely under-reported due to a cultural bias against discussing sexual violence, and the predominance of male interviewers and translators working on the project.

Conclusion

The Darfur Atrocities Documentation Project successfully applied survey methodology in the midst of a humanitarian crisis to achieve its aim to reliably document the nature and extent of the events that had occurred in Darfur. Secretary of State Powell's proclamation that genocide was unfolding in Sudan was a bold step to draw attention to the extreme suffering and terror inflicted upon the civilian population of Darfur. Unfortunately, while survey methodology can illumine dark corners of the world, it cannot solve the problems revealed, which remains the ongoing task of the international community.

References

Agresti, Alan and Finlay, Barbara (1997). *Statistical Methods for the Social Sciences*. Upper Saddle River, NJ: Prentice Hall.
Scheuren, Fritz (2004). "What is a Survey?" Available at: http://www.whatisasurvey.info

Notes

1. The views presented in this chapter are solely those of the author, and in no way represent the views or opinions of the United States Government or the U.S. Department of State.
2. For the lay reader, some basic definitions of terms used in this chapter may prove helpful. A survey is defined by Scheuren (2004) as "a method for gathering information from a sample of individuals. This 'sample' is usually just a fraction of the population being studied. In a bona-fide survey, the sample is not selected haphazardly or only from persons who volunteer to participate. It is scientifically chosen so that each person in the population will have a measurable chance of selection. This way, the results can be reliably projected from the sample to the larger population." Survey methodology refers to the

rules and procedures used to select the individuals in the sample, and the way the selected individuals are interviewed (e.g., in person, by telephone, through the mail, or over the internet).

3. Sampling methodology refers to the rules guiding the selection of individuals from a broader population (in this case, Darfuri refugees residing in Chad) for participation in a survey. The degree to which the responses gathered from the individuals in the sample reflect the broader population is largely determined by the validity of the sampling methodology used. In an ideal simple, random sample, each member of the population has an equal chance of being selected for an interview.

4. The Humanitarian Information Unit is an interagency division within Intelligence and Research's (INR) office of the Geographer and Global Issues dedicated to collecting, analyzing, and disseminating information on humanitarian emergencies worldwide.

5. Coding of open-ended responses is the process of creating categories of meaningful responses that capture the substance of what the respondent said, and applying numeric values to each category so that they may be tabulated and analyzed by a statistical program.

6. Event refers to a specific incident reported by the refugee. The coding process applied numeric values to a specific list of events, such as killing, rape, destruction of property, etc., so that the percentage of refugees experiencing each type of event could be reported.

7. Response categories refers to the list of predefined events and their associated codes used in the field by interviewers. The list was supplemented in the field at the conclusion of fifty interviews and again during the coding process in the United States, as described later in this chapter.

8. See final page of the "Darfur Refugees Questionnaire (DRQ)." A copy of the DRQ is located in Appendix I of this book.

9. Sampling frame refers to the list of units to be sampled in a survey. This can be a list of all people in the population or a list of other types of population clusters, such as cities or, in the case of this project, refugee camps and the refugees residing in each camp.

10. A stratified random sample as defined by Agresti and Finlay (1997) "divides the population into separate groups, called strata, and then selects a simple random sample from each stratum." In contrast to a simple random sample of the entire population, a stratified random sample ensures that each strata — whether defined by ethnicity, geography, or another variable — is proportionately represented in the final sample.

11. A Kish grid is a numerical table used to randomize the selection of individuals from a group. See page 1 of the "Darfur Refugees Questionnaire" in Appendix I of this book.

12. A syntax is a short string of computer code used to instruct a program, in this case the statistical software package SPSS, to operate in a specific manner.

CHAPTER 5

The Critical Link: Interpreters

HELGE NISKA

Prologue

In June 2004, I took part in a seminar arranged by the International Criminal Court (ICC) in The Hague on the use of interpreters in international court proceedings and in criminal investigations in the field. There, I gave a talk on the organization of interpreting services for immigrants and how the training of those interpreters is organized in Sweden. My talk must have had an impact on the organizers of the conference because only a few weeks later I received a telephone call from the Coalition for International Justice (CIJ), which had obtained my name from the ICC as someone with the kind of knowledge and experience in recruiting, testing, and training interpreters that would be helpful to the Darfur Atrocities Documentation Team (ADT) project CIJ was about to undertake. I accepted, and two weeks later I was on my way to Chad.

ADT Interpreters

Locating the Interpreters

A mission such as the CIJ was proposing would have been impossible without interpreters because few, if any, of the two dozen investigators knew

Arabic, let alone any of the many tribal languages of the refugees they were about to interview. Communicating via interpreters is part of the daily routine for nongovernmental organization (NGO) representatives, aid workers, and others in various parts of the world. Too often, though, bilingual "translators" are recruited haphazardly among people in the vicinity of the organization's headquarters, and only after some time, if at all, does it become apparent that something has to be done about the interpreting process (or "translation" as it is often called, even if it is oral). The ADT was different. From the inception of the project, the leadership team understood the critical need for properly recruited interpreters, and they were willing to provide the funds for the training of those interpreters. This showed impressive foresight.

Recruitment of the Interpreters

Most of the interpreters for the ADT were recruited by an assessment team that traveled to Chad a couple of weeks before the regular interviews were to start. On this team were two representatives from the U.S. Darfur Friendship Society. Thanks to these people, who seemed to know every expatriate from Darfur living in the Chadian capital N'Djamena, a large number of people were asked to gather for an information and assessment meeting at a hotel in the capital. Of these people, a dozen individuals were selected as being the most suitable candidates for working as interpreters with the ADT.

In addition to the people recruited in N'Djamena, I did some supplementary recruitment onsite at our headquarters in Abéché to find interpreters in languages that had been hard to find earlier. We finally ended up with interpreters in the following language combinations: English and Arabic (18), English and Zaghawa (9), English and Masalit (4), English and Fur (3), English and Tama (2), English and Jabal (1), English and Dinka (1), English and Maba (Borgo) (1), and English and French (1).

The Interpreters

From earlier experience, team members knew that male interpreters could be a constraint on women to talk freely, especially about delicate matters as rape and sexual abuse that we foresaw would be dealt with in the interviews. Also, half of the interviewers were female. But despite our efforts, we were not able to recruit any women with the necessary linguistic and educational background here to serve as interpreters.

ADT's expert on interviewing women who had been victims of sexual abuse, Jan Pfundheller, comments on the problems we faced and how we handled them. (She is a police officer from the United States who had also worked as an investigator for the International Criminal Tribunal for the former Yugoslavia.)

During the second briefing Helge (Niska) and I held privately with the interpreters, I explained that we had tried to secure female interpreters to conduct sexual assault interviews, but had been unable to find ladies with the language capabilities.

I knew from past experience that success in these interviews could rest with them. Thus, I decided to enlist them as well as train them. It went like this: "I know that you know there have been many ladies and girls who have been victimized in this way. It is very important that the world know of these situations. These types of crimes violate international law. These crimes also have an impact on your country and culture. You have told me yourselves in our talks that, if a lady is the victim of such things, her husband may divorce her and she may become only a servant in her parents home, no longer marriageable and no longer respected.

In order to translate these ladies' stories, you must be able to do several things. You must be able to repeat exactly what I ask the lady — using the correct translation for the English words in the local language. You must not interject any slang terms of your own. You must be able to be my voice in this matter with these ladies. And when the lady answers my question with her description of events, you must be able to translate exactly what she says into English.

As educated men who speak fine English, this may not sound difficult. But remember, you will hear me ask about things you would never speak of. The ladies will be telling things they would never tell their husbands or families. You know that no woman anywhere in the world wants to be the victim of such crimes.

I will convey to the ladies my appreciation and thanks that they shared these things with me. I will tell them I am sorry these things happened to them. But understand that there is something more important than those words from me. I will leave this place in a few weeks. You will remain. You are their countrymen. You are the educated men of their society. *Your* demeanor, *your* body language, and the manner in which *you* take your leave from these ladies at the completion of the interview will have a significant impact on them, as women, wives, and mothers.

Commenting on the above process and its ramifications, Pfundheller made the following observations:

These men and everyone in the region knew of the atrocities being committed. Many had seen them firsthand. I believe they came to understand just how much we cared, how we needed all of the facts, the verifications, the absolute core of truth. The number of animals stolen, the number of planes, the smells, the exact words, the color of the weaponry. I saw it in Bosnia and Kosovo in interpreters also, people who must have known that the horrors they were hearing were their own history, that the killed child could've been their own child, the rape victim could've been their sister or daughter. The reaction of these men tells me a great deal about the possibilities ahead. Although their skill levels varied, it was their desire and dedication to the task and their willingness to undertake such things that carried us forward.

Testing

According to widely acknowledged professional standards, an interpreter, besides possessing the necessary linguistic and communicative skills, is supposed to be neutral and unobtrusive, not letting his/her personal knowledge of the parties and circumstances color the interpreting. Under normal circumstances, the recruitment procedure of new interpreters can be a fairly long process, including various screening procedures and aptitude tests.[1] Such a battery of tests, however, could not be used in the very short time span at our disposal in Chad. What we did try to do, however, was to test the applicants in relation to some issues of a personal nature that can impact the interpreter's job. This was done in the form of an interview where the aim was to get a profile of the applicant's ability to work as an interpreter, taking into consideration the delicate nature of the job. Among the many issues taken up for discussion were education, ethical standards, expectations in taking the job ("Why do you want to be an interpreter with this project?"), contacts with the immigrant's/refugee's home country, politics (personal involvement in the conflict), religion, ethnicity, attitude toward authorities, the applicant's own situation, and reactions to criticism. Some were touched upon only briefly and some more in-depth depending on the situation.

Obviously, such issues as religion and politics have to be discussed with great caution in order to not violate the personal integrity of the applicant; nevertheless, they are issues that have to be addressed since they can influence the work of the interpreter.

The interview of the interpreters was conducted in English. The goal of the interviewing process was, besides assessing the applicants' knowledge of English, to filter out individuals who were too committed personally or politically to the conflict and thus might not be able to be neutral as they went about their jobs. It is worth noting that funding was not available to test the applicants' skills in the other languages concerned.

Joint Training: The Interpreter and Investigators

It was decided from the outset that the introductory training of both interpreters and interviewers should be done in joint training sessions. The idea behind this was that it was extremely important for the successful outcome of the project that the interpreters know as much as possible about the purpose of the mission and the methodologies of the investigation, including the interviewers' demands on the interpreter. If one knows how a person thinks, it is easier to interpret him or her. As for the interviewers, it was a natural way of learning the dos and don'ts of speaking through an interpreter while at the same time getting acquainted with the constraints that the ethical rules impose on the interpreter's work.

A typical introductory training session for interviewers and interpreters consisted of the following:

1. Introductions of the participants in the ADT (interpreters, interviewers, and staff).
2. Presentation on the focus of the ADT (Project Coordinator Stefanie Frease).
3. Background to the conflict in Darfur (U.S. State Department official).
4. Interviewing: Problems and issues, e.g., sexual assaults (Jan Pfundheller).
5. Interpreting: Rules for interpreting, rules for using interpreters (Helge Niska).
6. Methodology of the investigation, discussion of the questionnaire (U.S. State Department official).
7. Cultural awareness, e.g., social hierarchy in the tribes concerned (local staff members).

Such sessions lasted almost a full day including meal breaks and a necessary mid-day rest. One day is admittedly a very short time for a course in any subject area, but this was the time that was allocated for such. After the introductory session, sometimes on the same afternoon or evening, the investigators and "their" interpreters left for the interview location. But since the investigators arrived in small groups over a period of three days, most of the interpreters actually had the opportunity to sit in on the training session for several days in a row. This was obviously of great value for the interpreters.

The guidelines/rules that were given to the interpreters were as follows:

- The interpreter is neutral and impartial.
- The interpreter should only accept assignments for which he is competent.
- The interpreter must keep confidentiality at all times.
- The interpreter shall convey the message as exactly as possible (concealing nothing, adding nothing, changing nothing).
- The interpreter shall not accept any other duties during the interpreting session than to interpret.
- The interpreter shall continuously strive to improve his professional skills.

It was repeatedly stressed that the interpreters should only interpret ("translate orally") what the interlocutors (e.g., the interviewers and interviewees) were saying. The interpreter was told that if there is something the interlocutors did not understand, they needed to let the interpreter know this and vice versa. Furthermore, the interlocutors were informed that if they needed clarification, they should ask the original speaker via the interpreter. In other words, the interpreter was not allowed to answer questions on his own.

Satisfactory interpreting requires that the interpreter has (1) good linguistic knowledge in his/her working languages, (2) good factual knowledge of the subject areas involved, (3) knowledge of special terminology, and (4) correct interpreting technique. An additional prerequisite that came up during the training sessions was empathy. The interpreter, while being a neutral translator, must still be able to understand why people behave the way they do, and he must treat every client — in this case, refugee and investigator alike — with respect. This has to do with establishing and maintaining confidence, which is of utmost importance in such sensitive circumstances.

Adjusting the Role to the Circumstances

It is important to bear in mind that the interpreters were hired to help the primary parties — in this case, the investigator and the refugee — to converse with one another. While the interpreter was a necessary part of the communicative situation, it was the interlocutors who had to decide what the interpreter was to say. Thus, it was made clear in the training session that it was not for the interpreter to decide what is important or unimportant, proper or improper to say.

In this project, we introduced a very important exception to the general rule: In the first contact between the investigator and the interviewee, it was decided that the interpreter would take an active role in greeting and introducing the investigator to the refugee. The reasoning behind this was that the interpreter, having knowledge about the local customs and rules of politeness, was best suited at creating an atmosphere of confidence and trust.

Rules for Speaking through an Interpreter

Most of the investigators had previous experience speaking via an interpreter, but I thought it would be valuable to discuss the ground rules and compare them with the corresponding ethical rules for the interpreters. Among them were the following:

- Use simple language. The investigators were informed that most of the interpreters had not mastered English as they had their first language and, for many, English was their third or even fourth language. Thus, I stated that "you should avoid technical terms and jargon when possible. If you must use technical terms or legal terms, which are necessary to use in the investigation, be sure to explain them or be prepared to give an explanation if the interpreter asks for one." (The reciprocal obligation for the interpreters, I explained, was to immediately ask for clarification if there was something they didn't understand.)
- Be clear and concise, speak in short sentences. "The more long-winded you are," I informed them, "the more difficult it will be for the interpreters to understand you and the higher the risk of being misinterpreted."
- Speak directly to the interviewee. "Do not ask the interpreter to ask the refugee a question," I directed them.
- The interpreters are taught to use direct speech (to speak in first person), thus, when a refugee says, "My house was burnt down," the interpreter will say, "My house was burnt down."
- Don't use the interpreter as an expert. "Remember that it is you who is responsible for the material outcome of the interview — not the interpreter." Again, the interpreter has a corresponding rule: "Remember," I told the interpreters, "you are the language and translation expert, not an expert on the subject matter."

That said, an exception to this rule was agreed upon, and that was that the investigators had the right to consult with the interpreter in regard to cultural matters. The interpreters also had a right to intervene when they deemed it necessary, but it was stressed that this right was to be used with great caution.

Mid-Term Assessment

The investigating teams and their interpreters usually spent ten days in the interviewing location, and it was decided that the "headquarters" staff would do a mid-term assessment after each of the teams was in the field for several days or more. These trips were made either by small plane or by four-wheel vehicles. We usually had only a couple of hours at our disposal for each meeting because the teams were anxious to conduct as many interviews as possible. Nevertheless, the investigating teams always seemed happy to meet us and discuss their experiences.

The mid-term assessments were not conducted as joint meetings. Rather, we (the project coordinators, Pfundheller and myself) talked to the investigators and the interpreters separately. In this way we could get the opinions of each, and not only of their own work, but also of the experience of their co-workers. In general, there was a feeling of satisfaction over the results of the work and of the cooperation between investigators and interpreters. There were, though, exceptions. One interpreter had to be dismissed because of a lack of confidence by the investigators; there was a feeling that the interpreter did not only translate, but added his own opinions during the translations.

Mid-Term Assessment Interpreter Training

During the mid-term assessment, we also had time to have a short training session for the interpreters. The session consisted of debriefings that included discussions about each interpreter's field experiences. The discussion included any difficulties they faced as well as positive aspects and outcomes.

A frequent issue that was broached was how to cope with psychological stress. Difficult situations that the interpreters had encountered or were thinking about were acted out in role playing. Pfundheller took the role of the investigator and one of the interpreters played a refugee. I then commented on each situation from a technical and ethical point of view.

Feedback and Debriefing After the Initial Assignment

Upon the conclusion of the first team's work and prior to the work of the second team, there was a break in the investigations and everyone returned to headquarters in Abéché. I had thought that the interpreters would be exhausted after ten days in the bush and be grateful for a couple of days rest before the next assignment, but to my surprise and delight they actually insisted on more interpreter training. As a result, the fellows gathered at headquarters for two additional days of training.

The first day, we went through some of the points that the investigators had raised about the interpreting: (1) Respect for all parties. There had been occurrences where the investigator felt that the interpreter had treated a refugee with disrespect. (2) Interpreting technique. I addressed the critical need to not add, omit, or change anything. This rule had been broken on several occasions. (3) And, neutrality. Again, I stressed not to let their own knowledge or commitment influence the interpreting. This had become a big problem on one of the teams.

We had a good discussion about the necessity to heed the rules and about having the trust of the investigator. Another discussion was on how to avoid getting too involved with the personal fates of the refugees or the political implications of the investigation. To conclude the day, I presented a lesson on terminology, basics about concepts and terms, and I held a discussion as to why terminology is important. Then we examined terms related to medicine and law. I must say, I have rarely met such a devoted group of "students"; you could have heard a pin drop.

The following day we had a long role-playing session, once again with the invaluable help of Pfundheller as the investigator while the individual interpreters took turns playing the role of a refugee.

Conclusion

The investigators almost unanimously expressed their satisfaction with the interpreters' work and vice versa. Ultimately, the mission was accomplished. But there are a couple of issues that still need to be addressed. Many investigators said that this was the first time they had seen such an effort put into the recruiting and training interpreters for this type of field work, and that it had paid off. In light of that, it is a pity there isn't an international "interpretation service" agency in case there is a need of a mission of this sort again and thus "our" interpreters would be in line for a position.

Second, having been a teacher at an interpreting school for many years, many of the things that I encountered in this project forced me to rethink a lot of "truths" about interpreter training that I had lived by for so long. At my university, a basic course for public service interpreters (the kind of interpreting that comes closest to the Darfur project) spans a full academic year, plus an additional two semesters each for those seeking a specialization in legal *or* medical interpreting. Be that as it may, I now realize that it is possible to achieve satisfactory, if not perfect, results, and within a very limited amount of time and with a very limited group of people to recruit from, if (1) interpreters are recruited for work on a limited, clearly defined subject area, (2) individuals who meet, at least, the minimum criteria stipulated are recruited, and (3) interpreters and interviewers are trained together, and, in doing so, a feeling of cooperation and helpfulness between the interpreters and the users is achieved. I am quite convinced that even from such a modest start, it is possible to develop a good interpretation service.

Note

1. In fact, I have been instrumental in developing an ambitious recruitment test for community interpreters in Sweden, which consists of both oral and written tests of general knowledge about the societies and cultures concerned, basic translation skills, etc.

Moving into the Field and Conducting the Interviews: Commentary and Observations by the Investigators

SAMUEL TOTTEN AND ERIC MARKUSEN

Introduction

This chapter provides a discussion of the efforts of the twenty-four investigators who were on the the Darfur Atrocities Documentation Team (ADT). In doing so, it summarizes the predeployment briefings and training, the process of moving into the field, interactions with refugees, the investigators' impressions of the data being collected, problems encountered in the field, post-mission debriefing, some lighter moments, and final thoughts about the mission.

The Mission

Predeployment Briefing and Training in Abeche

Each four-person investigative team flew into N'Djamena, the capital of Chad, and was shuttled to the desert town of Abeche, in eastern Chad, which served as the operations base for the project. In a rented house on a small compound along a back street in the dusty town, the Coalition for International Justice (CIJ) welcomed the incoming investigators who arrived in small staggered groups over five weeks in July and August 2004.

The compound consisted of an unfurnished concrete four-room building with a surrounding mud wall and a covered verandah. There was an outside pit toilet that the local staff preferred and one inside toilet (that clogged regularly), a basic shower, and sink. Two local women were hired to cook, and all meals were prepared on top of a small wire basket filled with bits of coal. Eventually, a small propane burner was brought in to speed along the meals. CIJ purchased twenty foam sleeping mattresses from the local open-air market, which were placed in the two rooms the men used for sleeping and in the large room used by the women.

Jan Pfundheller, a seasoned investigator who was both a trainer for incoming teams and a field investigator, recalled, "We also purchased, at a dear price, three rough wooden tables and four wooden benches. They were our desks and tables. The electricity came on at 10 p.m. and went off at 5 a.m. This occurred on most nights, but not all. The heat was always, always stifling, and the flies always present."

In this compound, the investigators, along with their interpreters, received several hours of briefing and training organized by CIJ. U.S. State Department analyst Michael Orona provided an overview of the history of the conflict in Darfur, as well as the current situations in Darfur and along the Chad side of the Chad–Sudanese border. A Sudanese doctor/refugee discussed the culture and customs of the refugees. Stefanie Frease, the project director, described the overall project, explained the operational plan, provided location assignments, and discussed communications and safety procedures. Jonathan Howard from the State Department's Office of Research explained the methodology for conducting the interviews and went over the way the eight-page questionnaire (Darfur Refugees Questionnaire) devised for the investigation was to be filled out. He explained that the questionnaire had been developed in Washington, D.C. via a collaborative effort involving members of various nongovernmental organizations (NGOs) and staff from the U.S. State Department. Throughout, he emphasized the importance of the systematic, random selection of respondents. He also discussed the way in which to divide the huge refugee camps into quadrants, how to actually conduct randomized interviews, and how to code the questionnaire (see Chapter 4, "Survey Methodology and the Darfur Genocide"). Helge Niska, a linguistics professor from Sweden, explained the best approaches to use in working with interpreters. He also spent considerable time with the interpreters to ensure they understood the basics of interpreting and taught them vocabulary related to violent crime (see Chapter 5, "The Critical Link: Interpreters").

Since previous reports had indicated widespread rapes of Darfurian women, Pfundheller, a former investigator at the UN International Criminal Tribunal for the Former Yugoslavia (ICTY) with considerable experience in dealing with cases of sexual assault, provided a valuable tutorial on effective techniques to use with victims of such crimes. The investigators and interpreters were told that most victims of sexual assault have great difficulty talking about such traumatic experiences, and that interviewees may refer to such crimes by using euphemisms (e.g., the victims, themselves, might comment that "they humiliated us" or "they did the worst to us," while male respondents might say "they tried to marry our women").

The team members were informed that the approximately two hundred thousand people who were living in the camps in United Nations-issued tents and improvised shelters represented about 10 percent of the total number of people displaced by the conflict in Darfur as of summer 2004. These were the "lucky ones" who had escaped the horror of Darfur and who were now, for the most part, receiving food, water, and other aid from the United Nations and other humanitarian agencies.

Pfundheller noted that:

The toughest challenge in regard to providing a comprehensive briefing was the time constraints we faced, as it was imperative to get the investigators out to the field as soon as possible.

In every case, the investigators had made very long flights across many time zones. They landed in N'Djamena, the capital of Chad, spent from eight to twenty-four hours there waiting for transport to Abeche. They took tiny four-passenger planes to Abeche, which, depending on the wind, took between three and five hours. As soon as they arrived at the compound in Abeche and dropped their duffel bags, orientation began.

The incoming investigators had to deal with jet lag and the impact of the searing heat at the same time they underwent briefings and then immediately headed out to conduct interviews. Fortunately, everyone involved was a highly qualified professional and each of them felt that being on the ADT was something far more important than personal needs.

Moving into the Field

Following the day of briefings, teams of investigators were outfitted with walkie talkies and a Thuraya satellite phone and then departed for their sites — one or more of the ten refugee camps and numerous settlements in Eastern Chad near the border with Sudan. Some reached their sites via four-wheel drive vehicles, while others were transported by small four-seater aircraft.

Upon reaching their sites, teams set about establishing themselves in various ways. For example, the team sent to the southeastern town of Goz Beida, contacted the sheik of Goz Beida (who had provided the land for the establishment of the massive refugee camp on the outskirts of the village) in order to inform him of the focus and purpose of their work and to seek his imprimatur and support. Other teams contacted the officials of the refugee camp to which they had been assigned. (It should be noted that prior to the team's arrival, an advance team had visited all sites and met with local officials and United Nations and NGO representatives to advise them of the team's impending arrival.)

Once the teams set up their camps, they drove out to the dusty and massive refugee camps comprised of thousands of United Nations tents and various makeshift accommodations, where they met with the *umda* (the head of all sheiks) and the other sheiks residing in the camp to explain the mission and secure final permission to conduct the interviews. The meetings, generally over cups of hot, sweet tea, often took place on a tarp near the shade of a tree or collection of bushes, with all of the leaders sitting around the *umda* and scores of refugees — men, women, and children — standing as they listened to the conversations between the investigators, who spoke through their translators, and the *umda* and sheiks.

Once the introductions were made and permission was granted to work in the camps (as it was in every case), teams of two (an investigator and his/her interpreter) selected a section of the camp and counted off every tenth tent in order to conduct an interview. Once at the tent, if more than one adult was present, the method outlined by the State Department for randomly selecting the individual was used, and the person selected was asked if he/she would be willing to be interviewed. Once a person agreed, everyone else in the immediate area was politely asked to leave. The latter was to provide the interviewee with the opportunity to answer the questions as he/she saw fit without any pressure from family members or outsiders. In only a small number of cases did people decline to be interviewed — some individuals were so ill they did not have the energy or inclination to speak; while in other cases, particularly towards sunset when they were busy preparing meals, some simply apologized and said they didn't have the time to do so. When this occurred, the interviewer–interpreter team moved on to the next occupied tent and repeated the process.

At the outset of each interview, the investigator had his/her interpreter introduce, first, himself and then the investigator. Next, the investigator, through the interpreter, explained the nature and purpose of the interview. The interviewee was informed that the investigator and interpreter were there to speak with him/her about his/her experiences in the Darfur region of Sudan, and that his/her name, specific identity, and personal information would remain confidential. Further, it was explained that taking part in the interview did not guarantee compensation for losses or deaths experienced by his/her household, nor did it mean that the individuals in their household would necessarily be able to bring specific charges against anyone or testify at trials. Each interviewee was also told that the decision to participate in the interview was entirely voluntary, and that if he/she chose not to be interviewed, then such a decision would be respected.

The interviewer began by asking basic demographic information — name, age, ethnic group, and years of schooling. Next, using a series of laminated maps that had been provided to the investigators, respondents were asked to locate the town, village, or settlement from which they had been forcibly driven. Then, the respondents were asked questions about when and why they had left their villages; if they had been personally harmed (and if so, how); if other members of their family, or fellow villagers, had been harmed or killed (and if so, how); if property — including livestock, bags of grains and seeds, and household goods — were stolen or destroyed; if their home and/or village had been destroyed, partially or completely; if particular groups were singled out for harm; and if any members of their household or village had died on the journey to the camp or settlement in which they were now living in Chad. They were also asked to identify and describe the perpetrators of the attacks, note whether the attackers said anything to them during the attack, and explain why they thought they had been attacked. Finally, they were asked if, after fleeing their homes and villages, they had been attacked again and by whom (and how), and if they had witnessed or heard about attacks on other people and villages.

Interviews lasted between fifty minutes and two hours. The amount of time each interview took depended on the number of incidents the person experienced, as well as the depth and detail with which he or she was able to describe the events. When respondents said that they had been injured, follow-up questions were asked in order to obtain precise details. When respondents said they witnessed the injury or death of family members or fellow villagers, interviewers asked for the name, age, gender, and relationship of each victim; cause of death; as well as how the respondent knew of the injury or death (e.g., personally witnessing the attack, discovering the bodies after the perpetrators had departed, hearing about it from relatives or other villagers).

Interactions with the Refugees and the Type of Information Gathered

Many of the stories related during the interviews were difficult to listen to, for not only were the events described horrific, but the countenances, voices, and body language of the interviewees conveyed the great amount of suffering they had experienced. The investigators heard stories ranging from bombings by Antonov aircraft to the beatings of the interviewees and/or family members and others, the shooting of individuals to mass killings, and individual rapes to gang rapes of young women and mothers (often in front of family members). In addition to the trauma caused by the attacks on their homes and villages and the flight to Chad, the refugees were experiencing continuing hardship in the camps, and many infants and children showed signs of malnutrition.

Speaking of her various experiences in war-torn countries, investigator Linda Patrick made the following observation: "I found working in the refugee camps in Chad much harder than working in Kosovo and Bosnia. In Chad, the refugees were in areas that had no resources and, for the first time, I saw people who literally had nothing." Investigator Debbie Bodkin, a police officer from Canada with extensive experience conducting homicide investigations, recounted:

> My very first interview will stay with me forever. Our team was on the outskirts of the village of Bahai and our driver had gone into the town and brought back some recent refugees to speak with us. By the time we started it was dark and my interpreter and I sat on the porch of an abandoned school and did the interview by flashlight and candlelight while swatting the bugs away. The man we spoke to was wearing a dirty and torn *jalabia* and was so visibly sad it was hard to look at him without getting choked up. His pain was so fresh as he told us how he had watched his parents, wife, and child being killed. He cried throughout the interview, as did I. Even though he was hurting so badly, he still was gracious and thanked us for coming to try and help his people. His final words were, "Life is nothing anymore when you have no one."

Eric Markusen, an investigator who had also interviewed victims in a number of war zones, commented, "For me, personally, the most heart-wrenching aspect of this mission was asking the respondents for details of their murdered relatives — spouses, children, parents, cousins, aunts, uncles. Many lost four or five or more relatives, and recording names, ages, gender, relationship, and cause of death left me emotionally exhausted."

Speaking about a particularly moving moment, Pfundheller shared the following:

My last interview [one] day was with a beautiful ebony lady named Mohasin. She was clear and unflinching in her answers and conveyed the brutality of the village attack, the gang rapes, the slashing of the women, the killing of the village leaders. Men anally raped, then castrated and bleeding to death. She related the smells, the sounds, her fear, the village panic. She had a long wait in the sun to speak with me and yet she didn't seem to falter. At the end of the interview, I said to her what I had said to so many: "I thank you for speaking with me and telling me what happened. I am very sorry this happened to you." She responded to me in English, "Thank YOU my sister." I was completely surprised, and said, "You speak English." And she responded, "Yes, I am educated in English. Thank you for coming and hearing what happened; you are my sister." She squeezed my hand and then hugged me and walked away toward the tents. I got up, walked to the Land Rover, and got in the back. I put my head in my hands and sobbed.

One refugee told Sam Totten, one of the twenty-four investigators, a harrowing story of giving birth in the mountains while fleeing her burning village. Her husband and son had been killed in the village and then, in the mountains, four of her nephews and an aunt were murdered by Government of Sudan (GoS) soldiers and *Janjaweed* while they (the refugees) were cutting timber to make a shelter. The distraught young woman said, "I feel there is no justice in Sudan, maybe in the whole world. What can I believe in after losing my husband and son? And who will help me with my baby?"

Each investigator endeavored to interview an average of five refugees per day. The goal was for each team of four interviewers and four interpreters to conduct a total of two hundred interviews during their period in the field. In the end, local contingencies — such as bad weather, vehicle breakdowns, and security concerns — resulted in some teams being unable to meet that goal. Ultimately, the ADT conducted over twelve hundred interviews of which eleven hundred thirty-six were conducted using the random methodology and were, therefore, statistically analyzed later.

On top of interviewing between four to seven refugees a day, each investigator worked for about fourteen days consecutively — from around 6 a.m. to 5 to 6 p.m. Investigator Jamal Jafari observed that one of the most difficult aspects of conducting the interviews for him was "balancing a need to process the horrible stories we heard every day with the danger of becoming complacent after hearing up to fifty versions of similarly disturbing stories."

For each interview conducted during the day, the interviewers filled out a one-page "preliminary atrocity field coding sheet" that included approximately three dozen types of "event codes," such as reports of killing of family, nonfamily, and mass execution; rape of self or others; abduction; beating; property destruction (partial or total); property theft (e.g., food stores, livestock, household goods); racial epithets; aerial bombing; and death caused by the displacement and flight to Chad (e.g., starvation, disease, injury). There was also approximately one dozen "perpetrator codes," including such categories as Sudanese soldiers, *Janjaweed* militia, rebel militias, and foreigners.

A Sample of the Refugees' Experiences Related in the Interviews

As previously mentioned, all refugees were asked to describe the attacks against their villages. What is included herein typifies the sort of stories that each investigator heard throughout his/her time in the field.

A 25-year-old Masaleit woman from West Darfur recalled the following:

> They attacked our village at 6 a.m. First, I saw three black and green helicopters. They were shooting from the helicopters. Shooting villagers at random as they ran. I saw men, women, and children being shot and falling down. Then came four vehicles (green and black [GoS] vehicles). Men in cars wearing military uniforms. Then came about eighty horsemen [*Janjaweed*], also in same uniforms, same guns. [The attack was] six hours long.

Totten noted that the first interview he conducted was with a 23-year-old woman who related that she had been captured, beaten, and made to dance a lewd dance by several soldiers. She wouldn't talk about the specific harm they had done to her, but her extremely sad countenance and tentativeness to speak indicated that she had experienced more than she was willing to tell. The GoS soldiers called her a "Tora Bora (a term used to infer that the person supported the Black African Sudanese rebel groups) prostitute." Her cousin and her cousin's twelve children were killed in front of her.

Totten learned of numerous massacres that were carried out in an area north of Mukjar. "I was informed by one interviewee (and heard similar stories from others) that about one hundred fifty to one hundred seventy-five people were blindfolded, tied up, and put on trucks. They were told they were being taken to a town called Garsila, but in fact they were taken just north of Mukjar to a valley where they were unloaded and machine-gunned."

Investigator Larissa Wakim reported that:

One theme that came up in a number of interviews that I conducted, although I didn't hear this in many other investigators' accounts, nor have I read about it in other reports, was an accusation of gas attacks. Several interviewees spoke of oil drums dropped from airplanes, which exploded on impact. A green/blue gas was released and victims' eyes turned a bluish color before they died. Significantly, one man buried a number of bodies that he claimed had been killed by the gas, as they had no visible injuries or other obvious reasons for death. He, himself, had physical symptoms (including changed eye color), which he attributed to the attack. I am keen to know if this was something unique to the area where the people I interviewed came from or if others have heard similar accounts.[1]

Jafari remarked, "Like everyone else, I heard many horrendous stories. That said, some that stuck out included a woman who saw her neighbor's baby thrown up in the air and speared on a bayonet. She also witnessed the baby's father set on fire while still alive." Totten also reported the following:

A man from Ouorm reported to me that his village was attacked by Antonov airplanes and helicopters. "The Antonovs threw fire from above." GoS soldiers broke into his home and immediately shot and killed his son and shot his nephew, who ultimately died in Chad from his wounds. The soldiers were shouting, "Kill Nuba." The soldiers also took one of his wives and his five sons whom he never saw again and does not know if they are dead or alive. The man told me, "I lost everything but the clothes I have on now."

Totten was also informed by an interviewee that "those who fled their own towns after they were attacked by the GoS and the *Janjaweed* attempted to enter Delj, a town known to have water, where they were attacked and killed by the *Janjaweed*. The *Janjaweed* actually hid near the wells and waited for people to appear so they could kill them."

Rapes

While it is highly probable that the incidents of rape were under-reported, every investigator and interpreter heard stories of rape by GoS troops and the *Janjaweed*, which took place in the victims' homes, in the dirt pathways of their villages, and/or in the mountains where the survivors had fled. Speaking of such, Pfundheller related the following:

On our third day at Breidjing refugee camp, Brent (Pfundheller's husband, a veteran criminal investigator who also served on the ADT) and his interpreter spoke with one of the *umdas* in the camp. During the conversation, Brent asked if there had been sexual assaults in the *umda's* village. The *umda* confirmed that there had been many, and that although some of the victims had died as a consequence of the rapes, others from the village were in the camp. The *umda* said, "Our women have suffered greatly and suffer still. Please speak to them yourself."

The next morning, my interpreter and I accompanied Brent and his interpreter to the *umda's* tent. He had been called away to a meeting, but had left a sheik behind to speak with us. The sheik explained that the women were willing to talk with us. I told him that we would drive to a spot nearby just on the bank of the *wadi* where there were not so many people. We would wait for the ladies to come to us. He agreed and said he would tell them.

So we went down to the *wadi* and found two trees to sit under. I asked Brent to stay as I thought perhaps there would be eight or ten women and with that many I would need to split the interviews between us. Old ladies nearby came quickly to loan us their "*bombas*," the small stools of wood and woven goatskin they sit on to cook. [Extremely] grateful for their kindness, we settled in and waited. Soon we began to see women approach, walking over the small rise, toward us. They walked straight and tall, their bright clothes fluttering. And they came and came. I handed Brent my camera and told him to take some pictures, saying, "I think this is something very unusual."

Almost three hundred women and girls walked up in silence, and began sitting around me. I counted seventy-three who sat close in a circle under my tree.

Then, about seven to ten yards beyond, there were two hundred-plus more. The sheik approached and said, "Here are the women." I said, "Were all these women and girls raped?" He said, "Yes. These under the tree are willing to speak with you today, the others are a bit afraid to speak with you, but they wanted to come also so that you will know they also suffered in this way."

Knowing it would never be possible to interview such a group, but knowing I could not simply pick a few and send the others away without comment, I spoke with them. "Ladies," I said, "you honor me today by coming to speak with me. I will explain who I am and why I am here. My name is Jan and this man is Brent. We have come from America. America cares very deeply about what is happening in Darfur. My government has sent us to listen to you so you personally can tell us what is happening in Darfur. One of our government leaders, Colin Powell, came to Sudan, and he wants to know more about what has happened to you." (These silent ladies all murmured to each other at this point — clearly they considered Colin Powell's concern to be important). "I understand that you have all suffered and are suffering still. I would like to hear from every one of you about what has happened. That will not be possible, as we are here for only a very short time. So, I would like to speak to about ten of you, if that is possible, and if you agree. But from all of you I ask that you take with you my personal regards and the regards from America. I cannot promise you more food distributions or more medicine for the children. I cannot tell you that you will return to your homes. I can only promise you that what has happened to you will be told to my government, and then perhaps to the world. After I choose the ladies that will be interviewed, I must ask the remainder to go some distance away so that these ladies might have privacy in their interviews with Brent and me. But they will need your presence and your support later and you will need theirs. Thank you ladies."

Before the crowd of women left, I walked through the crowd thanking them. They held my hands, rubbed the skin on my forearms and touched my hair. We then picked several ladies at random and began our interviews, with the "ladies in waiting" sitting a distance away and approaching as their turns came.

A glimpse into the horror experienced by victims of rape is provided by excerpts from two interviews conducted by the ADT. When asked by an investigator what had happened to her and if she had been physically harmed in the attack on her village, a 25-year-old Masaleit woman from West Darfur described her ordeal: "Sixteen of us women [were] caught and raped there. I saw others being raped. [One was] raped vaginally, her breasts slashed. [A] stick was shoved in her vagina. [She was] very pregnant at the time. Four soldiers held her hands and feet, [and] took turns. [They also] shoved sticks far inside of her."

A younger Masaleit woman, also from West Darfur, related the following to an investigator:

I was running after this [attack] carrying my baby and my three-year-old daughter. Two pickups, Toyotas, followed me with soldiers. A soldier took my baby son and said, "I will kill him." I told the soldier, "You killed my husband, don't kill my boy." One other [soldier] said, "Don't kill the baby." My baby was laying near me, and my daughter was crying and trying to come to me, and they kicked her away. I was knocked down, and the first soldier had sex with me from the front. They were saying the government from Khartoum sent [them] and we [were to be] killed and raped and cleaned [from] their land. Ten soldiers rape[d] me and left me. I was bleeding and could not walk. They did this to me for nearly three hours. I was laying there while my village burned. A man fleeing from another village found me and took me and my children to Masteri.

All my village — maybe three hundred fifty houses — burned. We had one hundred cows, ten goats, 20 million Sudanese pounds — all taken or destroyed. The village was not defended, and no rebels [were] in the village.

Beatings, Torture, Injuries, and the Residual Effects

Beatings and torture were common occurrences as the GoS and *Janjaweed* attacked village after village, breaking into homes, accosting people or chasing them, and tracking them down in surrounding fields, hills, and mountains. Many refugees continued to suffer both physical and mental anguish long after the atrocities to which they had been subjected. As one investigator, Larissa Wakim, reported:

I interviewed one gentleman who had been detained and tortured by GoS forces in a prison after fleeing his village, which had been attacked. When he talked about the treatment at the prison, he became visibly upset; he was unable to look at either me or my interpreter; he was silent for short periods of time to collect his thoughts, and he ceased talking when people walked past and would not continue until they were gone and then he could talk freely again. He avoided questions about what had happened to him in prison, and I began to suspect that he had been sexually molested by his captors. He had been with a group of prisoners, and although he said that they had been beaten, he claimed he had not been. I pressed him gently on this, to clarify what he was saying, but he confirmed his story and was not willing to go into any more detail.

He had an excellent memory and had provided very detailed observations about the attack on his village and aspects of his detention. (This was another signal to me that there was more to his story than he was willing to share because of the lack of information about particular aspects of his incarceration in prison.) We explained that with the information he had given us, we would be in a stronger position to create increased international pressure on the GoS and hold accountable those responsible. As we concluded the interview, we told him that if there was anything else that he remembered and wanted to add he could. He declined, and thus we thanked him and left.

Several hours later, we were wandering through the camp at the end of our day, and the man came up to me and said he had things he had forgotten and wanted to add to his testimony. Firstly, he said he had forgotten to mention that when the town he had been captured in was itself attacked, he had seen helicopters and Antonov planes. Secondly, and more importantly, he wanted on the record that while in prison he had been mistreated — he had suffered a "man's beating." My interpreter was sure by the choice of words (and what we could see in the man's body language and demeanor) that he had indeed been sexually tortured in some way.

This incident deeply touched me. He was so ashamed, so embarrassed, so determined to erase those memories from his mind that he had been unable to talk about them in the first interview. Yet, he had obviously spent the afternoon thinking about the purpose of the project in collecting statements and had come to the conclusion that disclosing to us what had happened to him was worth that discomfort and pain. It was just such a poignant illustration of someone who was suffering enormous emotional and mental anguish and yet was prepared to open up to the system in the hope it would help him and others like him find some solace and justice.

Speaking of an interviewee's story that had touched him deeply, Jafari commented that:

> One man's story stuck with me particularly. He had lost a leg below the knee in one of the attacks. What stuck out was the fact that he made his living as a driver when nearly everyone else I met was a farmer. Here was the one man who definitely needed two legs for his livelihood and it's clear that even if he could return to Darfur, his life would never be the same. It wasn't the worst story I heard, but the most bitterly ironic.

Destruction of Livelihood

Any property that was not looted by the GoS and *Janjaweed* was destroyed by them. Houses and entire villages were burned to the ground, the carcasses of dead animals and human bodies were thrown into wells to poison them, and crops were razed and orchards chopped down.

A refugee who had been a man of great wealth in his village reported to Totten that the *Janjaweed* entered his orchard around midnight and cut down the entire grove that he had dedicated his life to planting and tending — "one hundred mango trees, tweny-five orange trees, and ten lemon trees."

Most of the refugees interviewed had a very detailed memory of their losses of livestock — how many camels, sheep, goats, and donkeys had been stolen by the GoS or *Janjaweed*. The same was true for the number of sacks of grain, vegetables, and other goods stolen and/or destroyed by the GoS and *Janjaweed*. Totten also recalled interviewing a middle-aged man who had been extremely wealthy in Darfur:

He owned scores of cows, donkeys, and camels, had huge orchards, and even owned a wide array of mechanical devices that he used in his farming. As I got up to leave following the interview, the man motioned toward the inside of his tent, which was totally empty except for a cot and one blanket — it was, in fact, one of the barest tents I observed out of the hundreds that I had seen in the camp — and simply asked, "What am I supposed to do now?" The refrain has haunted me for all these months, for I had no answer then, just as I have no answer now.

Reflecting on her contact with the children in the refugee camps, Vanessa Allyn, who served as a field-based coordinator for the CIJ project, observed that, "I can't help but think of how the children — reduced to nothing, with little food, clothing, or shelter — always seemed to be smiling. They were so resilient, and such an inspiration to see (especially for someone such as myself who lives in a very decadent yet dissatisfied culture)."

Slurs Directed at the Black African Sudanese Population

Time and again, investigators were informed by interviewees that the GoS and the *Janjaweed* called them disparaging and dehumanizing names, and also made comments that made clear they were not welcome in Sudan. For example, one man, who lost everything except the clothes on his back, reported that the *Janjaweed* screamed at him: "You are not a real Sudanese, you're black. We swore to drive you away from this country on al-Bashir's [the president's] orders. We are the real Sudanese. No blacks need stay here." Another man, whose father and mother were killed in their village, as well as the man's baby son, was told by the *Janjaweed*, "We are going to cut off your roots."

A refugee told Totten that following an attack on his village by Sudanese planes (Antonovs), the *Janjaweed* swooped in on horseback, and GoS troops raced in in land cruisers and burned the entire village down, killing over fifty people. As the *Janjaweed* carried out the attack, some screamed, "The President of Sudan ordered us to cleanse Darfur of the dirty slaves in order to establish the beginning of the Arab Union."

Problems Faced by ADT Personnel in the Field

Investigators and their translators, as well as other ADT personnel, faced a variety of problems. That is understandable in light of the fact that temperatures ranged from the relatively balmy 90 degree Fahrenheit (30 degrees Celsius) in the south to the searing 130 degrees Fahrenheit (50 degrees Celsius) in the north (which is located on the edge of the Sahara Desert), and that some groups had to cross flooded *wadis* and/or were located in areas in which torrential downpours were a common part of the day. Among some of the many problems encountered by various groups and individuals were, for example, various ailments (heat prostration took down several investigators and interpreters, but only for minimal amounts of time, and numerous people suffered from diarrhea and high fevers); two broken axles; numerous four-wheel vehicles stuck in flooded *wadis* (which, sometimes, took days to free up); difficulties with translators (a few translators were not very cooperative, including one who seemed to have an "agenda"); and key equipment that was sent to the wrong destination. Linda Patrick, who was based in northern Chad, stated that:

Certainly, a major problem was the 130 degree heat without any relief. [Before leaving home,] not knowing precisely how to prepare for those conditions or what to bring was of considerable concern. Water and rehydration was a key factor to survival and performance out in the heat. These unknowns for the first team [in the field] was a factor in settling into the actual interviews.

In regard to difficulties faced, Pfundheller provided the following observations:

The first day I arrived in Abeche, I went into the field with two officials from the U.S. State Department, one representative from the American Bar Association's CEELI Program, and three interpreters. We went to Kounoungo Refugee Camp. Now I know you don't drink the local water, but I had made the mistake of going to a tent for an interview and leaving my water bottle in the truck. Having ready access to your water bottle is important, especially if you've poured powdered Gatorade into it. It allows you to turn down any offer of anything else by saying, "I am drinking this special medicated water." This is greeted with nods of understanding. But there I was without the water bottle. The host offered me a cup of water. I could not say no without offending, so I took it. After several minutes, the host inquired if the water was all right. Again, not wanting to offend, I sipped about one tablespoon of water. Oh what a mistake. I followed that up with two or three liters of bottled water. But by midnight I was in the throes of the worst diarrhea I've ever suffered.

It didn't help that we were staying in the house of the local "governor," which was gracious of him, but we found the place to be full of bugs, devoid of furniture, and equipped with a western toilet that looked the part but had never been flushed. And there was no toilet paper. The next day I was taken back to base. I have no memory of that day other than our wonderful Sudanese doctor coming to me and telling me to immediately take Ciproflaxin (Cipro) or I would be in grave danger. I now have a deep respect for Cipro. It is a miracle, really.

Totten faced a different set of problems as a result of being caught out in the open during a sandstorm.

Early one morning while interviewing a refugee, winds began kicking up. At first, the wind was simply an annoyance as it resulted in people scurrying about the camp picking up loose items that were being blown about. But within minutes, the winds became fierce, creating funnels of sand that whirled through the camp, eventually engulfing the entire camp in a thick gauze of swirling sand. Rushing for the interviewee's open tent, the respondent, my interpreter, and I crawled in the tent, and quickly battened down the flaps, but even that did not stop the sand from blowing in and swirling around the tent. Within a half hour or so the winds died down, but the damage had been done. From that point on, I coughed incessantly, spitting out globs of sand-coated phlegm, and at night when I tried to sleep I would choke on the sand and phlegm in my lungs, and the only way I could avoid that was to prop myself up and try to sleep in a sitting position.

Once I got back to the States, I called the Center for Disease Control in Atlanta and was informed that the sand would eventually work its way out of my system in a month or so, which, indeed, it finally did.

I often find myself wondering how the refugees are managing, as they face such natural occurrences on top of everything else they are dealing with.

In regard to various teams' experiences with the flooded *wadis*, Pfundheller related the following.

By the time we were about to complete the mission, the rains had come. Torrential downpours. You would see it coming in the afternoon from far away, the black sky rolling toward you, then the lightning and thunder. We were out at border settlements, planning to return to Abeche the following day when the sky grew dark. The drivers explained that we were facing a major storm, and that staying an extra day would put us in danger of being stuck for several days. Since our return to Abeche was to be followed by an immediate departure to N'Djamena and then home, we decided to make a run for it. We quickly packed what was absolutely necessary and left the rest of our food, medicines, extra clothing, and most of the water with lovely Australian missionaries and their three children we had shared a compound with for two days.

When it began to rain, it just poured down. The sky was pure black. We had three cars and we stayed as close together as possible given the poor visibility. At each *wadi*, our lead translator/fixer/miracle worker would leap out, walk the *wadi* to determine if we might make it, then wave us across. There were moments of complete silence followed with shouts of joy when we made it. But when we reached Wadi Mura at about nine o'clock in the evening, we clearly knew it was the end of our luck as the *wadi* had become a raging river. A supply truck had already attempted to cross, but had been carried fifty or so yards down-stream where it tipped over spilling all the cargo. Other travelers were stuck with us on the east side of the river. The mud hut selling tea with camel's milk on our side of the wadi was grateful for the upswing in business.

We were forced to settle in for the night. The interpreters warned us not to venture away from the vehicles as the rains would bring snakes to the riverbanks and we might not see them until it was too late. So, stiff and exhausted, we did what we could to sleep in the vehicles. We shared our Land Rover with two lovely U.S. Congressional staffers visiting the region (one of whom, I recall, worked for Congressman Henry Hyde [R-IL]). They were upbeat and uncomplaining and completely suited to the task.

In the morning, we attempted to cross the wadi. Every vehicle that went before us got stuck. Thankfully, we had paid for "insurance." Insurance on the east side of Wadi Mura consisted of $80 (U.S.) to the group of locals. If you paid it in advance, it was $80, if you failed to pay it and got stuck, it would be double. Our driver said, "Pay it." We did and we were glad. Only fifteen yards from the east riverbank and we were stuck. The strong pressure of the water against the vehicle was a concern, especially as we looked downstream at the supply truck on its side. Soon the water was pouring through the Land Rover — four inches or so deep on the floorboards.

The insurance paid off, as the gang of river men rocked us and pushed us — with a dozen of their number pulling on a thick hemp rope to inch us forward.

In spite of the major logistical challenges, none of the hurdles proved insurmountable. This was undoubtedly due to the outstanding planning that went into the project, the Herculean efforts by CIJ staff in Washington, D.C. and the CIJ staff based in Abeche (and especially Stefanie Frease who served as coordinator of the entire project in Chad), and the *esprit de corps* felt by those involved with the project. Ultimately, none of the obstacles impeded the group's ability to reach the goal of collecting nearly twelve hundred interviews in Chad.

Impressions of the Data Being Collected

No one on the ground, of course, knew which elements of which crimes would be met by the data being gathered in the field. Nonetheless, in the evenings, team members shared and discussed some of what they were being told by the survivors. In regard to the issue of rape, Allyn commented that:

> One thing that really stood out in my mind was the clear intent to use rape as a weapon of war. The perpetrators knew that raped women would be cast away and/or that having Arab babies would tear at the fabric of the culture. After hearing a large number of rape and sexual slavery stories, it started to seem like killing the women would have been too simple, that it wouldn't have inflicted enough harm on the group as a whole. The high incidence and prevalence of rape in this situation seemed horrifyingly purposeful.
>
> Also, the targeting of males and male children seemed to indicate an attempt to eradicate a significant portion of the group and endanger the future existence of the group as a whole. The targeted killing of one gender (coupled with the debasement of the other), destruction of water sources, food supply, and shelter (in extremely harsh conditions) were all calculated efforts to make survival very, very difficult. When all of these factors began to coalesce, it didn't take long for me to see that what was occurring was definitely a case of crimes against humanity, if not genocide.

Patrick noted:

> All of the stories, no matter which camp we went to or where the victims were from in Darfur, related the same sort of information. The young men in all the villages were taken, beaten, killed if found, as if the attackers were trying to wipe out that generation of young men. Many of the young girls were beaten and raped as if the attackers were trying to impregnate them with their own traits.

Pfundheller reflected:

> During the course of the interviews I conducted with refugees, and in my conversations with my colleagues about the interviews they had conducted, it was so clear to me that what had taken place, and was continuing to take place (intentionally directing attacks against

a specific part of the civilian population — the black African Darfurians; willful killing; unlawful deportation and transfer of many
tens of thousands; intentionally directing attacks against buildings
that are dedicated to religion; committing mass rape, sexual slavery,
forced pregnancy) was clearly, completely, and undeniably genocide.
I don't think one of us left there thinking, "It's not as bad as I heard
before I came." I think we all left wanting to scream at the world to
"hurry, hurry up and make this stop. Can't you see what's happening
here, for God's sake? Don't let this happen again."

While Samuel Totten and Brenda Sue Thornton, the two investigators
who were based in Goz Beida with the first out in the field, discussed the
data they collected and pondered how the U.S. Department of State would
ultimately define the atrocities that were being perpetrated in Darfur, they
were of a like mind that whether they were called crimes against humanity
or genocide, there was a dire need for the international community to act
immediately to stanch the killing, rapes, beatings, and the wholesale theft
and destruction of property.

Lighter Moments

While the fieldwork was demanding, the weather trying, and the findings
sorrowful, most experienced some lighter moments in the field that helped
to relieve, even if only a little, the heavy burden and strain felt by most.
Many of these "lighter moments" resulted from the investigators' interactions with the children in the camps, who, despite the hardships they
had faced in Darfur and now in Chad, were relatively cheerful, extremely
friendly, and happy to see the friendly faces of foreigners.

Of her interaction with the children in the refugee camps, Patrick
remarked:

Meeting the children and seeing how they can adapt to anything and
be happy with the smallest of pleasures was a moving experience.
After the interviews, the children would gather around to learn English and wait for an empty water bottle, which they would put to a
hundred different uses. I saw children making toys from tin cans,
rubber thongs, and pieces of wood, and they were extraordinarily
functional toys and carts. I met some young boys who were making
bird catchers out of ordinary items, a small branch, donkey hair, and
a piece of fabric. They could actually catch birds with them.

Every day after interviewing, Totten looked forward to engaging in
banter with the children of "his" camp:

Every evening, my field partner, Brenda Sue Thornton, and I would meet back at our land cruiser, and before heading back to our camp-site we'd interact with the children who gathered around us. To entertain them, I generally engaged in one of two activities, which they seemed to look forward to each day with great anticipation. The first involved my asking them in a Bugs Bunny-like, cartoonish voice, "Da, what's up, doc?" which they'd repeat in unison and giggle and laugh uncontrollably.

The second was to teach them how to play tag and then play it with them. I was always the initial "it" and when I lunged to tag someone, they would scream and career off and scatter in all directions.

Over and above seeing the children's wonderful smiles and hear-ing their great waves of laughter, one of the most edifying aspects of these moments was always noticing a ring of adults on the periphery of the group smiling at the antics.

Speaking of some "down time," Pfundheller commented that:

One afternoon about two weeks into the mission and between field visits, Helge Niska, Vanessa Allen (our absolute ace intern), an inter-preter, and I were sitting on the verandah, swatting flies, sweating, listening to Finnish radio (in Finnish, which only Helge understood) and passing the day away. The interpreter was explaining what he knew of America — especially the World Wrestling Federation. We, in turn, explained baseball. And then we taught him the "alternate" national anthem ("Take Me Out to the Ball Game"). We sang and laughed and sang. It was wonderful.

Bodkin emphasized the importance of the friendships that developed among her fellow investigators and their interpreters:

Combining the unbearable heat and the emotional turmoil from hearing the heart-wrenching stories, the time in the field could have gotten the best of me if it weren't for the wonderful friendships that developed between me and the other members of my team. It was amazing how the tragedies we listened to all day somehow forced us to become like friends who had known each other for years. We shared very personal things about ourselves and could also sit together in silence quite comfortably. It was like leaving family mem-bers when it was time to go home.

Debriefing Sessions

As each set of team members concluded their work in the field and returned to the base camp in Abeche, they were debriefed about the data they collected, any difficulties encountered, the usefulness of the question-naire, the conditions in the camps, the cooperation of local officials and NGO personnel, the work of the interpreters, et al. Copious notes were taken during each debriefing session and many suggestions made by the first team were implemented for the benefit of the second team.

Final Thoughts

Despite the difficult living and working conditions, many were reluctant to leave the field, as they had become even more dedicated to doing what they could to help end the killing and other crimes being committed in Darfur.

Speaking for herself, but voicing the sentiments of many investigators, Patrick said, "To discover the truth and be able to provide that to our own government, who then passed it onto the UN Security Council gave me a great sense of accomplishment."

Jafari commented, "I was overwhelmed by the thanks received from some of the victims and local leaders for the work we were doing, but at the same time this was accompanied by guilt, knowing that even if the project had a great impact on United States policymakers, there was a good chance that not much would really change on the ground in the refugee camps or in Darfur."

Wakim commented that:

The hardest part of the job for me was the feeling that we were fiddling while Rome burned. When my interviews echoed the same stories that I had read about in countless reports in preparation for the trip, it really made me wonder what on earth could come of our work. And even if it did lead to a definitional decision on whether genocide was occurring, would it be enough for action to actually be taken?

Pfundheller offered the following observation:

I am so grateful to the Sudanese victims of this terrible crisis who were willing to give up time in their day to tell me what happened to them. Their lives have become so incredibly difficult. Every day is a struggle to survive in harsh conditions, unwanted immigrants in a foreign land, at the mercy of the elements, disease, hunger, and poverty. And they live with the memories of seeing their children/families/communities destroyed by their own government forces, who should have been protecting (not attacking) them. Just as all of the investigators did, I spoke with the victims first-hand. I didn't read the account of the horrors and wonder what license had been taken. I didn't hear from the person who heard it from the victim. I heard it from the victims themselves. And having heard it, knowing in my heart that I can and will stand up and say, "this happened" to whoever will listen, to whoever cares, and to those who do not. To give a louder voice to the victims and their horrific truths.

As for the international community's reaction to the findings of the ADT, Jafari observed, "I can hardly put my disappointment into words. I can't say at all that I am surprised. Sadly, I don't think the international community has learned one lesson from Rwanda. Until there is a new mechanism empowered to react quickly to such situations, the response will likely be the same with the next genocide."

Allyn speaking about the issue, commented:

The reaction has been appalling. I realize the machinery of the international community moves slowly, but there is no excuse for such an inadequate level of response. Not only is promised funding for aid not being delivered, but the reluctance to enforce more serious measures (such as a no-fly zone) will likely be an embarrassment in the future. The self-interest of UN Security Council members, be it China with oil interests, the United States with North–South peace agreement issues, or general international politics, are a shame upon each of them and the United Nations system as a whole.

I also feel that the reliance on AU [African Union] troops as some sort of piecemeal solution is an excuse to do less; there aren't enough of them, they have no mandate to stop violence perpetrated against IDP [internally displaced persons] camps or the refugees themselves (rather they are mandated NOT to intervene), and they aren't adequately supplied. It seems to come down to the same old racist/colonialist international attitude toward the "dark" continent: "It is an African problem, let the Africans solve it, and if they don't solve it, the people who are dying are just Africans anyway. Let them go on slaughtering each other until they learn their lesson or all die, but we aren't going to waste our precious western resources or lives on something like hopeless, chaotic Africa."

Speaking in a similar vein, Wakim observed that:

The cynical side of me is not surprised [about the failure of the international community to undertake meaningful action to stop the killing and dying in the months since U.S. Secretary of State Colin Powell declared what was taking place in Darfur constituted genocide]; just, once again, disappointed by the international community's inaction in the face of atrocity. Then, the human side of me feels helplessness, despair, and pure rage at our inability to raise ourselves', our neighbors', and our families' responsiveness into action that would translate into concrete improvements for Darfurians.

Bodkin, from her perspective as a homicide investigator, offered the following comments:

My heart breaks knowing that even though our work was successful in many ways, the horrors are still continuing now as I write this. I know there are politics and money involved in making changes which causes things to be done slowly, but there is something terribly wrong with our system if the rest of the world can't step in quicker and make the killing stop. As a police officer, when I am at work back home, once I obtain the evidence to show an offense is being committed, action is taken immediately to stop the offender and bring him to justice. I guess I naively believed that this would happen in Darfur as well.

Totten, a scholar of genocide, asserted, "If the international community continues to waver and equivocate, there is no doubt in my mind that ten years from now the international community will apologize to the victims of Darfur just as it did recently to the Tutsis on the tenth anniversary of the 1994 Rwandan genocide. But such apologies are as hollow as they get when something could have and should have been done to save the people in the first place."

Finally, reflecting on the mission, investigator Brenda Sue Thornton wrote:

Today, virtually one year later, a year after our work in Chad, I reflect back on one of the women interviewed, her child, and all of the other refugees that my partner Sam Totten and I interviewed. And I think that they are all still there, if alive, under the blazing sun, waiting daily for the world to understand what happened and to send help. The woman probably has no idea where here her other child is and no idea as to whether help will ever come. When asked about the project, the work that we did, this is the aspect I find the most troubling and saddening. Despite the documentation, despite countries knowing what went on and the status of these people, they are still there — waiting.

Note

1. Another investigator, Samuel Totten, a member of the same four-person team as Larissa Wakim, also was informed about gas attacks from aircraft. Notably, though Totten and Wakim were on the same team, they were each based at a different refugee camp — Totten was at Goz Beida and Wakim was at Goz Amer, both of which were located in southern Chad. The proximity of the refugee camps suggests that the refugees Totten and Wakim spoke with likely fled areas that were also within proximity.

PART 3

The Genocide Determination

CHAPTER 7

Making the Determination of Genocide in Darfur

STEPHEN A. KOSTAS

Introduction

During the summer of 2004, swelling domestic United States and international concern about the unfolding catastrophe in Darfur focused on whether the world, but particularly the United States, which had been so vocal about suffering in Sudan, would intervene to stop the atrocities. As in the past, much attention was also focused on whether governments would call the crimes by their proper name.

The reluctance of the Clinton administration to use the term genocide in relation to the former Yugoslavia and especially Rwanda in the mid-1990s had been roundly criticized and there was pressure not to make that mistake again. Commentators and scholars traced the source of that reluctance to a fear that once the administration did, it would face powerful pressure to intervene militarily. By late spring 2004, the Bush administration alternately described the situation in Darfur as a crisis, catastrophe, and ethnic cleansing, but resisted using the "g" word. The Legislative Branch, however, did not share the Executive Branch's hesitancy. In mid-July, both houses of Congress passed concurrent resolutions identifying the situation in Darfur as a genocide and calling on the Bush administration to do so as well.

The views expressed in his chapter are attributable to the author alone and do not necessarily reflect the views of the ICTY or the United Nations.

At the time, the U.S. State Department had teams of investigators[1] organized by the nongovernmental organization (NGO), the Coalition for International Justice (CIJ), on the Chad-Sudan border to interview people who had fled Darfur. The data collected by these teams of independent investigators, including a handful of State Department and U.S. Agency for International Development's (USAID) Office of Transition Initiatives (OTI) staff, was to be used by Secretary of State Colin Powell and his analysts to determine whether, in fact, genocide was occurring in Darfur.

In an effort to better understand what led the State Department to send investigators into the field and, ultimately, for Secretary Powell to reach the determination of genocide, Eric Markusen and I conducted two telephone interviews with Pierre-Richard Prosper, former U.S. Ambassador-at-Large for War Crimes, and I interviewed Lorne Craner, former Assistant Secretary for the State Department's Bureau of Democracy, Human Rights and Labor in person, in November 2005.

First Warnings about Darfur

By all accounts, Andrew Natsios' frequent warnings of a growing humanitarian crisis in Darfur first alerted the U.S. Department of State (State Department) to the gravity of the situation there. Natsios, head of USAID, made nine trips to Sudan between late 2003 and spring 2004 and repeatedly warned key officials at the State Department that conditions in Darfur were grave and deteriorating. His equally focused Assistant Administrator and longtime Sudan hand, Roger Winter, also made multiple trips to the region. In late October 2003, Natsios briefed the State Department about the murder of nine Sudanese USAID relief workers in Darfur.

In the view of many international actors at that time, Darfur was a humanitarian catastrophe, but the ethnic component of the attacks was not fully appreciated. By late spring 2004, however, UN Undersecretary-General for Humanitarian Affairs and Emergency Relief Coordinator, Jan Egeland (2004), warned the Security Council that the situation amounted to ethnic cleansing — a term with uncertain legal meaning, if any. The State Department itself estimated in June that more than three hundred thousand refugees would likely die from a lack of food and medicine without an immediate international response (Natsios, 2004).

Initially, the State Department had tried to address the mounting crisis in Darfur with "quiet diplomacy." President George W. Bush, Powell, and National Security Advisor Condoleezza Rice spoke with their counterparts in Sudan out of the public eye. Natsios joined the diplomatic effort when he visited Sudan in October 2003, delivering the administration's refrain that there would be no normalization of relations between Washington and

Khartoum until the atrocities in Darfur ended — a message carried during the North–South negotiations by the administration's Special Envoy to the Sudan, former Senator John Danforth (R-MO), and its chief North–South negotiator, Senior Representative on Sudan Charles Snyder. The situation in Darfur became a constant issue in United States–Sudan relations when, in December 2003, a short-lived ceasefire between rebel groups and the government of Sudan broke down and the government escalated violence against civilians.

By spring 2004, however, the Bush administration exchanged quiet diplomacy for more robust, confrontational rhetoric. Officials in the State Department also realized they needed to learn more about what was happening on the ground. More than a year after hostilities began in Darfur, some in the State Department believed they lacked sufficient information on the racial or ethnic dimensions to speak about it in terms other than as a humanitarian crisis born of battles between rebels and a progovernment militia. Some, though, were also concerned that speaking about the underlying racial or ethnic dimensions would undermine hard-won progress at the North–South bargaining table.

During early 2004, Craner held regular intelligence briefings with the Bureau of Intelligence and Research (INR) and the Central Intelligence Agency (CIA). Prosper recalls that "as we moved into the spring of 2004, it became a little clearer, at least from the information that was emerging from our people as well as NGOs, that there was a deliberate targeting and killing of the African population." With NASA satellite imagery acquired in April 2004, the State Department learned of the systematic destruction of Fur, Massalit, and Zaghawa villages — three hundred of five hundred seventy-six villages were completely destroyed and another seventy-six were partially destroyed (Igiri and Lyman, 2004, p. 11). In addition to seeing the amount of destruction taking place, Prosper recalls that the satellite images clearly revealed the selective targeting of black African villages. USAID posted these images on its website in an effort to persuade others of the extent of the damage and precision of the targeting.

After holding a number of meetings to examine satellite imagery and other intelligence on the region, Craner believed he had reached the limits of what he could learn without sending people to the region, and determined it was essential to get up-to-date information from the ground. In particular, Craner wanted detailed information about the population in the region, the distribution of ethnic groups, those responsible for the violence, the nature and scope of the violence, and the plight of the affected Darfurians.

Rwanda and Standing Orders

Why was the State Department willing to investigate an internal conflict in a remote and undeveloped part of Africa? Had the State Department learned from the history of willful blindness (or worse) that has frequently characterized United States policy toward large-scale violence in Africa? It has been widely reported that early in his presidency, George W. Bush was presented with a National Security Council (NSC) memorandum summarizing a three-year investigation into the Clinton administration's response to the genocide in Rwanda and warning of the likely outbreak of ethnic violence in Burundi. President Bush wrote firmly in the memo's margin: "NOT ON MY WATCH" (Power, 2002a, p. 511). Craner recounts that, from the beginning of his tenure as assistant secretary, he had standing instructions from Powell and Marc Grossman, Under Secretary of State for Political Affairs, that "there was not going to be another Rwanda," and, with that in mind, the State Department devoted significant time to ensuring that the situation in Burundi remained under control in the first two years of Bush's presidency. The scar of Rwanda on the State Department was genuine, according to Craner, who cited the chapters on Rwanda and Cambodia in Samantha Power's "A Problem from Hell" as influential frameworks for his thinking about the response to Darfur.

But exactly what "not another Rwanda" meant to the administration remained unclear. Did Craner's standing order from Powell signify that the Bush administration would not claim ignorance while a large-scale catastrophe unfolded? Did it require that in the face of overwhelming evidence, the United States would call genocide by its rightful name? Did it suggest that the United States would not cling to formalistic legal notions of State responsibility in response to such suffering — that is, merely calling on Khartoum to protect civilians from attack? Was it a pledge that the Bush administration would not let another genocide unfold?

Certainly, the State Department's use of the term genocide largely remained tethered to a formal legal determination of its requisite elements. Just as the State Department clarified ten years before, with full knowledge that Hutus had already killed over three hundred thousand Tutsis, "the use of the term 'genocide' has a very precise legal meaning ... [and] before we begin to use [the] term, we have to know as much as possible about the facts of the situation..." (Shelley, 1994). In a similar vein, Secretary Powell explained on June 30, 2004, more than a year after the Government of Sudan (GoS) began widespread attacks that killed more than seventy thousand black African Darfur civilians, "the genocide definition has to meet certain legal tests.... It is a legal determination. And, based on what we have seen, there were some indicators, but there was certainly no full accounting of all indicators that lead to a legal definition of genocide, in accordance with the terms of the genocidal treaties [sic]. That's the advice of my lawyers" (Powell, 2004a).

For Craner, "not another Rwanda" meant, at a minimum, that the State Department wouldn't remain willfully blind to the scale of violence in Darfur. Craner cited the efforts of foreign service officer Charles Twining, who was posted to the Thai–Cambodian border to interview refugees in 1975 and whose dispatches back to Washington were received with incredulity and disbelief until they were verified and expanded on by French and British reports (Power, 2002a, pp. 115–121). Then, as now, the State Department would only respond to information that it trusted before it would act to stop the violence, if it did at all. Prosper shared the sentiment, emphasizing, "again, we knew that the [civilian] population was being attacked, villages were being destroyed, we had reports of people being killed, raped, but we decided to get first-hand information rather than third- or fourth-hand through various organizations." Prosper stated that he was "not comfortable making a determination on what a human rights group was telling [him], because [he] had no idea what the methodology for reporting was."

At the time, Natsios was reporting credible information gathered by USAID workers in Sudan about the human costs of the conflict, and the State Department possessed sufficient satellite imagery and external reporting to conclude there were "indicators of genocide," as Prosper would eventually testify before the House of Representatives in late June 2004 (Prosper, 2004). Craner and Prosper both believed the State Department needed more information before it could "speak out conclusively" about genocide. Prosper wanted to avoid making a "half-statement" and believed that once a declaration was made on behalf of the United States, it couldn't be pulled back, so he wanted to ensure that they had solid information to support their statement that could then become "a catalyst for action."

Influences on United States Darfur Policy

Several events during spring 2004 coincided to sharpen the State Department's resolve to send an independent team to investigate the situation in Darfur. United States policy in Sudan was already of special interest to the Bush administration, and had an important domestic constituency — the evangelical Christian community. Evangelicals had taken an interest in the plight of black Christians in southern Sudan and there was a growing left–right coalition on Darfur. The Bush administration was playing the lead role in brokering a deal to end Sudan's decades-old civil war in the South.

Moreover, the Bush administration was eager to point to its leadership on Sudan policy to demonstrate that they could speak with authority on grave issues of human rights at a time when issues around the treatment of detainees, particularly at Guantánamo and Abu Ghraib, threatened to strip the administration's voice of legitimacy on human rights issues (Craner, 2004).

Importantly, both UN Secretary-General Kofi Annan and the Bush administration used the tenth anniversary of the 1994 genocide in Rwanda to focus their rhetoric on the unfolding crisis in Darfur. Marking the anniversary, Annan delivered an "Action Plan to Prevent Genocide," including a somber warning that reports on the situation in Darfur left him "with a deep sense of foreboding" (Annan, 2004). After largely pursuing quiet diplomacy with Sudan, President Bush (2004) used the occasion to issue a statement condemning the atrocities in Darfur, marking a shift in rhetoric for the administration.

The United States tried to coordinate an international strategy to abate the violence in Darfur at the 2004 UN Commission on Human Rights meeting in Geneva that spring. Represented by Richard S. Williamson, Ambassador for Special Political Affairs, the State Department pushed for an aggressive stance on Darfur, but was ultimately thwarted by a lack of political will in the European Union (EU). After a special session at the Commission to address the situation in Darfur was blocked, Williamson (2004) warned, "ten years from now, the sixtieth Commission on Human Rights will be remembered for one thing and one thing alone: Did we have the courage and strength to take strong action against the 'ethnic cleansing' in Darfur? We will be asked, 'Where were you at the time of the ethnic cleansing?' 'What did you do?'"

In late April, the United States delegation to the Commission on Human Rights proposed a draft resolution condemning the war crimes in Darfur, calling the situation "ethnic cleansing," and appointing a Special Rapporteur on the situation in Darfur. But, on the last day of the Commission meetings, the EU, which had previously joined the United States, backed down in the face of Sudanese pressure. Instead, the EU joined the African Union (AU) and sponsored a weaker resolution that appointed an independent expert, but failed to condemn the crimes against humanity, war crimes, or other violations of international humanitarian law committed by the Sudanese government. Only the United States voted against the resolution.

The United States was exasperated by international inertia, and Craner believed that if the United States could *authoritatively* call it "genocide," it might mobilize European governments to take a more aggressive approach. Craner suggested that Europe's problematically patient approach to conflicts in the Balkans, Rwanda, and Darfur resulted from a willingness to let the violence play out before intervening. To be sure, the United States has its own history of characterizing conflicts as intractable and intervention as futile (see, for example, Power, 2002a), but Craner suggested the Bush administration's Sudan policy revealed a different mindset that he admires, especially in the way Special Envoy Danforth and Special Representative Charles Snyder and Assistant Secretary for African Affairs Walter Kantsteiner pushed the North–South peace negotiations, and the determination with which Secretary Powell engaged the GoS.

Designing the Inquiry

During late winter 2004, Craner and Prosper began discussing methods to obtain better information about the situation in Darfur. With a background in polling, Craner pushed for better human intelligence using an empirical, survey-based method. Prosper, a former prosecutor for the International Criminal Tribunal for Rwanda, recalled how effectively refugee surveys were used to gather information about the conflict in Kosovo, a process that he had worked on creating when he was Special Counsel and Policy Adviser to his predecessor, Ambassador David Scheffer. Both Craner and Prosper realized they were heading into new territory for the State Department. Indeed, never before had investigation teams been sent to the field to survey refugees in order to determine, in a statistically and empirically formulated manner, the nature and scope of a conflict as it was unfolding.

The two approached the problem with a prosecutor's clinical analysis and a poll taker's empirical sensibility, deciding to launch a "limited investigation" by random sample survey of Darfur refugee camps along the Chad border. For Prosper, the investigation into what he repeatedly called a "purely" legal question was valuable because it would remove politics from the determination. Prosper recalled the prevailing attitude as one of, "Let's just get the facts, let's call it what it is, and let's deal with it."

Both Craner and Prosper shared the objective of determining whether genocide had been committed and emphasized its persuasive rhetorical significance. For Prosper, investigating for genocide permitted an answer to a difficult legal question and would allow the use of a mechanism to refer the matter to the United Nations Security Council. Craner, who does not come from a legal background, considered the legal question of genocide to be formalistic, and neither as interesting nor as important as determining the scope of the attacks and the needs of Darfurians. For Craner, investigating genocide provided a useful tool in statecraft, and would help to determine what was happening in Darfur in order to tailor a humanitarian response accordingly.

Although Prosper was concerned that the survey teams ask the right questions and get the information State Department lawyers needed, neither his office nor the Office of Legal Adviser had a hands-on role in constructing the questionnaire. There were meetings between lawyers from the Office of Legal Adviser and the National Security Council prior to the June 23, 2004 meeting that initially brought together State Department and NGO personnel to consider whether establishing this kind of unprecedented investigation was even possible, but once Craner learned what the lawyers needed, he didn't consult them on the questionnaire or on the Atrocities Documentation Team (ADT) process.

Insignificant Political Opposition to the Darfur Genocide Inquiry

Craner and Prosper insist there was little sustained opposition to launching the genocide inquiry. Craner reflected that, "Yes, there were people of rank that were obstacles, but it's really the story of good people … . It's the way things should work … . There should always be people that say, 'Wait a minute, let's take another look at this,' but this is really the story of Secretary Powell and others doing their job right."

From the beginning to the end, the decisions were primarily made within the State Department. "The President felt that Secretary Powell was in the best place to deal with this issue," Prosper suggests. As such, the process was primarily a "State Department-driven operation," although parts of the White House's National Security Council, such as the African Affairs group and the "democracy shop" were also involved. Funding and leadership from USAID, and, in particular, OTI staff, were essential to the success of the ADT. Prosper insists, "There was never resistance, anywhere. And everyone was supportive of us from the highest levels to try to figure out what it was."

Craner, though, does lament that there were some at the State Department who might have tried to claim ignorance of the situation in Darfur if the State Department had taken a different approach, but, at the highest levels, there was no opposition. What little opposition Craner alludes to appears to have come from the African Affairs Bureau and Bureau of International Organization Affairs. Media accounts during the spring and summer of 2004 included speculation that there was opposition within the African Affairs Bureau to publicly declaring genocide in Darfur because of the concern that it would derail the North–South peace talks on which they had worked for years (Snyder, 2004). Craner indicates there may be some truth to those stories, but that ultimately Powell, Grossman, and Snyder believed stability in

Darfur was essential to the success of the North–South peace accords. Craner also suggests Powell, Grossman, and the leadership in African Affairs believed that if the Government of Sudan was committing genocide in Darfur, they could not be trusted in the North–South negotiations.

In the State Department's Bureau for International Organization Affairs, some were concerned that finding genocide would trigger a referral to the International Criminal Court (ICC), a move seen to contribute to the court's legitimacy, against which the Bush administration had steadfastly fought. Craner indicates these early objections were dealt with by making it clear that the ICC was a distant consideration, many steps down the line. Craner himself didn't seem concerned about the potential for ICC referral, since it wouldn't amount to an endorsement of the ICC by the United States.

Craner insists the obstacles were overcome early in process of designing the ADT and that he and Prosper didn't require a political green light to design the inquiry. Craner and the Bureau of Democracy, Human Rights, and Labor (DRL) wanted to know what had happened in the region recently. Up-to-date information, it was thought, would help fashion appropriate responses. For example, if DRL learned that women were targeted for sexual violence, then they could adjust their humanitarian aid to meet specific related needs. DRL hoped to find out if it would be possible for the refugees to return to their land, if they would be able to farm, and if they had retained any cattle.

Both Craner and Prosper say that the Darfur genocide inquiry was viewed positively by the leadership in the State Department, where they described everyone as taking a "let the chips fall where they may" approach to the genocide inquiry and determination. Why did the State Department's Darfur policy appear so unitary when other problems have often elicited a more fragmented response? The answer remains unclear, but appears at least partly due to significant institutional investment in the North–South peace accords as a showcase for United States leadership, and the politically active domestic constituency for intervention in Sudan. Craner emphasizes the administration's commitment to securing the North–South peace agreement, and notes that numerous people inside and outside of government knew about Sudan and were invested in the success of State Department policy there.

Powell's visible leadership on the issue appears to have cleared any internal opposition. Already heavily invested in a successful Sudan policy, Powell was increasingly dismayed by Sudan's complete disregard for international calls to end the violence. Attempting to send the strongest signal to Khartoum, Powell arranged to visit Sudan with Kofi Annan at the end of June to inspect internally displaced persons (IDP) camps. According to

Prosper, Powell was "appalled by what he saw and what was hidden from him [on his visit], and he just really dug into the issue."

Sending the ADT into the Field

The State Department's lack of experience on the ground in Darfur posed a significant problem when the DRL began thinking about sending investigation teams. As Craner recalls, "There weren't many people to turn to with an understanding of the area — it was out in the middle of the desert." Few knew what to expect when they got there. Early on, Craner recognized that the staff at the U.S. Embassy in Chad was too small to conduct the investigations without outside help.

Lacking the staff and expertise required to conduct the investigations, Craner proposed the novel approach of using State Department–NGO hybrid teams, and called in NGOs with investigatory experience and regional knowledge.[2] There was initially some opposition within his Bureau and the rest of the State Department to putting NGOs in such a prominent role. Some at State viewed NGOs with deep skepticism and saw them as reliable critics of (any) State Department policy. Craner, who had himself served as the president of an NGO, viewed them as the best available option.

As the ADT went into the field, Craner relied on a DRL analyst and lawyer, Michael Orona, to work alongside CIJ's Stefanie Frease and address the myriad logistical problems that arose in the field. Craner praised Orona for his solid field judgment and knack for extricating himself from difficult situations.

Craner left the State Department at the end of July 2004, before the ADT investigators returned from Chad. He hadn't, though, found anything unexpected in the ADT data being communicated back from the field prior to his departure. He felt confident that the ADT data would be considered in good faith and that, if it supported a genocide determination, no political calculation would prevent that conclusion.

'Matching Facts to the Law:' Arriving at the Genocide Determination

Craner and Prosper presented the State Department's approach as dispassionate and clinical. The purpose was "to make a pure decision" — a "clean legal and factual analysis" free of "policy considerations." So, as Prosper explains, the key State Department decision-makers gathered all the available information and "analyzed the facts with the breadth of the law in mind — meaning, genocide, crimes against humanity, war crimes .... But after looking at it and looking at it carefully, it became abundantly clear to us that it fit [genocide]."

Once the ADT survey data came back to the State Department, several bureaus analyzed it for evidence of patterns of attack and destruction as well as elements of genocide. The ADT data was compiled into the now-public State Department report "Documenting Atrocities in Darfur," (Report) and communicated to Secretary Powell. With the data and the UN Convention on the Prevention and Punishment of Genocide (Genocide Convention) in hand, Powell telephoned Prosper at home on a Saturday night to walk through the facts and the law. The two analyzed the facts summarized in the Report and those they had already collected. As Prosper recalls, "The big issue inside the State Department during that period was the question of intent, [and for] that we had to rely [on information from] outside of the Report." Powell and Prosper had a long conversation about the actions of the government in Khartoum: "How they created these militias; they had the ability to rein them in and then did not; they acted in concert with the *Janjaweed* ... in attacking these villages ... the aerial bombardment and then *Janjaweed* would come in; and then the fact that the Government of Sudan would block humanitarian assistance to people in need." It was enough, Prosper says, "to form the intent."

The following day, Secretary Powell convened a conference call with his Chief of Staff Larry Wilkerson, Legal Adviser William Taft, IV, Assistant Secretary of International Organization Affairs Kim Holmes, Michael Kosack, who replaced Craner as acting head of DRL, Assistant Secretary of the African Affairs Bureau Constance Newman, and Deputy Assistant Secretary of the African Affairs Bureau Michael Ranneberger. The group again went through the facts and law, and the Secretary concluded, based on the available information and the understanding of the Genocide Convention, that genocide had been committed.

Prosper explained the factors that the group considered which pointed to genocide. First, they noted that villages of Africans were being destroyed and neighboring Arab villages were not. Large numbers of men were killed and women raped. Livestock was killed and water polluted. In IDP camps, the GoS was preventing medicines and humanitarian assistance from going in despite persistent international calls for access. Examining these factors, they concluded there was a deliberate targeting of the group with the intent to destroy it.

Prosper recalls the group examining the concepts of unlawful killing, causing of serious bodily and mental harm, and "the real one that got us, ... was the deliberate infliction of conditions of life calculated to destroy the group in whole, or in part." Looking at the IDP camps, Prosper and Powell could not find any "logical explanation for why the Sudan government was preventing humanitarian assistance and medicine" into the camps "other than to destroy the group." The GoS was seen as offering unbelievable excuses, leading Powell to conclude that there was a clearly intentional effort to destroy the people in the camps who were known to be almost exclusively black African.

There was no real opposition among the group to the genocide determination. Some wanted clarification of the Genocide Convention, but Prosper, who was trial prosecutor for the International Criminal Tribunal for Rwanda case against Jean-Paul Akayesu and secured the first conviction for genocide in an international court, was able to alleviate their concerns.

Prosper's experience as a prosecutor supported his understanding that genocidal intent could be inferred from the evidence as well as proved by express statements. As Prosper explains, Powell and he asked each other, if the GoS was not committing genocide then "what else are they trying to do?" "What else could their intent be but to destroy this group?" First, Powell and Prosper looked at the coordination and collaboration between the GoS and the *Janjaweed*. Then, Powell and Prosper examined how the government acted once they were shown to have knowledge of the perpetrators of violence, the targeting of black African tribes, and the scale of human destruction in Darfur. This part was most convincing. The Government of Sudan "had knowledge across the board. Let's *pretend* that it wasn't coordinated. They knew what was going on and not only did they do nothing to stop it, they intentionally obstructed assistance that would have bettered the situation. So, when you have knowledge, you take no steps to stop it, and then, when people are trying to help, you block the assistance, what else could you want other than for these people to die or to be destroyed."

To Powell the conclusion was clear. In the now well-known testimony before the Senate Foreign Relations Committee on September 9, 2004, Powell announced his determination "that genocide has been committed in Darfur and that the Government of Sudan and the *Janjaweed* bear responsibility — and that genocide may still be occurring" (Powell, 2004b).

Genocide, But No New Action

Yet, Powell followed his first-of-a-kind genocide determination by concluding "no new action is dictated by this determination" (Powell, 2004b). To many, this was a disappointment. But, it should not have come as much of a surprise. In June 2004, in an interview from Sudan, Powell said, "I can assure you that if all of the indicators lined up and said this meets what the treaty test of genocide is then I would have no reluctance to call it that. Now, if it were genocide, we would certainly increase international pressure, but whether we would do more than we are now doing is a question that I can't answer. [Calling it genocide] doesn't open any real new authorities to me, or give me any additional powers or responsibilities that I'm not now executing" (Powell, 2004a).

What did the U.S. Government hope would be accomplished by Powell's genocide determination? Prosper and Powell discussed the question of "what next" during their Saturday night phone call. They agreed that Article VIII of the Genocide Convention offered "a great tool" because it would allow the United States to call on the Security Council to take action that it considers appropriate for the prevention and suppression of acts of genocide. The treaty measure had never been invoked before.

Powell notified Kofi Annan of his intention to refer the matter to the Security Council, and the United States submitted a draft resolution the following day. The amended text, eventually adopted as Security Council Resolution 1564 (2004), called on the Secretary-General to "rapidly establish an international commission of inquiry, which would immediately investigate reports of human rights violations in Darfur, and determine whether acts of genocide had occurred there" (UN Security Council, 2004).

Was this increase in international pressure a legally, morally, or practically adequate response to a determination of genocide? Prosper confines his response to a legal analysis: "Well, this is a debate the international community will have to have in the future. The duty to respond and prevent has yet to be defined. I think what it really means is that you have to use the tools that are acceptable or available to you. It doesn't mean that every country has to launch a military offensive, but I think it ranges from diplomatic to military." As a legal matter, however, the State Department would not have deemed a diplomatic or military response to genocide as required since it does not recognize that the duty to prevent and to punish extends extraterritorially.

Instead, the Bush administration would stick to its self-described strong leadership and diplomatic role — condemning the conduct, pressing for action at the United Nations, and providing humanitarian assistance. Although Prosper believed that a military presence was needed, he suggests U.S. troops wouldn't have been accepted by the African Union. Instead, the United States "tried to empower the African Union" to restore peace. A year after the genocide determination, the African Union had deployed only about six thousand troops to Darfur — less than half the minimum number thought to be required — and they still lacked a United Nations mandate to protect civilians. Sending in American troops may have never been an option. On the campaign trail, candidate Bush told ABC News reporter Sam Donaldson, "I don't like genocide and I don't like ethnic cleansing, but I would not send our troops [to stop them]" (Power, 2002b).

Prosper considers the genocide determination to have mobilized the international community, but laments that "there's a lot more that could have and still could be done." Returning to its rhetorical significance, Prosper notes that the State Department's inquiry and genocide determination "finally got everyone on the same page." Before the ADT, "everyone was dodging the question. All these other countries, no one was taking leadership, no one was taking action. [The State Department] forced the issue, and put it on the Security Council calendar, forced the [UN] Commission of Inquiry investigation, and forced the passage of resolutions" that brought sanctions and peacekeepers to the region, and ultimately led the Security Council to refer the situation in Darfur to the ICC.

Conclusion

The State Department's decision to launch an empirical investigation into genocide and then determine that genocide had occurred — all while the conflict was ongoing — is a remarkable innovation in statecraft, stemming at least in part from the concern among key State Department officials that there must not be another Rwanda. The failure to prevent the Rwandan genocide seems to bear powerfully on thinking about Darfur. As welcome as the "never again" refrain is, the State Department's Darfur policy makes it hard to gauge its reach and impact.

In retrospect, it is clear that the Clinton administration's failure in Rwanda wasn't due to poor information, but to a lack of political will (Ferroggiaro, 2004; Power, 2004, pp. 373–384, 508–516). In the past, American leaders felt no pressure to act from the electorate. Power (2002a) explains, "Genocide in distant lands has not captivated senators, congressional caucuses, Washington lobbyists, [or] elite opinion to stop genocide, [which] has thus been repeatedly lost in the realm of domestic politics... . [So] officials at all levels of governments calculated that the political costs of getting involved in stopping genocide far exceeded the costs of remaining uninvolved" (pp. 508–509).

Was this calculus significantly different with Darfur? Craner and Prosper acknowledge the significance of having a powerful bipartisan domestic constituency interested and informed about the situation in Sudan. They suggest that poor information wasn't a barrier to action with respect to Darfur, and that the genocide determination was a tool to galvanize a political response. Was the ADT essential to the genocide determination? The answer appears to be *yes*. In Powell's statement to the Senate Foreign Relations Committee, he stated that the genocide determination derived from the ADT investigation and was supported by other information gathered by the State Department. Prosper suggests proof of genocidal intent, the key legal dispute within the State Department at the time, ultimately came from information other than the ADT data. But, even on the question of genocidal intent, the ADT data contributed significantly to State Department officials' evolving understanding of the GoS's role in the attacks. Although the ADT data may not have been considered the best proof of genocidal intent, it undoubtedly helped support the finding: 33 percent of interviewees heard racial epithets during their attack and black Africans were the overwhelming targets of violence while Arab villagers were spared. Having a wealth of trusted, internally verified facts about the scope and nature of the violence appears to have given the State Department the confidence it needed to make an authoritative statement about the genocide.

It isn't clear whether the investigation of Darfur atrocities and ultimate finding of genocide will make such an approach by the State Department more likely in future crises. Craner though, is enthusiastic about the potential use of social science methods to form State Department policy regarding ethnic conflict in the future. He is interested in developing a nongovernmental network of investigators, analysts, logisticians, and other experts ready for rapid deployment as crises arise. Such a mechanism is cheap by government standards; Craner estimates the ADT only cost "several hundred thousand dollars." As the ADT showed, this approach can generate detailed, up-to-date information about situations that critically demand a response. What policymakers do with that information is another question.

Acknowledgment

I thank Lorne Craner and Pierre-Richard Prosper for generously discussing the State Department's determination of genocide. For many helpful comments and suggestions, I am grateful to Nina Bang-Jensen, Edgar Chen, David Bosco, Stefanie Frease, Shaoli Sarkar, Anna Workman, Martin Mennecke, Eric Markusen, and Samuel Totten.

References

Annan, Kofi (2004). "Action Plan to Prevent Genocide," April 7, 2004. Available at: http://www2.unog.ch/news2/documents/newsen/sg04003e.htm

Bush, George W. (2004). "President Condemns Atrocities in Sudan." Statement by the President. Available at: http://www.whitehouse.gov/news/releases/2004/04/20040407-2.html

Craner, Lorne (2004). Testimony by Assistant Secretary Lorne Craner at a Hearing of the Committee on International Relations, U.S. House of Representatives, July 7, 2004. Available at: http://wwwc.house.gov/international_relations/108/cra070704.htm

Egeland, Jan (2004). "Sudan Envoy Warns of Ethnic Cleansing as Security Council Calls for Ceasefire," April 2, 2004. Available at: http://www.un.org/apps/news/storyAr.asp?NewsID=10307&Cr=sudan&Cr1=

Ferroggiaro, William (2004). "The U.S. and the Genocide in Rwanda 1994: Information, Intelligence and the U.S. Response," March 24, 2004. Available at: http://www.gwu.edu/~nsarchiv/NSAEBB/NSAEBB117/

Igiri, Cheryl O., and Lyman, Princeton N. (2004). "Giving Meaning to 'Never Again': Seeking an Effective Response to the Crisis in Darfur and Beyond." *CSR* No. 5, September 2004. Available at: www.ciaonet.org/wps/igc01/igc01_front.pdf

Natsios, Andrew (2004). Presentation to Joint United Nations–United States–European Union Donor Consultations on Darfur, Geneva, Switzerland, June 3, 2004. Available at: http://www.usaid.gov/press/releases/2004/pr040603_1.html

Powell, Colin L. (2004a). Interview on National Public Radio with Michele Norris, June 30, 2004. Transcript available at: http://www.state.gov/secretary/former/powell/remarks/34053.htm

Powell, Colin L. (2004b). "The Crisis in Darfur." Testimony before the Senate Foreign Relations Committee, September 9, 2004. Available at: http://www.state.gov/secretary/former/powell/remarks/36042.htm

Power, Samantha (2002a). *"A Problem from Hell:" America and the Age of Genocide.* New York: Basic Books.

Power, Samantha (2002b). "Genocide and America." *The New York Review of Books*, 49(4): n.p.

Prosper, Pierre-Richard (2004). Testimony before U.S. House of Representatives International Relations Committee, Subcommittee on Africa, June 24, 2004. Available at: http://wwwc.house.gov/international_relations/108/pro062404.htm

Shelley, Christine (1994). Department of State Daily Press Briefing, April 28, 1994. Available at: http://dosfan.lib.uic.edu/ERC/briefing/daily_briefings/1994/9404/940428db.html

Snyder, Charles (2004). "Sudan: Peace Agreement Around the Corner?" Testimony before the House International Relations Committee, Subcommittee on Africa, March 11, 2004. Available at: http://wwwc.house.gov/international_relations/108/sny031104.htm

UN Security Council (2004). United Nations Security Council Resolution 1564 of September 18, 2004. Available at: http://www.un.org/News/Press/docs/2004/sc8191.doc.htm

Williamson, Richard S. (2004). General Statement on Item 3 and 9 on Sudan, 60th Session of the United Nations Commission on Human Rights, April 23, 2004. Available at: http://www.humanrights-usa.net/statements/0423Sudan.htm

Notes

1. Referred to herein as the Atrocities Documentation Team, though that term first officially appeared when the State Department issued its report on September 9, 2004. See *infra*, note 3 and accompanying text.
2. For discussion, see Frease and Bang-Jensen, Chapter 3, this volume.

CHAPTER 8

A New Chapter of Irony:
The Legal Definition of Genocide and the
Implications of Powell's Determination

JERRY FOWLER

Legal scholar Diane Orentlicher once observed that the United Nations Convention on the Prevention and Punishment of the Crime of Genocide (UNCG) "has come to embody the conscience of humanity." She then acidly remarked that the Convention's "moral force is surely ironic" in light of the persistent failure of governments to enforce its terms (Orentlicher, 1999, p. 153). Darfur adds another sad chapter of irony in the Convention's history, given the dramatic incongruity between the sense of urgency that one might expect a plausible case of ongoing genocide to engender and the relatively lackadaisical international political response that actually has unfolded. As it turns out, this irony is embedded in the provisions of the Convention itself. After calling for international cooperation "to liberate mankind from such an odious scourge," the Convention proceeds to define the crime of genocide in terms that, from the perspective of "preventing" or "suppressing" genocide, are problematic. It then offers only the vaguest sense of what should be done when genocide is imminent or actually underway.

'To Liberate Mankind from Such an Odious Scourge'

Though there are examples of mass violence directed against identifiable groups dating back to antiquity, "genocide" as a term and a concept has a quite recent origin. Raphael Lemkin (1944), a Jewish lawyer who fled Poland after the German invasion in 1939, coined the word and introduced it in 1944. He derived it from the Greek for tribe or nation (*geno*) and the Latin for killing (*cide*). By genocide, Lemkin meant "a coordinated plan of different actions aiming at the destruction of essential foundations of the life of national groups, with the aim of annihilating the groups themselves" (p. 79).

In no small part due to the efforts of Lemkin himself, his new word soon gained currency (Power, 2002, pp. 30–85). It was mentioned in the 1945 Nuremberg indictment as a description of war crimes committed by the defendants being tried before the International Military Tribunal (International Military Tribunal, 1945, para. VIII(A)).[2] In December 1946, the General Assembly of the newly created United Nations adopted a resolution that described genocide as "a denial of the right of existence of entire human groups" that "shocks the conscience of mankind" and "affirm[s]" that genocide is "crime under international law" (Resolution 96(I)).

That resolution also set in motion the process that resulted in the adoption of the Genocide Convention on December 9, 1948. The Convention itself is rather a spare document — nineteen articles, of which the last nine are more technical than substantive, dealing with matters such as where states that become parties to the Convention shall deposit their instruments of ratification or accession (with the Secretary-General of the United Nations); how many states must become parties before the Convention comes into force (twenty, a number that was reached in late 1950); and where the original copy of the Convention would be held (in the UN archives).

The Convention's preamble invokes "international law" and "the spirit and aims of the United Nations," as well as the condemnation of genocide "by the civilized world." It echoes the General Assembly's view that international cooperation is necessary to free humanity from the "odious scourge" of genocide. To that end, Article I specifies "genocide, whether committed in time of peace or in time of war, is a crime under international law which [the Contracting Parties] undertake to prevent and to punish."

The heart of the substantive portion of the Convention is Article II, which defines genocide as a matter of international law. The definition has two essential components: specified physical acts (what lawyers would call the *actus reus*) and a particular state of mind (technically, a *mens rea*). The specified acts cannot constitute genocide unless they are committed with the requisite state of mind.

The specified acts are:

1. Killing members of the group.
2. Causing serious bodily or mental harm to members of the group. Deliberately inflicting on the group conditions of life calculated to bring about its physical destruction in whole or in part.
3. Imposing measures intended to prevent births within the group.
4. Forcibly transferring children of the group to another group.

The required state of mind, which distinguishes genocide from any other crime, is the "intent to destroy, in whole or in part, a national, ethnical, racial, or religious group, as such." Thus, merely intending to commit the specified acts is not enough. The perpetrators must also have a "specific" or "special" intent to destroy a protected group in whole or in part (Schabas, 2000, pp. 217–221). Establishing the subjective intent harbored in the minds of perpetrators can present vexing issues of proof, especially when events are unfolding in some inaccessible location. As discussed more fully below, the circumstances surrounding the commission of specific acts can provide evidence of the intent with which those acts are committed.

Several articles flesh out the central idea that genocide is an international crime and, therefore, punishable. Article III explains that not only genocide itself can be punished, but also "conspiracy to commit genocide, direct and public incitement to commit genocide, attempt to commit genocide, and complicity in genocide." According to Article IV, perpetrators are subject to punishment without regard to their status as "constitutionally responsible rulers" or holders of some other public office. In Article V, the parties "undertake" to pass whatever domestic legislation might be necessary to give effect to the terms of the Convention, specifically emphasizing punishment for genocide and the other crimes listed in Article III. For good measure, Article VI adds an unspecified "international penal tribunal"[3] as a possible venue for trying those accused of genocide, in addition to courts in the territory where the criminal acts were committed.[4] Article VII addresses the extradition of accused perpetrators from one country in order to stand trial in another.

As terse as the provisions related to punishment of genocide are, the Convention's other avowed goal — that of genocide prevention — gets even shorter shrift. Article VIII merely states that a party to the Convention "*may* call upon the competent organs of the United Nations to take such action under the Charter of the United Nations as they consider appropriate for the prevention and suppression of acts of genocide" (emphasis added). Tossing the ball in the UN's court, in other words, is permitted, but not required.

No other article refers to prevention, except for Article I's rather ambiguous statement that parties to the Convention "undertake to prevent" genocide. Exactly what obligation this language imposes is not clear. Particularly opaque is whether the undertaking to prevent genocide is directed at a state's own territory or territory under its control or whether it imposes some duty on parties to act wherever in the world genocide might be threatened or occur. Some scholars have asserted the latter (e.g., Toope, 2000, pp. 192–193). Yet the language of the Convention does not provide any indication that such an extensive obligation was contemplated. Indeed, it would be quite bizarre to think that the drafters intended in 1948 to make intervention in the internal affairs of other states obligatory for individual states or groups of states (through the broad interpretation of Article I), while recourse to the United Nations is merely optional (under the plain terms of Article VIII). Such a scheme diverges wildly from the structure for maintaining international peace and security established just three years earlier with the adoption of the UN Charter and the creation of the United Nations itself. And in the almost six decades since adoption of the Genocide Convention, there is scant evidence of state practice evincing a sense of obligation to prevent or suppress genocide in other countries pursuant to Article I.

When Bosnia argued to the International Court of Justice that all parties to the Convention had a duty under Article I to prevent genocide against it and its citizens, the ad hoc judge appointed by Bosnia itself could only observe, rather morosely, that "[t]he limited reaction of the parties to the Genocide Convention in relation [to past episodes of apparent genocide] may represent a practice suggesting the permissibility of inactivity" (International Court of Justice, 1993, para. 115). Likewise, the internal State Department memorandum to U.S. Secretary of State Warren Christopher that recommended in May 1994 that the United States begin to use the word "genocide" in relation to Rwanda noted that such a move "would not have any particular legal consequences" (United States Department of State, 1994).

Is, Is Not

The UN Genocide Convention provided the framework within which U.S. Secretary of State Colin Powell and the U.S. Government considered in mid-2004 the question of whether genocide was occurring in Darfur. Applying Article II's legal definition to the facts gathered by the Atrocities Documentation Team (ADT) and from other sources, they concluded that genocide had been committed and that the Government of Sudan and its militia allies — the so-called "*Janjaweed*" — were responsible (Powell, 2004a).

In announcing his determination, Secretary Powell pointed to murder, rape, and other physical violence committed against members of non-Arab ethnic groups. This violence corresponded with the acts specified in Article II(a) and (b) of the Convention — killing members of a group and causing serious bodily or mental harm to them. He also pointed to the destruction of foodstuffs and other means of survival of the targeted groups, coupled with obstruction by the Sudanese Government of the humanitarian assistance that the victims needed in order to survive. This conduct, which itself inflicted a large number of deaths on the targeted population in addition to those who perished from direct violence, corresponded with Article II(c) — deliberately inflicting conditions of life calculated to bring about a group's physical destruction, in whole or in part.

As for the "intent to destroy" required by Article II, Secretary Powell concluded that intent could be inferred from the Sudanese Government's deliberate conduct. Inferring intent from conduct in the absence of direct evidence is widely accepted. The International Criminal Tribunal for Rwanda (ICTR), for example, has listed a number of circumstances that are relevant to determining "intent to destroy," many of which are present in the case of Darfur: "The general context of the perpetration of other culpable acts systematically directed against that same group"; "the scale of atrocities committed"; the "general nature" of the atrocities; deliberately and systematically targeting members of some groups but not others; attacks on (or perceived by the perpetrators to be attacks on) "the foundation of the group"; "the use of derogatory language toward members of the targeted group"; "the systematic manner of killing"; and "the relative proportionate scale of the actual or attempted destruction of a group" (International Criminal Tribunal for Rwanda, 1998, paras. 523–524; International Criminal Tribunal for Rwanda, 2000, para. 166).

In this regard, Secretary Powell's testimony to the Senate Foreign Relations Committee emphasized that the scale and scope of the murder and rape of civilians as well as the actions of the Sudanese military and its militia allies were "a coordinated effort, not just random violence" (Powell, 2004b, p. 4). Additionally, in the report released along with the testimony, the ADT's investigation documented substantial use of racial epithets and derogatory language directed against members of non-Arab ethnic groups in conjunction with violence (United States Department of State, 2004, p. 4). Secretary Powell also noted Khartoum's failure to cease and desist from the attacks on the non-Arab groups and its continued obstruction of humanitarian aid even after having been repeatedly put on notice by other governments and the United Nations.

Invoking Article VIII of the Convention, Secretary Powell called upon the United Nations to undertake its own investigation. Thus, the only specific outcome of the genocide determination was the September 18 passage by the UN Security Council of Resolution 1564, which requested that the Secretary General appoint an International Commission of Inquiry to look into whether acts of genocide had, in fact, occurred and to identify perpetrators of violations of international humanitarian and human rights law. While awaiting the Commission's report, the Council decided "to remain seized of the matter."

At the end of January 2005, the Commission issued its report, which documented the Sudanese Government's role in organizing, arming, and training the *Janjaweed* militia. Page after page of the voluminous report laid responsibility for serious violations of international humanitarian and human rights law at the government's doorstep. The Commission concluded that the government and its allies bore primary responsibility for massive violence against civilians that had a pronounced ethnic dimension. Addressing the particular terms of the Genocide Convention, the Commission noted that its investigation

> collected substantial and reliable material which tends to show the occurrence of systematic killing of civilians belonging to particular tribes, of large-scale [actions] causing of serious bodily or mental harm to members of the population belonging to certain tribes, and of massive and deliberate infliction on those tribes of conditions of life bringing about their physical destruction in whole or in part (for example, by systematically destroying their villages and crops, by expelling them from their homes, and by looting their cattle). (International Commission of Inquiry, 2005, para. 507)

The Commission believed that this evidence could establish the physical acts enumerated in Article II(a) to (c) (International Commission of Inquiry, 2005, para. 518).[5]

But then the Commission explicitly "conclude[d] that the Government of Sudan has not pursued a policy of genocide" based on the absence of the required "intent to destroy." (International Commission of Inquiry, 2005).[6] Although the Commission acknowledged that the scale of atrocities, the systematic nature of the atrocities and racially motivated statements by perpetrators indicated genocidal intent, it asserted that "other more indicative elements" pointed to a lack of intent. The Commission identified three elements supposed to be "more indicative." (International Commission of Inquiry, 2005, para. 513).

First, in some unspecified number of villages, the attackers "refrained from exterminating the whole population" (ICI, 2005). As evidence, the Commission referred to one group of villages in which the Government Commissioner and the leader of the Arab militias executed about two

hundred twenty-seven people out of some twelve hundred who were captured after the attack. Apparently, fifteen of the executed were on a written list brought by the perpetrators, seven were village leaders (*omdas*),
and two hundred five were accused of being rebels. The Commission's reference to the fact that the perpetrators did not "exterminat[e] the *whole*
population" is puzzling. The plain language of the Convention includes an
intent to destroy a group "in part." The Commission itself had explained
in a previous paragraph that international case law establishes that "the
intent to destroy a group 'in part' requires the intention to destroy a 'considerable number of individuals' or 'a substantial part,' but not necessarily a 'very important part of the group'" (International Commission of
Inquiry, 2005, para. 492). The Commission failed to offer any reason why
two hundred twenty-seven out of twelve hundred is neither a "considerable number of individuals" (in relation to that sample) nor "a substantial part" of that sample, especially when the community leadership was
particularly targeted. Moreover, it seems to take at face value the perpetrators' reported assertion that the two hundred five murdered villagers
were rebels, leading the Committee to distinguish between "the intent …
to destroy an ethnic group as such" and "the intention to murder all those
men they considered to be rebels." Yet, on just the previous page, the Commission had included a number of quotes in which the perpetrators used
ethnic identity, racial epithets, and terms like *Torabora* (slang for *rebels*)
interchangeably (International Commission of Inquiry, 2005, n. 189).[7] The
whole point of the government's campaign against the civilian population of the non-Arab ethnic groups was equating ethnicity with rebellion,
rendering it nonsensical to distinguish an intent to destroy those ethnic
groups from an intent to murder rebels. The targets were, by the Sudanese
Government's apparent definition, one and the same.[8]

The second element cited by the Commission as indicating a lack of
genocidal intent is that the Sudanese Government collects survivors of
destroyed villages in camps for internally displaced persons (IDPs), where
it "generally allows humanitarian organizations to help the population
… by providing food, clean water, medicines, and logistical assistance"
(International Commission of Inquiry, 2005, para. 515). This element begs
the question of whether the direct violence (i.e., murdering and raping)
was of sufficient scale to evince the intent to destroy the targeted groups
"in part," even though there are survivors who are not murdered outright. And the Commission offers no rationale why this element would
be more indicative of intent than the scale and systematic nature of direct
violence. It also skirts the issues of government obstacles to humanitarian
aid, which were reduced but not eliminated only as a result of concerted
international pressure in mid-2004; continuing elevated mortality rates in

these camps and continuing attacks (meaning murder and rape) against those who venture out of the camps in search of essentials of life such as firewood, water, or food.

The third element identified by the Commission is that some unspecified number of villages with a mixed ethnic composition had not been attacked at the time the Commission was undertaking its investigation. It is difficult to know what to make of this assertion as the Commission makes no effort to contextualize it. For example, it does not quantify the number of untouched villages in relation to the number of villages destroyed, or by relating the number of inhabitants of such villages to the number of civilians who were subject to murder, rape, or displacement. As important, previously unharmed villages were being attacked and destroyed *during* the time that the Commission was researching and writing its report (Steidle, 2005).[9]

The Commission's final paragraph of analysis regarding intent is perhaps the most difficult to fathom. It recounts a single anecdote from "a reliable source" in which one man was not killed when "attackers" (there is no identification of the attackers) took two hundred camels from him. By contrast, the man's younger brother resisted the theft of his one camel and was shot dead. "Clearly," the Commission concluded, "in this instance the special intent to kill a member of a group to *destroy the group as such* was lacking, the murder being only motivated by the desire to appropriate cattle belonging to the inhabitants of the village" (International Commission of Inquiry, 2005, para. 517). Perhaps the requisite intent was indeed missing in that one instance. But the relationship of that one instance to the overall situation — in which "pillaging and destruction ... appears to have been directed to bring about the destruction of the livelihoods and means of survival of" the targeted populations (International Commission of Inquiry, 2005, para. 638) — is a mystery.

Weighing the Evidence

Although Secretary Powell and the Commission operated from a largely similar factual base, they reached diametrically opposite conclusions on the question of genocide. One explanation for this may be an issue that neither addressed explicitly — the weight of evidence necessary to reach a conclusion. In these circumstances, how much evidence of genocidal intent, in terms of quality and credibility, is necessary relative to evidence of a lack of intent?

The Commission hinted that it was applying an extremely high standard in assessing the evidence. "Courts and other bodies charged with establishing whether genocide has occurred," the Commission noted, "must, however, be very careful in the determination of subjective intent" (International Commission of Inquiry, 2005, para. 503). It then approvingly quoted the International Criminal Tribunal for the former Yugoslavia for the proposition that "[c]onvictions for genocide can be entered only where intent has been unequivocally established" (International Commission of Inquiry, 2005, para. 503). In essence, the Commission adopted for itself the standard that intent must be shown "beyond reasonable doubt" — the weight of evidence necessary to convict an individual in a criminal trial (Rome Statute, Article 66.3). This is the most exacting burden imaginable, an understandable burden for a prosecutor to bear when a court is deciding the life or liberty of an individual.

Viewed in the context of this burden, the Commission's analysis on the issue of genocidal intent is less mysterious. The three "elements" it cites, though not particularly compelling, do cast some doubt as to the existence of a genocidal intent on the part of the Sudanese Government. One might well conclude that the evidence of genocidal intent that is adduced in the Commission's report, though quite strong, does not establish such intent "beyond reasonable doubt."

But this standard is clearly wrong under these circumstances. The Commission was not a court of law, nor was it adjudicating the fate of individual defendants. The liberty of an accused defendant did not turn on its decision. Quite to the contrary, the Commission was only called upon to make a threshold finding on the basis of which the UN Security Council would decide whether to take additional action, including referring the situation to the International Criminal Court (ICC) for a full-fledged criminal investigation.

A review of the ICC Statute makes clear the Commission's error in applying the "beyond reasonable doubt" standard. The Statute contemplates several stages through which a case proceeds, each stage requiring that a separate weight of evidence be met. When a situation is referred to the ICC, the Prosecutor is required to initiate an investigation unless "there is *no reasonable basis* to proceed" (Art. 53.1) (emphasis added). Having conducted an investigation, the Prosecutor may seek an arrest warrant if he/she can establish *"reasonable grounds to believe* that the person has committed a crime within the jurisdiction of the Court" (Art. 58) (emphasis added). The Court next is called upon to confirm the charges, which it will do if the Prosecutor offers "sufficient evidence to establish *substantial grounds to believe* that the person committed the crime charged" (Art. 61) (emphasis added). Finally, at trial, an individual can only be convicted if the Court is "convinced of the guilt of the accused *beyond reasonable doubt"* (Art. 66.3) (emphasis added).

Between "no reasonable basis to proceed" and "beyond reasonable doubt" lies a continuum in which the required weight of evidence steadily, and appropriately, mounts as the process moves forward. To eliminate that continuum and require a Prosecutor to establish guilt beyond a reasonable doubt *as a condition* of launching an investigation would be nonsensical. Yet that is the standard of proof apparently applied by the Commission, in spite of the fact that its investigation was prefatory to any judicial action. The Commission's application of this standard is all the more erroneous in light of the constraints placed upon it by the amount of time available[10] as well as the continued commission of the very crimes it was supposed to investigate. It was not in any conceivable position to reach a conclusion "beyond reasonable doubt" on an issue as complex and problematic as genocidal intent.

Secretary Powell did not articulate what weight of evidence he looked for in making his determination. But the tenor of his analysis, which emphasized the necessarily limited nature of the ADT investigation and other information available, suggests that he was, in essence, asserting a *reasonable basis* for concluding that the Sudanese Government and its *Jan-jaweed* allies had committed genocide. The additional facts established by the Commission confirmed the existence of that reasonable basis.

Politics, Not Law

If a determination of genocide is to be a predicate for further action — whether the launching of a judicial investigation or the launching of humanitarian intervention or anything else — the weight of evidence necessary for supporting that finding cannot be "beyond reasonable doubt." That level of evidence will simply not be available until those in danger are long dead. Commissions or diplomats or politicians can take endless refuge behind every fig leaf of doubt. Outside of a formal judicial process, it only makes sense to speak of a reasonable basis to believe that genocide is occurring or threatened.

But the ultimate irony of the Genocide Convention is that, when it comes to "preventing" or "suppressing" genocide, a determination of genocide does not trigger any form of action whatsoever. If this was not already clear from the Convention's plain language, it was made starkly so by Secretary Powell's assertion on September 9, 2004 that "no new action is dictated by this determination" (Powell, 2004a, p. 5). Secretary Powell's affirmative determination and the Commission's negative determination had the same effect. The Genocide Convention, for all its supposed moral force, in actuality contributes little to prevention and suppression.

Secretary Powell's request to the United Nations, pursuant to the permissive provisions of Article VIII, to launch an investigation was made "with a view to ensuring accountability," that is, punishment. Yet punishment is not the same as prevention or suppression. It inevitably occurs, if at all, after the time for preventing or suppressing has passed. One may argue that a real enough threat of punishment may have a deterrent effect powerful enough to stop ongoing acts of genocide or prevent imminent acts. But that argument is purely theoretical and the continued deterioration of the situation in Darfur months after the Security Council referred the situation to the ICC suggests that the theory may be faulty.

Secretary Powell's request under Article VIII, Security Council Resolution 1564, the Commission's investigation, the Commission's analysis of genocidal intent, all were couched in the language of law drawn from the Genocide Convention and other legal instruments. But in a very real sense, the whole process was a burlesque of law. Essentially everything documented by the Commission was not only knowable, but actually known months and months before the Commission was even formed. Even as the Commission was conducting its investigation, the Government of Sudan was continuing to perpetrate the very crimes that the Commission was analyzing. During the whole time that the basic facts have been known, and even since the Commission released its report, no effective action has been taken by the so-called "international community" actually to stop the killing and the rape. It is as though one man is clubbing another on a street corner while bystanders respond with a prolonged reflection on whether the incident is premeditated murder or simple assault or even self-defense. Meanwhile, the crime continues.

Secretary Powell, near the end of his testimony in September 2004, told the Senate committee that "[w]e have been doing everything we can to get the Sudanese Government to act responsibly." He certainly deserves credit for going out of his way to identify himself with a difficult issue, and there are many officials in the State Department and elsewhere in the U.S. Government who have been working diligently on Darfur. But the definition of "everything we can" ultimately is a political question, not a legal one. And effective prevention and suppression of "genocide" — or other forms of mass atrocities against civilian populations — will not be through a sense of obligation under international law, but as the result of political pressure on governments by their citizens. As Samantha Power (2002) has argued, politicians will act to stop mass killing when the political cost of inaction outweighs the risk of acting (Power, 2002, pp. 510–511).

In preparation for the 2005 World Summit, held to mark the sixtieth anniversary of the United Nations, a draft General Assembly resolution was circulated that would have recognized an "*obligation*" of United Nations members to use various peaceful means "to help protect populations from genocide, war crimes, ethnic cleansing, and crimes against humanity." The draft also would have recognized a "shared *responsibility*" to take collective coercive action under the UN Charter if peaceful means fail and national authorities are "unwilling or unable to protect their populations."

In the end, the first passage was watered down to acknowledge a "responsibility" to use "appropriate diplomatic, humanitarian, and other peaceful means." The second passage jettisoned the notion of a responsibility to act and replaced it with the statement that "we are prepared to take collective action ... on a case-by-case basis ... should peaceful means be inadequate and national authorities are manifestly failing to protect their populations from genocide, war crimes, ethnic cleansing, and crimes against humanity." Being "prepared" to do something case-by-case is, in fact, consistent with actually *not* doing anything from case-to-case.

It may well be that the final language approved by the UN General Assembly represents a normative advance. It is certainly more explicit than anything in the Genocide Convention. It also broadens the circumstances in which action might be taken beyond the narrow category of genocide by adding war crimes, ethnic cleansing, and crimes against humanity, which might forestall endless arguments about the complex and problematic notion of genocidal intent. But the final language underscores that the prevention and suppression of genocide and other mass atrocities will never be accomplished by the international community or members of that community through a sense of legal obligation. It will happen, if at all, as a result of political or practical necessity. Only by recognizing and acting on this reality is there hope for ending the heartbreaking irony of a universally condemned crime that is allowed to transpire in broad daylight.

References

International Commission of Inquiry (2005). *Report of the International Commission of Inquiry on Darfur to the United Nations Secretary-General*. Geneva: United Nations.

International Court of Justice (1993). *Application of the Convention on the Prevention and Punishment of the Crime of Genocide (Bosnia and Herzegovina v. Yugoslavia (Serbia and Montenegro)), Further Requests for the Indication of Provisional Measures*. Separate Opinion of Judge Elihu Lauterpacht.

International Criminal Tribunal for Rwanda (2000). *Prosecutor v. Musema*. Judgment and Sentence.

International Criminal Tribunal for Rwanda (1998). *Prosecutor v. Akayesu*. Judgment and Sentence.

International Military Tribunal (1945). *United States of America et al. v. Hermann Goering et al.* Indictment (available at: http://www.yale.edu/lawweb/avalon/imt/proc/count.htm).

Lemkin, Raphael (1944). *Axis Rule in Occupied Europe: Laws of Occupation; Analysis of Government; Proposals for Redress*. Washington, D.C.: Carnegie Endowment for International Peace.

Orentlicher, Diane (1999). "Genocide," pp. 153-57. In Roy Gutman & David Rieff (Eds.) *Crimes of War*. New York: W.W. Norton.

Powell, Colin (2004a). *The Crisis in Darfur: Written Remarks Before the Senate Foreign Relations Committee*. September 9, 2004 (available at: http://www.state.gov/secretary/former/powell/remarks/36032.htm).

Powell, Colin (2004b). *The Crisis in Darfur: [Oral] Testimony Before the Senate Foreign Relations Committee*. September 9, 2004 (available at: http://www.state.gov/secretary/former/powell/remarks/36042.htm).

Power, Samantha (2002). *"A Problem from Hell:" America and the Age of Genocide.* New York: Basic Books.

Rome Statute of the International Criminal Court (1998). (available at: http://www.icc-cpi. int/library/about/officialjournal/Rome_Statute_120704-EN.pdf).

Schabas, W. (2000). *Genocide in International Law: The Crime of Crimes.* Cambridge, U.K.: Cambridge University Press.

Steidle, Brian (2005). "In Darfur, My Camera Was Not Enough." *The Washington Post*, March 2, p. B2 (available at: http://www.ushmm.org/conscience/alert/darfur/steidle).

Toope, Stephen J. (2000). "Does International Law Impose a Duty upon the UN to Prevent Genocide?" *McGill Law Journal*, 46(1): 187-94.

United Nations (1948). *Convention on Prevention and Punishment of the Crime of Genocide* (available at: http://www.unhchr.ch/html/menu3/b/p_genoci.htm).

United Nations General Assembly (2005). Resolution 60/1. UN Doc. A/Res/60/1.

United Nations General Assembly (1946). Resolution 96(I) (available at: http://www.un.org/ documents/ga/res/1/ares1.htm).

United States Department of State (2004). *Documenting Atrocities in Darfur.* Washington, D.C.: Bureau of Democracy, Human Rights and Labor and Bureau of Intelligence and Research (available at: http://www.state.gov/g/drl/rls/36028.htm).

United States Department of State (1994). *Action Memorandum: Has Genocide Occurred in Rwanda?* Washington, D.C. (available at: http://www.gwu.edu/%7Ensarchiv/NSAEBB/ NSAEBB53/rw052194.pdf).

Notes

1. The views expressed are those of the author and not necessarily those of the Committee on Conscience or the United States Holocaust Memorial Museum.

2. The four counts in the indictment charged the defendants with crimes against the peace, war crimes, crimes against humanity, and conspiracy to commit the other crimes.

3. This idea came to fruition in July 2002 with the creation of the International Criminal Court. By January 2006, 100 countries had become members of the court. Neither the United States nor Sudan is a member of the Court.

4. It is now widely, though not unanimously, accepted as a matter of customary international law that genocide is subject to "universal jurisdiction," meaning that the crime can be adjudicated in any national court without regard to territorial or other connections (Schabas, 1999, pp. 353–368).

5. The Commission also addressed the issue of whether the targeted "tribal" groups are of the type ("national, ethnical, racial or religious") protected by the Genocide Convention and concluded that they are (International Commission of Inquiry, 2005, paras. 508–512). This is a more complicated question than might first appear (see, e.g., Schabas, 2000, pp. 109–114), but does not ultimately seem to be an issue with regard to Darfur.

6. At the same time, the Commission conceded that individuals, including government officials, may, in fact, have acted with genocidal intent (para. 520) begging the difficult question of how many government officials must harbor such intent before it is attributed to the state itself.

7. "Epithets that eyewitnesses or victims reported to the Commission included the following: 'This is your end. The Government armed me.' 'You are Massalit (a non-Arab ethnic group), why do you come here, why do you take our grass? You will not take anything today.' 'You will not stay in this country.' 'Destroy the *Torabora*.' 'You are Zhagawa tribes [a non-Arab ethnic group], you are slaves.'"

8. The Commission, as well as the State Department's ADT, found little or no evidence of rebel activity in villages that were attacked by the Sudanese Government and its militia allies.

9. One of the pictures brought back from Darfur by Brian Steidle, a former U.S. Marine who served on the African Union monitoring team, is of the body of a boy who looks about two years old, killed when his village was attacked. The date stamp on the photo is 2005/01/15, ten days before the Commission submitted its report to the Secretary General.

10. The Secretary-General requested that the Commission report back to him within three months of its creation (International Commission of Inquiry, 2005, para. 1).

CHAPTER **9**

Prosecuting Gender Crimes Committed in Darfur: Holding Leaders Accountable for Sexual Violence

KELLY DAWN ASKIN

Introduction

Sex crimes have a devastating impact far beyond the individuals physically violated by the assaults — the assaults destroy lives, families, communities, and associated groups. Not only do those who survive the violence suffer an attack committed against the most intimate, sacred parts of their bodies, but they also are (especially if the crime committed against them is reported to authorities or becomes known) forced to endure additional psychological, familial, social, cultural, legal, and religious implications, both on themselves and on others. No other form of violence has such a broad-reaching, adverse impact on the victim and associated groups. Vile acts of, for example, amputating limbs, beheading, and torture instill horror, but the crimes do not routinely cast stigmas or impact marriageability.

To intensify fear and humiliation, rapes in many violent conflicts are committed publicly and by more than one assailant. Women's reproductive capacity — including their potential to bear children for the victims or the victimizers' groups — is one of numerous reasons females are singled out for sexual assault. Discriminatory laws, customs, and practices regulating female sexual activity/sexual purity impose additional harms, instead of protections. More detrimental consequences of sexual violence, such as HIV/AIDS and other contagious sexually transmitted diseases or infections, and damage to the reproductive system, are also common. Consequently, the shame and stigma are wrongly imputed to the victim/family of sex crimes. The historical practice of criminal justice systems (police, prosecutors, judges, legislators) marginalizing or ignoring rape crimes, or worse, revictimizing the victims; the sheer terror that threats of the crime evoke; the severe medical and reproductive repercussions; and the simple fact that for countless cowardly combatants, unlawfully attacking an unarmed woman or girl and raping her is more "attractive" than legitimately attacking an armed soldier/militia, are some of the reasons that sexual violence has become such an effective and potent instrument of war and vehicle of terror and destruction.

Rape and other forms of sexual violence have been prominent features of attacks committed by Government of Sudan (GoS) forces and their *Janjaweed* proxy against non-Arabs in all three states of Darfur. In fact, it is difficult to find a comprehensive report on the most serious crimes committed in Darfur that does not include sex crimes. Murder, rape, pillage, forced displacement, and razing of villages are part and parcel of ground attacks. If a village attack involves either GoS forces or their *Janjaweed* puppets and collaborators on the ground, rape virtually always forms part of the attack. Even in instances when the primary purpose of a particular attack is not to directly kill or displace civilians, but instead, for example, to steal their cattle, rape still routinely occurs. And when the primary purpose of an attack is to inflict maximum harm on the civilians and drive survivors into the desert and out of the territory, sex crimes are particularly rampant and vicious.[1]

A multitude of reports on crimes committed in Darfur have been published over the past two years, and analogous to other armed conflicts around the world, these reports confirm that sexual violence is committed both strategically and opportunistically in Darfur.[2] Opportunistic rapes are committed because the atmosphere of war — and the violence, lawlessness, chaos, and hatred it produces — creates the opportunity. Random rapes cause as much fear and trauma as the orchestrated crimes, sometimes more because of their unpredictability. Once it becomes clear that superiors do not disapprove of sexual violence, the opportunistic rapes typically then become more public, more frequent, and more violent, growing indistinguishable from and becoming part of the organized rapes committed at least in part to inflict widespread terror and harm on the targeted group.

Even if it cannot be proved that rape was officially encouraged or initially intended, when the crimes become well known and superiors fail to disapprove of the crimes and/or acquiesce and tolerate the abuse, it signals tacit approval. And the fact is that the entire world was informed repeatedly about the rapes in Darfur. Undoubtedly, the political and military leaders knew of them and their silence demonstrated official tolerance and even encouragement. By the time the government expressed purported outrage of the rapes, they had been raging unabated for some two years, hundreds of thousands had been killed, millions were displaced, and Darfur was in shambles as a result of the scorched earth policy of the GoS, with the conditions of life intentionally inflicted upon the black Darfuris so dire that women and girls have been forced to knowingly risk rape by venturing outside internally displaced persons (IDPs) camps for food and firewood in order to try to survive inside the camps.

Historical Treatment of Wartime Rape in Law and Society

Since recorded wartime history, rape has been a common characteristic of armed conflict. From Viking invasions to the Crusades to the First and Second World Wars, and the hundreds of international and noninternational armed conflicts in between, there is a litany of reports of rape and other sexual atrocities committed during the course of the conflicts. The literature is so replete with depictions of rape during war that it is exceptional to read in detail about one (war) without reading about the other (rape). Yet, until relatively recently, most reports depicted sexual assault as an inevitable consequence of war — a regrettable by-product of war or simply as a common feature of war, not as a serious crime, much less a means of attack, which could, in fact, significantly and dramatically impact the war.

Beginning in the Middle Ages, the customs of war gradually treated rape as a war crime, and not the legitimate right of a victor as part of the so-called spoils of war, as had been largely accepted until around the 1400s. For centuries, rape was considered primarily a crime committed against a man's property. By the end of the nineteenth century, wartime rape was widely criminalized, but seldom punished. Even by the mid-twentieth century, rape was regarded principally as a crime against honor or dignity, not a crime of violence.[3] And there is little indication that it was then considered as bad as — or worse than — death.

In contemporary laws, sexual violence is a crime under both customary laws and codified laws. More recently, the 1949 Fourth Geneva Convention and the 1977 Additional Protocols to the Geneva Conventions explicitly forbid wartime rape.[4] Furthermore, the laws of war strictly mandate that combatants direct attacks solely against military objectives, including other combatants; they can never lawfully direct attacks against civilians or civilian objects.[5] When militaries respect the laws of war and promote notions of honor and even perhaps punish their own soldiers who commit sex crimes, rape still occurs (as it does in law-abiding societies during peacetime). Even when rape is strictly forbidden by superiors who enforce the laws and take measures to prevent or punish the crime, and takes place less frequently and certainly less conspicuously, it remains a persistent occurrence (as do other war crimes). However, when targeting of civilians and the abuse of women is not expressly forbidden by the military and political leaders, and its perpetration is either explicitly or implicitly encouraged or just ignored, or, in some circumstances, even ordered, the regularity and brutality of the crime increases exponentially. This is the situation in most contemporary armed conflicts, including Darfur. Thus, while the sexual violence committed in Darfur is horrific, sexual depravity is not unusual during conflict situations, and sexual atrocities are not unique to Darfur. The universal recognition that rape is epidemic in armed conflict, and has been since time immemorial, puts all on notice, including leaders, about their frequent commission.

Sexual Violence in Darfur

Many reports have documented atrocities in Darfur and over a dozen reports documenting these crimes have focused *exclusively* on rape and other forms of sexual violence, indicating its perceived gravity, its pervasiveness, and its need for redress.[6] International and local human rights organizations, United Nations bodies and agencies, government agencies, monitors, and reporters have been among those expressing alarm over the persistent episodes of sexual violence committed during attacks on villages, while in flight, and inside and outside of IDP and refugee camps. Nonetheless, because of significant underreporting of the crime (due largely to discriminatory treatment of victims by law and society), the actual number of rapes undoubtedly greatly exceeds even the high numbers already reported. Male rapes and other forms of sexual violence (especially mutilation) are increasingly reported and also occur with far greater frequency than statistics indicate.

Sex crimes are almost always accompanied by other forms of violence or abuse, such as beatings, forced nudity, enslavement, inhumane conditions, and/or destruction of homes, families, communities, and livelihoods. Many victims are regularly killed after being raped, but some are left alive simply because many perpetrators consider rape worse than death.[7] Damage to reproductive health and pregnancy are also regular features of rapes, with self-induced abortions to terminate the pregnancies not uncommon.

In 2004, the United Nations appointed five independent Commissioners to investigate and report on the most serious crimes perpetrated in Darfur. The Commission of Inquiry (COI) into crimes committed in

Darfur released its report in January 2005, concluding that atrocity crimes had been committed in all three states of Darfur by both GoS forces and *Janjaweed* militia. In summarizing its conclusion on the crimes committed on a widespread and systematic basis throughout Darfur, the report stated the following:

> Based on a thorough analysis of the information gathered in the course of its investigations, the Commission established that the Government of the Sudan and the *Janjaweed* are responsible for serious violations of international human rights and humanitarian law amounting to crimes under international law. In particular, the Commission found that Government forces and militias conducted indiscriminate attacks, including killing of civilians, torture, enforced disappearances, destruction of villages, rape and other forms of sexual violence, pillaging and forced displacement, throughout Darfur. These acts were conducted on a widespread and systematic basis, and, therefore, may amount to crimes against humanity.[8]

The COI Report outlined the most common patterns of rape crimes, which had been previously documented and which were then confirmed by the Commissioners' own investigations:

> First, deliberate aggressions against women and girls, including gang rapes, occurred during the attacks on the villages. Second, women and girls were abducted, held in confinement for several days and repeatedly raped during that time. Third, rape and other forms of sexual violence continued during flight and further displacement, including when women left towns and IDP sites to collect wood or water. In certain areas, rapes also occurred inside towns. Some women and girls became pregnant as a result of rape.[9]

As other reports similarly conclude, rape, gang rape, sexual slavery, and pregnancy (as a result of rape) were recurring themes in attacks throughout hundreds of villages in North, West, and South Darfur.

The most extensive documentation of crimes committed in Darfur, including sex crimes, was collected by the Coalition for International Justice and U.S. State Department's Atrocities Documentation Project in July and August 2004, during which over eleven hundred interviews were conducted in refugee camps in Chad and in several other unofficial makeshift camps just inside the Chad–Sudanese border.[10] Testimony of sexual violence obtained by the Atrocities Documentation Team (ADT) includes the following (names of villages typically phonetic; numbers used are to identify witness statements.):[11]

- In western Darfur (near Beida) in June 2003, a Massalit man saw the *Janjaweed* cut out the stomachs of pregnant women. If the fetus was male, the *Janjaweed* hit the fetus against a tree; if female, the fetus was left in the dirt. The witness stated his sister was also raped. (41)
- In western Darfur (near Foro Borunga) in June 2003, a Fur man said his wife was raped by seven GoS soldiers, and thirteen other women were also raped during the attack. He saw horsemen take a baby from a woman's back, tear off its clothes and slice its stomach; another woman's baby daughter was smashed against a tree and killed. He witnessed approximately twenty male and seven female babies being killed. (6)
- A Fur woman fled an attack on her village in Darfur (near Bendesi) in August 2003. She witnessed a twelve-year-old girl being gang raped by five men; the girl died soon after the attack. The witness also heard of many children being abducted as slaves or cowherders. (4)
- During an attack in West Darfur (near Gokor) in November 2003, a Massalit woman was among forty women captured and gang raped by seven soldiers during an aerial and ground attack. Some males were also sexually assaulted. (336)
- A Massalit woman in West Darfur (near Senena) in December 2003 said twenty girls were captured by GoS soldiers and gang-raped (vaginally and anally) for three days. Three girls had nails put in their vaginas (one of whom died), two other girls had their vaginas sewn up, and five became pregnant from the rapes. All were unmarried. (491)
- In West Darfur (near Genena) in December 2003, a Massalit woman stated that she and six other women were taken to a GoS base (Dongeta) where they were held for three days and repeatedly gang raped (vaginally and anally, sometimes with sticks) while tied naked and spread eagle. The witness saw the bodies of three naked elderly women with foreign objects thrust in their vaginas. She also said another woman told her she had been tied to a tree and forced to watch her daughter being raped. (497)
- A Massalit woman in West Darfur (near El Geneina) in February 2004 saw GoS soldiers catch sixteen women with babies. They broke the baby boys' necks in front of the mothers and beat mothers with their own babies like whips until the babies died. (482)
- In Northern Darfur (near Karnoi) in January 2004, a pregnant Zaghawa woman and four girls (ages 12, 13, 15, and 16) were

abducted and raped by five to six soldiers each night, until their release five days later. (161)

- A Zaghawa woman in North Darfur (near Karnoi) had her village attacked in March 2004 and she and eight other women were abducted and raped. After a month, an officer with two stars on his shoulder made the soldiers let the women go. (170)

The ADT's interviewers also recorded testimony of epithets or slurs directed at the victims during the course of the sexual assaults. Rape often lasts for long periods of time and the perpetrators tend to communicate some of the reasons behind the attacks. Some of the rape testimony collected by the ADT, which includes racial or gendered comments, follows:

- During an aerial and ground attack on a village in North Darfur (near Karnoi) in June 2003, a female Zaghawa survivor reported that she was told, "We want to kill the men and take the women to be our wives." (542)
- During an attack in western Darfur (near Masteri) in November 2003, a Massalit woman was raped by ten soldiers who said that the government "sent them to kill and rape and clean their land." (287)
- During a ground attack in western Darfur (near Seleya) in November 2003, a Eregnan man reported hearing, "We will kill all men and rape women. We want to change the color. Every woman will deliver red. Arabs are the husbands of those women." (533)
- During a village attack in western Darfur (near Kruink) in November 2003, a male Massalit witness reported seeing twelve women raped and mutilated (breasts and vaginas cut) by GoS and *Janjaweed*, and being told, "You have no country here, you must leave and go to Chad." (325)
- A Massalit woman in West Darfur (near El Geneina) in December 2003 saw Arabs take eight male babies by their feet and slam them into the ground until they died; the *Janjaweed* told women being raped, "We rape you to make a free baby, not a slave like you." (489)
- A Fur male reported that in December 2003, a few months before his village in West Darfur (near El Geneina) was attacked, *Janjaweed* raped his daughter and two other girls (ages 14, 15, and 16) and said, "We will take your women and make them ours. We will change the race." (575)
- During an attack on her village in western Darfur (near Misterei) in January 2004, a Massalit woman reported that she was one of sixteen women caught and raped by four soldiers during an

aerial/ground attack. Three other rapes she witnessed included girls having their breasts slashed, two girls died from the gang rapes. The attackers told her, "If you like this, stay in Sudan; if you don't, go to Chad." (259)

- A Zaghawa woman in North Darfur (near Kotum) in March 2004 stated that sixteen girls from her village were abducted and gang raped. A perpetrator said, "From now and for twenty years, we will kill all the blacks and all of the Zaghawa tribe." (803)
- A Massalit woman in South Darfur (near Garsila) had her village attacked in June 2004 by GoS and *Janjaweed*. Despite being four months pregnant, she fled, but was caught running by five men. They beat her with a whip, causing her to lose her baby. The attackers said, "Black prostitute, whore, you are dirty blacks." (1056)

These are only a fraction of the reports of various forms of sexual violence inflicted on the black indigenous population in Darfur, but they demonstrate the consistency of the reasons behind the attacks, the regularity with which the rape crimes occur, and the calculated use of rape as an instrument to terrorize and destroy the targeted group. The gendered nature of many attacks — targeting fetuses or babies because of their sex and targeting some women because of their reproductive capacity or pregnancy — should not be minimized. Interviewees time and again told stories of black Darfurians being raped, raped by gangs or with foreign objects, or having breasts, vaginas, or penises mutilated. They also told of pregnant women having their wombs sliced open or women having their pregnancies forcibly aborted by beatings or other abusive treatment; babies, particularly male babies, being murdered; women made pregnant by the rapes; men and women forced into nudity; and women and girls being abducted and sexually enslaved. Males are often targeted in armed conflicts because they are viewed as the fighters or potential fighters, females are often targeted because they are viewed as the repositories of culture and the (re)producers of generations, or simply as the gender intended to serve and service men as is their perceived legitimate right. The form and nature of the violence often reflects these attitudes.

In the most progressive societies, impediments to reporting, investigating, and prosecuting rape still abound. In conservative and religious societies like Sudan, the obstacles multiply. As mentioned earlier, the misplaced shame and stigma of rape crimes and the revictimization by criminal justice systems, in particular, cause the crime to be underreported. When extremist laws or practices, such as the Islamic laws operating in Darfur, require women or girls to prove a rape by the testimony of four male witnesses and be subjected to an insensitively or crudely conducted government medical exam, there is little incentive, and many disincentives, to reporting the crime. This is particularly true as the survivor may be charged with *zena*, adultery or having sex outside of a marital relationship, if she cannot prove the rape, especially if she is pregnant. This could result in public whippings and imprisonment, perhaps even a death sentence. At a minimum, it might result in the survivor being cast out of the community and precluded from marriage. In addition, the dysfunctional and discriminatory court system in Darfur (not to mention that the courts are controlled by the government, which is considered responsible for the atrocities) further reduces reporting of sex crimes.[12]

Rape as Genocide and a Crime against Humanity

Since the mid-1990s, many articles and books have focused on how rape and other forms of sexual violence can be and have been prosecuted as war crimes, crimes against humanity, and genocide.[13] Crimes include rape, enslavement, sexual slavery, torture, persecution, mutilation, enforced sterilization, forced pregnancy, forced abortion, forced nudity, sexual humiliation, forced marriage, cruel treatment, and inhumane acts, some of which are explicitly listed in the International Criminal Court (ICC) Statute, and others implicitly covered under the "or any other form of sexual violence of comparable gravity" language of the ICC Statute.[14] Judgments in the International Criminal Tribunal for the former Yugoslavia (ICTY) and the International Criminal Tribunal for Rwanda (ICTR) have also convicted individuals of rape as crimes against humanity and instruments of genocide.[15] Because, as noted previously, there is already a plethora of information available on how gender-related crimes can be successfully prosecuted, these issues will be given only cursory treatment here.

The ICC can prosecute gender-related crimes under Article 6 (genocide), Article 7 (crimes against humanity), and Article 8 (war crimes) of the Statute. The specifically enumerated gender crimes in the Statute are rape, enforced prostitution, sexual slavery, forced pregnancy, enforced sterilization, and other forms of sexual violence of comparable gravity. Additionally, gender persecution and trafficking of women and children are also explicitly referred to in the Statute.[16]

Under the UN Convention on the Prevention and Punishment of Genocide (UNCG) and the ICC Statute, genocide means any of the acts listed in subparagraphs (a) through (e) committed with intent to destroy, in whole or in part, a national, ethnical, racial, or religious group, as such. The five prohibited acts are: (a) killing members of the group, (b) causing serious bodily or mental harm to members of the group, (c) deliberately inflicting on the group conditions of life calculated to bring about its physical destruction in whole or in part, (d) imposing measures intended to prevent births within the group, or (e) forcibly transferring children of the group to another group.

"Killing members of a group," prohibited in (a) is undoubtedly the most widely recognized means of committing genocide, although all five subarticles share equal prohibition. The other subarticles do not necessarily involve death, or even outright violence, as a means of destruction of a group. Rape as an instrument of genocide most often invokes subarticle (b) intending to destroy a protected group by causing serious bodily or mental harm to members of that group, and (d) imposing measures intended to prevent births within a group.[17] Rape, along with torture and enslavement, including sexual torture and sexual slavery, regularly takes longer to commit than other crimes, and the extended time and proximity together often, as previously noted, prompt statements by the perpetrator(s), which can be useful in discerning genocidal intent. The *Akayesu* Judgement of the ICTR is the seminal decision recognizing rape as an instrument of genocide.[18]

The ICTY and ICTR have also convicted persons for rape as a crime against humanity when the crimes formed part of a widespread or systematic attack directed against a civilian population. It is the attack which must be either widespread or systematic, not the rapes, although rape itself is frequently both widespread and systematic. Systematic rape does not mean each rape is meticulously organized and planned — it refers, among other things, to a plan or policy to sexually abuse women, which is often carried out by implicitly or explicitly encouraging or granting free reign to commit the crime.

There is every indication that the official policy of the GoS and *Janjaweed* forces is to wage, jointly or separately, concentrated and strategic attacks against black Darfurians by a variety of means, including through killing, raping, pillaging, burning, and displacement. Various forms of sexual violence regularly formed part of these attacks. As emphasized by the COI report: "The findings of the Commission confirm that rape and sexual abuse were perpetrated during attacks by *Janjaweed* and soldiers. This included the joint attacks by Government soldiers and *Janjaweed* attacks."[19] BBC News reported the following regarding the attack of one village: "More than one hundred women have been raped in a single attack carried out by Arab militias in Darfur in Western Sudan ... . Another one hundred fifty women ... have been abducted."[20] Rape crimes have been documented in dozens of villages throughout Darfur and committed in similar patterns, indicating that rape itself is both widespread and systematic.

The information available on crimes in Darfur suggest that the ICC can prosecute rape as a crime against humanity and an instrument of genocide, and that other forms of sexual violence, particularly forced pregnancy, sexual mutilation, and sexual slavery, are also common forms of attack and destruction in Darfur.

Individual and Superior Responsibility

The ICC can prosecute both physical perpetrators and others responsible for sexual violence, including civil and military leaders and others who ordered, instigated, aided or abetted, or otherwise facilitated the crimes (individual responsibility) or who knew or had reason to know about crimes committed by subordinates under their control, but failed to prevent, halt, or punish the crimes (superior responsibility). In most situations, the persons most responsible for orchestrating war and the atrocities committed therein are not the physical perpetrators or even those physically present at the crime sites, unless they are military/militia leaders. More specifically, in the ICC Statute, individual criminal responsibility grants the court jurisdiction over persons who commit a crime, individually or jointly, or who order, solicit, or induce a crime, or who aid, abet, assist, or otherwise facilitate a crime. Participating in a common criminal purpose may also incur individual criminal responsibility.[21] Command and superior responsibility is invoked for military leaders and other superiors who (1) knew or should have known of crimes, or consciously disregarded information about them, and (2) where the crimes were committed by subordinates under their effective responsibility/authority/command and control, and they failed to take all necessary and reasonable measures within their power to prevent or repress the crimes or to submit the crimes to the relevant competent authorities for investigation and prosecution.[22]

In the jurisprudence of the World War II trials, as well as the ad hoc tribunals (ICTY and ICTR), and as incorporated in the ICC Statute,[23] crimes may be punished under the Joint Criminal Enterprise (JCE) theory of responsibility (also known as the common purpose doctrine). Essentially, a JCE is considered a form of commission, a form of individual criminal responsibility. A joint criminal enterprise is composed of a plurality of persons, participating in some way (through assistance or other contribution) to a common plan/design/purpose, which amounts to or involves a crime within the jurisdiction of the Court. The common plan can be agreed upon in advance, can materialize extemporaneously, and can be inferred from the facts.[24]

The ICTY has identified three distinct, but often overlapping, forms of JCE. JCE I is the basic form, in which all co-defendants share the same criminal intent/goal. They knowingly participate in some way and intend the result. JCE II is the systemic form. It is a subset of JCE I and has primarily been applied to concentration camps or situations where there is an orchestrated campaign of persecution or oppression. In JCE II, there is an organized system of ill treatment, and defendants have awareness of the nature of the system and an intent to further that system. There is some form of participation in the system, but their participation does not have to be significant. JCE III is the extended form, where responsibility for crimes committed beyond the common plan can be incurred. This happens when a perpetrator — not necessarily the defendant — commits a crime outside the common purpose, but the act is a natural or foreseeable consequence of the criminal endeavor. Here, a defendant willingly takes a risk that additional predictable crimes will be committed. The various forms may, and often do, overlap or occur parallel to each other.[25]

In a culture of mass atrocity, it may sometimes be difficult to determine which crimes were part of the agreed upon enterprise and which were outside the scope of the intended crimes, but foreseeable nonetheless. Yet, in most situations of mass violence and oppression, rape and other common forms of sexual violence will not be mere foreseeable consequences; rather, they should be considered integral parts of the destruction, of the physical and mental violence intentionally inflicted on the targeted group. The fear and terror inflicted by sexual violence rivals and sometimes exceeds that of murder, as it is a crime calculated to inflict maximum harm on the targeted group. Treating sex crimes as simply foreseeable (JCE III), but killing, beating, torturing, and burning as intended (JCE I) or part of a system of ill treatment (JCE II), would distort the historical record and ignore the gravity and potency of the crimes. Thus, rape crimes should be prosecuted under JCE I and II, with JCE III rape prosecutions restricted to the situations where the joint criminal plan was very specific (e.g., summary execution of all boys over 13 years old in a village) and the rapes which occur are truly not planned, but are nonetheless foreseeable.[26]

In Darfur, the evidence suggests that GoS political and military leaders participated in a Joint Criminal Enterprise with their *Janjaweed* collaborators, whom the GoS armed, supplied, and directed for at least the first two years. Initially, many attacks were joint GoS and *Janjaweed* attacks, until virtually all black African villages had been attacked, and then the GoS appears to have largely left it to the *Janjaweed* and regular bandits to complete the destruction on the ground. From February 2003 to March 2005, in particular, a common mode of attack in Darfur was for a GoS plane or helicopter to bypass Arab villages and wage an attack (or surveillance) on black villages, in concert with or followed by ground attacks by government forces or government supported *Janjaweed* militia. During the course of these attacks, civilian huts were destroyed, men, women, and children killed, women and girls raped, animals and other property stolen, child cattle herders and others abducted, and survivors forced into the inhospitable desert.

Aerial and ground attacks also commonly targeted life sources, such as water and food supplies, shelter, arable land, crops, livestock, and medical supplies.[27] In the context of Darfur, with temperatures soaring to 130 degrees Fahrenheit in the harsh desert environment in the daytime, but dropping dramatically some nights, such destruction was especially effective and quite naturally resulted in death and illness. Starvation, dehydration, exposure, infection, and disease were intended results of the intentional destruction of life sources and forced displacement.

The *ad hoc* Tribunals have not significantly developed the concept of command/superior responsibility beyond that promulgated by the post World War II trials, as most indictees in the Yugoslav (ICTY) and Rwanda (ICTR) Tribunals have been found guilty of individual responsibility. Indeed, the courts have found not only that many leaders regularly failed in their duty to prevent or punish crimes committed by subordinates, but also more egregiously, they incurred individual responsibility for facilitating the commission of the crimes. As might be expected, leaders who orchestrate, authorize, condone, encourage, or otherwise assist criminal activity do not then tend to endeavor to stop the crimes they orchestrated or punish those who committed the crimes they themselves authorized. Therefore, the ICTY and ICTR have tended to either convict on individual responsibility and dismiss the superior responsibility charges or find that the superior responsibility crimes were subsumed within the crimes incurring individual responsibility. Thus, the notion seems to be that if one orders a crime, one should not also be held responsible for failing to punish the subordinate who carried out one's orders.

Ignoring crimes committed by subordinates initially might fall under superior responsibility, failure to act. But when the silence continues, a potent message is sent to subordinates that superiors do not disapprove of their crimes, and this signals tacit approval, invoking individual responsibility. Additionally, Joint Criminal Enterprise (JCE), being a form of commission, is a form of individual responsibility, not superior responsibility. Still, when there is insufficient evidence available to prove that a leader participated in a JCE or facilitated the commission of a crime, holding him/her responsible for his/her duty to prevent or punish crimes committed by his/her *defacto* or *dejure* subordinates under his/her command and control remains a viable option.

The ICC Prosecutor, Luis Moreno-Ocampo, has consistently stated that his office intends to focus on leaders bearing the greatest responsibility for the most serious crimes. For Sudan, then, the ICC will likely indict less than a dozen civil and military leaders (used here to encompass *Janjaweed/* militia) for war crimes, crimes against humanity, and possibly genocide in Darfur. There is little dispute that war crimes and crimes against humanity, including sex crimes, have been committed. Many genocide experts have concluded that genocide has also been committed in Darfur.[28] The COI report unconvincingly reached a different conclusion, which caused the Government of Sudan to imply the Commission had exonerated it of all serious criminal activity. The U.S. Government has called the crimes in Darfur a genocide and, despite its hostility to the ICC, did not veto a Security Council resolution referring the situation in Darfur to the ICC.[29]

Holding Leaders Accountable for Sex Crimes

As noted previously, the ICC has indicated it intends to focus principally on investigating those holding the highest level of responsibility for justiciable crimes. Leaders have a duty to protect the civilian population and provide justice to those who have been victims of crimes. In Darfur, GoS leaders have not only failed this duty, but also they are implicated in committing or otherwise facilitating the atrocities. In *Kvocka*, the ICTY Trial Chamber emphasized that special measures needed to be taken to ensure that women placed in vulnerable positions during armed conflict are protected from sexual violence. It further noted that after reports or knowledge of such crimes, persons in positions of authority are placed on notice; to prevent being held accountable, extra measures must be taken to prevent sex crimes.[30] Even if one took the dubious view that consistent reports of rape crimes in conflicts throughout the world over the past one thousand years, much less the explosion of rape reports filed during wars over the last decade, did not put leaders on notice that sexual assaults are common means of destroying a village or harming the targeted group, the recurring reports every month of rape crimes in Darfur certainly did put the political and military leaders in Sudan on notice that rape was a frequent occurrence in Darfur. In reports by the United Nations, of which Sudan is a member, the prevalence of rape is highlighted and raised as a grave concern.

A wide range of United Nations experts have repeatedly noted that rape crimes flourish in Darfur with the full knowledge of the government. For example, Louise Arbour, the UN's High Commissioner for Human Rights, who is also the former Chief Prosecutor of the ICTY and ICTR, as well as former member of the Supreme Court of Canada, stressed, "There is a credible base of evidence that there is a severe, severe, serious amount of sexual violence that is not being properly addressed."[31] On June 21, 2005,

Jan Egeland, the UN Undersecretary for Humanitarian Affairs, reported that "in Darfur, rape is systematically used as a weapon of warfare."[32] Mukesh Kapila, the UN Coordinator for Sudan, discussed the mass rape committed in Darfur and emphasized: "It is more than just a conflict. It is an organized attempt to do away with a group of people."[33] Sima Samar, the UN Special Rapporteur for Human Rights in Sudan, stated that "'gender-based violence continues unfortunately with impunity'" and that the government's excuses were unacceptable.[34] And Juan Mendez, UN Special Advisor to the Secretary-General on the Prevention of Genocide, emphasized that even by September 2005, "the rape of women remained too prevalent."[35]

It is relatively straightforward to hold persons criminally responsible for sex crimes when they commit them physically, directly order the crimes (and there is documentation or other evidence), or they are physically present at crime sites and either encourage or otherwise aid and abet the crimes. As noted previously, it is also largely accepted that the most culpable government and military leaders do not have to be physically present at crime sites to be held accountable for the policies they dictated in directing a widespread or systematic attack against a targeted civilian group. Nonetheless, an attack on village after village may involve murder, torture, rape, pillage, and forced displacement; yet, in prosecutions, all but the sex crimes will typically be attributed to the leaders as part of their official policy.

While in theory it should not be particularly complicated to hold political/civilian or military leaders criminally responsible, either as individuals or as superiors, for sexual violence when the crimes are widespread or systematic, not to mention notorious, in practice there has been enormous reluctance to hold leaders and nonphysical perpetrators accountable for sex crimes, as opposed to other crimes. In general, the attitude seems to be that leaders do not have to be physically present at crime sites to be held responsible for the carnage that ensues during the course of carrying out a plan or policy to harm the targeted group, whereas sex crimes are regularly treated by investigators, prosecutors, and judges as different/private/special crimes, outside the scope of any intended attack. The notion — held by many investigators, prosecutors, trial attorneys, and judges — appears to be that leaders should not be held accountable for *sex* crimes unless there is incontrovertible proof that they ordered the crimes, or knew about them and *personally* intended their commission. This attitude is not only legally and factually inaccurate, it is morally untenable, provides a flawed, sexist historical record of the events, and denies justice to half the population. Failing to hold leaders accountable for sex crimes when they occur regularly and consistently over weeks and months, much less years, suggests that the crimes are not considered serious or are deemed personal/private issues.

It also ignores consistent and credible reports that conclude that wartime rapes are used strategically as weapons of war or instruments of terror.

That said, the ICTY has recognized that leaders can be held accountable for sex crimes when they were neither present nor ordered the crimes. For example, in the *Plavsic* case before the ICTY, a former leader of *Republika Srpska,* pled guilty to one count of persecution as a crime against humanity, in exchange for dropping the other seven charges, including the genocide counts. To accept a guilty plea, the Chamber had to be satisfied that the guilty plea was informed, voluntary, and unequivocal, and that there was a sufficient factual basis that the crimes were committed and that the person pleading guilty participated in them. Plavsic's guilty plea on the persecution as a crime against humanity charge, accepted by the Tribunal, included acknowledging responsibility for rape crimes.[36] The persecution count accused Plavsic of participating in a Joint Criminal Enterprise to plan, instigate, order, and aid or abet the persecution of non-Serbs in Bosnia–Herzegovina. The means of persecution included killing, raping, torturing, forcibly displacing, and committing other inhumane acts against civilians and destroying civilian property. Accepting the guilty plea and convicting Plavsic of persecution as a crime against humanity, the Chamber noted that she was neither as influential nor powerful as many other leaders, and played a lesser role in facilitating the crimes. Nonetheless, she incurred responsibility for rape and other crimes for acquiescing in them. As Plavsic herself stated, "[A]lthough I was repeatedly informed of allegations of cruel and inhuman conduct against non-Serbs, I refused to accept them or even to investigate."[37] She thus bore individual responsibility for the crimes, being a leader who knowingly participated in a joint criminal endeavor to persecute non-Serbs. She may not have specifically intended the rapes, but nonetheless she had knowledge of them and made no effort to indicate disapproval, to complain, or to initiate preventive measures, thus incurring individual responsibility for the crimes.[38]

To be sure, the orchestrators of mass atrocity in Darfur know what is happening on the ground and receive full and detailed reports of events. The political, military, and militia leaders have no doubt that when they order an attack, the violence that will ensue will take many diverse forms, including rape. In the extraordinary event that they were so naïve that they did not know initially, they certainly knew after reports were issued, and still the leaders continued urging or ignoring unlawful attacks on civilians with full knowledge that rape — and other crimes — would form part of the attacks.

The Government of Sudan has not made a secret of its intent to refuse to cooperate with the ICC, which also may include denying visas to ICC investigators and prosecutors to enter the country. Thus, there will be some difficulty in investigating crimes within Darfur itself, at least until Sudan is forced or induced to cooperate with the Court. Nevertheless, refugees who are victims of and witnesses to crimes in Darfur are in dozens of countries around the world, over two hundred thousand in Chad alone, and many would undoubtedly be willing to give evidence to the Court. States Parties to the ICC — one hundred countries as of November 2005 — are required by the ICC Statute to cooperate with the Court, and many of these countries have valuable intelligence information on evidence of crimes and the most culpable parties. The UN Security Council, African Union, European Union, UN bodies and agencies, and nongovernmental organizations can also play a positive role in assisting the Court. To be sure, the obstacles confronting the ICC are many, but with perseverance, integrity, and creativity, the challenges can be overcome and the people of Darfur can receive some measure of justice for the atrocities committed against them.

Notes

1. See, for example, Human Rights Watch, "Sexual Violence and its Consequences among Displaced Persons in Darfur and Chad," *HRW Briefing Paper,* 12 April 2005; *Medecins sans Frontieres,* "The Crushing Burden of Rape: Sexual Violence in Darfur," 8 March 2005; *Report of the International Commission of Inquiry on Darfur to the United Nations Secretary-General,* January 25, 2005; Gingerich, Tara and Leaning, Jennifer, "The Use of Rape as a Weapon of War in the Conflict in Darfur, Sudan," Physicians for Human Rights, October 2004; Human Rights Watch, "Empty Promises? Continuing Abuses in Darfur, Sudan," 11 August 2004; Amnesty International, "Darfur: Rape as a Weapon of War: Sexual Violence and its Consequences," Amnesty International, 19 July 2004.

2. Most recently, see Kristof, Nicholas D., "Sudan's Department of Gang Rape," *New York Times,* 22 November 2005; Fisher, Jonah, "A Culture of Impunity in Darfur," BBC News, 26 September, 2005; Report of the UN Special Advisor on the Prevention of Genocide, Visit to Darfur, Sudan 19–26 September, 2005, dated 4 October 2005, available at: http://www.protectdarfur.org/Pages/Download_D ocs/Special _Advisor_Report 1005.pdf

3. The historical treatment of the laws and customs of war concerning rape, from customary law to codified law, is discussed in detail in Askin, Kelly Dawn (1997). *War Crimes Against Women: Prosecution in International War Crimes Tribunals.* Transnational Publisher, pp. 18–48.

4. Geneva Convention (IV) Relative to the Protection of Civilian Persons in Time of War, 6 U.S.T. 3516, 75 U.N.T.S. 287 [Fourth Geneva Convention]; Protocol Additional to the Geneva Conventions of 12 August 1949, and Relating to the Protection of Victims of International Armed Conflicts, June 8, 1977, 1125 U.N.T.S. 3, 16 I.L.M. 1331 (entered into force December 7, 1978) [Additional Protocol I]; Protocol Additional to the Geneva Conventions of August 12, 1949, and Relating to the Protection of Victims of Non-International Armed Conflicts, June 8, 1977, S. Treaty Doc. No. 100-2, 1125 U.N.T.S. 609 (entered into force December 7, 1978) [Additional Protocol II].

5. Protocol I, supra, arts. 35, 48–60. While the laws of war accept that civilians may be killed or injured during activities directed against military objectives, as collateral damage, nonetheless civilians cannot be the object of or the target of an attack. Further, many precautions are required to be taken to minimize the risk of civilians being injured during an attack against military objects.

6. See, for example, Amnesty International, "Sudan: Surviving Rape in Darfur," AFR 54/097/2004, 9 August 2004; Amnesty International, "Darfur: Rape as a Weapon of

War: Sexual Violence and its Consequences," AFR 54/076/2004, 19 July 2004; Amnesty International, "Sudan: Mass Rape, Abduction and Murder," AFR 54/125/2004, 10 Dec. 2004; Amnesty International, "Sudan: Systematic Rape of Women and Girls," AFR 54/038/2004, 15 April 2004; Amnesty International, "Sudan: Rape as a Weapon of War," AFR 54/088/2004, 19 July 2004; Medecins Sans Frontieres, "The Crushing Burden of Rape, Sexual Violence in Darfur," 8 March 2005; Human Rights Watch, "Darfur: Women Raped Even After Seeking Refuge," 12 April 2005; UNICEF, "Darfur Region in Crisis: Girls and Women Terrorized by Widespread Rape in Darfur," 20 October 2004; Refugees International, "Rape, Islam and Darfur's Women Refugees and War Displaced," 24 August 2004; Fritz, Mark, "In Darfur, Wood-Gathering Women Walk Through a Minefield of Rape," 19 August 2004, International Rescue Committee; Hampton, Tracy, "Agencies Speak Out on Rape in Darfur," *Journal of American Medical Associations*, 294(5): 3, August 2005; Kristof, Nicholas D., "A Policy of Rape," *New York Times*, 5 June 2005; Polgreen, Lydia, "Darfur's Babies of Rape are in Trial from Birth," *New York Times*, 11 February 2005; Dixon, Robyn, "In Sudan, Rape's Lasting Hurt," *Los Angeles Times*, 15 September 2004; Wax, Emily, "'We Want to Make a Light Baby:' Arab Militiamen in Sudan Said to Use Rape as Weapon of Ethnic Cleansing," *The Washington Post*, 30 June 2004, A01; Dealey, Sam, "Rape is a Weapon in Darfur, but Sudan's Government Doesn't Want to Hear About It," *Sudan Times*, 28 August 2005, citing TIME/US ed.; BBC News, "Mass Rape Atrocity in West Sudan," 19 March 2004; BBC News, "UN attacks Darfur 'fear and rape,'" 25 September 2004; Sengupta, Somini, "Rampage of Rape in Sudan Continues Undeterred," *New York Times*, 27 October 2004; SOAT, "Darfur: Abduction and Rape in Nyala," 20 September 2005; Masciarelli, Alexis and Eveleens, Ilona, "Sudanese Tell of Mass Rape," BBC News, 10 June 2004.

7. For example, Refugees International reported: "'As you have raped me, please don't leave me alive ... kill me with your gun' begged Almina to her rapist. 'May shame kill you' was the reply of the *Janjaweed* militiaman who raped her." *Refugees International, Rape, Islam, and Darfur's Women Refugees and War-Displaced*, 24 August 2004.

8. Report of the International Commission of Inquiry on Darfur to the United Nations Secretary-General, January 25, 2005, p. 3 [COI Report], available at: http://www.un.org/News/dh /sudan/com_i nq_darfur.pdf

9. COI Report, supra, paras. 334–336.

10. See U.S. Department of State, Documenting Atrocities in Darfur, September 2004, available at: http://www.sta te.gov/g/drl/rls/36 028.htm. See also other chapters in this book, especially Part 2: Chapter 3 (Bang-Jensen and Frease), Chapter 4 (Howard), and Chapter 6 (Totten and Markusen).

11. Unpublished statements collected by the CIJ/USAID Atrocities Documentation Project (on file with author).

12. See especially, Access to Justice for Victims of Sexual Violence, Report of the UN High Commissioner for Human Rights, 29 July 2005, pp. 13–26, available at: http://www.ohchr.org/en glish/press/doc s/20050729Darfurreport.pdf

13. In addition to the writings of many other academics, legal experts, or journalists, I have also already written on various ways to prosecute gender crimes. See, for example, Askin (1997), *War Crimes Against Women, supra cit*; Askin, Kelly D. (1999), "Sexual Violence in Decisions and Indictments of the Yugoslav and Rwandan Tribunals: Current Status," *American Journal of International Law*, vol. 93, pp. 97–123; Askin, Kelly (1999), "Crimes Within the Jurisdiction of the International Criminal Court," *Criminal Law Forum*, vol. 10, pp. 33–59; Askin, Kelly D. (1999). "Women and International Humanitarian Law," pp. 41–87, in Kelly D. Askin and Dorean M. Koenig (Eds.), *Women and International Human Rights Law*, Vol. I, Transnational; Askin, Kelly D. (1999), "The International War Crimes Trial of Anto Furundzija: Major Progress Toward Ending the Cycle of Impunity for Rape Crimes," *Leiden Journal of International Law*, vol. 12; Koenig, Dorean M. and Askin, Kelly D. (2000). "International Criminal Law and the International Criminal Court Statute: Crimes Against Women," pp. 3–29, in Kelly D. Askin and Dorean M. Koenig (Eds.), *Women and International Human Rights Law*, Vol. II, Transnational; Askin, Kelly Dawn (2000). "Women's Issues in International Criminal Law: Recent Developments and the Potential Contribution of the ICC," pp. 47–63, in Dinah Shelton (Ed.), *International Crimes, Peace, and Human Rights: The Role of the International Criminal Court*,

Transnational; Askin, Kelly D. (2001). "Comfort Women — Shifting Shame and Stigma from Victims to Victimizers," *International Criminal Law Review*, Vol. I; Vandenberg, Martina and Askin, Kelly (2001). "Chechnya: Another Battleground for the Perpetration of Gender Based Crimes," *Human Rights Review*, 2(3): 140–156; Askin, Kelly D. (2003). "The Quest for Post-Conflict Gender Justice," *Columbia Journal of Transnational Law*, 41(3): 509–521; Askin, Kelly D. (2003). "The Kunarac Case of Sexual Slavery: Rape and Enslavement as Crimes Against Humanity," pp. 806-817, in Andre Klip and Goran Sluiter (Eds.), *Annotated Leading Cases of International Criminal Tribunals*, Vol. 5, Intersentia; Askin, Kelly D. (2003). "Prosecuting Wartime Rape and Other Gender-Related Crimes Under International Law: Extraordinary Advances, Enduring Obstacles," *Berkeley Journal of International Law*, vol. 21, pp. 288–367; Askin, Kelly D. (2004). "The International Criminal Tribunal for Rwanda and Its Treatment of Crimes Against Women," pp. 33-88, in John Carey et al. (Eds.), *International Humanitarian Law: Challenges*, Vol. 2, Transnational; Askin, Kelly D. (2005). "Gender Crimes: *Jus Cogens* Violations and Universal Jurisdiction," pp. 57-66, in Evelyn A. Ankumah and Edward K. Kwakwa (Eds.), *African Perspectives on International Criminal Justice*, Africa Legal Aid; Askin, Kelly D. (2005). "Gender Crimes Jurisprudence in the ICTR," *Journal of International Criminal Justice*, vol. 3, pp. 1007–1018; Askin, Kelly D. (2005). "The Jurisprudence of International War Crimes Tribunals: Securing Gender Justice for Some Survivors," pp. 125–154, in Helen Durham and Tracey Gurd (Eds.), *Listening to The Silences: Women and War*, Martinus Nijhoff.

14. Rome Statute of the International Criminal Court, 1998 Sess., U.N. Doc. A/CONF.183/9 (1998) (entered into force July 1, 2002) [ICC or Rome Statute], at art. 7.

15. See, for example, *Prosecutor v. Jean Paul Akayesu*, Judgement, ICTR-96-4-T, 2 September 1998 [Akayesu Trial Chamber Judgement]; *Prosecutor v. Kunarac et al*, Judgement, IT-96-23-T and IT-96-23/1, 22 February 2001 [Kunarac Trial Chamber Judgement]; de Brouwer, Anne-Marie L.M. (2005). Supranational Criminal Prosecution of Sexual Violence: The ICC and the Practice of the ICTY and the ICTR, Intersentia.

16. ICC Statute, supra, art. 6, art. 7(1)(g), and art. 8(b)(xxii) and 8(e)(vi). Under the crimes against humanity provisions of the Statute, "enslavement" is specifically noted to include "the exercise of such power in the course of trafficking in persons, in particular women and children" (art. 7(2)(c)) and "persecution" explicitly includes gender-based persecution (art. 7(1)(h).

17. See, for example, Askin (1997), *War Crimes Against Women, supra cit*.

18. Akayesu Trial Chamber Judgement, *supra cit*.

19. COI Report, *supra cit*, para. 338.

20. BBC News, "Mass rape atrocity in West Sudan," 19 March 2004.

21. ICC Statute, *supra cit*, art. 25.

22. ICC Statute, *supra cit*, art. 28 (the requirements for military commanders and other superiors are slightly different.)

23. ICC Statute, *supra cit*, art. 25(3)(d).

24. *Prosecutor v. Tadic, Judgement*, IT-94-1-A, 15 July 1999 [Tadic Appeals Chamber Judgement], at para. 227.

25. See, for example, *Prosecutor v. Tadic*, Judgement, IT-94-1-A, 15 July 1999 [Tadic Appeals Chamber Judgement], at paras. 195–229; *Prosecutor v. Kvocka*, Judgement, IT-98-30-T, 2 November 2001, at paras. 77–119 [Kvocka Trial Chamber Judgement], *Prosecutor v. Kvocka*, Judgement, IT-98-30-A, 28 February 2005, at paras. 77–119 [Kvocka Appeals Chamber Judgement]; *Prosecutor v. Ntakirutimana*, Judgement, ICTR-96-10A and ICTR-96-17A, 13 December 2004, at paras. 461–468; *Prosecutor v. Milutinovic et al.*, Decision on Dragoljub Odjanic's Motion Challenging Jurisdiction — Joint Criminal Enterprise, IT-99-37-AR72, 21 May 2003 [Ojdanic Joint Criminal Enterprise Appeal Decision]; *Prosecutor v. Stakic*, Judgement, IT-97-24-T, 31 July 2003, paras. 438–442 [Stakic Trial Chamber Judgement]; *Prosecutor v. Krnojelac*, Judgement, IT-97-25-A, 17 September 2003, paras. 64–124 [Krnojelac Appeals Chamber Judgement]; *Prosecutor v. Vasiljevic*, Judgement, IT-98-32-A, 25 February 2004, paras. 94–111 [Vasiljevic Appeals Chamber Judgement]; *Prosecutor v. Brdjanin*, Decision on Interlocutory Appeal, IT-99-36-A, 19 March 2004 [Brdjanin Interlocutory Appeal Decision]. See also *Rwamakuba v. Prosecutor*, ICTR-44-AR72.4, Decision on Interlocutory Appeal Regarding Application of Joint Criminal

Enterprise to the Crime of Genocide, 22 October 2004 [Rwamakuba Interlocutory Appeal Decision on JCE and Genocide].

26. See, for example, the Krstic Trial Chamber Decision, *supra cit*, where the summary execution of all fighting-age men and boys in Srebrenica was held to be a joint criminal enterprise (JCE I), but the rape crimes committed during the course of the JCE deemed foreseeable (JCE III) under the circumstances of mass violence and persecution.

27. See, for example, Physicians for Human Rights, "Destroyed Livelihoods, A Case Study of Furawiya Village, Darfur, Preliminary Briefing," 2005, available at: http://www.phrusa. org/research/sud an/pdf/darf ur_briefin g.pdf

28. See, for example, some of the reports on Darfur crimes included on the following websites: http://www.prevent genocide.org/; http: //www. darfurgeno cide .org/; http://www. genocidewatch.org/Never%20Again.htm; http://www.sav edarfur.org

29. United Nations Doc. SC Res. 1593, S/RES/1593, 31 March 2005.

30. Kvocka Trial Chamber Judgement, *supra cit*, para. 318.

31. BBC News, "UN attacks Darfur 'fear and rape,'" 25 September 2004. The Commission of Inquiry made a similar statement: "On their part, the authorities failed to address the allegations of rape adequately or effectively." *COI Report, supra cit*, para. 336.

32. See http://www.wluml.org/english/newsfulltxt.shtml?cmd%5B157%5D=x-157-249107. Accessed September 13, 2005.

33. "Mass Rape Atrocity in West Sudan," BBC News, 19 March 2004.

34. *Sudan Times*, "Sudan Failed to Try Darfur War Crimes — UN Rights Official," 23 October 2005.

35. Jonah Fisher, "'Culture of Impunity' in Darfur," BBC News, 26 September 2005.

36. See *Prosecutor v. Plavsic*, Plavsic Sentencing Judgement, IT-00-39 and 40/1, 27 February 2003, at paras. 27, 29, 34, 120, 126 [Plavsic Sentencing Judgement].

37. Plavsic Sentencing Judgement, *supra cit*, para. 51.

38. Plavsic Sentencing Judgement, esp. at paras. 55, 121.

PART 4

The Significance of the Darfur Atrocities Documentation Project: A Precedent for the Future?

The Perspective of 'Outsiders'

CHAPTER 10

The Darfur Atrocities Documentation Project: A Precedent for the Future?

A Perspective from Washington, D.C.

TAYLOR B. SEYBOLT

The Darfur Atrocities Documentation Project (ADP) was both a great success and a disturbing failure. The project and the report, "Documenting Atrocities in Darfur," had great value in at least three respects. First, the Project played a pivotal role in the U.S. Government's declaration of genocide in Darfur. Second, Secretary of State Colin Powell's and President George W. Bush's evocations of the UN Convention on the Prevention and Punishment of the Crime of Genocide (UNCG) in response to the report helped to keep Darfur on Washington's political agenda. Third, the field interviews and timely analysis of data in mid-2004 showed that a determination of genocide can be made before it is too late to respond. Despite all this, the Darfur Atrocities Documentation Project led to virtually no action to stop the genocide. The combination of high-level attention and near complete lack of action bodes poorly for future efforts to respond effectively to ongoing mass killing.

A Pivotal Role

The single most important reason the ADP grabbed the attention of Washington was that it was "plugged in." It originated within the government, had a strong champion in the State Department, and issued its findings as a State Department document. No other investigation led by a nongovernmental organization could claim the same advantage.

The U.S. Agency for International Development's Office of Transitional Initiatives (USAID/OTI), located in the executive branch of government, approached several nongovernmental organizations (NGOs) in early 2004, asking them to document the violence in Darfur in a systematic way. The legislative branch of government got in on the act when the U.S. House of Representatives and the Senate passed a "sense of the Congress" resolution (a resolution that is not legally binding) in early July 2004, calling on the Secretary of State to make a determination of whether genocide was taking place (H. Amdt. 651 to H.R. 4754).

Despite this official encouragement, NGOs and government officials were skeptical that such a documentation project could be done. Lorne Craner, Assistant Secretary of State for Democracy, Human Rights and Labor, did not accept their skepticism. He convened a series of meetings and insisted that a government–NGO investigation take place. The Coalition for International Justice (CIJ) took on the challenge and the Office of Transitional Initiatives paid the costs. Without Craner's forceful advocacy, from a position of authority within the executive branch of government, the documentation project would not have happened (correspondence with Bang-Jensen, 2005).

In addition to being plugged in, the report had an effect on the political establishment because it reinforced an already fervent call for attention to Darfur. The administration of President George W. Bush had declared its interest in Sudan from the beginning of its first term in the White House, largely in response to great concern among its supporters on the "Christian Right" with the ill treatment of Christians in southern Sudan, at the hands of Muslims from the north. (Although the religious persecution perspective was overly simplistic and oriented toward the southern provinces, not the western Darfur provinces, it served to raise Sudan's profile in Washington.) Concern in Washington and New York was great enough that U.S. Secretary of State Colin Powell visited Darfur in June 2004, as did United Nations Secretary-General Kofi Annan.

A number of NGOs across the ideological spectrum raised the alarm about Darfur. Some engaged in fieldwork to document killing, rape, and expulsion of civilians. For instance, Physicians for Human Rights (PHR), a premiere organization in the use of medical expertise to document human rights violations, conducted an investigation along the Sudan/Chad border in May 2004, together with the Open Society Justice Initiative (OSJI). The investigation led PHR to call for intervention to stop the genocide before CIJ even put its team together (PHR, 2004a; PHR, 2004b, p. 5). Other groups engaged in different kinds of political pressure tactics. For example, the Save Darfur Coalition, a group of over one hundred faith-based organizations, issued a call for action in August 2004 and continued to facilitate citizen involvement through the summer of 2006. Suggested actions ranged from prayer vigils to school education days to writing letters to Congressional members and the President (Save Darfur Coalition, 2006).

Be that as it may, the final reason the report was taken so seriously was its rigorous methodology, discussed in previous chapters of this book. The population sampling technique and the size of the sample, combined with satellite imagery of destroyed villages, was more convincing than "dozens" of interviews conducted by other organizations and the episodic coverage by news media. A determination of genocide by one government against another, after all, must be based on the best possible evidence at the time.

On the Political Agenda

Based in part on the evidence compiled by the ADP, on September 9, 2004, Secretary of State Powell testified to the Senate Foreign Relations Committee that the Government of Sudan was committing genocide against the people of Darfur. (It is interesting to note that the report itself does not use the word "genocide.") He was pushing on an open door. Two days earlier the House and Senate had passed concurrent resolutions citing the 1948 UNCG and declaring genocide in Darfur (H. Con. Res. 467; S. Con. Res. 133). President Bush repeated the accusation of genocide in front of heads of state from around the world, who were gathered at the UN General Assembly on September 21, 2004.

The momentum gained from consensus within the government, together with continued interest from domestic political constituents, kept the violence in Darfur near the top of Washington's political agenda for an unusually long time. President Bush reaffirmed the finding of genocide at the June 2005 summit meeting of the Group of Eight (G-8). Condoleezza Rice, who replaced Colin Powell as Secretary of State in 2005, visited Darfur in July. Her deputy, Robert Zoellick, visited Sudan four times between April and November, 2005. The Congress constantly engaged in legislative action regarding Darfur, including the allocation of money for aid and calls for the imposition of sanctions on individuals responsible for crimes against humanity. In November 2005, the Senate passed the "Darfur Peace and Accountability Act of 2005" (S. 1462). The Act, described in more detail later, called for the United States to support the African Union Mission in Sudan (AMIS) and to take diplomatic and economic measures to try to stop the ongoing violence.

The sustained attention has been rather extraordinary for a crisis with no obvious security or economic ramifications for the United States and where there are virtually no U.S. military personnel deployed (except for one or two advisors to AMIS). Humanitarian crises such as Darfur usually elicit no more than a sad shake of the head and some emergency assistance money from official Washington. For evidence of common reaction to atrocities, one need look no farther than the brutal war in southern Sudan for most of its 21-year duration, the devastating conflict in the Democratic Republic of Congo in the late 1990s, or the present crisis in northern Uganda.

Of course the relationship between Sudan and the United States is more complex than the issue of Darfur alone. The U.S. Government is heavily engaged with the new Sudanese "government of national unity" to promote implementation of the Comprehensive Peace Agreement that ended the long-running war in southern Sudan. The two governments also cooperate on counter-terrorism efforts. The importance of Sudan as a source of regional instability, a producer of oil, and a player in the arena of transnational terrorism help to explain Washington's attention. Nevertheless, among these many interests, the particular concern with violence against civilians in Darfur has persisted.

A Timely Report

One often hears that the definition of genocide has a serious drawback in practice — by the time we know an event is genocidal, it is too late to do anything. The ADP and other calls for action proved that claim wrong. When the report was published and the U.S. Government declared genocide, a tragic number of people already had been killed or died as a consequence of being driven from their homes. Yet, many more people were still alive and in peril. More than a year after the report, there is still the opportunity to save the lives of people who are caught up in the violence and who are the target of *Janjaweed* and army raids.

If foreign governments and international organizations do not take action to protect civilians, it is likely that many more people will perish. The *Janjaweed* militia have not been reigned in by the Sudanese Government; the government and the Darfur rebels are stalled on the battlefield and have made no progress at the negotiating table; the main rebel group, the Sudanese Liberation Army (SLA), is fracturing, making command and control even less certain than it was; and civilians, foreign aid workers, and African Union peacekeepers continue to be attacked. The situation is clearly ripe for more violence. It is also ripe for action to stop the killing. The documentation of genocide did not come too late.

The question of being able to identify a genocide before it is too late to react will remain open, not least because most governments and the United Nations do not officially believe the events in Darfur constitute genocide. The United States is the only country to declare genocide. The UN Commission of Inquiry on Darfur described widespread massacres and forcible expulsion, but decided they did not meet the genocidal standard of intent to kill members of a group because of their group membership (United Nations, 2005). Perhaps it will remain true that most policymakers will recognize genocide only after most of a targeted group has been wiped out, in which case it *will* be too late to act. The lesson of the ADP is that this need not be the case. But people in a position of power must be willing to live up to the obligations of the Genocide Convention (UNCG) that their governments have signed.

Ultimately, Not Enough

One cannot help but be concerned about the political precedent that has been set. The U.S. Government clearly recognized in September 2004 that genocide was underway in Darfur. It has done next to nothing in response. No other country has done any better, and the United Nations has proven ineffective.

The President of the United States referred to "crimes my government has concluded are genocide" in the General Assembly of the United Nations (Bush, 2004). That statement obligates the United States, as a signatory of the Convention on the Prevention and Punishment of Genocide, under international law to try to prevent the continuation of genocide and to punish individuals found guilty of genocidal crimes. Yet, the Bush administration has not taken military action, such as imposing a no-fly zone to prevent the aerial bombardment of villages before the militia attacks. It has not taken economic action, such as blacklisting oil tankers that dock at the port of Sudan. (The United States does not buy Sudanese oil, but in the global petroleum market those same tankers carry oil from other locations to the United States.) It has not taken diplomatic action, such as appointing a presidential envoy, like former Senator John Danforth who helped to broker the Comprehensive Peace Agreement between the North and South. Furthermore, the United States failed to act in the UN Security Council to support referral of the matter to the International Criminal Court (ICC), to which it is ideologically opposed. (It should be noted that the United States did not block the referral to the ICC, preferring instead to abstain from the vote.) The Bush administration's declaration of genocide has proved to be a substitute for action, not a call to action.

The U.S. Congress did no better until 15 months after its declaration of genocide. Most of the legislative action on Darfur since the resolutions "declaring genocide in Darfur, Sudan" did not consist of the passage of laws, but of proposals, counter-proposals and debate — cheap talk. The legislation that was passed before November 2005 was largely to provide humanitarian aid. While the people of Darfur desperately need aid, what they need more is protection.

Finally, on November 18, 2005, the Senate passed a bill intended to help protect civilians and to punish individual perpetrators. Specifically, it called for the rapid expansion of the size and mandate of AMIS and for NATO, the European Union, and the United States to provide the resources necessary for expansion. It insisted that the U.S. President work to impose a countrywide arms embargo, deny access to U.S. ports for ships that export Sudanese oil, and impose targeted sanctions on individuals responsible for genocidal crimes. It also called on the President to appoint a high-level envoy to lead diplomatic efforts (S. 1462). If all of those provisions are implemented, they could make a real difference on the ground.

The United States is not alone in deserving criticism for inaction. No government has been able to bring itself to do more than make pronouncements or take small, weak measures. Some countries, such as China and Russia, are openly hostile to the idea of pressuring Sudan to stop the killing. UN Security Council resolutions on Darfur — while well intentioned — all have had no effective enforcement mechanisms built into them.

Sadly, the lack of action should not surprise us. Governments are most likely to act when they perceive threats to their primary interests or an opportunity to promote their primary interests. When secondary or tertiary interests are at stake, we can expect to see only weak responses, especially when taking action involves risks. Preventing and punishing genocide and mass killing in most parts of the world is still a weak interest for states, despite recent progress in the international human rights debate on state sovereignty and the "responsibility to protect" individuals. The perpetrators of genocide and mass killing, in contrast, have very strong interests at stake. To stop atrocities, outsiders must act swiftly, be willing to take risks, and be prepared to pay possibly significant costs in blood and treasure. Until governments see living up to their obligations under the UNCG as a strong interest, we can expect to witness continued passivity in the face of inhumane brutality.

Even projects that are able to shape political debate, as the Darfur Atrocities Documentation Project did, depend on political leaders to decide and to act. The most troubling aspect of the rhetoric in Washington is that governments with the power to act now understand that it is acceptable to allow mass killing even when they cannot deny knowledge of it. The excuse of ignorance, behind which governments hid during the Rwandan genocide, is not available in Sudan. Once again, when faced with genocide, governments and their people are content with discussion and humanitarian aid. The people of Darfur need peace or long-term protection so they can return safely to their land and start their lives over again.

References

Beng-Jensen, Nina (2005). Personal correspondence, October, 18.

Bush, George (2004). "President Speaks to the United Nations General Assembly," September 21. Available at: http://www.whitehouse.gov/news/releases/2004/09/20040921-3.html

House Amendment 651 to House of Representatives 4654 (H. Amdt. 651 to H.R. 4754). July 7, 2004. Available at: http://thomas.loc.gov/cgi-bin/bdquery/D?d108:2:./temp/~bd6ZRg::|/bss/d108query.html

House Concurrent Resolution 467 (H. Con. Res. 467), September 7, 2004. Available at: http://thomas.loc.gov/cgi-bin/query/D?c108:3:./temp/~c108AY5l6K::

Physicians for Human Rights (2004a). "PHR Calls for Intervention to Save Lives in Sudan: Field Team Compiles Indicators of Genocide." Available at: http://www.physiciansforhumanrights.org/research/sudan/sudan_genocide_report.pdf

Physicians for Human Rights (2004b). *Annual Report 2003-04*. Cambridge, MA: Author. Available at: http://www.physiciansforhumanrights.org/about/reports.html

Save Darfur Coalition (2005). Available at: http://savedarfur.org/

Senate 1462(S. 1462). November 18, 2005. Available at: http://thomas.loc.gov/cgi-bin/query/D?c109:2:./temp/~c109pC6QEw::

Senate Concurring Resolution 133 (S. Con. Res. 133), September 7, 2004. Available at: http://thomas.loc.gov/cgi-bin/bdquery/D?d108:10:./temp/~bd5ODp::|/bss/108search.html|

United Nations (2005). *Report of the International Commission of Inquiry on Darfur to the United Nations Secretary General, 25 January 2005*. Available at: http://www.un.org/News/dh/sudan/com_inq_darfur.pdf

Samuel Totten interviews a Darfur refugee in Goz Beida, Chad (July, 2004).

Section of the Cariari refugee camp, on the border between Chad and Sudan, which contained tens of thousands forced from their villages in Darfur. Photo by Eric Markusen.

Section of the Cariari refugee camp, where camp authorities were unable to provide tents, but only tarps to cover personal belongings. Photo by Eric Markusen.

An elderly woman in the Iridimi refugee camp after being interviewed by the Atrocities Documentation Team. Photo by Eric Markusen.

The daily line up for water in the Goz Beida refugee camp.

CHAPTER 11

From Rwanda to Darfur: Lessons Learned?

GERALD CAPLAN

Introduction

Even before the 1994 Rwandan genocide ended, some began wondering when "the next Rwanda" would be. Not "if," but when. Despite Indonesia in 1965, Burundi in 1972, and Cambodia from 1975 to 1978, genocide had receded in the public consciousness. From the late 1960s, it is true, memory of the Holocaust was in full bloom. But the Holocaust was treated as almost a self-contained phenomenon separate from "ordinary" genocide. Indeed, the Herero's extermination by the Germans in southwest Africa in 1904 was unknown beyond a few experts, and any attention paid to the earlier Armenian genocide was mainly the crusade of Armenians. As for the post-Holocaust massacres of half-a-million Communists in Indonesia, the slaughter by the Tutsi army of perhaps two hundred thousand Hutu in Burundi, including all those with secondary education, and the deaths by beating, starving, or torture by the Khmer Rouge of a million and a half Cambodians, none quite seemed to meet the standards set down in the 1948 Convention on the Prevention and Punishment of Genocide (UNCG).

Rwanda was different. Rwanda was a "classic UNCG genocide," fulfilling all the conditions, and it reminded the world that a half-century after the world first vowed "never again," genocide had not disappeared. What

171

Primo Levi had said of the Holocaust was now said about Rwanda: It happened, so it will happen again. For some, it happened soon enough. For them, Srebrenica in 1995 seemed "another Rwanda," and indeed, the international Criminal Tribunal for the former Yugoslavia eventually decided that the murder of eight thousand Muslim Bosnian males by Bosnian Serb soldiers and militias was indeed genocide. But this has been a controversial issue. Cold-bloodedly murdering eight thousand Bosnian Muslims was beyond question an egregious war crime, even a crime against humanity, but, some wondered, did it belong in the same category as killing one million Armenians or six million Jews?

Rwanda, however, left no room for ambiguity. Ironically, the seeming absence of genocide since 1945 had made most observers refuse to take seriously in advance that an actual genocidal conspiracy was being hatched in Rwanda before 1994. Once it was over, it seemed all but inevitable that others could, and would, follow. For many, early in the new millennium, Darfur seemed well on its way to becoming "the next Rwanda." The urgent question then emerged: Had Rwanda taught the world any lessons that might help prevent Darfur from following in its path?

Three Lessons from Rwanda

Assuming, of course, that there really are any lessons at all that the past can teach the future, it is possible to isolate three from the unmitigated catastrophe of 1994 Rwanda. Of these, the first, and most obvious, is profoundly disheartening to all those who favor intervention in crises where no interests beyond the humanitarian are at stake. The second and third are apparently, or potentially, encouraging. To seek a ray of hope out of a genocide borders on the desperate, but in the curious universe of those who study genocides in order to prevent them, what else is there to hold on to?

The horror of the Rwandan genocide extends beyond its intrinsic bestiality. What's also notable is, first, how swiftly it became evident that this was a "perfect storm" of a genocide, and, second, how easily it could have been prevented. (Before addressing the betrayal of Rwanda by the "international community," genocide prevention activists must not forget that it could have been prevented most successfully if the Hutu conspirators who plotted to "cleanse" Rwanda of its Tutsi citizens had simply called off their plot.) Yet the genocide was not formally named as such by the vast majority of governments and institutions, including the United Nations and the Organization of African Unity, until the one hundred days of slaughter had virtually come to an end. Moreover, not only was the genocide not prevented, it was not even marginally mitigated. From the first day to the last, not a single reinforcement arrived in Rwanda to bolster the puny United Nations force of four hundred that was trying desperately to save the relatively few Tutsi that it could.

Thus, the first lesson from Rwanda — the harsh unwelcome reminder (as if the world needed another) — was that the global powers-that-be are capable of almost infinite callousness and indifference to human suffering if geopolitical or political interests are not at stake. Calls for forceful intervention based strictly on humanitarian grounds, as we have learned the hard way once again in Darfur, are simply irrelevant to those with the means to intervene.

Here, I refer essentially to the UN Security Council, and within that body to the remarkably powerful five Permanent Members (P5) who alone hold a veto over all its resolutions. Since United Nations missions can only be authorized by the Security Council, and since any one of the P5 can veto any resolution, the leverage of the United States, Britain, France, Russia, and China can hardly be exaggerated. Those who have begged for a more assertive response in both Rwanda and Darfur understand the immutability of this phenomenon.

Often, middle powers are looked to as a means to exert pressure on the inner sanctum of the P5. Canada, northern Europe, and the Scandinavian countries are all seen, sometimes naïvely, as being less in the thrall of self-interest and more open to humanitarian projects. In trying to leverage action for Darfur, activists placed considerable hope on these countries. The role of Belgium in 1994, though, shows both the leverage that a middle power can play and the perverse use it can make of that leverage.

For one hundred ten years prior to the Rwandan genocide, no external power played a more deplorable role in Africa than Belgium — a tiny country responsible for giant crimes against humanity. Its impact on Congo, Rwanda, and Burundi was catastrophic. The turbulent history of the entire Great Lakes region in the twentieth century would have been profoundly different if it had not been for Belgian colonial rule. And in 1994, just as the genocide was exploding across Rwanda, the Belgian Government sought to bring pressure on the Security Council to withdraw (in its entirety) its six-month old UN Assistance Mission for Rwanda (UNAMIR). In light of the fact that ten of Belgium's United Nations troops had been murdered by Rwandan Government soldiers less than a day after the genocide was triggered by the shooting down of the Rwandan president's plane, the Belgian government decided it was politically impossible for its troops to remain in Rwanda. Their withdrawal very substantially undermined UNAMIR's capacity, and its lethal consequences were not merely theoretical. In fact, it immediately and directly led to the death of some twenty-five hundred Rwandans being protected by Belgian troops at the Ecole Technique

Officielle (ETO) school compound in the capital, Kigali. At least the Belgian Government had the good sense to feel humiliated by the decision to abandon Rwanda at its moment of greatest need and, thus, sought to cover its guilt by prodding the entire world to share its culpability.

To the everlasting sorrow of Rwanda, the Belgians found the administration of U.S. President Bill Clinton ready and willing. Largely for their own entirely short-term partisan reasons, with pathological United Nations-hating Republicans breathing down their necks, the Clintonites were unprepared to have anything whatsoever to do with sending a new United Nations mission to a tiny African country which, as is invariably said, almost no American could even find on a map. Among the P5, France was the only country genuinely concerned about Rwanda for its own perverse reasons of francophone solidarity, and it was stealthily seeking a way to intervene on behalf of the Hutu extremist *genocidaire* government. It was left to U.S. Ambassador to the UN, Madeleine Albright, to lead a vigorous movement in the Security Council to literally decimate UNAMIR's twenty-five hundred-odd force. Britain, for reasons British journalist-historian Linda Melvern is still trying to unravel, fell in solidly behind the Americans. Russia and China were largely uninterested, a situation that would change significantly in the case of Darfur. At the end of the genocide's second week, with an estimated one hundred thousand or more Tutsi and almost all prominent moderate Hutu already dead, and the genocide gaining daily momentum, the Security Council voted to reduce the UNAMIR mission to two hundred fifty men. UN Force Commander Romeo Dallaire, furious and sick at heart, disobeyed this explicit instruction and managed to retain four hundred men for the duration of the genocide.

Even now, it is impossible to recapitulate these events without feeling they cannot possibly be true. But as virtually all authorities on the subject agree, and as the Security Council's reaction to Darfur a decade later makes entirely clear, they were only too true, and their lesson was clear. There seemed barely any depths to which the members of the "international community" would not sink if it was deemed necessary to its national interests, even if that interest was nothing more nor less than, in Belgium's case, covering up a cowardly abandonment of a people at ultimate risk, or for the United States, winning an impending election. Political expediency was all, and human need seemed completely irrelevant.

However, two other lessons of the international reaction, distressing as they were at the time, seemed to offer a certain hope for intervention in future crises. First, were the lies told by both U.S. President Bill Clinton and UN Secretary-General Kofi Annan when later apologizing for their inaction during the 100 days. Both claimed that they were insufficiently aware of the situation at the time. These claims, on the part of both men, have been repudiated beyond a shadow of a doubt. They knew everything, or at least everything they wanted to know. Nevertheless, their very disingenuousness permitted the inference that the next time "another Rwanda" loomed, if it could attain a sufficiently high public profile, the Security Council would no longer have the excuse of ignorance and, thus, have little alternative but to intervene. This apparent truth initially gave heart to the movement to intervene in Darfur.

Second, as already noted, almost no one in an official position at the time agreed to characterize Rwanda as a genocide and, led again by the Clinton administration, actually denied that a genocide was, in fact, in progress. This refusal to affirm the obvious was tied directly to the Clintonites' electoral fears. Government lawyers studying the 1948 Genocide Convention appear to have decided that accepting the genocide label would trigger a major obligation on the administration to intervene actively. That such an interpretation was highly debatable is neither here nor there. It was perfectly possible to argue that a mere Security Council resolution satisfied the wording of the UNCG. But Clinton's advisors chose not to adopt this reading. Their judgment powerfully affected Clinton's public stance.

Television captured a moment of true self-debasement when a U.S. State Department spokesperson, Christine Shelly, tried to explain to reporters that Rwanda was the scene of "acts of genocide" but not of genocide. When pushed to indicate how many "acts of genocide" constitute one full genocide, Shelly, obviously humiliated beyond words, explained that she wasn't authorized to deal with that question. (To her everlasting chagrin, several documentaries on the genocide include footage of her disastrous performance, unforgivingly immortalizing her forever.) The difference between this pathetic moment and subsequent American reactions to Darfur under President Bush could hardly have been more glaring.

And indeed, Clinton's position that there was no full-blown genocide in Rwanda unwittingly provided the glimmer of hope out of an act of unsurpassed political opportunism. If Rwanda was "not quite" a genocide, and therefore intervention was not obligatory, it surely followed logically that if a genocide were declared in future, would it not mean that intervention was mandatory, inescapable? That logic, combined with the prospect that if a disaster was well-enough publicized, the world would have little choice but to move in, offered some real hope that the "next Rwanda" would not be betrayed and abandoned as the original Rwanda had been.

The Next Rwanda

Then came Darfur. Less than a decade after Hutu Power was defeated, the world had found its "next Rwanda." It is irrelevant to the argument of this essay that genocide authorities (including those represented in the present volume) disagree about whether the conflict is a genocide or not. All agree that it has had many of the dimensions of a genocide, that it is an appalling catastrophe, and that robust intervention is demanded. As we know, no such intervention has occurred, and as of this writing (Summer 2006), the situation seems to have deteriorated substantially and become even more complex — the almost inevitable consequence of the world's meager response to date. From the point of view of the hopes raised by two of the optimistic lessons from Rwanda, the response of the "international community" to the crisis in Darfur can only be considered a giant, tragic set-back. It is not too much to say that Darfur shows that only the first despairing lesson — the bottomless cynicism and self-interest of the major powers — remains valid, while the hopes have been largely destroyed.

After all, by the middle of 2004, at the very latest, everyone who counts knew that an overwhelming political and humanitarian man-made disaster had befallen western Sudan. On April 7, when he rightly should have been in Kigali for the commemoration of the tenth anniversary of the Rwandan genocide, Kofi Annan was instead in Geneva unveiling a new five-point plan for genocide prevention and announcing that the world must not permit Darfur to become "another Rwanda." Everyone who counts soon either visited Khartoum to plead with the Government of Sudan that was orchestrating the crisis, or popped in at a displaced persons or refugee camp in Darfur or across the border in Chad. When Annan and Colin Powell make a stop somewhere, you know that it is already a major story. It may not have competed with the Michael Jackson trial, but even in the mainstream media, Darfur stories, features, and opinion pieces were remarkably common for a crisis so remote and complex.

The crisis in Darfur, in other words, was fairly big news. This was unlike Rwanda. Clinton and Annan knew all about Rwanda, but media coverage for many weeks was both minimal and distorted ("tribal savagery") so the public remained largely uninformed. Yet despite Darfur's profile, the Security Council was effectively paralyzed by the conflicting interests of the veto-casting P5. This time China, thirsty for Sudan's oil, and Russia, anxious to sell arms to a genocidal government, also played spoiler roles. The Council passed a series of powder-puff resolutions each threatening the killers in Khartoum that if they did not rein in their *Janjaweed* forces they would be forcefully confronted with yet another resolution. Perhaps not since a representative of Rwanda's *genocidaire* government retained his position on the Security Council through the entire 1994 genocide has the Security Council appeared to be more of a joke than over Darfur.

The Role of the United States

Yet there was another reason for hope. For reasons already documented in this book, both the Congress and Executive Branch of the U.S. Government publicly declared that Darfur constituted a genuine genocide under the 1948 Convention. Such a radical and dramatic step was unprecedented in United States history. Both chambers of Congress (the House and the Senate) hastily and unanimously passed their own resolutions declaring Darfur to be a genocide with barely an explanation, let alone debate, and President Bush and Secretary of State Colin Powell each eventually followed with their own concurring declarations. To the genocide prevention community, this seemed the moment they had so long dreamed of and planned for. What would be the point of making this declaration unless significant action was being planned? It was true the Bush administration, and others, were modestly generous in providing humanitarian aid to the displaced and the refugees as well as funding for the Africa Union Mission to Darfur. But now, surely, with these declarations, was the long-awaited moment of qualitative escalation. Now we would see the kind of forceful intervention denied Rwanda that was crucial if the travesty in Sudan was to end.

In fact, all that was needed was to pay heed to the second part of Colin Powell's statement before the U.S. Senate Foreign Relations Committee. Yes, the United States had decided, upon looking at evidence of the investigation it had specifically commissioned (the exact opposite of Rwanda) that a genocide was taking place before the eyes of the world. Powell had no doubt what the world expected next, and said so explicitly: "Mr. Chairman, some seem to have been waiting for this determination of genocide to take action. In fact, however, no new action is dictated by this determination. We have been doing everything we can to get the Sudanese Government to act responsibly. So, let us not be preoccupied with this designation of genocide. These people are in desperate need and we must help them. Call it a civil war. Call it ethnic cleansing. Call it genocide. Call it 'none of the above'. The reality is the same: There are people in Darfur who desperately need our help" (Powell, 2004).

How was this possible? Had the historic declaration of genocide been nothing more than an opportunistic political ploy by the Bush administration to assuage some domestic pressure groups? Could even the Bush neocons [neoconservatives] be so cynical as to play politics with genocide? If not, how could this wholly unanticipated development be explained? How could the esteemed Colin Powell participate in this destructive exercise, which has done so much to debase the currency of the Genocide Convention?

Within mere months of the U.S. Government's determination of genocide in Darfur, a new Bush administration betrayal of Darfur was exposed. First came the revelation that the CIA had sent a plane to Khartoum to ferry the head of Sudanese intelligence, General Salah Abdallah Gosh, to Washington for discussions with his American peers on the "war against terror." Sudan, it appears, had become "a crucial intelligence asset to the CIA" (Goldenberg, 2005). Nevermind that General Gosh's name is widely assumed to be among the fifty-one leading Sudanese officials named by the UN-appointed International Commission of Inquiry on Darfur. The "war on terrorism" obviously trumps genocide.

Later we learned just how close this tie really was. In October 2005, *Guardian* reporter Jonathan Steele reported the following:

> Question: When do Bush administration officials cuddle up to leaders of states that the U.S. describes as sponsors of international terrorism? Answer: When they are in Khartoum. I know because I saw it the other day.... We were attending the closing dinner of a two-day conference of African counter-terrorism officials, to which the U.S. and U.K. were invited as observers. The western spooks were less than happy to have the western press on hand, especially as their names were called out. But loss of anonymity was a small price for the excellent cooperation both agencies believe Sudan is giving to keep tabs on Somalis, Saudis, and other Arab fundamentalists who pass through its territory....
>
> [The dinner] was in the garden of the headquarters of Sudan's intelligence service, not far from the Nile. Up stepped a senior CIA agent. In full view of the assembled company, he gave General Salah Abdallah Gosh, Sudan's intelligence chief, a bear hug. The general responded by handing over a goody-bag, wrapped in shiny green paper. Next up was the [British] M16 official, with the same effusive routine (Steele, 2005, n.p.).

There are still Darfur activists who believe that despite close working relationships between the Bush administration and precisely those Sudanese leaders against whom the International Criminal Court intends to issue warrants, the United States can still be relied on as an ally in pressuring Khartoum to end its war against the black Africans. I wish I could agree. The Khartoum Government is as canny as it is treacherous, and blithely uses its leverage to continue getting away with murder in Darfur. It now has trump cards with the Americans, the Chinese, and the Russians. Those of us who urge intervention on strictly humanitarian grounds have no comparable influence whatsoever. The result is virtually preordained: The death and rape and suffering in western Sudan will continue.

Are there now lessons from Darfur, having seen that the only lesson from Rwanda that proved relevant was the most despairing one? It is almost too disheartening even to ask. But for those committed to genocide prevention or to interventions on strictly humanitarian grounds, tough questions must again be asked, creative new directions and mechanisms sought. The alternative is too ghastly to contemplate.

References

Goldenberg, Suzanne (2005). "Ostracized Sudan Emerges as Key American Ally in 'War on Terror.'" *Guardian Weekly*, May 6–12, p. 7.

Powell, Colin (2004). "The Crisis In Darfur." Written remarks presented before the Senate Foreign Relations Committee, Washington, D.C., September 9, 2004. http://www.state.gov/secretary/former/powell/remarks/36032.htm

Steele, Jonathan (2005). "Darfur Wasn't Genocide and Sudan is Not a Terrorist." *Guardian*, October 7, pp. n.p.

CHAPTER 12

Proving Genocide in Darfur: The Atrocities Documentation Project and Resistance to Its Findings

GREGORY H. STANTON

The U.S. Secretary of State, Colin Powell, on September 9, 2004 declared "that genocide has occurred in Darfur and the Government of Sudan and the *Janjaweed* bear responsibility, and genocide may still be continuing."[1]

The State Department has not historically been forward leaning in making findings of genocide, as was notoriously evident during its refusal to apply the term "genocide" to Rwanda in 1994 until most of the eight hundred thousand victims had been murdered. For Darfur, however, the State Department's Bureau of Democracy, Human Rights and Labor, and the Ambassador for War Crimes Issues, Pierre-Richard Prosper, adopted an exemplary strategy of proof. Prosper was the prosecutor in the *Akayesu* case,[2] which resulted in history's first conviction after trial by an international criminal tribunal applying the Genocide Convention. The State Department's strategy demonstrated the careful investigation and solid legal analysis that made Prosper such a formidable prosecutor at the International Criminal Tribunal for Rwanda (ICTR).

The Atrocities Documentation Project

Prosper knew that proof of genocide must be based on authoritative facts. He arranged for the State Department's Bureau of Democracy, Human Rights and Labor to commission a thorough investigation by experts recruited by the Coalition for International Justice (CIJ), and funded by the U.S. Agency for International Development's Office of Transition Initiatives. The result was the Darfur Atrocities Documentation Project (ADP), the first use of systematic social science survey research to prove commission of genocide and crimes against humanity. An interviewing tool was formulated and tested, and systematic random sampling methods were then used to interview over eleven hundred eyewitnesses in Sudanese refugee camps in Chad, a sample large enough to be a statistically significant representation of the estimated two hundred thousand Darfuri refugees in Chad. The interviewing teams were carefully chosen and given full support for the project. Then Prosper and the State Department Legal Advisers' Office applied international law to the facts without determining in advance what the conclusion would be. The legal conclusions were properly separated from their political consequences.

The results of the CIJ report were shocking. Over 60 percent of the people interviewed had witnessed the killing of a family member. Two-thirds had witnessed the killing of a nonfamily member. Over 80 percent had witnessed destruction of a village. Two-thirds had witnessed aerial bombing of villages by the Sudanese government. And perhaps most chillingly, one-third had heard racial epithets used while they or their relatives were being murdered or raped. Assailants often shouted, "Kill the slaves," and "We have orders to kill all the blacks." Over two hundred fifty thousand black Africans have died in Darfur and over two million people have been displaced from their homes. The State Department Report stated that as of September 2004, Arab *Janjaweed* militias, supported by Sudanese government bombing, had burned to the ground over six hundred villages.

The Finding of Genocide

Genocide, as defined by the UN Genocide Convention, is "the intentional destruction, in whole or in part, of a national, ethnical, racial, or religious group, as such." Was the killing "intentional?" Yes. According to the elements of crimes defined by the Statute of the International Criminal Court, genocide must be the result of a policy, which may be proved by direct orders or evidenced by systematic organization. Was the killing in Darfur systematically organized by the al-Bashir regime[3] using government-armed *Janjaweed* militias, bombers, and helicopter gunships? Yes. Were the victims chosen because of their ethnic and racial identity? Yes.

Fur, Massalit, and Zaghawa black African villages were destroyed, while Arab villages nearby were left untouched. The State Department report concludes that the "primary cleavage is ethnic: Arabs against Africans."[4] Does this conclusion constitute the intentional destruction, in part, of ethnic and racial groups? Yes. In short, the violence in Darfur is genocide, and it continues. The atrocities committed by the Sudanese Government and *Janjaweed* militias in Darfur meet all three requirements for genocide:

1. **The atrocities are intentional, evidenced by the systematic nature of their destruction** of major parts of the Fur, Massalit, Zaghawa, and tribal groups through killing and mass rape. The widespread expression of ethnic and racial intent to destroy by the perpetrators was strongly proven by the CIJ survey. The intent is specific — it is aimed at partial destruction of specific ethnic and racial groups. The fact that some members of the groups have been spared and allowed to flee to refugee and internally displaced persons (IDPs) camps is irrelevant to this finding of specific intentionality, contrary to the finding of the UN Commission of Inquiry. This is a case of "ethnic cleansing" being accomplished through genocide. The two crimes are not mutually exclusive.

2. **The crimes are directed against groups protected by the Genocide Convention**. The Fur, Massalit, and Zaghawa are ethnic groups who have their own languages, cultures, and preferential kinship systems, distinguishing them from the Arab perpetrators not by color, but by ethnicity. The claim by the Sudanese Government that both perpetrators and victims are alike is simply false. The fact is that the African groups being attacked are culturally distinctive, and their attackers certainly recognize the distinctions when they refer to their victims as "blacks" and/or "slaves."

3. **The crimes include all the acts of genocide enumerated in the Genocide Convention:** Widespread mass killings of people targeted because of their ethnic identity; mass rape, causing serious bodily or mental harm to members of the groups; deliberately inflicting on the groups destruction of crops, poisoning of wells, and other conditions of life calculated to bring about their physical destruction in whole or in part; imposing measures intended to prevent births by the group (directly declared by rapists who tell their victims, "Now you will bear light-skinned children."); and kidnapping the children of the group and forcing them into slavery.

The al-Bashir regime in Sudan has mastered genocide and ethnic cleansing, having combined these crimes before in the Nuba Mountains and in southern Sudan, where over two million black Africans died over the course of the twenty-one-year-long civil war between the North and the South.[5] In the South, the government wants to confiscate rich oil reserves under the lands of the Nuer, Dinka, Shilluk, Nuba, and other black African groups. In Darfur, the regime is driven by the racist ideology of the "Arab Gathering," a secretive elite reminiscent of the Ku Klux Klan or Nazi Party, that wants to "arabize" Sudan and drive out black Africans in order to confiscate their grazing lands, water resources, and cattle herds.

One of the most insidious aspects of the Sudanese Government's genocide in Darfur is that its policy of direct mass murder is complemented by a longer-term strategy of what Helen Fein has named "genocide by attrition."[6] Alex De Waal calls it "famine that kills."[7] Mass murder by starvation has been a method of genocide for centuries, perfected by the Turks in Armenia in 1915 and by Stalin in 1933 Ukraine. It has been the strategy of choice of the Sudanese government, both in the South and in Darfur. It is a shrewd strategy because death comes slowly for many of its victims and denial is easy. All a government need do is arm and support militias, which drive a self-sufficient people off their land through terror, herd them into displaced persons and refugee camps, then systematically impede aid from getting to them, letting them slowly die of starvation and disease. The deaths can then be blamed on "famine," "disease," "ancient tribal conflicts," or "civil war," or most cynically, "failure of the international community to provide needed relief."

Resistance and Denial

There was dissent regarding the classification of genocide within the State Department's Office of the Legal Adviser from die-hard deniers, including George Taft, who was one of the State Department lawyers who notoriously opposed calling the Rwandan genocide by its proper name for over two months in 1994. Even after more than two hundred fifty thousand people had died in Darfur, Taft told me personally in Washington, D.C., on August 16, 2005 (witnessed by the former U.S. Ambassador to Rwanda, David Rawson), that the Darfur mass murders do not constitute genocide, and he opposed use of the term *genocide* for Darfur. Fortunately, the State Department's Legal Adviser, William H. Taft IV, and Secretary of State Colin Powell had already exercised better legal judgment in September 2004 as a result of the findings of the ADP and had determined that the mass killing in Darfur was genocide.

The legal deniers' main argument is that the killings don't fit the definition of genocide. Such "definitionalist" denial, which is based on technical legal doubt about proof of one of the elements of the crime of genocide (usually intent), is most common among lawyers and policymakers who want to avoid intervention beyond provision of humanitarian aid. It results in "analysis paralysis," which the State Department/CIJ ADT and report brilliantly overcame. Nevertheless, the European Union, the Secretary-General of the United Nations, and even Human Rights Watch and Amnesty International still avoid calling the crimes in Darfur by their proper name. There are five reasons for such reluctance.

1. Among journalists, the general public, diplomats, and lawyers who haven't read the Genocide Convention, there is a common misconception that a finding of genocide would legally require action to suppress it. Under this misconception and having been informed that the United States would take no action in Rwanda in 1994, State Department lawyers ordered avoidance of the word. They made their legal conclusion fit the Procrustean bed of United States policy.

   Unfortunately, the Genocide Convention carries no such legal compulsion to act. It legally requires only that states–parties to the Convention pass national laws against genocide and then prosecute or extradite those who commit the crime. Article VIII of the Convention says they also "*may* call upon the competent organs of the United Nations to take such action under the Charter of the United Nations as they consider appropriate for the prevention and suppression of acts of genocide" (emphasis added). But, they are not legally required to do so. Article I of the Genocide Convention creates a moral obligation to prevent genocide, but it does not dictate military intervention or any other particular measure.

2. Another misconception is the "all or none" concept of genocide. The "all or none" school considers killings to be genocide only if the intent is to destroy a national, ethnic, racial, or religious group "in *whole*." Their model is the Holocaust. They ignore the "in part" in the definition in the Genocide Convention. This school would render the Convention for the *Prevention* and Punishment of the Crime of Genocide (emphasis added) functionally useless, since genocide could only be found after an entire group was dead. It would also limit applicability of the Convention to just three cases: Armenia, the Holocaust, and Rwanda; a mistake that Dr. Alain Destexhe made in his 1994 book on the Rwandan genocide.[8]

3. Since the 1990s, a new obstacle to calling genocide by its proper name has been the distinction between genocide and "ethnic

cleansing." Genocide and "ethnic cleansing" are sometimes portrayed as mutually exclusive crimes, but they are not. Professor William Schabas, for example, says "it is incorrect to assert that ethnic cleansing is a form of genocide, or even that in some cases, ethnic cleansing amounts to genocide."[9] He argues that the specific intent of "ethnic cleansing" is *expulsion* of a group, whereas the specific intent of "genocide" is its *destruction*, in whole or in part. He illustrates with a simplistic distinction: In "ethnic cleansing," borders are left open and a group is driven out; in "genocide," borders are closed and a group is killed. The fallacy of the distinction arises from the misconception that an act or policy can have only one specific intent. Any prosecutor knows that the same act may have several intents and constitute the basis for several criminal charges. The Sudanese Government has at least two intents in Darfur. One is to destroy a significant part of the Fur, Massalit, and Zaghawa population of Darfur. That is genocide. The other intent of the Sudanese Government and their *Janjaweed* militias is to drive Fur, Massalit, and Zaghawa black African farmers off of their ancestral lands, *using* terror caused by mass murder, mass rape, mass starvation, and concentration camps run by *Janjaweed* and Sudanese army guards. That is "ethnic cleansing." Thus, *both* ethnic cleansing and genocide are underway in Darfur.

4. Another way to avoid use of the term "genocide" is to confuse motive with intent. An example is the claim that the motive of the perpetrator is merely "ethnic cleansing" of a territory, not "genocide," which requires the specific intent to *destroy*, in whole or in part, a national, ethnic, racial, or religious group. The UN Commission of Experts report of 2005 made this mistake. Ironically, the Commission report even included a paragraph saying motive and intent should not be confused, an exhortation the Commission promptly violated.[10] Even if a stated or otherwise evident motive of a perpetrator is to drive a group off its land ("ethnic cleansing"), the methods used to terrorize the group may include killing part of the group and other acts enumerated in the Genocide Convention, resulting in the destruction of the group, in whole or in part. That is what is happening in Darfur. That is genocide.

5. The most important diplomatic argument against using the term *genocide* was that it would antagonize the Sudanese Government, cut off United States ability to act as a mediator in "the peace

process," and jeopardize Sudanese cooperation in the war on terror. George Taft explicitly stated this view to me when I discussed the State Department's determination with him. This *realpolitik* argument has been especially effective in frightening diplomats who fear upsetting the peace processes between North and South, and now between Darfur rebels and the Sudanese government. In 2005 and 2006, the argument has become: "Don't upset the fragile new order in Khartoum put in place by the agreements settling the civil war in the South. Let's concentrate on getting the Darfur 'rebels' to reach a similar agreement with Khartoum in Abuja under the African Union. And by all means don't jeopardize Sudanese cooperation with the United States in the war on terror." Most recently that policy was demonstrated when the chief of the Sudanese intelligence service, Salah Abdallah Gosh, one of the main planners of the Darfur genocide, was flown by executive jet to confer with the CIA in Langley, Virginia.[11]

Overcoming Appeasement

Meanwhile, the ethnic cleansing of Darfur is nearly complete, and genocidal massacres and rapes continue daily.[12] Diplomats repeatedly and naïvely avoid antagonizing genocidists, ignoring the fact that they are serial killers. Policies toward them based on fear lead only to appeasement and further genocide. Unfortunately, such appeasement now seems to be the main illusion driving U.S. policy.

It is time for the United States to recognize that seven thousand African Union military observers without a robust mandate cannot protect civilians in Darfur. We should seek a Chapter VII UN Security Council resolution mandating the African Union to protect civilians in Darfur, and calling on United Nations members to quickly provide it with strong military and financial resources. If the resolution cannot pass the Security Council, or if the African Union refuses the mandate, the United States and NATO should declare a no-fly zone over Darfur and enforce it with AWACS planes, NATO jets, and helicopter gunships. If Sudanese Government bombers and gunships violate it and continue to bomb and machine-gun villagers in Darfur, the planes should be shot down. NATO should also prepare a heavy infantry force to intervene if *Janjaweed* militias continue their reign of ethnic cleansing, mass rape, and genocide.

Those who are bystanders to genocide are guilty of complicity. In genocide, only the stars are neutral.

Notes

1. Hearing of the U.S. Senate Foreign Relations Committee, 9 September 2004.
2. Jean-Paul Akayesu was a bourgmestre (mayor) in the Taba commune of Gitarama. On 2 September 1998, the ICTR found him guilty of "genocide, direct and public incitement to commit genocide, and crimes against humanity (extermination, murder, torture, rape, and other inhumane acts.)" One of the court's most significant findings was that systematic mass rape is an act of genocide under Article 2 (b) of the Genocide Convention ("Causing serious mental or bodily harm to members of the group") when it is intended to destroy the group (ICTR-96-4-1).
3. Lieutenant General Omar Hassan Ahmed al-Bashir took power in a military coup by the National Islamic Front (NIF) in 1989, when he became Prime Minister, and he has been President since October 1993.
4. State Department Report, page 1, Summary.
5. Eric Reeves (2005), "Darfur: Genocide Before Our Eyes," in J. Apsel, Ed., *Darfur: Genocide Before Our Eyes*, New York: Institute for the Study of Genocide, p. 28.
6. Helen Fein (1993). "Accounting for Genocide after 1945: Theories and Some Findings," *International Journal of Group Rights*, I:79, p. 106.
7. Alex De Waal (2005, rev. ed.). *Famine that Kills. Darfur, Sudan.* London: Oxford University Press.
8. Alain Destexhe, M.D. (2004). *Rwanda, essai sur le genocide.* Paris: Editions Complexe.
9. William Schabas (2000). *Genocide in International Law.* Cambridge, U.K.: Cambridge University Press, p. 200.
10. Report of the International Commission of Inquiry on Darfur to the United Nations Secretary-General Pursuant to Security Council Resolution 1564 of 18 September 2004, 25 January 2005, paragraph 493: "Of course, this special intent must not be confused with motive, namely the particular reason that may induce a person to engage in criminal conduct. For instance, in the case of genocide, a person intending to murder a set of persons belonging to a protected group, with the specific intent of destroying the group (in whole or in part), may be motivated, for example, by the desire to appropriate the goods belonging to that group or set of persons, or by the urge to take revenge for prior attacks by members of that group, or by the desire to please his superiors who despise that group. From the viewpoint of criminal law, what matters is not the motive, but rather whether or not there exists the requisite special intent to destroy a group."
11. *The New York Times*, June 18, 2005.
12. See daily news updates at: http://savedarfur.org/go.php?q=latestNews.html and http://www.genocidewatch.org/SUDAN2003Page.htm

CHAPTER 13

'Atrocity Statistics' and Other Lessons from Darfur

SCOTT STRAUS

Introduction

The Darfur crisis has demonstrated, yet again, that an international commitment to prevent genocide does not meaningfully exist. That conclusion may not be surprising, but for those who need reminding, Darfur reveals the hollowness of the post-Holocaust promise of "never again." In Darfur, for nearly three years, the Sudanese Government together with militia proxies committed widespread, systematic violence against the region's black African population. The violence was public and often executed in broad daylight. The violence was massive: Arab perpetrators displaced more than two million black Africans and claimed the lives of more than two hundred thousand civilians. The early stages of the conflict did not attract much international concern; however, starting in mid-2004, Darfur received considerable attention in the U.S. press. Eventually, the violence led to unprecedented government focus in the United States, including the first time that an administration authoritatively accused another state of committing genocide while the genocide was happening.[1] Yet, as we know, despite the public nature of the violence, despite excellent information, and despite civil society and government attention, there developed no concrete policy to stop the violence. Genocide persisted, yet again. The question of why deserves our attention.

My brief commentary here has two principal objectives. First, I want to explore some reasons why the international response to Darfur was so lackluster. Darfur's lessons are not those from Rwanda of a decade earlier. Unlike Rwanda, Darfur did generate considerable attention from citizens, scholars, and policymakers as the crisis unfolded. Unlike Rwanda, policymakers did not shy away from employing the term *genocide*. Darfur demonstrated that visibility and labeling violence *genocide* are not enough to trigger international intervention. Second, I want to highlight some important developments that emerged during the Darfur crisis. Chief among them, in my view, is the Darfur Atrocities Documentation Team (ADT). The ADT systematically collected evidence about patterns of violence in the midst of an unfolding crisis. Such documentation sets an important precedent. If a cogent policy to prevent genocide emerges over time, that policy should include social scientific documentation of atrocities. The ADT is a benchmark for future projects of this sort, and I want to highlight some important aspects of the project.

In the end, the international response to the Darfur crisis was a failure. Despite the renewed international attention to genocide in the wake of Rwanda and Bosnia, the international community did not act decisively to stop the systematic destruction of human lives. At the same time, there were important developments that happened during the Darfur crisis. For those who are interested in developing a more sophisticated and effective approach to stopping genocide, the task is to understand both what went wrong, but also what went right. The remainder of my commentary is one step in that direction.

Defining the Crime of Crimes

Genocide is the "crime of crimes," as is often said. The UN Convention on the Prevention and Punishment of Genocide (UNCG) was one of the first major international human rights treaties. The Convention itself differs from other treaties because it obligates signatories to "undertake to prevent" genocide. Yet the term *genocide* is a contested concept. Policymakers and scholars disagree about what constitutes genocide. Some believe genocide is the attempt to destroy whole groups, in particular ethnic, racial, and religious groups. Others believe that genocide is the attempt to destroy groups "in part" (as per the UNCG). Still others argue that genocide should not be limited to racial, religious, and ethnic groups; political, economic, and other social groups also are victims of genocide.[2] The definitional debate is not likely to disappear soon. Darfur shows us why the conceptual disagreement matters.

As others in this book have shown, a major sticking point as the Darfur crisis unfolded was whether to label the violence *genocide*. After coming under pressure to use the word *genocide*, the Bush administration commissioned a study (hence, triggering the ADT). Later, the UN Security Council established a Commission of Inquiry (COI). Both investigations found broadly similar patterns of violence in Darfur. Yet, after reviewing the ADT results, Secretary of State Powell made a genocide determination, while the authors of the COI did not. We might take issue with the logic of the United Nations report, as Jerry Fowler aptly does in Chapter 8, "A New Chapter of Irony: The Legal Definition of Genocide and the Implications of Powell's Determination." But the difference of opinion is also rooted in ambiguity about what genocide is and what genocide is not.

Recognizing and resolving that ambiguity are critical to devising a future strategy for preventing genocide. If major international actors disagree about what genocide is, then "genocide" becomes a difficult term around which to galvanize major international action. Pierre-Richard Prosper (U.S. State Department, Ambassador-at-Large for War Crimes) is quoted as having wanted to make a pure legal determination about whether the violence in Darfur constituted "genocide." The sentiment is valid, but a "pure" genocide standard does not yet exist.

Atrocity Statistics

The ADT did more than lay bare definitional disagreements. In particular, the ADT established and executed an innovative methodology for systematically documenting patterns of violence in the midst of a humanitarian emergency. The survey produced, in the words of Jonathan Howard (State Department Office of Research), "atrocity statistics." (See Chapter 4, "Survey Methodology and the Darfur Genocide") The term *atrocity statistics* is jarring, but the idea is extremely important. Systematic documentation should be a critical aspect of any response to a potential genocide. The ADT establishes an important precedent and, as such, I want to highlight a few important dimensions of the project.

First, the members of the ADT team designed a questionnaire to determine whether genocide was taking place. In so doing, the survey's authors operationalized genocide; they thought through what kind of evidence would be needed to make a genocide determination. The survey included questions about what respondents heard during attacks; analysts could, in turn, examine the responses to measure the perpetrators' intent. Both the survey questions and the responses are important for developing a more precise understanding of genocide and for helping outsiders recognize when genocide is occurring. Whether future surveys replicate the same questions or develop new ones, the ADT survey is a benchmark in this regard.

Second, the ADT developed a creative sampling methodology that others may use in the future. As Howard describes well in his chapter, the ADT researchers sampled randomly, and they did so using an innovative "random route" technique. Anyone who has done field research on atrocities — whether the research is done in the name of journalism, scholarship, or a particular project — knows that asking questions about violence is never neutral. Often local elites want outsiders to come away with a particular version of events; in other instances, those who have suffered have a particular experience that they want to share. However, the ADT mandate was to document how widespread and systematic the violence was. In so doing, the investigators sought to understand how representative particular patterns of violence were and to do so they sampled randomly. Genocide and social science methods are not often paired. However, the ADT did pair them, and to great effect.

Third, the sample size was impressive. Like randomization, a large sample size mattered. Often international human rights organizations are limited in the scope of their investigations. Given financial, travel, or time constraints, human rights reports often are based on dozens of field interviews. By contrast, the ADT conducted more than eleven hundred interviews. The result was unusually comprehensive documentation of the character and extent of violence in Darfur. Future researchers may well find reason to improve on the methods, but the ADT set a standard for systematic, social scientific collection of evidence.

The ADT also was significant because it showed that with enough professionalism, resources, and dedication such an effort can succeed. No one should underestimate the difficulty of quickly executing a large-scale research project in the middle of an emergency in an area as remote as eastern Chad. The logistical challenges are formidable, as Stefanie Frease and Nina Bang-Jansen make clear in Chapter 3, "Creating the ADT: Turning a Good Idea into Reality." Finding transportation, healthcare, money, food, shelter, and the like all require time and focus. Translation is also fundamental. The ADT brought experience and professionalism to bear on the project. I make the point because, based on my experiences in other contexts, notably Rwanda, I know how difficult and important the logistical and translation issues are.[3] The same is true for designing and carrying out a survey of more than eleven hundred refugees. The ways in which the ADT handled these issues provide a roadmap for future projects of this sort.

Not Just Political Will

Yet, as we know, despite the professionalism and excellence of the ADT project, despite the team's findings, and despite Secretary Powell's historic genocide determination, little international action materialized to halt the violence in Darfur. Why? The standard answer concerns political will. When it is absent, politicians will not act and, thus, citizens must force genocide onto the national agenda. Much of this common wisdom comes from Rwanda, where the genocide received scant domestic attention at the time the violence occurred. However, Darfur's lesson is different. Darfur shows us that raising the profile of an issue and generating domestic political will are insufficient to galvanize a policy to halt genocide.

For a humanitarian emergency and for a complex crisis in a remote part of Africa, Darfur was a remarkably salient foreign policy issue. As the crisis developed, an unusual and bipartisan coalition of civil society groups emerged, calling for action. Editorialists in newspapers around the nation wrote about Darfur, and a vibrant student movement formed on college campuses around the country. U.S. Government officials were broadly responsive. Congress passed a historic resolution calling the violence in Darfur "genocide." Secretary of State Powell made a high-profile visit to the region. Powell later commissioned the ADT study, he reviewed the results, and he made a genocide determination. President George W. Bush followed suit. The genocide declarations were historic: Never before had a sitting government so authoritatively labeled an ongoing crisis *genocide*. There was, in short, real visibility to the issue, sustained pressure, and apparent political movement on the issue.

What then was the problem? Any answer must be speculative at this stage, but the evidence does point in a couple important directions. For one, the Genocide Convention incorporates a definition of genocide that leaves considerable room for uncertainty about how to identify genocide. But more than that, as Fowler argues in Chapter 8, the Convention does not establish concrete mechanisms for stopping genocide. Signatories to the treaty "undertake to prevent" and "suppress" genocide; the Convention also includes language allowing member states to "bring genocide" to the Security Council for action (which the United States did). But specific enforcement mechanisms beyond such language are nonexistent. The Genocide Convention is unusual amongst international human rights treaties for its comparatively strong language. Darfur, however, shows that the Convention is weaker than many imagined. If international inaction is to be avoided in the future, revisiting the Convention — and its definitions and mechanisms for prevention — is in order.

But there is another arguably more significant issue. Darfur shows that international politics — and particularly politics at the United Nations — matter. One reason that Darfur did not get traction at the United Nations was that China, especially, and Russia strongly opposed more forceful intervention to stop the violence. China has significant oil interests in Sudan; China also bristles when human rights trump sovereignty in the international arena. Russia also does not want human rights to be a standard for military intervention. With China and Russia firmly opposed to forceful action in Darfur, the UN Security Council became a dead end for generating a policy to halt the violence. Both China and Russia are permanent members of the Security Council and, as such, each has the ability to veto resolutions. Politics within the Security Council, thus, became a fundamental obstacle to forceful UN action on the issue. That matter needs to be taken seriously.

But Darfur also had fairly little traction in Europe. Diplomatic fallout from the war in Iraq is probably partly the reason. By the time Secretary of State Colin Powell made a genocide determination and requested action from the Security Council, his actions lacked some of the credibility that they had prior to Iraq. In the end, the United States was largely alone when pressing for forceful international action on Darfur. Preventing genocide is and should be a multilateral issue. Moreover, given its commitments in Iraq and Afghanistan, the United States was in no position to initiate a new troop deployment. Certainly the United States could have done more, but Darfur shows that a strategy to stop genocide needs to take international politics seriously. In the United States, an effective approach to preventing genocide might start with lobbying policymakers and generating political will, but the issue does not end there.

Those in civil society, academia, and government — as well as ordinary citizens — who care about genocide, successfully learned many of Rwanda's lessons. When the crisis in Darfur broke, many lobbied for action, and many urged the government to make a genocide determination. The international response to Darfur represents another failure and, as happened after Rwanda, we should try to understand the reasons behind the failure in order to prepare for the next potential genocide. The international community, such as it exists, may still be a long way from having a concrete and effective strategy to prevent genocide, but examining what went wrong *and* what went right in Darfur might change that in the future.

Notes

1. Scott Straus, "Darfur and the Genocide Debate," *Foreign Affairs* 84:1 (2005), pp. 123–133.

2. For a longer discussion, see Scott Straus, "Contested Meanings and Conflicting Impera-tives: A Conceptual Analysis of Genocide," *Journal of Genocide Research* 3:3 (2001), pp. 349–375.
3. For a discussion of my research in Rwanda, see Scott Straus, *The Order of Genocide: Race, Power, and War in Rwanda,* Ithaca, NY: Cornell University Press (forthcoming).

PART 5

Analysis of the Rationale and Reasoning Behind the U.S. ADP and Genocide Determination

The U.S. Investigation into the Darfur Crisis and Its Determination of Genocide: A Critical Analysis

SAMUEL TOTTEN

Introduction

In July and August 2004, the U.S. State Department sponsored a field investigation (the Darfur Atrocities Documentation Project or ADP) whose express purpose was to ascertain whether genocide had been and/or was continuing to be perpetrated in Darfur. By that point in time, the Darfur crisis had been declared "the worst humanitarian disaster in the world" by Jan Egeland, the UN Under-Secretary for Humanitarian Affairs (UN, 2004, p. 1); the United States Holocaust Memorial Museum's Committee on Conscience had issued a genocide warning with regard to the killings and death in Darfur; and both the U.S. House of Representatives and U.S. Senate had declared the crisis to be a case of genocide.

Following an analysis of the data collected by the Darfur Atrocities Documentation Team (ADT), Secretary of State Colin Powell declared, on September 9, 2004, in a statement to the Senate Foreign Relations Committee, that genocide had been perpetrated in Darfur.

In the year and a half since the investigation and subsequent declaration by Powell, heated debate has erupted over the motives and value of the ADP

199

as well as the validity of the genocide determination. Some have asserted that while crimes against humanity have been perpetrated in Darfur, genocide has not. What follows is a discussion of the stated purpose, methodology, and findings of the ADP as well as the debate over the motives behind the ADP and the determination of genocide by the U.S. Government.

Findings

Ultimately, the State Department statistically analyzed eleven hundred thirty-six interviews conducted during the month-long ADP. Following the compilation and analysis of the survey data,[1] the State Department's Bureau of Intelligence and Research reported that "analysis of the refugee interviews points to a pattern of abuse against members of Darfur's non-Arab communities" (U.S. State Department, 2004a, p. 3). More specifically, the interviewees reported personally witnessing or experiencing the following:

- Killing of family member (61 percent)
- Killing of nonfamily member (67 percent)
- Shooting (44 percent)
- Death from displacement (28 percent)
- Abduction (25 percent)
- Beating (21 percent)
- Rape (16 percent)
- Hearing racial epithets (33 percent)
- Village destruction (81 percent)
- Theft of livestock (89 percent)
- Aerial bombing (67 percent)
- Destruction of personal property (55 percent)
- Looting of personal property (47 percent)

(U.S. Department of State, 2004a, p. 1).[2]

Significantly, the State Department report noted that "numerous credible reports corroborate the use of racial and ethnic epithets by both the *Janjaweed* and GoS military personnel: 'Kill the slaves! Kill the slaves!' and 'We have orders to kill all the blacks' are common" (U.S. Department of State, 2004a, p. 4).

In regard to those who carried out the attacks against the black Africans and their villages, the refugees' responses indicated the following:

- Both the *Janjaweed* and the GoS military (48 percent)
- The GoS alone (26 percent)

- The *Janjaweed* alone (14 percent)
- Unknown (12 percent)

(U.S. Department of State, 2004a, p. 4).

The Factors Resulting in Major Conclusion(s) of the Investigation

Once the study was completed, the findings and analysis were turned over to U.S. Ambassador-at-Large for War Crimes Pierre-Richard Prosper and U.S. Secretary of State Colin Powell. Kostas (Chapter 7), who interviewed Prosper in order to ascertain how the United States came to the "genocide determination," reports that "Craner and Prosper presented the State Department's approach as dispassionate and clinical. The purpose was 'to make a pure decision' — a 'clean legal and factual analysis' free of policy considerations — [...and in doing so] 'analyzed the facts with the breadth of the law in mind — meaning, genocide, crimes against humanity, war crimes...'" (p. 120).[3]

In a series of wide-ranging telephone conversations and meetings (between Powell and Prosper, and Powell and various Assistant Secretaries within the State Department) in which the participants compared and contrasted the findings of the ADP with the wording in the UN Convention on the Prevention and Punishment of Genocide (UNCG), it was gradually determined that genocide had been, and possibly continued to be, perpetrated in Darfur.

In speaking with Kostas and Eric Markusen during the course of a telephone interview, Prosper noted that he and Powell had a long and detailed discussion regarding the important but always sticky issue of "intent" (e.g., the genocidal "intent" of the perpetrators). Among the issues they discussed in regard to this matter were the following: "How they [the GoS] created these militias [the *Janjaweed*]; how they [the GoS] had the ability to rein them [the militias] in and then did not; how they [the GoS troops] acted in concert with the *Janjaweed* ... in attacking these [black African] villages ... the aerial bombardment and then *Janjaweed* would come in; and then the fact that the Government of Sudan would block humanitarian assistance to people in need" (quoted in Kostas, Chapter 7, p. 121). The aforementioned actions (and, in certain cases, lack of actions) led the State Department to infer "intent."

Prosper also spelled out the factors that the State Department officials considered in coming to their determination of genocide, and among the most significant were the following:

- The villages of the black Africans were attacked and destroyed while nearby Arab villages were not.

- A large number of men were killed, while a large number of women were raped.
- The means to existence, such as livestock and water, were, respectively, killed and polluted.
- The GoS prevented both medical care (and medicine) as well as humanitarian assistance from being delivered to the internally displaced persons (IDPs) camps where people were dying from a lack of food, water, and medical attention (Kostas, p. 121).

Based on the above factors, Powell, Prosper, and the other State Department personnel involved in the determination "concluded that there was a deliberate targeting of the groups with the intent to destroy" (Kostas, Chapter 7, p. 121). Speaking about the latter, Prosper stated that while examining and discussing the concepts of unlawful killing, causing of serious bodily and mental harm, all of which are actions that constitute an act of genocide under the UNCG, "... the real one that got us ... was the deliberate infliction of conditions of life calculated to destroy the group in whole, or in part... . [In regard to the situation in the IDP camps, Prosper and Powell could not find any] logical explanation for why the Sudan government was preventing humanitarian assistance and medicine [into the camps] other than to destroy the group" (quoted in Kostas, p. 121). Kostas notes that "[t]he Government of Sudan was seen as offering unbelievable excuses, leading Powell to conclude that there was a clearly intentional effort to destroy the people in the camps who were known to be almost exclusively black African" (pp. 121–122).

Finally, and tellingly,

Prosper's experience as a prosecutor supported his understanding that genocidal intent could be inferred from the evidence as well proved by express statements. As Prosper explains, Powell and he asked each other if the Government of Sudan was not committing genocide then "what else are they trying to do?" "What else could their intent be but to destroy this group?" First, Powell and Prosper looked at the coordination and collaboration between the Government of Sudan and the *Janjaweed*. Then, Powell and Prosper examined how the government acted once they were shown to have knowledge of the perpetrators of violence, the targeting of black African tribes, and the scale of human destruction in Darfur. This part was most convincing: The Government of Sudan "had knowledge across the board. Let's pretend that it wasn't coordinated. They knew what was going on and not only did they do nothing to stop it, they intentionally obstructed assistance that would have bettered the situation. So when you have knowledge, you take no steps to stop it, and then when people are trying to help you block the assistance, what else could you want other than for these people to die or to be destroyed?" (Kostas, p. 122).

On September 9, 2004, in testimony before the U.S. Senate Foreign Relations Committee, Secretary of State Colin Powell stated that based on a consistent and widespread pattern of atrocities (killings, rapes, the burning of villages) committed by the *Janjaweed* and government forces against non-Arab villagers, the State Department had concluded that "genocide has been committed in Darfur and that the Government of Sudan and the *Janjaweed* bear responsibility — and genocide may still be occurring" (p. 4). Continuing, Powell stated that:

- The United States was continuing to press the GoS to rein in the *Janjaweed* and that the GoS needed to "stop being complicit in such raids" (U.S. Department of State, 2004b, p. 2).
- The United States continued to strongly support the work of the African Union (AU) monitoring mission in Darfur and, in fact, "initiated the mission through base camp setup and logistics support by a private contractor" (U.S. Department of State, 2004b, p. 2).
- The United States had also called for an "expanded AU mission in Darfur through the provision of additional observers and protection forces" and "identified $20.5 million in FY04 funds for initial support of this expanded mission" (U.S. Department of State, 2004b, p. 3).

Then, acting under Article VIII of the UNCG, Powell reported that the United States was calling on the United Nations to initiate a full investigation into the situation in Darfur. In doing so, he said, "We believe in order to confirm the true nature, scope, and totality of the crimes our evidence reveals, a full-blown and unfettered investigation needs to occur" (U.S. Department of State, 2004b, p. 4).

Finally, Powell, in part, concluded his statement with these words: "Mr. Chairman, some seem to have been waiting for this determination of genocide to take action. *In fact, however, no new action is dictated by this determination.* We have been doing everything we can to get the Sudanese Government to act responsibly. So, let us not be preoccupied with this designation of genocide. These people are in desperate need and we must help them" (italics added) (U.S. Department of State, 2004b, p. 5).

Strengths and Limitations of the Investigation, the Genocide Finding, and Action Based upon the Genocide Finding

The strengths of the ADP were many. More specifically, a methodologically sound study resulted from the thought, effort, and expertise put into the development of the questionnaire and the way the investigation was carried out. As part of the methodology, each and every one of the twenty-four investigators asked the same set of questions listed on the questionnaire and documented the findings using the same coding methods. Second, the number of interviews conducted constituted a number large enough to result in statistically significant findings. (For a discussion of this matter, see the U.S. Department of State's *Documenting Atrocities in Darfur*. Washington, D.C., 2004.) Also, "the final data set used for the *Documenting Atrocities in Darfur* report represented three successive waves of data entry" (J. Howard, see Chapter 4, p. 68). More specifically, as Jonathan Howard, an analyst with the U.S. Department of States' Office of Research, reports:

> As successive teams of interviewers rotated through Chad, the Office of Research hired an international public opinion research company to create a data set from the remaining questionnaires. [T]he company's team of professional coders read each questionnaire thoroughly, verifying and correcting if necessary the interviewer's field codes. In all three rounds of data entry, a fifth of the questionnaires were randomly selected and recorded by an additional analyst to ensure accuracy in the coding process.
>
> Each questionnaire's demographic information, event codes, and attendant information were entered into the data set. Every questionnaire was entered by two different data entry specialists, or double-punched, to verify that the correct information had been entered. Once the two data entry specialists separately entered the data from a questionnaire, a computer compared the two and flagged any discrepancies.
>
> From the final data set, two databases were created. The first was the respondent database in which each line of data represents an individual refugee with all related demographics and event codes for that refugee. Eleven hundred thirty-six refugees are represented in the refugee database. The respondent data set was used to generate the atrocity percentages in the final report.... .
>
> Because each respondent may have experienced the same event multiple times — numerous refugees had experienced several attacks during their journey to Chad — during the analysis stage, it was necessary to write a syntax to prevent the statistical software

from counting multiple events toward the total for the survey population.... .

A second event database was also created in which the multiple events from each refugee's story were separated so that each line of data in the event database reported a single event. Ten thousand three hundred and four events are represented in the event database.... .

From the outset, the team decided to adopt a conservative approach to reporting the data collected during the documentation mission. To this end, during all three stages of data entry, events were coded as either eyewitness or hearsay. Eyewitness events were those reported to have been directly witnessed by the respondent, while hearsay events took place outside the respondent's presence. The atrocity statistics eventually reflected only events reported as eyewitnessed by the the refugees (pp. 68–69).

The efforts of the State Department's people on the ground in Chad and involved in the analysis of the data were seemingly impeccable. Indeed, State's personnel were serious, hardworking, dedicated, and demanding. From the outset, they seemed determined to collect and analyze the data in the most methodologically sound and accurate manner possible. Furthermore, the investigaors on the ground were highly professional in their approach to the work at hand and were seemingly intent on collecting as much data as possible under extremely trying conditions, and doing so in a way that accurately reflected the experiences of each interviewee.

Be that as it may, there were certain weaknesses and limitations to the investigation. First, the most obvious limitation was that the investigation was conducted solely in Chad versus in Darfur *and* the refugee camps in Chad. Had the ADT been provided access to both those black Africans in IDP camps in Darfur as well as those who remained in any villages that had not been destroyed (and, for that matter, those Arab villagers, who were not attacked but may have witnessed the attacks on the black Africans), the data would have been much richer. Entry into Darfur for the purpose of an investigation was not, it seemed, an option — or at least not one that the U.S. Government wanted to pursue — either due to the danger it might present to the interviewers and/or the cost of either alienating the Sudanese Government or being rebuffed. Second, the respondents were largely limited to those from the most western states of Darfur, as well as those refugees who, for the most part, had the least distance to travel to Chad. Again, the data would have been richer had the investigators been able to interview a wider swath of the black African population in Darfur. Third, as the interviews were being conducted in the first two weeks of the ADT, various investigators found that there were certain categories/

codings not listed on the questionnaire (e.g., questions about disappearances, sexual violence other than rape, separation by gender, targeting of the elderly, rebel activity in and/or near the villages) that they were collecting information about. As a result, the coordinators of the ADT took such concerns and suggestions and passed them on to other investigators spread out along the Chad/Sudanese border. The question that remains is this: Were the other investigators informed in a timely manner about the additional categories? And if not, did the investigators of their own accord add additional categories where they saw fit? If only some of the investigators added additional categories, then there is the problem that the information collected, in respect to new categories, was incomplete. That said, *the major categories that the State Department used to make the determination of genocide were included on the questionnaire every investigator used and, thus, the latter concern did not have any bearing at all on the final determination of genocide.* Finally, the process of delineating the data on the questionnaires could have been much more detailed (and uniform) had the investigators been directed to write up the most detailed narratives possible versus delineating the findings, as many did, by simply highlighting and succinctly commenting on key points.

According to sources within the U.S. State Department, the final determination of genocide was arrived at in a methodical and deliberate manner in which the evidence gathered during the investigation was compared to the exact wording and concepts delineated in the UNCG. Be that as it may, numerous scholars have called into question the motive(s) behind the determination of genocide. Some have not only questioned the motives, but have questioned and/or attempted to refute the validity of the determination.

Prior to highlighting some of the many debates surrounding the motives and validity of the determination, this author (who happens to think that the determination of genocide was the correct one to make and who, it should be noted, was one of the twenty-four investigators with the ADP) wishes to raise some issues that have been discussed in other chapters. First, numerous authors have indicated that the Bush administration felt pressed to display its concern over Darfur. In fact, as Kostas notes: "U.S. policy in Sudan was already of special interest to the Bush administration and had an important domestic constituency — the evangelical Christian community. Evangelicals had taken an interest in the plight of black Christians in southern Sudan and there was a growing left-right coalition on Darfur (p. 115)."[4] Furthermore, as Lorne Craner explained, "The Bush administration was eager to point to its leadership on Sudan policy to demonstrate that they could speak with authority on grave issues of human rights at a time when issues around the treatment of detainees, particularly at Guantánamo and Abu Ghraib, threatened to strip the administration's voice of legitimacy on human rights issues" (quoted in Kostas, p. 116). The latter points raise several questions: Was the determination of genocide truly as "dispassionate and clinical" (cum "apolitical") as some within the Bush administration claim? Was there possibly a bias going into the investigation that genocide would be found (or, at the least, was there, as strange as this sounds, an ardent hope that it would be found), and did that somehow tip the scale in favor of such a determination? And was there already a plan that if a genocide determination was made the White House would simply pass the matter onto the United Nations, thus, being able to claim, as it did, that the United States need not do any more than it had already done? At this point in time, such questions are simply that, questions; however, they do merit further examination and study. It should be duly noted that the aforementioned questions are not raised to question the validity of the determination of the genocide, but to acknowledge that there may have been certain factors at work that favored a particular determination — that is, a certain propensity that may have tipped the scales, so to speak, in favor of making such a determination versus not doing so.[5]

There are a host of other questions that also come to mind: In *"A Problem from Hell:" America and the Age of Genocide*, Samantha Power (2002) reports that George W. Bush, after being elected and while reading about the Clinton administration's failure in Rwanda, "wrote in firm letters in the margin of the memo: 'NOT ON MY WATCH'" (p. 511). Power (2002) goes on to comment, "While he [George W. Bush] was commander in chief, he was saying, genocide would not recur" (p. 511). While he has obviously reneged on the promise he made to himself, there is the possibility that he may have thought that by declaring genocide (something the Clinton administration failed to do regarding Rwanda — and, in fact, as is well known, even went so far as to warn its officials/bureaucrats from using the so-called "g-word"), the Bush administration was, at least in part, trying to do something.

As for others, Alex de Waal (2005), an expert on the Sudan, has raised two questions about the genocide determination and his own responses to each of the questions further complicate the issue regarding possible motive(s) behind the determination:

> Is the U.S. Government's determination that the atrocities in Darfur qualify as "genocide" an accurate depiction of the horrors of that war and famine? Or is it the cynical addition of "genocide" to America's armoury of hegemonic interventionism — typically at the expense of the Arabs? The answer is both. The genocide finding is accurate according to the letter of the law.[6] But it is no help to understanding what is happening in Darfur, or to finding a solution. And this

description merely serves the purposes of a philanthropic alibi to the U.S. projection of power.

In addressing the political nature of the determination of genocide, de Waal (2005) asserts that:

The September 9, [2004] determination is the first time the Genocide Convention has been used to diagnose genocide (rather than prosecute it) ... What does the United States determination signify? At one level, it is the outcome of a very specific set of political processes in Washington, D.C., in which interest groups were contending for control over U.S. policy toward Sudan. In this context, the call to set up a State Department inquiry into whether there was genocide in Darfur was a tactical maneuver destined to placate the anti-Khartoum lobbies circling around Congress (an unlikely alliance of liberal journalists and human rights advocates, and the religious right), while buying time for those in the State Department committed to pushing a negotiated settlement.... .

But at another level, the genocide determination reveals much about the United States role in the world today, and the unstated principles on which United States power is exercised. Those principles are shared by both the advocates of U.S. global domination and their liberal critics, and are revealed in the commonest narrative around genocide, which takes the form of a salvation fairy tale, with the United States playing the role of the savior.... .

For six decades, Americans have been dreaming of redeeming that historic fatal tardiness [i.e., in regard to responding to the Nazi-perpetrated Holocaust], and dispatching troops in time to save the day. Their failure to do so in Rwanda and Bosnia ten years ago sparked another round of soul searching and led directly to the Kosovo bombing campaign and the Darfur genocide determination.

de Waal's criticism that the September 9th determination was the first time the Genocide Convention had been used to diagnose genocide, *rather than prosecute it*, is, at least in this author's mind, misplaced. Indeed, it seems as if the use of the UNCG for the purpose of diagnosing genocide should, at least when it's used in a serious and conscientious manner, be praised rather than criticized. (Furthermore, the findings of the ADP led the United States to refer the matter to the UN, and the UN, following its investigation, referred the matter to the International Criminal Court (ICC). As a result of the latter, the ICC is now conducting an investigation into the atrocities in Darfur for the express purpose of bringing suspected perpetrators to trial. Thus, in fact, the ADP has contributed to the current effort to bring the perpetrators to trial.) Indeed, why shouldn't the

UNCG be used to diagnose genocide? Too often scholars, political analysts, activists, politicians, and the media posit guesses (some of which are wild guesses) in regard to whether a crisis constitutes genocide or not, and that is problematic. Is it not better to gather solid data — granted, preferably early on, and certainly much earlier than the United States did *vis-a-vis* Darfur — prior to making a determination? That is not to say that the international community should wait until a genocide determination is made to act to stanch mass killing. Indeed, whenever any threat or actual outbreak of mass killing takes place, then strong, effective measures should be taken to halt it immediately. It is, however, to say that an accurate determination is preferable to guess work.

As for de Waal's point that the pressure to establish a State Department investigation was "a tactical maneuver destined to placate the anti-Khartoum lobbies circling around Congress…, while buying time for those in the State Department committed to pushing a negotiated settlement," a question that comes to mind is, "What is the evidence for such an assertion?" If, though, even for the sake of argument, one assumes de Waal is correct, a question that arises is: "Just how significant is his point?" First, it is almost a given that most countries are going to attempt to negotiate a settlement before resorting to military means. And generally, that is a good idea. That said, negotiating with actors that are intransigent and not likely to negotiate in good faith is not only a waste of time but unconscionable when large numbers of people are being killed during the negotiation process. As we now know, the ongoing attempt to negotiate with both the GoS and the rebel groups has largely proved fruitless over a period of several years. Furthermore, it quickly became apparent that "talk" by the international community served, once again, as a substitute for action and, as it did, the killing and dying (both as a result of murder and genocide by attrition) in Darfur continued unabated. That was and is unconscionable. It seems, to this author at least, that a better "target" for de Waal to have taken aim at would have been the incessant talk carried out by the international community rather than the implementation of the ADP.[7]

Undoubtedly, intervention to halt the killing would have been preferable (at least to some, including this author) to the ongoing negotiations that got nowhere, as well as the ADP, but that was not in the cards for the United States in light of its ongoing "war against terrorism" in Afghanistan and Iraq. That is, it is dubious that the Pentagon would have readily — or, for that matter, even begrudgingly — agreed to send troops into another potential quagmire, especially when the armed services were already having difficulty recruiting enough personnel for the war in Iraq. Over and above that, the so-called "Somalia factor" still haunts many within the U.S. Government. The latter is a result of the October 1993 disaster in which U.S. troops attempting to capture top advisors to Mohammed Farah Aideed were attacked by Somalia militia, and eighteen U.S. soldiers were killed and seventy-three wounded. A Black Hawk helicopter pilot was also kidnapped, and a dead U.S. soldier was dragged through the streets of Mogadishu. Finally, some prognosticators have also ventured that, in light of the United States and Sudanese collaboration on the "war on terror," the Bush administration would not countenance an intervention that would put such cooperation at risk.

Furthermore, if de Waal is correct that the ADP was used as a ploy to stave off criticism while focusing on negotiations, it is also true that governments are not known for acting in the most altruistic manner possible. It is also a fact that governments act for a multiplicity of motives, some more — and some less — altruistic than others. Also, aside from totalitarian states, governments are not monolithic entities and some branches and/or departments of a government may address issues and make decisions that are not necessarily shared or in accord with another branch or department. And aside from all that, what is so grievous if the ADP was initiated under pressure and not for the best of reasons? Is that any reason to dismiss an investigation that was handled in a highly professional manner and that resulted in an analysis that was methodologically sound? At the very least, the United States was doing something besides talking.[8]

Another possible motive behind the ADP, which de Waal does not take into consideration, was the fact that sanctions had been threatened time and again by the UN, but such threats were never carried out and, thus, soon became little more than "paper tigers." This continued to happen despite the fact that the United States introduced resolutions aimed at Sudan only to have them watered down by various members of the UN Security Council, purportedly, to avoid "upsetting Khartoum." The point is that it is just as likely that the United States may have carried out the ADP, as Craner suggests (see Kostas, p. 116), in the hope that it might have moved the international community to action. And if so, that could hardly be construed as a questionable or despicable aim. de Waal is undoubtedly correct that the Darfur crisis did release, as he says, "another round of soul searching." But is that necessarily bad? This author would submit that it is not. Would de Waal, one wonders, prefer the opposite reaction?

Granted, some critics of the ADP have asserted that the ADP was largely a cosmetic action — something fairly innocuous in the place of real action. Possibly. But then who would have thought that a finding of genocide would constitute an innocuous action? Still, the fact is, sadly, in many ways (and particularly in light of the lack of action by the United States to truly push the international community to halt the killing and death in Darfur) the assertion that it was largely cosmetic is difficult (if not impossible) to refute. Again, the only saving grace is that the finding based on ADP data has led to the current attempt by the ICC to bring the perpetrators to trial. Still, that has done virtually nothing to protect the victims of the GoS and the *Janjaweed* over the past year and a half.

de Waal's assertion that the United States conducted the investigation in order to enact a "salvation fairy tale" so that it could play " the role of the savior" is, at least in one sense, so outlandish that it is utterly absurd. Possibly many at State and some within the Executive Branch felt that the investigation constituted a kind of salvation affair, but in the long run no one, it seems, including Powell and Bush, could conclude that the United States, in any way whatsoever, played the role of savior — and that is true for the simple but profound fact that the United States did the very minimum it could to *prevent* the killing and rape of the black Africans of Darfur: The minimum this side of doing nothing, that is; but, then again, if it had done nothing in the face of genocide, it would have been totally excoriated.

de Waal (2005) sees the determination of genocide as even more problematic than the motive(s) behind the investigation, and that has to do, as he puts it, with "… the fact that the group labeled as *genocidaire* in this [the Darfur] conflict are 'Arab' is no accident" (p. 7). More specifically, he asserts that

> There's no covert master plan in Washington to brand Arabs genocidal criminals, but rather an aggregation of circumstance that has led to the genocide determination. It has special saliency in the shadow of the United States "global war on terror," misdirected into the occupation of Iraq and seen across the Arab and Muslim worlds as a reborn political Orientalism.
>
> After 11 September 2001, the United States sees Muslim Arabs as actual or potential terrorists targeting the homeland. After 9 September 2004…, Arabs (and perhaps all Muslims, too) are actual or potential *genocidaires*, and their targets are Africans. It's sad but predicable that too many Africans will fall for this trap and that the brave efforts of the African Union to build a continental architecture for peace and security will be impaled on an externally constructed divide (pp. 7–8).

The latter argument of de Waal's is likely to attract considerable debate. Be that as it may, one, at the least, has to question the validity of his assertion and argument in light of the fact that the Bush administration has reached out to the GoS, an Arab-run government, for help in its fight against terrorism. More specifically, in May of 2005, the CIA flew Salah Gosh, head of Sudan's National Security and Intelligence Service, to CIA headquarters in Langley to confer with top CIA administrators. At the time, the CIA must have known that Gosh was enmeshed in the Darfur crisis and likely issuing directives to the GoS troops and *Janjaweed*.[9] The point is, to paint the United States with such large swaths of opprobrium is somewhat misdirected — and, some would no doubt claim, sorely so.

It must also be pointed out, though, that the relationship between the United States and Sudan in the so-called "war on terror" raises the very real issue of just how much pressure the United States is really willing to place on the Sudanese Government. Desperate for allies on the antiterrorism front, it is highly unlikely that the United States will risk losing out on major assistance in the area of intelligence gathering, especially in such an area as "fecund" as Sudan.

Howard Adelman, a philosophy professor who has written extensively about genocide and issues of intervention, is another who vehemently disagrees with the United States' determination of genocide and has also raised a host of questions regarding the motives of the United States. Among some of the many questions he has raised are: "What influence did the desire not to repeat American inaction on Rwanda have on characterizing Darfur as genocide?" "What was the influence of the Christian lobby on the resolutions?" and "What was the influence of the immanence of the 2004 election?" (Adelman, 2005, p. 1).[10]

There is no point in repeating the previous discussion in regard to whether or not the United States had honorable or ulterior motives in carrying out the investigation. As for Adelman's criticism of the determination, he cites all of the actors who were and are in disagreement with it (e.g., the UN, the EU, Doctors Without Borders, and others), and asserts that the atrocities and other actions constitute, at worst, crimes against humanity. Over-reliance on the UN Commission of Inquiry's (COI) findings, however, may be ill-advised.[11]

As for Doctors Without Borders, Adelman asserts that such a reputable group, whose leader called for an intervention early on during the 1994 Rwandan genocide and whose personnel have been on the ground for extended periods of time in Darfur, should be duly recognized when it claims that genocide has not been perpetrated in Darfur. But that is dubious advice for two reasons. First, Doctors Without Borders never conducted its own investigation to ascertain whether the crisis in Darfur constituted genocide or not. Second, Doctors Without Borders did not provide empirical, let alone conclusive, evidence to support its pronouncement. On a different front, it is also true that Adelman has a relatively close relationship with the AU and that he has previously asserted that he believes that calling for an international intervention undermines the will and efforts of the AU. Ultimately, it is only known by him how the latter affects his stance in regard to how the atrocities and death in Darfur should be categorized.

One of the fiercest critics of the determination of genocide by Powell and Bush was (and continues to be) Professor Eric Reeves of Smith College in Northampton, Massachusetts. Actually, Reeves agrees with the determination. It is the lack of action following the determination that has resulted in his caustic criticism. In a piece entitled "Secretary of State Colin Powell's Genocide Determination: What It Does, and Doesn't, Mean for Darfur," Reeves (2004) asserts that "... by arguing in yesterday's testimony before the Senate Foreign Relations Committee that the obligation to 'prevent' genocide entails so very little, Powell has done what his State Department spokesmen have done for months; he has made it less likely that the Genocide Convention will ever be used as a tool to serve the primary purpose for which it was created" (p. 1). Continuing, Reeves (2004) argues that:

> ... Powell's genocide determination may actually signal the end of the Genocide Convention as a tool of deterrence and prevention. For if a finding of this sort, rendered in light of the most conspicuous evidence of ongoing genocide, prompts no action, then the precedent created during yesterday's Senate testimony by the U.S. Secretary of State is wholly unfortunate.
>
> The insistence that, despite a genocide finding, "no new action is dictated" reflects in part United States impotence at the UN, a function in many ways of diplomatic capital expended on the war in Iraq. Indeed, under questioning by Senators on the Foreign Relations Committee, it became painfully clear that the new U.S. draft resolution being circulated at the UN Security Council is not so much a draft as a plea. The proposed resolution is vague, without a clear or explicit threat of sanctions, and establishes no meaningful new benchmarks for Khartoum.
>
> This provides a certain ghastly clarity in the new world of the twenty-first century — even genocide, even the crime that defined the actions in Rwanda and Eastern Europe during the Holocaust, does not entail any special response or effort of prevention. If this indeed marks the end of any particular obligations under the Genocide Convention, we may legitimately wonder whether the price paid for Powell's determination is not exorbitantly high (pp. 2–3).[12]

Reeves is certainly justified in his disappointment in and criticism of the United State's assertion that it had done all it could for the targeted population in Darfur and in its subsequent lack of action following the determination. Indeed, once the U.S. Government declared Sudan had committed genocide, it (the United States), aside from providing hundreds of millions of dollars, did the minimum it could (e.g., refer the matter to

the UN Security Council), without totally losing face. Furthermore, its justification that it had done everything it could do was not only disingenuous but a brazen lie. Be that as it may, Reeves' assertion that Powell and,
thus, the United States, had "made it less likely that the Genocide Convention will ever be used as a tool to serve the primary purpose for which it
was created" is, or so it seems, nothing short of hyperbole. Of course, only
time will tell if Reeves is correct, but "ever" is a long time. Even if the international community takes another hundred years or more to act in good
faith when it comes to genocide and makes effective use of the UNCG to
prevent or halt genocide then all will not have been for naught. Be that
as it may, one can certainly empathize with Reeves' sense of utter disappointment and share his dismay at the disastrous impact that the United
States' timid and unconscionable response will not only have on the black
Africans of Darfur, but is likely to have on a wide range of other groups
that will, inevitably, face major human rights violations, including crimes
against humanity and genocide, in the future.

As for Reeves' criticism of Powell's assertion that "no new action is dictated," Powell, of course, was talking about any action by the United States.
Legally, Powell was absolutely correct. Be that as it may, many are bound
to find Powell's (and the United States') position morally questionable, at
best. Others are likely to counter that preventing and/or halting genocide
should be a shared responsibility and not something to be left to a single
nation, no matter how powerful it is. Still, when all is said and done — and
not even taking into consideration the possibility of unilateral intervention — Reeves was correct in asserting that the United States could have
done a lot more than it did.

Reeves is also highly critical of the lack of "teeth" in the resolution that
the United States submitted to the UN Security Council. As Reeves (2004)
put it, "What is most striking about Powell's testimony concerning the proposed U.S. resolution for the Security Council is its utter lack of enforcement provisions" (p. 7). One can hardly argue with Reeves' grievance, and
this author sees no point in doing so. Again, the "actions" (or lack thereof)
following the genocide finding left a lot to be desired, and that is a gross
understatement. And, in the two years since the declaration, such lack of
action is what has caused the most consternation among the critics of the
U.S. Government in regard to its approach to Darfur.

Finally, Reeves blasts the U.S. Government for its tardy response to the
ongoing crisis in Darfur:

> Powell ... attempt[s] to suggest that the State Department responded
> in a timely fashion to the threat of genocide. This is not true. Ample
> evidence was available at the end of 2003, clearly suggesting that

genocide was occurring (by December 2003 the nature of the fall offensive by Khartoum and the *Janjaweed* became fully known). Human rights reports, alluded to at one point in Powell's testimony, were filled with details suggesting that genocide was unfolding. Certainly by February of 2004, as attacks on the African tribal populations of Darfur again dramatically increased, there was more than enough evidence to justify a genocide investigation. And yet the State Department deployed an investigative team only in July, almost half a year later. This was shamefully belated action — shamefully" (pp. 6–7).

Reeves' criticism is both fair and justified. The investigation could — and should — have taken place earlier. A government truly dedicated to genocide prevention would have seen to that. That said, to bring to fruition such an investigation is not within the purview of any single individual within government and, thus, it takes a good amount of time to move the idea through the various channels. One must also take into account the fact that there was a lot of in-fighting within State over Darfur and it no doubt took a great deal of effort and time to overcome objections to such an investigation. This is not in any way whatsoever to condone the tardiness of the investigation, but simply to acknowledge the reality of how governments work. Such a reality underscores the need for the establishment of a strong antigenocide regime that is buffeted as little as possible by partisan politics and *realpolitik*. Currently, however, that is solely a goal and dream of genocide scholars and many human rights activists — and, skeptics, of course, might venture that it is little more than an utopian idea. Again, time will tell.

Gérard Prunier, an expert on East Africa, the Horn, Sudan, and the Great Lakes of Africa, and the author of *Darfur: The Ambiguous Genocide* (2005), has also weighed in on the motives of the investigation, the genocide determination, and the aftermath of the latter. In regard to the motive(s) behind the investigation, Prunier seems to suggest that the ever-increasing pressure — from constituents, nongovernmental organizations, Congress, and others — for the U.S. Government to act may have prompted Bush to support a "genocide investigation" into the Darfur crisis:

On 1 June 2004, the members of Congress who sympathized with the SPLA sent President Bush a list of twenty-three names of *Janjaweed* supporters, controllers, and commanders who were either members of the GoS or closely linked to it. The message was clear — do something about these people. President Bush seemed to have been embarrassed by the implicit demand, all the more because supporters of the anti-Khartoum legislation tended to be more "on the left" (insofar as this political category has relevance in U.S. politics) within both parties and within the fairly tight Black Caucus. President Bush could not be expected to care too much about "the left," but unfortunately for him there was a core group of anti-Khartoum activists at the opposite end of the political spectrum, from where he drew most of his electoral support. Many fundamentalist Protestant organizations had rallied to the anti-Khartoum lobby activated by Nina Shea. Then by mid-2004 vocal Jewish groups, such as the Committee for the Holocaust Memorial (sic), in Washington had joined in the indignant chorus of protests about Darfur. The President thus found himself under pressure from an array of public opinion elements too wide to be ignored during an election year. But since the "realists" in the intelligence community kept insisting that Khartoum was too important to be harshly treated, these contradictory pressures led the White House to compromise on all fronts — supporting the Naivasha negotiations, [and] not putting too much practical pressure on Khartoum, but nevertheless passing legislation, which could be used as a sword of Damocles in case of noncompliance.... . (pp. 139-140).

Continuing, Prunier (2005) drops a bombshell, of sorts, especially if the assertion is true: "This author was assured that Secretary of State Colin Powell had practically been ordered to use the term 'genocide' during this (sic) high-profile 9 September 2004 testimony to the Senate Committee on Foreign Relations, but that he also been (sic) advised in the same breath that this did not oblige the United States to undertake any sort of drastic action, such as a military intervention" (p. 140). Prunier's source for the latter assertion was a "[c]onfidential interview with a high-ranking member of the U.S. administration, [in] Washington [in] October 2004" (p. 191). It is certainly possible, of course, that Powell had received a "push" in that direction. Be that as it may, there are three sticking points with Prunier's statement. First, it comes from an unidentified source and cannot readily be followed up. That, of course, does not mean it isn't true, but prevents verification of it. Second, Prunier uses the words "practically been ordered." So, Powell, ostensibly, was not ordered to do so, but was strongly encouraged, pressured, prodded, or goaded to do so. Third, Prunier uses the words "advised to add." "Advised," of course, is not the same as being told, directed, or ordered to do so. The questions that arise from such wording are many, including but not limited to the following: Was Powell, in fact, "practically ordered" to use the word "genocide," and did he cave in to the pressure and/or act the part of the "good soldier?" *Or,* was the analysis of the data collected by the ADT persuasive "enough" that Powell felt comfortable using the word "genocide" on his own accord. Or, was the analysis of the data persuasive enough that Powell did not feel guilty using the word "genocide" when all but ordered to do so? The same sorts of questions, of course, are germane to his statement about the United States not being obligated to do any more than it already had done *vis-a-vis* Darfur.

Prunier concludes by asserting that "President Bush tried to be all things to all men on the Sudan/Darfur question. Never mind that the result was predictably confused. What mattered was that attractive promises could be handed around without any sort of firm commitment being made. Predictably, the interest level of U.S. diplomacy on the Sudan question dropped sharply as soon as President Bush was reelected" (p. 140). Prunier is certainly correct in regard to his comment about a lack of "firm commitment" being made in the aftermath of the determination. As for U.S. diplomatic efforts concerning Darfur, they have actually waxed and waned time and again over the course of the past two years. There have been spikes of interest (most recently in pushing for the deployment of UN troops and NATO involvement in Darfur), but there have also been mixed messages issued by Bush's underlings in the State Department (e.g., in regard to whether the situation in Darfur still constitutes genocide and whether there is a need to push for tough sanctions on Khartoum and/or to prod the UN to undertake an intervention). Ultimately, Prunier *is* correct in suggesting that "talk over action" has been the *modus operandi* of the Bush Administration's approach to protecting the black Africans of Darfur.

Ramifications of the ADP

The development and implementation of the ADP, aside from the determination based on the data collected by its team, has numerous ramifications. And, of course, the genocide determination by the U.S. Government does as well. As one might surmise, some are positive and some are negative.

First, the development and implementation of the ADP set a precedent of sorts in regard to the way in which an individual nation can develop and conduct an official investigation for the express purpose of attempting to ascertain whether genocide is being perpetrated in some part of the world. Indeed, it proves that it can be done fairly quickly, efficiently, effectively, and relatively inexpensively. That, in and of itself, is significant, for far too often in the past, individual nations, the media, human rights activists, and the international community have relied more on guess work and piecemeal information seeping in from different sources than carefully collected and analyzed data in order to ascertain the nature of a violent crisis.

Second, the precedent has now been established for an individual nation to conduct an investigation into atrocities while they are being perpetrated for the express purpose of ascertaining whether genocide has been perpetrated or not. While this may appear to be of little note, its nothing of the sort. If nothing else, and this is significant, there is no excuse for nations with the financial wherewithal to fail to conduct such investigations when it appears as if a situation may be spiraling towards crimes against humanity or genocide. In other words, a new bar has been set in making a genocide determination. Now, it is up to human rights activists, NGOs, genocide scholars, and others to insist on such investigations.

Third, the ADP has provided a solid model for one essential component of an antigenocide regime. Such investigations should become an integral part of any antigenocide regime, and due to the ADP it is not a component that will need to be developed from scratch. In light of the fact that the ADP was not perfect (but what is), developers of future investigations can learn from both the strengths and weaknesses of the ADP.

As for the genocide determination, a precedent has been set in which one sovereign nation (the United States) has accused another sovereign nation (Sudan) of having committed genocide while the atrocities were still ongoing. This, in and of itself, was a historic occasion. The determination broke, if you will, a certain "barrier" of individual nations not making such an accusation when they were not only justified in doing so, but had a moral obligation, if signatories to the UNCG, to do so.

Be that as it may — and ironically and sadly — there is also the danger, as numerous scholars and commentators have asserted, that, in the end, the genocide determination by the United States could prove counterproductive. More specifically, the fact that the determination was made and then the matter was simply and solely referred to the UN Security Council does not bode well for those in favor of a proactive stance against genocide. Indeed, the fact that the determination did not result in *any concrete action* by the United States to attempt to halt the ongoing genocide may, in the short-run (but even here we are talking about the precious and fragile lives of untold numbers of people) — if not the long run — result in minimizing the "weight" and significance of such a finding. That is, other nations and international bodies may now perceive such determinations simply as a matter of course and of no great consequence.

As the cliché goes, only time will tell. That said, de Waal (2005) made the interesting point that "although Colin Powell insisted the U.S. policy towards Sudan would remain unchanged — thereby seeming to defeat the purpose of making the determination in the first place — there is no doubt that declaring genocide creates legal and political space for intervention" (p. 6).[13] It is, of course, still possible for a military intervention to take place in Darfur. While most would agree that if an intervention is eventually carried out, it will have been horrifically late in coming; but, it is crucial to recognize and appreciate the fact that some two million displaced persons are still at the mercy of the GoS and the *Janjaweed* and are in need of all the help they can get in staving off even more terror and mayhem. And if an intervention does take place, then the genocide determination by the United States may well have served the important purpose, at least in part, of having "created the legal and political [and one might add, moral] space" for doing so.

Conclusion

Aside from continuing to provide humanitarian aid, which was not, of course, inconsequential, the only other major action that the United States undertook following its determination of genocide was, as previously noted, to refer the matter to the UN Security Council. In doing so, it called for a more comprehensive study of the Darfur crisis. At the time, many scholars and activists raised the issue of whether another study was really needed, especially in light of the fact that no one — other than Khartoum, perhaps — doubted that grave crimes against humanity had been perpetrated against the black Africans and that they continued to perish each and every week in huge numbers due to the actions of the GoS and *Janjaweed*.

Again, a question that has been asked by many, though largely rhetorical, was: Did the U.S. actually do all it could? The answer to the latter was, and continues to be, an emphatic "no"! Among some of the many options that the United States could have pursued but chose not to — due no doubt to *realpolitik* — were the following: Push implacably for a multilateral effort to establish a no-fly zone over Darfur and/or do it alone; apply unrelenting pressure on the UN Security Council to establish a strong, Chapter VII mandate that would allow the AU troops (and others) to truly protect the black Africans at risk; apply equally unrelenting pressure on the AU to allow UN troops to join the AU troops in Darfur; provide the AU with top-notch training of its recruits and troops prior to their deployment to Darfur; provide the AU with ample military materiel and equipment, along with a guarantee of fuel and personnel to service equipment, such as four-wheel vehicles, planes, etc., versus providing dribbles of military support; serve notice to Khartoum that if it continued to interfere and/or outright block humanitarian aid from reaching the IDP camps, the repercussions would be serious and long-term — and then act on such in a timely and effective manner. Noticeably absent from this list is the possibility of the United States actually sending its own troops to Darfur, either as a multilateral or unilateral effort supported or not supported by the UN Security

Council. Again, as discussed previously, this, realistically, was never, at least as far as the Bush Administration was concerned, a real option. The point is, though, there is plenty that the United States could have done — and still can and should do — but it hasn't. And that is nothing short of shameful.

References

Adelman, Howard (2005). "Reading History Backwards: Rwanda and Darfur." Abstract of a Talk Presented at the 2005 Conference of the International Association of Genocide Scholars, Boca Raton, FL.

de Waal, Alex (2005). "What Does Adding the 'Genocide' Label to the Darfur Crisis Really Mean?" *Index on Censorship.* Available from: www.indexonline.org/en/news/articles/2005/1/international-true-meanings-and-consequences.shtml

Howard, Jonathan (2006). "Survey Methodology and the Darfur Genocide." In Samuel Totten and Eric Markusen (Eds.), *Genocide in Darfur: Investigating Atrocities in the Sudan.* New York: Routledge.

John F. Kennedy Library and Foundation (2004). "The Crisis in Darfur with Jennifer Leaning, Eric Reeves, Alex de Waal, and William Schulz." December 9. Available at: www.jfklibrary.org/forum_darfur.html

Kostas, Stephen A. (2006). "Making the Determination of Genocide in Darfur." In Samuel Totten and Eric Markusen (Eds.), *Genocide in Darfur: Investigating the Atrocities in the Sudan.* New York: Routledge.

Physicians for Human Rights (2006). *Darfur: Assault on Survival: A Call for Security, Justice and Restitution.* Cambridge, MA: Author.

Prunier, Gérard (2005). *Darfur: The Ambiguous Genocide.* Ithaca, NY: Cornell University Press.

Reeves, Eric (2004). "Secretary of State Colin Powell's Genocide Determination: What It Does, and Doesn't Mean for Darfur." September 10. Available at: www.sudanreeves.org

United Nations (2004). "Sudan: World's Worst Humanitarian Crisis — Press Release." March 22. New York: United Nations.

United Nations (2005). *Report of the International Commission of Inquiry on Darfur to the United Nations Secretary-General.* New York: Author.

U.S. Department of State (2004a). *Documenting Atrocities in Darfur.* Washington, D.C.: Bureau of Democracy, Human Rights and Labor and Bureau of Intelligence and Research.

U.S. Department of State (2004b). "Secretary of State Colin L. Powell, The Crisis in Darfur, Written Remarks, Senate Foreign Relations Committee." September 9. Washington, D.C: Author.

Notes

1. The field data for the eleven hundred thirty-six interviews were compiled using a standardized data entry process that involved the collection and coding of detailed information from each refugee respondent's set of answers. The researchers then used a statistical program to aggregate the data and analyze the results" (U.S. State Department, 2004, pp. 7–8).

2. "Reported atrocities were included in the data set only if the respondent directly witnessed the event. For the purpose of this study [*Documenting Atrocities in Darfur*], a respondent is considered to have 'directly witnessed' an atrocity if she or he was an eyewitness to the event, visually confirmed the death of victims, or, in cases of rape, was directly told about the atrocity by the victim. Hearsay accounts were excluded from the data set" (U.S. State Department, 2004, p. 1).

3. A key question that arises is whether political appointees are truly capable of being "dispassionate and clinical" when making such a judgment. Furthermore, can any decision made by governmental officials/entities truly be considered "pure?" That is, are not all decisions political in one way or another?

4. For an informative and detailed discussion as to what prompted the State Department to investigate the internal conflict in Sudan, see Stephen A. Kostas' "Making the Genocide Determination."

5. While State Department officials were conferring and coming to a decision as to whether the atrocities in Darfur constituted crimes against humanity or genocide, rumors leaked out from State that the final decision could "go either way." This suggests, if the rumors were correct, that there might not have been a foregone conclusion of genocide. It also suggests that the State Department officials, including Colin Powell, were determined to make the most accurate determination they possibly could.

6. Speaking of the atrocities committed by the GoS and the *Janjaweed*, de Waal (2005) asserts that "they have killed, burned, raped, and starved their way across the central belt of Darfur. In doing so, they have killed thousands of people and deliberately starved thousands more. They have also managed to stop a running insurgency that was rapidly seizing control of the entire region" (p. 2). He also asserts that "Powell is correct in law. According to the facts as known and the law as laid down in the 1948 Genocide Convention, the killings, displacement, and rape in Darfur are rightly characterized as 'genocide.' But his finding has significant political implications" (de Waal, 2005, pp. 2–3). Elsewhere, de Waal has asserted that "famine in Sudan is a crime, and has been a crime for the last 20 years, and the form of genocide that we are seeing in Darfur is, I would argue, a famine crime" (quoted in John F. Kennedy Library and Foundation, p. 5).

7. Some have also suggested that the United State's initiation of the ADP was a cynical ploy by the Bush Administration to "try to have it both ways." That is, it allowed the Bush Administration to assert that it was attempting to defend and protect human rights in Darfur, while also allowing it, in the end — especially by not pushing for an intervention — to attempt to solidify its relationship with the GoS.

8. This author is not so naïve as to think or believe that the investigation *might not have* been used as a sign of showing concern in a way that was not all that costly in terms of financial, political, or human capital (meaning lives lost) and, thus, used in place of calling for — if not leading — a major intervention to halt the killing. That is another issue, and one that needs to be addressed. And, if the latter is true, then the initiation of the ADP certainly was a problematic, if not sordid, affair.

9. Tellingly, Gosh reportedly is the number two person on the United Nation's list that was forwarded to the ICC of those who are suspected of having a hand in the killings in Darfur.

10. For a discussion of these and related questions (e.g., What is the evidence for genocide in Darfur? Why have other states not fallen into line with the United States in characterizing Darfur as genocide? What impact did the characterization of the crisis in Darfur as genocide have on the effort to get the Security Council to endorse sanctions against Sudan?), see Adelman's "Reading History Backwards: Rwanda and Darfur," a talk he presented at the 2005 International Association of Genocide Scholars conference in Boca Raton, Florida.

11. Debb Bodkin, a police officer based in Canada and the only person who served as an investigator for both the ADP and the Commission of Inquiry (COI), told this author that the data collected by the COI was unsystematic and not as focused as the ADP's. More specifically, in recent correspondence with the author, Bodkin commented as follows:

> "During our briefing [about the COI] in Geneva, we were given no format or indication as to how the investigation and interviews were to be conducted. As a result every investigator conducted his/her investigation and interviews in whatever fashion he/she preferred. I cannot believe that with the vast difference in expertise of each investigator there would be any semblance of consistency in regard to the gathering of evidence…. The United Nations investigation did not have any laid-out parameters whatsoever and, as a result, an untrained interviewer could easily ask questions in a manner that would elicit whatever response the interviewer hoped to obtain…. [Also,] each investigator was open to choose who they interviewed and how…. As far as the soundness of the COI, when I compare it to any of the sexual assault or homicide investigations that I was part of during my police service in Waterloo, Ontario, it would not [have gone forward] due to the

low probability of a conviction, mainly because of the fact that the investigators did not meet the required adequacy standards to be conducting interviews and did not have the knowledge, skills, or ability to be doing so ..." (e-mail sent to the author, April 15, 2006).

Furthermore, Bodkin asserted that while the COI team was in Geneva, prior to entering the field, Antonio Cassese, who oversaw the COI, inferred that the COI would not result in a finding of genocide. More specifically, Bodkin, in recent correspondence with the author, conveyed the following: "Commissioner Antonio Cassese, who had traveled to Khartoum and some parts of Darfur for a few days and had conducted some interviews, stated that he felt that we would find that there were two elements of genocide missing: (1) target group (victims are from mixed tribes) and (b) mens rea (intent). He talked for a while and my personal opinion was that he was telling us that the outcome of the investigation would show that it was not genocide that was occurring. He did not specify how long he had visited nor how many interviews he had conducted, but I don't believe either was extensive. I felt it was very inappropriate for him to plant this opinion in the investigators' minds prior to starting the investigation and other investigators felt uncomfortable about it as well.... The female Commissioner (Hina Jilani from Pakistan) stated: 'Go with an open mind.' During the briefing, I got the distinct impression that there was some tension between Commissioner Cassese and Commissioner Jilani as their comments often conflicted with one another and he was expressing what he thought our findings would be, whereas she always made comments about us doing our job open-mindedly" (e-mail received by the author on April 15, 2006).

Adding more fuel to the claim that the UN's Commission of Inquiry's findings are, at best, problematic is Gérard Prunier's cogent observation that "the Report of the UN Commission of Inquiry on the Darfur Violence was the latest but perhaps not only the final example of the world body ... acting ... in a ... show of egregious disingenuousness. The report documented violations of international human rights by "people who might have acted with genocidal intentions;" yet the situation was not genocide ..." (p. 143).

12. Reeves' (2004) criticism does not stop there. Continuing, he states that "despite his finding of genocide on the part of Khartoum, Powell preemptively pardons the regime by saying 'we are not trying to punish them.' But shouldn't genocidaires be punished? Shouldn't there be, as Powell explicitly suggests elsewhere, be an international tribunal to punish the crimes of genocide in Darfur and those guilty of this monstrous crime? ... How can Powell simultaneously find the regime guilty of genocide, but then declare that 'we are not trying to punish the Sudanese Government' and indeed we may have 'a mutual interest with the Sudanese Government?'" (p. 4). Actually, Powell's words could be understood in various ways (and, thus, could be misconstrued). Possibly he was "pardoning" the regime, but that seems dubious. At worst, Powell seemed to be apologizing for the genocide finding while also stating that the United States wanted to maintain, even if shaky, relations with Sudan. Or, Powell may have simply misspoke when he used the words "not trying to punish Sudan." Or, possibly, Powell was trying to send a distinct message: Sudan had better reign in its troops and the *Janjaweed* if it did not want the United States to come down hard on Sudan. Of course, in retrospect, we now know that, if the latter were the actual meaning of the words they were idle for, again, the United States has done little to nothing since September 2004 to halt the killing and death in Darfur.

13. de Waal perceived the creation of such a space as a negation, playing into the hands of the United States "hegemonic" push across the globe.

Contributors

Editors

Samuel Totten, a scholar of genocide studies, is based at the University of Arkansas, Fayetteville. He is also a member of the Council of the Institute on the Holocaust and Genocide (Jerusalem). Totten was one of the twenty-four investigators on the Darfur Atrocities Documentation Team.

Totten is one of the founding editors of *Genocide Studies and Prevention (GSP): An International Journal,* and is the new editor of the acclaimed series *Genocide: A Critical Bibliographic Review.* For four years (2001 to 2005), he served as the book review editor of the *Journal of Genocide Research.*

Totten most recently edited, co-edited and/or has written the following books on genocide: *Century of Genocide: Critical Essays and Eyewitness Accounts* (New York: Routledge, 2004); *Genocide at the Millennium* (New Brunswick, NJ: Transaction Publishers, 2005); and *The Prevention and Intervention of Genocide: An Annotated Bibliography* (New York: Routledge, 2006).

Among the most recent articles on genocide Totten has published: "The Intervention and Prevention of Genocide: Sisyphean or Doable?" *Journal of Genocide Research,* June 2004, 6(2); "The U.S. Government Darfur Genocide Investigation" (with Eric Markusen), *Journal of Genocide Research,* June 2005, 7(2); and "Investigating Allegations of Genocide in Darfur: The U.S. Atrocities Documentation Team and the UN Commission of Inquiry" (with Eric Markusen) in Joyce Apsel (Ed.) *Darfur: Genocide Before Our Eyes.* New York: Institute for the Study of Genocide, 2005.

Eric Markusen (MSW, University of Washington; Ph.D., University of Minnesota) is Professor of Sociology and Social Work at Southwest Minnesota State University and a Senior Researcher with the Department of Holocaust and Genocide Studies of the Danish Institute for International Studies.

He is European Liaison for the International Association of Genocide Scholars, co-editor of *Genocide Studies and Prevention*, the official journal of the International Association of Genocide Scholars, and served as associate editor for the two-volume *Encyclopedia of Genocide*. Markusen has written about nuclear weapons policy; the nature of modern war; the Holocaust; and the genocides in Cambodia, Bosnia, Rwanda, and Sudan.

He traveled extensively in the former Yugoslavia during and after the wars of the 1990s and has made many visits to meet with officials at the International Criminal Tribunal for the Former Yugoslavia. In 1998 and 1999, he conducted field investigations in both Ethiopia and Eritrea of alleged war crimes committed during their border war. Markusen served as an investigator on the Atrocities Documentation Team.

Authors

Kelly Dawn Askin currently serves as Senior Legal Officer, International Justice, with Open Society Justice Initiative. She was also a 2004–2005 Fulbright New Century Scholar on the Global Empowerment of Women and Fellow, Yale Law School. She has taught or served as a visiting scholar at Notre Dame, Washington College of Law, Harvard, and Yale. Additionally, she served as Executive Director of the International Criminal Justice Institute and American University's War Crimes Research Office. She has also served as an expert consultant, legal advisor, and international law trainer to prosecutors, judges, and Registry at the International Criminal Tribunal for the former Yugoslavia, the International Criminal Tribunal for Rwanda, the Serious Crimes Unit in East Timor, the International Criminal Court, and the Special Court for Sierra Leone.

She has lectured in over sixty-five countries and has published extensively in international criminal law, international humanitarian law, and gender justice. Among her publications are *War Crimes Against Women: Prosecution in International War Crimes Tribunals* (1997), and the three-volume treatise *Women and International Human Rights Law* (1999, 2001, 2002).

Nina Bang-Jensen most recently served as the Executive Director of the Coalition for International Justice (CIJ), a nongovernmental organization that has offices in Washington, D.C. and The Hague, The Netherlands. For ten years, CIJ provided support to the two international *ad hoc* war crimes tribunals for the former Yugoslavia and Rwanda in the form of legal and technical assistance, advocacy, public education, and independent reporting. For 6 years, beginning in 2000, CIJ provided similar assistance to hybrid (international–domestic) tribunals, including the United Nations-established Serious Crimes Unit in East Timor, the Special Court for Sierra Leone, and the newly emerging tribunal in Cambodia. In 2004, at the request of the U.S. Government, CIJ assembled and led a team of investigators from eight countries that interviewed over eleven hundred refugees from Darfur along the Chad border. The information collected by that team lead directly to the first official genocide determination and referral to the United Nations by the U.S. Government under the Genocide Convention.

Prior to joining CIJ, Bang-Jensen served as counsel to a U.S. senator and as chief counsel to a Senate subcommittee. In 1989 and 1990, she was the Deputy Director for the President's Commission on Aviation Security and Terrorism, which investigated the bombing of Pan Am 103. She received her undergraduate degree, *magna cum laude,* from Princeton University and its Woodrow Wilson School for Public and International Affairs, studied diplomatic history in Denmark as a Marshall scholar, and received her law degree from the Georgetown University Law Center. She has taught about human rights enforcement as an adjunct professor of law at Georgetown University and serves on the boards of a number of human rights organizations.

Gerald Caplan, a Canadian, has a Ph.D. in African history from the School of Oriental and African Studies, University of London. He is author of *Rwanda: The Preventable Genocide*, the report of the International Panel of Eminent Personalities appointed by the Organization of African Unity to investigate the Rwandan genocide; founder of "Remembering Rwanda"; and co-editor with Eric Markusen of a special issue of the *Journal of Genocide Research* devoted to the tenth anniversary of the Rwandan genocide. He teaches a course on the genocide in Rwanda.

Robert O. Collins is Professor of History, Emeritus, at the University of California/Santa Barbara (UCSB). Educated at Dartmouth College, Balliol College, Oxford, and Yale University, he has taught at Williams College, Columbia University, and UCSB for forty years where he served as Dean of the Graduate School (1970 to 1980) and Director of the UCSB Center in Washington, D.C. (1992 to 1994). He has lectured in numerous American, European, Middle Eastern, and African universities and been a consultant to the Sudan government, the High Executive Council of the Southern Sudan Regional Government, 1975 to 1983, and Chevron Overseas Petroleum Inc., 1981 to 1991. He first went to the Sudan in 1956, a month after independence, and has returned regularly to live, travel widely in every part of the Sudan, and carry out his historical research both in the archives and in the field, particularly southern Sudan.

Between 1962 and 1994, he published seven histories of the Sudan, southern Sudan, and the Nile. Among the books he has published (with Millard Burr) are *Requiem for the Sudan: War, Drought, and Disaster Relief, 1983–1993* (1994); *Africa's Thirty Years War: Chad, Libya, and the Sudan, 1963–1993* (1999); *Revolutionary Sudan: Hasan al-Turabi and the Islamist State, 1989–2000* (2003); and *The Nile* (2002). His latest books include *Alms for Jihad: Charities and Terrorism in the Islamic World* and *Revolution and Civil Wars in the Sudan: Twenty Collected Essays on the Sudan, Southern Sudan, and Darfur, 1962–2004* from Cambridge and Tsehai Publishers.

Jerry Fowler, a graduate of Princeton University and Stanford Law School, is staff director of the Committee on Conscience, which guides the genocide prevention efforts of the United States Holocaust Memorial Museum. His publications include "Out of that Darkness: Preventing Genocide in the 21st Century," in Samuel Totten, William S. Parsons, and Israel W. Charny (Eds.), *Century of Genocide: Critical Essays and Eyewitness Accounts* (New York: Routledge, 2004). He also directed the short film, *A Good Man in Hell: General Romeo Dallaire and the Rwanda Genocide.* Fowler has taught at George Mason University Law School and George Washington University Law School. For the 2006–2007 academic year, he will be William F. Podlich Distinguished Visitor and Visiting Scholar at Claremont McKenna College in Claremont, California.

Stefanie Frease, as Director of Programs for the Coalition for International Justice, led the Atrocities Documentation Team in Chad in the summer of 2004. She has spoken widely on the crisis in Darfur, Sudan, and on other international justice-related matters. At CIJ, she led advocacy efforts on East Timor and assisted in the establishment of the UN's Serious Crimes Unit in East Timor. She is currently on a leave of absence while working at the International Criminal Court (ICC) in The Hague, The Netherlands as Project Manager/Field Investigations. Prior to joining CIJ, Frease worked in the investigation division of the Office of the Prosecutor at the International Criminal Tribunal for the former Yugoslavia from 1995 to 2000. Frease received a graduate degree from the School of International and Public Affairs, Columbia University, and an undergraduate degree from the Jackson School of International Studies, University of Washington. The chapter in this book was written while the author was with CIJ, and the views expressed are the author's alone and do not necessarily reflect the views of the ICC.

Jonathan P. Howard is a research analyst specializing in African public opinion research for the U.S. Department of State. Howard served as the survey methodologist for the Darfur Atrocities Documentation Project, designing the sampling methodology, overseeing initial survey implementation in the field, briefing interviewers, and compiling and analyzing the resulting data. He holds bachelor's degrees in political science and philosophy from Wheaton College, as well as a master's in Comparative Politics from the University of Virginia.

Stephen Kostas is an International Bar Association Fellow at the Appeals Chamber of the UN International Criminal Tribunal for the Former Yugoslavia (ICTY). Previously he was a law clerk for H. E. Judge Theodor Meron at the ICTY. He has a Juris Doctorate degree from the University of Chicago, and a Ph.D. from Johns Hopkins University. He worked pro bono for the Coalition for International Justice.

Andrew S. Natsios served as Administrator of the U.S. Agency for International Development (USAID) from May 2001 to January 2006. During that period, he also served as Special Coordinator for International Disaster Assistance and Special Humanitarian Coordinator for the Sudan. In earlier service to USAID, Natsios held the positions of director of the Office of Foreign Disaster Assistance and assistant administrator for the Bureau for Food and Humanitarian Assistance (now the Bureau of Democracy, Conflict and Humanitarian Assistance).

From 1975 to 1986, Natsios also served in the Massachusetts House of Representatives. He is a graduate of Georgetown University and Harvard University's Kennedy School of Government, where he received a master's degree in public administration. He has written numerous articles on foreign policy and humanitarian emergencies as well as two books: *U.S. Foreign Policy and the Four Horsemen of the Apocalypse* (Center for Strategic and International Studies, 1997), and *The Great North Korean Famine* (U.S. Institute of Peace, 2001).

Natsios left his position as administrator of USAID to become a professor at Georgetown University's Edmund A. Walsh School of Foreign Service.

Helge Niska is lecturer, project manager, developer of study programs, and examiner of community and conference interpreters at the Institute for Interpretation and Translation Studies (TÖI), Stockholm University, Sweden. He teaches theory and practice of terminology, and theory of interpreting. Niska has served as an expert on public service interpreting services and interpreter training in numerous locales, including Chad, Scandinavia, the Baltic states, and South Africa.

Scott Straus is an Assistant Professor of Political Science and International Studies at the University of Wisconsin, Madison, where he teaches classes on genocide, human rights, and African politics. Straus is the author of two forthcoming books on Rwanda: *The Order of Genocide: Race, Power, and War in Rwanda*, from Cornell University Press, Ithaca, New York, and, with Robert Lyons, *Intimate Enemy: Images and Voices of the Rwandan Genocide*, from Zone Books, Cambridge, Massachusetts. Straus also recently published an article on Darfur in *Foreign Affairs*, and he has published in the *Journal of Genocide Research* and *Patterns of Prejudice*. He co-authored, with David Leonard, *Africa's Stalled Development: International Causes and Cures* (Lynne Rienner, 2003) and translated Jean-Pierre Chrètien's *The Great Lakes of Africa: Two Thousand Years of History* (Zone Books, 2003). Before starting in academia, Straus was a freelance journalist based in Nairobi, Kenya.

Taylor B. Seybolt is a Senior Program Officer at the United States Institute of Peace (USIP), in Washington, D.C., where he is engaged in making grants to civil society organizations in Sudan to strengthen the prospects of consolidating peace. Prior to joining USIP in 2002, he spent three years as the director of the Conflicts and Peace Enforcement Project at the Stockholm International Peace Research Institute (SIPRI) in Stockholm, Sweden. From 1997 to 1999, he was a research fellow at the Belfer Center for Science and International Affairs at Harvard University's Kennedy School. He holds a Ph.D. in political science from MIT. He is the author of *Knights in Shining Armor? The Success and Failure of Humanitarian Intervention* (SIPRI/Oxford University Press, forthcoming 2006). He was not involved with the Darfur Atrocities Documentation Project.

Gregory H. Stanton (Juris Doctorate from Yale Law School, 1982) was a law professor at Washington and Lee University School of Law from 1985 to 1991, Chair of the American Bar Association Young Lawyers Division Committee on Human Rights, and a member of the ABA's Standing Committee on World Order Under Law. Currently, he is the James Farmer Visiting Professor of Human Rights at the University of Mary Washington, Fredericksburg, Virginia.

Stanton served in the State Department from 1992 to 1999, where he wrote UN Security Council Resolutions 955 and 978, which established the International Criminal Tribunal for Rwanda. He founded the Cambodian Genocide Project in 1981 and has since worked to bring Khmer Rouge leaders to justice. In 2003 to 2005, he drafted rules of procedure and evidence for the mixed UN/Cambodia tribunal.

Stanton is President of Genocide Watch and Chair of the International Campaign to End Genocide. He is also Vice President of the International Association of Genocide Scholars.

Afterword

As scholars who have each devoted decades to researching, writing, and teaching about genocide, we are proud to have served as two of the twenty-four investigators on the Darfur Atrocities Documentation Team (ADT). As we commented in the Introduction to this book, we regard this initiative as being truly historic for several reasons. The ADT was the first official investigation by a government into allegations of genocide committed by another government while the killing and dying were still underway. Data collected by the ADT were instrumental in the U.S. Government's unprecedented declaration that the Government of Sudan and its *Janjaweed* allies were guilty of genocide. The data collected by the ADT also served as the basis for the U.S. Government invoking, for the first time, Chapter VIII of the United Nations' Convention on the Prevention and Punishment of the Crime of Genocide to call on the UN Security Council to conduct an official criminal investigation of alleged genocide. As a result of Resolution 1564, passed on September 18, 2004, the Security Council established the UN Commission of Inquiry, whose report, released just a few months later, led the Security Council, in Resolution 1593, to refer the situation in Sudan to the International Criminal Court — both actions being unprecedented in the history of the United Nations.

Contributors to this book have identified other important aspects of the ADT Project. Andrew Natsios, the former Administrator of the U.S. Agency for International Development (USAID), writes that evidence collected by the ADT "will be critical in helping prosecute Sudanese individuals guilty of planning and executing the execution and widespread killings." He also notes that the ADT "was an important step toward institutionalizing USAID's role as a government *tripwire* for identifying and addressing protection problems and human rights violations and pushing for accountability of those responsible" (emphasis added). Nina Bang-Jensen and Stefanie Frease, both formerly with Coalition for International Justice, document how the ADT represents a unique, creative, and productive collaboration between U.S. Government agencies and nongovernmental organizations in addressing critical human rights violations. "Outsider" Gregory Stanton, a Yale-educated attorney involved in the establishment of the International Criminal Tribunal for Rwanda, notes that the ADT constituted "the first use of systematic social science survey research to prove commission of genocide and crimes against humanity." "Outsider" Taylor Seybolt of the U.S. Institute for Peace points out that the ADT had "great value" insofar as it played a "pivotal role" in the U.S. Government's declaration of genocide in Darfur, helped keep the issue of Darfur alive on the United States political agenda, and — perhaps most importantly — showed that "a determination of genocide can be made before it is too late to respond."

Furthermore, as Gerald Caplan reminds us in his "outsider's" essay, compared with the intentional avoidance by the international community and the United States to call the 1994 genocide in Rwanda by its proper name in order to justify inaction, the responses to the Darfur tragedy show some progress. If nothing else, for the first time, instead of looking the other way, both the United States and the United Nations made the crucial decision to put forth the time, effort, and funding to undertake criminal investigations of an ongoing case of mass killing that could lead to prosecution of its perpetrators.

It is our (the editors') hope that the ADT may eventually come to be regarded as an important milestone in (1) the struggle against impunity for perpetrators of heinous international crimes, (2) the effort to replace the rule of force with the rule of law, and, most significantly, (3) the campaign to prevent genocide.

That hope, however, is obviously tarnished by the fundamental fact that, as this book goes to press in Summer 2006, there has not been any discernible improvement in the conditions under which helpless civilians in Darfur struggle to survive — and that is despite the declaration of genocide by the United States, the issuance of the UN's Commission of Inquiry's report, and the subsequent referral of the Darfur situation to the International Criminal Court. Indeed, it sickens us to think about the victims still being hunted down, killed, and raped even after they have sought safety and shelter in the internally displaced persons (IDPs) camps in Darfur and the refugee camps in Chad.

We cannot disagree with Taylor Seybolt's assertion that "the Bush administration's declaration of genocide has proved to be a substitute for action, not a call to action." Other observers who were not associated with the ADT or this book also have made such an accusation. Not long after the ADT's results were made public and Secretary of State Colin Powell made his declaration of genocide, Danish researchers Martin Mennecke and Elisabeth Moltke warned that "investigating [whether the conflict should be labeled 'genocide' or some other serious crime] runs the risk of becoming a mere substitute for stopping the widespread killings by means of political pressure or intervention" (Mennecke and Moltke, 2004, p. 1). The same point was reiterated more recently by Julie Flint and Alex de Waal (2005) in their book, *Darfur: A Short History of a Long War*, in which they conclude that the debate over the "g" word became "a hindrance to action" (p. 102).

One has to muse as to why neither the United States nor the United Nations has acted effectively to stem the ongoing atrocities in Darfur. Is it due, as some suggest, to both the United States and the United Nations not wanting to "endanger" the peace accord that Sudan signed with the rebels in the South, which ended the twenty year war that engulfed some two million lives? Is it due, as others suggest, to the fact that the United States already has its hands full with its current war efforts in Afghanistan and Iraq? Is it due to Western countries not wishing to engage in battle with a Muslim state, fearing an onslaught of terrorist activity by *Al Qaeda* and other groups, if not outright warfare with various Muslim states? Is it due to the fact that Sudan suddenly is playing "ball" with the United States in the latter's "war against terrorism"? Is it because both China, which has heavy petroleum interests in Sudan, and Russia, which has a large arms deal with Sudan, have threatened, time and again, to veto any sanctions against Sudan — and thus neither the United States nor the United Nations wants to go head-to-head with such powers? Is the United States' unwillingness to intervene militarily the result of the so-called "Somalia factor," which resulted in the deaths of U.S. military personnel when the United States attempted to subdue rebel forces there in 1993? Or, is it, as some have surmised, due to the fact that few really care about the victims because they are black Africans, and thus "expendable"?

The lack of action is likely a result of some combination of these reasons and more. Thus, once again, both *realpolitik* and a lack of political will, along with an unconscionable lack of caring, have come to the fore during a genocidal event — one which, unlike the genocide in Rwanda (1994), *was* declared a genocide while underway. And, we are painfully aware of the fact — pointed out by both Gerald Caplan and Gregory Stanton in their commentaries herein — that accusing the Sudanese Government of genocide has not stopped the United States from treating some members of that government in a respectful, business-as-usual, and even friendly manner. There, again, is *realpolitik* in action.

Like our ADT colleagues around the world, when we returned from Chad, we waited anxiously to see if, when, and how Secretary of State Powell would announce his conclusions on the question of genocide. We were relieved (as there were some fears that Powell would simply avoid taking a stand on the issue) when he told the world that he had concluded that the Sudanese Government was guilty of genocide. But our relief turned to dismay when, in the same testimony, shortly after his declaration of genocide, he asserted that no changes in U.S. policy were required. Our feelings were echoed by Eric Reeves, of Smith College, who has closely followed the unfolding genocide in Darfur. Writing the day after Secretary Powell's declaration of genocide, Reeves (2004) warned that "this provides a certain ghastly clarity in the new world order of the twenty-first century: Even genocide, even the crime that defined the actions in Rwanda and Eastern Europe during the Holocaust, does not entail any special response or effort of prevention. If this indeed marks the end of any particular obligations under the Genocide Convention, we may legitimately wonder whether the price paid for [Sectretary] Powell's determination is not exorbitantly high" (n.p.).

Our enthusiasm for the Security Council referral of Darfur to the International Criminal Court (ICC), which the ADT Project played a crucial role in making possible, is diminished by the suspicion that the Government of Sudan is unlikely to cooperate with the Court. As Reeves (2005), who regards the present regime in Khartoum as being guilty of "serial genocide" for their mass killing campaigns against specified groups in the Nuba mountains in 1992 and in the southern oil regions in 1997, notes, "It is not in the self-interest of genocidaires to cooperate in their own prosecution …" (n.p.). "Indeed," Reeves observes, "the very existence of an ICC investigation creates incentives for the NIF [the ruling regime in Khartoum] to sustain prevailing levels of insecurity in Darfur as a means of hampering possible investigation, even as such insecurity is now the most powerful tool of human destruction" (n.p.).

In the final analysis, while investigation and efforts to prosecute constitute a necessary move forward by the international community in regard to facing (versus ignoring) the horror and danger of massive atrocities, particularly those slouching towards crimes against humanity and/or genocide, they are far from sufficient. What was and still is needed but not yet available is a robust military intervention that is comprised of a highly trained force with an adequate number of troops and ample resources and the support to carry out the mission of halting the killing, rape, and destruction that continues to be carried out by Government of Sudan troops and the *Janjaweed*.

So, the question remains: Is there anything that anyone can do to attempt to halt the ongoing genocide in Darfur? It is a tough question to answer.

And, to be truthful, it is not as if everyone has cast a blind eye to Darfur. Professor Eric Reeves has written over one hundred detailed articles on Darfur and cast them out to the world via his Internet website. *The New York Times* columnist Nicholas Kristof has written one article after another on various facets of the atrocities being perpetrated in Darfur as well as pieces that lambaste, in no uncertain terms, the Bush White House, the UN Security Council, the European Union, and others for their lack of attention to the Darfurian tragedy. The U.S. Holocaust Memorial Museum's Committee on Conscience, which issued an early genocide warning regarding the situation in Darfur, has sponsored panel after panel on Darfur and has issued — and continues to issue — important updates regarding the crisis.

We (co-editors Totten and Markusen) initiated a letter-writing campaign over the Internet, urging concerned citizens to write letters to a host of officials (everyone from their Congressional representatives to President Bush and U.S. Secretary of State Condeleezza Rice to UN Secretary-General Kofi Annan and UN Special Advisor on the Prevention of Genocide Juan Mendez). The Save Darfur Committee, an alliance of over one hundred thirty diverse faith-based, humanitarian, and human rights organizations, has organized letter-writing campaigns and protests, and issued updates on both the plight of the black Africans of Darfur and how the international community has reacted (and not reacted) to the ongoing bloodshed in Darfur. University students across the United States have organized letter-writing campaigns, protests in front of Congress and the White House, and teach-ins. Samuel Totten has initiated his own Darfur petition campaign and has obtained over five thousand signatures from scholars, church leaders, and community members across the United States. One student group in Texas reports that it has collected over ten thousand signatures calling on the United States and the United Nations to do something more than pass anemic resolutions. Church groups and synagogues across the United States have educated their own congregants about the tragedy in Darfur and urged them to contact their representatives in Congress to do something besides talk about the situation. And that is just a fraction of what has taken place over the past two years or so.

That is all well and good, but the question that remains is: What good has it all done? First, it has kept the issue of Darfur alive and in the news. Second, it has educated large masses of people (young and old alike) about Darfur and what is happening there as well as what is not being done to prevent ongoing killing, deaths by attrition, and mass rape. Third, the concern by certain politicians (be they in the United States, Canada, or Europe) regarding the Darfur crisis may be a direct result of the ongoing letter-writing campaigns. The slow but sure increase in the number of African Union (AU) troops being deployed in Darfur and the assistance and supplies provided the AU by the United States, the European Union, NATO, Canada, and others might also be a result of ongoing pressure applied on various governmental and intergovernmental officials and bodies.

All of that is good, but it still is not enough, and thus the question that remains is this: *What can be done to halt the killing, raping, and dying? The simple but profound answer is to apply much more pressure, pressure that is systematic, ongoing, and relentless, all aimed at prodding the United Nations, regional organizations, and individual nations to act and to act now.* Quite frankly, it is not enough to simply sign a petition, write a single letter, give some money, wear a wristband, or write a single article. Each and every individual who detests the thought of genocide must attempt to keep the pressure on the powers that be, and that means not being satisfied or complacent by carrying out a single action or two.

Some may, and indeed have, claimed that the ADT Project was a cover for real action by the U.S. Government, and thus little more than a Pyrrhic victory of sorts for those who want to see genocide prevented in a timely and effective manner. Truthfully, for at least some of us who were members of the ADT, it certainly feels that way. But another way of looking at it — and not through rose-colored glasses, but with the view that change is slow, despicably so when it comes to the protection of peoples' human rights in many developing countries — the ADP is simply, but profoundly, one more piece of an extremely complex and thorny puzzle, a puzzle called the prevention and intervention of genocide. Thus, if nothing else, and this, in and of itself, is significant, the ADT Project has established, once and for all, that an investigation into suspected genocide can be undertaken during the actual period the atrocities are being perpetrated.

Finally, though, the upshot is this: No matter what the atrocities (mass murder of men, women, and children; mass rape of girls and women; and/or wholesale destruction of villages and wells) in Darfur (or any place else for that matter) are deemed (e.g., crimes against humanity or genocide), the victim population should not have to wait for assistance and protection until an investigatory body has completed its study and analyzed its data. Indeed, any time, anywhere that there is the danger of an outbreak of massacres, the international community must act to prevent such from becoming a reality. Furthermore, when massacres actually occur is not the time to study the problem or solely refer the matter to the ICC, but rather it is the time to halt the killing. Until that lesson is learned and acted upon, we fear that the world is going to witness more Darfurs in the years ahead.

References

Mennecke, Martin and Moltke, Elisabeth (2004). "From Rwanda to Darfur — When 'Genocide' Prevents 'Genocide Prevention.'" *The Aegis Review on Genocide,* Summer/Autumn, 1(3): 1-4.

Reeves, Eric (2005). "Khartoum Triumphant: Managing the Costs of Genocide in Darfur: The International Community Has Failed to Prevent, and Gives No Promise of Punishing, the Ultimate Crime." December 17, 2005, (n.p.). Available at: http://www.sudanreeves.org/index

Reeves, Eric (2004). "Secretary of State Colin Powell's Genocide Determination: What It Does, and Doesn't, Mean for Darfur." September 10, 2004, (n.p.). Available at: http://www.sudanreeves.org/modules

Appendices

Darfur Refugee Questionnaire

Questionnaire Serial: ☐☐☐☐☐☐

Camp: [ ] **Date:** [ ] **Time Started:** [ ] **Time Completed:** [ ]

| **Interviewer:** | | **Organization (NGO):** | |
| **Interpreter:** | | **Language Used:** | |

Location of Interview: *Describe nearby landmarks / paths / locating information*

INTRODUCTION

Hello. My name is _____. I work with _____, and we are talking with refugees about their experiences in the Darfur region of Sudan. If you are willing, we would like to have a brief conversation with a member of your household who will be selected at random. The experiences you share with us will be kept confidential, and will be used by the _____ to prepare a report. Your name, and all information you give us, will remain confidential and will not be released in any reports. Participation in this survey does not guarantee compensation for losses/deaths experienced by your household, nor does it mean that the individuals in your household will be able to testify at trials or bring specific charges against anyone. We understand you may not want to talk about your experiences; if so, we respect your decision.

HOUSEHOLD CONSENT

Would one of you be willing to speak with us? *Interviewer: Circle Response.*	1. Yes 2. No	INTERVIEWER: **If members of the household decline to be interviewed, thank them and walk away. Mark "NO" and use a new questionnaire for the next interview.**

RESPONDENT SELECTION

QA. How many members are there in your household, i.e. living here at the moment? Please include children. *Interviewer: Record Number.* ☐

QB. Among these members, how many children are there below 18 years of age? *Interviewer: Record Number.* ☐

QC. *Interviewer: Record the names of the adults, and choose one using the Kish-grid table.*

No.	Age	Name	A	B	C	D	E	F	G	H	I	J
1			1	1	1	1	1	1	1	1	1	1
2			1	2	1	2	1	2	1	2	2	2
3			1	3	2	1	3	2	1	3	1	1
4			1	2	3	4	1	2	3	4	2	4
5			5	4	3	2	1	5	4	3	1	3
6			1	2	3	4	5	6	1	2	4	6
7			3	2	1	7	6	5	4	3	1	6
8+			1	2	3	4	5	6	7	8	2	8

RESPONDENT CONSENT

Would you be willing to speak with us? *Interviewer: Circle Response.*	3. Yes 4. No	INTERVIEWER: If the selected person declines to be interviewed, thank them and walk away. Mark "NO" and use a new questionnaire for the next interview.

RESPONDENT DEMOGRAPHICS

Name:		Father's Name:	
Date of Birth:		Place of Birth:	
Gender:	1. Male 2. Female	Ethnicity:	1. Zaghawa 2. Fur 3. Masaleit 4. Other_____ 9. Don't Know / Refused
Tribe:		Clan:	
Type/ Years of School:	1. 0 2. 1-3 3. 4-6 4. 7-8 5. 9-12 6. 12+ 7. Islamic School 8. Other _____ 9. DK/ Ref. 1.	(If Female) Maiden Name:	
		What did you do? Did you work outside the home?	

RESPONDENT LOCATION

Q1. Which district do you come from? *Interviewer: circle district.*	1. North Darfur 2. West Darfur 3. South Darfur

Q2. Name of Interviewee's Town or Village:

In your language, what do you call your town/village? (Write the name as it sounds)	What is your town/village called in Arabic? (Write the Arabic name as it sounds)	Is your town/village known by any other name(s)? (Write the name/names as it sounds)

Q3. Proximity of Interviewee's Town or Village to the nearest large town.

Name of nearest large town in local language: (Write the name as it sounds)	Name of nearest large town in Arabic: (Write the Arabic name as it sounds)	How far is it to this town from your home village/town? (Write the number of kilometers)	What direction is this large town *from* your home village/town? (Write the direction as explained by interviewee)

Q4. Proximity of Interviewee's Town or Village to the nearest main road.

Name of nearest main road in local language: (Write the name as it sounds)	Name of nearest main road in Arabic: (Write the Arabic name as it sounds)	How far is it to this main road from your home village/town? (Write the number of kilometers)	What direction is this main road *from* your home village/town? (Write the direction as explained by interviewee)

INTERVIEWER: Preliminary Atlas Coordinates:
OFFICE: Final Atlas Coordinates:

RESPONDENT NARRATIVE

Q5. When did you leave your village? *Date or days since departure.*

Q6. Why did you leave your village?

Q7. What happened to you? Were you physically harmed?

Incident Location:		Incident Date:	
Perpetrator Name(s):		Perpetrator Phys. Desc.:	

Q8. Did those who harmed or attacked you say anything to you? Did the attackers say anything to each other during the event?

Q9. Were any members of your household harmed? In what way?

Incident Location:		Incident Date:			
Victim Name(s):		Ages:		Gender:	
Perpetrator Name(s):		Perpetrator Phys. Desc.:			

Q10. Did those who harmed or attacked your family say anything to them? Did the attackers say anything to each other during the event?

Q11. Were your household's water or food stores taken away or destroyed? If so, how? Were your cattle stolen? Did they have your brand?

Incident Location:		Incident Date:	
Perpetrator Name(s):		Perpetrator Phys. Desc.:	

Q12. Did your household own property or things that were destroyed or stolen?

Item List:			
Incident Location:		**Incident Date:**	
Perpetrator Name(s):		**Perpetrator Phys. Desc.:**	

Q13. Did you see any one else in your village being harmed or taken away? How were they harmed? Where were you when this was happening?

Victim Names:		Type of Harm:			
Incident Location:		**Incident Date:**			
Victim Name(s):		**Ages:**		**Gender:**	
Perpetrator Name(s):		**Perpetrator Phys. Desc.:**			

Q14. Was your village attacked / destroyed? If so, how and to what extent (e.g. burning/ shelling, partial/complete)? Were you and members of your family herded together and kept in groups before being expelled?

Q15. During the attack, were there any particular groups or types of people who were singled out for harm?

Incident Location:		**Incident Date:**	
Perpetrator Name(s):		**Perpetrator Phys. Desc.:**	

Q16. Were there any particular groups or types of people who were spared from harm?

Incident Location:		**Incident Date:**	
Perpetrator Name(s):		**Perpetrator Phys. Desc.:**	

Q17. Why do you think they did this to you, your household, or your village?

Q18. Since leaving your village, have any members of your household or village died on the journey to this camp? If so, how?

Incident Location:		Incident Date:			
Victim Name(s):		Ages:		Gender:	

Q19. Since leaving your village, have you *personally witnessed* attacks on other people or villages?

Victim Names:		Type of Harm:			
Incident Location:		Incident Date:			
Victim Name(s):		Ages:		Gender:	
Perpetrator Name(s):		Perpetrator Phys. Desc.:			

Q20. Since leaving your village, have you *heard about* attacks on other people or villages?

Victim Names:		Type of Harm:			
Incident Location:		Incident Date:			
Victim Name(s):		Ages:		Gender:	
Perpetrator Name(s):		Perpetrator Phys. Desc.:			

INTERVIEWER OBSERVATIONS:

Q I A. In what type of shelter did the respondent live?	1. Tent 2. Hut 3. Straw / stick enclosure 4. Plastic sheeting 5. Nothing 6. Other_____

Q I B. Were there any people present during the interview?	1. No one 2. Spouse 3. Children only 4. Family members 5. Small crowd 6. Large crowd 7. Other_____

Q I C. Did the respondent check with others for information to answer any question?	1. Yes 2. No

Q I D. Do you think anyone influenced the respondent's answers during the interview?	1. Yes 2. No

Q I E. Did you observe anyone intimidating the respondent during the interview?	1. Yes 2. No

Q I F. Did the respondent appear nervous during the interview or for any specific question?	1. Yes – whole interview 2. Yes – Question #_____ 3. No

Q I G. Did the respondent have difficulty answering any question?	1. Yes – Question #_____ Type of Difficulty _____ 2. No

FOR THE INTERVIEWER

Q I H. How did your presence influence neighbors?	1. No interest 2. Interest – looks 3. Interest – questions 4. Suspicion 5. Fear 6. Gathered

Q I I. Were you approached by any community / camp / militia representatives during the interview?	1. Yes (Specify) _____ 2. No

Q I J. Were you threatened during the interview?	3. Yes – Verbal threat. 4. Yes – Physical threat. 5. No

PRELIMINARY ATROCITY FIELD CODING

EVENT CODE	PERP. CODE	DATE	NUMBER OF VICTIMS	LOCATION	COMMENTS

EVENT CODES:

1. Killing — Family
2. Killing — Nonfamily
3. Killing — Mass (Specify # in comments)
4. Killing — Summary / displayed
5. Rape — Self
6. Rape — Other
7. Rape — With object
8. Abduction
9. Beating — Self
10. Beating — Others
11. Property destruction — Complete village
12. Property destruction —Partial village
13. Property destruction — Complete house
14. Property destruction — Partial house
15. Property destruction — Food stores
16. Property destruction — Personal items
17. Property theft — Looting
18. Property theft — Cattle
19. Property theft — Food stores
20. Whipping
21. Knifing
22. Branding
23. Sexual humiliation
24. Racial epithets
25. Reported rape
26. Reported killing
27. Aerial bombing
28. Attack from Sudanese military
29. Collateral damage — Property
30. Collateral damage — Killing
31. Collateral damage — Injury
32. Death from displacement – Starvation / dehydration
33. Death from displacement — Disease
34. Death from displacement — Infirmity
35. Other (*specify in comments*)

PERPETRATOR CODES:

1. *Jenjaweed* militia
2. Arab villagers
3. Black villagers
4. Sudanese soldier(s)
5. Sudanese police
6. JEM militia
7. SLA militia
8. Camp / humanitarian workers
9. Foreigners
10. Others (*specify in comments*)

Documenting Atrocities in Darfur

State Publication 11182
Released by the Bureau of Democracy, Human Rights and Labor, and the
Bureau of Intelligence and Research
September 2004

Summary

The conflict between the Government of Sudan (GoS) and two rebel groups that began in 2003 has precipitated the worst humanitarian and human rights crisis in the world today. The primary cleavage is ethnic: Arabs (GoS and militia forces) versus non-Arab villagers belonging primarily to the Zaghawa, Massalit, and Fur ethnic groups. Both groups are predominantly Muslim.

A U.S. Government project to conduct systematic interviews of Sudanese refugees in Chad reveals a consistent and widespread pattern of atrocities committed against non-Arab villagers in the Darfur region of western Sudan. This assessment is based on semistructured interviews with eleven hundred thirty-six randomly selected refugees in nineteen locations in eastern Chad. Most respondents said government forces, militia fighters, or a combination of both had completely destroyed their villages. Sixty-one percent of the respondents witnessed the killing of a family member; sixteen percent said they had been raped or had heard about a rape from a victim. About one-third of the refugees heard racial epithets while under attack. Four-fifths said their livestock was stolen; nearly half asserted their personal property was looted. This assessment highlights incidents and atrocities that have led to the displacement of large portions of Darfur's non-Arabs.

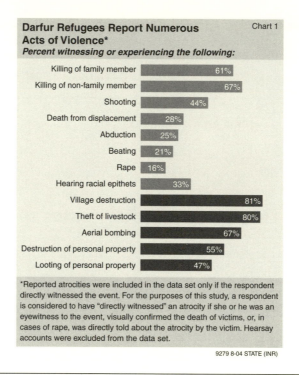

Figure A.1 Key findings of the Atrocities Documentation Team.

An Atrocities Documentation Team (ADT), assembled at the initiative of the U.S. Department of State's Bureau of Democracy, Human Rights and Labor (DRL), conducted interviews in Chad in July and August 2004. The team was primarily composed of independent experts recruited by the Coalition for International Justice (CIJ), and also included experts from the American Bar Association (ABA), DRL, and the State Department's Bureau of Intelligence and Research (INR) as well as the U.S. Agency for International Development (USAID). INR was responsible for compiling the survey data and producing the final report. USAID met the costs of the CIJ and ABA.

Humanitarian Crisis

As of August 2004, based on available information, more than four hundred five villages in Darfur had been completely destroyed, with an additional one hundred twenty three substantially damaged, since February 2003. Approximately two hundred thousand persons had sought refuge in eastern Chad as of August, according to the UN High Commissioner for Refugees (UNHCR); the UN Office for the Coordination of Humanitarian

Affairs reports another 1.2 million internally displaced persons (IDPs) remain in western Sudan. The total population of Darfur is six million. The lack of security in the region continues to threaten displaced persons. Insecurity and heavy rains continue to disrupt humanitarian assistance. The UN World Food Program provided food to nearly nine hundred forty thousand people in Darfur in July. Nonetheless, since the beginning of the Darfur food program, a total of eighty-two out of one hundred fifty-four concentrations of IDPs have received food, leaving seventy-two locations unassisted. Relief and health experts warn that malnutrition and mortality are likely to increase as forcibly displaced and isolated villagers suffer from hunger and infectious diseases that will spread quickly among densely populated and malnourished populations (Figure A.1).

The health situation for the two hundred thousand refugees in Chad is ominous. The U.S. Centers for Disease Control and Prevention estimate that one in three children in the refugee settlements in Chad is suffering from acute malnutrition and that crude mortality rates are already well above emergency threshold levels (one per ten thousand per day).

Human Rights Crisis

The non-Arab population of Darfur continues to suffer from crimes against humanity. A review of eleven hundred thirty-six interviews shows a consistent pattern of atrocities, suggesting close coordination between GoS forces and Arab militia elements, commonly known as the *Janjaweed*. ("*Janjaweed*" is an Arabic term meaning "horse and gun.").

Despite the current cease-fire and UN Security Council Resolution 1556, *Janjaweed* violence against civilians has continued (cease-fire violations by both the *Janjaweed* and the rebels have continued as well). Media reports on August 10, 16, and 19 chronicled GoS–*Janjaweed* attacks in western Darfur. In addition to their work on the survey, the interviewers had the opportunity to speak with newly arrived refugees who provided accounts that tended to confirm press reports of continuing GoS participation in recent attacks. Refugees who fled the violence on August 6 and 8 spoke with the team, providing accounts consistent with media reports: Joint GoS military and *Janjaweed* attacks; strafing by helicopter gun ships followed by ground attacks by the GoS military in vehicles and *Janjaweed* on horseback; males being shot or knifed; and women being abducted or raped. Respondents reported these attacks destroyed five villages. Multiple respondents also reported attacks on the IDP camp of Arja.

The United Nations estimates the violence has affected 2.2 million of Darfur's 6 million residents. The GoS claims it has been unable to prevent *Janjaweed* atrocities and that the international community has exaggerated the extent and nature of the crisis. The GoS has improved international relief access to IDPs in Darfur since July, but problems, including lack of security and seasonal rains, have hampered relief programs. Survey results indicate that most Sudanese refugees state that *Janjaweed* militias and GoS military forces collaborate in carrying out systematic attacks against non-Arab villages in Darfur.

Ethnographic Background

Darfur covers about one-fifth of Sudan's vast territory and is home to one-seventh of its population. It includes a mixture of Arab and non-Arab ethnic groups, both of which are predominantly Muslim (see Figure A.3). The Fur ethnic group (Darfur means "homeland of the Fur") is the largest non-Arab ethnic group in the region. Northern Darfur State is home to the nomadic non-Arab Zaghawa, but also includes a significant number of Arabs, such as the Meidab. Sedentary non-Arabs from the Fur, Massalit, Daju, and other ethnic groups live in Western Darfur State. The arid climate and the competition for scarce resources over the years have contributed to recurring conflict between nomadic Arab herders and non-Arab farmers, particularly over land and grazing rights. Various ethnic groups have fought over access to water, grazing rights, and prized agricultural land as desertification has driven herders farther south.

Political and Military Conflict

Ethnic violence affected the Darfur region in the 1980s. In 1986, Prime Minister Sadiq al-Mahdi armed the ethnic-Arab tribes to fight John Garang's Sudanese People's Liberation Army (SPLA). After helping the GoS beat back an SPLA attack in Darfur in 1991, one of these Arab tribes sought to resolve ancient disputes over land and water rights by attacking the Zaghawa, Fur, and Massalit peoples. Arab groups launched a campaign in Southern Darfur State that resulted in the destruction of some six hundred non-Arab villages and the deaths of about three thousand people. The GoS itself encouraged the formation of an "Arab Alliance" in Darfur to keep non-Arab ethnic groups in check. Weapons flowed into Darfur and the conflict spread. After President al-Bashir seized power in 1989, the new government disarmed non-Arab ethnic groups, but allowed politically loyal Arab allies to keep their weapons.

In February 2003, rebels calling themselves the Darfur Liberation Front (DLF) attacked GoS military installations and the provincial capital of Al Fashir. The DLF complained of economic marginalization and demanded a power sharing arrangement with the GoS. In March 2003, the DLF changed its name to the Sudan Liberation Movement/Army (SLM/A), intensified its military operations, unveiled a political program for a "united democratic Sudan," and bolstered its strength to some four thousand rebels. The Justice and Equality Movement, with fewer than one thousand members, was established in 2002, but has since joined the SLM/A in several campaigns against GoS forces.

The GoS has provided support to Arab militia attacking non-Arab civilians, according to press and nongovernment organizations (NGO) reports. Refugee accounts corroborated by United States and other independent reporting suggest that Khartoum has continued to provide direct support for advancing *Janjaweed*. Aerial bombardment and attacks on civilians reportedly have occurred widely throughout the region; respondents named more than one hundred locations that experienced such bombardment (see Figure A.4). The extent to which insurgent base camps were co-located with villages and civilians is unknown. The number of casualties caused by aerial bombardment cannot be determined, but large numbers of Darfurians have been forced to flee their villages. According to press and NGO reports, the GoS has given *Janjaweed* recruits salaries, communication equipment, arms, and identity cards.

Current International Response

On July 30, 2004, the UN Security Council adopted Resolution 1556, which demanded that the GoS fulfill commitments it made to disarm the *Janjaweed* militias and apprehend and bring to justice *Janjaweed* leaders and their associates; it also called on the GoS to allow humanitarian access to Darfur, among other things. The United Nations placed an embargo on the sale or supply of materiel and training to nongovernmental entities and individuals in Darfur. The resolution endorsed the African Union (AU) deployment of monitors and a protection force to Darfur. It requested the UN Secretary-General to report on GoS progress in thirty days and held out the possibility of further actions, including sanctions, against the GoS in the event of noncompliance.

The Security Council has expressed its deep concern over reports of large-scale violations of human rights and international humanitarian law in Darfur. The main protection concerns identified by the United Nations and corroborated by the ADT include threats to life and freedom of movement, forced relocation, forced return, sexual violence, and restricted access to humanitarian assistance, social services, sources of livelihood, and basic services. Food security has been precarious and will probably worsen as the rainy season continues. Many displaced households no longer can feed themselves because of the loss of livestock and the razing of food stores.

Relief agencies' access to areas outside the state capitals of Al Junaynah, Al Fashir, and Nyala was limited until late May. Visits by UN Secretary-General Kofi Annan and U.S. Secretary of State Colin Powell in June 2004 brought heightened attention to the growing humanitarian crisis. As a result, the GoS lifted travel restrictions and announced measures to facilitate humanitarian access. Nonetheless, serious problems remain, specifically capacity, logistics, and security for relief efforts. USAID's Disaster Assistance Response Team and other agencies have deployed additional staff to increase emergency response capacity.

Refugee Interviews and Survey Results

The Atrocities Documentation Team (ADT) conducted a random-sample survey of Darfurian refugees in eastern Chad in July and August 2004. The team interviewed eleven hundred thirty-six refugees, many of whom had endured harsh journeys across the desolate Chad–Sudan border.

A plurality of the respondents were ethnic Zaghawa (46 percent), with smaller numbers belonging to the Fur (8 percent) and Massalit (30 percent) ethnic groups. Slightly more than half the respondents (56 percent) were women (see Figure A.3).

Analysis of the refugee interviews points to a pattern of abuse against members of Darfur's non-Arab communities, including murder, rape, beatings, ethnic humiliation, and destruction of property and basic necessities. Many of the reports detailing attacks on villages refer to government and militia forces, preceded by aerial bombardment, acting together to commit atrocities. Respondents said government and militia forces wore khaki or brown military uniforms. Roughly one-half of the respondents noted GoS forces had joined *Janjaweed* irregulars in attacking their villages. Approximately one-quarter of the respondents said GoS forces had acted alone; another 14 percent said the *Janjaweed* had acted alone. Two-thirds of the respondents reported aerial bombings against their villages; four-fifths said they had witnessed the complete destruction of their villages. Sixty-one percent reported witnessing the killing of a family member. About one-third of the respondents reported hearing racial epithets while under attack; one-quarter witnessed beatings. Large numbers reported the looting of personal property (47 percent) and the theft of livestock (80 percent).

Most reports followed a similar pattern:

1. GoS aircraft or helicopters bomb villages.
2. GoS soldiers arrive in trucks, followed closely by *Janjaweed* militia riding horses or camels.
3. GoS soldiers and militia surround and then enter villages, under cover of gunfire.
4. Fleeing villagers are targets in aerial bombing.
5. The *Janjaweed* and GoS soldiers loot the village after most citizens have fled, often using trucks to remove belongings.
6. Villages often experience multiple attacks over a prolonged period before they are destroyed by burning or bombing.

When describing attacks, refugees often referred to GoS soldiers and *Janjaweed* militias as a unified group. As one refugee stated, "The soldiers and *Janjaweed*, always they are together." The primary victims have been non-Arab residents of Darfur. Numerous credible reports corroborate the use of racial and ethnic epithets by both the *Janjaweed* and GoS military personnel; "Kill the slaves, Kill the slaves," and "We have orders to kill all the blacks," are common. One refugee reported a militia member stating, "We kill all blacks and even kill our cattle when they have black calves." Numerous refugee accounts point to mass abductions, including persons driven away in GoS vehicles, but respondents usually do not know the abductees' fates. A few respondents indicated personal knowledge of mass executions and grave sites.

A subset of four hundred respondents were asked about rebel activity in or near their villages. Nearly nine in ten said there was no rebel activity before the attack. Nine percent noted rebels were in the vicinity; 2 percent said the rebels were present in their villages. The overwhelming majority (91 percent) said their village was not defended at all against the attack. One percent asserted their village had been successfully defended and another 8 percent cited an unsuccessful defense (Figure A.2).

Respondents reported ethnic tensions in the region had risen over the past few years. For example, markets in which non-Arabs and Arabs had previously interacted have become segregated, and almost all villages are now said to be ethnically homogenous. According to many of the interviewees, GoS soldiers and *Janjaweed* attacked villages because of their non-Arab populations; men of fighting age have been abducted, executed, or both; and women and girls have been abducted and raped.

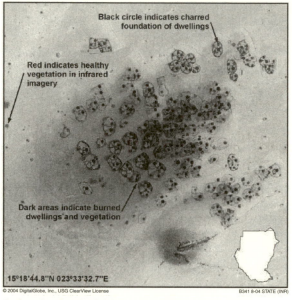

Black circle indicates charred foundation of dwellings

Red indicates healthy vegetation in infrared imagery

Dark areas indicate burned dwellings and vegetation

15°18'44.8"N 023°33'32.7"E

© 2004 DigitalGlobe, Inc., USG ClearView License

B341 8-04 STATE (INR)

A refugee interviewed in Bahai camp reported that his home in Darurja was destroyed in February 2004 by *Janjaweed* who torched his village, stole his cattle and belongings, and raped 5-10 young women. The *Janjaweed* said "we will kill all blacks—this is not your homeland."

Figure A.2 Example of a destroyed village in Darfur. (With permission, DigitalGlobe Inc, USG Clearview License, 2004.)

Refugee Interviews and Survey Methodology

This report is based on results from personal interviews conducted by three teams between July 12 and August 18, 2004. DRL, USAID, and the Coalition for International Justice jointly designed the questionnaire in conjunction with other NGOs. INR provided technical assistance on questionnaire design and survey methodology. The teams used a semi-structured interviewing approach that permitted the refugees to give the broadest possible accounts of the events they had experienced. The interviews were conducted in nineteen locations in eastern Chad, including UNHCR camps and informal settlements.

Refugees were selected using a systematic, random sampling approach designed to meet the conditions in Chad. Interviewers randomly selected a sector within a refugee camp and then, from a fixed point within the sector, chose every tenth dwelling unit for interviewing. All adults were listed within the dwelling unit, and one adult was randomly selected. This methodology ensures the results are as representative as possible in light of refugee conditions. Interviews took place in private, with only the refugee, a translator, and the interviewer present.

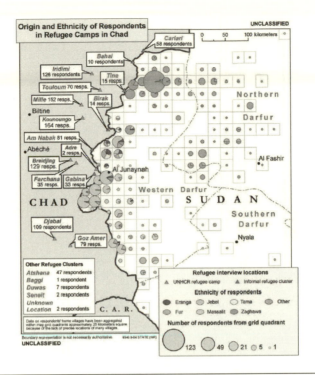

Figure A.3 Origins and ethnicities of refugees interviewed by the Atrocities Documentation Team.

Several characteristics of the survey must be underscored. First, accounts of atrocities may be dated, depending on when the individual refugee fled his or her village. Second, the data may actually undercount the extent of atrocities because mass attacks often leave few survivors. Third, most respondents come from villages within fifty miles of the border in Western Darfur and Northern Darfur States. Fourth, it is very likely that rapes are underreported because of the social stigma attached to acknowledging such violations of female members of one's family.

The results are broadly representative of Darfurian refugees in Chad, but may not be representative of internally displaced persons still in Darfur because they were not included in the sample. A margin of error for this sample cannot be calculated because of the lack of accurate demographic information about the refugee camps and settlements. The methodology was designed to achieve as broadly representative a sample as was feasible under the prevailing conditions. Dates of events reported by refugees frequently utilized the Islamic calendar; these dates were then converted to dates on the Gregorian calendar (Figure A.3).

The field data for the eleven hundred thirty-six interviews were compiled using a standardized data entry process that involved the collection

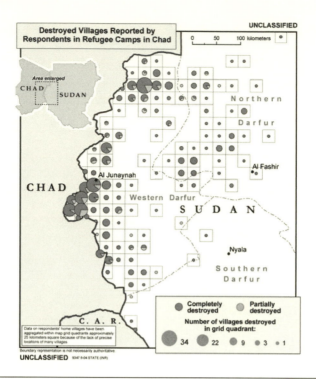

Figure A.4 Partially and completely destroyed villages reported to the ADT.

and coding of detailed information from each refugee respondent's set of answers. The researchers then used a statistical program to aggregate the data and analyze the results (Figure A.4).

APPENDIX **3**

The Crisis in Darfur

U.S. SECRETARY OF STATE COLIN L. POWELL

Testimony before the Senate Foreign Relations Committee
Washington, D.C.
September 9, 2004
(9:35 a.m. EDT)

SECRETARY POWELL: Thank you very much, Mr. Chairman. It's a pleasure to be back before the committee as you conduct these deliberations on one of the most difficult situations the international community is facing, and that's the tragedy in Darfur where, as you noted, so many hundreds of thousands of people are at risk, so many hundreds of thousands of people have been forced from their homes, from their villages to camps, and where there is an absolute need for the international community to come together and speak with one voice as to how we deal with this situation.

   Mr. Chairman, I do have a prepared statement that I would like to offer for the record and then I will draw from that in my opening remarks.

CHAIRMAN LUGAR: It will be published in full and please proceed as you wish.

SECRETARY POWELL: Mr. Chairman and members of the committee, let me thank you for this opportunity to testify on the situation on Darfur, and let me begin by reviewing a little history. The violence in Darfur has complex roots in traditional conflicts between Arab nomadic herders and African farmers. The violence intensified during 2003 when two groups — the Sudan Liberation Movement and the Justice and Equality Movement — declared open rebellion against the Government of Sudan because they feared being on the outside of the power and wealth-sharing agreements that were being arranged in the north-south negotiations, the "Naivasha discussions," as we call them. Khartoum reacted aggressively, intensifying support for Arab militias to take on these rebels and support for what are known as the *Janjaweed*. The Government of Sudan supported the *Janjaweed*, directly and indirectly, as they carried out a scorched-earth policy toward the rebels and the African civilian population in Darfur.

Mr. Chairman, the United States exerted strong leadership to focus international attention on this unfolding tragedy. We first took the issue of Sudan to the United Nations Security Council last fall. President Bush was the first head of state to condemn publicly the Government of Sudan and to urge the international community to intensify efforts to end the violence. In April of this year, the United States brokered a ceasefire between the Government of Sudan and the rebels, and then took the lead to get the African Union to monitor that ceasefire.

As some of you are aware, I traveled to the Sudan in midsummer and made a point of visiting Darfur. It was about the same time that Congressman Wolf and Senator Brownback were there, as well as Secretary-General Kofi Annan. In fact, the Secretary-General and I were able to meet in Khartoum to exchange our notes and to make sure that we gave a consistent message to the Sudanese Government of what was expected of them.

Senator Brownback can back me up when I say that all of us saw the suffering that the people of Darfur are having to endure. And Senator Corzine was just in Darfur recently. He can vouch for the fact that atrocities are still occurring. All of us met with people who had been driven from their homes by the terrible violence that is occurring in Darfur; indeed, many of them having seen their homes and all their worldly possessions destroyed or confiscated before their eyes.

During my visit, humanitarian workers from my own Agency — USAID — and from other nongovernmental organizations told me how they are struggling to bring food, shelter, and medicines to those so desperately in need — a population, as you noted, Mr. Chairman, of well over a million.

In my midsummer meetings with officials of the Government of Sudan, we presented them with the stark facts of what we knew about what is happening in Darfur from the destruction of villages to the raping and the killing to the obstacles that impeded relief efforts. Secretary-General Annan and I obtained from the Government of Sudan what they said would be firm commitments to take steps, and to take steps immediately, that would remove these obstacles, help bring the violence to an end, and do it in a way that we could monitor their performance.

There have been some positive developments since my visit, since the visit of Senator Brownback, Congressman Wolf, and the Secretary-General.

The Sudanese have met some of our benchmarks, such as improving humanitarian access, engaging in political talks with the rebels, and supporting the deployment of observers and troops from the Africa Union to monitor the ceasefire between Khartoum and the rebels.

The AU [African Union] Ceasefire Commission has also been set up and is working to monitor more effectively what is happening in Darfur. The general who is in charge of that mission, a Nigerian general by the name of General Okonkwo, is somebody that we know well. He is the same Nigerian general who went into Liberia last year and helped stabilize the situation there — a very good officer, a good commander who knows his business.

The AU's mission will help to restore sufficient security so that these dislocated, starving, hounded people can at least avail themselves of the humanitarian assistance that is available. But what is really needed is enough security so that they can go home, not be safe in camps. We need security throughout the countryside. These people need to go home. We are not interested in creating a permanent displaced population that survives in camps on the dole of the international community.

And what is really needed to accomplish that is for the *Janjaweed* militias to cease and desist their murderous raids against these people — and for the government in Khartoum to stop being complicit in such raids. Khartoum has made no meaningful progress in substantially improving the overall security environment by disarming the *Janjaweed* militias or arresting its leaders.

So we are continuing to press the Government of Sudan and we continue to monitor them. We continue to make sure that we are not just left with promises instead of actual action and performance on the ground. Because it is absolutely clear that as we approach the end of the rainy season, the situation on the ground must change, and it must change quickly. There are too many tens upon tens of thousands of human beings who are at risk. Some of them have already been consigned to death in the future because of the circumstances they are living in now. They will not make it through the end of the year. Poor security, inadequate capacity, and heavy rains, which will not diminish until later this month, continue to hamper the relief effort.

The United Nations estimates that there are over 1.2 million internally displaced persons (IDPs) in Darfur. In July, almost one million IDPs received food assistance. About two hundred thousand Sudanese refugees are being assisted by the UNHCR and partner organizations across the border in Chad. The World Food Program expects two million IDPs will need food aid by October.

The U.S. Government provision of aid to the Darfur crisis in the Sudan and Chad totaled $211 million as of September 2, 2004. This includes $112 million in food assistance, $50 million in nonfood assistance, $36 million for refugees in Chad, $5 million for refugee programs in Darfur, and $6.8 million for the African Union mission.

The United States also strongly supports the work of the AU monitoring mission in Darfur. In fact, we initiated the mission through base camp set-up and logistics support by a private contractor that we are paying for. The AU mission is currently staffed with one hundred twenty-five AU monitors now deployed in the field, and those monitors have already completed twenty investigations of ceasefire violations and their reports are now being written up and being provided to the AU and to the UN and to the international community.

The AU monitoring staff is supported by a protection force of three hundred five troops, made up of a Rwandan contingent of one hundred fifty-five, who arrived on August 15, and a Nigerian contingent of one hundred fifty, who arrived on August 30th. Recognizing the security problems in Darfur, the United Nations and the United States have begun calling for an expanded AU mission in Darfur through the provision of additional observers and additional protection forces so their presence can spread throughout this very, very large area that is about, oh, 80 percent the size of the state of Texas. It is not a simple geographic or monitoring or military mission. It is very complex. Khartoum seems to have expressed a willingness to consider such an expanded mission.

I am pleased to announce, Mr. Chairman, that the State Department has identified $20.5 million in FY04 funds for initial support of this expanded AU mission. We look forward to consulting with the Congress on meeting additional needs that such a mission might have.

As you know, as we watched the month of July — as you watched through the month of July, we felt that more pressure was required. So we went to the United Nations and asked for a resolution. And we got that resolution on July 30th, after a bit of debate, but it was 13-0 with two abstentions.

This resolution, 1556, demands that the Government of Sudan take action to disarm the *Janjaweed* militia and bring *Janjaweed* leaders to justice. It warns Khartoum that the Security Council will take further actions and measures, which is the UN term for sanctions. "Measures" is not a softer word. It includes sanctions and any other measures that might be contemplated or available to the international community. And it warned

Khartoum that the United Nations, through its Security Council, will take actions and measures if Sudan fails to comply.

That resolution urges the warring parties to conclude a political agreement without delay and it commits all states to target sanctions against the *Janjaweed* militias and those who aid and abet them as well as others who may share responsibility for this tragic situation. Too many lives have already been lost. We cannot lose any more time. We in the international community must intensify our efforts to help those imperiled by violence, starvation, and disease in Darfur.

But the Government of Sudan bears the greatest responsibility to face up to this catastrophe, rein in those who are committing these atrocities, and save the lives of its own citizens. At the same time, however, the rebels have not fully respected the ceasefire and we are disturbed at reports of rebel kidnapping of relief workers. We have emphasized to the rebels that they must allow unrestricted access of humanitarian relief workers and supplies, and that they must cooperate fully, including cooperating with the AU monitoring mission.

We are pleased that the Government of Sudan and the rebels are currently engaged in talks in Abuja, hosted by the AU. These talks are aimed at bringing about a political settlement in Darfur. The two sides have agreed on a protocol to facilitate delivery of much-needed humanitarian assistance to rebel-held areas, and are now engaged in discussions of a protocol on security issues.

These negotiations are difficult. We expect that they may be adjourned for a period of time after these initial agreements and we are some ways away from seeing a political resolution between the two sides. We are urging both sides to intensify negotiations in order to reach a political settlement. And I have personnel from State Department who are on the ground in Abuja on a full-time basis to assist the negotiators in their work.

When I was in Khartoum earlier in the summer, I told President al-Bashir, Vice President Taha, Foreign Minister Ismail, the Minister of Interior and others, that the United States wants to see a united, unified, prosperous, democratic Sudan. I told them that to that end we are fully prepared to work with them. I reminded them that we had reached an historic agreement on June 5th — an agreement that we had worked on for so long — an agreement between the Government of Sudan and the Sudan People's Liberation Movement, the so-called North–South agreement. And this North–South agreement covered all of the outstanding issues that had been so difficult for these parties to come to agreement on; they had come to agreement on. [sic]

Since then, the parties have been engaged in final negotiations on remaining details. However, the parties now are stuck on the specifics of a formal ceasefire agreement and have not yet begun the final round of implementation modalities. Special Envoy Sumbeiywo met recently with the parties, but could not resolve the remaining ceasefire-related issues. Khartoum appears unwilling to resume talks at the most senior level, claiming that it must focus on Darfur. That would be fine if its focus were the right focus, but it is not. The SPLM [Sudan People's Liberation Movement] is more forward leaning, but still focused on negotiating details. We believe that a comprehensive agreement would bolster efforts to resolve the crisis in Darfur by providing a legal basis for a political solution and by opening up the political process in Khartoum.

President Bashir has repeatedly pledged to work for peace, and he pledged that again when I met with him earlier in the summer. But President Bush, this Congress, Secretary-General Annan and the international community want more than promises. We want to see dramatic improvements on the ground right now. Indeed, we wanted to see them yesterday.

In the meantime, while we wait, we are doing all that we can. We are working with the international community to make sure all those nations who have made pledges of financial assistance and other kinds of assistance meet their pledges. We are not yet satisfied with the response from the international community to meeting the pledges that they have made. In fact, the estimated needs have grown and the donor community needs to dig deeper. America has been in the forefront of providing assistance to the suffering people of Darfur and will remain in the forefront. But it is time for the entire international community to increase their assistance.

The United States has pledged $299 million in humanitarian aid through FY05, and $11.8 million to the AU mission, and we are well on our way to exceeding these pledges. Clearly, we will need more assistance in the future and we are looking at all of our accounts within the Department to see what we can do. And when we are beyond our ability to do more from within our current appropriations, we will have to come back to the Congress and make our requests known.

Secretary-General Annan's August 30th report called for an expanded AU mission in Darfur to monitor commitments of the parties more effectively, thereby enhancing security and facilitating the delivery of humanitarian assistance. The Secretary-General's report also highlighted Khartoum's failure to rein in and disarm the *Janjaweed* militia, and noted that the Sudanese military continued to take part in attacks on civilians, including aerial bombardment and helicopter strikes.

We have begun consultation in New York on a new resolution that calls for Khartoum to fully cooperate with an expanded AU force and for cessation of Sudanese military flights over the Darfur region. It also provides for international overflights to monitor the situation in Darfur and requires the Security Council to review the record of Khartoum's compliance to determine if sanctions, including on the Sudanese petroleum sector, should be imposed. The resolution also urges the Government of Sudan and the SPLM to conclude negotiations, the Lake Naivasha negotiations, on a comprehensive peace accord.

And, Mr. Chairman, there is, finally, the continuing question of whether what is happening in Darfur should be called genocide.

Since the United States became aware of atrocities occurring in Sudan, we have been reviewing the Genocide Convention and the obligations it places on the Government of Sudan and on the international community and on the state parties to the genocide convention.

In July, we launched a limited investigation by sending a team to visit the refugee camps in Chad to talk to refugees and displaced personnel. The team worked closely with the American Bar Association and the Coalition for International Justice, and was able to interview eleven hundred thirty-six of the 2.2 million people the United Nations estimates have been affected by this horrible situation, this horrible violence.

Those interviews indicated, first, a consistent and widespread pattern of atrocities: Killings, rapes, burning of villages committed by *Janjaweed* and government forces against non-Arab villagers; second, three-fourths of those interviewed reported that the Sudanese military forces were involved in the attacks; third, villagers often experienced multiple attacks over a prolonged period before they were destroyed by burning, shelling, or bombing, making it impossible for the villagers to return to their villages. This was a coordinated effort, not just random violence.

When we reviewed the evidence compiled by our team, and then put it beside other information available to the State Department and widely known throughout the international community, widely reported upon by the media and by others, we concluded, I concluded, that genocide has been committed in Darfur and that the Government of Sudan and the *Janjaweed* bear responsibility — and that genocide may still be occurring. Mr. Chairman, we are making copies of the evidence that our team compiled available to you and to the public today. We are putting it up on our website now, as I speak.

We believe in order to confirm the true nature, scope, and totality of the crimes our evidence reveals, a full-blown and unfettered investigation needs to occur. Sudan is a contracting party to the Genocide Convention and is obliged under the Convention to prevent and to punish acts of genocide. To us, at this time, it appears that Sudan has failed to do so.

Article VIII of the Genocide Convention provides that Contracting Parties may, I will quote now, "may call upon the competent organs of the United Nations to take action, such action under the Charter of the United

Nations as they," the competent organs of the United Nations, "as they consider appropriate, actions as they consider appropriate for the prevention and suppression of acts of genocide or any of the other acts enumerated in Article III" of the Genocide Convention.

Because of that obligation under Article VIII of the Convention, and since the United States is one of the contracting parties, today we are calling on the United Nations to initiate a full investigation. To this end, the United States will propose that the next UN Security Council Resolution on Sudan request a United Nations investigation into all violations of international humanitarian law and human rights law that have occurred in Darfur, with a view to ensuring accountability.

Mr. Chairman, as I have said, the evidence leads us to the conclusion, the United States to the conclusion, that genocide has occurred and may still be occurring in Darfur. We believe the evidence corroborates the specific intent of the perpetrators to destroy "a group in whole or in part," the words of the Convention. This intent may be inferred from their deliberate conduct. We believe other elements of the convention have been met as well.

Under the 1948 Convention on the Prevention and Punishment of the Crime of Genocide, to which both the United States and Sudan are parties, genocide occurs when the following three criteria are met:

First, specific acts are committed, and those acts include killing, causing serious bodily or mental harm, deliberately inflicting conditions of life calculated to bring about physical destruction of a group in whole or in part, imposing measures to prevent births, or forcibly transferring children to another group. Those are specified acts that, if committed, raise the likelihood that genocide is being committed.

The second criteria: These acts are committed against members of a national, ethnic, racial, or religious group; and the third criterion is, they are committed "with intent to destroy, in whole or in part, the group, as such."

The totality of the evidence from the interviews we conducted in July and August, and from the other sources available to us, shows that the *Janjaweed* and Sudanese military forces have committed large-scale acts of violence, including murders, rape, and physical assaults on non-Arab individuals. Second, the *Janjaweed* and Sudanese military forces destroyed villages, foodstuffs, and other means of survival. Third, the Sudan government and its military forces obstructed food, water, medicine, and other humanitarian aid from reaching affected populations, thereby leading to further deaths and suffering. And finally, despite having been put on notice multiple times, Khartoum has failed to stop the violence.

Mr. Chairman, some seem to have been waiting for this determination of genocide to take action. In fact, however, no new action is dictated by this determination. We have been doing everything we can to get the

Sudanese Government to act responsibly. So, let us not be too preoccupied with this designation. These people are in desperate need and we must help them. Call it civil war; call it ethnic cleansing; call it genocide; call it "none of the above." The reality is the same. There are people in Darfur who desperately need the help of the international community.

I expect, I more than expect, I know that the government of Khartoum in Khartoum will reject our conclusion of genocide anyway. Moreover, at this point, genocide is our judgment and not the judgment of the international community. Before the Government of Sudan is taken to the bar of international justice, let me point out that there is a simple way for Khartoum to avoid such wholesale condemnation by the international community, and that way is to take action — to stop holding back, to stop dissembling.

The government in Khartoum should end the attacks and ensure its people — all of its people — are secure, ensure that they are all secure. They should hold to account those who are responsible for past atrocities, and ensure that current negotiations taking place in Abuja, and also the Naivasha accords, are successfully concluded. That is the only way to peace and prosperity for this war-ravaged land.

Specifically, Mr. Chairman, the most practical contribution we can make to the security of Darfur in the short term is to do everything we can to increase the number of African Union monitors. That will require the cooperation of the Government of Sudan.

And I am pleased that the African Union is stepping up to the task. It is playing a leadership role and countries within the African Union have demonstrated a willingness to provide a significant number of troops. And this is the fastest way to help bring security to the countryside through this expanded monitoring presence, so we can see what is going on and act to prevent it.

In the intermediate and long term, the security of Darfur can best be advanced by a political settlement at Abuja, and by the successful conclusion of the peace negotiations between the SPLM and the Government in Sudan, the Lake Naivasha accords.

Mr. Chairman, I will stop here and take your questions. Thank you.

Convention on the Prevention and Punishment of the Crime of Genocide

Adopted by Resolution 260 (III) A of the United Nations General Assembly on 9 December 1948.

Article 1

The Contracting Parties confirm that genocide, whether committed in time of peace or in time of war, is a crime under international law, which they undertake to prevent and to punish.

Article 2

In the present Convention, genocide means any of the following acts committed with intent to destroy, in whole or in part, a national, ethnical, racial or religious group, as such:

(a) Killing members of the group.
(b) Causing serious bodily or mental harm to members of the group.
(c) Deliberately inflicting on the group conditions of life calculated to bring about its physical destruction in whole or in part
(d) Imposing measures intended to prevent births within the group.
(e) Forcibly transferring children of the group to another group.

Article 3

The following acts shall be punishable:

- (a) Genocide
- (b) Conspiracy to commit genocide
- (c) Direct and public incitement to commit genocide
- (d) Attempt to commit genocide
- (e) Complicity in genocide

Article 4

Persons committing genocide or any of the other acts enumerated in Article 3 shall be punished, whether they are constitutionally responsible rulers, public officials or private individuals.

Article 5

The Contracting Parties undertake to enact, in accordance with their respective Constitutions, the necessary legislation to give effect to the provisions of the present Convention and, in particular, to provide effective penalties for persons guilty of genocide or any of the other acts enumerated in Article 3.

Article 6

Persons charged with genocide or any of the other acts enumerated in Article 3 shall be tried by a competent tribunal of the State in the territory of which the act was committed, or by such international penal tribunal as may have jurisdiction with respect to those Contracting Parties, which shall have accepted its jurisdiction.

Article 7

Genocide and the other acts enumerated in Article 3 shall not be considered as political crimes for the purpose of extradition.

The Contracting Parties pledge themselves in such cases to grant extradition in accordance with their laws and treaties in force.

Article 8

Any Contracting Party may call upon the competent organs of the United Nations to take such action under the Charter of the United Nations as they consider appropriate for the prevention and suppression of acts of genocide or any of the other acts enumerated in Article 3.

Article 9

Disputes between the Contracting Parties relating to the interpretation, application or fulfillment of the present Convention, including those relating to the responsibility of a State for genocide or any of the other acts enumerated in Article 3, shall be submitted to the International Court of Justice at the request of any of the parties to the dispute.

Article 10

The present Convention, of which the Chinese, English, French, Russian, and Spanish texts are equally authentic, shall bear the date of 9 December 1948.

Article 11

The present Convention shall be open until 31 December 1949 for signature on behalf of any Member of the United Nations and of any nonmember State to which an invitation to sign has been addressed by the General Assembly.

The present Convention shall be ratified, and the instruments of ratification shall be deposited with the Secretary-General of the United Nations.

After 1 January 1950, the present Convention may be acceded to on behalf of any Member of the United Nations and of any nonmember State, which has received an invitation as aforesaid.

Instruments of accession shall be deposited with the Secretary-General of the United Nations.

Article 12

Any Contracting Party may at any time, by notification addressed to the Secretary-General of the United Nations, extend the application of the present Convention to all or any of the territories for the conduct of whose foreign relations that Contracting Party is responsible.

Article 13

On the day when the first twenty instruments of ratification or accession have been deposited, the Secretary-General shall draw up a process-verbal and transmit a copy of it to each Member of the United Nations and to each of the nonmember States contemplated in Article 11.

The present Convention shall come into force on the ninetieth day following the date of deposit of the twentieth instrument of ratification or accession.

Any ratification or accession effected subsequent to the latter date shall become effective on the ninetieth day following the deposit of the instrument of ratification or accession.

Article 14

The present Convention shall remain in effect for a period of ten years as from the date of its coming into force.

It shall thereafter remain in force for successive periods of five years for such Contracting Parties as have not denounced it at least six months before the expiration of the current period.

Denunciation shall be effected by a written notification addressed to the Secretary-General of the United Nations.

Article 15

If, as a result of denunciations, the number of Parties to the present Convention should become less than sixteen, the Convention shall cease to be in force as from the date on which the last of these denunciations shall become effective.

Article 16

A request for the revision of the present Convention may be made at any time by any Contracting Party by means of a notification in writing addressed to the Secretary-General.

The General Assembly shall decide upon the steps, if any, to be taken in respect of such request.

Article 17

The Secretary-General of the United Nations shall notify all Members of the United Nations and the nonmember States contemplated in Article 11 of the following:

- (a) Signatures, ratification and accessions received in accordance with Article 11.
- (b) Notifications received in accordance with Article 12.
- (c) The date upon which the present Convention comes into force in accordance with Article 13.
- (d) Denunciations received in accordance with Article 14.

(e) The abrogation of the Convention in accordance with Article 15.

(f) Notifications received in accordance with Article 16.

Article 18

The original of the present Convention shall be deposited in the archives of the United Nations.

A certified copy of the Convention shall be transmitted to all Members of the United Nations and to the nonmember States contemplated in Article 11.

Article 19

The present Convention shall be registered by the Secretary-General of the United Nations on the date of its coming into force.

Personnel, Darfur Atrocities Documentation Project

Coalition for International Justice (CIJ)

Bang-Jensen, Nina   *Executive Director, Coalition for International Justice*
Frease, Stefanie   *Director of Programs, Coalition for International Justice*
Allyn, Vanessa   *Program Associate, Coalition for International Justice*
Barry, Sophie   *Freelance Videographer*
Niska, Helge   *Coordinator/Trainer — Interpretation*
Pfundheller, Jan   *Coordinator/Trainer — Investigations*
Thornton, John   *Coordinator — Operations*
De Guzman, Diane   *Coordinator — Field Operations*
   (consultant to American Bar Association)

CIJ Investigators

Belair, Maria
Bodkin, Debbie
Caine, Philip
Chaffee, Devon
Curlett, Chad
Davidson, Michael
Fricke, Adrienne
Gulick, Karen
Jafari, Jamal
Loewenstein, Andrew

Marcus, Maxine
Markusen, Eric
Momeni, Mercedeh
Parker, Tom
Patrick, Linda
Paul, Diane
Pfundheller, Brent
Pfundheller, Jan
Stefanovic, Michael
Stemmler, Louise
Takatsuno, Jocelyne
Thornton, Brenda Sue
Thornton, John
Totten, Samuel
Wakim, Larissa

Additional Investigative Personnel

Orona, Michael	*U.S. Department of State participant*
Gilbride, Karen	*U.S. Department of State participant*
Howard, Jonathan	*U.S. Department of State participant*
Wax, Rachel	*Office of Transition Initiatives/USAID*
Inman, Molly	*Assessment mission representative of American Bar Association's Central European and Eurasian Law Initiative*

Index